A WORLD BIBLIOGRAPHY
OF ORIENTAL BIBLIOGRAPHIES

A

WORLD BIBLIOGRAPHY

OF

ORIENTAL BIBLIOGRAPHIES

by THEODORE BESTERMAN

REVISED AND BROUGHT UP TO DATE BY

J. D. PEARSON

ROWMAN AND LITTLEFIELD
TOTOWA, NEW JERSEY

A WORLD BIBLIOGRAPHY OF BIBLIOGRAPHIES

FIRST PUBLISHED
OCTOBER 1939–MARCH 1940

SECOND EDITION
MARCH 1947–NOVEMBER 1949
(REPRINTED 1950)

THIRD EDITION
FEBRUARY 1955–JUNE 1956
(REPRINTED IN REDUCED FACSIMILE 1960)

FOURTH EDITION
MARCH 1965–1966
(REPRINTED 1971)

A WORLD BIBLIOGRAPHY OF ORIENTAL BIBLIOGRAPHIES

FIRST PUBLISHED 1975

© 1939, 1947, 1955, 1965, 1975

by THEODORE BESTERMAN

Library of Congress Cataloging in Publication Data

Besterman, Theodore, 1904–
    A world bibliography of Oriental bibliographies.

    Includes volumes cited in the 4th ed. of the author's
A world bibliography of bibliographies, first published
1965-1966, plus additional volumes published down to 1973.

    I. Bibliography—Bibliography—Asia.   I. Pearson,
James Douglas, 1911–   II. Title.
Z3001.A1B47 [DS5] 016.01695 75-17936
ISBN 0-87471-750-7

PRINTED IN ENGLAND

BY

CHENEY & SONS LTD BANBURY OXFORDSHIRE

PREFACE

THE fourth edition of *A World bibliography of bibliographies*, which extends to 1963, sets out some 6562 volumes for Asian and Oceanic subjects, a vast number indeed, but the bibliographical activity of the past decade has naturally kept pace with political developments, and the number of additional volumes now recorded, published down to 1973, amounts to 4471, so that the total has increased by some 68 per cent. In addition, well over a hundred titles in WBB4 have been modified in some way, usually to indicate continuations. It is remarkable that only one title has been removed, as it appears to be a ghost. The exact figures for the contents of this new work are:

General (Asia and Africa combined)	297
Asia (general)	840
West Asia	3046
South Asia	3778
South-east Asia	1256
Pacific region	422
East Asia	1394
Total	11033

In compiling this work the principles set out by Theodore Besterman in his Introduction have been rigidly adhered to. Every bibliography has been examined personally, except for some few titles that have defied discovery. These may be recognised by the absence of the terminal figure in square brackets for the estimated number of titles listed. An asterisk placed at the end of the description indicates reproduction from typescript; one at the beginning denotes a union catalogue.

The entries have been arranged first under geographical divisions and thereafter, as the case requires, in regional or subject subdivisions or both, as shown in the table of contents.

The additions have been collected from a great many libraries, beginning with that of the School of Oriental and African studies in London, and proceeding through other libraries in London and elsewhere in the United Kingdom to the Library of Congress and other depositories in the United States and Canada, and in Holland. It is not possible to enumerate the many libraries and curators of collections who have given freely of their time and knowledge in providing full facilities to the compiler. Such assistance is traditionally furnished by members of the profession all over the world. A deep sense of gratitude is felt for this help. My wife has helped me search for titles in libraries, and has typed a large part of the manuscript.

Finally, the compiler would wish to echo, in the words of Hemachandra quoted by Theodore Besterman, the hope that "noble-minded scholars" will correct errors "committed through the dullness of my intellect in the way of wrong interpretations and mis-statements".

J. D. P.

CONTENTS

GENERAL
(Asia and Africa combined)

TROPICS

i. *General*

TROPICAL abstracts. Royal tropical institute [Koninklijk instituut voor de tropen]:Amsterdam.

i. 1946.
ii. 1947.
iii. 1948.
iv. 1949.
v. 1950.
vi. 1951.
vii. 1952.
viii. 1953. pp.876.xxxvii. [3141.]
ix. 1954. pp.936.xliv. [3641.]
x. 1955. pp.936.xlviii.[3646.]
xi. 1956. pp.916.li. [3434.]
xii. 1957. pp.864.liv. [3075.]
xiii. 1958. pp.864.xlvi. [2990.]
xiv. 1959. pp.864.xlix. [3072.]
xv. 1960. pp.864.lxxiv. [3244.]
xvi. 1961. pp.864.lxxxviii. [3224.]
xvii. 1962. pp.872.cxli. [3212.]
xviii. 1963. pp.868. [3006.]
xix. 1964. pp.864.126. [3000.]
xx. 1965. pp.852.168. [2821.]
xxi. 1966. pp.824.180. [2693.]
xxii. 1967. pp.197.824. [2630.]
xxiii. 1968. pp.193.816. [2663.]
xxiv. 1969. pp.138.852. [2868.]
xxv. 1970. pp.852.158. [3088.]
xxvi. 1971. pp.904.163. [3253.]
xxvii. 1972. pp.880.153. [3065.]
xxviii. 1973. pp.928. [3090.]
in progress

THEO[DORE] L[EWIS] HILLS, A select annotated bibliography of the humid tropics. International geographical union: Special commission on the humid tropics: Montréal &c. 1960. pp.[ii].xiii. 238. [3000.]*

RESEARCH catalogue of the American geographical society [New York]. Polar regions, oceans, tropics. Boston 1962. pp.xx.10049–10436. [8134.]
this is a photographic reproduction of catalogue cards; the figure in square brackets refers to these cards.

ii. *Subjects*

Agriculture

J[OHN] C[HRISTOPHER] WILLIS, Literature of tropical economic botany and agriculture. II. 1904–08 to 1907–10. [Colombo 1911]. pp.45. [1500.]

SELECTED list of publications on tropical agriculture. Pan american union: Washington 1930. ff.[i].90. [1000.]*

BIBLIOGRAPHY of tropical agriculture. International institute of agriculture: Rome.
1931. pp.[v].70. [400.]
1932. pp.iii–viii.88. [400.]
1933. pp.iii–viii.140. [750.]
1934. pp.vii.247. [1000.]
1935. pp.vii.256. [1250.]
1936. pp.vii.327. [1500.]
1937. pp.vii.420. [1750.]
1938. pp.vii.466. [2000.]
1939. pp.iii.497. [1500.]
1940. pp.iii.302. [1000.]
1941–1942. pp.iii.365. [1000.]
no more published.

PERIODICALS and books relating to tropical agriculture and forestry. Science library: Bibliographical series (no.75): [1933]. ff.[i].6. [98.]*

Botany

J[OHN] C[HRISTOPHER] WILLIS, Literature of tropical economic botany & agriculture. II.1904–1908 to 1907–1910. [Colombo] 1911. pp.45. [1500.]

HELEN V[IRGINIA] BARNES and JESSIE M[AY] ALLEN, A bibliography of plant pathology in the tropics and in latin America. Department of agriculture: Bibliographical bulletin (no.14): Washington 1951. pp.vi.78. [2395.]

TROPICAL vegetation. List of references, India, Burma & Ceylon 1948–1954. Unesco: South Asia science co-operation office: [New Delhi 1956]. pp.[iii].12. [300.]*

Economics

DOCUMENTATIEBLAD. Koninklijk instituut voor de tropen: Afdeling tropische producten: Amsterdam 1946 &c.

Forestry

PERIODICALS and books relating to tropical agriculture and forestry. Science library: Bibliographical series (no.75): [1933]. ff.[i].6. [98.]*

TROPICAL rain forests. Science library: Bibliographical series (no.681): 1949. ff.2. [37.]*
— Supplement. . . . (no.784): [1963]. pp.7. [145.]*

Housing

PRELIMINARY BRAB bibliography of housing and building in hot-humid and hot-dry climates. National research council: Building research advisory board: [Washington] 1953. pp.[iii].32. [250.]*

— Supplement. University of Texas: Bureau of engineering research: Special publication (no.27): Austin.*

    1953 . . . (no.27). pp.viii.115. [750.]
    1954 . . . (no.28). pp.xi.160. [1500.]

[P. BOTTOMLEY *and others*], Une bibliographie choisie et analytique de l'habitat en milieu tropical. Commission du Pacifique sud: Document technique (no.76): Nouméa 1955.pp.v.44. [250.]

LITERATURE on building and housing in the tropics. Royal tropical institute [Koninklijk instituut voor de tropen]: Amsterdam 1962. pp.[iii].91. [300.]*

Medicine

TROPICAL diseases bulletin. Tropical diseases bureau [*afterwards:* Bureau of hygiene and tropical diseases].

    i–ii. November 1912–1913. pp.vi.766+vi. 705.lxv. [5000.]
    iii–iv. 1914. pp.vi.622.v.lxxxii+vi.589.lix. [5500.]
    v–vi. 1915. pp.vi.541.lxxiv+vi.655.lxi. [5000.]
    vii–viii. 1916. pp.vii.528.lxxx+vii.624.lvii. [5000.]
    ix–x. 1917. pp.vi.562.lxxiv+[v].423.lxiii. [4500.]
    xi–xii. 1918. pp.iv.526.lxxix+iv.498.lx. [4000.]
    xiii–xiv. 1919. pp.iii.431.lviii.viii+iii.453. lvii. [3500.]
    xv–xvi. 1920. pp.iv.529.lxxx+iv.533.lxxiv. [4000.]
    xvii–xviii. 1921. pp.iv.500.lxxiv+iv.483. lxxviii. [4000.]
    xix. 1922. pp.iv.970. [2000.]
    xx. 1923. pp.iv.1076. [2500.]
    xxi. 1924. pp.iv.1083. [2500.]
    xxii. 1925. pp.iv.1094. [2500.]
    xxiii. 1926. pp.iv.1009. [2500.]
    xxiv. 1927. pp.iv.1100. [3000.]
    xxv. 1928. pp.iv.1077. [3000.]
    xxvi. 1929. pp.iv.1107. [3000.]
    xxvii. 1930. pp.iv.1096. [3000.]
    xxviii. 1931. pp.iv.1100. [3000.]
    xxix. 1932. pp.iv.941. [3000.]
    xxx. 1933. pp.iv.970. [3000.]
    xxxi. 1934. pp.iv.958. [3000.]
    xxxii. 1935. pp.iv.969. [3000.]
    xxxiii. 1936. pp.iv.1032. [3500.]
    xxxiv. 1937. pp.iv.1022. [3500.]
    xxxv. 1938. pp.iv.988. [3000.]
    xxxvi. 1939. pp.iv.1096. [3500.]
    xxxvii. 1940. pp.iv.948. [3000.]
    xxxviii. 1941. pp.iv.783. [2500.]
    xxxix. 1942. pp.iv.953. [3000.]
    xl. 1943. pp.iv.1009. [3000.]
    xli. 1944. pp.iv.1137. [3500.]

    xlii. 1945. pp.vi.1113. [3500.]
    xliii. 1946. pp.vi.1271. [4000.]
    xliv. 1947. pp.vi.1191. [3500.]
    xlv. 1948. pp.vi.1224. [4000.]
    xlvi. 1949. pp.vi.1295. [4000.]
    xlvii. 1950. pp.vi.1334. [4000.]
    xlviii. 1951. pp.vi.1260. [4000.]
    xlix. 1952. pp.vi.1261. [4000.]
    l. 1953. pp.vi.1186. [3500.]
    li. 1954. pp.vi.1426. [4000.]
    lii. 1955. pp.vi.1345. [4000.]
    liii. 1956. pp.vi.1500. [4000.]
    liv. 1957. pp.vi.1484. [4000.]
    lv. 1958. pp.vi.1589. [4000.]
    lvi. 1959. pp.vi.1363. [4000.]
    lvii. 1960. pp.vi.1328. [4000.]
    lviii. 1961. pp.vi.1412. [4000.]
    lix. 1962. pp.vi.1224. [3000.]
    lx. 1963. pp.vi.1172. [3000.]
    lxi. 1964. pp.vii.1337. [2500.]
    lxii. 1965. pp.vii.1363. [2500.]
    lxiii. 1966. pp.vii.1494. [3000.]
    lxiv. 1967. pp.vii.1470. [3000.]
    lxv. 1968. pp.vii.1598. [3306.]
    lxvi. 1969. pp.vii. 1435. [2551.]
    lxvii. 1970. pp.vii.1552. [2985.]
    lxviii. 1971. pp.vii.1616. [2683.]

in progress

E. G. NAUCK [*and others*], Tropical medicine and parasitology. Office of military government for Germany: Field information agencies technical: Fiat review of german science, 1939–1946: Wiesbaden 1948. pp.[viii].253. [1350.]
the text is in german.

Trade and manufactures

AN INDUSTRIAL technical library for a tropical country. International cooperation administration: Office of industrial resources: Washington [1957]. pp.[ii].106. [1250.]*

Water

REVIEWS of research on arid zone hydrology. Unesco [United nations educational, scientific and cultural organization]: Arid zone programme (no.1): Paris [1953]. pp.212. [1650.]

COLONIES, COLONIZATION

    Imperialism, Mandates
    British commonwealth
    French territories
    Portuguese territories

CATALOGUS van de boeken en kaarten, uitmakende de bibliotheek van het Departement van koloniën. 's Gravenhage 1884. pp.viii.711.xlix. [7500.]

— Nieuwe uitgave. [By Alexander Hartmann]. 1898. pp.[iii].viii.1000. [10,000.]
— — Verfolg. 1923 &c.
in progress.

BULLETIN bibliographique colonial. Première année, — no.1. Quinzaine coloniale; Supplément: 1900. pp.xi. [400.]
printed on grey paper.

A[PPLETON] P[RENTISS] C[LARK] GRIFFIN, List of books (with references to periodicals) relating to the theory of colonization, government of dependencies, protectorates, and related topics. Library of Congress; Washington 1900. pp.vi.131. [2500.]
— — Second edition. 1900. pp.viii.156. [3000.]

BULLETIN bibliographique colonial. Première année. Union coloniale française: 1902. pp.100. [846.]
no more published.

BIBLIOTHÈQUE de la Société d'études coloniales. Catalogue. Bruxelles 1902. pp.liii. [1250.]
— [another edition]. Catalogue de la bibliothèque. Institut colonial international: 1908.pp.86. [1650.]

VICTOR TANTET, Catalogue méthodique de la bibliothèque du Ministère des colonies. Melun 1905. pp.xxiv.652. [3000.]
— — Table alphabétique [par noms d'auteurs]. By O. Wirth. 1905. pp.653–680.

SELECT list of references on the military and naval defense of colonies and dependencies. Library of Congress: Washington 1910. ff.4. [17.]★

RACCOLTA cartografica. Direzione centrale degli affari coloniali: Roma 1911. pp. viii.372. [770.]

HUBERT HENOCH, Die deutsche kolonialliteratur im jahre ... (Im nachtrag: Kolonialliteratur fremder völker.) Berlin.
1911. pp.118. [5000.]
1913. pp.116. [5000.]

LIST of references on the commercial and economic conditions in the colonies. Library of Congress: Washington 1914. ff.4. [45.]★

H[UGO] MARQUARDSEN, Die kolonial-kartensammlung des Reichs-kolonialamts. Mitteilungen aus den deutschen schutzgebieten (1915, no.2, beilage): Berlin 1915. pp.iv.60. [750.]

WINIFRED C. HILL, A select bibliography of publications on foreign colonisation—german, french, italian, dutch, portuguese, spanish, and belgian—contained in the library. Royal colonial institute: Bibliographies (no.1): 1915. pp.48. [1500.]

LIST of recent books on colonization. Library of Congress: Washington 1916. ff.2. [17.]★

LIST of references on inter-colonial relations. Library of Congress: Washington 1918. ff.10. [83.]★

TH. SIMAR, Catalogue de la bibliothèque, 1914–1921 ... suivi d'un appendice bibliographique sur la colonisation en général. Ministère des colonies: Bruxelles 1922. pp.186. [2500.]

EVANS LEWIN, Select bibliography of recent publications in the library ... illustrating the relations between Europeans and coloured races. Royal colonial institute: Bibliographies (no.3): 1926. pp.62. [1250.]★
— — Addenda. 1927. ff.2. [40.]★

ALFRED [ALBERT] MARTINEAU, [PAUL] ROUSSIER and [JOANNÈS MARTIAL MARIE HIPPOLYTE] TRAMOND, Bibliographie d'histoire coloniale (1900–1930). Société de l'histoire des colonies françaises: 1932. pp.iii–xvi.669. [7500.]

LOWELL JOSEPH RAGATZ, Colonial studies in the United States during the twentieth century. [1932]. pp.[ii].48. [475.]
— — [second edition]. Washington 1934. pp. [iii].48. [550.]

LOWELL JOSEPH RAGATZ, A list of books and articles on colonial history and overseas expansion published in the United States in 1931 and 1932. [1933]. pp.[iii].41. [500.]
the same text, in each case with an additional preface, was reissued in Washington (1933), Toronto (1934) and Melbourne (1935).
— — 1933–1935. [1936]. pp.iv.91. [1500.]

LOWELL JOSEPH RAGATZ, A bibliography of articles ... on colonies and other dependent territories appearing in american geographical and kindred journals ... Washington.
  i. through 1934. [1935]. pp.vii.122. [2000.]
  ii. Compiled by Janet Evans Ragatz. 1935 through 1950. pp.viii.149. [2300.]

KOLONIEN im deutschen schrifttum. Eine uebersicht über deutsches koloniales schrifttum unter berücksichtigung nur volksdeutscher autoren. Reichskolonialbund: Berlin 1936. pp.62. [500.]

LISTE sélectionnée d'ouvrages sur la question des matières premières et des colonies et sur les problèmes connexes. ... Édition revisée: Société des nations: Bibliothèque: Listes bibliographiques (no.6): Genève 1937. pp.[ii].24. [150.]★

KOLONIALES schrifttum. Reichskolonialbund: Deutsche kolonialbibliothek: Beriln.
  i. 1938.
  ii. 1939. pp.[ii].28. [1300.]
  iii. 1940.
  iv. 1941. pp.[ii].259. [3000.]
  v. 1942. pp.256. [3000.]

LOWELL JOSEPH RAGATZ, A list of books and articles on colonial history and overseas expansion published in the United States, 1900–1930. Ann Arbor 1939. pp.[iii].45. [600.]★

KOLONIALES schrifttum in Deutschland. Kolonialpolitisches amt: Koloniale politik: München 1941. pp.vii.110. [2000.]

P. A. BOWER, Colonial economics. Oxford university: Nuffield college: Select reading lists for colonial studies (no.2): Oxford 1946. pp.vi.51.★
[—] — [another edition]. The economics of 'underdeveloped' areas. Compiled by Arthur Hazlewood. 1954. pp.102. [623.]
— — Second . . . edition. 1959. pp.xii.157. [1027.]

BIBLIOGRAPHIES on non-self-governing areas: a selected list of references. Library of Congress: Washington 1946. ff.17. [90.]★

HELEN F[IELD] CONOVER, Non-self-governing areas, with special emphasis on mandates and trusteeships. A selected list of references. Library of Congress: General reference and bibliography division: Washington 1947. pp.[ii].ix.467. [3603.]★

C[HARLES] K[INGSLEY] MEEK, Colonial law. A bibliography with special reference to native african systems of law and land tenure. Nuffield college [Oxford]: 1948. pp.xiii.59. [813.]

READING list on colonial development and welfare. Colonial office: 1951. pp.12. [150.]★

MARINA NIKOLAEVNA TALANTOVA and SH. M. GERMAN, Углубление кризиса колониальной системы империализма после второй мировой войны. Рекомендательный указатель литературы. Государственная ордена Ленина библиотека СССР имени В. И. Ленина: Москва 1955. pp.59. [220.]

A[LEKSANDR] A[LEKSANDROVICH] POPOV, Распад колониальной системы империализма. Рекомендательный указатель литературы. Государственная . . . публичная библиотека имени М. Е. Салтыкова–Щедрина: Ленинград 1959. pp.108. [476.]

CATALOGUE of the Colonial Office library, London. Boston 1964.
  i. Author catalogue. Pre-1950 accessions. A-J. pp.[iii]. 531.
  ii. — K–Z. pp.545.
  iii. Author and title catalogue. Post-1950 accessions. A–Ear. pp.737.
  iv. — Eas–Jam. pp.752.
  v. — Jan–Ref. pp.738.
  vi. — Reg–Z. pp.743.

  vii. Subject catalogue. Pre-1950 accessions. A–In. pp.ix. 904.
  viii. — Io–Z. pp.840.
  ix. Subject catalogue. Post-1950 accessions. A–Citr. pp.683.
  x. — Cits–Gg. pp.688.
  xi. — Gh–Mas. pp.697.
  xii. — Mat–Rur. pp.680.
  xiii. — Rus–Z. pp.709.
  xiv. Classified catalogue. Post-1950 accessions. A–Hj. pp.798.
  xv. — Hk–Z. pp. 698.
— First supplement 1963–1967. 1967. pp.vii. 894. [18,900.]
— Second supplement 1972.
  i. Author catalogue. pp.626. [13,143.]
  ii. Classified catalogue. pp.591. [12,411.]
there are 176,000 cards reproduced in the pre- and post-1950 catalogues. The pre-1950 subject catalogue is copied from a sheaf-catalogue.

[Imperialism. see also Colonies.]

A FEW standard books on imperialism, expansion, government of dependencies, etc. Library of Congress: Washington 1916. ff.2. [30.]★

LOWELL JOSEPH RAGATZ, The literature of european imperialism, 1815–1939. A bibliography. Washington [1944]. pp.ix.153. [8000.]★

Mandates. [see also Colonies.]

BRIEF list of references on mandatories and protectorates. Library of Congress: [Washington] 1919. ff.4. [40.]★

A LIST of references on mandates. Library of Congress: [Washington] 1924. ff.31. [372.]★

LISTE d'ouvrages relatifs au régime des mandats et aux territoires sous mandat catalogués à la bibliothèque de la Société des nations. Genève 1930. pp.106. [3000.]
— — Premier supplément. 1934. pp.56. [1000.]

A. YAARI [and others], A post-war bibliography of the near eastern mandates. A preliminary survey of publications on the social sciences dealing with Iraq, Palestine and Trans-Jordan, and the Syrian states . . . to Dec. 31, 1929. American university of Beirut: Social science series (no.1): Jerusalem 1933 &c.
in progress.

British commonwealth

DAS ZEITUNGSWESEN der britischen kolonien. [Berlin 1926]. pp.156. [1000.]

[ULRICH] PHILIP MAYER, Reading list on rural conditions and betterment in the British colonies. Oxford university: Nuffield college: 1947. pp.vii. 121. [1085.]

BIBLIOGRAPHY of current periodical abstracts and indexes published in the British Commonwealth and contained in the Science museum library. [1948]. pp.12. [125.]

A[RTHUR] R[EGINALD] HEWITT, Union list of commonwealth newspapers in London, Oxford and Cambridge. University of London: Institute of commonwealth studies: 1960. pp.ix.101. [2426.]

[PATRICIA MARIE PUGH], Papers of sir Charles Woolley, MSS. Brit. Emp. s 276. Oxford colonial records project: [Oxford 1965]. ff.26. [294.]*

COMMONWEALTH directory of periodicals; a guide to scientific, technical and professional journals published in the developing countries of the Commonwealth. Commonwealth secretariat: 1973. pp.ix.157. [971.]

French territories

HENRI MAGER, Annuaire de la presse coloniale. 1891. pp.242. [4750.]
— [another edition]. Annuaire de la presse française des colonies et de l'étranger. 1892. pp.480. [1500.]

ÉNUMÉRATION des travaux sur productions et cultures coloniales publiés par le professeur [Frédéric Heim] et ses collaborateurs. [Conservatoire national des arts et métiers:] Chaire d'agriculture et productions agricoles: [1931]. pp.54.

FAVITZKI DE PROBOBYSZ, Répertoire bibliographique de la littérature militaire et coloniale française depuis cent ans. 1935. pp.xi.303. [7943.]

F. BLONDEL, Bibliographie géologique et minière de la France d'outre-mer. Édition définitive. Bureau d'études géologiques et minières coloniales: Publications (no.11): 1941. pp.x.422+[iii].423-1038. [12,500.]

F. M[AIRIER] D'UNIENVILLE, Annuaire mondial des journaux ... et associations culturelles de langue française hors de France. Mauritius 1953. pp.[vi].200. [2500.]

BULLETIN bibliographique. Ministère de la France d'outre-mer: Direction des affaires économiques et du plan: Service des statistiques (later Ministère de l'économie et des finances: Institut national de la statistique et des études économiques: Secrétariat d'état aux affaires étrangères:) 1948 &c.
in progress.

P[IERRE] WATTEL, Bibliographie des mémoires de l'Institut des territoires d'outre-mer. Commission belge de bibliographie: Bibliographia belgica (no.11): Bruxelles 1955. pp.95. [903.]

CATALOGUE bibliographique de la documentation réunie au Service d'information. Ministère d'état: Départements & territoires d'outre-mer: Service de documentation: Paris 1966. ff.[v].113.67. [1000.]*

GUIDE bibliographique sommaire d'histoire militaire et coloniale française. Ministère des armées: État-major de l'armée de terre: Service historique: Paris 1969. pp.522. [3971.]

Portuguese territories

JOAQUIM HELIODORO DA CUNHA RIVARA, Catálogo dos manuscriptos da Bibliotheca pública eborense.... Tomo I, que comprehende a noticia dos codices e papeis relativos ás cousas da America, Africa e Asia. Lisboa 1856. pp.[v].459. [5000.]

A[RTHUR] C[OKE] BURNELL, A tentative list of books and some mss. relating to the history of the Portuguese in India proper. Mangalore 1880. pp.vi.133. [500.]
15 copies privately printed.

[PEDRO WENCESLAU DE] BRITO ARANHA, Subsidios para a historia do jornalismo nas provincias ultramarinas portuguezas. Sociedade de geographia: Lisboa 1885. pp.27. [175.]

FRANCISCO JOSÉ DINIZ, Repertoria alphabético e synóptico de todas as leis, decretos, portarias e officios do Ministerio de marinha e ultramar. Lisboa 1887. pp.91. [600.]

ERNESTO JULIO DE CARVALHO E VASCONCELLOS, Relação de diversos mappas, cartas, planas e vistas pertencentes a este ministerio. Ministerio da marinha e ultramar: Lisboa 1892. pp.55.[vii]. [150.]

[—] SILVA LEAL, Jornaes indo-portuguezes. Lisboa 1898. pp.44. [138.]

Z. CONSIGLIERI PEDROSO, Catálogo bibliográphico das publicações relativas aos descobrimentos portugueses. Academia das sciencias: Lisboa 1912. pp.xi.134. [900.]

GEORG SCHURHAMMER, Die zeitgenössischen quellen zur geschichte portugiesisch-Asiens und seiner nachbarländer ... zur zeit des hl. Franz Xavier (1538-1552). Katholische universität Jôchi Daigaku, Tôkyô: Xaveriusreihe (vol.i): Leipzig 1932. pp.xlvii.521. [6236.]
— — Unveränderter neudruck ... mit vollständigem index und supplement bis 1962. Institutum historicum S. I.: Bibliotheca (vol.xx): Rom 1962. pp.v.xlvii.653. [6236.]

[AMADEU CUNHA], Catálogo bibliográfico da Agência geral das colónias. Ministério das colónias: Lisboa 1943. pp.3-305. [750.]

MATERIALS in the National archives relating to portuguese possessions in Africa and in the Atlantic. National archives: Reference information circular (no.18): [Washington] 1943. pp.4. [large number.]*

CATÁLOGO das edições de cartas geográficas e hidrográficas. Ministério das colónias: Junta das missões geográficas e de investigações coloniais: Lisboa 1949. ff.[30]. [300.]

[LUÎS SILVEIRA], Catálogo didascálico das publicações. Ministério do ultramar: Junta das missões geográficas e de investigações do ultramar: Lisboa [1952]. pp.26. [300.]

PERIÓDICOS portugueses de interesse ultramarino actualmente en publicação. Centro de documentação cientifica ultramarina: Lisboa 1959. pp.[iii]. 89. [450.]*

BIBLIOGRAFIA científica da junta de investigações do ultramar. Centro de documentação científico ultramarina: Lisboa 1960. pp.371. [1697.]

[IDALINO DA COSTA BROCHADO and others], Bibliografia henriquina. Comissão executiva das comemorações do v centenário da morte do infante d. Henrique: Lisboa 1960. pp.iii–xi.327+ [v].385. [4661.]

ECONOMIC DEVELOPMENT

POINT four. A selected bibliography of materials on technical cooperation with foreign governments. Department of state: Division of library and reference services: Bibliography (no.54): Washington 1950. pp.[ii].10. [100.]*

READING lists on certain under-developed countries. International labour office: Library: Bibliographical reference list (no.55): Geneva 1952. pp.28. [100.]*

LISTE d'ouvrages et de rapports sur l'assistance technique: le "point quatre"; le plan de Colombo; le programme de l'Organisation des états américains; le programme élargie d'assistance technique des Nations Unies. Bureau international du Travail: Bibliothèque: Liste bibliographique sommaire (no.2): 1952. pp.4. [35.]*

TECHNICAL assistance. International labour office: Library: Bibliographical reference list (no.59): Geneva 1953. pp.28. [400.]*

GUIDE to documents by the regional economic commissions on economic development and related subjects. United Nations: Department of economic affairs: New York 1953. pp.[ii].35. [200.]*

INDEX of documents issued for general distribution by the Technical assistance administration. United nations: New York 1953. pp.15. [75.]*
— [another edition]. Index of final reports [&c.]. 1954. pp.iii.40. [250.]*

ARTHUR HAZLEWOOD, The economics of 'underdeveloped' areas. An annotated reading list of books, articles, and official publications: Institute of commonwealth studies: 1954. pp.xii.90. [623.]
— — Second ... edition. 1959. pp.xii.157. [1027.]

BIBLIOGRAPHIE der entwicklungspläne [und -vorhaben]. Bremer ausschuss für wirtschaftsforschung: Bremen 1954. pp.22.
— 8. ausgabe. 1962. pp.95.

ECONOMIC problems of underdeveloped areas. External research, a listing of recent studies. Department of state: Office of intelligence research: [Washington] 1956. pp.[iv].59. [1000.]*

BIBLIOGRAPHY on industrialization in underdeveloped countries. Bibliographie de l'industrialisation dans les pays sous-développés. Bibliografía sobre la industrialización en los países insuficientemente desarrollados. Bibliographical series (no. 6): United nations headquarters library: [New York] 1956. pp.xi.216. [2290.]*

JEAN VIET, Assistance to under-developed countries. ... An annotated bibliography. United nations educational, scientific and cultural organization: Social science clearing house: Reports and paper in the social sciences (no.8): Paris 1957. pp.84. [869.]*

SOCIAL factors in economic growth. With particular reference to underdeveloped countries. Unesco: Current sociology (vol.vi, no.3): Paris 1957. pp.[ii].173–237. [419.]

LITERATUR über entwicklungsländer. Friedrich-Ebert-stiftung: Schriftenreihe: A. Sozialwissenschaftliche schriften: Eine zusammenstellung des wichtigen schrifttums deutscher, englischer und französischer sprache 1950–1959. Hannover.
   i. 1950–1959. pp.xviii.702. [10,000.]
   ii. — russischer sprache 1950–1959. 1961. pp.[v].88. [850.]
   iii. — deutscher, englischer und französischer sprache 1960. Bearbeitet von Ingrid Heidermann. pp.xxiii.373. [4750.]
   iv. — russischer sprache 1960. Bearbeitet von Eva Braun und Miroslav Petruszek. 1963. pp.[xii].112. [1050.]
   v. — deutscher, englischer und französischer sprache 1961. Bearbeitet von Vera Lamberg. 1966. pp.xxiv.455. [6000.]
   vi. — russischer sprache 1961. 1966. pp.xiii. 135. [1530.]

vii. — deutscher, englischer und französischer sprache 1962. Bearbeitet von G. Dommick-Herdina. 1967. pp.xxvi.495. [8250.]

viii. — russischer sprache 1962. Bearbeitet von Miroslav R. Petruszek. 1967. pp.xv. 115. [1200.]

HELGA and DIETER DANCKWORTT, Entwicklungshilfe — entwicklungsländer. Ein verzeichnis von publikationen in der Bundesrepublik Deutschland und Westberlin 1950–1959. Carl Duisburg-gesellschaft: Köln [1960]. pp.[ii].471. [3665.]*

JALEEL AHMAD, Natural resources in low income countries. An analytical survey of socio-economic research. [Pittsburgh] 1960. pp.xxv.118. [502.]*

INDUSTRIALIZATION and economic development. Literature recommendations. International cooperation administration: Office of industrial resources: Washington [1960]. pp.[iii].29. [150.]*

SELECTED references on industrial development. International cooperation administration: Office of industrial resources: Technical aids branch: Washington 1961. pp.ix.140. [600.]*

BIBLIOGRAPHIE des études démographiques relatives aux pays en voie de développement (ouvrages parus depuis 1945). Institut national de la statistique et des études économiques: Service de coopération: [Paris] 1961. ff.110. [700.]*

ENTWICKLUNGSLÄNDER-STUDIEN. Bibliographie der entwicksländer-forschung. Deutsche stiftung für entwicklungsländer: Bonn.
  i.
  ii.
  iii.
  iv. 1965–7. pp.[vii].124.193. [467.]*
  v. 1968. pp.[vii].104.218. [591.]*
  vi. 1969. pp.[vii].98.271. [699.]*
  vii. 1970. pp.[iv].85.225. [550.]*
  viii. 1972. pp.[xiv].86.208. [500.]*
  also published as "vorabdrücke" (pre-prints) in larger format.

[RICHARD M. BIRD], Bibliography on taxation in underdeveloped countries. Law school of Harvard university: Cambridge 1962. pp.[viii]. 75. [2100.]

READING list, United nations conference on the application of science and technology for the benefit of the less developed areas. Agency for international development: Communications resources division: [Washington] 1962. pp.[ii].90. [1400.]*

SELECTED readings and source materials on economic development . . . assembled by the Economic development institute. International bank for reconstruction and development: Washington [1962]. pp.vi.66. [394.]

SAUL M. KATZ and FRANK MCGOWAN, A selected list of U.S. readings on development. Agency for international development: Washington 1963. pp. xvii.363. [1195.]

MARIAN CRITES ALEXANDER-FRUTSCHI, *ed.* Human resources and economic growth. An international annotated bibliography on the role of education and training in economic and social development. Stanford research institute: International development center: Menlo Park, Cal. 1963. pp.xv.398. [1150.]

ALAN A. SPITZ and EDWARD W. WEIDNER, Development administration. An annotated bibliography. Honolulu [1963]. pp.xi.116. [340.]*

JACK BARANSON, Technology for underdeveloped areas; an annotated bibliography. International series of monographs in library and information science: Oxford &c. 1967. pp.vii.81. [319.]

S. K. MISRA, Building and planning in developing countries; a partially annotated bibliography. National swedish institute for building research: Stockholm 1967. pp.71. [446.]*

A PRACTICAL bibliography for developing areas: a selective annotated and graded list of United States publications in the social sciences. Agency for international development: Department of state: Washington [1967?] pp.xxiii.202+xxix. 332. [8,600.]

M. M. MEHTA, Documentary material on human resources development (with special reference to Asia and the Far East). United nations: Asian institute for economic development and planning: Bangkok 1968. pp.523.39. [4000.]*

JOHN BRODE, The process of modernization. An annotated bibliography on the sociocultural aspects of development. Cambridge, Mass. 1969. pp.xi.378. [5000.]*

CATALOGUE of Institute of developing economies 1959–1968. Tokyo 1969–70. pp.xxv.808+xxvii. 753+v.519. [30,000.]

PHILIP G. ALTBACH and BRADLEY NYSTROM, Higher education in developing countries; a select bibliography. Occasional papers in international affairs (no.24): Center for international affairs: Harvard university [Cambridge, Mass.] 1970. pp.[ix].116. [1750.]

GARTH N. JONES [and others], Planning, development, and change; a bibliography on development administration. Honolulu 1970. pp.xi.180. [1590.]*

SELECT bibliography on british aid to developing countries. 3rd revised edition. Foreign and commonwealth office: Overseas development administration library: [London] 1971. ff.[ii].pp. 23. [259.]*

J. A. DOWNEY, A guide to information on developing countries in U.S. government publications, 1962–1971. Institute of development studies library: Occasional guides (no.2): Brighton [1973?] pp.vii.82. [400.]*

R. P. MARSDEN, Bibliography of public enterprise, with special reference to the developing countries. Based on the collections of professor A. H. Hanson. University of Leeds 1973. pp.x.97. [1820.]

RURAL migration in less developed countries: a preliminary bibliography. Occasional guides (no.3): Institute of development studies library: Brighton [1973]. pp.vi.62. [480.]*

DEVELOPMENT administration and assistance; an annotated bibliography. P.A. prints and reprints (no.45): Department of state: Agency for international development: Communication resources division: Washington 1963. pp.vi.176. [1115.]*

ÚMPE bibliography regarding problems of developing countries. Библиография к вопросам развивающихся стран, Bibliografie k otázkám rozvojových zemí. Ústav pro mezinárodní politiku a ekonomii. Institute of international politics and economics: Praha [1963?].pp.64. [420.]

BIBLIOGRAPHIE over het derde wereldblok. Recueil bibliographie tiers-monde. [Title also in english, french, italian, spanish, portuguese.]

Universitair instituut voor de overzeese gebieden: Institut universitaire des territoires d'Outremer: Antwerpen 1964. pp.iv.157. [1000.]

BIBLIOGRAPHY on canadian aid to the developing countries. Bibliographie sur l'aide canadienne aux pays en voie d'expansion. Overseas institute of Canada: Ottawa 1964. pp.ii.8. [82.]*

ECONOMIC and social development plans: Africa, Asia and Latin America. Dag Hammarskjold library: United nations, New York 1964. pp.v.25. [Asia: 128]*

TECHNICAL co-operation; a monthly bibliography. 1964 &c.
in progress.

JACK MEZIROW and DAVID EPLEY, Adult education in developing countries; a bibliography. International education clearinghouse of the Graduate program in international and development education: School of education: University of Pittsburgh: Pittsburgh 1965. pp.vii.120. [1350.]*

ELOISE G. REQUA and JANE STATHAM, The developing nations: a guide to information sources concerning their economic, political, technical and social problems. Management information guide (5): Detroit 1965. pp.339. [880.]

HOWARD S. WHITNEY, HASSAN A. RONAGHY and others, Bibliography on cooperatives and social and economic development. Supplement prepared by Anna Marie Taylor. International cooperative training center: University extension division, University of Wisconsin: Madison 1966. pp.[iv].91. [1450.]*

ASIA

ASIA

i. *General*

ANTONIO DE LEÓN [PINELO], Epitome de la biblioteca oriental i occidental, nautica i geográfica. Madrid 1629. pp.[lxxxviii].186.xiii. [oriental: 600.]

— — Edición bibliófilos argentinos: Buenos Aires [1919]. pp.xxxiii.facsimile. [1].
300 copies printed.

— — Añadido, y emmendado nuevamente [by Andres Gonzales de Barcia Carballido y Zuñiga]. 1737–1738. pp.[cxliv].coll.536.pp.537–539.ff.540–560[sic,561].[ii] + [ii].coll.561–912.ff.913–920. [xxi–xxviii(sic,xxxii)].coll.921–1191.ff.1192–1199. mcc–mccxxxviii+[ii].coll.1200–1729.pp.133. [oriental: 7500.]

JOH[ANN] HEINRICH HOTTINGER, Promtuarium; sive, bibliotheca orientalis: exhibems catalogum sive, centurias aliquot, tam authorum, quàm librorum hebraicorum, syriacorum, arabicorum, ægyptiacorum, æthiopicorum, &c. Heidelbergæ 1658. pp.[viii].332.46. [2000.]

GEORG MATTHIAS KÖNIG, Bibliotheca vetus et nova, in qua hebræorum, chaldæorum, syrorum, arabum, persarum, ægyptiorum, græcorum & latinorum per universum terrarum orbem scriptorum, theologorum, jctorum. . . . oratorum, poetarum, &c. patria, ætas, nomina, libri, sæpiùs etiam eruditorum de iis elogia, testimonia & judicia . . . ordine alphabetico digesta . . . recensentur. Altdorfi 1678. pp.[xii].888. [20,000.]
one of the British museum copies contains voluminous ms. notes.

JOHANN DAVID MICHAELIS, Orientalische und exegetische bibliothek. Frankfurt am Mayn.

   i. 1771. pp.[xxviii].252. [18.]
   ii. 1772. pp.[iv].255. [10.]
   iii. 1772. pp.[iv].252. [15.]
   iv. 1773. pp.[iv].252. [20.]
   v. 1773. pp.[iv].252. [15.]
   vi. 1774. pp.[iv].251. [15.]
   vii. 1774. pp.[viii].248. [18.]
   viii. 1775. pp.[iv].224. [17.]
   ix. 1775. pp.[iv].234. [21.]
   x. 1776. pp.[iv].228. [19.]
   xi. 1776. pp.[iii].220. [12.]
   xii. 1777. pp.[vi].196. [14.]
— Anhang zum zwölften theil. 1778. pp.[vii]. 200.
   xiii. 1778. pp.[iv].252. [18.]
   xiv. 1779. pp.[iii].156. [10.]
— Anhang zum vierzehnten theil. 1779. pp.224.
   xv. 1780. pp.[iv].188. [14.]
   xvi. 1781. pp.[iii].292. [9.]
   xvii. 1781. pp.[iv].188. [11.]
   xviii. 1782. pp.[iv].196. [11.]
   xix. 1782. pp.[iv].204. [10.]

   xx. 1782. pp.[iv].199.[v]. [12.]
   xxi. 1783. pp.[iv].193.[xi]. [19.]
   xxii. 1783. pp.[iv].204. [15.]
   xxiii. 1785. pp.[iv].188. [17.]
   xxiv. Sieben-fachs register über die 23. vorhergehenden theile. [By Johann Georg Schmidt and Johann Wilhelm Stüber]. 1789. pp.xiv.348.
[continued as:]
Neue orientalische und exegetische bibliothek.
   i. 1786. pp.[viii].231. [23.]
   ii. 1786. pp.[iv].260. [18.]
   iii. 1787. pp.[iv].244. [20.]
   iv. 1787. pp.[iv].209. [15.]
   v. 1788. pp.[iv].252. [16.]
   vi. 1789. pp.[iv].236. [17.]
   vii. 1790. pp.
   viii. 1791. pp.[vi].254. [12.]
   ix. Fortgesetzt von Thomas Christian Tychsen. 1793. pp.[viii].246. [16.]

[ADAM CLARKE], A bibliographical dictionary containing a chronological account, alphabetically arranged, of the most curious, scarce, useful, and important books, in all departments of literature, which have been published in latin, greek, coptic, hebrew, samaritan, syriac, chaldee, æthiopic, arabic, persian, armenian, &c. from the infancy of printing. 1802–1804. pp.[vi].288+[iv].300+[iv]. 300+iv.312+vi.296+viii.343. [25,000.]

[—] — The bibliographical miscellany; or, supplement to the Bibliographical dictionary. 1806. pp.vii.324+xii.323. [2000.]

[CHARLES] H[ENRI] TERNAUX-COMPANS, Bibliothèque asiatique et africaine . . . jusqu'en 1700. 1841. pp.vi.347. [3184.]

WISSENSCHAFTICHER jahresbericht über die morgenländischen studien. Zeitschrift der deutschen morgenländischen gesellschaft: Leipzig.
   1859–1861. Von Richard Gosche. . . . (vol. xx, supplement): 1868. pp.viii.310. [1926.]
   1862–1867 . . . (vol.xxiv, supplement, heft 1): 1871. pp.[vii].208. [933.]
   1876–1877. . . . Herausgegeben von Ernst [Wilhelm Adalbert] Kuhn und Albert Socin . . . vol.xxxiii, Supplement): 1879. pp.xvi.132+[ii].184. [2793.]
   1878. Herausgegeben von Ernst Kuhn. 1881. [1503.]
   1879 . . . Herausgegeben von Ernst Kuhn und [Friedrich] August Müller. 1881. pp.[iii].183. [1397.]
   1880. . . . (vol.xxxiv, Supplement): 1883. pp.[iii].223. [1752.]
   1881. 1885. pp.[iii].154. [1166.]

the second part for 1862–1867, and the issue for 1868–1875 were not printed. The first issue, for 1846, was published in the society's Jahrbuch for that year.

Those for 1847, 1849–58 appeared in the Zeitschrift, vols. 2–17. Issues for 1907–19 appeared in the Zeitschrift, vols. 62–74, but contained no lists of books.

J[ULIUS] TH[EODOR] ZENKER, Bibliotheca orientalis. Manuel de bibliographie orientale. Leipzig 1846–1861. pp.xlvii.264+xv.616. [8831.]

[PAUL TRÖMEL], Bibliographie für linguistik und orientalische literatur. No.1[–4]. Leipzig 1856–1858. pp.88. [1000.]

PROGRÈS des études relatives à l'Égypte et à l'orient. [Edited by J. D. Guigniaut]. Ministère de l'instruction publique: Recueil de rapports sur les progrès des lettres et des sciences en France: Sciences historiques et philosophiques: 1867. pp.[iii].xi.213. [500.]

CARL HEINRICH HERRMANN, Bibliotheca orientalis et linguistica. Verzeichniss der vom jahre 1850 bis incl. 1868 in Deutschland erschienenen bücher, schriften und abhandlungen orientalischer und sprachvergleichender literatur. Bibliotheca philologica (pars 1): Halle a S. 1870. pp.[iv].182. [6000.]
also issued with a french subtitle and a Paris imprint.

REVUE bibliographique de philologie et d'histoire. [Edited by Ernest Leroux].
   i. 1874. pp.[iii].240. [3000.]
   ii. 1875. pp.[iii].235. [1000.]
   iii. 1876. pp.152. [1000.]

P[IETER] A[NDREAS] M[ARTIN] BOELE VAN HENSBROEK, De beeofening der oostersche talen in Nederland en zijne overzeesche bezittingen 1800–1874. Bibliographisch overzicht. Feestgave ter gelegenheid van het driehonderd-jarig bestaan der Leidsche hoogeschool: Leiden 1875. pp.xx.108.viii.34.[xlii]. [1750.]
also published in two other issues, one independently (pp.iv.108), the other under the auspices of the Vereeniging ter bevordering van de belangen des boekhandels (pp.vi.107).

KARL FRIEDERICI, Bibliotheca orientalis, oder eine vollständige liste der im jahre ... in Deutschland, Frankreich, England und den colonien erschienenen bücher, ... u.s.w. über die sprachen, religionen, antiquitäten, literaturen, geschichte und geographie des ostens. London &c.
   1876. pp.86. [1727.]
   1877. pp.[iv].92. [1654.]
   1878. pp.[iv].108. [2084.]
   1879. pp.[iv].60. [966.]
   1880. pp.[iv].62. [1007.]
   1881. pp.[iv].76. [1301.]
   1882. pp.[iii].79. [1284.]
   1883. pp.[iv].83. [1573.]
also issued with english titlepages, except the last two issues, the titlepages of which are bi-lingual; no more published.

LIST of periodicals and publications received in the library of the Asiatic society of Bengal. Calcutta 1878. pp.6.[100.]

LITERATUR-BLATT für orientalische philologie. Unter mitwirkung von Johannes Klatt ... herausgegeben von Ernst Kuhn. Leipzig.
   i. 1883–1884. pp.[iv].476. [3000.]
   ii. 1884–1885. pp.[iv].406. [4898.]
   iii. 1885–1887. pp.iv.261.128. [4608.]
   iv. [1886]. pp.[ii].224. [3676.]
no more published; vol.iv contains an index to the whole.

ORIENTALISCHE bibliographie (Oriental bibliography). Berlin.
   i. [1887]. Herausgegeben von [Friedrich] A[ugust] Müller. 1888. pp.[iii].300. [4635.]
   ii. 1888. 1889. pp.[vi].419. [6318.]
   iii. 1889. 1890. pp.iv.304. [5409.]
   iv. 1890. 1891. pp.iv.298. [5436.]
   v. 1891. 1892. pp.iv.290. [5343.]
   vi. 1892. Herausgegeben von E[rnst Wilhelm Adalbert] Kuhn. 1893. pp.v.324. [5375.]
   vii. 1893. 1894. pp.vii.371. [6039.]
   viii. 1894. 1895. pp.vii.372. [6086.]
   ix. 1895. Herausgegeben von Lucian Scherman. 1896. pp.vii.388. [6282.]
   x. 1895 [sic, 1896]. 1897. pp.vii.318. [5639.]
   xi. 1897. 1898. pp.vii.322. [5510.]
   xii. 1898. 1899. pp.vii.326. [5489.]
   xiii. 1899. 1900. pp.viii.345. [5678.]
   xiv. 1900. 1901. pp.vii.381. [6203.]
   xv. 1901. 1902. pp.vii.335. [6136.]
   xvi. 1902. 1903. pp.ix.324. [5884.]
   xvii. 1903. 1904. pp.viii.361. [6595.]
   xviii. 1904. 1905. pp.x.385. [6774.]
   xix. 1905. 1906. pp.vii.376. [6705.]
   xx. 1906. 1908. pp.viii.385. [6821.]
   xxi. 1907. 1909. pp.iv.402. [7184.]
   xxii. 1908. 1910. pp.vii.330. [5955.]
   xxiii–xxiv. 1909–1910. 1912–1915. pp.vi.737. [13,155.]
   xxv. 1911. 1917–1922. pp.vi.427. [7307.]
   1926. 1928. pp.ii.82. [1352.]
no more published.

LUZAC AND CO's oriental list [Luzac's oriental list].
   i–lx. 1890–1949.
   lxi. 1950. pp.xii.98.x. [1500.]
   lxii. 1951. pp.xii.98.x. [1500.]
   lxiii. 1952. pp.xii.70.xii. [1000.]
   lxiv. 1953. pp.xii.72. [1000.]
   lxv. 1954. pp.x.66.viii. [1000.]
   lxvi. 1955. pp.x.82.xii. [1000.]
   lxvii. 1956. pp.x.76. [1000.]
   lxviii. 1957. pp.xi.74.xiii. [1000.]
   lxix. 1958. pp.92.xii. [1500.]
   lxx. 1959. pp.96. [1500.]
   lxxi. 1960. pp.80.xii. [1500.]

lxxii. 1961. pp.80.xii. [1500.]
lxxiii. 1962. pp.88.xii. [1500.]
lxxiv. 1963. pp.92.xii.[1750.]
in progress; originally a monthly, then a quarterly.

V[LADIMIR] I[ZMAILOVICH] MEZHOV, Библіографія Азіи, 2-я серія. Вся Азія, исключая Сибири. С.-Петербургъ 1891-1894. pp.[iii].ii. iii.230+[iii].ix.231-389+vii.257. [15,290.]

LUZAC & CO., Bibliographical list of books on Africa and the east published in England between . . . 1889, and . . . 1892. 1892. pp.79. [500.]

[HENRI AUGUSTE OMONT, *ed.*], Choix de manuscrits, d'imprimés, de cartes et de médailles exposés à l'occasion du Congrès des orientalistes. 1897. pp.[iii].98. [400.]

ORIENTALISTISCHE litteratur-zeitung [literaturzeitung]. Berlin [vols.xiii &c.: Leipzig].
  i. 1898. Edited by F[elix] E[rnst] Peiser. pp.vi.coll.411. [1000.]
  ii. 1899. pp.vi.coll.427. [1000.]
  iii. 1900. pp.vi.coll.479. [1000.]
  iv. 1901. pp.vi.coll.515. [1500.]
  v. 1902. pp.vii.coll.507. [1500.]
  vi. 1903. pp.vii.coll.519. [1500.]
  vii. 1904. pp.vi.coll.495. [1500.]
  viii. 1905. pp.vi.coll.584. [2000.]
  ix. 1906. pp.vi.coll.676. [2500.]
  x. 1907. pp.viii.coll.656. [2500.]
  xi. 1908. pp.viii.coll.564. [2500.]
  xii. 1909. pp.iv.coll.568. [2500.]
  xiii. 1910. pp.iv.coll.568. [2500.]
  xiv. 1911. pp.iv.coll.576. [2500.]
  xv. 1912. pp.iv.coll.576. [2500.]
  xvi. 1913. pp.iv.coll.576. [2500.]
  xvii. 1914. pp.iv.coll.512. [2000.]
  xviii. 1915. pp.iv.coll.384. [1000.]
  xix. 1916. pp.iv.coll.384. [1000.]
  xx. 1917. pp.iv.coll.384. [1000.]
  xxi. 1918. pp.iv.coll.304. [1000.]
  xxii. 1919. pp.iv.coll.288. [1000.]
  xxiii. 1920. pp.iv.coll.288. [1000.]
  xxiv. 1921. Edited by Walter Wreszinski pp.iv.coll.336. [1000.]
  xxv. 1922. pp.vi.coll.528. [2500.]
  xxvi. 1923. pp.vi.coll.632. [3000.]
  xxvii. 1924. pp.vi.coll.756. [4000.]
  xxviii. 1925. pp.x.coll.1028. [5000.]
  xxix. 1926. pp.x.coll.1044. [5000.]
  xxx. 1927. pp.xvi.coll.1152. [5000.]
  xxxi. 1928. pp.xvi.coll.1160. [5000.]
  xxxii. 1929. pp.xii.coll.960. [5000.]
  xxxiii. 1930. pp.xiv.coll.1084. [5000.]
  xxxiv. 1931. pp.xii.coll.1104. [5000.]
  xxxv. 1932. pp.x.coll.804. [4000.]
  xxxvi. 1933. pp.x.coll.772. [4000.]
  xxxvii. 1934. pp.x.coll.774. [4000.]
  xxxviii. 1935. Edited by Richard Hartmann. pp.x.coll.774.[4000.]

  xxxix. 1936. pp.x.coll.772. [4000.]
  xl. 1937. pp.ix.coll.772. [4000.]
  xli. 1938. pp.viii.coll.776. [4000.]
  xlii. 1939. pp.viii.coll.776. [4000.]
  xliii. 1940. pp.vi.coll.500. [3000.]
  xliv. 1941. pp.vi.coll.492. [3000.]
  xlv. 1942. pp.vi.coll.484. [3000.]
  xlvi. 1943. pp.vi.coll.492. [3000.]
  xlvii. 1944. pp.iv.coll.254. [1500.]
  xlviii. 1953. pp.vi.coll.558. [3500.]
  xlix. 1954. coll.562. [3500.]
  l. 1955. pp.vi.coll.562. [3500.]
  li. 1956. pp.vi.coll.562. [3500.]
  lii. 1957. pp.vi.coll.562. [3500.]
  liii. 1958. pp.vi.coll.594. [3500.]
  liv. 1959. pp.vi.coll.658. [4000.]
  lv. 1960. pp.vi.coll.658. [4000.]
  lvi. 1961. pp.vi.coll.658. [4000.]
  lvii. 1962. Edited by Fritz Hintze. pp.vi.coll. 658. [4000.]
  lviii. 1963. pp.vi.coll.626. [3750.]
  lix. 1964. pp.vi.coll.626. [3750.]
  lx. 1965. pp.vii.coll.630. [3800.]
  lxi. 1966. pp.vii.coll.622. [3700.]
  lxii. 1967. pp.vii.coll.622. [3700.]
  lxiii. 1968. pp.vii.coll.622. [3700.]
  lxiv. 1969. pp.vii. coll.622. [3700.]
  lxv. 1970. pp.vii.coll.620. [3700.]
  lxvi. 1970. pp.vii.coll.622. [3700.]
  lxvii. 1972. pp.vii.coll.622. [3700.]
in progress.

L'IMPRIMERIE hors l'Europe, par un bibliophile. Paris 1902. pp.[iii.]203. [3500.]

LIST of grammars, dictionaries,etc. of the languages of Asia, Oceania, Africa in the New York public library. New York 1909. pp.201. [6000.]

GIUSEPPE GABRIELI, Bibliografia degli studi orientalistici in Italia dal 1912 al 1934. Roma 1935. pp.xlviii.171. [2500.]

D. N. EGOROV, Библиография востока. Вып. I. История (1917-1925). Научная ассонцация востоковедения при ЦИК. СССР: Москва 1928. pp.[ii].300. [1510.]

U[PENDRA] N[ATH] GHOSHAL, Progress of greater indian research (1917-1942). (Afghanistan, central Asia, Tibet, Mongolia, Manchuria, Burma, Siam, Cambodia, Champa, Java, Bali, Borneo, Celebes, Sumatra, Malaya and Ceylon). Greater India society: Calcutta 1943. pp.[iii].viii.114.viii. [200.]

JOSEPH A. DAGHER [YŪSUF AS'AD DĀGHIR], L'orient dans la littérature française d'après guerre, 1919-1933. Beyrouth 1937. pp.[vi].xvii[*sic*, xviii]. 306. [5239.]

CHARLES ANDRÉ JULIEN, Renseignements bibliographiques et pratiques sur les arts et la civilisation de l'Inde, du Cambodge, de la Chine et du Japon. 1927. pp.19. [150.]

ROB[ERT] STREIT, Bibliotheca missionum. Vierter [–fünfter] band. Asiatische missionsliteratur 1245–1599 [–1699]. Internationales institut für missionswissenschaftliche forschung: Aachen 1928–1929. pp.24.626+24.1114. [5100.]
subsequent volumes of the series deal with individual parts of Asia.

ASIATICA. A monthly record of literature dealing with the east and with Africa.
  i. 1928. pp.318. [2000.]
  ii. (nos. 1–4). 1929. Edited by C[harles Hertel] Egerton. pp.[iii].250. [1500.]
no more published.

ANTONIO R. RODRÍGUEZ MOÑINO, Bibliografía hispano-oriental. Apuntes para un catálogo de los documentos referentes a Indias orientales . . . que se conservan en las colecciones de la Academia de la historia. Madrid 1931. pp.3–61. [153.]

Библиография востока. Bibliography of the Orient. Выпуск 1–6. Институт востоковедения: Академия наук СССР: Ленинград 1932–4. [large number.]
no more published.

[OLGA PINTO and LIONELLO LANCIOTTI], Contributo italiano alla conoscenza dell'oriente. Repertorio bibliografico dal 1935 al 1958. Commissione nazionale italiana per l'Unesco: Firenze (1962). pp.3–280. [4000.]

CUMULATIVE bibliography of asian studies 1941–1965. Association of asian studies. Boston.
  Author bibliography. 1969. pp.xi.716+724+788+766. [105,000.]
  Subject bibliography. 1970. pp.xvi.749+iv.752+iv.725+iv.734. [110,000.]
  — 1966–1970.
  Author bibliography. 1973. pp.viii.726+758+758. [61,000.]
  Subject bibliography. 1972. pp.xv.797+v.750+ix.738. [61,000.]
also published as annual volumes.
in progress.

ORIENT-LITERATUR in Deutschland und Österreich, 1945–1950. Westdeutsche bibliothek: Marburg [1950]. pp.46. [610.]

I. H. BAQAI, Books on Asia. Asian relations conference, march–april 1947: Indian council of world affairs: New Delhi [1947]. pp.[iii].111. [800.]

BERTOLD SPULER, Hinweise für das studium der orientalistik mit bibliographischen nachweisen. Notdrucke für universitäten: Wolfenbüttel-Hannover 1946. pp.16. [126.]

ASIEN-BIBLIOGRAPHIE. Asien-bücherei: Frankenau. (Bad Wildungen).*

i. 1949. [Edited by] Wilhelm Brandes. ff.18.16. [477.]
ii. 1950. ff.30.28.27.25. [1454.]
iii. 1951. ff.28.28.20.30. [1000.]
iv. 1952. ff.32.24.22.34.27. [1600.]
v. 1953.ff.27.28.23.31. [600.]
vi. 1954. ff.33.30.32.24. [740.]
vii. 1955. ff.26.24.34.27. [700.]
viii. 1956. ff.24.31.23.25. [750.]
ix. 1957. ff.29.27.38. [488.]
x. 1958. ff.33.22.31.34. [721.]
xi. 1959. ff.34.33.36.53. [1020.]
xii. 1960. ff.35.47.36. [799.]
xiii. 1961. ff.38.41.33.38. [831.]
xiv. 1962. ff.32.28.50. [661.]
xv. 1963. ff.25.55.42. [896.]
xvi. 1964. ff.53.32.31. [826.]
xvii. 1965. ff.39.37. [456.]
1966 volume not published.
xviii. 1967. ff.56.46. [639.]
xix. 1968. ff.32.43.38. [807.]
xx. 1969. ff.30.37.41. [830.]
xxi. 1970. ff.35.58.32. [955.]
xxii. 1971. ff.34.40.28. [788.]
xxiii. 1972. ff.30.33.35. [846.]
in progress.

SUPPLEMENT to the Consolidated list of publications in the ECAFE library. United nations: Economic commission for Asia and the far east: Bangkok.*
  1950.
  1951.
      [continued as:]
Asian bibliography.
  i. 1952. pp.[44]. [300.]
  ii. 1953. pp.[46]. [300.]
  iii. 1954. pp.[iii].iii.33. [200.]
  iv. 1955. pp.61. [500.]
  v. 1956. pp.58. [550.]
  vi. 1957. pp.63. [600.]
  vii. 1958. pp.88. [850.]
  viii. 1959. pp.86. [850.]
  ix. 1960. pp.v.47.vi.53. [900.]
  x. 1961. pp.v.42.v.42. [850.]
  xi. 1962. pp.v.37.v.40. [750.]
  xii. 1963. pp.v.38.v.36. [750.]
  xiii. 1964. pp. v.81. [800.]
  xiv. 1965. pp.vi.63.vi.65. [1200.]
  xv. 1966. pp.vi.54.vii.71. [1250.]
  xvi. 1967. pp.vi.70.vii.86. [1500.]
  xvii. 1968. pp.vi.79.vii.88. [1600.]
  xviii. 1969. pp.vii.73.ix.97. [1600.]
  xix. 1970. pp.vii.79.vii.88. [1600.]
  xx. 1971. pp.viii.87.vii.73. [1600.]
  xxi. 1972. pp.vii.78.vii.83. [1500.]

LIST [Monthly list] of titles added to the catalogue. University of London: School of oriental and african studies: Library: 1951 &c.*
in progress.

[VADIME ELISSEEFF], Bibliographie sommaire des ouvrages d'orientalisme en langue japonaise (parus entre 1938 et 1950). Maison franco-japonaise: Bulletin (n.s.i): Tōkyō 1952. pp.[ii].ii.219. [1500.]

BIBLIOGRAPHIA asiatica. Asien-bücherei: Frankenau Hessen (Bad Wildungen).*

   i. 1953. ff.12.13.16.16. [1500.]
   ii. 1954. ff.16.15.17.14. [1500.]
   iii. 1955. ff.12.15.13.13. [1250.]
   iv. 1956. ff.12.12.12.13. [1000.]
   v. 1957. ff.12.14.11.14. [1250.]
   vi. 1958. ff.13.11.13.13. [1000.]
   vii. 1959. ff.10.12.17. [500.]
   viii. 1960. ff.12.12.14. [500.]
   ix. 1961. ff.12.12.11.10. [750.]
   x. 1962. ff.11.13.
   xi. 1963. ff.10.16.12. [1130.]
   xii. 1964. ff.9.11.13. [948.]
no more published?

THE FAR EAST and south-east Asia. A cumulated list of periodical articles [of periodical articles on the far east, (south Asia) and south east Asia]. University of London: School of oriental and african studies: Library.*

   1954–1955. pp.vi.50. [900.]
   1955–1956. pp.vi.80. [1250.]
   1956–1957. pp.[xiii].122. [2000.]
   1957–1958. pp.xvi.126. [2000.]
the annual cumulations are set out here; first issued under the title of Monthly list of periodical articles on the far east [&c.]

L. KING QUAN [LAO–CHING KUAN], Introduction to Asia. A selective guide to background reading. Library of Congress: Reference department: Washington 1955. pp.x.214. [811.]

W[ILLIAM] A[RTHUR] C[HARLES] H[ARVEY] DOBSON, *ed.* A select list of books on the civilization of the orient. Prepared by the Association of british orientalists. Oxford 1955. pp.xii.80. [1000.]

BOOKS and articles on oriental subjects published in Japan. Tōhōgakkai: [Tokyo].

   [i] 1954. pp.41. [500.]
   [ii.] 1955. pp.50. [800.]
   [iii.] 1956. pp.49. [800.]
   [iv.] 1957. pp.48. [370.]
   [v.] 1958. pp.ii.69. [480.]
   [vi.] 1959. pp.73. [700.]
   vii. 1960. pp.96. [800.]
   viii. 1961. pp.114. [700.]
   ix. 1962. pp.138. [800.]
   x. 1963. pp.132. [1200.]
   xi. 1964. pp.160. [1900.]
   xii. 1965. pp.184. [2000.]
   xiii. 1966. pp.210. [2200.]
   xiv. 1967. pp.233. [2400.]
   xv. 1968. pp.228. [2400.]
   xvi. 1969. pp.221. [2400.]
   xvii. 1970. pp.229. [2400.]
   xviii. 1971. pp.233. [2400.]

BIBLIOGRAPHIE de l'orientalisme japonais, rédigée par la Société franco-japonaise des études orientales sous la direction de Ishida Mikinosuke. Tokyo, Paris.

   1955 (premier semestre). 1958. pp.vi.56. [340.]
   1955 (suite)—1956.1962. pp.ii.151. [559.]

P. K. GARDE, Directory of reference works published in Asia. Répertoire des ouvrages de référence publiés en Asie. Unesco bibliographical handbooks (5): Paris 1956. pp.xxvii.139. [1619.]

A SELECT bibliography of books, films, filmslides, records and exhibitions about Asia. United States national commission for Unesco: Washington 1957. pp.vi.47. [393.]

G[ALINA] P[ETROVNA] BOGATOVA, Освоим природные богатства Сибири и Дальнего Востока. Беседа о книгах. Государственная ... библиотека СССР имени В. И. Ленина: За новые нспехи в шестой пятилетке: Москва 1956. pp.30. [50.]

WIESLAW KOTAŃSKI and BARBARA MAJEWSKA, Bibliografia polskich prac orientalistycznych (1945–1955). Polska akademia nauk: Komitet orientalistyczny: Warszawa 1957. pp.92. [707.]

DOCUMENTS on asian affairs. Select bibliography. Indian council of world affairs [ii &c.: and Indian school of international studies]: Bibliographical series (no. 5 &c.): New Delhi.*

   i. 1957.... (no.5). ff.[i].ix.150. [1250.]
   ii. 1957.... (no.9). ff.[i].iii.ix.174. [2000.]
   iii. 1958.... (no.7). ff.[i].xii. pp.236. [4000.]
   iv. 1959.... (no.8). ff.[i].xix. pp.280. [3500.]
   vi. 1960....

REPERTORIO delle attività italiane intese a promuovere e diffondere la conoscenza della civiltà orientale. Commissione nazionale italiana [per la Unesco]: Progetto maggiore sul mutuo apprezzamento dei valori culturali dell'oriente e dell'occidente: Roma 1958. ff.[359]. [4000.]*

E[KATERINA] I[VANOVA] ARSENTEVA, Путешественники исследователи Азии. Рекомендательный указатель литературы для учащихся 6–8 классов. Государственная ... публичная библиотека имени М. Е. Салтыкова-Щедрина: Ленинград 1958. pp.44. [70.]

JACQUELINE SENNY, Contributions à l'appréciation des valeurs culturelles de l'orient: traductions françaises de littératures orientales. Commission belge de bibliographie: Bibliographia belgica (no.37): Bruxelles 1958. pp.300. [2466.]

STEFAN STRELCYN and BARBARA RUSZCZYC, Pismo i ksǎżka orientalne. Katalog wystawy. Polski komitet do spraw Unesco: Grupa robocza projektu "Wschód-Zachód": Warszawa 1958. pp.76. [431.]

HYMAN KUBLIN, An introductory reading guide to Asia. The Asia society: New York 1958. pp. [iii].21. [115.]
— Revised edition. 1959. pp.24. [145.]

ASIA: a selected list of books dealing with Asia or written by asians which are currently available for loan from the city of Sydney public library. Sydney 1959. ff.2.76. [1500.]*

QUARTERLY check-list of oriental studies: an international index of current books, monographs, brochures & separates. American bibliographic service: East Northport 1959 &c.*
  i. 1959. pp.62. [676.]
  ii. 1960. pp.62. [723.]
  iii. 1961. pp.75. [859.]
  iv. 1962. pp.63. [770.]
  v. 1963. pp.71. [901.]
  vi. 1964. pp.62. [774.]
  vii. 1965. pp.70. [851.]
  viii. 1966. pp.76. [922.]
  ix. 1967. pp.68. [823.]
  x. 1968. pp.68. [850.]
reprint of vols. 1–10, 1959–68, New York, London, 1971.

U.S.S.R. Academy of sciences. Institute of oriental studies. Books published in 1957. Moscow 1959. pp.109. [26.]

BALDOON DHINGRA, Vie et pensée de l'Asie. Bibliographie pour la jeunesse. Bruxelles 1959. pp.56. [185.]

BALDOON DHINGRA, A guide to asian life and thought for young people. An annotated bibliography. World assembly of youth: Brussels 1959. pp.46. [200.]

RICHER by Asia. A selected bibliography of books and other materials for promoting west-east understanding among young adults. American library association: Chicago 1959. pp.vii.64. [100.]

ASIA and Africa. A select bibliography for schools. University of London: School of oriental and african studies: [1960]. pp.15. [105.]
— Second edition. [1963.] pp.18. [158.]

PARKER WORLEY, Asia today. A bibliography. Trenton state college: Roscoe L. West library: [Trenton] 1960. ff.[i].35. [300.]*

S. M. VOYAKINA, Страны Азии. Рекомендательный указатель литературы. Государственная библиотека СССР имени В. И. Ленина: Москва 1960. pp.137. [600.]

V. MACHWE, ed. Documentation on Asia. Indian council of world affairs and Indian school of international studies: New Delhi 1960 &c.
  i.
  ii.
  iii. 1962.1969.pp.ix.461. [4633.]*
in progress.

A SELECT bibliography: Asia, Africa, eastern Europe, Latin America. American universities field staff: New York 1960. pp.ix.536. [Asia: 2748.]
— Supplement 1961. pp.iv.76. [Asia: 122.]
— — 1963. pp.iv.68. [Asia: 172.]
— — 1965. pp.iv.82. [Asia: 181.]
— — 1967. pp.iv.80. [Asia: 157.]
— — 1969. pp.[iv.]98. [Asia: 219.]
— — 1971. pp.[iv.]90. [Asia: 263.]

ANNE G. BLANKINSHIP, A bibliography of juvenile holdings in the Library of Congress in classifications DS (history of Asia), DS 5–DS 902. Catholic university of America: Washington 1961. ff.[ii].96. [226.]*

G. M. WICKENS, ed. Book list on Asia including parts of Africa for Canadians. Canadian national commission for UNESCO: Ottawa [1961]. pp.xiv.46. [500.]

Литература о странах Азии и Африки. Ежегодник. Акабемия наук СССР: Институт народов Азии: Москва.
  1961.1964. pp.224. [3378.]
  1962. 1965. pp.276. [3824.]
  1963. 1967. pp.268. [3698.]

Литература о странах Азии, Африки и Океании. 1964–1966 гг. Академия наук СССР *and* Ииститут научной информации и Фундаментальная библиотека общественных наук *and* Институт востоковедения: Москва 1972. pp.520. [8077.]

A. N. KONONOVA, ed. Литература на языках стран Азии и Африки. Аннотированный каталог новых поступлений, 1959. Академия наук СССР: Библиотека [&c.]: Ленинград 1962. pp.432. [1750.]

Новая советская и иностранная литература по странам зарубежного востока. Фундаментальная библиотека общественных наук им. В. П. Волгина: Москва.*
  1961. pp.243.268.206.215.221.183.195.225. 190.184.195.178. [24,551.]
  1962. pp.162.169.184.197.220.242.170.181. 216.187.206.193. [25,037.]
  1963. pp.205.199.212.247.172.158.277.218. 184.181.200.185. [28,113.]
  [continued as:]

Новая советская и иностранная литература
по странам Азии и Африки.

    1964.   pp.186.156.184.203.208.180.187.184.
       169.189.186.217. [26,191.]
    1965.   pp.182.231.214.228.164.212.197.215.
       164.190.207. [25,973.]
    1966.   pp.184.216.164.163.149.179.163.179.
       183.171.180.188. [27,944.]
    1967.   pp.166.169.172.163.168.159.144.156.
       178.180.220.233. [27,018.]
    1968.   pp.184.210.189.181.177.227.210.205.
       212.212.227.226. [30,222.]
        [*continued as:*]
Новая литература по странам Азии и
Африки.
   and divided into three sections: General works;
Africa, Near and middle east; South and south-east
Asia; Far east.

    1969.   pp.20.91.89+18.97.91+27.102.115+
      20.94.107 + 21.95.103 + 19.84.81 + 19.89.
      103 + 22.112.138 + 20.78.99 + 25.99.95
      +23.109.118 + 23.102.105. [32,986.]
    1970.   pp.16.93.110 + 20.111.123 + 27.103.
      126 + 35.100.131 + 30.97.118 + 30.105.
      133 + 42.141.114 + 31.112.120 + 19.107.
      119 + 26.107.115 + 34.119.139 + 28.109.
      140. [39,043.]
    1971.   pp.26.100.109 + 33.130.137. + 27.107.
      129 + 36.103.124 + 29.117.131 + 18.92.
      93 + 22.118.138 + 17.112.144 + 26.101.
      139 + 24.111.129 + 14.84.113 + 20.104.
      116. [41,179.]
    1972.   pp.17.85.135 + 29.101.109 + 15.77.
      118 + 18.90.128. + 24.102.137 + 24.91.107
      + 29.102.134 + 32.158.181 + 15.96.117+
      21.102.135 + 16.86.126. [31,430.]
in progress.

RENÉ FAYT, Les civilisations afro-asiatiques. Sug-
gestions bibliographiques particulièrement destinées au personnel enseignant. Commission nationale belge de l'Unesco: [Brussels 1963]. pp.91.
[299.]

I. M. AKSELROD and E. R. BOCHKAREVA, Художественная литература зарубежного Востока. Библиография переводов на языки
народов СССР, 1918–1960. Академия наук
СССР: Институт народов Азии: Москва
1963. pp.132. [2200.]

EVE APOR and HILDA ECSEDY, Hungarian
publications on Asia and Africa 1950–1962; a
selected bibliography. Library of the Hungarian
academy of sciences. East-west committee of the
Hungarian national commission for Unesco:
Budapest 1963. pp.106. [Asia: 717.]

A SURVEY of japanese bibliographies concerning
asian studies. Centre for east asian cultural studies:
Tokyo 1963. pp.[iii].200.xvii. [1000.]

W[ILLIA]M THEODORE DE BARY and AINSLEE
THOMAS EMBREE, *edd.* A guide to oriental classics.
New York 1964. pp.xi.199. [800.]

DEUTSCHE übersetzungen asiatischer, orientalischer und afrikanischer autoren. Verzeichnis der
seit 1955 erschienenen werke. Deutsche bibliothek
in Frankfurt a. M.: 1964. pp.46. [450.]

EUROPE informed. An exhibition of early books
which acquainted Europe with the east. Sixth
international colloquium on luso-brazilian studies:
[Boston] 1966. pp.x.192. [242.]

AINSLIE T. EMBREE [*and others*]. A guide to paper-
backs on Asia, selected and annotated. Asia
society: New York 1964. pp.iv.i.89. [550.]
— Supplement. 1966. pp.iv.18. [225.]

G[ODFREY] RAYMOND NUNN, Resources for
research on Asia at the university of Hawaii and in
Honolulu. Occasional papers (no.1) of East-west
library, East-west center: University of Hawaii:
Honolulu 1965.

MICHAEL FODOR, The east. Books in western
languages. International federation of library
associations: London 1965. pp.8.107. [287.]
title also in french and spanish.

AINSLIE T. EMBREE [*and others*], Asia; a guide to
basic books. Asia society: [New York] 1966. pp.
[vi].57. [300.]

O[LGA] E[MANUILOVNA] LIVOTOVA and V[ILEN]
B[ORISOVICH] PORTUGAL, Востоковедение в
изданиах Академии наук 1726–1917. Библиография. Академия наук СССР: Институт
народов Азии: Москва 1966. pp.144. [1813.]

CYNTHIA T. MOREHOUSE, Paperbound books on
Asia. (Sixth revised edition in print, September,
1965). Newsletter of the Association for asian
studies (vol.xi, supplement no.1): Ann Arbor
1966. pp.v.114. [3000.]*

J[AMES] D[OUGLAS] PEARSON, Oriental and
asian bibliography; an introduction with some
reference to Africa. London 1966. pp.xvii.261.
[332.]

A SELECTED bibliography of books, films, filmslides, records, and exhibitions about Asia. United
States national commission for the United nations
educational, scientific and cultural organisation:
Washington 1967. pp.v.47. [500.]

AINSLIE T. EMBREE, *ed.*, Asia; a guide to paper-
backs. Revised edition. Asia society: New York
1968. pp.iii.178. [1000.]

MILLI BAU, Asien: ein wegweiser durch das
schrifttum. München 1967. pp.95. [450.]

YA. YA. BYCHKOV, Книги главной редакции восточной литературы издательства "Наука" 1957–1966; аннотированный каталог. Москва 1968. pp.304. [1325.]

FRIEDMAR GEISSLER, Die veröffentlichungen des Instituts für orientforschung und seiner mitarbeiter. Berlin 1968. pp.40. [565.]

MILTON W. MEYER, Asia: an introductory bibliography. Third edition, revised. Los Angeles 1968. pp.iii.75. [3000.]★
— Fourth edition, revised. 1971. pp.[iv].21. [600.]★

WINSTON L. Y. YANG and TERESA S. YANG, Asian resources in american libraries; essays and bibliographies. Occasional publication (no.9): Foreign area materials center: University of the state of New York: New York 1968. pp.viii.122. [650.]★

JEAN MULLER and ERNST ROTH, Aussereuropäische druckereien im 16 jahrhundert; bibliographie der drucke. Bibliotheca bibliographica aureliana (xxii): Baden-Baden 1969. pp.176. [Asia: 117.]

ELEAZAR BIRNBAUM, Books on Asia from the near east to the far east; a guide for the general reader. Toronto [1971]. pp.xv.341. [2000.]

G[ODFREY] RAYMOND NUNN, Asia: a selected and annotated guide to reference works. Cambridge, Mass. and London 1971. pp.xiii.233. [966.]

ORIENTALICA published in Poland. Polish society for oriental studies. Warsaw [1972?]. pp.70. [107.]

HANS-JÜRGEN CWIK, Deutschsprächige publikationen des jahres 1969 über Asien und Ozeanien. Publications of 1969 on Asia and Oceania in german language. Documentatio Asiae (no.1): Institut für asienkunde: Dokumentationsleitstelle: Hamburg 1971. pp.[iii.]ii.70. [571.]★

ii. *Academic writings*

COLUMBIA university masters' essays and doctoral dissertations on Asia 1875–1956. East asiatic library: Columbia university libraries: New York 1957. pp.[iv].ii. 96. [1500.]★

THE UNIVERSITY of Chicago doctoral dissertations and masters' theses on Asia, 1894–1962. University of Chicago: Library: Far eastern library: Chicago [1962.]. pp.[ii].iv.52. [630.]★

CURTIS W. STUCKI, American doctoral dissertations on Asia, 1933–1962, including appendix of master's theses at Cornell university. Cornell university: Southeast program: Data paper (no.50): Ithaca, N.Y. 1963. pp.204.

DONN V. HART, An annotated bibliography of theses and dissertations on Asia accepted at Syracuse university 1907–1963. Syracuse university library: Syracuse 1964. pp.xii.46. [161.]

EXTERNAL research: Asia (studies in progress). A list of current social science research by private scholars and academic centers. External research staff (Office of external research): U.S. Department of state: Washington.
　　ER 2.22—1964. pp.[iv].83. [900.]★
　　　2.25—1966. pp.[v].124. [1200.]★
　　　2.26—1967. pp.iv.84. [1600.]★
　　　2.27—1968. pp.iv.117. [1700.]★
no more published.

B[ARRY] C[AMBRAY] BLOOMFIELD, Theses on Asia accepted by universities in the United Kingdom and Ireland 1877–1964. London 1967. pp.xi.127. [2571.]

CURTIS W. STUCKI, American doctoral dissertations on Asia, 1933–June 1966, including appendix of master's theses at Cornell university 1933–June 1968. Cornell university: Southeast Asia program: Data paper (no.71): Ithaca N.Y. 1968. pp.vii.304. [3689.]★

THÈSES & mémoires relatifs au tiers monde (moins l'Afrique). Faculté de droit et des sciences économiques de Paris: Centre de documentiaton africaine.★
　　1968. ff.30. [150.]
　　1969. ff.34. [200.]
in progress.

ENID BISHOP, Australian theses on Asia. A union list of higher degree theses accepted by Australian universities to 31 December 1970. Occasional paper (12). Faculty of asian studies: Australian national university: Canberra 1972. pp.[iv].iv.35. [306.]

Докторские и кандидатские диссертации защищенные в Институте востоковедения Академии наук СССР с 1950 по 1970 гг. Москва 1972. pp.244. [754.]★

iii. *Periodicals*

M. LEWICKI [*and others*], Katalog czasopism i wydawnictw ciągłych orjentalistycnych znajdujących się w Polsce. Lwów 1933. pp.[x].66. [420.]★

PERIODICALS received in the library. International labour office: Bibliographical reference list (no.41): Geneva 1951. pp.5. [91.]
limited to the periodicals of Asia.

LIST of scientific & other periodicals published in the indo-pacific area. 2nd edition. Indo-pacific fisheries council: Bangkok 1953. pp.50. [400.]

[SERGE ELISSEEFF, *ed.*], Huit cents revues d'Asie. Bibliothèque nationale: Département des périodiques and Commission de la République française pour l'Unesco: 1960. pp.[ii].208. [800.]

ROGER PÉLISSIER and DANIELLE LE NAN, 2,000 revues d'Asie. Sous la direction de Serge Elisséeff. Maison des sciences de l'homme: Paris 1964. pp.xiii.477. [2263.]★

CHECK-LIST of periodicals currently received. ECAFE library: Bibliographical bulletin (no.2): Revision 1. Bangkok 1965. pp.[i].128.

S. S. BULATOV, *ed.*, Периодические издания стран Азии и Африки. Катапог фондов Библиотеки Академии наук СССР и Государственной публичной библиотеки им. М. Е. Саптыкова-Щедрина (физикоматематические, естественные и технические науки). Ордена трудового красного знамени библиотека Академии наук СССР. Ленинград 1967.

ASIEN und Ozeanien behandelnde zeitschriften und ihre bestände in bibliotheken der Bundesrepublik Deutschland (ZGV Asien); zusammengestellt und als manuskript gedruckt vom Institut für asienkunde, Dokumentations-leitstelle. Hamburg 1970. pp.iv.181. [1605.]

PERIODICALS in asian studies in the University of British Columbia library. Prepared by Asian studies division. List of catalogued books: supplement (no.2): Reference publication (no.22): Vancouver 1967. pp.91. [900.]★
— [Another edition.] Supplement (no.2a). 1971. ff.[iii].pp.158. [2200.]★

LIST of current serials received from Asia. National lending library for science and technology: Boston Spa [1967]. pp.48. [2800.]★

FRITZ FEUEREISEN and ERNST SCHMACKE, Die presse in Asien und Ozeanien; ein handbuch für wirtschaft und werbung. München-Pullach 1968. pp.303. [Asia:538.]

INDEX indo-asiaticus. Edited by S. Chandhuri. Calcutta (New Delhi).
   i. 1968. pp.[vi].24.16.8.
   ii. 1968. pp.[viii].48.
   iii. 1968. pp.[viii]. 80.
   iv. 1968. pp.44.
   v. 1969. pp.104.
   vi. 1969. pp.28.viii.
   vii. 1969. pp.iv.76.
   viii. 1969. pp.48.
   ix. 1970. pp.[x].48.36.
   x.
   xi.
   xii. 1970. pp.84.
   xiii–xiv. 1971. pp.112.
each issue contains contents lists of a varying number of orientalist journals, with other bibliographical material.

iv. *Library catalogues*

[ANDREAS MÜLLER], Catalogus librorum sinicorum Bibliothecæ electoralis brandenburgicæ [Andreæ Mülleri Greiffenhagii]. [Cologne 1683]. pp.[6].[150.]
not limited to chinese books.

CHARLES STEWART, A descriptive catalogue of the oriental library of the late Tippoo sultan of Mysore. Cambridge 1809. pp.[iii].viii.96.364. [750.]

U[LRICH] J[ASPER] SEETZEN, Verzeichniss der für die orientalische sammlung in Gotha zu Damask, Jerusalem u.s.w. angekauften orientalischen manuscripte und gedruckten werke. Leipzig 1810. pp.20.27.40.

[W. MARSDEN], Bibliotheca marsdeniana philologica et orientalis. A catalogue of books and manuscripts collected with a view to the general comparison of languages, and to the study of oriental literature, by William Marsden. 1827. pp.[iii].310. [6000.]

CATALOGUE of the printed books in the Royal asiatic society's library. 1830. pp.76.23. [678.]

каталогъ книгамъ, рукописемъ и картамъ, на китайскомъ, маньчжурскомъ, монгольскомъ, тибетскомъ и санскритскомъ языкахъ, находящимся вь библіотекѣ Азіятскаго департамента. Санкшетербургъ 1843–1844. pp.[iv].102+[ii].69.13. [1100.]

[BERNHARD DORN and REINHOLD ROST], Catalogue des manuscrits et xylographies orientaux de la Bibliothèque impériale publique. St. Pétersbourg 1852. pp.[ii].xliv.719. [901.]
300 copies printed.

CATALOGUE of books in the Astor library relating to the languages and literature of Asia, Africa and the oceanic islands. New York 1854. pp.[viii].424.[1500.]★
the preface is dated 1855.

[ALOYS SPRENGER], A catalogue of the Bibliotheca orientalis sprengeriana. Giessen 1857. pp.vii.111. [1972.]
the collection was acquired by the Preussische staatsbibliothek, Berlin.

INDEX librorum orientalium et latinorum Publicae bibliothecae melitensis. Melitae 1857. pp.[iii].253. [oriental: 150.]

JULES THONNELIER, Catalogue de la bibliothèque d'un orientaliste. ... Tome Ier. 1864. pp.xi.318. [1857.]
no more published.

CATALOGUE de la bibliothèque orientale de feu M. J. Mohl. Paris 1876. pp.xv.192.

CATALOGUE de la bibliothèque orientale de feu M. Jules Thonnelier. Paris 1880. pp.viii.564. [4200.]

[FRIEDRICH AUGUST MÜLLER], Katalog der bibliothek der Deutschen morgenländischen gesellschaft. Leipzig 1880–1881. pp.xvi.216+84. [1300.]
— — Zweite auflage. Erster band. Drucke. ... Bearbeitet von R[ichard] Pischel, A. Fischer, G. Jacob. 1900. pp.xviii.726. [10,000.]

WALTER ARNOLD BION, Catalogue of the library of the Asiatic society of Bengal. Calcutta 1884. pp.[ii].418. [7500.]

CATALOGUE of the library of the Royal asiatic society. 1893. pp.viii.537. [10,000.]
— — [Another edition]. Catalogue of printed books published before 1932 in the library of the Royal asiatic society. 1940. pp.vii.542. [20,000.]

E. LAMBRECHT, Catalogue de la bibliothèque de l'École des langues orientales vivantes. Tome premier. Linguistique. I. Philologie. II. Langue arabe. École des langues orientales vivantes: Publications (4th ser., vol.i): 1897. pp.xi.623. [oriental languages: 337.]

[R. HANITSCH], Catalogue of the Rost collection in the Raffles library. Singapore 1897. pp.[iv].47. [900.]

TIELE'S KAMER. Lijst der boeken uit de nalatenschap van ... C. P. Tiele. Rijks-universiteit: Bibliotheek: Leiden 1902. pp.vi.135. [2000.]

[GEORGE S. A.] RANKING, Catalogue of books in oriental languages in the library of the Board of examiners. Calcutta 1903. pp.[v].37.[ii].25.[ii].25. [ii].19.[ii].10.[ii].14.[ii].3.[1500.]
— — Index 1905. pp.[ii].54.

G. P. ROUFFAER and W. C. MULLER, Catalogus der koloniale bibliotheek van het Kon. instituut voor de taal-, land- en volkenkunde van Ned. Indië en het Indisch genootschap. 's-Gravenhage 1908. pp.ix.1053. [15,000.]
— — Eerste supplement. Door W. C. Muller. 1915. pp.viii.426. [6000.]
— — Tweede supplement. 1927. pp.viii.459. [6500.]
— — Derde supplement. 1937. pp.viii.438. [6000.]
— — Vierde supplement. 1966. pp.ix.801. [11,000.]
— — Vijfde supplement. 1972. pp.xi.728. [10,000.]

A CATALOGUE of printed books in european languages in the library of the Asiatic society of Bengal. Calcutta 1908–1910. pp.[ii].195+[ii]. 197–380+[ii].381–523+[ii].525–664. [12,500.]

BERLINER titeldrucke. Verzeichnis der von der Königlichen bibliothek zu Berlin und den preussischen universitätsbibliotheken erworbenen neueren druckschriften. [C.] Orientalische titel. Berlin.
    1910. pp.[ii].125. [922.]
    1911. pp.[ii].89. [805.]
    1912. pp.[ii].91. [609.]
    1913. pp.[ii].50. [330.]
    1914. pp.[ii].38. [249.]
    1915–1916. [not published.]
    1917. no.1. pp.16. [119.]
    1918. [not published.]
    1919. no.1. pp.24. [199.]
    1920. [not published.]
    1921. no.1/2. pp.50. [605.]
    — Register, 1917–1921. pp.11.
no more published.

[WALTER GOTTSCHALK], Katalog der handbibliothek der orientalischen abteilung. Preussische staatsbibliothek [Berlin]: Leipzig 1929. pp.xiii.573. [4300.]

CATALOGUE de la bibliothèque de feu Clément Huart dans la bibliothèque de l'université de Taihoku. Bibliographia taihokuana (no.1): Taiwan 1929. pp.[iii].153. [2000.]

ELIZABETH STROUT, Catalogue of the library of the American oriental society. Yale university: Library: New Haven 1930. pp.vii.308. [5000.]

LIBRARY catalogue of the Geographical association: Asia. Geographical association: Sheffield 1955. pp.44. [700.]

MATERIALS on the Pacific area in selected libraries of the Los Angeles region; a second checklist. Claremont colleges library: Claremont, Calif.*
    i. Books in western languages, including bound pamphlets and maps. 1943. ff.iii. pp.ii.ff.2–286.
    ii. Periodicals and serials in thirty-six California libraries. 1944. ff.ii.pp.ii.ff.2–86. [1500.]
    iii. Books in chinese and japanese languages. ff.iii.pp.ii.ff.2–63. [500.]
a preliminary checklist was published in 1939.

ZUGANGSVERZEICHNIS der bibliothek der Deutschen morgenländischen gesellschaft, dezember 1931–mai 1934. pp.112. [1800.]

DICTIONARY catalog of the oriental collection in the New York public library, Reference department: Boston 1960. 16 vols. pp.iv. 15,166. [318,000 cards.]

CATALOGUE presenting our holdings in the sixteenth imprints with the principal rare acquisitions in 1961. Exhibited in commemoration of the 31st anniversary of Tenri central library. Tenri 1961. pp.35. [188.]

RESEARCH catalogue of the American geographical society [New York]. Asia. Boston 1962. pp.xx.8461–9072+[ii].9073–9678. [25,551.] *this is a photographic reproduction of catalogue cards; the figure in square brackets refers to these cards.*

Новая советская и иностранная литература по странам зарубежного востока, Москва 1961–3.

[*continued as:*]

Новая советская и иностранная литература по странам Азии и Африки. 1964–8.

[*continued as:*]

Новая литература по страиам Азии и Африки. [divided into three series, general works; Africa, near and middle east; south and south-east Asia, far east.]

in progress, details given at cols. 52–3 supra.

LIBRARY catalogue of the School of oriental and african studies, university of London. Authors. Boston 1963.

 i. A–Bof. pp.[iv].973. [20,000.]
 ii. Bog–Enm. pp.[ii].967. [20,000.]
 iii. Enn–Imo. pp.[ii].942. [24,000.]
 iv. Imp–Ly. pp.[ii].938. [20,080.]
 v. M–Nuo. pp.[ii].914. [20,000.]
 vi. Nur–Sal. pp.[ii].948. [20,000.]
 vii. Sam–Tonf. pp.[ii].911. [10,000.]
 viii. Tong–Z. pp.[ii].775. [16,000.]
 — Titles.
 ix. A–Dh. pp.[ii].909. [19,000.]
 x. Di–Iq. pp.[ii].873. [20,000.]
 xi. Ir–Nota. pp.[ii].892. [19,000.]
 xii. Note–Shy. pp.[ii].805. [17,000.]
 xiii. Si–Z. pp.[ii].771. [16,000.]
 — Subjects.
 xiv. General. pp.[ii].753. [16,000.]
 xv. Africa. pp.[ii].618. [13,000.]
 xvi. Middle east, A–Iran. pp.[ii].844. [18,000.]
 xvii. Middle east, Iraq–Z. pp.[ii].696. [14,000.]
 xviii. South Asia, A–Indian. pp.[ii].568. [12,000.]
 xix. South Asia, Indo–Z. pp.[ii].829. [17,000.]
 xx. South east Asia and the Pacific is. pp.[ii]. 535. [11,000.]
 xxi. Far east pp.[ii].558. [11,000.]
 —Manuscripts and microfilms.
 xxii. pp.1–83. [231.]
 —Chinese catalogue.
 xxiii. Titles, A–Let. pp.[ii].646. [13,500.]
 xxiv. Titles, Li–Z. pp.[ii].664. [14,000.]
 xxv. Authors, A–Liu(J). pp.[ii].819. [17,000.]
 xxvi. Authors, Liu (K)–Z. pp.[ii].744. [16,000.]
 xxvii. Subjects. pp.994. [21,000.]
 — Japanese catalogue.
 xxviii. A–Z. pp.760. [16,000.]
 — First supplement. 1968.

Author catalogue.
 i. A–Ha. pp.iv.668. [14,000.]
 ii. He–Perin. pp.655. [14,000.]
 iii. Periodicals–Z. Catalogue of manuscripts and microfilms. pp.690. [13,500.]
Title index.
 iv. A–G. pp.701. [15,000.]
 v. H–O. pp.637. [13,000.]
 vi. P–Z. pp.710. [15,000.]
Subject catalogue.
 vii. General. pp.318. [7,000.]
 viii. Africa. pp.540. [11,000.]
 ix. Middle East. pp.609. [13,000.]
 x. South Asia. pp.570. [12,000.]
 xi. South-east Asia and Pacific islands. pp.234.
 xii. Far east. pp.285. [6000.]
Chinese catalogue.
 xiii. Authors. A–Ling. pp.598. [12,500.]
 xiv. — Lin–Yu. pp.608. [13,000.]
 xv. Titles. A–Z. pp.568.368. [20,000.]
 xvi. Subjects. Japanese catalogue. pp.718. [15,000.]
— Second supplement. 1973.
Author catalogue.
 i.
 ii.
 iii.
Title index.
 iv. A–G. pp.865. [18,000.]
 v. H–O. pp.834. [17,500.]
 vi. P–Z. pp.940. [20,000.]
Subject catalogue.
 vii. General. pp.622. [13,000.]
 viii. Africa. pp.652. [14,000.]
 ix. Near and middle east. A–Ir. pp.441. [9000.]
 x. — Is–Z. pp.463. [10,000.]
 xi. South Asia. pp.587. [12,000.]
 xii. South-east Asia.
 xiii. Far east.
this is a photographic reproduction of catalogue cards; the figures in square brackets refer to these cards.

LESLEY FORBES, Catalogue of books printed between 1500 and 1599 in the library of the School of oriental and african studies. 1968. pp.ix.193. [360.]*

DAVID E. HALL, *ed.*, Union catalogue of asian publications 1965–1970. School of oriental and african studies: University of London. 1971. pp.xi.596+602+602+612. [77,400.]*

— — 1971 supplement. 1973. pp.704. [20,000.]*

v. *Cartography*

A CATALOGUE of maps of the british possessions in India and other parts of Asia. Published by order of her majesty's Secretary of state for India in council. 1870. pp.60. [400.]

— — [another edition]. 1874. pp.20. [600.]

ELENCO dei documenti orientali e delle carte nautiche e geographiche che si conservano negli archivi di stato di Firenze e di Pisa. R. soprintendenza degli archivi toscani: Firenze 1878. pp.32. [maps: 16.]

[J. L. POWER], Catalogue of maps in the Intelligence division, War office. . . . Vol.II. Asia. 1890. pp.[v].307. [2000.]

ASIA, Australia, and the Pacific map catalog. Army map service: Washington [1954]. *consists largely of key-maps.*

TULLIA GASPARRINI LEPORACE, Mostra "L'Asia nella cartografia degli occidentali." Catalogo descrittivo. Comune di Venezia: VII centenario della nascita di Marco Polo: [Venice 1954]. pp.[vi].96. [86.]

vi. Films

VIOLET M. BELL and others, A guide to films, filmstrips, maps & globes, records on Asia, selected and annotated. Asia society: [New York] 1964. pp.ii.87. [251.]
— Supplement, including a new section on slides. Leonard W. Ingraham and others. 1967. pp.[iv].i.64. [574.]

WINIFRED HOLMES, Orient: a survey of films produced in countries of arab and asian culture. British film institute: Unesco 1959. pp.[184.] [348.]

FILMS on Asia available in Canada. Canadian film institute and National film board of Canada: Ottawa 1959. pp.23. [286.]

VIOLET M. BELL and others, A guide to films, filmstrips, maps & globes, records on Asia, selected and annotated. Asia society: [New York] 1964. pp.ii.87. [251.]
— Supplement, including a new section on slides. Leonard W. Ingraham and others. 1967. pp.[iv].i.64. [574.]

viii. Subjects

Anthropology

SEIICHI IZUMI, Cultural anthropology in Japan, by the Committee for the publication of cultural anthropological studies in Japan. Tokyo 1967. pp.vi.112. [587.]

Art

CHARLES ANDRÉ JULIEN, Renseignements bibliographiques et pratiques sur les arts et la civilisation de l'Inde, du Cambodge, de la Chine et du Japon. 1927. pp.19. [150.]

BENJAMIN ROWLAND, Outline and bibliographies of oriental art. Cambridge, Mass. 1938. pp.[ii].ff.3–41. [500.]

— — Revised edition. The Harvard outline and reading lists for oriental art. 1958. pp.[v].74. [1500.]

Bible

FRANZ CARL ALTER, Bibliographische nachrichten von verschiedenen ausgaben orientalischer Bibletexte, und der kirchenväter. Wien 1779. pp.[vi].222.[iv]. [Bible: 750.]

JACQUES LE LONG, Bibliotheca sacra. . . . Partis secvndae de versionis librorvm sacrorvm primvm de versionibvs orientalibvs. Halae 1781. pp.xvi. 226. [1000.]

Book art

[FRANZ UNTERKIRCHER *and others*], Buchkunst des morgenlandes. Katalog der ausstellung. Nationalbibliothek: Wien 1953. pp.70. [201.]

Buddhism

[OTTO KISTNER], Buddha and his doctrines. A bibliographical essay. 1869. pp.iv.32. [900.]

E[WARD] B[YLES] COWELL and J[ULIUS] EGGELING, Catalogue of buddhist sanskrit manuscripts in the possession of the Royal asiatic society (Hodgson collection). pp.56.

SAMUEL BEAL, The buddhist Tripitaka as it is known in China and Japan. A catalogue and compendious report. 1876. pp.[iv].117. [1000.]

RĀJENDRALĀLA MITRA, The sanskrit buddhist literature of Nepal. Calcutta 1882. pp.xlvii.340. [85.]
a catalogue of mss. given to the library of the Asiatic society of Bengal by Brian Houghton Hodgson.

CECIL BENDALL, Catalogue of the buddhist sanskrit manuscripts in the university library. Cambridge 1883. pp.lvi.225. [500.]

BUNYIU NANJIO, A ctaalogue of the chinese translation of the buddhist Tripitaka, the sacred canon of the Buddhists in China and Japan. Oxford 1883. pp.xxxvi.coll.480.

[SIR] E[DWARD] DENISON ROSS, Alphabetical list of the titles of works in the Chinese buddhist Tripitaka, being an index to Bunyiu Nanjio's catalogue and to the 1905 Kioto reprint of the Buddhist canon. Archaeological department of India: Calcutta 1910. pp.[iv].xcviii. [1750.]

HANS LUDWIG HELD, Deutsche bibliographie des Buddhismus . . . als religionswissenschaft. München &c. 1916. pp.viii.192. [2544.]
reprinted 1973.

IDA A[UGUSTA] PRATT, Buddhism. A list of references in the New York public library. New York 1916. pp.vii.78. [1750.]

BIBLIOGRAPHIE bouddhique. Buddhica [vols.i–iii only].

　i. 1928–1929. pp.xii.64. [315.]
　ii. 1929–1930. pp.xi.97. [634.]
　iii. 1930–1931. pp.ix.89. [586.]
　iv–v. 1931–1933. pp.[ii].x.150. [885.]
　vi. 1933–1934 . . . [With] index général des tomes i–vi. pp.xii.152. [637.]
　vii–viii. 1934–1936. pp.xii.183. [910.]
　ix–xx. 1936–1947. pp.ix.167. [1585.]
　xxi–xxiii. 1947–1950. pp.viii.213. [2316.]
　xxiii bis. Rétrospective . . . et index général des tomes vii–xxiii. 1955. pp.[viii]. 166.
　xxiv–xxvii. 1950–1954. pp.xv.261. [2744.]
　xxviii–xxxi. 1954–1958. [1961]. pp.xvii.364. [3983.]
　xxxii. Index général des tomes xxiv–xxvii et xxviii–xxxi. 1967. pp.215.

CLARENCE H. HAMILTON, Buddhism in India, Ceylon, China and Japan. A reading guide. Chicago 1931. pp.viii.107. [150.]

HAKUJU UI [and others] A complete catalogue of the tibetan buddhist canons (Bkah-hgyur and Bstan-hgyur). Tôhoku imperial university: Sendai 1934. pp.[ix].2.3.703.5+[iii].125. [4569.]

ARTHUR C. MARCH, A buddhist bibliography. Buddhist Lodge: 1935. pp.xi.258. [2210.]
limited to works in english; 500 copies printed.
— — Annual supplement.
　i. 1936. pp.259–274. [94.]
　ii. 1937. pp.275–284. [39.]
　iii. 1938. pp.285–297. [52.]
　iv. 1939. pp.297–305. [38.]
　v. 1940. pp.307–316. [35.]
no more published.

C. REGAMEY, Buddhistische philosophie. Bibliographische einführungen in das studium der philosophie (vol.20/21): Bern 1950. pp.86. [1000.]

SIBADAS [ṢIVA-DĀSA] CHAUDHURĪ, A bibliographical survey of the contributions of the Royal asiatic society of Bengal towards the study of Buddhism: 1748–1949. Journal of the Royal asiatic society of Bengal: Letters (vol.xvi, no.1, supplement): [Calcutta 1950]. pp.xxvi. [245.]

YENSHO KANAKURA [and others], A catalogue of the Tohoku university collection of tibetan works on Buddhism. Tohoku university: Seminary of indology: Sendai [1953]. pp.531.[xlii].

BANDŌ SŌJUN [and others], A bibliography of japanese Buddhism. Cultural interchange institute for Buddhists: Tōkyō 1958. pp.xiii.181. [1660.]

BIBLIOGRAPHY on Buddhism. Edited by the commemorative committee for prof. Shirishō Hanayama's sixty-first birthday. Tokyo 1961. pp. xiii.869.

PIERRE BEAUTRIX, Bibliographie du bouddhisme. Publications de l'Institut belge des hautes etudes bouddhiques: serie "bibliographies" (no.2): Bruxelles.
　i. Editions de textes. 1970. ff.iii.206. [1072.]

SIBADAS CHAUDHURI, Contributions to a buddhistic bibliography. Second series. Journal of the Asiatic society (vol.v, nos.1+2, &c.): Bibliographical supplement: Calcutta 1965–8. pp.30. [317.]

HEINZ MODE, HANS-JOACHIM PENKE, BURCHARD THALER, edd., Bibliography of literature on buddhist topics published on the territory of the G.D.R. since 1945. Supplement to "Buddhist yearly". Halle 1966. pp.71. [543.]*

YUSHIN YOO, Buddhism; a subject index to periodical articles in english, 1728–1971. Metuchen, N.J. 1973. pp.xxii.162. [1261.]*

Carpets

LIST of references on oriental rugs. Library of Congress: Washington 1918. ff.3. [41.]*

Censuses

INTERNATIONAL population census bibliography (no.5): Population research center: Department of sociology: University of Texas: Austin 1966. pp.x.[292.] [1500.]*
— Supplement 1968. Census bibliography (no.7). [Asia: 76.]

Communism

SHEN-YU DAI, Contemporary world communism and the communists developments in Asia; a bibliographical guide. Fort Collins, Colorado 1963. pp.15. [201.]*

Co-operation

ANNOTATED bibliography of literature produced by the co-operative movements in southeast Asia. International co-operative alliance: New Delhi [1963]. ff.[ii.74]. [300.]
—Supplement.
　1967. pp. .19.
　1968. pp.16.27. [160.]*
　1969. pp.18.36. [200.]*
　1970. pp.34.75. [450.]*
　1971. pp.59.47. [450.]*

Current affairs

SELECT articles on current affairs. Indian council of world affairs: Library: Bibliographical series: New Delhi*.
　i. 1956. By B. C. Tewari. ff.[ii].xii.pp.149. [2000.]
　ii. 1957. ff.[ii].xiii.pp.155. [2000.]

iii. 1958. ff.[i.]xii.pp.236. [3000.]

iv. 1959. Compiled by B. C. Tewari and Shaukat Ashraf. ff.[ii].xix.pp.280. [3500.]

v.

vi.

vii.

viii.

ix.

x.

xi. 1966. 1971. pp.xxvii.323. [3000.]

DOCUMENTATIO Asiae. Eine reihe selektiver bibliographien zu aktuellen themen des heutigen Asien und Ozeanien. A series of selective bibliographies on current problems of present-day Asia and Oceania. Dokumentations-leitstelle am Institut für asienkunde. 1971 &c.
entered also separately.

Dictionaries

MOHAMMAD WAJID, Oriental dictionaries; a select bibliography. Library promotion bureau: Karachi 1967. pp.xii.54. [345.]

Drama

LIST of works in the New York public library relating to the oriental drama. [New York 1906]. pp.6. [175.]

Economics

WALTER T. LORCH, Entwicklungshilfe und ausländische investitionen in Asien. Development aid and foreign investments in Asia. Documentatio Asiae (no.2). Institut für asienkunde: Dokumentations-leitstelle: Hamburg.*

i. 1972. pp.x.100. [788.]

Education

SELECT list of references on oriental students in the United States. Library of Congress: Washington 1910. ff.5. [27.]*

Family planning

FAMILY PLANNING, internal migration and urbanization in ECAFE countries; a bibliography of available materials. Asian population studies series (no.2): United nations: New York 1968. pp.v.66. [869.]

Government

SHEN-YU DAI, Comparative asian government and politics; an annotated bibliography. Fort Collins, Colorado 1963. pp.13. [68.]*

History

B. L. KANDEL, История зарубежных стран. Библиография русских библиографий, опубликованных с 1857 до 1965 год. Москва 1966. pp. 256. [Asia and Africa 44; Asia 192].

International organization

HAROLD S. JOHNSON and BALJIT SINGH, International organization; a classified bibliography. Asian studies center: South Asia series: Michigan state university: East Lansing 1969. ff.v.263. [4500.]

Leaders

SHEN-YU DAI, Leaders of modern Asia; a select bibliography of biographic works. Fort Collins, Colorado 1963. pp.6. [75.]*

Librarianship

G. RAYMOND NUNN, Asian libraries and librarianship: an annotated bibliography of selected books and periodicals, and a draft syllabus. Metuchen, N.J. 1973. pp.vii.137. [353.]*

Literature

Литература стран зарубежной Азии. Государственная . . . библиотека СССР имени В. И. Ленина: [Moscow] 1964. ff.8. [122.]*

Liturgies

J. M. SAUGET, Bibliographie des liturgies orientales (1900–1960). Pont. institutum orientalium studiorum: Roma 1962. pp.143. [1572.]

'Mandeville, sir John'

J[OHANN] VOGELS, Die ungedruckten lateinischen versionen Mandeville's (Wissenschaftliche beilage zum Programm des Gymnasiums zu Crefeld, Ostern 1886). Crefeld 1886. pp.23. [20.]

HENRI CORDIER, Jean de Mandeville. Leide 1891. pp.38. [100.]

Music

WOLFGANG LAADE, Gegenwartsfragen der musik in Afrika und Asien; eine grundlegende bibliographie. Collection d'études musicologiques: Baden-Baden 1971. pp.110. [98.]

Nationalism

SHEN-YU DAI, Nationalism and revolution in Asia; an annotated bibliography. Fort Collins, Colorado 1963. pp.22. [112.]*

Odorico da Pordenone

HENRI CORDIER, Les voyages en Asie au XIVe siècle du bienheureux Odoric de Pordenone. . . . Introduction. 1891. pp.[v].xiv.clviii. [146.]

Planning

DIANA CHANG, Asia and Pacific planning bibliography. University of Hawaii libraries and Pacific urban studies and planning program: Honolulu.*
i. 1971. pp.29. [500.]
ii. 1971. pp.29. [500.]
iii.
iv.
v. 1974. pp.226. [2500.]

Printing

PRINTING design and production from ... Malaya, Burma, Ceylon, India, Pakistan, Iran, Turkey. American institute of graphic arts: [New York 1963]. pp.72. [120.]
an exhibition catalogue.

Religion

H[ARRY] DANIEL SMITH, Profile of a library in transition. A bibliographical survey of history of religious resources. Syracuse university: Program of south Asia studies: Syracuse 1966.*
i. History of religions in south Asia. pp.205. [2800.]
ii. History of religions in Africa (exclusive of judaism, christianity and islam). pp.85. [1360.]
iii. History of religions in islamic areas. pp.v.63. [720.]

Social education

HARRY H. L. KITANO, Asians in America; a selected bibliography for use in social work education. Council on social work education: New York 1971. pp.vii.79.

Social sciences

N. K. GOIL, ed., Asian social science bibliography, with annotations and abstracts, 1966. Institute of economic growth, Delhi: Delhi, etc. 1970. pp. xxiii.490. [1972.]

Soils

BIBLIOGRAPHY. (Annotated bibliography.) Commonwealth bureau of soils: Commonwealth agricultural bureaux: Farnham Royal.*
708. Bibliography on the soils of South Africa (1962–1920). ff.8. [55.]
709. Bibliography on the soils of northern and southern Rhodesia and Malawi.
810. Bibliography on soils and agriculture of Libya (1961–1933). pp.18. [74.]
820. Bibliography on soils of Turkey (1963–1930). pp.5. [38.]
853. Bibliography on soils of Fiji (1960–1935). pp.3. [17.]
913. Bibliography on soils and agriculture of the Sudan republic (1964–1935). pp.15. [115.]
958. Bibliography on soils of China (1965–1930). pp.20. [188.]
973. Bibliography on desert soils of India, Pakistan & Afghanistan (1962–1945). pp.3 [15.]
974. Bibliography on desert soils of Israel and Jordan (1964–1954). [41.]
1076. Bibliography on soils and land-use in Vietnam and Cambodia (1966–1930). pp.9. [46.]
1085. Bibliography on the soils of Malawi, Rhodesia and Zambia (1966–1957). Supplement to no.709. pp.6. [28.]
1099. Selective bibliography on fertilizing in north Africa and the near east (1966–1956). pp.8. [39.]
1160. Bibliography on soils and agriculture in Borneo (1967–1932). pp.5. [29.]
1186. Bibliography on soils, land use and land classification in the Philippines (1965–1931). pp.9. [55.]
1297. Bibliography on soils of Indonesia. pp.16. [88.]
1381. Bibliography on soils of Malaysia, Singapore and Brunei (1969–1956). pp.12. [67.]
1383. Bibliography on soils and agriculture of the Pacific islands excluding Hawaii (1969–1933). pp.20. [117.]
1385. Bibliography on soils and vegetation of New Guinea. pp.5. [22.]
1479. Bibliography on soils of South Africa (1970–1962). Supplements no.708. 1971. Commonwealth agricultural bureaux (Farnham Royal]. 1971. pp.7. [32.]
1552. Some references to the soils of Tanzania (1971–1962). 1972. pp.6. [27.]
1596. Some references to soils and agriculture of the Sudan republic (1973–1964). 1973. pp.7. [30.]

ix. Oriental literatures

1. Bibliographies

GIUSEPPE GABRIELI, Manoscritti e carte orientali nelle biblioteche e negli archivi d'Italia. Dati statistici e bibliografici delle collezioni, loro storia e catalogazione. Biblioteca di bibliografia italiana (vol.x): Firenze 1930. pp.ix.89. [400.]

ENRIQUE SPARN, Las mayores colecciones de manuscritos orientales existentes en las bibliotecas del mundo. Cordoba (Rep. Arg.) 1935. pp.25. [114.]

[SIR] F[RANK] C[HALTON] FRANCIS, Oriental printed books and manuscripts. Catalogues of British museum (no.3): 1951. pp.14. [50.]

J[AMES] D[OUGLAS] PEARSON, Oriental manuscripts in Europe and north America; a survey. Bibliotheca asiatica (7). Zug, Switzerland 1971. pp.lxxx.515. [2100.]

2. Manuscripts

Austria

DANIEL DE NESSEL, Catalogus sive recensio specialis omnium codicum manuscriptorum græcorum, nec non linguarum orientalium, Augustissimæ bibliothecæ cæsareæ vindobonensis. Vindobonæ &c. 1690. pp.[xv].448.36.56.164.179.188. [oriental: 275.]

—— [another edition]. Bibliotheca acroamatica ... comprehendens recensionem specialem omnium codicum msctorum græcorum, hebraicorum, syriacorum, arabicorum, turcicorum, armenicorum, æthiopicorum, mexicanorum, sinensium, &c. ... Bibliothecæ cæsareæ vindobonensis. ... Nunc autem ... in hanc concinnam epitomen redacta et luci publicæ restituta à Jacobo Friderico Reimanno. Hanoveræ 1712. pp. [xciv].112.808. [oriental: 276.]

MICHAEL TALMAN, Elenchus librorum orientalium manuscriptorum ... a ... Aloysio Ferdinando Marsigli ... partim in ultimo bello turcico, et partim in itinere Constantinopolim suscepto collectorum coëmptorúmque. Viennæ Austriæ 1702. pp.[iv].63. [400.]

Belgium

DOCUMENTS relatifs aux civilisations orientales. Exposition' Bibliothèque royale de Belgique: Bruxelles 1938.

Ceylon

A DESCRIPTIVE catalogue of pali, sanskrit, sinhalese, siamese, english, and other books in the Oriental library [located in the Octagon]. Kandy 1925. pp.13. [400.]

Denmark

CODICES orientales Bibliothecæ regiæ Havniensis ... enumerati et descripti. Havniæ.

i. Codices indici ... enumerati et descripti a N. L. Westergaard. Subjungitur index codicum indicorum et iranicorum Bibliothecæ universitatis Havniensis. 1846. pp.x. 122. [366.]

ii. Codices hebraici et arabici ... 1851. pp.xi. 188. [355.]

iii. Codices persici, turcici, hindustanici variique alii ... enumerati et descripti ab A. F. Mehren. 1857. pp.v.92. [240.]

France

[ÉTIENNE FOURMONT and GUILLAUME DE VILLEFROY], Catalogus codicum manuscriptorum Bibliothecæ regiæ. Tomus primus [complectens codices manuscriptos orientales]. Parisiis 1739. pp.[iv].458.[xliv]. [2000.]

LÉON FEER, Papiers d'Eugène Burnouf conservés à la Bibliothèque nationale. 1899. pp.[iv].xxvi.197. [500.]

E[DGAR] BLOCHET, Catalogue des manuscrits mazdéens (zends, pehlvis, parsis et persans) de la Bibliothèque nationale. Besançon 1900. pp.[iii]. 132. [5000.]

Germany

SEBASTIAN GOTTFRIED STARCKE, Bibliotheca manuscripta Abrahami Hinckelmanni ... sicuti pleraque ex parte constat ex codicibus orientalibus. Hamburgi [1695]. pp.[iv].28. [191.]

HEINRICH LEBERECHT [ORTHOBIUS] FLEISCHER, Catalogus codicum manuscriptorum orientalium Bibliothecæ regiae dresdensis. ... Accedit Friderici Adolphi Eberti ... Catalogus codicum manuscriptorum orientalium Bibliothecæ ducalis guelferbytanæ. Lipsiæ 1831. pp.xiii.106. [1000.]

[G. H. A. VON EWALD], Verzeichniss der orientalischen handschriften der Universitäts-bibliothek. Tübingen 1839. pp.32. [60.]

AENOTH. FRID. CONST. [LOBEGOTT FRIEDRICH CONSTANTIN VON] TISCHENDORF, Anecdota sacra et profana ex oriente et occidente allata sive notitia codicum græcorum, arabicorum, syriacorum, copticorum, hebraicorum, æthiopicorum, latinorum. Lipsiae 1855. pp.x.vi.220. [100.]

ANTON KLETTE and JOSEF STAENDER, Chirographorum in Bibliotheca academica bonnensi servatorum catalogus. Volumen II quo libri descripti sunt præter orientales relicui. Bonnæ 1858–1876. pp.x.250. [856.]

FR[IEDRICH] AUG[UST] ARNOLD and AUGUST MÜLLER, Verzeichnis der orientalischen handschriften der Bibliothek des hallischen Waisenhauses. Halle 1876. pp.16. [88.]

JOHANN GILDEMEISTER, Catalogus librorum manu scriptorum orientalium in bibliotheca Academica bonnensi servatorum. Bonnae 1864–1876. pp.[vi].154. [200.]

[E. WEST and others], Verzeichniss der orientalischen handschriften aus dem nachlasse des professor dr. Martin Haug. München 1876. pp.[iii]. 48.[vi]. [400.]

[WILHELM BRAMBACH and others], Die handschriften der grossherzoglich badischen hof- und landesbibliothek in Karlsruhe. II. Orientalische handschriften. Karlsruhe 1892. pp.viii.61. [115.]

WILHELM PERTSCH, Die orientalischen handschriften der Herzoglichen bibliothek zu Gotha.
. . . Anhang: die orientalischen handschriften mit
ausnahme der persischen, türkischen und arabischen. Gotha 1893. pp.x.65. [89.]

K. VOLLERS, Katalog der islamischen, christlich-
orientalischen, jüdischen und samaritanischen
handschriften. Katalog der handschriften der
Universitäts-bibliothek (vol.ii): Leipzig 1906. pp.
xiii.509. [1250.]

CARL BROCKELMANN, Katalog der orientalischen
handschriften. . . . Teil 1. Die arabischen, persischen, türkischen, malaiischen, koptischen, syrischen, äthiopischen handschriften. Katalog der
handschriften der Stadtbibliothek (vol.iii): Hamburg 1908. pp.[iii].xxi.246. [400.]

GUSTAV RICHTER, Verzeichnis der orientalischen
handschriften der Staats- und universitäts-bibliothek Breslau. Leipzig 1933. pp.viii.63. [400.]

JÖRG KRAEMER, Persische miniaturen und ihr
umkreis. Buch- und schriftkunst arabischer, persi-
scher, türkischer und indischer handschriften aus
dem besitz der früheren Preussischen staats- und
der Tübinger universitätsbibliothek. Austellung.
Tübinger kunstverein: Tübingen [1956]. pp.x.52.
[73.]

Great Britain

JOANNES URI [Part ii: ALEXANDER NICOLL],
Bibliothecæ bodleianæ codicum manuscriptorum
orientalium, videlicet hebraicorum, chaldaico-
rum, syriacorum, æthiopicorum, arabicorum,
persicorum, turcicorum, copticorumque catalogus. Oxonii 1787–1835. pp.[ii].ii.98.327.[xli]+
[iv].143+[ii].viii.145–730. [2500.]

[SAMUEL GUISE], A catalogue of oriental manuscripts, collected in Indoostan. By mr. Samuel
Guise . . . from the year 1777 till 1792. [c.1795].
pp.31. [361.]

[SAMUEL GUISE], A catalogue and detailed
account of a very valuable and curious collection
of manuscripts, collected in Hindustan by Samuel
Guise . . . including all those that were procured by
monsieur Anquetil du Perron. 1800. pp.15. [127.]

[JOHN LEE], Oriental manuscripts purchased in
Turkey. [1830]. pp.[ii].22. [116.]
[—]—[second edition]. 1840. pp.72. [250.]

[SIR WILLIAM OUSELEY], Catalogue of several
hundred manuscript works in various oriental
languages. 1831. pp.viii.24. [725.]

J[OSEPH] B. B. CLARKE, A historical and descriptive catalogue of the european and asiatic manuscripts in the library of the late dr. Adam Clarke.
1835. pp.xi.3–236. [350.]

[ROBERT CURZON], Catalogue of materials for
writing, . . . rolled and other manuscripts and
oriental manuscript books, in the library of the
honourable Robert Curzon. 1849. pp.[iv].33.
ff.34–43. [200.]

T. PRESTON, Catalogus Bibliothecæ burck-
hardtianæ, cum appendice librorum aliorum
orientalium in bibliotheca Academiæ cantabrigiensis asservatorum. Cantabrigiæ 1853. pp.[iv].
64. [300.]

[D. FORBES], Catalogue of oriental manuscripts,
chiefly persian, collected within the last five and
thirty years by Duncan Forbes. 1866. pp.[iii].92.
[291.]

D[AVID] S[AMUEL] MARGOLIOUTH, Catalogue of
the oriental manuscripts in the library of Eton
college. Oxford 1904. pp.35. [220.]

[MUHAMMAD HIDĀYAT HUSAIN], List of arabic
and persian mss. acquired on behalf of the
government of India by the Asiatic society of
Bengal during 1903–1907. [Calcutta 1908.] pp.
[ii].61. [1106.]
——1908–1910. [By Nazir Ahmad and Hazir
Razawi]. [1911]. pp.[ii].62. [540.]
not limited to arabic and persian mss.

EDWARD G[RANVILLE] BROWNE, A descriptive
catalogue of the oriental mss. belonging to the
late E. G. Browne. Cambridge 1932. pp.xxii.325.
[1000.]

J[AMES] D[OUGLAS] PEARSON, Oriental manuscript collections in the libraries of Great Britain
and Ireland. Royal asiatic society: 1954. pp.vi.90.
[large number.]

India

WILLIAM TAYLOR, A catalogue raisonnée [sic]
of oriental manuscripts in the library of the (late)
College, Fort Saint George. Madras 1857–1862.
pp.xxviii.viii.v.xxiii.678 + xxi–xcv.xv.902 + [v].
lviii.802. [16,500.]

T. S. CONDASWAMI IYER, Alphabetical catalogue
in the vernacular and english characters of the
oriental manuscripts in the library of the Board
of examiners. Vol.1. Madras 1861. pp.[v].231.
[2500.]
no more published.

EDWARD REHATSEK, Catalogue raisonné of the
arabic, hindostani, persian, and turkish mss. in the
Mulla Firuz library. [Bombay] 1873. pp.[iv].ix.
279. [550.]
—— Supplementary catalogue . . . and descriptive catalogue of the avesta, pahlavi, pazend and
persian mss. . . . By S. A. Brelvi and Ervad B. N.
Dhabhar. 1917. pp.[ii].ix.[vii].v.xliv.v–xiv.3–79.
[250.]

MAHĀMAHOPĀDHYĀYA HARAPRASĀDA ŚĀSTRĪ, Catalogue of manuscripts in the Bishop's college library. Calcutta 1915. pp.[iii].57. [124.]

BAMANIJ NASARVANJI DHABHAR, Descriptive catalogue of all manuscripts in the First Dastur Meherji Rana library, Navsari. Bombay 1923. pp.[iv].170. [425.]

KALI PRASAD, Catalogue of oriental manuscripts in the Lucknow university library, Lucknow (India). [Lucknow] 1951. ff.[iii]. pp.75. [1164.]

Italy

STEPHANUS EVODIUS ASSEMANUS, Bibliothecae mediceae lavrentianae et palatinae codicum mms. [sic] orientalivm catalogvs. Antonio Francisco Goria curante. Florentiae 1742. pp.lxxii.492. [lvii]. [750.]

ANTONIO MARIA BISCIONIO, Bibliothecae medi-ceo-lavrentianae catalogvs. ... Tomvs primvs, codices orientales complectens. Florentiae 1752. pp.lvi.200.122. [500.]

SIMONE ASSEMANI, Catalogo de' codici mano-scritti orientali della Biblioteca naniana. Padova [1784-]1787-1793. pp.[viii].221+xxiv.447. [125.]

PAULINUS A SANCTO BARTHOLOMAEO, Musei borgiani velitris codices manuscripti avenses, peguani, siamici, malabarici, indostani. Romae 1793. pp.xii.266. [24.]

DAVIDE SAMUELE, [&c.] יד יוסף [Catalogue de la bibliothèque de littérature hébraïque et orientale de feu mʳ Joseph (Giuseppe) Almanzi]. Padoue 1864. pp.91.120.

HENRICUS [ENRICO] NARDUCCI, Catalogus codi-cum manuscriptorum praeter orientales qui in bibliotheca Alexandrina Romae adservantur. Romae 1877. pp.vii.184. [235.]

CATALOGHI dei codici orientali di alcune biblio-teche d'Italia. Firenze 1878. pp. iv.474. [972.]
catalogues of the Vittorio Emanuele, Angelica and Alessandrina libraries in Rome were also published separately.

ELENCO dei documenti orientali e delle carte nautiche e geografiche che si conservano negli archivi di stato di Firenze e di Pisa. R. sop
rainten-denza degli archivi toscani: Firenze 1878. pp.31. [oriental: 64.]

GIUSEPPE GABRIELI, La fondazione Caetani per gli studi musulmani. Notizia della sua istituzione a catalogo dei suoi mss. orientali. R. Accademie nazionale dei Lincei: Roma 1926. pp.96.vi. [300.]

[EUGÈNE TISSERANT], Catalogo della Mostra di manoscritti e documenti orientali tenuta dalla Biblioteca apostolica vaticana e dall'Archivio segreto. Città del Vaticano 1935. pp.40. [150.]

CARLO BERNHEIMER, Catalogo dei manoscritti orientali della Biblioteca estense [Modena]. Ministero della pubblica istruzione: Indici e cata-loghi (n.s., no.iv): Roma 1960. pp.xiii.112. [92.]

Netherlands

HENRICUS ARENTIUS [HENDRIK ARENT] HAMAKER, Specimen catalogi codicum mss. orientalium bibliothecae Academiae lugduno-batave. Lugduni Batavorum 1820. pp.viii.265. [12.]

R[EINHART] P[IETER] A[NNE] DOZY [vols.iii–iv: PIETER DE JONG and M[ICHAEL] J[OHANNES] DE GOEJE; V: M. J. DE GOEJE; vi: M[ARTIN] TH[EODOR] HOUTSMA], Catalogus codicum orientalium biblio-thecae Academiae lugduno batavae. Lugduni Batavorum 1851–1877. pp.[iii].xxxvi.367+[iv]. 323 + [iv].394 + [v].350 + vii.328 + [vii].234. [2850.]

[HENRICUS ENGELINUS] WEIJERS, Catalogus codi-cum orientalium bibliothecae Academiae regiae scientiarum. ... Edidit P[ieter] de Jong. Lugduni Batavorum 1862. pp.xx.319. [265.]

EXPOSITION de manuscrits orientaux, d'objets et documents relatifs à l'histoire des études orientalistes à l'université de Leiden. Organisée à l'occasion du XVIIIe congrès international des orientalistes au musée de "Lakenhal". [Leiden] 1931. pp.viii.48. [258.]

LEVINUS WARNER and his legacy. Three centuries Legatum Warnerianum in the Leiden university library. Catalogue of the commemorative exhibition held in the Bibliotheca Thysiana ... 1970. Leiden 1970. ff.[3].pp.77. [60.]

Portugal

RENÉ BASSET, Notice sommaire des manuscrits orientaux de deux bibliothèques de Lisbonne. Société de géographie; Lisbonne 1894. pp.31. [15.]

Russia

каталогъ санскритскимъ, монгольскимъ, тібетскимъ, маньджурскимъ и китайскимъ кни-гамъ и рукописямъ, въ библіотекѣ Импера-торскаго казанскаго университета храня-щимся. Казан. 1834. pp.[v].30. [189.]

[BARON] D[AVID] GÜNZBURG [and others], Les manuscrits arabes ... karchounis, grecs, coptes, éthiopiens, arméniens, géorgiens et bâbys de l'Institut des langues orientales. Institut des langues orientales: Collections scientifiques(vol.vi): Saint-Pétersbourg 1891. pp.xxiii.271. [3000.]

Scandinavia

NILS LINDHAGEN, W. G. ARCHER and B. W. ROBINSON, Oriental miniatures and manuscripts in scandinavian collections. Catalogue. . . . Translation by Axel Poignant. Nationalmuseum: Utställninggskatalog (no.240): Stockholm 1957. pp. [64. 282.]

Sinai

MURAD KAMIL, Catalogue of all manuscripts in the monastery of St. Catherine on mount Sinai. Wiesbaden 1970. pp.ix.213. [oriental: 2621]

Sweden

CARL JOHANN TORNBERG, Codices orientales Bibliothecæ regiæ Universitatis lundensis. Lundæ 1850. pp.[vi].40. [50.]

w. RIEDEL, Katalog över Kungl. bibliotekets orientaliska handskrifter. Kungliga biblioteket [Stockholm]: Handlingar: Bilagor (n.s., vol.iii): Uppsala 1923. pp.xi.68. [150.]

Tadzhikistan

A. M. MIRZOEV and A[LEKSANDR] N[IKOLAEVICH] BOLDYREV, Каталог восточных рукописей Академии наук Таджикской ССР.
i. Сталинабад 1960. pp.323. [288.]
ii.
iii. Под редакцией и при участии . . . А. М. Мирзоева и М. И. Занда. Душанбе 1968. pp.239. [338.]
iv. 1970. pp.279. [403.]

Turkestan

A[LEKSANDR] A[LEKSANDROVICH] SEMENOV Описание таджикских, персидских, арабских и тюркских рукописей фундаментальной библиотеки Среднеазиатского государственного университета им. В. И. Ленина. Ташкент 1956. pp.88. [199.]

Turkey

FEHMI EDHEM and IVAN STCHOUKINE [IVAN VASILEVICH SHCHUKIN], Les manuscrits orientaux illustrés de la bibliothèque de l'université de Stamboul. Institut français d'archéologie de Stamboul: Mémoires (vol.i): Paris 1933. pp.[iv].68.

United States

MUHAMMAD AHMAD SIMSĀR, Oriental manuscripts of the John Frederick Lewis collection in the Free library of Philadelphia. A descriptive catalogue. Philadelphia 1937. pp.xix.248. [153.]

MANUSCRIPTS & papyri. An exhibition arranged for the XXVII international congress of Orientalists. Ann Arbor 1967. pp.iv.21. [80.]

Uzbekistan

ALEKSANDR ALEKSANDROVICH SEMENOV, ed. Собрание восточных рукописей академии наук Узбекской ССР. Академия наук Узбекской ССР: Институт востоковедения: Ташкент 1952–1957. pp.440+590+556–560. [3462.]

3. Miscellaneous

HUGO BUCHTHAL and OTTO KURZ, A hand list of illuminated oriental christian manuscripts. Warburg institute: Studies (vol.xii): 1942. pp.120. [555.]

JOSÉ MILLÁS VALLICROSA, Las traducciones orientales en los manuscritos de la Biblioteca catedral de Toledo. Consejo superior de investigaciones científicas: Instituto Arias Montano: Madrid 1942. pp.[v].375. [100.]
deals with translations from oriental languages.

LOUIS B[ENSON] FREWER, Manuscript collections (excluding africana) in Rhodes house library, Oxford. Bodleian library, Oxford 1970. pp.62. [Asia: 443]

ÉMILE VANDEWOUDE and ANDRÉ VANRIE, Guide des sources de l'histoire d'Afrique du nord, d'Asie et d'Océanie conservées en Belgique. Conseil international des archives: Guide des sources de l'histoire des nations (B.III/1). Archives générales du royaume: Bruxelles 1972. pp.622. [very large number.]

C. STUART CRAIG, The archives of the Council for world mission (incorporating the London missionary society): an outline guide. School of oriental & african studies: Library: 1973. pp.[22]. [large number.]

WEST ASIA

ANCIENT NEAR EAST

i. *General*
ii. *Scholars*
iii. *Sumerian. Accadian (Babylonian, Assyrian). Cuneiform*
iv. *Hittites*
v. *Ancient Egypt*
   1. *General*
   2. *Subjects*
   3. *Egyptian literature*
   4. *Papyri*
   5. *Coptic*
vi. *Semitic languages and studies*
vii. *Mandaean*
viii. *Samaritan*
ix. *Ugaritic*

i. *General*

STELLA VIRGINIA SEYBOLD, History of literature. Part I: ancient chaldean literature [II: egyptian literature]. Special reading list (no. 8): Public library: Cincinnati 1902. pp.4. [Chaldean: 32.]

WESTERN ASIA. Council for old world archaeology: COWA surveys and bibliographies: Cambridge, Mass.*
   i. 1957. pp.22. [347.]
   ii. 1960. pp.28. [471.]
   iii. 1966. pp.34. [701.]
in progress.

MANFRED MAYRHOFER, Die Indo-Aryer im alten Vorderasien, mit einer analytischen bibliographie. Wiesbaden 1966. pp.160. [900.]

LOUIS L. ORLIN, Ancient near eastern literature: a bibliography of one thousand items of the cuneiform literatures of the ancient world. Partially annotated, and with a special section on literary contacts and interrelations between Greece and the near east. Ann Arbor 1969. pp.xx.113. [1002.]*

ii. *Scholars*

Albright, William Foxwell

HARRY M[EYER] ORLINSKY, An indexed bibliography of the writings of William Foxwell Albright. American schools of oriental research: New Haven 1941. pp.[ii].xxiv.66. [500.]*

Barton, George Aaron

BEATRICE ALLARD BROOKS, A classified bibliography of the writings of George Aaron Barton. Bulletin of the american schools of oriental research: Supplementary studies (no.4): New Haven 1947. pp.24. [400.]

Jastrow, Morris

[ALBERT TOBIAS CLAY and JAMES ALAN MONTGOMERY], Bibliography of Morris Jastrow. Philadelphia 1910. pp.12. [160.]
privately printed.

Menant, Joachim

[J. MENANT], Publications assyriennes de m. Joachim Menant. [1884]. pp.4. [28.]

iii. *Sumerian. Accadian (Babylonian, Assyrian). Cuneiform.*

CARL BEZOLD, Kurzgefasster überblick über die babylonisch-assyrische literatur, nebst ... einem index zu 1700 thontafeln des British-museum's. Leipzig 1886. pp.xv.395. [2500.]

C[ARL] BEZOLD, Catalogue of the cuneiform tablets in the Kouyunjik collection of the British Museum. London.
   i. 1889. pp.xxxi.420. [2191.]
   ii. 1891. pp.xxiv.421–900. [2192–8162.]
   iii. 1893. pp.xii.901–1370. [8163–14230.]
   iv. 1896. pp.xii.1371–1952. [6319.]
   v. 1899. pp.xxx.1953–2387. Preface, introduction, indexes and appendices.
—— Supplement, by L. W. King. 1914. pp.xxxviii.285. [3349.]
—— — A list of fragments rejoined in the Kuyunjik collection of the British Museum (revised and enlarged). 1960. [2727.]
—— Second supplement, by W. G. Lambert & A. R. Millard. 1968. [2516.]

HOPE W. HOGG, Survey of recent publications on Assyriology. Edinburgh [1908]. pp.48. [200.]
covers the period 1904–1907.
—— Second period, 1908–1909. 1910, pp.71. [300.]

C[LAUDE] H[ERMANN] W[ALTER] JOHNS. A short bibliography of works on the babylonian stories of creation and the flood, [s.l. 1913]. pp.[3]. [12.]

IDA A[UGUSTA] PRATT, Assyria and Babylonia. A list of references in the New York public library. Compiled ... under the direction of Richard [James Horatio] Gottheil. New York 1918. pp.vi.143. [2750.]

ERNST F[RIEDRICH] WEIDNER, Die Assyriologie 1914–1922. Wissenschaftliche forschungsergebnisse in bibliographischer form. Leipzig 1922. pp.x.192. [2000.]
—— Namenregister. [1923.] pp.193–200.

R[EGINALD] CAMPBELL THOMPSON, A catalogue of the late babylonian tablets in the Bodleian library. Oxford 1927. ff.[ii].80. [125.]*

T. FISH, Catalogue of sumerian tablets in the John Rylands library. Manchester 1932. pp.vii.160. [884.]

BIBLIOGRAPHIE analytique de l'assyriologie et de l'archéologie du proche-orient. Section A. L'archéologie. Leyde.

i. 1954–1955. Par L. Vanden Berghe et H. F. Mussche. 1956. pp.xv.131. [750.]
ii. 1956–1957. 1960. pp.x.178. [1750.]

BIBLIOGRAPHIE analytique de l'assyriologie et de l'archéologie du proche-orient. Section PH. La philologie. Leyde.
i. 1954–1956. Par L. Vanden Berghe et L. de Meyer. pp.xii.108. [950.]

TOM B[ARD] JONES and JOHN W. SNYDER, Sumerian economic texts from the third Ur dynasty. A catalogue. Minneapolis [1961]. pp.xix.421. [354.]*

ERLE LEICHTY, A bibliography of the cuneiform tablets of the Kuyunjik collection in the British Museum. London 1964. pp.xiii.289. [25,000.]

RYKLE BORGER, Handbuch der Keilschriftliteratur.
i. Repertorium der sumerischen und akkadischen texte. Berlin 1967. pp.x.672. [Very large number.]

MANFRED DIETRICH, OSWALD LORETZ, WALTER MAYER, Nuzi-bibliographie. Alter orient und altes testament: Sonderreihe, Veröffentlichungen zur kultur und geschichte des alten orients (band 11): Neukirchen-Vluyn 1972. pp.ix.172. [1000.]*

RICHARD S. ELLIS, A bibliography of mesopotamian archaeological sites. Wiesbaden 1972. pp.xxiv.113. [700.]*

iv. *Hittites*

G[EORGES] CONTENAU, Eléments de bibliographie hittite. 1922. pp.vii.139. [950.]
a supplement by the author appears in Babyloniaca *(1927–1928), x.1–68, 137–144.*

BENJAMIN SCHWARTZ, The Hittites. A list of references in the New York public library. New York 1939. pp.vii.94. [1750.]

EMMANUEL LAROCHE, Catalogue des textes hittites. Etudes et commentaires (75): Paris 1971. pp.xii.273. [833.]

v. *Ancient Egypt*

1. *General*

H[EIMANN] JOLOWICZ, Bibliotheca aegyptiaca. Repertorium über die ... in bezug auf Agypten ... erschienenen schriften. Leipzig 1858. pp.viii.244. [2675.]
—— Supplement 1. 1861. pp.[iv].76. [768.]

PROGRÈS des études relatives à l'Égypte et à l'orient. [Edited by Joseph Daniel Guigniaut]. Ministère de l'instuction publique: Recueil de rapports sur les progrès des lettres et des sciences en France: Sciences historiques et philologiques: 1867. pp.[ii].xi.213. [500.]

CESARE A. DE CARA, Notizia de'lavori de egittologia e di lingue semitiche pubblicati in Italia in questi ultimi decennii. Prato 1886. pp.[iv].103. [100.]

GIACOMO LUMBROSO, Progressi della egittologia greco-romana negli utlimi venticinque anni. Roma [printed] [1893]. pp.36. [750.]

JEAN CAPART, Bulletin critique des religions de l'Égypte. Bruxelles.
1904. 1905. pp.72. [200.]
1905. 1906. pp.[iii].73–160. [250.]
1906–1907. 1909. pp.[iii].161–276. [300.]
1908–1909. 1913. pp.[iii].277–382. [300.]
1904–1909. ... Avec une liste de publications de m. Capart ... et index du Bulletin ... par ... J. Janssen. Leiden 1939. pp.xxxv.400. [1000.]

REFERENCE catalogue of works upon the great pyramid of Egypt, and closely allied subjects the property of S. Allen Warner, 1907. pp.3–6 [125.]

SELECT list of references on ancient Egypt. Library of Congress: Washington 1912. ff.10. [99.]*

SEYMOUR [MONTEFIORE ROBERT ROSSO] DE RICCI. Esquisse d'une bibliographie égyptologique. 1919, pp.67. [1000.]

WILLIAM BURT COOK, Catalogue of the egyptological library and other books from the collection of the late Charles Edwin Wilbour. Brooklyn museum: Brooklyn, N.Y. 1924. pp.vi.795. [6000.]

IDA A[UGUSTA] PRATT, Ancient Egypt. Sources of information in the New York public library. Compiled ... under the direction of Richard [James Horatio] Gottheil. New York 1925. pp.xv.486. [10,000.]
—— Ancient Egypt, 1925–41. A supplement. 1942. pp.vii.340. [7500.]

JOHN WARNER, A list of books illustrating the story of ancient Egypt in the Newport public libraries. University extension lectures committee: Special reading lists (no.2): Newport 1926. pp.16. [125.]

HENRI MUNIER, Catalogue de la bibliothèque du Musée égyptien du Caire. Service des antiquités de l'Égypte: Le Caire 1926–1928. pp.vii.coll.496+497–1010. [14,000.]

EGYPTOLOGY. Second edition. [National book council:] Bibliography (no.88): 1928.pp.[4].[125.]

MIRON GOLDSTEIN, Internationale bibliographie der altaegyptischen medizin, 1850–1930. Berlin 1933. pp.[48]. [243.]

CHARLES BACHATLY, Bibliographie de la préhistoire égyptienne (1869–1938). Société royale de géographie d'Égypte: Publications: Le Caire 1942. pp.x.77. [836.]

ANNUAL egyptological bibliography. Bibliographie égyptologique annuelle. International association of Egyptologists: Leiden.

    i. 1947. Compiled by Jozef M[arie] A[ntoon] Janssen. pp.86. [331.]
    ii. 1948. pp.87–224. [373.]
    iii. 1949. pp.225–335. [452.]
    iv. 1950. pp.337–463. [459.]
    v. 1951. pp.465–631. [504.]
    vi. 1952. pp.633–819. [551.]
            [continued as:]

Bibliographie égyptologique annuelle. Association internationale des Égyptologues.

    1947–1956. pp.1608. [4981.]
    1957. pp.xii.170. [575.]
    1958. pp.x.231. [681.]
    1959. pp.x.218. [667.]
    1960. pp.x.272. [784.]
    Indexes 1947–56, by Jozef M. A. Janssen. Leiden 1960. pp.xviii. 475.
    1961–1963. pp.xix.270. [785.]
    1962. Compiled by Jozef M. A. Janssen and M. S. H. G. Heerma van Voss. 1964. pp.x.205. [670.]
    1963. Compiled by M. S. H. G. Heerma van Voss. 1968. pp.xi. 185. [617.]
    1964. 1968. pp.x.177. [570.]
    1965. 1969. pp.x.171. [540.]
    1966. Compiled by M. S. H. G. Heerma van Voss and Jac. J. Janssen. 1971. pp.xxii.193. [651.]
    1967. Compiled by Jac. J. Janssen. 1972. pp.x.197. [647.]

J[ACQUES] PIRENNE, Introduction bibliographique à l'histoire du droit égyptien jusqu'à l'époque d'Alexandre le grand. Le statut des hommes libres pendant la première féodalité dans l'ancienne Égypte. Wetteren 1948. pp.33–143. [1000.]

WARREN R[OYAL] DAWSON, Who was who in Egyptology ... from the year 1700 to the present day, but excluding persons now living. Egypt exploration society: 1951. pp.x.172. [1500.]

JEAN SAINTE-FARE GARNOT, Religions égyptiennes antiques. Bibliographie analytique, 1939–1943. 1952. pp.viii.279. [2800.]

H[ENRY] L[ESLIE] MAPLE, A bibliography of Egypt, consisting of works printed before A.D.1801. Pietermaritzburg 1952. ff.84. [1000.]

P[IERRE] L[OUIS] COLLIGNON and E[RIC] F[OULGER] WILLS, An index to the essays dealing with ancient Egypt, the Celts and the Basques by dr. J. Rendel Harris & miss Helen T. Sherlock. [Winscombe 1953]. pp.70. [65.]

J[EAN] LECLANT and GISÈLE CLERC, Inventaire bibliographique des Isiaca (IBIS). Répertoire analytique des travaux relatifs à la diffusion des cultes isiaques, 1940–1969. Études préliminaires aux religions orientales dans l'empire romain (tome 18): A-D. Leiden 1972. pp.xvii.191, pls. xxi. [346.]

MICHEL MALAISE, Inventaire préliminaire des documents égyptiens découverts en Italie. Études préliminaires aux religions orientales dans l'empire romain (21): Leiden 1972. pp.xvi.400, pls.64. [large number.]

2. Subjects

Archaeology

BERTHA PORTER and ROSALIND L[OUISA] B[EAUFORT] MOSS, Topographical bibliographical bibliography of ancient egyptian hieroglyphic texts, reliefs, and paintings. Oxford.

    i. The Theban necropolis. 1927. pp.xix.212. [6000.]
    — Second edition. 1960– . pp.503+ .
    ii. Theban temples. 1929. pp.xviii.204. [6000.]
    iii. Memphis (Abu Rawâsh to Dahshûr). 1931. pp.xxii.255. [7000.]
    iv. Lower and middle Egypt (delta and Cairo to Asyut). 1934. pp.xxviii.295. [8000.]
    v. Upper Egypt: sites (Deir Rifa to Aswân, excluding Thebes and the temples of Abydos, Dendera, Esna, Edfu, Kôm Ombo and Philae). 1937. pp.xxiv.292. [8000.]
    vi. Upper Egypt: chief temples (excluding Thebes), Abydos, Dendera, Esna, Edfu, Kôm Ombo, and Philae. 1939. pp.xx.264. [7000.]
    vii. Nubia, the deserts, and outside Egypt. 1951. pp.xxxvi.454. [12,500.]

BERTHA PORTER, ROSALIND L[OUISA] B[EAUFORT] MOSS and ETHEL W. BURNEY, Topographical bibliography of ancient egyptian hieroglyphic texts, reliefs and paintings. 2nd ed. Oxford.

    i. The Theban necropolis, Part 1: Private tombs. 1960. pp.xx.493. [viii]. [457.]
    ii. Theban temples. 1972. pp.xxxvi.586. [large number.]
    — Part 2: Royal tombs and smaller cemeteries. 1964. pp.xxxviii.494–887. [xx]. [large number.]

Architecture

MIRPAH G. BLAIR, History of architecture. Part 1: Ancient egyptian architecture. Public library: Special reading list (no.7): Cincinnati 1901. pp.4. [60.]

Champollion, family of

[JEAN JACQUES] CHAMPOLLION-FIGEAC, Notice sur les manuscrits autographes de Champollion le jeune, perdus en l'année 1832 et retrouvés en 1840. 1842. pp.47. [13.]

[HENRI JOSEPH] ADOLPHE ROCHAS, Notices biographiques et littéraires sur Champollion le jeune et mm. Champollion-Figeac. 1856. pp.17. [75.]

Cleopatra

GEORG HERMANN MOELLER, Die auffassung der Kleopatra in der tragödienliteratur der romanischen und germanischen nationen. Ulm 1888. pp.[iii].94. [30.]

GEORG HERMANN MÖLLER, Beiträge zur dramatischen Cleopatra-literatur. Schweinfurt 1907. pp.39. [127.]

THEODORE [DEODATUS NATHANIEL] BESTERMAN, A bibliography of Cleopatra. 1926. pp.8. [189.] *the British museum pressmarks are added in ms. to one of the copies in that library.*

Mathematics

RAYMOND CLARE ARCHIBALD, Bibliography of egyptian mathematics, with special reference to the Rhind mathematical papyrus. Mathematical association of America: Oberlin, O. 1927. pp.[ii]. 84. [250.]
—— Supplement [1929]. pp.[ii].85–106. [50.] *the Library of Congress copy contains a duplicated leaf for corrections and additions.*

Medicine

MIRON GOLDSTEIN, Internationale bibliographie der altaegyptischen medizin, 1850–1930. Berlin 1933. pp.[48]. [243.]

Mummies

WARREN R. DAWSON, A bibliography of works relating to mummification in Egypt. Institut d'Égypte: Mémoires (vol.xiii): Le Caire 1929. pp.[v].51. [163.]

Numismatics

ROBERT MOWAT, Bibliographie numismatique de l'Égypte grecque et romaine. [1900]. pp.7. [125.]

3. *Egyptian literature* [see also *Coptic literature.*]

[JEAN FRANÇOIS CHAMPOLLION, *the younger*], Catalogo de' papiri egiziani della biblioteca Vaticana. [Translated by Angelo Mai]. Roma 1825. pp.viii.79. [35.]
[—] — Die aegyptischen papyrus der Vaticanischen bibliothek. Aus dem italienischen des Angelo Mai [or rather, from his translation], von Ludwig Bachmann. Leipzig 1827. pp.vi.30. [35.]

EDWARD HINCKS, Catalogue of the egyptian manuscripts in the library of Trinity college. Dublin 1843. pp.[ii.]32. [19.]

THÉODULE DEVÉRIA, Catalogue des manuscrits égyptiens écrits sur papyrus, toile, tablettes et ostraca ... qui sont conservés au Musée égyptien du Louvre. 1881. pp.[iv].272. [1000.]

HORATIUS [ORAZIO] MARUCCHI, Monumenta papyracea aegyptia bibliothecae Vaticanae. Romae 1891. pp.ix.137. [138.]

STELLA VIRGINIA SEYBOLD, History of literature. ... II. Egyptian literature. Public library: Special reading list (no.8): Cincinnati 1902. pp.4. [24.]

BERTHA PORTER and ROSALIND L. B. MOSS, Topographical bibliography of ancient egyptian hieroglyphic texts, reliefs and paintings. Oxford 1927 &c.
details of this work are entered under Archaeology: Egypt, above.

A[LAN] W[YNN] SHORTER, Catalogue of egyptian religious papyri in the British museum. Copies of the book Pr(t)-m-hrw from the XVIIIth to the XXIInd dynasty. British museum.
i. Description of papyri with text. 1938. pp.xiv.127. [27.]

S. R. K. GLANVILLE, Catalogue of demotic papyri in the British museum.
i. A theban archive of the reign of Ptolemy I, Soter. 1939. pp.liii.75. [17.]

4. *Papyri*

[JEAN FRANÇOIS CHAMPOLLION, *the younger*], Catalogo de' papiri egiziani della biblioteca Vaticana. [Translated by Angelo Mai]. Roma 1825. pp.viii.79. [35.]
[—] — Die aegyptischen papyrus der Vaticanischen bibliothek. Aus dem italienischen des Angelo Mai [or rather, from his translation] von Ludwig Bachmann. Leipzig 1827. pp.vi.30. [35.]

EDWARD HINCKS, Catalogue of the egyptian manuscripts in the library of Trinity college. Dublin 1843. pp.[ii].32. [19.]

THÉODULE DEVÉRIA, Catalogue des manuscrits égyptiens écrits sur papyrus, toile, tablettes et ostraca ... qui sont conservés au Musée égyptien du Louvre. 1881. pp.[iv].272. [1000.]

KATALOG rekopisów egipskich, koptyjskich i etiopskich. Catalogue des manuscrits égyptiens, coptes et éthiopiens. Manuscrits égyptiens décrits par Tadeusz Andrzejewski, manuscrits coptes décrits par Stefan Jakobielski, manuscrits éthiopiens décrits par Stefan Strelcyn. Catalogue des manuscrits orientaux des collections polonaises (tome iv). Polska akademia nauk: Zakład orientalistyki: Warsawa 1960. pp.65. [egyptian: 9].

URSULA KAPLOWY-HECKEL [teil ii: KARL-THEODOR ZAUZICH), Ägyptische handschriften. Herausgegeben von Erich Lüddeckens. Verzeichnis der orientalischen handschriften in Deutschland (band xix): Wiesbaden 1971. pp.xx.310+xxii.217. [1046.]

E. A. E. REYMOND, Catalogue of the demotic papyri in the Ashmolean museum.
i. 1973.

5. Coptic literature

CARL HEINRICH TROMLER, Bibliothecae coptoiacobiticae specimen. Lipsiae 1767. pp.78. [200.]

GEORG ZOEGA, Catalogus codicum copticorum manu scriptorum qui in Museo borgiano Velitris adservantur. Romac. 1810. pp.xxi.663. [312.]

PAUL [ANTON] DE LAGARDE, Die koptischen handschriften der Goettinger bibliothek. Königliche gesellschaft der wissenschaften: Historisch-philologische klasse: Abhandlungen (vol.xxiv, no.1): Göttingen 1879. pp.62. [20.]

W[ILLEM] PLEYTE and P[IETER] A[DRIAAN] A[ART] BOESER, Manuscrits coptes du Musée d'antiquités des Pays-Bas [Rijksmuseum van oudheden] á Leide. Leide 1897. pp.[ix].490.

W[ALTER] E[WING] CRUM, Catalogue of the coptic manuscripts in the British museum. 1905. pp.xxiii.624. [1252.]

J[EAN] B[APTISTE] CHABOT, Inventaire sommaire des manuscrits coptes de la Bibliothèque nationale. 1906. pp.21. [190.]
the British museum copy contains ms. notes and corrections.

ADULPHUS HEBBELYNCK and ARNOLDUS VAN LANTSCHOOT, Codices coptici vaticani barberiniani borgiani rossiani. Bibliothecae apostolicae vaticanae codices manu scripti: [Vatican] 1937. pp.xxxv.698. [103.]

P. V. ERNSHTEDT, Коптские тексты Государственного Эрмитажа. Академия наук СССР: Отделение литературы и языка: Москва-Ленинград 1959. pp.192. [77.]

KATALOG rękopisów egipskich, koptyjskich i etiopskich. Catalogue des manuscrits égyptiens, coptes et éthiopiens . . . Manuscrits coptes décrits par Stefan Jakobielski . . . Catalogue des manuscrits orientaux des collections polonaises (tome iv): Zakład orientalistyki: Warzawa 1960. pp.65. [coptic: 19.]

ANTOINE KHATER and O. H. E. KHS-BURMESTER, Catalogue of the coptic and christian arabic mss. preserved in the cloister of saint Minas at Cairo. Publications de la Société d'archéologie copte: Bibliothèque de manuscrits (1): Le Caire 1967. pp.xviii.85,pls.12.21. [195.]

DAVID M. SCHOLER, Nag Hammadi bibliography 1948–1969. Nag Hammadi studies: Leiden 1971. pp.xvi.201. [2425.]

vi. Semitic languages and studies

CESARE A. DE CARA, Notizia de' lavori de egittologia e di lingue semitiche pubblicati in Italia in questi ultimi decennii. Prato 1886. pp.[iv].103. [100.]

[VICTOR CHAUVIN], Bibliographie biographique des sémitistes depuis le XVIe siècle jusqu'à nos jours. [Liége 1893]. pp.28. [150.]

HERBERT LOEWE, Catalogue of the printed books and of the semitic and jewish mss. in the Mary Frere hebrew library at Girton college. Cambridge [1916]. pp.[iii].xii.40. [250.]

MARIA HÖFNER, Verzeichnis der schriften von Enno Littmann. Tübingen 1945. pp.27. [451.]

WOLF LESLAU, Bibliography of the semitic languages of Ethiopia. Public library: New York 1946. pp.[ii].94. [1250.]

HENRI FLEISCH, Introduction à l'étude des langues sémitiques. Éléments de bibliographie. Université de Paris: Institut des études islamiques: Initiation à l'Islam (vol.iv): 1947. pp.148. [350.]

WILLIAM SANFORD LA SOR, A basic semitic bibliography (annotated). Fuller theological seminary: Bibliographical series (no.1): Wheaton, Ill. [1950.] pp.viii.56. [300.]

J[OHANNES] H[ENDRIK] HOSPERS, ed., A basic bibliography for the study of the semitic languages. Leiden 1873.
i. pp.xxv.401. [5500.]

vii. Mandaean

R[OBERT] PAYNE SMITH, Catalogi codicum manuscriptorum Bibliothecae bodleianae pars sexta, codices syriacos, carshunicos, mandaeos, complectens. Oxonii 1874. pp.x.coll.680. [Mandaean: 3.]

[H. ZOTENBERG], Manuscrits orientaux. Catalogues des manuscrits syriaques et sabéens (mandaïtes) de la Bibliothèque nationale. 1874. pp.viii.248. [Mandaean: 25.]

SVEND AAGE PALLIS, Essay on mandaean bibliography, 1560–1930. 1933. pp.xi.240. [850.]

viii Samaritan literature

STEPHANUS EVODIUS ASSEMANUS and JOSEPH SIMONIUS ASSEMANUS, Bibliothecæ apostolicæ codicum manuscriptorum catalogus. . . . Partis primae tomus primus, complectens codices ebraicos et samaritanos. Romæ 1756. pp.lxxvi.499. [500.]

[SALOMON MUNK *and others*], Manuscrits orientaux. Catalogues des manuscrits hébreux et samaritains de la Bibliothèque impériale. [1866]. pp. viii.263. [samaritan: 14.]

A. E. [Y.] HARKAVY, Описаніе самаритянскихъ рукописей, хранящихся въ Императорской публичной библіотекѣ. Санктпетербургъ 1875. pp.[xii].536. [202.]

G[EORGE] MARGOLIOUTH, Descriptive list of the hebrew and samaritan mss. in the British museum. 1893. pp.[iv].134. [1250.]

G[EORGE] MARGOLIOUTH [part iv: L. LEVEEN], Catalogue of the hebrew and samaritan manuscripts in the British museum. 1899–1935. pp. [vii].283 + [vii].492 + v.155 + [ii].157–378 + [ii]. 375–610+xv.208. [2500.]

DAVID SOLOMON SASSOON, אהל דוד [Ohel Dawid]. Descriptive catalogue of the hebrew and samaritan manuscripts in the Sassoon library, London 1932. pp.lxiii.566+[v].567–1112.[276].5. [samaritan: 60.]

EDWARD ROBERTSON, Catalogue of the samaritan manuscripts in the John Rylands library. Manchester 1938. pp.xii.coll.xiii–xxxviii.412. [1000.]

— Volume II. The Gaster manuscripts. Manchester 1962. pp.xiv.cols.xv–xxii.314. pls.12. [367.]

L[EO] A[RY] MAYER, Bibliography of the Samaritans, edited by Donald Broadribb. Supplements to Abr-Nahrain (vol.1): Leiden 1964. pp.vi.49. [750.]

ix. Ugaritic

M. DIETRICH [*and others*], Ugarit-bibliographie, 1928–1966. After Orient und Altes Testament (20): Neukirchen-Vluyn 1973. pp.xii.420+ 421–824+824–1275+860. [15,000.]*

HEBREW

i. Hebrew Language

JOHANN CHRISTOPH WOLF, דעת ספרי שרשים siue historia lexicorum hebraicorum, quae tam a Judaeis quam Christianis . . . in lucem uel edita, uel promissa sunt, uel in bibliothecis adhuc latentia deprehendentur. Accedit appendix de lexicis biblicis, quae nomina hebraica aliarumve lingvarum in Veteri vel Novo instumento [*sic*] obvia latine exponunt. Vitembergae 1705. pp.240.[xiv]. [150.]

GEORG HEINRICH GÖTZE, Elogia philologorum quorundam hebræorum, collectore Georgio Heinrico Goezio. Lubecæ 1708. pp.[viii].116. [175.]

[FRIEDRICH HEINRICH] WILHELM GESENIUS, Geschichte der hebräischen sprache und schrift. Eine philologisch-historische einleitung in die sprachlehre und wörterbücher der hebraischen sprache. Leipzig 1815. pp.viii.232. [100.]

LEOPOLD DUKES, Literaturhistorische mittheilungen ueber die ältesten hebräischen exegeten, grammatiker und lexicographen. Stuttgart 1844. pp.ix.199. [350.]

MORITZ STEINSCHNEIDER, Bibliographisches handbuch über die theoretische und praktische literatur für hebräische sprachkunde. Ein selbstständiger anhang zu Gesenius' Geschichte der hebräischen sprache und Le-Long-Masch's Biblioth. sacra. Leipzig 1859. pp.xxxvi.160. [2294.]

—— Zweite auflage, nebst zusätze [*sic*] und berichtigungen. Jerusalem 1937. pp.[iii].xxxvi. 160.132. [3500.]
this edition consists of a photographic reproduction of the original work, with additions and corrections by the author, N. Porges and M. Grunwald.

B[ER] BOROKHOV, די ביבליאטייק פון יידישן פילאלאגי [Vilna 1913]. pp.[ii]. coll.72. [501.]

MOSES BENSABAT AMZALAK, Portuguese hebrew grammars and grammarians. Lisbon 1928. pp.33. [25.]

MAX ZELDNER, A bibliography of methods and materials of teaching Hebrew in the light of modern language methodology. Education committee of New York: New York 1951. pp.[v].v. 98. [1500.]

URIEL WEINREICH and BEATRICE WEINREICH, Yiddish language and folklore. A selective bibliography for research. Janua linguarum (no.10): 's-Gravenhage 1959. pp.66. [481.]

ii. Manuscripts. Inscriptions

1. Manuscripts

STEPHANUS EVODIUS ASSEMANUS and JOSEPH SIMONIUS ASSEMANUS, Bibliothecæ apostolicæ codicum manuscriptorum catalogus. . . . Partis primæ tomus primus, complectens codices ebraicos et samaritanos. Romæ 1756. pp.lxxvi.499. [500.]

GIOVANNI BERNARDO DE ROSSI, Mss. codices hebraici biblioth. I. B. de-Rossi . . . accurate ab

eodem descripti. Parmae 1803. pp.viii.192+192
+222. [2000.]

*this collection is now in the Biblioteca palatina,
Parma.*

[EPHRAIM MOSES] PINNER, Prospectus der der
Odessaer gesellschaft für geschichte und alter-
thümer gehörenden ältesten hebräischen und rab-
binischen manuscripte. Odessa 1845. pp.92. [45.]

ALBREICHT KRAFFT and SIMON DEUTSCH, Die
handschriftlichen hebräischen werke der K. k.
hofbibliothek zu Wien. Bibliotheca palatina:
Catalogus codicum manuscriptorum (part 2):
Wien 1847. pp.viii.190.[vi]. [195.]

[M. H. HOHLENBERG, JUSTUS OLSHAUSEN and
AUGUST FERDINAND MICHAEL MEHREN], Codices
hebraici et arabici Bibliothecae regiae hafniensis.
Hafniae 1851. pp.xi.188. [hebrew: 50.]

J[ULIUS] GOLDENTHAL, Die neuerworbenen
hanschriftlichen hebräischen werke der K. k. hofbibliothek zu Wien. Bibliotheca palatina: Catalogus codicum manuscriptorum (part 3): Wien
1851. pp.[viii].91.[v]. [39.]

M[ORITZ] STEINSCHNEIDER, Conspectus codd
mss. hebraeorum in Biblotheca bodleiana.
Appendicis instar ad catall. liborum et mss. hebr.
... digessit M. Steinschneider. Berolini 1857. pp.
viii.32. [500.]

a facsimile was published at Berlin in 1931.

M[ORITZ] STEINSCHNEIDER, Catalogus codicum
hebraeorum bibliothecae Academiae Lugduno-
Batavae. Lugduni-Batavorum 1858.pp.xxviii.424.
[250.]

F. LEBRECHT, Handschriften und erste ausgaben
des Babylonischen talmud. ... Abtheilung 1:
handschriften. Wissenschaftliche blätter aus der
Veitel Heine Ephraim'schen lehranstalt (no.1):
Berlin 1862. pp.viii.114. [100.]
no more published.

[SALOMON MUNK and others]. Manuscrits orientaux. Catalogues des manuscrits hébreux et samaritains de la Bibliothèque impériale. [1866.] pp.
viii.263. [hebrew: 1750.]

JONAS GURLAND, Kutze beschreibung der
mathematischen, astronomischen und astrolo-
gischen hebräischen handschriften der Firko-
witsch'schen sammlung in der Kayserlichen
öffentlichen bibliothek zu St. Petersburg. Neue
denkmäler der jüdischen literatur (no.2): St.
Petersburg 1866. pp.[iv].57. [100.]

E[DWARD] H[ENRY] PALMER, A descriptive catalogue of the arabic, persian and turkish manuscripts in the library of Trinity college, Cambridge.
With an appendix, containing a catalogue of the
hebrew and samaritan mss. in the same library [by
William Aldis Wright]. Cambridge, London
1870. pp.vii.235. [hebrew: 31.]

M[ORITZ] STEINSCHNEIDER, Verzeichniss karai-
tischer und anderer hebräischer handschriften [im
besitze des herrn J[erocham] Fischl). Berlin 1872.
pp.[ii].34.

MORITZ STEINSCHNEIDER, Die hebræischen hand-
schriften der K. hof- und staatsbibliothek in
Muenchen. Catalogus codicum manu scriptorum
Bibliothecae regiae monacensis (vol.i, part 1):
Muenchen 1875. pp.228. [2000.]
——Zweite ... auflage. 1895. pp.x.277.
[2500.]

B. ZUCKERMANN, Catalogus bibliothecae semi-
narii jud.-theol. Vratislaviensis, continens CXC
codicum mss. hebr. rarissimorum et CCCLXIII
bibliorum editionum descriptionem. ... Editio
secunda. Vratislaviae 187. pp.[ii].x.65.[ii]. [453.]

S[ALOMON] M[ARCUS] SCHILLER-SZINESSY, Catalogue of the hebrew manuscripts preserved in the
University library, Cambridge. Volume 1. ...
Cambridge 1876. pp.[viii].248. [250.]
no more published.

A. [E. Y.] HARKAVY and H[ERMANN] L[EBERECHT]
STRACK, Catalog der hebräischen Bibelhand-
schriften der Kaiserlichen öffentlichen bibliothek
in St. Petersburg. St. Petersburg &c. 1875. pp.
[iv].xxxv.297. [175.]

MORITZ STEINSCHNEIDER, Catalog der hebräischen handschriften. Catalog der handschriften in
der Stadtbibliothek (vol.i): Hamburg 1878. pp.
xx.220. [500.]

MARCO MORTARA, Catalogo dei manoscritti
ebraici della biblioteca della Communita israelitica
di Mantova. Livorno 1879. pp.72. [200.]

MORITZ STEINSCHNEIDER, Verzeichniss der hebräischen handschriften. Königliche bibliothek:
Handschriften-verzeichnisse (vol.ii): Berlin 1878–
1897. pp.viii.149+viii.172. [500.]

BERNARDINO PEYRON, Codices hebraici manu
exarati Regiae bibliothecae que in Taurinensi
athenaeo asservantur. Taurini &c. 1880. pp.li.
327.[1000.]

S[AMUEL] LANDAUER, Katalog der hebräischen,
arabischen, persischen und türkischen handschriften der Kaiserlichen universitäts-und landesbibliothek. Strassburg 1881. pp.[iv].75. [125.]

[JOSEPH SIMON], Les manuscrits hébreux de la
bibliothèque de la ville de Nîmes. Versailles
[printed] [1881]. pp.15. [15.]

AD[OLF] NEUBAUER, Catalogue of the hebrew
manuscripts in the Jews' college, London. Oxford
1886. pp.viii.64. [250.]
privately printed.

S[OLOMON] J[OACHIM] HALBERSTAM, Catalog
hebräischer handschriften. Wien 1890. pp.168.
[411.]

formerly in the Judith Montefiore college, Ramsgate, and now in the Jews' college, London.

GUSTAVO SACERDOTE, Catalogo dei codici ebraici della Biblioteca casanatense. Firenze 1897. pp.192. [1000.]

AD[OLF] NEUBAUER [vol.ii: and ARTHUR ERNEST COWLEY], Catalogue of the hebrew manuscripts in the Bodleian library and in the college libraries of Oxford. Catalogi codd. mss. Bibliothecae bodleianae pars xii: Oxford 1886–1906. pp.xxxii. coll.1168+pp.xvi.coll.536.pp.537–544+vol. of facsimiles. [4000.]

G[EORGE] MARGOLIOUTH, Descriptive list of the hebrew and samaritan mss. in the British museum. 1893. pp.[iv].134. [1250.]

GUSTAVO SACERDOTE, I codici ebraici della Pia casa dei neofiti. Roma 1893. pp.41. [100.]

E. DEINARD, Or mayer. Catalogue of the old hebrew manuscripts and printed books of the library of Hon. M. Sulzberger of Philadelphia, Pa. New York 1896. pp.100. [394.]

G[EORGE] MARGOLIOUTH [part iv: J. LEVEEN], Catalogue of the hebrew and samaritan manuscripts in the British museum. 1899–1935. pp. [vii].283 + [vii].492 + v.155 + [ii].157–378 + [ii].375–610+xv.208. [2500.]

K[ARL] V[ILHELM] ZETTERSTÉEN, Verzeichnis der hebräischen und aramäischen handschriften der Kgl. universitätsbibliothek zu Upsala. Lund 1900. pp.22. [38.]

C[ARL] BROCKELMANN, Verzeichnis der arabischen, persischen, türkischen und hebräischen handschriften der Stadtbibliothek. Breslau 1903. pp.v.53. [80.]

HARTWIG HIRSCHFELD, Descriptive catalogue of the hebrew mss. of the Montefiore library. 1904. pp.xii.190. [1000.]
reprinted 1969. The mss. are housed at Jews' college, London.

[MOÏSE SCHWAB], Les manuscrits et incunables hébreux de la bibliothèque de l'Alliance israélite. [1904.] pp.40. [manuscripts: 130.]

S[ALOMON] MUNK, Manuscrits hébreux de l'Oratoire à la Bibliothèque nationale de Paris. Notices inédites. Franckfort-sur-le-Mein 1911. pp.88. [48.]

H. BRODY, Die handschriften der Prager jüdischen gemeindeibibliothek, "Talmud-Thora" religionsschule der israelischen Kultusgemeinde zu Prag: Bericht (2, 4, 5): Prag. 1911–14.

CARLO BERNHEIMER, Catalogue des manuscrits et livres rares hebraïques de la Bibliothèque du Talmud Tora de Livourne. Livourne [1914] pp.xiii. cols.250 [1150.]

ARTHUR ZACHARIAS SCHWARZ, Die hebräischen handschriften der K. k. hofbibliothek zu Wien. (Erwerbungen seit 1851). Kaiserliche akademie der wissenschaften: Sitzungsberichte: Philosophisch-historische klasse (vol.clxxv, no.5): Wien 1914. pp.136. [150.]

[E. N. ADLER], Catalogue of hebrew manuscripts in the collection of Elkan Nathan Adler. Cambridge 1921. pp.xii.228. [4000.]
pages 156a–d appear between 156 and 157; this collection is now in the library of the Jewish theological seminary, New York.

DAVID SIDERSKI, La stèle de Mésa. Index bibliographique. 1920. pp.33. [262.]

DAVID SIDERSKI, L'inscription hébraïque de Siloé. Essai bibliographique. 1924. pp.15. [124.]

MEYER ABRAHAM, Catalogue des manuscripts et incunables de l'École rabbinique de France. Société des études juives: 1924. pp.[i].27. [153.]

ARTHUR ZACHARIAS SCHWARZ, Die hebräischen handschriften der Nationalbibliothek in Wien. Nationalbibliothek: Museion (vol.ii): Wien &c. 1925. pp.xx.272. [750.]

HERBERT LOEWE, Catalogue of the manuscripts in the hebrew character collected and bequeathed to Trinity college library by the late William Aldis Wright. Cambridge 1926. pp.xx.165. [250.]

J. MILLAS I VALLICROSA, Documents hebraics de jueus catalans. Institut d'estudis catalans. Seccio historico–arqueologica: Barcelona 1927. pp.107. [33.]

ARTHUR ZACHARIAS SCHWARZ, Nikolsburger hebräische handschriften. New York 1929. pp.12. [10.]

G[ERSHOM] SCHOLEM and B. [YISSACHAR] JOEL, Catalogus codicum hebraicorum quot conservantur in Bibliotheca hieroslymitana quae est judaeorum populi et universitatis hebraicae. Pars prima: Cabbala. Supplementum specialiter additum ad "Kirjath sepher" ephemeridis bibliographicae tomum vii: Hierosolymis 1930. pp.xii. 248. [157.]

ARTHUR ZACHARIAS SCHWARZ, Die hebräischen handschriften in Österreich (ausserhalb der Nationalbibliothek in Wien). Teil 1: Bibel-Kabbala. Leipzig 1931. pp.viii.211. [1000.]

DAVID SOLOMON SASSOON, אהל דוד (Ohel Dawid). Descriptive catalogue of the hebrew and samaritan manuscripts in the Sassoon library, London 1932. pp.lxiii.566+[v].567–1112.[276].5. [1500.]

LISTE des manuscrits des commentaires bibliques de Raschi. Société des études juives: 1932. pp.55. [400.]

[GERSHOM] GERHARD SCHOLEM, Einige kabba-
listische handschriften im Britischen museum.
Jerusalem 1932. pp.56. [3.]

CARL BERNHEIMER, Codices hebraici Byblio-
thecae ambrosianae. Fontes ambrosiani (vol.v.):
Florentiae 1933. pp.xvi.211. [122.]
250 copies printed.

LEON NEMOY, Catalogue of hebrew and yiddish
manuscripts and books from the library of
Sholem Asch presented to Yale university by
Louis M. Rabinowitz. Yale university library
miscellanies (vol. v). New Haven 1945. pp.xxii.69.
[331.]

[DAVID JASSINE], Exposition de ... manuscrits,
incunables et autres éditions rares de la Biblioteca
iudaica simonseniana de Copenhague. Musée d'art
juif: 1952. pp.64. [181.]

HUMBERTUS CASSUTO, Codices vaticani hebraici.
Bybliotheca vaticana: [Rome] 1956. pp.[vii]. 199.
[1000.]

LIST of photocopies in the institute. State of
Israel: Ministry of education and culture: The
institute of hebrew manuscripts: Jerusalem.
1. Hebrew manuscripts in the libraries of
Austria and Germany, by N. Allony and D. S.
Loewinger, 1957. pp.viii.80. [835.]
2. Belgium, Denmark, the Netherlands, Spain
and Switzerland, by N. Allony and E. (F.) Kupfer,
1964. pp.xii.202. [1691.]
3. The Vatican, by N. Allony and D. S.
Loewinger. 1968. pp.xi.141. [801.]

ABRAHAM I. KATSH, Catalogue of hebrew manuscripts preserved in the USSR. Acquired (on
microfilm) by Abraham I. Katsh, curator, New
York university library of judaica and hebraica.
i. New York 1957. ff [v]. 62. [165]*
ii. Ginze Russiyah. Contains facsimiles of
Genizah manuscripts ... from the Antonin Cairo
Genizah collection in Leningrad. New York
university libraries. Occasional papers (nos. 3, 4).
ff. xi.138. [424.]*

THE JOHN Rylands library, Manchester: catalogue of an exhibition of hebrew manuscripts and
printed books together with other items of jewish
interest. Manchester 1958. pp.28. [73.]

MICROCARD catalogue of the rare hebrew
codices, manuscripts and ancient prints in the
Kaufman collection. Hungarian academy of
sciences (Magyar tudományos akademia): Oriental library (Keleti Könyvtár): Publications (vol.
iv): Budapest 1959. pp.5–44. [200.]

MARIA LUISA GENGARO, FRANCESCO LEONI and
GEMMA VILLA, Codici decorati e miniati del-
l'Ambrosiana, ebraici e greci. Fontes ambrosiani
(vol.xxxiii-A): Milano 1959. pp.3–253. [hebrew:
24.]

AARON FREIMANN, Union catalog of Hebrew
manuscripts and their location. New York.*
i. Index by Menahem Hayyim Schmelzer ...
American academy for jewish research: 1973.
pp.xxxiv.280. [5876.]
ii. 1964. pp.[iii].462. [11,861.]
reproduced from catalogue cards.

D. S. LOEWINGER and B. D. WEINRYB, Catalogue
of hebrew manuscripts in the library of the Jue-
disch-theologisches seminar in Breslau. Publication of the Leo Baeck institute, New York:
Wiesbaden 1965. pp.xiii.303. [405.]

RAFAEL EDELMANN, Hebraica from Denmark:
manuscripts and printed books in the collection of
the Royal library, Copenhagen. pp.[16]. [32.]

ERNST RÓTH and LOTHAR TETZNER, Hebräische
handschriften, teil 2. Herausgegeben von Hans
Striedl. Verzeichnis der orientalischen handschriften in Deutschland (band vi, 2): Wiesbaden
1965. pp.xx.416. [656.]

VALERIA ANTONIOLI MARTELLI and LUISA
MORTARA OTTOLENGHI, Manoscritti biblici ebraici
decorati provenienti de biblioteche italiane
pubbliche e private. Catalogo della mostra
ordinata presso la Biblioteca Trivulziana, Castello
Sforzeseo, Milano, 2/28 marzo 1966. Milano 1966.
pp.101. [vi]. [50.]

BEZALEL NARKISS, Hebrew illuminated manuscripts. Jerusalem, New York 1969. pp.176. [60.]

HEBRAICA Ambrosiana. I. Catalogue of un-
described hebrew manuscripts in the Ambrosiana
library, by Aldo Luzzatto. II: Description of
decorated and illuminated hebrew manuscripts in
the Ambrosiana library, by Luisa Mortara
Ottolenghi. Milano 1972. pp.[xii].164. [85.]

L. FUKS and R. G. FUKS-MANFELD, Catalogue of
the manuscripts of the Bibliotheia Rosentha-
liana, University library of Amsterdam. Hebrew
and judaic manuscripts in Amsterdam public
collections (1): 1973.

ALEJANDRO DÍEZ MACHO, Mannscritos hebreos
y arameos de la Biblia: contribución al estudio de
las diversas tradiciones del texto del Antiguo
Testamento. Studia ephemeridis "Augistinianum"
(5): Roma 1971. pp.314. [large number.]

Genizah

B[ENZION] HALPER, Descriptive catalogue of
genizah fragments in Philadelphia. Dropsie college: Philadelphia 1924. pp.235. [487.]
*nearly all the manuscripts are now in the Dropsie
college library.*

RICHARD GOTTHEIL and WILLIAM H. WORRELL,
edd. Fragments from the Cairo genizah in the
Freer collection. New York 1927. pp.xxxi.273.
[50.]

J. SCHIRMANN, Die poetischen genizafragmente in der jüdischen gemeindebibliothek Berlin. [s.l. c.1930]. pp.16. [90.]

SHAUL SHAKED, A tentative bibliography of Geniza documents. Prepared under the direction of D. H. Baneth and S. D. Goitein. École pratique des hautes études: 6me section: Sciences économiques et sociales: Études juives (v): Paris, The Hague 1964. pp.355. [3000.]

Dead sea manuscripts

WILLIAM SANFORD LASOR, Bibliography of the Dead sea scrolls 1948–1957. Fuller theological seminary: Fuller library bulletin (no.31): Pasadena 1958. pp.92. [2983.]

CHRISTOPH BURCHARD, Bibliographie zu den handschriften vom Toten meer. Zeitschrift für die alttestamentliche wissenschaft: Beihefte (no.76): Berlin 1959. pp.xv.118. [1556.]
—— II. Berlin 1965. pp.xx.360. [2903.]

MICHAEL YIZHAR, Bibliography of Hebrew publications on the Dead Sea scrolls, 1948–1964. Harvard theological studies (xxiii): Cambridge 1967. pp.[vi]. [275.]

B. JONGELING, A classified bibliography of the finds in the desert of Judah, 1958–1969. Studies on the texts of the desert of Judah (vol. vii): Leiden 1971, pp.xiv.140. [1500.]

iii. Printing

*GIOVANNI BERNARDO DE ROSSI, De hebraicae typographiae origine ac primitiis, seu de antiquis ac rarissimis hebraicorum liborum editionibus seculi xv disquisitio historico-critica. Parmae 1776. pp.[viii.]100. [71.]
reissued at Erlangen in 1778.

GIOVANNI BERNARDO DE ROSSI, De typographia hebraeo-ferrariensi commentarius historicus, quo ferrarienses Judaeorum editiones hebraicae, hispanicae, lusitanae recensentur et illustrantur. Parmae 1780. pp.xvi.112. [43.]
—— Editio altera. [Edited by Wilhelm Friedrich Hufnagel]. Erlangae 1781. pp.xxxii.136. [43.]

GIAMBERNARDO DE ROSSI, Annali ebreo-tipografici di Sabbioneta sotto Vespasiano Gonzaga. Parma 1780. pp.32. [31.]
—— Annales typographiae ebraicae Sabionetenses appendice aucti. Ex italicis latinos fecit m. Io. Frid. Roos. Erlangae 1783. pp.xvi.52. [36.]

*GIOVANNI BERNARDO DE ROSSI, Annales hebraeo-typographici sec. xv. Parmae 1795. pp. xxiv.184. [155.]

GIOVANNI BERNARDO DE ROSSI, Annales hebraeo-typographici ab an. MDI ad MDXL. Parmae 1799. pp.[iv].64.4. [525.]

G[IOVANNI] BERNARDO DE ROSSI, Annali ebreo-tipografici di Cremona. Parma 1808. pp.24. [52.]

GAETANO ZACCARIA [ANTONUCCI], Catalogo di opere ebraiche, greche, latine ed italiane stampate dai celebri tipografi Soncini ne' secoli xv e xvi. Fermo 1863. pp.85. [125.]
150 copies printed.
—— Serie di opere ebraiche imprese [&c.]. . . . 3ª edizione assistita de Crescentino Giannini. 1870. pp.122.69. [100.]
not limited to hebrew works.

E[LIAKIM] CARMOLY, Annalen der hebräischen typographie von Riva di Trento (1558–1562). Zweite auflage. Frankfurt a. M. 1868. pp.16. [34.]

FEDERIGO SACCHI, I tipografi ebrei dei Soncino. Studii bibliografici. Cremona 1877. pp.71. [200.]
on cover: 'Parte prima'; no more published.

MOÏSÉ SOAVE, Dei Soncino, cèlebri typografi Italiani. Venzenia 1878. pp.50. [175.]
the British museum copy has ms. additions.

MOÏSE SCHWAB, Les incunables orientaux et les impressions orientales au commencement du xvie siècle. 1883. pp.[iii].139. [530.]
limited to works in hebrew.

GIACOMO MANZONI, Annali tipografici dei Soncino. Tomo II [–IV, fascicolo I]. Bologna 1883–1886. pp.iv.164+xxiv.136+504+[iv].127. [150.]
no more published.

H[ENRI AUGUSTE] OMONT, Alphabets grecs & hébreux. 1885. pp.15. [hebrew: 27.]

LEONELLO MODONA, Degli incunaboli e di alcune edizioni ebraiche rare o pregevoli nella biblioteca della R. università di Bologna. Brescia 1890. pp.15. [40.]

A[BRAHAM ADOLF] BERLINER, Aus meiner bibliothek. Beiträge zur hebräischen bibliographie u. typographie. Frankfurt a. M. 1898. pp.vi.77. xxxv. [72.]

EDUARD BIBERFELD, Die hebräischen druckereien zu Karlsruhe und ihre drucke. Karlsruhe i. B 1898. pp.40. [64.]

F[RIEDRICH] C[LEMENS] EBRARD, Ausstellung hebräischer druckwerke, Zweite ... auflage. Stadtbibliothek: Frankfurt a. M. 1902. pp.40. [196.]

*ARON FREIMANN, Über hebräische inkunabeln. Leipzig 1902. pp.[ii.]9. [100.]

ARON FREIMANN, Annalen der hebräischen druckerei in Wilhermsdorf. Berlin 1903. pp.16. [150.]

MAGNUS WEINBERG, Die hebräischen druckereien in Salzbach. Frankfurt a. M. 1904. pp.190. [539.]

*[MOÏSE SCHWAB], Les manuscrits et incunables hébreux de la bibliothèque de l'Alliance israélite. [1904]. pp.40. [incunabula: 13.]

DAVID WERNER AMRAM, The makers of hebrew books in Italy. Philadelphia 1909. pp.xvii.417. [2000.]

*UMBERTO CASSUTO, Incunaboli ebraici di Firenze. Firenze 1912. pp.[ii.]36. [43.]

GUIDO SONNINO, Storia della tipografia ebraica in Livorno. Torino 1912. pp.[ii].105. [567.]

ELKAN NATHAN ADLER, A gazetteer of hebrew printing. 1917. pp.23. [500.]

*ARON FREIMANN, Die hebräischen inkunabeln der stadtbibliothek. Frankfurt a. M. 1920. pp.16. [59.]

*MOSES BENSABAT AMZALAK, A tipografia hebraica em Portugal no século xv. Coimbra 1922. pp.47. [20.]
150 copies printed.

*MEYER ABRAHAM, Catalogue des manuscrits et incunables de l'École rabbinique de France. Société des études juives: Publications: 1924. pp.[i].27. [153.]

KARL J. LÜTHI, Hebräisch in der Schweiz. Bern 1926. pp.[vi].48. [400.]
300 copies printed.

J. S. DA SILVA ROSA, אלפי מנשה 1627-1 Januari-1927. Catalogus der tentoonstelling in het portugeesch israëlietisch seminarium 'Ets haim' te Amsterdam ter herinnering aan het...eerste.. te Amsterdam gedrukte hebreeuwsche boek. Amsterdam 1927. pp.30. [66.]

JOSHUA BLOCH, Hebrew printing in Riva di Trento. Public library: New York 1933. pp.[iii]. 15. [35.]

B[ERNHARD] FRIEDBERG, [&c.] תולדותהדפוס העברי מדינות • History of hebrew typography in Italy, Spain-Portugal, Turkey and the orient.... With bibliography of all existing hebrew incunabula. Antwerp 1934. pp.[vii].141. [300.]
200 copies printed.

ARON FREIMANN, A gazetteer of hebrew printing. Public library: New York 1946. pp.86. [1250.]
a bibliography of the first productions of the several hebrew presses.

[I. ADLER], Le livre hébraïque, incunables—publications israéliennes. Exposition organisée avec le concours de la Bibliothèque nationale 1962. pp.3–120. [incunables: 39].

SHOSHANA HALEVY, The printed hebrew books in Jerusalem during the first half century (1841–1891). Publication of the Ben-Zvi institute: Bibliography: Jerusalem 1963, pp.202. [662.]

ELI ESHKENAZI, STRAKHILL GICHEV, Опис на еврейските старопечати книги в България. Descriptive catalogue of the old printed hebrew books in Bulgaria. Tom i–xviв. Част 1-до 1540 г. Българска академия на науките: София 1966. pp.172. [26.]

ABRAHAM YAARY, Hebrew printing at Constantinople; its history and bibliography. Supplement to Kirjath sepher (vol.xlii): Jerusalem 1967. pp.303. [758.]

iv. Catalogues of printed books

JOHANN BUXTORF, De abbreviaturis hebraicis liber novus & copiosus: cui accesserunt operis talmudici brevis recensio. ... Item bibliotheca rabbinica nova. Basilea 1613. pp.[xvi].335. [1000.]
—— Editione ... secunda. 1640. pp.[xvi]. 472. [viii]. [1250.]
—— Editione ... novissima. Herbornae Nassaviae 1708. pp.[xxviii].304.217.[x]. [1500.]

JULIUS BARTOLOCCIUS, [&c.] ... קרית ספר Bibliotheca magna rabbinica de scriptoribus, & scriptis hebraicis, ordine alphabetico hebraicè. & latinè digestis. ... Edita a D. Carolo Ioseph Imbonato. [Vol.v: Bibliotheca latino-hebraica... avctore ... Carolo Ioseph Imbonato]. Romæ 1675–1694. pp.[xxiii].831 + [xv].924 + [xi].1003 + [xvi].lxxvi.684 + [xiii].549.278.[v]. [25,000.]

JOH[ANN] DAVID HOHEISEL, Pseudonymorum hebraicorum hexecontas. Gedani [1708]. pp.34. [60.]

JOHANN CHRISTOPH WOLF, Bibliotheca hebræa, sive notitia tum auctorum hebr. cujuscunque ætatis, tum scriptorum quæ vel hebraice primum exarata vel ab aliis conversa sunt, ad nostram ætatem deducta. Accedit in calce Jacobi Gaffarelli Index codicum cabbalistic. mss. quibus Jo. Picus, Mirandulanus comes, usus est. Hamburgi &c. 1715–1733. pp.[vi].40.1161.[xxxv].24 + [x].1484 + [viii].1226.[lx] + [xii].1226.[lxxii]. [10,000.]
the titles of the several volumes vary.

[GABRIEL GRODDECK], לקט פלוני אלמוני id est spicilegium aliquot librorum anonymorum et pseudonymorum, qui lingua rabbinica partim impressi, partim manuscripti reperiuntur. Trajecti ad Rhenum 1728. pp.196. [519.]

[FRIEDRICH OPPERGELT], Aufrichtige nachricht von den jüdischen lehrern, und ihren zur exegesi u. antiqvitæt gehörigen schriften....Nebst einer kleinen bibliotheca rabbinica. Halle im Magdeburgischen 1730. pp.[xxiv].264. [1000.]

ANTONIO MARIA BISCIONI, Bibliothecae ebraicae graecae, florentinae sive Bibliothecae mediceolavrentianae catalogvs. Florentinae 1757. pp.vi.308 + 559. [hebrew: 1000.]
the second volume sets out the hebrew works.

JOSEPH RODRIGUEZ DE CASTRO, Biblioteca española. Tomo primero, que contiene la noticia de los escritores rabinos españoles desde la epoca conocida de su literatura hasta el presente. Madrid 1781. pp.[xxxiv].668.[clxviii]. [2500.]

HERMANN FRIEDRICH KOECHER, Nova bibliotheca hebraica secvndvm ordinem Bibliothecae hebraicae b. Io. Christoph. Wolfi disposita, analecta literaria hvivs operis sistens. Iena 1783–1784. pp.[iv].130+[xvi].276. [2000.]

G[IOVANNI] B[ERNARDO] DE' ROSSI, Dizionario storico degli autori ebrei e delle loro opere. Parma 1802. pp.viii.192+170. [1750.]
— — Historisches wörterbuch der jüdischen schrifsteller . . . übersetzt von C. H. Hamberger. Leipzig 1839. pp.xvi.336. [1750.]
— — — Ausführliches sach- und namenregister . . . von Heimann Jolowicz, . . . herausgegeben von Ad[olf] Jellinek. 1846. pp.32.

[GIOVANNI BERNARDO DE ROSSI], Libri stampati di letteratura sacra ebraica ed orientale della biblioteca del dottore G. Bernardo de-Rossi. Parma 1812. pp.84. [3000.]

COLLECTIO Davidis, i.e. catalogus celeberrimae illius bibliothecae hebraeae quam . . . collegit r. Davides Oppenheimerus. Hamburgi 1826. pp. xvi.744. [4100.]

M[ORITZ] STEINSCHNEIDER, Catalogus liborum hebraeorum in Bibliotheca bodleiana. Berolini 1852–1860. pp.[iii].coll.cxxxii.pp.[ii.].coll.3104. pp.c. [15,000.]
the author published a supplement in the Centralblatt für bibliothekswesen (1894), xi.484–508.

המזכיר . . . Hebræische bibliographie. Blätter für neuere und ältere literatur des Judenthums. Berlin.
    i. 1858. Redigirt von M[oritz] Steinschneider. pp.[ii].ii.132. [750.]
    ii. 1859. pp.[ii].ii.112.[iv]. [500.]
    iii. 1860. pp.viii.120.8. [500.]
    iv. 1861. pp.iv.156. [750.]
    v. 1862. pp.iv.152. [750.]
    vi. 1863. pp.vi.148. [500.]
    vii. 1864. pp.iv.136. [400.]
    viii. 1865. pp.iv.152. [400.]
    ix. 1869. Herausgegeben von Julius Benzian. pp.vi.176. [1500.]
    x. 1870. pp.iv.174. [1500.]
    xi. 1871. pp.vi.142. [1000.]
    xii. 1872. pp.vi.134. [750.]
    xiii. 1873. pp.viii.140. [500.]
    xiv. 1874. pp.viii.136. [750.]
    xv. 1874. pp.viii.136. [1000.]
    xvi. 1876. pp.viii.136. [1000.]
    xvii. 1877. pp.viii.136. [1000.]
    xviii. 1878. pp.viii.136. [1000.]
    xix. 1879. pp.viii.136. [1000.]

    xx. 1880. pp.vi.138. [1000.]
    xxi. 1881–1882. pp.viii.136. [1000.]
not published 1866–1868; no more published.

G. WOLF, Catalog der bibliothek des sel. herrn dr. Bernhard Beer. Berlin 1863. pp.lii.161.120. [4000.]

SAMUEL DAVIDE LUZZATTO, &c. יד יוסף [Catalogue de la bibliothèque de littérature hébraïque et orientale de feu mr Joseph (Giuseppe) Almanzi]. Padoue 1864. pp.91.120.

[LEOPOLD] ZUNZ, Literaturgeschichte der synagogalen poesie. Berlin 1865. pp.xi.666. [5000.]
— — Nachtrag. 1867. pp.[iii.]76. [750.]
— — Mafteach ha-pijutim. Index . . . von Ad[olph] Gestetner. Zunz-stiftung: 1889. pp. viii.127.

[JOSEPH ZEDNER], Catalogue of the hebrew books in the library of the British museum. 1867. pp.viii.891. [10,0000.]
— — Catalogue of hebrew books in the British museum acquired during the years 1868–1892. By S. Van Straalen. 1894. pp.vii.532. [4650.]

קרות ספר Ausführlicher bibliographischer catalog der reichhaltigen sammlungen hebräischer und jüdischer bücher und handschriften, nachgelassen vom rabbiner Jakob Emden, vom oberrabbiner M. J. Lewenstein, in Paramaribo, und anderen. Amsterdam 1867. pp.224. [761.]

M[EYER MARCUS] ROEST, Catalog der Hebraica und Judaica aus der L[ippmann] Rosenthal'schen bibliothek. Amsterdam 1875. pp.vii.910+[ii]. 911–1218.[ii].504. [7500.]
based on notes by Rosenthal.

R[APHAEL] N[ATHAN] RABBINOVICZ, Kritische uebersicht der gesammt- & einzelausgaben des Babylonischen talmuds seit 1484. München 1877. pp.132. [100.]

CATALOG einer sammlung hebräischer und jüdischer bücher und handschriften grösstentheils nachgelassen von Jacob Lehmans und Joseph Bernard Lehmans. Amsterdam 1879. pp.92.

I[SAAC] A. BENJACOB, [&c.] אוצר הספרים [Оцаръ га-сефаримъ (сокровище книгъ). Библіографія всеобщей еврейской письменности]. Вильна 1880. pp.xxiv.678. [15,000.]

WILLIAM ZEITLIN, Bibliotheca hebraica post mendelssohniana. . . . Erste lieferung. St. Petersburg 1881. pp.80. [750.]
A-Hurwitz only; no more published.
— — Zweite . . . auflage. Leipzig 1891–1895. pp.[iii.]iv.548. [3000.]

CYRUS ADLER, Catalogue of a hebrew library . . . of the late Joshua I. Cohen. Baltimore 1887. pp.47. [350.]
privately printed.

HEIMANN JOSEPH MICHAEL, &c. אוֹר הַחַיִּים
[(Or ha-chajim). Umfassendes bibliographisches
und literar-historisches wörterbuch des rabbi-
nischen schriftthums]. [Edited by Elieser Loeb
and Abraham Berliner]. Frankfurt a. M. 1891.
pp.viii.617. [1230.]

A[LBERT] LÖWY, Catalogue of Hebraica and
Judaica in the library of the corporation of the
city of London. 1891. pp.xi.231. [1500.]

SAMUEL WIENER, Bibliotheca Friedlandiana.
Catalogus librorum impressorum hebraeorum in
Museo asiatico Academiae scientiarum rossicae
asservatorum. Petropoli 1893–1918. pp.iv.630.
[5139.]
— Fasc. vii. Editio altera, Jerusalem 1963.
pp.631–656 [5140–5507A.]
— Catalogue des livres hébraïques (édités
jusqu'à l'an 1892) de la bibliothèque de l'Institut
des études orientales de l'Académie des sciences de
l'URSS, livraison viii, par Joseph Bender,
rédigée par Paul Kokowzoff. 2ème tirage. pp.657–
689.iii. [5508–5905.] Vol. I, partes i–vi.

GUSTAVO SACERDOTE, Deux index expurgatoires
de livres hébreux. Versailles 1895. pp.31. [65.]

רְשִׁימַת סִפְרֵי יִשְׂרָאֵל [Catalog der hebräi-
schen bücher in der bibliothek des professors D.
Chwolson (Daniil Avraamovich Khvolson)].
Wilna 1897. pp.[v].142.

ERICH BISCHOFF, Kritische geschichte der Thal-
mud-übersetzungen aller zeiten und zungen.
Frankfurt a. M. 1899. pp.112. [200.]

CATALOGUE of the Leopold Strouse rabbinical
library. Johns Hopkins library: Baltimore 1900.
pp.3–28. [400.]

SOLOMON GOLDSCHMIDT, Verzeichniss der judaica aus der bibliothek des herrn dr. H. B. Levy
in Hamburg. Hamburg 1900.

M. ZUCKERMANN, Katalog der Israelitschen
gemeindebibliothek zu Hannover. Hannover
1901. pp.x.123. [1000.]

S[AMUEL] WIENER, [&c.) רְשִׁימַת הַגָּדוֹת פֶּסַח
Bibliographie der Oster-haggadah, 1500–1900.
Académie impériale des sciences: St.-Pétersbourg
1902. pp.12.54.vii. [900.]
*the hebrew titlepage is dated 1901; a facsimile
appeared New York 1949.*

W[ILHELM] ZEITLIN, Anagramme, initialen und
pseudonyma neu-hebräischer schriftsteller und
publizisten. Frankfurt a.M. 1905. pp.18. [400.]

I[SRAEL] ABRAHAMS, Bibliography of Hebraica
and Judaica (Autumn 1904–Autumn 1905).
Oxford 1905. pp.42. [500.]
— — 1905–1906. 1906. pp.46. [600.]

MAX WEISZ, Katalog der hebräischen handschriften und bücher in der bibliothek des professors dr. David Kaufmann. Frankfurt a. M.
1906. pp.[iv.]199.80.[ii]. [2250.]
*this library is now in the possession of the Magyar
tudományos akademia, Budapest.*

[ARON FREIMANN], Bibliothek der Israelitischen
religionsschule zu Frankfurt am Main. Katalog.
Frankfurt a. M. 1909. pp.[iv].69.201. [Hebrew:
3118.]

SAMUEL POZNAŃSKI, Die karaïsche literatur der
letzten dreissig jahre. Frankfurt a. M. 1910. pp.40.
[45.]

BERNARD WACHSTEIN, Katalog der Salo Cohn'-
schen schenkungen. Bibliothek der Israelitischen
kultusgemeinde: Wien 1911–1914. pp.xviii.215
+xiii.178. [1338.]
— — Zuwachsverzeichnis.
    1924–1925. pp.[ii].60.7. [1100.]
    1926–1927. pp.67.11. [1171.]
    1928–1929. pp.82.15. [1435.]
    1930–1931. pp.145.14. [1675.]

CARLO BERNHEIMER, Catalogue des manuscrits
et livres rares hébraïques de la bibliothèque du
Talmud Tora de Livourne. Livourne [1915]. pp.
xiii.coll.254+portfolio of plates. [1000.]

BERNHARD WACHSTEIN, &c. מִפְתַּח הַסְּפָרִים
[Zur bibliographie der gedächtnis- und trauer-
vortraege in der hebräischen literatur]. Israeli-
tische kultusgemeinde Wien: Bibliothek: Veröffentlichungen (vols.iii–vi): Wien 1922–1932.
pp.[vi].xvi.72+[ii].xvii.52+xxxiv.115+v.63.40.
[5000.]

MEYER ABRAHAM, Catalogue des manuscrits et
incunables de l'École rabbinique de France.
Société des études juives: 1924. pp.[i].27. [153.]

EPHRAIM DEINARD, [&c.] קֹהֶלֶת אַמֶּרִיקָא
Koheleth America. Catalogue of hebrew books
printed in America from 1735–1925. St. Louis
[1926].

GERHARD SCHOLEM, Bibliographia kabbalistica.
Verzeichniss der gedruckten die jüdische mystik
(gnosis, kabbala, sabbatianismus, frankismus,
chassidismus) behandelnden bücher und aufsätze
von Reuchlin bis zur gegenwart. Mit einem anhang: bibliographie des Zohar und seiner kom-
mentare. Kabbala (vol.ii): Leipzig 1927. pp.xviii.
230. [1550.]
reissued in 1933.

B[ERNHARD] FRIEDBERG, בֵּית עֵקֵד סְפָרִים ...
Bet eked sepharim. Lexique bibliographique de
tous les ouvrages de la littérature hébraïque et
judéo-allemande, y compris les ouvrages arabes,
grecs, italiens, espagnols-portugais, persans, sa-

maritains et tartares en caractères hébraïques, imprimés et publiés de 1475 à 1900. Anvers 1928–131. pp.[viii].844. [17,500.]

— — Second edition. Bet eked sepharim. Bibliographical lexicon of the whole hebrew and jewish-german literature, inclusive of the arab, greek, french-provencal, italian, latin, persian, samaritan, spanish-portuguese and tartarian works, printed in the years 1474–1950 with hebrew letters. Published by Baruch Friedberg. [Tel Aviv 1951–1956]. pp.[viii].340+[iv].341–708+[iv].709–1048 +[iv].1049–8420. [25,000.]

A[RTHUR] E[RNEST] COWLEY, A concise catalogue of the hebrew printed books in the Bodleian library. Oxford 1929. pp.vii.816. [12,500.]

JOSEPH I. GORFINKLE. A bibliography of Maimonides. New York 1932. pp.16. [200.]

SAUL CHAJES, **השם אוצר בדויי** Thesaurus pseudonymorum quæ in litteratura hebraica et judaeo-germanica inveniuntur. Israelitisch-theologische lehransalt: Veröffentlichungen der Oberrabbiner dr. H. P. Chajes-preisstiftung [vol.iv]: Wien 1933: pp.xiv.335.**ד** [vi].66. [2500.]

ISRAEL SCHAPIRO, **אוצר תרגומים עברים מספרות הגרמגית** Bibliography of hebrew translations of german works. New York 1934. pp.79. [450.]

KATALOG der bibliothek des verewigten prof. dr. Ludwig Blau. Budapest 1936. pp.76.38. [2500.]

GERSHOM [GERHARD] SCHOLEM, **עלך קיבטרס לשלום** [Desiderata in kabbala and jewish mysticism].[Jerusalem 1937]. ff.5. [31.]

MITCHELL M. KAPLAN, Panorama of ancient letters. Four and a half centuries of hebraica and judaica. Bibliographical notes and descriptions of 1,000 rare books and manuscripts, forming a part of the Mitchell M. Kaplan collection, presented to New York university jewish culture foundation. New York 1942. pp.[vi].316. [1012.]

ABRAHAM I[SAAC] KATSH. The Solomon Rosenthal collection of Hebraica . . . presented to New York university. [New York] 1942. pp.[xv].53. [xxi]. [496.]*

LEON NEMOY, Catalogue of hebrew and yiddish manuscripts and books from the library of Sholem Asch presented to Yale university by Louis M. Rabinowitz. Yale university library miscellanies (vol.v): New Haven 1945. pp.xxii.69. [331.]

SPECIAL list of books in medieval hebrew poetry and liturgy. College of the city of New York: Davidson library of Judaica: New York 1948. pp.34. [500.]

ALEX LEDERER and BEN-ZION ROSENZWEIG, The Henry and Mollie Cohen collection of Hebraica and Judaica. A check list of the books in the hebrew language. University of Texas: Library: Austin 1951. ff.33. [225.]
the collection forms part of the university library.

[DAVID JASSINE], Exposition de . . . manuscrits, incunables et autres éditions rares de la Biblioteca iudaica simonseniana de Copenhague. Musée d'art juif: 1952. pp.64. [181.]

. . . רשימת ספרים לספריות עברית· List of books for standard hebrew libraries. World club for hebrew libraries: Jerusalem 1957. pp.[viii]. **גד.**[viii].48. [1862.]

MARTIN J. BUSS, Old Testament dissertations 1928–1958. Facsimile produced by microfilm/xerography. [1958?]. pp.x.57. [650.]*

MENAHEM M. KASHER and JACOB B. MANDELBAUM, *edd.* Sarei ha-elef: a millennium of hebrew authors (4260–5260: 500–1500 C.E.). A complete bibliographical compendium of hebraica written during the thousand-year period between the close of the Talmud and the beginning of the Shulhan aruch. New York 1959. pp.[9].555. [3,500.]

CATALOG of hebrew and yiddish titles of the jewish collection. New York public library: Reference department: Boston 1960. pp.10147–10854+10855–11532+11533–12120. [44,500.]

PHILIP FRIEDMAN, Bibliography of books on the jewish catastrophe and heroism in Europe. Yad washem, remembrance authority of disaster and heroism, Jerusalem: Yivo institute for jewish research, New York: Joint projects: Bibliographical series (2): Jerusalem 1960, pp.x.433. [1246.]

MICROCARD catalogue of the rare hebrew codices, manuscripts and ancient prints in the Kaufman collection. Hungarian academy of sciences [Magyar tudományos akadémia]: Oriental library [Keleti könyvtár]: Publications (vol.iv): Budapest 1959. pp.5–44. [200.]

JACOB ISRAEL DIENSTAG, **ביאור מלות ההגיון להרמב"ם** Maimonides' Treatise on logic. An annotated bibliography. Jerusalem 1960. pp.7–34.

ABRAHAM YAARI, **ביבליוגרפיה של הגדות פסח מראשית הדפוס ועד היום בצירוף עשרים וחמשה עילומי רפים מתור הגדות יק רות מציאות** Bibliography of the Passover Haggadah from the earliest printed edition to 1960. [Jerusalem 1960]. pp.ixi.207.xx.xi.

Y. YOSEF COHEN and M. PIEKARZ, פרומים
1917–1960: יהודיים בברית־המועצות.
Jewish publications in the Soviet Union, 1917–
1960. [Jerusalem 1961]. pp.143.502.vi.

HEBRAICA & judaica. The Theodore E. Cummings collection. An exhibit. University of California: [Los Angeles 1963]. pp.[ii].12. [80.]

[HARRY J. HIRSCHHORN], מה נשתנה··· Mah nishtana. A selection of ... Passover hagadot. Kol Ami museum: Highland Park, Ill. 1964. pp. ix.117. [119.]

DICTIONARY catalog of the Klau library, Cincinnati. Hebrew union college—Jewish institute of religion: Boston 1964.
Vols. 28–32. Hebrew titles. pp.640+631+607 +644+599. [54,691 cards.]

HEBRAICA at the university of Chicago. [An exhibition.] Chicago 1965. pp.22. [52.]

WILLIAM M. BRINNER, Sutro library hebraica: a handlist. California state library 1966. pp.xiii.82. [167.]*

PETER NICKELS, Targum and New Testament: a bibliography together with a New Testament index. Pontifical biblical institute: Rome 1967. pp.xi.88. [123.]*

I. ISAACSON, Check-list of hebraica and judaica in the library of the university of the Witwatersrand. Johannesburg 1967–70. pp.3.38+[iii]. 39+ [iii].35. [2000 catalogue entries.]

CATALOGUE of hebrew books. Harvard university library: Cambridge, Mass. 1968. pp.vii. 595+598+561+574. [48,862 cards.]
— Supplement 1972. [13,000 titles.]
1. Classified listing. Appendix: Judaica in the Houghton library. pp.xxxii, 593. 193. [15,878 cards.]
2. Authors and selected subjects. pp.715. [15,015.]
3–5. Titles. pp.615+634+631. [39,452.]

YOHAI GOELL, Bibliography of modern hebrew literature in english translation. Jerusalem &c. 1968. pp.vii. 110.[xxii]. [3312.]

v. Translations

MORITZ STEINSCHNEIDER, Die hebraeischen uebersetzungen des mittelalters und die Juden als dolmetscher. Ein beitrag zur literaturgeschichte des mittelalters, meist nach handschriftlichen Quellen. Berlin 1893. pp.xxxiv.1077. [1250.]
320 copies printed; a facsimile was issued Graz 1956.

ISRAEL SCHAPIRO, אוצר תרגומים עברים
מספרות האנגלית Bibliography of hebrew translation of english works. New York 1929. pp.[iii]. 3. [250.]

MARTIN HOWARD SABLE, Traducciones hebreas en la edad media. Universidad nacional autonoma: México 1952. pp.99. [200.]

ISRAEL SCHAPIRO אוצר תרגומים עברים
מספרות הגרמנית Bibliography of hebrew translations of german works. New York 1934. pp.79. [450.]

[PHILIPPA TRAVIS], A bibliographical guide to shabbat and to festivals. Modern hebrew literature in translation. Jewish agency: Youth leaders guide: [1960]. pp.[ii].46. [500.]*

vi. Miscellaneous

CHRISTIAN FRIEDRICH SCHNURRER, Biographische und litterarische nachrichten von ehmaligen lehrern der hebräischen litteratur in Tübingen. Ulm 1792. pp.vi.274. [250.]

HERM[ANN] L[EBERECHT] STRACK, Lehrbuch der neuhebräischen sprache. ... Abriss der neuhebräischen litteratur. Karlsruhe &c. 1884. pp.xii. 132. [400.]

A[BRAHAM ADOLF] BERLINER, Censur und confiscation hebräischer bücher im Kirchenstaate. Auf grund der inquisitions-akten in der Vaticana und Valicellana dargestellt. Frankfurt a. M. 1891. pp. [ii].65. [1250.]

LIST of writings based on the life of David, king of Israel. Library of Congress: Washington 1920. ff.5. [49.]*

BERNHARDT WACHSTEIN, I[SRAEL] TAGLICHT and ALEXANDER KRISTIANPOLLER, Die hebräische publizistik in Wien. Historische kommission der israelitischen kultusgemeinde in Wien: Quellen und forschungen zur geschichte der Juden in Deutschösterreich (vol.ix): Wien 1930. pp.c.297.x.105.16. [5000.]
this is an index of the hebrew periodicals published in Vienna.

vii. Scholars, etc.

Abrahams, Israel

DUDLEY WRIGHT, Select bibliography of the works of Israel Abrahams. Vienna 1927. pp.29. [750.]

Abramowitz, Shalom Jacob

EPHIM H. JESHURIN, ששלום יעקב אברא־
מאוויץ מענדעלע מוכר ספרים׳ ביבלי־
אגראפיע, Sholem Iankew Abramovitch Mendele Moicher Sforim, bibliography. Buenos Aires 1958. pp.39. [633.]

Adler, Cyrus

EDWARD DAVIDSON COLEMAN and JOSEPH REIDER, A bibliography of the writings and addresses of Cyrus Adler, 1882–1933. Philadelphia 1933. pp.[iv].367–445. [586.]

Agnon, S. J.

YONAH DAVID, Books and essays on S. J. Agnon and his works (bibliography). Jerusalem 1972. pp.100. [1500.]

Ashkenazi, Touvia

A BIBLIOGRAPHICAL list of writings, 1922–1954, with published biographical notes. Washington 1954. ff.2–103. [150.]*

Ben-Gurion, David

SAMUEL LACHOWER, כתבי דוד בן־גוריון; ביבליוגרפיה תר"ע־תשי"ט The writings of David Ben-Gurion. A bibliography 1910–1959. Foreword by Yehuda Erez. Tel-Aviv 1960. pp. 28.155. [2836.]

Bensabat Amzalak, Moses

ARMANDO GONÇALVES PEREIRA, L'activité scientifique du professeur Moses Bensabat Amzalak. Lisbonne [1933]. p.25. [131.]

Ben-Zvi, Ishak

SHLOMO SHUNAMI, The writings of Izhak Ben-Zvi. A bibliography, 1904–1958. General federation of jewish labour in Israel: Israel library association: Jerusalem 1958. pp.[x].38. [882.]

Bialostozky, Benjamin J.

EPHIM H. JESHURIN, ב ·· י· ביאלאסטאצקי ביבליאגראפיע B. J. Bialostozky bibliography. New York 1958. pp.xxv. [500.]

Brahinsky, Mani Leib

EPHIM H. JESHURIN, Mani Leib bibliography. מאני לייב ביבליאגראפיע· New York 1955. pp.23.

Cahan, Abraham

EPHIM H. JESHURIN, ... אב· קאהאן ביבליאגראפיע· Abraham Cahan bibliography. New York 1941. pp.64. [410.]

Cassuto, Umberto

[MILKA CASSUTO], Bibliografia delle pubblicazioni scientifiche di Umberto Cassuto. Collegio rabbinico italiano: [Florence] 1931. pp.[ii].12. [565.]

Chajes, Hirsch Perez

MORITZ ROSENFELD and SAUL CHAJES, Bibliographie der schriften, reden und vorträge von Hirsch Perez Chajes. Wien 1932. pp.48. [483.]

Charney, Samuel

EPHIM H. JESHURIN, שמואל ניגער ביבליאג־ ראפיע· Samuel Niger (Charney) bibliography. New York 1956. pp.12.

Dahood, Mitchell J.

ERNEST R. MARTINEZ, Hebrew-ugaritic index to the writings of Mitchell J. Dahood: a bibliography, with indices of scriptural passages, hebrew and ugaritic words and grammatical observations. Scripta Pontificii instituti biblici (116): Rome 1967. pp.120. [135.]

Dupont-Sommer, André

[A. DUPONT-SOMMER], Titres et travaux. 1958. pp.31. [160.]

Edelstadt, David

EPHIM H. JESHURIN, דוד עדעליסטאט ביבליאגראפיע David Edelstadt bibliography. New York 1953. pp.23. [250.]

Friedlaender, Israel

BOAZ COHEN, Israel Friedlaender. A bibliography of his writings. New York 1936. pp.40. [154.]

Gaster, Moses

B[RUNO] SCHINDLER, Gaster centenary publication. Royal asiatic society of Great Britain and Ireland: 1958. pp.[viii].40. [281.]

Kaplan, Mordecai Menahem

GERSON D. COHEN, Bibliography of the writings of professor Mordecai M. Kaplan. New York 1953. pp.33. [260.]

Kohut, George Alexander

EDWARD D. COLEMAN, A bibliography of George Alexander Kohut. New York 1935. pp.82. [700.]

Lutzky, Aaron

EPHIM H. JESHURIN, א לוצקי ביבליאגרא־ פיע· A. Lutzky bibliography. New York 1959. pp.24. [300.]

Luzzatto, Moses Hayyim

SIMON GINZBURG, The life and works of Moses Hayyim Luzzatto. Dropsie college: Philadelphia 1931. pp.vii.189. [176.]

Luzzatto, Samuele Davide

[ISAIA LUZZATTO], Index raisonné des livres de correspondance de feu Samuel David Luzzatto. Padoue 1878. pp.xv.136. [1211.]
300 copies printed.

ISAIA LUZZATTO, Catalogo ragionato degli scritti sparsi di Samuele Davide Luzzatto. Padova 1881. pp.xvi.488. [600.]
300 copies printed.

Meyerhof, Max

THE WORKS of Max Meyerhof; a bibliography. Hebrew University: School of Oriental Studies: Jerusalem 1944. pp.32. [320.]

Nieto, David

MOSES BENSABAT AMZALAK, David Nieto. Noticia biobibliográfica. Lisboa 1923. pp.37. [15.]
100 copies printed.

Peretz, Yitzhok Leibush

EPHIM H. JESHURIN, Solomon Ettinger, Alexander Zederbaum, Yitzhok Leibush Peretz bibliographies. Buenos Aires 1957. pp.32. [Peretz: 150.]

Pereyra, Abraham Israel

MOSES BENSABAT AMZALAK, Abraham Israel Pereyra. Notícia biobibliografica. Lisboa 1927. pp.21. [5.]

Reisen, Abraham

SALOMON SLUTSKY, אברהם רייזען— ביבליאגראפיע Abraham Reisen—bibliography. [New York] 1956. pp.328. [1000.]

Rivkin, B. [pseud. *Baruch Abraham Weinrib*.]

EPHIM H. JESHURIN, ביבליאגראפיע ב ·ריוקין B. Rivkin bibliography. New York 1953. pp.32. [500.]

Rogoff, Hillel

EPHIM H. JESHURIN, הלל ראגאף ביבליאג־ ראפיע· Harry Rogoff bibliography. New York 1958. pp.32. [150.]

Rosenfield, Morris

Z. SZAJOWSKI, Morris Rosenfield (1862–1923) and his time. Catalogue of the exhibition. Yivo institute for jewish research, New York, 1962. ff.x.49. [1227.]★

Rossi, Giovanni Bernardo de

[G. B. DE ROSSI], Memorie storiche sugli studi e sulle produzioni del dottore G. Bernardo de-Rossi. Parma 1809. pp.112. [122.]

Schechter, Solomon

ADOLPH S. OKO, Solomon Schechter. . . . A bibliography. Cambridge 1938. pp.xxi.103. [400.]

Schwab, Moïse

P[AULA] HILDENFINGER, Bibliographie des travaux de m. Moïse Schwab, 1905. pp.39. [410.]
reproduced from handwriting.

Shatzky, Jacob

M. KOSOVER and M. UNGER, A bibliography of the writings of Jacob Shatzky. New York 1939. pp.[ii].81. [579.]

Shatzky, Jacob

EPHIM H. JESHURIN, ד·ר יעקב שאצקי ביבליאגראפיע' אפרופן אויף זיין טויט· Dr Jacob Shatzky bibliography, evaluations postmortem. Buenos Aires 1958. pp.10. [100.]

Sheps, Elias

EPHIM H. JESHURIN, א· אלמי (אליהו חיים שעפס) ביבליאגראפיע •- Eli A. Almi bibliography. [Buenos Aires 1961]. pp.38. [200.]

Steinschneider, Moritz

A[BRAHAM ADOLF] BERLINER, Die schriften des dr. M. Steinschneider. Berlin 1886. pp.[ii].32. [500.]

Warshawski, Mark

EPHIM H. JESHURIN, מארק וואַרשאַוואָסקי ביבליאגראפיע· Mark Warshawski bibliography. New Yor [*sic*] 1958. pp.8. [100.]

Zunz, L.

M. ST[EINSCHNEIDER], Die schriften des dr. L. Zunz. Berlin 1857. pp.16. [49.]
—— [another edition]. Hebräische bibliographie (no.82, beigabe): Berlin 1874. pp.8. [74.]

PALESTINE. ZIONISM. ISRAEL

i. *Palestine*
ii. *Zionism*
iii. *Israel*

i. Palestine

TITUS TOBLER, Bibliographia geographica Palestinae. Zunächst kritische uebersicht gedruckter und ungedruckter beschreibungen der reisen ins heilige land. Leipzig 1867. pp.v.265. [2500.]
—— [supplement]. Bibliographia geographica Palestinae ab anno CCCXXX usque ad annum M. Dresdae 1875. pp.27. [1000.]

v[ASILY] N[IKOLAEVICH] KHITROVO, Палести-на и Синай. (Библіографическій указатель русскихъ книгъ и статей о святыхъ мѣстахъ востока, преимущественно палестинскихъ и синайскихъ). Часть I. Выпускъ I[–2]-й. С.-Петербургъ 1876–1886. pp.[v].vi.152+[iii]. 78. [800.]

no more published.

[ALEXANDER B. MCGRIGOR], Contributions towards an index of passages bearing upon the topography of Jerusalem, from writings prior to the eleventh century. Glasgow 1876. pp.xi.90. [1000.]

privately printed.

S[TEPAN IVANOVICH] PONOMAREV, Іерусалимъ и Палестина въ русской литературѣ, наукѣ, живописи и переводахъ. (Матеріалы для библіографіи.) Императорская академія наукъ: Сборникъ отдѣленія русскаго языка (vol.xvii, no.2): Санктпетербургъ 1877. pp.[ii]. xxi.128. [924.]

issued simultaneously in vol.xxx of the Academy's Записки, *and also separately.*

BIBLIOTHECA palaestinensis. Catalogus librorum aliquot selectorum de terra sancta . . . quos collegit dr. Th. B[orret]. [Amsterdam] 1884. pp.103. [2500.]

[AUGUSTE MOLINIER and CARL KOHLER], Itinerum bellis sacris anteriorum series chronologica. . . . I.30–600. Itinera hierosolymitana (vol.ii): Genevae 1885. pp.267. [3000.]

no more published.

REINHOLD RÖHRICHT, Bibliotheca geographica Palestinae. Chronologisches verzeichniss der auf die geographie des heiligen landes bezüglichen literatur von 333 bis 1878 und versuch einer cartographie. Berlin 1890. pp.[ii].xx.744. [5000.]
— — Verbesserte und vermehrte neuausgabe mit einem vorwort von David H. K. Amiran. Jerusalem 1963. pp.xvi.816. [4262.]

A[THANASY IVANOVICH] PAPADOPOULOS-KERA-MEUS, Ἱεροσολυμιτικη βιβλιοθηκη ἤτοι καταλογος των ἐν ταις βιβλιοθηκαις του ἁγιωτατου ἀποστολικου τε και καθολικου ὀρθοδοξου πατριαρχικου θρονου των Ἱεροσολυμων και πασης Παλαιστινης ἀποκειμενων ἑλληνικων κωλικων. Πετρουπολει 1891–1915. pp.[xviii].623 + [vi].448 + 449–894 +[vi].440+[vii].600+[ii].650.[10,000.]

MORITZ STEINSCHNEIDER, Jüdische schriften zur geographie Palästinas (x–xix jahrh.). Jerusalem 1892. pp.70. [154.]

REINHOLD RÖHRICHT, Die Deutschen im heiligen lande. Chronologisches verzeichniss derjenigen Deutschen, welche als Jerusalem-pilger und kreuzfahrer sicher nachzuweisen oder wahrscheinlich anzusehen sind (*c.*650–1291]. Innsbruck 1894. pp. iv.169. [1250.]

SYSTEMATISCHE bibliographie der Palästina-literatur. Deutscher verein zur erforschung Palästinas: Leipzig &c.

   i. 1895–1904. Bearbeitet von Peter Thomsen. 1908. pp.xvi.204. [2918.]

   [continued as:]

Die Palästina-literatur. Eine internationale bibliographie.

   ii. 1905–1909. 1911. pp.xx.316. [3755.]
   iii. 1910–1914. 1916. pp.xx.388. [3754.]
   iv. 1915–1924. 1927. pp.xx.756. [8437.]
   v. 1925–1934. [1936–]1938. pp.x.ii.988. [11,252.]
   vi. 1935–1939. [1953–]1956. pp.viii.15.832. [9189.]
   vii. 1940–1945. 1972. pp.xi.783. [11,506.]
   Band A. 1878–1894. [1957–]1960. pp.xxii. 905. [12,818.]

KLEOPAS M. KOIKULIDES, Καταλοιπα χειρογραφων Ἱεροσολυμιτικης βιβλιοθηκης. Ἱεροσολυμοις 1899. pp.207.[1000.]

GIROLAMO GOLUBOVICH, Bibliotheca bio-bibliografica della terra santa e dell'oriente francescano. Quaracchi.

   i. 1215–1300. 1906. pp.viii.479. [500.]
   ii. Addenda al sec. XIII, e fonti pel sec. XIV. 1913. pp.vii.641. [500.]
   iii. 1300–1332. 1919. pp.vii.496. [500.]
   iv. 1333–1345. 1923. pp.vii.503. [500.]
   v. 1346–1400. 1927. pp.iii–xii.441. [500.]

ANTONIO CIRELLI, Gli annali di terra santa . . . e bibliografia di terra santa. Documenti francescani (vol.ii): Quaracchi 1918. pp.xvi.725. [1000.]

LEO GOLDHAMMER, Kleiner führer durch die Palästina-literatur. Palästina-amt: Broschüre (no.1): Wien 1919. pp.23. [100.]

LEONARDUS LEMMENS, Acta S. congregationis de propaganda fide pro terra sancta. Pars I. 1622–1720 [II. 1721–1847]. Biblioteca-bio-bibliografica della terra santa e dell'oriente francescano (new ser., vols.i–ii): Quaracchi 1921–1922. pp.xxxii.429 +xxxvi.333. [500.]

MOSHEH STEKELIS, Prehistory in Palestine. A bibliography. Jerusalem 1932. pp.[v].45. [379.]

A. YAARI [*and others*], A post-war bibliography of near eastern mandates. A preliminary survey of publications on the social sciences dealing with Iraq, Palestine and Trans-Jordan . . . to Dec. 31, 1929. American university of Beirut: Social science series (no.1): Jerusalem 1933 &c.

A LIST of references on the Balfour declaration and the mandate for Palestine. Zionist archives and library: [New York] 1941. ff.9. [150.]★

RECENT printed material received by the archives [Recent material on zionism and Palestine; Articles

on zionism and Palestine in current periodicals].
Zionist archives and library: New York.★
  i. 1939–1943. ff.[84]. [1000.]
  ii. 1944. ff.[43]. [1000.]
  iii. 1944–1945. ff.[79]. [1500.]
  iv, no.1. 1945–1946. ff.13. [250.]
    [*continued as:*]
Palestine and zionism. A cumulative author,
title and subject index. Palestine foundation fund:
Zionist archives and library: New York.
  i. 1946. [Edited by Sophie A. Udin]. pp.x.150.
    [2500.]
  ii. 1947. pp.x.171. [3000.]
  iii. 1946–1948. pp.[xiv].469. [12,500.]
  iv. 1949. [Edited by Sylvia Landress]. pp.x.
    212. [4000.]
  v. 1950. pp.[x]. 194. [4000.]
  vi. 1951. pp.x.211. [4000.]
  vii. 1952. pp.x.223. [4500.]
  viii. 1953. pp.x.243. [5000.]
  ix. 1954. pp.xi.226. [4500.]
  x. 1955. pp.xi.193. [4000.]
  xi. 1956. pp.x.181. [4000.]
*no more published; only the annual cumulations
have been set out.*

REGISTER of the Palestine press. Public information office [*c.*1945]. pp.38. [100.]

A. KONIKOFF, Selected bibliography of eastern
Palestine. Jerusalem 1946. pp.16. [300.]
issued as a supplement to the author's Transjordan
(*1946*).

PALESTINE: 1915–1946. A select, annotated bibliography. [House of commons: Library: Biblio-
graphy(no.3): 1946] ff.10. [98.]★

MAP catalogue. Third edition. Palestine command: Survey directorate: H.Q. Palestine 1947.
ff.[i].24. [500.]★

FIRST world war. Campaign in Egypt and
Palestine. Imperial war museum: Library: [1952].
pp.11. [150.]

A[LFRED] L. FONTAINE, Monographie cartographique de l'isthme de Suez, de la péninsule du
Sinaï, du nord de la chaîne arabique, suivie d'un
catalogue raisonné sur les cartes de ces régions.
Société d'études historiques et géographiques de
l'isthme de Suez: Mémoires (vol.ii): Le Claire
1955. pp.iii–xx.238. [300.]

A BIBLIOGRAPHICAL list of works about Palestine
and Jordan. Second edition. Bibliographical lists of
the arab world (no.2): National library, Cairo,
1964. pp.338.144.[x]. [1324.]

MAHMUD EL-AKHRAS, Palestine-Jordan bibliography, 1900–1970. Jordan library association:
Amman 1972. pp.354. [2746.]

  ii. *Zionism.*

УКАЗАТЕЛЬ литературы о Сіонизмѣ. С.-Пе-
тербургъ 1903. pp.[iii].x.214. [4000.]

WILLIAM ZEITLIN, תו־זכרון לעיון,‎ Bibliotheca
sionistica. Hebräische schriften über zionismus
[1852–1905]. Frankfurt a. M. 1909. pp.[ii].34.
[264.]

LIST of references on Zionism. Library of
Congress: [Washington] 1916. ff.12. [184.]★

CATALOGUE of books and pamphlets in english,
yiddish and hebrew on zionism. Zionist organization: [New York 1919]. pp.40. [200.]

ISRAEL COHEN, Zionism. Second edition.
[National book council:] Book list (no.87): 1932.
pp.[4]. [125.]
— — Third edition. 1937. pp.[4]. [100.]

OSCAR BRAUNFELD. A concise bibliography of
Zionism and Palestine. Universities' zionist council: [Cambridge] 1947. pp.18. [250.]

ZIONISM. Public library of South Australia:
Research service: [Adelaide] 1957. ff.5. [71.]★

G. HERLITZ, List of files. The executive of the
World zionist organization. The central zionist
archives: Jerusalem.
  i. The Central Zionist Office, Vienna: Z1
    ("Erez Israel" bureau des Zionistischen
    congresses), 1897–1905. 1960. ff.[ix].26.26.
    [iv]. [533.]★
  ii. The Central Zionist Office, Cologne: Z2
    (Zionistisches central bureau), 1905–1911.
    1961. ff.iv.iii.36.39, iii,vi. [654.]★
  iii. The Central Zionist office, Berlin. Z3.
    (Zionisches central bureau), 1911–1920.
    1964. ff.vii.iv.161. [1708]★

ZIONIST LITERATURE: new publications received
in the library. Central Zionist archives: World
Zionist organisation: Jerusalem. New Series, 1959
&c.
in progress.

THE CENTRAL Zionist archives. World Zionist
organisation: Jerusalem, 1970. pp.31. [595 collections.]

        iii. *Israel*

  1. *General*
  2. *Academic writings*
  3. *Periodicals*
  4. *Subjects*

        1. *General*

רשימה של פרסומי הממשלה ירושלים'
תש"ב- List of government publications. State
archives and library: Jerusalem 1952. pp.64.
[100.]
— [another edition]. 1954. pp.84. [200.]

ILSE R. WOLFF, Israel. Library association: Special subject list (no.20): 1957. pp.7. [50.]*

[ISRAEL ADLER], Le livre hébraïque, incunables—publications israéliennes. Exposition organisée avec le concours de la Bibliothèque nationale. 1962. pp.3–120. [israeli: 266.]

ISRAEL government publications. Compiled by the State archives. Jerusalem.
published at varying intervals.

ACCESSIONS list: Israel. The library of congress: Public law 480 project. American libraries book procurement center. Tel-Aviv.
  i. 1964. pp.2.157.xxxv. [1800.]
  ii. 1965. pp.2.196.xxxviii. [2400.]
  iii. 1966. pp.2.397.xxxvii. [4500.]
  iv. 1967. pp.2.510.liii. [6000.]
  v. 1968. pp.2.519.lxxxvii. [6000.]
  vi. 1969. pp.[ii].440.lxxiii. [5200.]
  vii. 1970. pp.[ii].406.lxi. [4800.]
  viii. 1971. pp.[ii].416.xxvii. [4800.]
  ix. 1972. pp.[ii].431.xcvii. [5200.]
  x. 1973. pp.[ii].85.xxix. [1000.]
no more published.

CATALOGUE of maps. Ministry of labour survey of Israel. Tel Aviv 1964. pp.iii.27. [32.]

ENTWICKLUNGSHILFE Israel; publikationen und institutionen. Israel development aid; publications and institutions. Deutsche Stiftung fur entwicklungsländer: Bonn, 1965. pp.70. [192].*

GUIDE to the archives in Israel. Israel archives association: Jerusalem, 1966. pp.158. [very large number.]

YONAH ALEXANDER, Israel: selected annotated and illustrated bibliography. Gilbertsville 1968. pp.[viii].116.[xiv]. [900.]

BERNARD REICH, Israel in paperback. Middle east studies association: Bibliographic series (ii): New York 1971. pp.ii.26.ix. [150.]*

S. LANDRESS, Selected books on Israel—issued on the occasion of the 25th anniversary of the state of Israel. Jewish book council: National jewish welfare board: New York 1972.

2. *Academic Writings*

MIRIAM STEKELIS, Publications of the Keren hayesod 1920–1935. Jerusalem 1935. pp.40. [306].

Hebrew university

רשימת הפירסומים המדעיים של
העובדים האקדימיים; במדעי־הרוח
משפטים מטמטיקה ומדעי הטבע וחק־
A לאות תש״ז־ חשי״ב׳ ירושלם׳ תשי״ב.

list of publications in humanities, law, science and agriculture 1946–1952, by members of the academic staff. [Jerusalem 1953]. pp.192. [1500.]

ABSTRACTS of theses approved for the degree of Doctor Philosophiae (Ph.D.) (vol. 1) and Doctor juris (Jur.D.) in the Hebrew University of Jerusalem . . . Jerusalem.
  1961–2. 1964. pp.xi.132. [107.]
  1962/3–1965/6. 1968. pp.viii.84.87.viii. [82.]

BAR-ILAN university. Publications by faculty members, 1959–1964. Select bibliography. Ramat Gan 1965. pp.64. [1013.]

PUBLICATIONS, 1960–1970. Negev institute for arid zone research. [Beer-Sheva] 1971. ff.54. [559.]*

FRANK JOSEPH SHULMAN, American and british doctoral dissertations on Israel and Palestine in modern times. Ann Arbor 1973. pp.vii.25. [530.]*

3. *Periodicals*

*[KAETHE LEWY and EMANUEL PFEFFERMANN], Union list of serials in Israel libraries. Pure and applied sciences excluding medicine. Israel national commission of Unesco: Sub-committee for documentation in the natural sciences: Jerusalem 1955. pp.vi.23. [2500.]

NEWSPAPERS and periodicals appearing in Israel. State of Israel: Government press office [Jerusalem?] 1967. pp.37. [369.]*

RUTH TRONIK, Israeli periodicals & serials in english & other european languages; a classified bibliography. Metuchen N.V. 1974. pp.xiii.193. [1100.]*

4. *Subjects*
Archaeology

MILKA CASSUTO SALZMANN, Selected bibliography. Publications on archaeological excavations and surveys in Israel, January, 1964–June, 1967. Atiqot, english series, supplement to volume viii, Jerusalem 1969. pp.29. [250.]

Education

JOSEPH M. BENTWICH, L'éducation en Israël. Unesco: Revue analytique de l'éducation (vol.x, no.6): 1958. pp.20. [110.]

H. D. EVERS, S. VON SCHWERIN, H. WEILER, Erziehungswesen in Ceylon, Israel und Nigeria; eine bibliograhphie. Arbeitsstelle für kulturwissenschaftliche forschung: Freiburg i. Br. 1962. pp.45. [Israel: 103.]

Kibbutz

FRANCIS D. HORIGAN, The israeli kibbutz. Psychiatric, psychological, and social studies with emphasis on family life and family structure. A survey of literature. Public health service: National institutes of health: Psychiatric abstracts series (no.9): Bethesda, Md. [1962]. ff.62. [100.]*

ERIK COHEN, Bibliography of the Kibbutz. A selection of recent sociological and related publications on collective settlements in european languages. Giv'at Haviva, 1964. pp.26. [300.]

Medicine

MEDICAL centre, 1939-1944. Hebrew university: Jerusalem [1944]. pp.[viii].84.[viii]. [500.]
this is a bibliography of writings by members of the staff.

Science

ISRAEL science bibliography. A guide to books, dissertations and periodicals published in Israel. Jerusalem, 1954. li,ii.
no more published?

*[KAETHIE LEWY and E. PFEFFERMANN], Union list of serials in Israel libraries. Pure and applied Sciences excluding medicine. Israel national commission of Unesco: Sub-committee for documentation in the natural sciences: Jerusalem 1955. pp.vi.123. [2500.]

CATALOGUE des publications scientifiques d'-Israel 1948-1955. 1955. pp.[x].164. [3235.]

[HANNAH FARKAS, ed.], Catalogue des publications scientifiques d'Israel, 1948-1955. Paris 1955. pp.[viii.].166. [3235.]
an exhibition catalogue.

CATALOGUE of scientific publications by Israel scientists 1948-1955. Research council:[Jerusalem 1956]. pp.259. [3235.]
also issued in a french edition.

SERIAL HOLDINGS of the Weizmann institute of science. Rehovot 1959. pp.[v].48. [1500.]*
— [another edition]. 1960. pp.[v].62. [1750.]*

Water

BIBLIOGRAPHY of hydrology. Israel. International association of scientific hydrology: Jerusalem.*

   -1948. 1956. pp.55. [131.]
   1949-1956. 1958. pp.42. [142.]

EASTERN CHRISTIANITY. SYRIAC

   i. *Eastern Churches*
   ii. *Nestorius*
   iii. *Christian oriental languages*
   iv. *Syriac*

i. *Eastern Churches*

[INNOKENTY OF KHERSON], Историческое обозрѣніе богослужебныхъ книгъ греко-россійской церкви. Кіевъ 1836. pp.205.

A[LEKSY IOANNOVICH] SPERANSKY, Систематическій каталогъ книгъ одобренныхъ и допущенныхъ Учебнымъ комитетомъ при Свитѣйшемъ синодѣ къ употребленію въ духовныхъ семинаріяхъ. Съ 1. янв. 1875 г. по. 1. іюля 1898 г. Саратов 1898. pp.[vi].47. [1205.]

AURELIO PALMIERI, Nomenclator litterarius theologicae orthodoxae russicae et graecae recentioris. Volumen I. A-E. Academia velehradensia [Akademie velehradska]: Operum (vol.iii): Pragae 1910. pp.[ii].267. [2000.]
only A-Bystrickij was published.

JOHN T. DOROSH, The eastern orthodox churches. A list of references to publications printed in the roman alphabet with indication of location. Washington 1946. pp.216.*

DEAN TIMOTHY ANDREWS, The eastern orthodox church. A bibliography. Greek archidiocese of north and south America: Publications (no.5): Brookline, Mass. [1953]. pp.32. [313.]
—— Second edition. [1957.] pp.79.

LIST of the writings of professors of the Russian orthodox theological institute in Paris, 1948-1954. Paris [1954.]. pp.98.
actually covers the period 1925-1954.

IOANNĒS N. KARMIRĒS, Ἡ Ἑλληνικὴ Θεολογικὴ βιβλιογραφία τῆς τελευταλας δεκαετίας (1945-1955). Ἰσταμπούλ 1957. pp.20. [500.]

DONALD ATTWATER, A list of books about the eastern churches. Newport, R.I. 1960. ff.xvii.22.*

JOYCE ELIZABETH SOUTHAN, A survey of periodicals relevant to byzantine studies in several London libraries. University of London: Institute of classical studies 1968. pp.xi.20. [124.]*

ii. *Nestorius*

CHRISTIAN PESCH, Zur neuern literatur über Nestorius. Stimmen aus Maria-Laach: Ergänzungsheft (no.115): Freiburg i. B. 1914. pp.[iii]. 30. [50.]

P. Y[OSHIRŌ] SAEKI, Catalogue of the nestorian literature and relics. Tokyo 1950. pp.[ii].50. [763.]

iii. *Christian oriental languages*

FELIX HAASE, Christlich-orientalische handschriftenkataloge. Sonderabdruck aus dem werke Ehrengabe deutscher wissenschaft dargeboten van Katholischen gelehrten, Herausgegeben von Franz Fessler. Freiburg im Breisgau 1920. pp.15. [235.]

iv. *Syriac literature*

HEBEDIESU ['ABHDĪSHŌ 'BAR BĔRĪKHĀ], ܐ
ܚܘܣܝܐ ܕܐܒܕܝܫܘ [&c.]. Ope domini nostri incipimus scribere tractatum continentem

catalogum librorum Chaldæorum, tam ecclesiasticorum, quàm profanorum ... latinate donatum ... ab Abrahamo Ecchellensi. Romæ 1653. pp.29.270.[xxxi]. [500.]

JOSEPH SIMONIUS ASSEMANUS, Bibliotheca orientalis clementino-vaticana, in qua manuscriptos codices syriacos, arabicos, persicos ... Bibliothecae vaticanae addictos, recensuit ... Joseph Simonius Assemanus ... Tomus I[–III]. De scriptoribus syris orthodoxis [monophysitis, nestorianis]. Romæ 1719–1728. pp.xlii.649+ [clxxii].548 + [xxxvi].709 + [xxxii].cmlxiii. [1500]. pp.[viii].328+[xvi].329–594. [1800.]
— — Orientalische bibliothek, oder nachrichten von syrischen schrifstellern, in einen auszug gebracht von August Friedrich Pfeiffer. Erlangen 1776–1777.

STEPHANUS EVODIUS ASSEMANUS and JOSEPH SIMONIUS ASSEMANUS, Bibliothecæ apostolicæ vaticanæ codicum manuscriptorum catalogus. ... Partis primæ tomus secundus[–tertius], complectens codices chaldaicos sive syriacos. Romæ 1758–1759. pp.xxiv.556+587. [1500.]

[JOSIAH FORSHALL and FRIEDRICH ROSEN], Catalogus codicum manuscriptorum orientalium qui in Museo britannico asservantur. Pars prima, codices syriacos et carshunicos amplectens. 1838. pp.xi.40. [syriac: 2000.]
— — Catalogue of syriac manuscripts ... acquired since the year 1838. ... By W. Wright. 1870–1872. pp.[v].399+[iii].401–1037+[v]. xxxviii.1039–1354. [1500.]
— — Descriptive list of the syriac and karshuni mss. ... acquired since 1873. ... By G[eorge] Margoliouth. 1899. pp.iv.64. [250.]

R. PAYNE SMITH, Catalogi codicum manuscriptorum Bibliothecae bodleianae pars sexta, codices syriacos, carshunicos, mendaeos, complectens. Oxonii 1864. pp.x.coll.680. [syriac. 5000.]

[H. ZOTENBERG], Manuscrits orientaux. Catalogues des manuscrits syriaques et sabéens (mandaïtes) de la Bibliothèque nationale. 1874. pp. viii.248. [syriac: 2500.]
— — Notice sur les manuscrits syriaques de la Bibliothèque nationale acquis depuis 1874. ... Par J[ean] B[aptiste] Chabot. [1896]. pp.19. [100.]

[CARL E[DUARD] SACHAU, Kurzes verzeichniss der Sachau'schen sammlung syrischer handschriften ... nebst übersicht des alten bestandes. Königliche bibliothek: Berlin 1885. pp.xxviii.35. [500.]

AGNES SMITH LEWIS, Catalogue of the syriac mss. in the convent of S. Catherine on Mount Sinai. Studia sinaitica (no.i): 1894. pp.xii.132. [279.]

J[EAN] B[APTISTE] CHABOT, Notice sur les manuscrits syriaques conservés dans la bibliothèque du Patriarcat grec orthodoxe de Jérusalem. 1894. pp.47. [50.]

[JEAN BAPTISTE CHABOT],Καταλογος συνοπτικος των ἐν τη βιβλιοθηκη του Ἱερου Κοινου του Π. Ταφου ἀποκειμενων συριακων χειρογραφων ὑπο [or, rather, translated by] Κλεόπα M. Κοιχυλίλου. Βερολινῳ 1898. pp.24. [50.]
the author's name is given in the preface, but incorrectly, as Chapot; the original work appears in the Journal asiatique *(1894), 9th ser.iii.92–134.*

[CARL] EDUARD SACHAU, Verzeichniss der syrischen handschriften. Königliche bibliothek: Handschriften-verzeichnisse (vol.xxiii): Berlin 1899. pp.xv.448+[vii].499–944. [1000.]

WILLIAM WRIGHT, A catalogue of the syriac manuscripts preserved in the library of the university. Cambridge 1901. pp.xxx.548+[iv].549–1290. [250.]

ADDAÏ SCHER, Catalogue des manuscrits syriaques et arabes conservés dans la Bibliothèque épiscopale de Séert (Kurdistan). Mossoul 1905. pp.102. [syriac: 123.]

ADDAÏ SCHER, Notice sur les manuscrits syriaques et arabes conservés à l'archevêché chaldéen de Diarbékir. 1907. pp.82. [syriac: 115.]

ADDAÏ SCHER, Notice sur les manuscrits syriaques et arabes conservés dans la bibliothèque de l'évêché chaldéen de Mardin. 1908. pp.36. [syriac: 83.]

FRÉDÉRIC MACLER, Notice des manuscrits syriaques conservés dans la bibliothèque du couvent des Syriens jacobites de Jérusalem. [?1924]. pp.28. [24.]

JACQUES VOSTÉ, Catalogue de la bibliothèque syro-chaldéenne du couvent de Notre-dame des semences près d'Alqos (Iraq). Rome &c. 1929. pp.144. [600.]

A[LPHONSE] MINGANA, Catalogue of the Mingana collection of manuscripts now in the possession of the trustees of the Woodbrooke settlement, Selly Oak, Birmingham. Cambridge.
i. Syriac and garshūni manuscripts. 1933. pp.viii.coll.1256. [2000.]
ii. Christian arabic manuscripts and additional syriac manuscripts. 1936. pp.vii.208. [600.]
iii. Additional christian arabic and syriac manuscripts. 1939. pp.xxvii.138. [191.]

ISSAC ARMALET [ISḤAQ ARMALAH], الطرقة في
مخطوطات دير الشرقة، تأليف اسحق
ارملة السرياني. Catalogue des manuscrits de
Charfet. [1936]. pp. 15. ٥٢٦. [1000.]

D[AVID] S[AMUEL] MARGOLIOUTH and G[EOF-
FREY] WOLEDGE, A. Mingana. A biography and
bibliography. Aberdeen [printed] 1939. pp.16.
[90.]

SEVERINUS GRILL, Vergleichende religions-
geschichte und kirchenväter. Beigabe: Die
syrischen handschriften des National-bibliothek
in Wien. Heiligenkreuzer studein (nr.11): Horn
1959. pp.65. [7.]

N. V. PIGULEVSKAYA, Каталог сирийских рукописей Ленингарада. Палестинский сборник
(Выпуск 6–69). Москва, Ленинград 1960.
pp.230. [78.]

LIST of Old Testament Peshitta manuscripts
(preliminary issue). Edited by the Peshitta institute, Leiden University, Leiden 1961. pp.xi.114.
[549.]

CYRIL MOSS, Catalogue of syriac printed books
and related literature in the British museum. 1962.
pp.[viii].coll.1174.205.271. [7500.]

JULIUS ASSFALG, Syrische handschriften: syrische,
karšunische, christlich-palästinische, neusyrische
und mandäische handschriften. Verzeichnis der
orientalischen handschriften in Deutschland (vol.
v): Wiesbaden 1963. pp.xxiii.255. [1000.]

JULES LEROY, les manuscrits syriaques à peintures
conservés dans les bibliothèques d'Europe et
d'Orient. Contribution à l'étude de l'iconographie
des églises de langue syriaque. Institut français
d'archéologie de Beyrouth: Bibliothèque arché-
ologique et historique [tome lxxvii]: Paris 1964.
pp.494+159 (album, plates). [62.]

ARN. VAN LANTSCHOOT, Inventaire des manu-
scripts syriaques des fonds vatican (409–631),
Berberini oriental et Neofiti. Studi e testi (243):
Citta del Vaticano 1965. pp.v.199. [240.]

IGNATIUS ORTIZ DE URBINA, Patrologia syriace.
Altera editio emendata et aucta. Pont. institutum
orientalium studiorum: Roma 1965. pp.268.
[large number.]

MODERN NEAR EAST (WEST ASIA)

    i. *General*
    ii. *Academic writings*
    iii. *Subjects*
    iv. *Scholars, etc.*

i. *General*

ANDRÉ LEVAL, Voyages en Levant pendant les
XVIIᵉ, XVIIIᵉ et XVIIIᵉ siècles. Essai de bibliographie.
Budapest 1897. pp.30. [125.]

SELECT list of references on the near east. Library of Congress: Washington 1906. ff.5. [25.]*

VOJISLAV M. JOVANOVIČ, Енглеска библиогра-
фија о источном нитању у Европи. Српска
краљевска академија: Сноменик (no.xlvii=
Други разред, no.40): Београду 1908. pp.[iii].
111. [1521.]

—— [another issue]. An english bibliography
on the near eastern question, 1481–1906. By
Voyslav M. Yovanovitch. Servian royal academy:
Second series of monuments (no.xlviii): Belgrade
1909. pp.[v].111. [1521.]

LIST of works in the New York public library
relating to the near eastern question and the balkan
states, including european Turkey and modern
Greece. New York 1910. pp.166. [5500.]

FRITZ REGEL, Die deutsche forschung in türkisch
Vorderasien. [Länder und völker der Türkei
(no.7):] Leipzig 1915. pp.48. [500.]

LIST of references on the relations of the United
States with the orient and the Barbary states
from 1781–1789. Library of Congress: [Wash-
ington] 1921. ff.6. [34.]*

MINNIE M[AY] NEWMAN, Handbook on racial
and nationality backgrounds. Section 1. Peoples
of the near east. New York 1922. ff.[i].vi.23.
[300.]*

EDWARD MEAD EARLE, Problems of the near east.
Carnegie endowment for international peace:
International relations clubs: Bibliography series
(no.2): [New York] 1924. pp.23. [400.]

A POST-WAR bibliography of the near eastern
mandates. A preliminary survey of publications
on the social sciences dealing with Iraq, Palestine
and Trans-Jordan, and the Syrian states, from
Nov. 11 1918 to Dec. 31 1929. . . . Stuart C[arter]
Dodd . . . general editor. American university of
Beirut: Faculty of arts and sciences: Publications:
Social science series (no.1).
    Arab   fascicle.   1933.   pp.[ii].ix.56.iv.i.
    [1941.]
    Arabic periodicals. 1933. pp.ix.[ii].545.[viii].
    [3023.]
    English fascicle. 1932. pp.[iii].xiv.248. [4681.]
    Franch fascicle. 1934. pp.xvi.[ii].210. [3359.]
    German fascicle. [*not published*?]
    Hebrew fascicle. 1933. pp.[v].xix.228. [2391.]
    Italian fascicle. 1933. pp.xx.80. [1100.]
    Miscellaneous oriental languages. 1936. pp.xii.
    45. [246.]

BIBLIOGRAPHY of periodical literature on the near and middle east. Reprinted from the Middle east journal. Washington.

1947. pp.[iv].111–122.229–244.351–368.475–490. [1119.]

1948. pp.[iv].104–127.228–253.363–380.495–506. [1167.]

1949. pp.106–123.229–242.359–372.485–494. [215.]

includes index, v–viii.

1950. pp.126–142.265–275.373–383.505–516. [763.]

1951. pp.122–136.259–267.397–406.528–536. [733.]

1952. pp.115–124.270–280.368–378.491–502. [793.[

1953. pp.121–130.265–277.404–414.570–580. [946.]

1954. pp.112–125.233–249.356–374.480–496. [1036.]

1955. pp.99–115.219–236.347–360.469–485. [980.]

1956. pp.104–116.217–234.334–351.452–469. [995.]

1957. pp.108–121.219–234.344–359.455–471. [959.]

1958. pp.111–126.227–246.352–365.484–498. [971.]

1959. pp.112–124.219–231.345–354.474–486. [800.]

1960. pp.111–123.233–242.354–364.490–500. [666.]

1961. pp.111–121.235–245.354–363.481–490. [551.]

1962. pp.115–124.265–274.394–402.557–566. [595.]

1963. pp.200–212.339–347.466–484. [589.]

1964. pp.133–139.267–276.391–403.529–544. [1324.]

1965. pp.117–126.248–257.   . 543–554. [1268.]

1966. pp.145–156.264–277.420–431.563–568. [1450.]

1967. pp.286–298.432–444.544–558. [1729.]

1968. pp.114–127.246–262.387–409.539–565. [2804.]

1969. pp.119–142.261–284.413–431.565–578. [2782.]

1970. pp.113–132.261–281.397–417.563–584. [2997.]

1971. pp.133–149.287–302.445–462.561–581. [2391.]

1972. pp.105–120.227–242.363–378.475–492. [2226.]

1973. pp.109–128.   . 421–438.
in progress.

CATALOGUE de la bibliothèque de la Banque de Syrie et du Liban. 1948. pp.[ix].174. [3000.]

LIST of books, reports and periodicals in the library on middle eastern countries. International labour office: Bibliographical reference list (no. 56): Geneva 1952. pp.11. [200.]*

SHIRLEY HOWARD WEBER, Voyages and travels in the near east [and adjacent regions] ... in the Gennadius library in Athens. American school of classical studies at Athens: Princeton.

1800. 1953. pp.ix.208. [860.]

1801–1900. 1952. pp.x.52. [1206.]

ERMANNO ARMAO, Catalogo ragionato della mia biblioteca. Opere di consultazione, Venezia, Albania, oriente mediterraneo. Firenze 1953. pp. xiii.316. [800.]

HENRY FIELD, Bibliography on southwestern Asia. Coral Gables, Fla.*

[i]. 1953. pp.xvi.106. [3016.]

ii. 1955. pp.xviii.126. [3292.]

iii. 1956. pp.xxviii.230. [6113.]

iv. 1957. pp.xlvi.464. [12,149.]

v. 1958. pp.xxxii.275. [6739.]

vi.1959. pp.xxxvi. 328. [8364.]

vii. 1962. pp.xxxix.305. [7492.]

— — Subject index to i–v.

i. Anthropogeography, by Edith W. Ware. 1961. pp.ix.157.

ii. Zoology, by Bernard J. Clifton. 1960. pp.vii.83.

iii. Botany, by Robert C. Foster. 1959 pp.vi.27.

— — Supplement. By Henry Field, Edith M. Laird and (viii:) Bernard J. Clifton.

i. 1968. pp.ii.92. [450.]

ii.

iii.

iv. Anthropogeography, maps, botany and zoology. 1969. pp.i.78. [1900.]

v.

vi.

vii. Anthropogeography, botany and zoology. 1972. pp.iv.97. [2500.]

viii. Botany and zoology. 1972. pp.iv.68. [1700.]

EXTERNAL research; a listing of recently completed studies. Near east (Middle east). External research staff: Office of intelligence research and analysis: Department of state: Washington.*

1954–55. pp.4. [100.]

1956.

1957. pp.8. [125.]

1958. pp.10. [150.]

1959. pp.11. [160.]

1960. pp.12. [160.]

1961. pp.11. [160.]

1962. pp.13. [170.]

1963–64. pp.13. [170.]

[*continued as:*]

EXTERNAL research: Middle east; a list of current social science research by private scholars and academic centres.

    1965. pp.24. [270.]
    1966. pp.28. [330.]
    1967. pp.18. [350.]
    1968. pp.25. [370.]
       no more published?

BERTOID SPULER and LUDWIG FORRER, Der vordere orient in islamischer zeit. Wissenschaftliche forschungsberichte: Geisteswissenschaftliche reihe (vol.21): Bern 1954. pp.248. [3500.]

A SELECTED bibliography of articles dealing with the middle east. Hebrew university: Economic research institute: Jerusalem.

    [i]. 1939–1950. 1954. pp.viii.95. ﬨﬦ [1442.]
    ii. 1951–1954. 1955. pp.x.83. ﬦ [1163.]
    iii. 1955–1958. 1959. pp.x.64. ﬦ [850.]

RICHARD ETTINGHAUSEN. A selected and annotated bibliography of books and periodicals in western languages dealing with the near and middle east, with special emphasis on medieval and modern times. Middle east institute: Washington 1954. pp.[ii.]viii.137. [2080.]*

MATERIALS in the National archives relating to the middle east. National archives: Reference information papers (no.44): [Washington] 1955. pp.56. [large number.]*

CURRENT research on the middle east. The Middle east institute, Washington.

    1955. Edited by Harvey P. Hall and Ann W. Noyes. pp.[viii].196. [1017.]
    1956. Edited by William Sands and John Hartley. pp.[vi].90. [1018–1335.]
    1957. Edited by William Sands and Kathleen H. Brown. pp.[vi].104. [1336–1612.]

H. B. SHARABI, A handbook on the contemporary middle east ... with annotated bibliographies. Georgetown university: Washington 1956. pp.ix. 113. [500.]*

JAMĀL MOUHASSEB [AL-MUHĀSB], ، المكتبة

مراجع منتقاه من الكتب العربية الصادرة فى

الاردن، سورية، العراق ولبنان [:on cover] Al Maktabah. A selective arabic bibliography for Iraq, Jordan, Lebanon and Syria. Harissa, Lebanon [printed] 1956–1958. ff.40+32+16. [400.]

BIBLIOGRAPHY, balkans and middle east area. Armed forces staff college: Library: Norfolk, Va. 1957.ff.[i].15. [150.]*

J. E. GODCHOT, Les constitutions du proche et du moyen-orient. Paris 1957. pp.ii.442.
    Texts of 16 constitutions and 575 titles in "bibliographies sommaires".

[HENRY] ROBIN FEDDEN, English travellers in the near east. British council: British book news: Bibliographical series of supplements (no.97): 1958. pp.44. [75.]

A[LEXANDER] R[OLLO] C[OLIN] BOLTON, Soviet middle east studies: an analysis and bibliography. Royal institute of international affairs: Chatham house memoranda: 1959.

    i. Introduction and general indexes. pp.[v]. 36. [150.]
    ii. Arabs and the arab world. pp.xvi.44. [80.]
    iii. The arabian peninsula. pp.vi.17. [27.]
    iv. Egypt. pp.x.29. [55.]
    v. Iraq. pp.xi.18. [32.]
    vi. Palestine (Israel) and Jordan. pp.ix.19. [31.]
    vii. The Sudan. pp.ix.23. [30.]
    viii. Syria and Lebanon. pp.v.17. [26.]

RODERIC H. DAVISON, The near and middle east: an introduction to history and bibliography. American historical association. Service center for teachers of history: Publication (no.24): Washington [1959]. pp.[ii].48. [125.]

HERBERT F. STEEPER, Middle east. Office of education: International educational relations: Keep tab on the lab (vol.ii, no.2): Washington 1960. pp.10. [150.]*

FLORENCE LJUNGGREN and MOHAMMED HAMDY, Annotated guide to journals dealing with the Middle East and North Africa. Cairo 1964. pp.viii. 107. [354.]

L. C. WRIGHT, The middle east; an annotated guide to resource materials. 1966. pp.26. [62.]*

CURRENT British research in middle eastern studies. Centre for middle eastern & islamic studies: University of Durham.

    1969. Compiler: Peter Beaumont. pp.89. [300.]
    1971. Compiler: Howard Bowen-Jones. pp.92. [250.]

THE 1969 [&c.] bibliography of the middle east: a complete and classified list of all the books published in about ten middle eastern countries. Syrian documentation papers: Damascus.

    1969. ff.176.[iv]. [548.]*
    1970. ff.[iii].153+154–316. [881.]*
    in progress.

URI DOTAN, A bibliography of articles on the Middle East 1959–1967. Edited by Avigdor Levy. Tel Aviv university: The Shiloah center for middle eastern and african studies: The Shiloah centre teaching and research aids (2): Tel Aviv 1970. pp.227.ff.[iv]. [2902.]
    title-page, preface and contents list also in Hebrew.

ORIENT-PRESS: bollettino bibliografico di studi orientalistici.

i. 1970. pp.159. [3174.]
in progress? lists contents of periodicals and 'sammelbände'.

HARRY N. HOWARD [*and others*], Middle east and north Africa: a bibliography for undergraduate libraries. Occasional publication (no.14): Foreign area materials center: University of the state of New York, State education department and National council of associations for international studies: Williamsport 1971. pp.xviii.80. [1192.]

J. L. MURRAY, and (1973 ii-) D. W. DRAKAKIS SMITH. Recent publications on the middle east. Department of geography: University of Durham.

1971. pp.[15].21. [750.]
1972. pp.14.17. [600.]
1973. pp.14.10. [500.]
1974. pp.18.
in progress.

DEREK HOPWOOD and DIANA GRIMWOOD-JONES, *edd.* Middle east and islam; a bibliographical introduction. Middle east libraries committee: Bibliotheca asiatica (9): Zug 1972. pp.viii.368. [3191.]

V[INCENT] J. CREASI [*and others*], Selected annotated bibliography of environmental studies of Iraq, Jordan, Lebanon and Syria, 1960–1969.

RICHARD BEVIS, Bibliotheca cisorientalia [*sic*]. An annotated check list of early english travel books on the near and middle east. Boston 1973. pp.xix.317. [2000.]*

ii. *Academic writings*

LIST of publications of the Faculty of arts and sciences of the American university of Beirut. American university of Beirut: Publications: Social science series (no.4 = Minor studies, 1942, A): [Beirut] 1942. pp.[ii].15. [300.]

LISTE des publications. Institut français de Damas: Damas 1948. pp.14.i. [60.]

BIBLIOGRAPHIE de l'Université Saint-Joseph de Beyrouth. Beyrouth 1951. pp.207. [1500.]

WALTER CROSBY EELLS, American doctoral dissertations on education in countries of the middle east. Middle east institute: Washington 1955. ff.28. [200.]*

SUHA TAMIM, A bibliography of A.U.B. faculty publications. American university of Beirut: Beirut 1967. pp.xxxii.401. [5000.]

GEORGE DIMITRI SELIM, American doctoral dissertations on the arab world 1883–1968. Library of congress: Washington 1970. pp.xvii.103. [1032.]

NAWAL MIKDASHI, Masters' theses: 1909–70. American university of Beirut: Jafet memorial library: Beirut 1971. ff.97.13. [1478.]*

A LIST of theses and dissertations of iraqis kept in the Central library, University of Baghdad. Baghdad 1967. ff.[ii].163.iii. [600.]*
— — Supplement 1. Compiled by Nazar M. A. Qassim. 1969. ff.[ii].86. [350.]

iii. *Subjects*
Agriculture

BIBLIOGRAPHY on agricultural economics and planning in the near east region. Sixth session of the Near east commission on agricultural planning and agricultural statistics. 1972.

H. DOST, Bibliography on land and water utilization in the middle east. Agricultural university: Wageningen 1953. ff.v.115.*

Archaeology

COWA bibliography. Area 15—Western Asia.*
i. 1957. pp.22. [347.]
ii. 1960. pp.10.28. [471.]
iii. 1966. pp.31.34. [701.]

Crusades

C. KLIMKE, Die quellen zur geschichte des vierten kreuzzuges. Breslau. pp.[iii].105. [50.]

COUNT [PAUL ÉDOUARD DIDIER] RIANT, Inventaire critique des lettres des croisades. . . . I–II. 768–1100. 1880. pp.xi.233. [165.]

IVAN MIKHAILOVICH MARTINOV [MARTUINOV], Dernières publications relatives aux croisades et à l'orient latin. 1880. pp.20. [22.]

BIBLIOGRAPHIE de l'orient latin. [Société de l'orient latin].
i. 1878–1880. 1881. pp.75. [1200.]
ii. 1881–1883. 1885. pp.[iv].165. [2300.]

[COUNT PAUL ÉDOUARD DIDIER RIANT], Inventaire sommaire des manuscrits relatifs a l'histoire et à la géographie de l'orient latin. 1. France. A. Paris. Gênes [printed] 1882. pp.81. [2000.]
150 copies printed.

[COUNT PAUL É. D. RIANT], Inventaires des matériaux rassemblés par les Bénédictins au XVIIIe siècle pour la publication des historiens des croisades (collection dite de dom Berthereau, Paris, Bibl. nat. fr. 9050–9080). Gênes [printed] 1882. pp.28. [750.]

HANS EBERHARD MAYER, Bibliographie zur geschichte der kreuzzüge. Hannover 1960. pp.iii-xxxii.272. [5362.]

AZIZ S[URYAL] ATIYA, The crusade, historiography and bibliography. Bloomington 1962. pp.170. [1500.]

Economics

POINT FOUR. Near east and Africa: a selected bibliography of studies on economically under-developed countries. Department of state: Division of library and reference services: Bibliography (no.56): Washington 1951. pp.ii.136. [2050.]

A SELECTED bibliography of articles dealing with the middle east. Hebrew institute: Economic research institute: Jerusalem.
[i]. 1939–1950. 1954. pp.viii.95. [v]. [1442.]
ii. 1951–1954. 1955. pp.x.83. [vi]. [1163.]
iii. 1955–1958. 1959. pp.x.64. [vi]. [850.]

ALI M. S. FATEMI, PANOS KOKOROPOULOS, ABBAS AMIRIE, Political economy of the middle east; a computerized guide to the literature. Department of economics: University of Akron: Akron 1970. ff.[xxiv].pp.346.326.49. [25,000.]*

Geology

M. A. AVNIMELECH, Bibliography of Levant geology, including Cyprus, Hatay, Israel, Jordania, Lebanon, Sinai and Syria. Jerusalem 1965–9. pp.x.192+xi.184. [13,500.]

Greek manuscripts

H[ENRY] O[CTAVIUS] COXE, Report to her majesty's Government, on the greek manuscripts yet remaining in libraries of the Levant. 1858. pp.[ii].88. [6000.]

V[ICTOR] GARDTHAUSEN, Catalogus codicum graecorum sinaiticorum. Oxonii 1886. pp.xi.295. [1250.]

PORPHYRY USPENSKY, Описаніе греческихъ рукописей Монастыря святой Екатерины на Синаѣ. Томъ I. С.-Петербургъ 1911. pp. xxviii.664. [2000.]
no more published.

Land tenure

NEAR east and South Asia: bibliography. A bibliography of materials dealing with the near east and south Asia in the Land tenure center library: University of Wisconsin: Madison 1971. pp.74. [850.]*
— Supplement. 1972.

Locusts

DONALD JAY, Annotated bibliography on locusts in southwestern Asia. Edited by Henry Field. Field research projects: Coconut Grove, Fla. 1969. pp.ii.29. [301.]*

Peasants

LOUISE E. SWEET and TIMOTHY J. O'LEARY, edd., Circum-mediterranean peasantry: introductory bibliographies. Behavior science bibliographies: New Haven 1969. pp.xxvi.106. [1500.]

Public administration

BIBLIOGRAPHY of publications on public administration and management. Regional co-operation for development: Secretariat: Tehran 1967. pp.5.ii.310. [2488.]

Science

LISTE de [des] travaux scientifiques publiés au moyen-orient. Unesco: Centre de coopération scientifique — moyen-orient: Le Caire.
i–ii. 1948. ff.37+65. [1200.]*
iii–iv. 1949. pp.59+72. [1400.]
v–vi. 1950. pp.78+76. [2336.]
Index des noms d'auteurs cités dans les listes 1, 2, 3, 4, 5 & 6, December 1951, pp.27.
vii. 1951. pp.77. [1063.]
viii. 1952. pp.86. [1046.]
ix. 1953. pp.64. [930.]
x. 1954. pp.74. [1145.]
xi. 1955. pp.84. [1110.]
xii. 1955. pp.130. [1268.]
[*continued as:*]
Résumés analytiques des travaux scientifiques et techniques publiés en Égypte et travaux reçus de l'Afghanistan, Chypre, Iran, Irak, Liban, Pakistan, Soudan et Syrie. National research council of Egypt: Bulletin of the scientific and technical documentation centre (part 2): Cairo.
i. 1955. pp.[59]. [705.]
ii. 1956. pp.150. [1755.]
iii. 1957. pp.158. [1839.]
iv. 1958. pp.149. [1743.]
v. 1959. pp.144. [1167.]
vi. 1960.
vii. 1961. pp.61. [495.]

V[INCENT] J. CREASI [*and others*], Selected annotated bibliography of environmental studies of Iraq, Jordan, Lebanon and Syria, 1960–1969.

Social sciences

MIDDLE east social science bibliography. Books and articles on the social sciences published in arab countries of the Middle east in 1955–1960. UNESCO Middle east science cooperation office: Cairo 1961. pp.v.152. [1270.]*

iv. Scholars, etc.

Amari, Michele

GIUSEPPE SALVO COZZO, Le opere a stampa di Michele Amari. Palermo 1909. pp.[iii].xlvi–cviii. [302.]

Bargès, Jean Joseph Léandre

[J. J. L. BARGÈS], Titres scientifiques et ouvrages de m. l'abbé Bargès. [1867]. pp.4. [24.]
reproduced from handwriting.

Bell, Gertrude

WINIFRED COTTERILL DONKIN, Catalogue of the Gertrude [Margaret Lowthian] Bell collection in the library of King's college. University library: Publications (no.1): Newcastle upon Tyne 1960. pp.64. [750.]

Brockelmann, Carl

OTTO SPIES, Verzeichnis der schriften von Carl Brockelmann. Leipzig 1938. pp.26. [600.]

Burton, sir Richard Francis

NORMAN M[OSLEY] PENZER, An annotated bibliography of sir Richard Francis Burton. 1923. pp. xvi.351. [500.]
500 copies printed.

Dāġir, Yūsof As'ad

[Y. A. DĀĠIR], L'oeuvre scientifique et littéraire de mʳ Joseph A. Dagher. Harissa [printed] 1951. pp.8. [26.]

[Y. A. DAGIR], Joseph A. Dagher, curriculum vitae. Beirut [c.1960]. pp.25. [180.]

Dehérain, Henri

[H. DEHÉRAIN], Notice sur les travaux de m. Henri Dehérain. 1898. pp.14. [30.]

Field, Henry

HENRY FIELD, Bibliography: 1926–1958. [Coconut Grove, Fla.] 1958. pp.91. [458.]★
— — 1926–1964. [Miami] 1964. pp.vi.112. [594.]★
— — 1926–1966. Ann Arbor 1966. pp.vii.112. [631.]★
— — 1966–1971. Nos. 624–727. Field research projects: Miami 1971. pp.22. [104.]
— — 1972–1973.

Fourmont, Etienne

[E. FOURMONT], Catalogue des ouvrages de monsieur Fourmont l'aîné. Amsterdam 1731. pp.[xxxvi].123. [121.]

Goldziher, Ignáz

BERNARD HELLER, Bibliographie des oeuvres de Ignace Goldziher. École nationale des langues orientales vivantes: Publications (6th ser., vol. i): 1927. pp.xvii.101. [592.]
supplements by Alexander Scheiber and I. Kratschovsky appear in the Ignace Goldziher memorial volume (Budapest 1948), i.419–431.

Hartmann, Richard

HEINZ H. GIESECKE, Richard Hartmann bibliographie. Festgabe zum 70 geburtstag. Leipzig 1951. pp.28. [416.]

Houdas, Octave

[O. HOUDAS], Résumé des travaux et publications de m. Octave Houdas. [c.1900]. pp.4. [33.]

Huart, Clément Imbault

[C. I. HUART], Notice des travaux et publications de Cl. Huart. Chalon-sur-Saône [printed] [c.1900]. pp.4. [50.]

Krachkovsky, Ignatiy Iulianovich

A. N. SAMOYLOVICH, Библиография печатных работ академика Игнатия Юлиановича Крачковского. (К 30-летию научной деятелности.) Академия наук СССР: Труды Института востоковедения (xix): Москва, Ленинград 1936. pp.62. [395.]

Laoust, Henri

[H. LAOUST], Titres et publications de Henri Laoust. [Macon] 1955. p.10. [25.]

Lawrence, Thomas Edward

T. GERMAN-REED, Bibliographical notes on T. E. Lawrence's Seven pillars of wisdom and Revolt in the desert. 1928. pp.[v].16. [5.]
375 copies printed.

G., Annotations on some minor writings of 'T. E. Lawrence'. 1935. pp.28. [60.]
500 copies printed.

ELIZABETH W. DUVAL, T. E. Lawrence. A bibliography. New York 1938. pp.[ii].96. [159.]
500 copies printed.

THOMAS EDWARD LAWRENCE. A list of references by and on col. T. E. Lawrence in the Imperial war museum library. [1952.]. pp.3. [30.]★

T. E. LAWRENCE. Fifty letters, 1920–35. An exhibition. University of Texas: Humanities research center: [Austin 1962]. pp.36. [50.]

DAVID G. DISBURY, T. E. Lawrence (of Arabia); a collector's booklist. Egham 1972. pp.[76]. [396.]★

Littmann, Enno

MARIA HÖFNER, Verzeichnis der schriften von Enno Littmann. Tübingen 1945. pp.27. [451.]

THE library of Enno Littmann, 1875–1958, professor of oriental languages at the university of Tübingen, with an autobiographical sketch. Introduction by dr. Maria Höfner. Catalogue (no.307): Brill, Leiden 1959. pp.xxiv.355. [4351.]

Massignon, Louis

Y[OUAKIM] MOUBARAC, Bibliographie de Louis Massignon. Institut français: Damas 1956. pp.56. [613.]

Meyerhof, Max

THE WORKS of Max Meyerhof. A bibliography. Hebrew university: School of oriental studies: Jerusalem 1944. pp.32. [400.]

Minorsky, Vladimir Fedorovich

A LIST of works (1901–40) by V. Minorsky. Cambridge [printed Calcutta] [1941]. pp.[ii].22. [111.]
SOAS copy corrected by Minorsky himself and brought down to 1951.

Mžik, Hans von

BIBLIOGRAPHIE der schriften des universitäts-professors dr. Hans von Mžik. Wien 1936. pp.16. [70.]

Nöldeke, Theodor

ERNST [WILHELM ADALBERT] KUHN, Übersicht der schriften Theodor Nöldeke's. Giessen 1907. pp.48. [628.]

E[NNO] LITTMANN, Der wissenschaftliche nach-lass von Th. Nöldeke. Leipzig [1933]. pp.36. [246.]

Postel, Guillaume

FRANÇOIS SECRET, Bibliographie des manuscrits de Guillaume Postel. Genève 1970. [250.]

Rondot, Edouard

[E. RONDOT], Exposé des titres et travaux scien-tifiques de m. Éduard Rondot. Bordeaux [print-ed] 1888. pp.39. [52.]

Sauvaget, Jean

JANINE SOURDEL-THOMINE and DOMINIQUE SOURDEL, Index analytique de l'œuvre de Jean Sauvaget. Institut français: Mémorial Jean Sau-vaget (vol.ii): Damas 1961. pp.xxvii.187. [5000.]

Sbath, Paul

[P. SBATH], Publications du r. p. Paul Sbath. [Cairo 1939]. pp.xiii. [18.]

ISLAM. MUHAMMAD

i. *General*
ii. *Subjects*

i. *General*

MUŞŢAFA IBN ʿABD ALLĀH, Lexicon biblio-graphicum et encyclopædicum. . . . Ad codicum vindobonensium, parisiensium et berolinensium fidem primum edidit, latine vertit et commen-tario indicibusque instruxit Gustavus Fluegel. Oriental translation fund: Leipzig 1835–1858. pp.[ii].xxiii.520+[ii].   xii.660+[ii].xx.648+[ii]. xxvi.591+x.661+viii.680+xiv.1258. [25,000.]
other editions are set out at Turkish literature: general.

WILLIAM SLOAN, Digest of principles of maho-medan law, decided by the Privy council and the Supreme and Sudder courts of Madras, Calcutta, Bombay, and the North-Western Provinces, from the year 1793 to 1859. Madras 1860. pp.xii.173. [1000.]

MORITZ STEINSCHNEIDER, Polemische und apolo-getische literatur in arbischer sprache, zwischen Muslimen, Christen und Juden, nebst anhängen verwandten inhalts. Mit benutzung handschrift-licher quellen. Deutsche morgenländische gesell-schaft: Abhandlungen für die kunde des morgen-landes (vol.vi, no.3): Leipzig 1877. pp.xii.456. [500.]

[EMIL GRATZL], Katalog der ausstellung von handschriften aus dem islamischen kulturkreis. München 1910. pp.37. [204.]

EDWARD G[RANVILLE] BROWNE, A hand-list of the muhammadan manuscripts, including all those written in the arabic character, preserved in the library of the university. Cambridge 1900. pp.xviii.440. [1541.]
—— A supplementary hand-list. 1922. pp.xii. 348. [1250.]
—— A second supplementary hand-list of the muḥammadan manuscripts in the university & colleges of Cambridge. By A[rthur] J[ohn] Arberry. 1952. pp.82. [450.]

K. A. INOSTRANTSEV and YA. I. SMIRNOV, Матеріалы для библіографіи мусульманской археологіи изъ бумагъ барона В. Г. Тизен-гаузена. Санктпетербургъ 1906. pp.viii.79–348. [4000.]

I[DA] A[UGUSTA] PRATT, List of works in the New York public library relating to muhamma-dan law. Prepared . . . under the direction of R[ichard James Horatio] Gottheil. [New York 1907]. pp.10. [225.]

VICTOR CHAUVIN, Bibliographie des ouvrages arabes ou relatifs aux Arabes publiés dans l'Europe chrétienne de 1810 à 1885. . . .
xi. Mahomet .Liège 1909. pp.[iii].255. [1000.]
xii. Le mahométisme. [Completed by Louis Polain.] 1922. pp.vi. 467. [1831.]

GIUSEPPE GABRIELI, Manuale di bibliografia musulmana. Parte prima. Bibliografia generale. Ministero delle colonie: Manuali coloniali: 1916. pp.iii–ix.491. [4000.]
no more published.

E[DGARD] BLOCHET, Inventaire de la collection de manuscrits musulmans de m. Decourdemanche. 1916. pp.112. [275.]
the collection forms part of the Bibliothèque nationale.

MAULAVÎ ABDUL ḤAMID ['ABD UL-ḤAMÎD], Catalogue of the arabic and persian manuscripts in the Oriental public library at Bankipore. Volume v[–VI]. Tradition. Patna 1920–1925. pp.viii.214+vii.231. [364.]

D. GUSTAV PFANNMÜLLER, Handbuch der Islamliteratur. Berlin &c. 1923. pp.viii.436. [4000.]

MAULAVÎ ABDUL ḤAMÎD ['ABD UL-ḤAMÎD], Catalogue of the arabic and persian manuscripts in the Oriental public library at Bankipore. Volume x. . . . Theology. Patna 1926. pp.vii.150. [161.]

C[HARLES] A[MBROSE] STOREY, Persian literature. A bio-bibliographical survey. 1927 &c.
details of this work are entered under Persian literature, below.

MAULAVI ABDUL MUQTADIR ['ABD UL-MUK-TADIR], Commentaries on the Qurân, Ḥadîs, law, theology and controversial works. Catalogue of the arabic and persian manuscripts in the Oriental public library at Bankipore (vol. xiv, Persian mss.): Patna 1928. pp.xi.182. [234.]

GIORGIO LEVI DELLA VIDA, Elenco dei manoscritti arabi islamici della Biblioteca vaticana: vaticani, barberiniani, borgiani, rossiani. Studi e testi (vol.lxvii): Città del Vaticano 1935. pp.iii. xxxix.347.41. [2500.]

ABSTRACTA islamica. Revue des études islamiques.
    i–v. 1927–1936. pp.381. [1500.]
    vi. 1938. pp.153. [800.]
    vii. 1940. pp.147. [1000.]
    viii. 1947. pp.126. [1200.]
    ix. 1951. pp.164. [1500.]
    x. 1953. pp.[136]. [1200.]
    xi. 1955–1957. pp.[244]. [2500].
    xii. 1958. pp.227. [2205.]
    xiii. 1959. pp.134. [1281.]
    xiv. 1960. pp.149. [1687.]
    xv. 1961. pp.193. [2331.]
    xvi. 1962. pp.168. [1784.]
    xvii. 1963. pp.190. [1978.]
    xviii. 1964. pp.133. [1339.]
    xix. 1965. pp.141. [1499.]
    xx. 1966. pp.178. [1920.]
    xxi. 1967. pp.205. [1999.]
    xxii. 1968. pp.170. [1660.]
    xxiii. 1969. pp.162. [1664.]
    xxiv. 1970. pp.133. [1392.]
    xxv. 1971. pp.158. [1848.]
    xxvi. 1972. pp.162. [1961.]
in progress.

A DESCRIPTIVE catalogue of the islamic manuscripts in the Government oriental manuscripts library, Madras. Madras 1939 &c.

JEAN SAUVAGET, Introduction à l'histoire de l'orient musulman. Éléments de bibliographie. Initiation à l'Islam (vol.i): 1943. pp.[iii].203. [1300.]
— — Édition refondue . . . par Cl[aude] Cahen. 1961. pp.vi.258. [1500.]

H. L. GOTTSCHALK [*and others*], Catalogue of the Mingana collection of manuscripts now in the possession of the trustees of the Woodbrooke settlement, Selly Oak, Birmingham. Volume IV. Islamic arabic manuscripts. Compiled and edited by Derek Hopwood. Birmingham (1948–) 1963. pp.ii.415. [2016.]

CLAUDE L. PICKENS Jr., Annotated bibliography of literature on Islam in China. Society of friends of the moslems in China: Hankow 1950. pp.[v.] 72. [350.]

GUILLERMO GUASTAVINO GALLENT and CARLOS RODRÍGUEZ JOULIA SAINT-CYR, Catálogo de materias (obras relativas al Islam y Africa) de la Biblioteca general del protectorado. Tetuán 1952. pp.611. [5810.]

A BASIC bibliography on Islam. FAO/52/4/2184. [1952?] pp.24. [319.]*

GAMAL-EDDINE HEYWORTH-DUNNE [JAMES HEYWORTH DUNNE], A basic bibliography on Islam. Muslim world series (no.4): Cairo [1952]. pp.52. [383.]

GEORGES [GEORGEI] VAJDA, Index général des manuscrits arabes musulmans de la Bibliothèque nationale de Paris. Institut de recherche et d'histoire des textes: Publications (vol.iv): 1953. pp. ix.744. [6000.]

BURTON BENEDICT, A short annotated bibliography relating to the sociology of muslim peoples. McGill university: Institute of islamic studies: Montreal 1955. ff.115. [500.]*

ZAGORKA JANC, Исламски рукописи из југословенских колекција. Музеј примењене уметности: Београд 1956. pp.50. [68.]

AHMAD HASAN DANI, Bibliography of the muslim inscriptions of Bengal down to a.d. 1538. Asiatic society of Pakistan: Journal (vol.ii, appendix): Dacca 1957. pp.ix.147. [264.]

J[AMES] D[OUGLAS] PEARSON and JULIA F. ASHTON, Index islamicus 1906–1955. A catalogue of articles on islamic subjects in periodicals and other collective publications. Cambridge [1958]. pp.xxxvi. 897. [26,076].
reprinted Cambridge, 1961 and London, 1972.
— — Supplement, 1956–1960. By J. D. Pearson. 1962. pp.xxviii.316. [7296.]
— — Second supplement, 1961–1965. 1957. pp.xxx.342. [8135.]

—— Third supplement, 1966–1970. By J. D. Pearson and Ann Walsh. London, 1972. pp.xxxvi. 384. [8000.]

RUDOLF LOEWENTHAL, Russian materials on Islam and islamic institutions: a selective bibliography. Department of state: External research paper (no.133.1): [Washington] 1958. pp.vi.34. [377.]*

MU'ĪN UL-DĪN AḤMAD KHĀN, A bibliographical introduction to modern islamic development in India and Pakistan, 1700–1955. Asiatic society of Pakistan: Journal (vol.iv, appendix): Dacca 1959. pp.[iii].vii.170. [895.]

BIBLIOTHÈQUE. Centre national pour l'étude des problèmes du monde musulman contemporain: Catalogues (no.1): Bruxelles 1960. pp.[iv].60. [695.]

ALI IBRAHIM HASSAN, An authentic annotated bibliography & methods of research of islamic & egyptian mediaeval history. Cairo 1963. pp.203. [large number.]

JEAN SAUVAGET's Introduction to the history of the muslim east; a bibliographical guide. Based on the second edition as recast by Claude Cahen. Berkeley and Los Angeles 1965. pp.xxii. 252. [large number.]

BISERA NURUDINOVIĆ. Bibliografija jugoslovenske orijentalistike. Bibliography of yugoslav orientalistics. 1945–1960. Orijentalni institut u Sarajevu: posebna izdanja (vi): Sarajevo 1968. pp.242. [1850.]*

ISLAM in paperback. American institute of islamic studies: Bibliographic series (no.1): Denver 1969. pp.vi.58. [xii]. [250.]

DEREK HOPWOOD and DIANA GRIMWOOD-JONES, edd., Middle east and Islam; a bibliographical introduction. Middle east libraries committee: Bibliotheca asiatica (9): Zug 1972. pp.viii.368. [3191.]

C[HARLES] L. GEDDES, An analytical guide to the bibliographies on Islam, Muhammad, and the Qur'an. Bibliographic series (no.3): American institute of islamic studies: Denver 1973. pp. [viii].102. [211.]*

ii. *Subjects*

Archaeology

ANNUAL bibliography of islamic art and archæology, India excepted. Jerusalem.
    i. 1935. Edited by L. A. Mayer. 1937. pp.[ix]. 64. [600.]
    ii. 1936. 1938.
    iii. 1937. 1939. pp.[ix].96. [900.]

ISLAMIC art and archaeology. Cambridge.*
    1954. Compiled by J[ames] D[ouglas] Pearson and D. S. Rice. 1956. p.iii.38. [355.]
    1955.1960. pp.[ii].iii.65. [478.]

Architecture

K[EPPEL] A[RCHIBALD] C[AMERON] CRESWELL, A provisional bibliography of the muhammadan architecture of India. Bombay 1922. pp.[ii].81–108. 165–179. [750.]

K. A. C. CRESWELL, A provisional bibliography of the moslem architecture of Syria and Palestine. [s.l. 1927]. pp.69–94. [300.]

K. A. C. CRESWELL, A bibliography of muslim architecture in north Africa (excluding Egypt). Hespéris (vol.xli, supplement): 1954. pp.67. [750.]

K[EPPEL] A[RCHIBALD] C[AMERON] CRESWELL, A bibliography of the muslim architecture of Egypt. Art islamique (vol.iii): Le Caire 1955. pp.64. [750.]

K[EPPEL] A[RCHIBALD] C[AMERON] CRESWELL, A bibliography of the architecture, arts and crafts of Islam to 1st Jan. 1960. [Cairo] 1961. pp.xxiv.coll. 1330.pp.xxv. [15,000.]
—— Supplement, January 1960 to January 1972. Cairo 1973. pp.xiii.coll.366.pp.ix. [4500.]

Arms & armour

K[EPPEL] A[RCHIBALD] C[AMERON] CRESSWELL, A bibliography of arms and armour in Islam. Royal asiatic society: James G. Forlong fund (vol.xxv): 1956. pp.79. [497.]

Art

ANNUAL bibliography of islamic art and archæology, India excepted. Jerusalem.
    i. 1935. Edited by L. A. Mayer. 1937. pp.[ix]. 64. [600.]
    ii. 1936. 1938. pp.ix.80. [750.]
    iii. 1937. 1939. pp.[ix].96. [900.]

ISLAMIC art and archaeology. Cambridge.*
    1954. Compiled by J[ames] D[ouglas] Pearson and D. S. Rice. 1956. pp.iii.38. [355.]
    1955. 1960. pp.[ii].iii.65. [478.]

HARRIET DYER ADAMS, Selective bibliography of hispano-islamic art in Spain and northern Africa, 711–1492. New York university: [New York 1939]. ff.[iv].79. [1200.]

K[EPPEL] A[RCHIBALD] C[AMERON] CRESWELL, A bibliography of the architecture, arts and crafts of Islam to 1st Jan. 1960. [Cairo] 1961. pp.xxiv.coll. 1330. pp.xxv. [15,000.]
—— Supplement. 1973. pp.208.

Astronomy

FRANCIS J[AMES] CARMODY, Arabic astonomical and astrological sciences in latin translation. A critical bibliography. Berkeley &c. 1956. pp.vi. 193. [2000.]

Ibadis

[GUSTAVE] A[DOLPHE] DE C[ALASSANTI] MOTY-LINSKI, Bibliographie du Mzab, les livres de la secte abadhite. Alger 1885. pp.62. [90.]

Isma'ilis

W. IVANOV, A guide to ismaili literature. Royal asiatic society: Prize publication fund (vol.xiii): 1933. pp.xii.138. [691.]

W. IVANOW, Ismaili literature; a bibliographical survey. A second amplified edition of "A guide to ismaili literature", London 1933. Ismaili society series (A no. 15): Tehran 1963. pp.xv.245. [929.]

Koran

W[ILLIAM] B[EDWELL], Index assvratorvm mvhammedici Alkorani. That is, a catalogue of the chapters of the turkish Alkoran, as they are named in the arabicke ... together with their several interpretations. [s.l.] 1615. pp.[14]. [114.] this is a reissue, with a separate titlepage, of Mohammedis imposturae, 1615.

JACOB GEORG CHRISTIAN ADLER, Descriptio codicvm qvorvndam cvficorvm partes Corani exhibentivm in Bibliotheca regia hafniensi. Altonae 1780. pp.34. [6.]

VICTOR CHAUVIN, Bibliographie des ouvrages arabes ou relatifs aux Arabes publiés dans l'Europe chrétienne de 1810 a 1885. .... x. Le Coran et la tradition. Liège 1907. pp.[iii].146. [400.]

C[HARLES] A[MBROSE] STOREY, Persian literature. A bio-bibliographical survey. ... Section I. Qur'ānic literature. 1927. pp.xxiii.57. [750.]

C[HARLES] A[MBROSE] STOREY, Catalogue of the arabic manuscripts in the library of the India office. Volume II. I. Qur'ānic literature. 1930. pp.[iii].95. [167.]

MAULAVI MUINUDDIN NADWI [MU'ĪN UD-DĪN NADWĪ], Catalogue of the arabic and persian manuscripts in the Oriental public library at Bankipore. Volume XVIII. ... Quranic science. Patna 1930–1932. pp.vii.187+v.181. [373.]

THE KORAN in slavonic. A list of translations. Compiled by the Slavonic division of the New York public library. New York 1937. pp.[ii].10. [16.]

GIORGIO LEVI DELLA VIDA, Frammenti coranici n carattere cufico, nella biblioteca vaticana-(codici vaticani arabi 1605, 1606). Biblioteca apostolica vaticana: Studi e testi (no.132): Città del Vaticano 1947. pp.xi.57. [74.]

Medicine

SAMI HAMARNEH, Bibliography on medicine and pharmacy in medieval Islam. Mit einer einführung, Arabismus in der geschichte der pharmazie, von Rudolf Schmitz. Veröffentlichungen der Internationalen gesellschaft für geschichte der pharmazie (neue folge: 25). Stuttgart 1964. pp.204. [1000.]

Numismatics

L[EO] A[RY] MAYER, Bibliography of moslem numismatics, India excepted. Royal asiatic society: Oriental translation fund (vol.xxxv): 1939. pp.116. [1500.]
—— Second ... edition. 1954. pp.xi.283. [2092.]

Painting

E[DGARD] BLOCHET, Inventaire et description des miniatures des manuscrits orientaux conservés à la Bibliothèque nationale. Paris 1900. pp.278. [176.]

[KEPPEL ARCHIBALD CAMERON CRESWELL], A provisional bibliography of painting in muhammadan art. [1922.] pp.11. [200.]

SIR THOMAS W[ALKER] ARNOLD, The Library of A. Chester Beatty. A catalogue of the Indian miniatures. Revised and edited by J. V. S. Wilkinson. London 1936. pp.xliii.87+pls.52+vii.pls.53–100. [18.]

K[EPPEL] A[RCHIBALD] C[AMERON] CRESWELL, A bibliography of painting in Islam. Institut français d'archéologie orientale: Art islamique (vol.i): Le Caire 1953. pp.100. [1000.]

M. BAQIR, ed., Miniatures. Labore museum collections. Vol. I. Edited, with introduction and text of plates nos. 5 and 8–10. Art treasures of Pakistan: The Panjabi Adabi academy publication (no.30). Lahore 1964. pp.28. [10.]

IVAN STCHOUKINE [and others], Illuminierte islamische handschriften. Verzeichnis der orientalischen handschriften in Deutschland (band xvi): Wiesbaden 1971. pp.vii.pls.54.pp.340. [111.]

Sufism

MAULAVI ABDUL HAMID ['ABD UL-ḤAMĪD] [vol.xvi: MAULAVI ABDUL MUQTADIR ('ABD UL-MUQTADIR)], Catalogue of the arabic and persian manuscripts in the Oriental public library at Bankipore. Volume XIII [xvi]. Ṣūfīsm. Patna 1928–1929. pp.viii.185+vii.142. [212.]

A. J. ARBERRY, Catalogue of the arabic manuscripts in the library of the India office. II. Ṣūfism and ethics. 1936. pp.[ii].97–198. [250.]

ARAB COUNTRIES
Arabia, Arabs

CARL FERDINAND HOMMEL, Bibliotheca jvris rabbinica et Saracenorvm arabica. Byrvthi 1762. pp.63.[xviii]. [250.]

JEAN GAY, Bibliographie des ouvrages relatifs à l'Afrique et à l'Arabie. San Remo &c. 1875. pp.xi.312. [Arabia: 400.]
a photographic reprint was issued Amsterdam 1961.

[JEAN BAPTISTE] B[ERNARD] ROY, MHAMMED BEL KHODJA [MUḤAMMAD IBN AL-KHAWAJAH] and MOHAMMED EL ḤACHAICHI [MUḤAMMAD IBN 'UTHMĀN AL-ḤASHA'ISHĪ], Extrait du catalogue des manuscrits et des imprimés de la bibliothèque de la Grande mosquée de Tunis. . . . Histoire. Secrétariat général du Gouvernement Tunisien: Tunis 1900. pp.[iii].iii.85. [250.]

LIST of works relating to Arabia and the Arabs. Public library: New York 1911. pp.70. [2000.]

LIST of references on the Moors in Spain. Library of Congress: Washington 1926. ff.4. [34.]*

MAULAVI ABDUL HAMID ['ABD UL-ḤAMĪD], Catalogue of the arabic and persian manuscripts in the Oriental public library at Bankipore. Volume XIX. . . . Jurisprudence. Patna 1931–1933. pp.viii.172+vii.169. [473.]

REUBEN LEVY, Catalogue of the arabic manuscripts in the library of the India office. . . . Vol.ii. III. Fiqh. 1937. pp.[ii].199–336. [500.]

THE ARABIAN peninsula. A selected, annotated list of periodicals, books and articles in english. Prepared under the direction of the Near east section, Division of orientalia. Library of Congress: Reference Department: Washington 1951. pp.xi. III. [719.]
reprinted, New York 1969.

GAMAL-EDDINE [JAMES] HEYWORTH-DUNNE, Bibliography and reading guide to Arabia. Muslim world series (no.1): Cairo [1952]. pp.16. [146.]

HENRY FIELD, Anthropogeographical bibliography of the Persian gulf area. [s.l.] 1952. ff.[i].17. [250.]*

A SELECTED and annotated bibliography of economic literature on the arabic speaking countries of the middle east, 1938–1952. American university of Beirut: Economic research institute: Beirut 1954. pp.ix.199. [2000.]
— Supplement.
   1953. pp.xii.79. [750.]
   1954. pp.xiii.64. [620.]

1955. pp.xiii.103. [1000.]
1956. pp.xiii.91. [900.]
1957. pp.xiii.111. [1100.]
1958. pp.xiii.69. [660.]
1960. pp.xiii.74. [720.]
1961. pp.xiii.88. [850.]
1962. pp.xiii.42. [400.]

[B. Y. BOUTROS-GHALI], Arab league bibliography. Carnegie endowment for international peace: James Thomson Shotwell library: Washington [1955]. ff.[i].4. [75.]*

A[LFRED] L. FONTAINE, Monographie cartographique de l'isthme de Suez, de la péninsule du Sinaï, du nord de la chaîne arabique, suivie d'un catalogue raisonné sur les cartes de ces régions. Société d'études historiques et géographiques de l'isthme de Suez: Mémoires (vol.ii): Le Caire 1955. pp.iii–xx.238. [300.]

JEAN T. BURKE, An annotated bibliography of books and periodicals in english dealing with human relations in the arab states of the middle east, with special emphasis on modern times (1945–1954). American university: Beirut 1956. pp.iii–xiv.117. [1453.]

MIROSLAV KAFTAN and VILÉM NOVÝ, Arabský svět. Výběrový sezam publikací à clánků. Universita: Knihovna: Čteme a studujeme (1956, no.9): Praze 1956. pp.16. [100.]

ERIC MACRO, Bibliography of the Arabian peninsula. Coral Gables. Fla. 1958. pp.xiv.80. [2380.]*

RUDOLF LOEWENTHAL, Russian materials on Arabs and arab countries. Department of state: External research paper (no.133.3): [Washington] 1958. pp.iv.14. [163.]*

FAHIM I[SSA] QUBAIN, Inside the arab mind. A bibliographic survey of literature in arabic on arab nationalism and unity. With an annotated list of english-language books and articles. Middle east research associates: Arlington, Va. [1960]. pp.ix. 100. [200.]

A BIBLIOGRAPHICAL list of works about the Arabian peninsula. Bibliographical lists of the arab world (no.10): The National library: Cairo 1963. pp.79.101. [450.]

THE ARAB history (a bibliographical list). National library & archives: Cairo 1966. pp.[vii]. 292. [1900.]

A CUMULATION of a selected and annotated bibliography of economic literature on the arabic-speaking countries of the middle east, 1938–1960. Cumulated at the School of oriental & african studies, University of London, from the bibliography prepared by the Economic research institute, American university of Beirut. Boston 1967. pp.viii.358. [10,700.]

LA REVUE bibliographique du moyen orient. Les plus importants ouvrages édités en Iraq, Jordanie, Kuwait, Liban, Syrie et R.A.U. avec les plus intéressantes nouvelles littéraires et scientifiques de ces pays. Damas-Beyrouth, nov. 1968. &c.
in progress?

CARLOS RODRIGUEZ JOULIA SAINT-CYR, Ensayo de bibliografia menor hispanomusulmana; hojas y folletos impresos de los siglos xvi, xvii y xviii. Madrid 1970. pp.xix.377. [1600.]

SELECT bibliography on arab islamic civilization and its contribution to human progress. Bibliographical series (no.3): Kuwait 1970.

BRITISH books on the arab world; an exhibition arranged by the British council. [London 1971.] pp.48. [900.]

ARAB culture and society in change; a partially annotated bibliography of books and articles in english, french, german and italian. Compiled by the staff of CEMAM "Centre d'études pour le monde arabe moderne", Saint Joseph's university, Beirut: Beirut 1973. pp.xli.318. [4954.]

J. H. STEVENS and R. KING, A bibliography of Saudi Arabia. University of Durham: Centre for middle eastern and islamic studies: Occasional papers series (no.3): [Durham] 1973. pp.[vi].81. [1079.]*

CHARLES L. GEDDES, The arab-israeli dispute—an annotated bibliography of bibliographies. Bibliographic series (no.7); American institute of islamic studies: University of Denver. 1973. ff.7. [26.]*

Bahrain

A BIBLIOGRAPHY on Bahrain. UNESCO regional office: Beirut 1973. ff.16. [86.]*

Egypt

i. *Bibliography*
ii. *General*
iii. *Modern Egypt*
iv. *Subjects*
v. *Suez*

i. *Bibliography*

C[HARLES] L. GEDDES, An analytical guide to the bibliographies on modern Egypt & the Sudan. American institute of islamic studies: Bibliographic series (no.2): Denver 1972. pp.78. [135.]*

ii. *General*

PRINCE IBRAHIM HILMY, The literature of Egypt and the Soudan. . . . A bibliography comprising printed books, periodical writings and papers of learned societies, maps and charts, ancient papyri, manuscripts. 1886–1888. pp.viii.398+459. [17,500.]

the titlepage of the second volume is usually found in the form of a cancel.

[K. VOLLERS], Catalogue de la section européenne. 1. l'Égypte. [Publications de la Bibliothèque khédiviale (vol.iv)]: Le Caire 1892. pp.vii.205. [1500.]
— — Deuxième édition. [By Bernhardt Moritz]. . . . (vol.xiii): 1901. pp.xiii.589. [5000.]

SELECT list of references on Egypt, 525 B.C. to the present time. Library of Congress: Washington 1908. ff.8. [36.]

BIBLIOGRAPHIE géographique de l'Égypte. Publiée sous la direction de m. Henri Lorin. Société royale de géographie d'Égypte: [Cairo].
  i. Géographie physique et géographie humaine. Par Henriette Agrel [*and others*]. 1928. pp.xvi.472. [6158.]
  ii. Géographie historique. Par Henri Munier. 1929. pp.[iii].271. [2700.]

HENRI MUNIER, Catalogue de la bibliothèque du Musée égyptien du Caire. Service des antiquités de l'Égypte. Le Caire 1928. pp.vii.1010. [20,000.]
— — 1927–1958. Par Dia' Abou-Ghazi et Abd el-Mohsen el-Khachab. Le Caire 1966–. pp.xi.618+619–1204+1205–1818.
A-L published to 1970.

CATALOGUE of the collection of h.h. the late prince Ibrahim Hilmy (european section). Egyptian university library: Cairo 1936. pp.ix.267. [12,500.]
— — (Arabic, Turkish & Persian section.) pp.182. [3500.]

H[ENRY] MUNIER, Tables de la Description de l'Égypte, suivies d'une bibliographie sur l'expédition française de Bonaparte. Société royale de géographie d'Égypte: Le Caire 1943. pp.381. [631.]
includes indexes to La décade égyptienne *and* Mémoires sur l'Égypte.

JEAN ÉDOUARD GOBY, Bibliographies de savants et d'érudits ayant publié sur des questions relatives à l'Égypte. Société d'études historiques et géographiques de l'isthme de Suez: Matériaux documentaires (no.1): [Ismailia] 1950. pp.20. [200.]*

iii. *Modern Egypt*

A LIST of publications, maps, and plans. Ministry of public works: Cairo 1901. pp.31. [600.]
continued with various changes of title, the current one being:

List of maps and publications for sale at the Survey of Egypt map rooms. 1952. loose-leaf. [1000.]

> R. C. R. OWEN, Catalogue of route, road, general reports, parliamentary papers and books in the Intelligence department reference libraries, Khartoum and Cairo. London 1906. ff.iii.pp.217. [4500.]

RENÉ MAUNIER, Bibliographie économique, juridique et sociale de l'Égypte moderne (1798–1916). Société Sultanieh d'économie politique: Travaux spéciaux (no.1): Le Caire 1918. pp.xxxii.372. [6695.]

BRIEF list of references on England and Egypt. Library of Congress: [Washington] 1920. ff.5. [65.]*

IDA A[UGUSTA] PRATT, Modern Egypt. A list of references to material in the New York public library. New York 1929. pp.v.320. [6000.]

JEAN DENY, Sommaire des archives turques du Caire. Société royale de géographie d'Égypte: Publications spéciales: Le Caire 1930. pp.vii.638. [large number.]

GABRIEL GUÉMARD, Histoire et bibliographie critique de la Commission des sciences et arts et de l'Institut d'Egypte. Le Caire 1936. pp.129. [1000.]

LISTE des ouvrages imprimés en Égypte de 1936 à 1942. American legation: Despatch (no.57, enclosure no.1): Cairo 1942. ff.[iii].38. [750.]*

[CHARLES KUENTZ and JEANNE KUENTZ ARCACHE], Catalogue. Institut français d'archéologie orientale: Exposition du livre français en Égypte: Le Caire 1946. pp.vii.204. [2000.]

MARCEL M. ANAWATI and CHARLES KUENTZ, Bibliographie des ouvrages arabes imprimés en Égypte en 1942, 1943 et 1944. Institut français: Bibliographie arabe: Le Caire 1949. pp.xvi.614.lv. [854.]
Continued in Mélanges de l'Institut dominicain d'études orientales.

ANGLO-EGYPTIAN relations since the 1936 treaty, and the Sudan. House of Commons: Library: Bibliographies (no.72): 1951. pp.20. [121.]*

GAMAL-EDDINE [JAMES] HEYWORTH-DUNNE, Select bibliography on modern Egypt. Muslim world series (no.2): Cairo [1952]. pp.41. [167.]

JEAN ELLUL, Index des communications et mémoires publiés par l'Institut d'Égypte (1859–1952). Le Caire 1952. pp.iii–xvi.194. 2. [2000.]
the publications of the Institute égyptien are also listed.

[S. M. EL-HIFNY and M. A. HUSSEIN, *edd.*], Egypt. Subject catalogue. Egyptian national library: Cairo 1957. pp.xiv.416+viii.414–771. [11,000.]

ARABIC publications; five years bibliography 1956–1960. Afro-Asian distribution centre: Arabic book division: Cairo 1962. pp.ix.762. [8048.]

Egyptian publications bulletin. iii. A cumulative list of publications in foreign languages deposited during August 1955 to December 1966, together with its relevant indexes. 1963. pp.[iii].75. [554.]

Egyptian publications bulletin: A cumulative list of publications deposited.
1961–2.
   i. Arabic publications. pp.[x].698. [5330.]
   ii. Publications in foreign languages.
1963.
   i. [Arabic publications]. 1964. pp.[vii].476. [3240.]
   ii. Publications in foreign languages. 1964. pp.vii.52. [280.]
1964.
   i. [Arabic publications]. 1966. pp.[viii].504. [3346.]
   ii. Publications in foreign languages. 1966. pp.75. [342.]
1961–5.
   i–ii. [Arabic publications]. pp.vii.1031+ 1032–1776. [14,301.]
   iii. Publications in foreign languages. 1966. pp.iii.204. [1272.]
1966–7.
   i.
   ii. Publications in foreign languages. 1968. pp.v.161. [784.]
   iii. Children and school publications. 1968. pp.vii.30.142. [1087.]
1968. The annual volume.
   i. Publications in the arabic language. 1969. pp.vi.436. [589.]
   ii. Publications in foreign languages. 1969. pp.vii.68. [290.]
      [*Continued as:*]
Egyptian publications bulletin. The U.A.R. national bibliography.
1969. The annual volume. 1970. pp.[viii].436. 71. [3466.]
1970. The annual volume. 1971. pp.[viii].722. 117. [4915.]
in progress.

ACCESSIONS list, middle east. Library of Congress: American libraries book procurement center: Cairo.*
   1962. pp.358. [2800.]
   i. 1963. pp.[iv].344. [2000.]
   ii. 1964. pp.360. [4000.]
   iii. 1965. pp.454. [3200.]
   iv. 1966. pp.390. [3100.]
   v. 1967. pp.299. [2400.]
   vi. 1968. pp.312. [2500.]
   vii. 1969. pp.481.xxxviii. [3800.]
   viii. 1970. pp.494.xxxx. [4000.]
   ix. 1971. pp.414.xxvi. [3200.]
   x. 1972. pp.337. xxv. [2700.]
   xi. 1973. pp.311. [2400.]
in progress; includes works published outside

Egypt. Since volume iii, the index has been produced as a separate fascicle. Vols. i and ii contained semi-annual lists of serials in the issues for june and december, vol. iii in that for june only; since vol. iv an annual list of serials has formed the whole or part of the july number.

ALY IBRAHIM HASSAN, An authentic annotated bibliography & methods of research of islamic & egyptian mediaeval history. Cairo 1963. pp.203. [large number.]

ABDEL RAHMAN ZAKI, A bibliography of the literature of the city of Cairo. Société de géographie d'Égypte: le Caire 1964. pp.21.19. [1000.]

GUIDE to U.A.R. government publications at the A.U.C. library. American university in Cairo library: Cairo 1965. pp.20.41. [500.]*

LEGAL deposit monthly bulletin. January 1969 &c. The National library: Cairo.
in progress.

'Ā'IDAH IBRĀHĪM NUSAIR, Arabic books published in the U.A.R. "Egypt" between 1926 and 1940; a study and a bibliography. Cairo 1969. pp.vi.400. 2.6. [5000.]

HELEN ANNE B. RIVLIN, The Dār al-wathā'iq in 'Ābdīn palace at Cairo as a source for the study of the modernization of Egypt in the nineteenth century. Leiden 1970. pp.vi.134. [large number.]

iv. *Subjects*

Agriculture

DRY farming in India, Egypt and South Africa. Science library: Bibliographical series (no.287): 1935 [1937]. single sheet. [22.]*

LIST of publications in English issued by the ministry. Ministry of agriculture: Extension service section: [Cairo] 1937. pp.16. [400.]

M. EWIEDA, Selected bibliography from foreign and arabic periodicals dealing with agricultural development and related fields. Institute of national planning: Memo. (no.734): Cairo 1967. pp.x.136. [850.]*

Economics

M. EWIEDA, classified index to articles of the periodicals for the years 1965 and 1966. Institute of national planning: Memo. (no.824): Cairo 1968.
See also Egypt: general.

Education

[MOHAMED KHAIRY HARBY *and others*], L'éducation en Égypte. Unesco: Revue analytique de l'éducation (vol.ix. no.8): 1957. pp.12. [47.]

M. HASHAD and M. AFIFI, Guide to selected references on educational and manpower planning and related subjects. Institute of national

planning: Memo. (no.709): Cairo 1966. pp.[ii]•120. [800.]*

Fellah

LYMAN H. COULT and KARIM DURZI, An annotated research bibliography of studies in arabic, english, and french of the fellah of the egyptian Nile 1798–1955. Coral Gables, Fla. 1958. pp.v.144. [831.]*

Geology

LIST of publications of the Mines & quarries department, Geological survey of Egypt and Petroleum research board, to which is appended a list of Survey department papers. Cairo 1948. pp.10. [150.]

ELIAS HABIB KELDANI. A bibliography of geology and related sciences concerning Egypt. Department of survey and mines: Cairo 1941. pp.xxix.428. [2939.]

Patents

RECUEIL égyptien périodique de la propriété industrielle, commerciale et intellectuelle et des sociétés. Le Caire.

    1929–1932. pp.324. [342.]
    1932–1933. pp.137. [305.]
    1933–1934. pp.135. [305.]
    1934–1935. pp.147. [294.]
    1935–1936. pp.151. [309.]
    1936–1937. pp.163. [369.]
    1937–1938. pp.161. [358.]
    1938–1940. pp.177. [428.]
no more published.

Press

MARTIN [P. W.] HARTMANN, The arabic press of Egypt. 1899. pp.[vi].94. [168.]

LIST of current periodicals [and newspapers]. National library: Cairo 1959. pp.88. [450.]

Science

C[HARLES] DAVIES SHERBORN, Bibliography of scientific and technical literature relating to Egypt, 1800–1900. Preliminary edition. Ministry of finance: Survey department: Cairo 1910. pp.[ii].ii. ff.2–156. [3500.]
12 copies printed.

*UNION catalogue of scientific periodicals in Egypt up to end of 1949. Fouad I national research council: Cairo 1951. pp.383. [3175.]

CLASSIFIED list of egyptian scientific papers. Fouad I national research council [ii–iii: Al-Ma'had al-qawmī lil-buḥūth]: Cairo.
    i. 1951. pp.55. [500.]
    ii. 1952.
    iii. 1953.
no more published.

World war I

FIRST world war. Campaign in Egypt and Palestine. Imperial war museum: Library: [1952]. pp. 11. [150.]

World war II

SECOND world war. Military operations. African theatre. Part 1. Libya and Egypt. Imperial war museum: Library: [1954]. pp.9. [150.]

v. Suez, isthmus of

BIBLIOGRAPHIE de l'isthme de Suez et des régions voisines pour les années 1939 à 1950. Société d'études historiques et géographiques de l'isthme de Suez: Matériaux documentaires (no.3): [Ismailia] 1951. pp.38. [250.]

A[LFRED] L. FONTAINE, Monographic cartographique de l'isthme de Suez, de la péninsule du Sinaï, du nord de la chaîne arabique, suivie d'un catalogue raisonné sur les cartes de ces régions. Société d'études historiques et géographiques de l'isthme de Suez: Mémoires (vol.ii): Le Caire 1955. pp.iii–xx.238. [300.]

Suez canal

THE SUEZ crisis. A chronological reading list. Department of state: Library division: Bibliographic list (no.144): [Washington] 1956. ff.15. [150.]*

Iraq

A. YAARI [and others], A post-war bibliography of the near eastern mandates. A preliminary survey of publications on the social sciences dealing with Iraq ... to Dec. 31, 1929. American university of Beirut: Social science series (no.1): Jerusalem 1933 &c.

WHAT to read about Iran, Iraq and Afghanistan. East and west association: [New York] 1942. pp.8. [33.]*

ROSEMARY BOXER, A bibliography of material on the development of modern Iraq. Development board of Iraq: Baghdad [1953]. pp.47. [800.]

FIRST world war. Mesopotamian campaign. Imperial war museum: Library: [1953]. pp.7. [100.]*

A BIBLIOGRAPHICAL list of works about Iraq. Second edition. Bibliographical lists of the arab world (no.5): The national library: Cairo 1964. pp.87.172. [649.]

GURGUIS AWWAD, A dictionary of iraqi authors during the nineteenth and twentieth centuries (1800–1969 A.D.). Baghdad, 1969. pp.487+510+704. [Very large number.]

CLASSIFFIED catalog of government publications available in the Central library, Baghdad university. Baghdad 1969. ff.53.14.3.14. [750.]*

E[SSAM] M[UHAMMAD] MAHMOOD and A[BDUL HALIM] AL-LAWAND, Mosul printed from 1861–1970. Mosul 1971. pp.158. [1500.]

EXTERNAL research: a listing of recently completed studies. South Asia, Iran, Iraq. External research staff: Office of intelligence research and analysis: Department of state: Washington. ERS list no.10.9. October 1957.
no more published?

A GUIDE to literature of Iraq's natural resources. UNESCO institute for applied research: Abu Graeb 1969. pp.133.

Jordan

RAPHAEL PATAI, Jordan, Lebanon and Syria: an annotated bibliography. Human relations area files: Behavior science bibliographies: New Haven 1957. pp.vii.289.[xii]. [1605.]

DARTHULA M. CARRAWAY, Annotated bibliography of climatic maps of Jordan. Weather bureau: Washington 1961. pp.v.10. [33.]*

A BIBLIOGRAPHICAL list of work about Palestine and Jordan. Second edition. Bibliographical lists of the arab world (no.2): National library: Cairo 1964. pp.338.144.[x]. [1324.]

MAHMUD EL-AKHRAS, Palestine-Jordan bibliography 1900–1970. Jordan library association: Amman 1972. pp.354. [2740.]

THE 1970 general directory of the press and periodicals in Jordan and Kuwait and all information concerning advertising in these countries. Syrian documentation papers: Damascus [1970]. ff.61. [22.]*

Kuwait

SORAYA M. KABEEL, Selected bibliography on Kuwait and the Arabian gulf. Kuwait university libraries department: Bibliographic series (no.1): Kuwait 1969. pp.xiv.104. [1300.]*

THE 1970 general directory of the press and periodicals in Jordan and Kuwait and all information concerning advertising in these countries. Syrian documentation papers: Damascus [1970.] ff.61. [22.]*

Lebanon

CATALOGUE des cartes de la Syrie, du Liban et des régions limitrophes publiées par le Service géographique du Levant et par l'Institut géographique national. Beyrouth 1941. pp.12. [200.]

IBRAHIM MAOUAD, Bibliographie des auteurs libanais de langue français. Commission libanaise de l'Unesco: Beyrouth 1948. pp.[v].57. [534.]

RAPHAEL PATAI, Jordan, Lebanon and Syria: an annotated bibliography. Human relations area files: Behavior science bibliographies: New Haven 1957. pp.vii.289.[xii]. [1605.]

Oman

R. KING and J. H. STEVENS, A bibliography of Oman 1900–1970. University of Durham: Centre for middle eastern and islamic studies: Occasional papers series (no.2): [Durham] 1973. pp.ii.ff.14. [172.]★

A BIBLIOGRAPHY on Oman. UNESCO regional office: Beirut 1973. ff.2. [9.]★

Qatar

A BIBLIOGRAPHY on Qatar. UNESCO regional office: Beirut 1973. ff.4. [22.]★
—[Another edition.] 1974. ff.11. [56.]★

Syria

PAUL MASSON, Éléments d'une bibliographie française de la Syrie (géographie, ethnographie, histoire, archéologie, langues, littératures, religions). Congrès français de la Syrie: Marseille 1919. pp.xix.529. [4534.]

A. YAARI [and others], A post-war bibliography of the near eastern mandates. A preliminary survey of publications on the social sciences dealing with . . . the syrian states . . . to Dec. 31, 1929. American university of Beirut: Social science series (no.1): Jerusalem 1933 &c.

RAPHAEL PATAI, Jordan, Lebanon and Syria: an annotated bibliography. Human relations area files: Behavior science bibliographies: New Haven 1957. pp.vii.289. [xii]. [1605.]

[HENRI LAOUST], Liste des publications, 1929–1959. Institut français de Damas: Damas 1959. pp.24. [100.]

A BIBLIOGRAPHICAL list of works about Syria. Second edition. Bibliographical lists of the arab world (no.3): The National Library: Cairo 1965 pp.192.166. [965.]

CATALOGUE des cartes de la Syrie, du Liban et des régions limitrophes publiées par le Service géographique du Levant et par l'Institut géographique national. Beyrouth 1941. pp.12. [200.]

LOUIS FARÈS, Répertoire général des publications périodiques de la République arabe syrienne. Mis-à-jour en avril/mai 1968, avec une documentation complète concernant les moyens de publicité en Syrie. Damas [1968]. ff.101. [83.]★

Yemen

ERIC MACRO, Bibliography on Yemen and notes on Mocha. Coral Gables, Fla. 1960. pp.vii.63. [894.]

THE tribes of Yemen: A list of western language books and periodical articles containing information on the tribes of Yemen. U.S. Department of state: Bureau of intelligence and research: External research paper (146): Washington 1964. pp.9. [102.]★

ARABIC

i. *Language*
ii. *Literature*

E. LAMBRECHT, Catalogue de la bibliothèque de l'École des langues orientales vivantes. Tome premier. Linguistique. I. Philologie.—II. Langue arabe. École des langues orientales vivantes: Publications (4th ser., vol.i): 1897. pp.xi.623. [arabic: 3196.]

ARDUINO KLEINHANS, Historia studii linguae arabicae et Collegii missionum Ordinis fratrum minorum in conventu ad S. Petrum in Monte Aureo Romæ erecti. Biblioteca bio-bibliografica della terra santa e dell' oriente francescano (new ser., vol.xiii): Quaracchi 1930. pp.xii.508. [500.]

[HENRI PÉRÈS], Langue et littérature arabes. Notions essentialles de bibliographie. Alger [printed] 1932. pp.27. [395.]

AZIMUDDIN AHMAD ['AZIMU'D-DĪN AḤMAD] and MAULAVI MUINUDDIN NADWÎ [MU'ĪNU'D-DĪN NADWĪ], Catalogue of the arabic and persian manuscripts in the Oriental public library at Bankipore. Volume xx (arabic mss.). Philology. Patna 1936. pp.vii.229. [159.]

WOLF LESLAU, Modern south arabic languages. A bibliography. Public library: New York 1946. pp.29. [195.]

HENRI PÉRÈS, L'arabe dialectal algérien et saharien. Bibliographie analytique avec un index méthodique. Institut d'études supérieures islamiques: Bibliothèque (no.xiv): Alger 1958. pp.141. [486.]

HENRI PÉRÈS, Dictionnaires arabes: en arabe et en français. École pratique d'études arabes d'Alger: Collection (no.21): Alger 1960. pp.19. [73.]

HARVEY SOBELMAN, *ed*. Arabic dialect studies. A selected bibliography. Modern language association [&c]: Center for applied linguistics: Washington 1962. pp.vi.100. [400.]★

WAGDY RIZK GHALI, Arabic dictionaries; an annotated comprehensive bibliography. Cairo 1971. pp.258. [707.]

ii. *Literature*

1. *Bibliographies*
2. *General*
3. *Library catalogues*
4. *Periodicals*
5. *Manuscripts*
6. *Arab writers*
7. *Literary characters*
8. *Subjects*
9. *Translations*

1. *Bibliographies*

JOSEPH A. DAGHER [YŪSUF AS'AD DĀGHIR],
فهارس المكتبة العربية ·فى الخافقين، تأليف
يوسف اسعد زاغر. [*on cover.*] Répertoire
bibliographique de la bibliothèque arabe. Beyrouth 1947. pp. . [500.]

GEORGES VAJDA, Répertoire des catalogues et
inventaires de manuscrits arabes. Centre national
de la recherche scientifique: Institut de recherche et
d'histoire des textes (no.2): 1949. pp.vi.49. [377.]

A[UGUSTE] J. W. HUISMAN, Les manuscrits arabes
dans le monde; une bibliographie des catalogues.
Leiden 1967. pp.x.99. [1000.]

SA'ID M. AL-HAJRASI, Bibliographical guide to
reference works in the arab world. Cairo 1965.
pp.xxvi.130. [183.]*

ABDUL KARIM ALAMIN and ZAHIDA IBRAHIM,
Guide to arabic reference books. Baghdad 1970.
pp.[vii].267. [401.]

2. *General*

CATALOGUS centuriae librorum rarissimorum
manuscript. & partim impressorum, arabicorum,
persicorum, turcicorum . . . qua . . . bibliothecam
publicam academiæ Upsalensis auxit . . . Ioan.
Gabr. Sparvenfeldius. Upsaliæ 1706. pp.[vi].74.
[120.]

JO[HANN] HENR. [HEINRICH] CALLENBERG, Specimen bibliothecae arabicae, qua libris arabici
editi recensentur. Halae 1756. pp.16. [50.]

GIAMBERNARDO DE ROSSI, Dizionario storico
degli autori arabi piu celebri e delle principali loro
opere. Parma 1807. pp.vii.196.[iv]. [1000.]

CHRISTIAN FRIEDRICH SCHNURRER, Bibliotheca
arabica. Halae ad Salam 1811. pp.xxiii.530. [2000.]
*pages 515a–518a are inserted between pages 514
and 515.*
—— Table alphabétique. [By Victor Chau-
vin]. [1892]. pp.cxvii.
also forms part of Chauvin's Bibliographie des
ouvrages arabes.

T[HOMAS] X[AVIER] BIANCHI, Notice sur le premier ouvrage d'anatomie . . . suivi du catalogue
des livres turcs, arabes et persans, imprimés à
Constantinople, depuis l'introduction de l'imprimerie, en 1726–27 jusqu'en 1820–1821. pp.[ii].40.
[68.]
*one of the copies in the Bibliothèque nationale
contains a ms. supplement.*

J[OHANN] H[EINRICH] MÖLLER, Catalogus librorum tam manuscriptorum quam impressorum qui
jussu divi Augusti, ducis Saxo-Gothani a beato
Seetzenio in oriente emti in bibliotheca Gothana
asservantur. . . . Tomus primus. Gothae 1826. pp.
vi.270.28. [965.]

[CHRISTIAN MARTIN FRÄHN], Хронологической списокъ ста сочиненій, преимущественно
историческаго и географическаго содержанія,
на арабскомъ, персидскомъ и туредкомъ
языкахъ, недостающихъ большею частію въ
европейскихъ библіотекахъ. С.-Петербургъ
1834. pp.[ii].24. [120.]
—— [another edition]. Казань 1834. pp.[viii].
24. [120.]
—— [another edition]. Indications bibliographiques relatives pour la plupart à la littérature
historico-géographique des Arabes, des Persans,
et des Turcs, spécialment destinées à nos employés
et voyageurs en Asie. St. Pétersbourg 1845.
pp.[iv].lv.87. [244.[

JULIUS THEODOR ZENKER, Bibliotheca orientalis·
Pars I. Libros continens arabicos, persicos, turcicos,
inde ab arte typographica inventa ad nostra usque
tempora impressos. [Fasciculus I. Libri arabici].
Lipsiae 1840. pp.[iii].90. [750.]
no more published.

A CATALOGUE of valuable collection of oriental
literature, collected by James Bruce. 1842. pp.36.
[97.]
*this is the auction catalogue of a collection now in the
Bodleian library, which has a copy containing notes
and an index in ms.*

T[HOMAS] X[AVIER] BIANCHI, Catalogue général
et détaillé des livres arabes, persans et turcs imprimés a Boulac en Égypte depuis l'introduction de
l'imprimerie dans ce pays, en 1822, jusqu'en 1842.
1843. pp.43. [243.]

IBN NADĪM, Kitâb al-fihrist, mit anmerkungen
herausgegeben von Gustav Flügel. Nach dessen
tode besorgt von Johannes Roediger und August
Mueller. Leipzig 1871–2. pp.xxii.43.361+viii.
279. [very large number.]

T. PRESTON, Catalogus Bibliothecae burckhard-
tianæ, cum appendice librorum aliorum orientalium in bibliotheca Academiæ cantabrigiensis
asservatorum. Cantabrigiæ 1853. pp.[iv].164.
[300.]
the Burckhardt collection is wholly arabic.

[BERNHARD] DORN, Catalogue des ouvrages arabes, persans et turcs, publiés a Constantinople, en Égypte et en Perse, qui se trouvent au Musée asiatique de l'Académie. St.-Pétersbourg 1866. pp.[ii].64. [387.]

[JULIUS EUTING], Arabische literatur. Katalog der Kaiserlichen universitäts- und landesbibliothek: Strassburg 1877. pp.[vii].111. [1250.]

CLÉMENT [IMBAULT] HUART, Bibliographie ottomane. Notice des livres turcs, arabes et persans imprimés a Constantinople.

    1294–1296 (1877–1879). pp.31. [91.]
    1297–1298 (1880–1881). pp.48. [218.]
    1299–1301 (1882–1884). pp.[iii].88. [452.]
    1302–1303 (1885–1886). pp.69. [344.]
    1304–1305 (1887–1888). pp.[iii].62. [300.]
    1306–1307 (1889–1890). pp.[iii].54. [303.]

F. F. ARBUTHNOT, Arabic authors. A manual of arabian history and literature. 1890. pp.xiv.247. [500.]

IBN KHAYR AL-ISHBĪLĪ, Index librorum de diversis scientiarum ordinibus quos a magistris didicit Abu Bequer ben Khair ... arabice nunc primum ediderunt indicibus additis Franciscus Codera ... et J. Ribera Târrago ... Caesaraugustae 1894–5. pp.463+xiii.465–582. [900.]

VICTOR CHAUVIN, Bibliographie des ouvrages arabes ou relaufs aux Arabes publiés dans l'Europe chrétienne de 1810 a 1885. Liège.

    i. Préface.—Table de Schnurrer.—Les proverbes. 1892. pp.cxvii.72. [175.]
    ii. Kalílah. 1897. pp.vii.239. [1000.]
    iii. Louqmâne et les fabulistes.—Barlaam.—'Antar et les romans de chevalerie. 1898. pp.[iii].151. [250.]
    iv–vii. Les mille et une nuits. 1900–1903. pp.[iii].228 + xii.297 + [iii].204 + [iii].192. [350.]
    viii. Syntipas. 1904. pp.[iii].219. [100.]
    ix. Pierre Alphonse.—Secundus.—Recueils orientaux. — Tables de Henning et de Mardrus. — Contes occidentaux. — Les maqâmes. 1905. pp.[iii].136. [250.]
    x. Le Coran et la tradition. 1907. pp.[iii].146. [400.]
    xi. Mahomet. 1909. pp.[iii].255. [1000.]
    xii. Le mahométisme. [Completed by Louis Polain.] 1922. pp.vi.467. [1831.]

corrections and additions by A. Fischer appeared in the Centralblatt für bibliothekswesen *(1893), x.82–93.*

A[LEXANDER] G[EORGE] ELLIS, Catalogue of arabic books in the British museum. 1894–1901. pp.[iii].coll.986+pp.[iii].coll.864. [10,000.]
—— Indexes. By A[lexander] S. Fulton. 1935. pp.[iv].coll.454.

—— Supplementary catalogue. ... By A. S. Fulton and A. G. Ellis. 1926. pp.[iv].coll.1188. [5000.]
—— Second supplementary catalogue ... By Alexander S. Fulton and Martin Lings. 1959. pp.ix.coll.1131. [10,000.]

FRANCISCO PONS BOIGNES, Ensayo bio-bibliogràfico sobre los historiadores y geógrafos arábigo-españoles. Madrid 1898. pp.[v].515. [303.]

CARL BROCKELMANN, Geschichte der arabischen litteratur. 1898–1902. pp.xii.528+xi.714. [very large number.]
—— Erster (-dritter) supplementband. Leiden 1937–42. pp.xix.973+xix.1045+xi.1326.
—— Zweiter den supplementbänden angepasste auflage. 1943–9. pp.ix.676+xiv.687.

ASHRAF 'ALĪ, A catalogue of the arabic books and manuscripts in the library of the Asiatic society of Bengal. Calcutta [1899–] 1904. pp.[ii].153.

MORITZ STEINSCHNEIDER, Die arabische literatur der Juden. Ein beitrag zur literaturgeschichte der Araber, grossenteils aus handschriftlichen quellen. Frankfurt a. M. 1902. pp.liv.348.32. [2000.]

I[DA] A[UGUSTA] PRATT, List of works in the New York public library relating to arabic poetry. Prepared ... under the direction of R[ichard James Horatio] Gottheil. [New York 1908]. pp.25. [750.]

CATALOGUE of arabic, persian and urdu books in the Imperial library. Calcutta 1915. pp.[ii].12. *limited to the arabic books.*

[ALFRED BEL], Catalogue des livres arabes de la bibliothèque de la mosquée d'El-Qarouiyîne à Fès. Fès 1918. pp.16. 165 [1500.]

JOSEPH SCHACHT, Aus den bibliotheken von Konstantinopel und Kairo [vol.ii: Aus kairiner bibliotheken; vol.iii: Aus orientalischen bibliotheken]. Preussische akademie der wissenshcaften: Abhandlungen: Philosophisch-historische klasse (1928, no.8; 1929, no.6; 1931, no.1): Berlin 1928–1931. pp.76+36+57. [1250.]

JOSEPH ELIAN SARKIS [YŪSUF ILYĀN SARKĪS], Dictionnaire encyclopédique de bibliographie arabe, comprenant ... le nom de tous les ouvrages imprimés, tant en orient qu'en occident et en Amérique. Le Caire 1928–1930. coll. 224 pp.1012.152.18. [25,000.]

[HENRI PÉRÈS], Langues et litérature arabes. Notions essentielles de bibliographie. Alger [printed] 1932. pp.27. [395.]

INDICE e inventarios. Alta comisaría de España en Marruecos: Biblioteca general del protectorado: Sección arabe: Tanger 1940. pp.[iv]. 224 [2500.]
the text is in arabic.

HENRI PÉRÈS, Littérature arabe moderne, grands courants. Bibliographie. Alger 1940. pp.32. [400.]

GEORG GRAF, Geschichte der christlichen arabischen literatur. Studi e testi (118 &c). Città del Vaticano. [very large number.]
    i. Die übersetzungen. 1944. pp.xliv.662. [185.]
    ii. Die schriftsteller bis zur mitte des 15 jahrhunderts. 1947. pp.xxxi.512. [147.]
    iii. Die schriftsteller von der mitte des 15. bis zum ende des 19 jahrhunderts. Melchiten, Maroniten. 1949. pp.xxxiii.525. [121.]
    iv. Die schriftsteller von der mitte des 15 bis zum ende des 19 jahrhunderts. Syrer, Armenier, Kopten, missionsliteratur, profanliteratur. 1951. pp.xxxvi.342. [225.]
    v. Register. 1953. pp.196.
the figures in brackets refer to sections, each of which may contain notices of several works or, indeed, of several authors.

JOSEPH ASSAD DAGHER, Éléments de bio-bibliographie de la littérature arabe conforme aux programmes officiels de l'enseignement. Liban–Syrie–Iraq–Egypte. Saida 1950–56. pp.xxxii.356+xxii.864. [very large number.]

M[ARCEL] M. ANAWATI and CHARLES KUENTZ, Bibliographie des ouvrages arabes imprimés en Égypte en 1942, 1943 et 1944. Institut français: Bibliographie arabe: Le Caire 1949. pp.xvi.614. lv. [854.]

[RADĪ AL-DĪN AHMAD IBN ISMĀʿĪL], A twelfth-century reading list. A chapter in arab bibliography. By [or rather, edited by] A[rthur] J[ohn] Arberry. Chester Beatty monographs (no.2): 1951. pp.27. [117.]

FIESTA del libro hispano-árabe 1951. (Exposición de manuscritos y documentos arabes y encuadernaciones.) Tetuán 1951. pp.[40]. [137.]

FEHMI EDHEM KARATAY, Istanbul üniversitesi kütüphanesi arapça basmalar alfabe kataloğu. Istanbul üniversitesi yayınlarından (no.501): Istanbul 1951–3. pp.857. [6500.]

AHMED MOHAMMED MEKINASI, Catálogo de autores y títulos de la biblioteca general del protectorado, sección arabe. Alta comisaria de España en Marruecos: Delegación de educación y cultura: Dirección de archivos y bibliotecas del protectorado: Tetuán 1952. pp.[ii].611. [10,000.]

EXPOSITION de pièces et oeuvres du fonds arabe de la bibliothèque nationale et universitaire de Strasbourg. [Strasbourg 1959]. ff.16. [150.]*

JOSEPH A. DAGHER, Democracy in arabic literature (short bibliography). [Beirut 1959.] pp.68. [500.]

ACCESSIONS list, middle east, library of congress. American libraries book procurement center: Cairo 1962 &c.*
details set out under Egypt.

RAOUF SHAFIK GHALI. A classified list of selected books for school libraries. 1962/63–1967/68. School library association: Cairo 1969. pp.318. [2809.]

IBN AL-NADĪM, The Fihrist of al-Nadīm, a tenth-century survey of muslim culture. Bayard Dodge, editor and translator. New York & London 1970. pp.xxxv.570+571–1149. [very large number.]

FUAT SEZGIN, Geschichte des arabischen shrifttums. Leiden.
    1. Qur'anwissenschaften, Hadit, Geschichte, Fiqh, Dogmatik, Mystik, bis ca. 430 h. 1967. pp.xv.936.
    3. Medizin, Pharmazie, Zoologie, Tierheilkunde, bis ca. 430 h. 1970. pp.xxi.498.
    4. Alchimie, Chemie, Botanik, Agrikultur bis ca. 430 h. 1971. pp.xiii.399.

BULLETIN of arab publications 1970.

[MIROSLAV KREK], Typographia arabica. The development of arabic printing as illustrated by arabic type specimens. Exhibition held at the Rapaporte treasure hall. Brandeis university library: Waltham 1971. ff.iii.43. [96.]*

JERZY GUTKOWSKI, Guide to arabic sources. The library: Institute of islamic studies: McGill university: Montreal 1973. ff.19. [82.]*

3. *Library catalogues*

BIBLIOTHÈQUE de m. le baron Silvestre de Sacy. Paris.
    1. Livraison
    i. Imprimés: philosophie, théologie, sciences naturelles. 1842. pp.12.lxiv.436. [1795.]
    bound up with:
    iii. Manuscrits. Tables générales. 1842. pp.[v].63. [364.]
    2. Livraison
    ii. Sciences medicales et arts utiles; psychologie; sciences morales; linguistique; littérature et beaux arts; histoire littéraire. 1846. pp.xxiii.416. [1796–3910.]
    3. Livraison
    iii. Imprimés. Sciences sociales; sciences historiques; polygraphie. 1847. pp.xxxi. 472. [3911–6022.]

ABDUR RAHMAN, *Maulavi* and ABDUL MAJID RUSHDI, *Maulavi*. Catalogue of books of the Islamia college library, Calcutta. Government of Bengal: Alipore 1935, pp.xxv.244. [6000.]

[A. BUSTANI], Biblioteca general del Protectorado, sección árabe. Indice e inventarios. Tanger 1940. pp.[ii].224. [1000.]

[M. WAHBY], Catalogo de las obras en lenguas árabe y europeas existentes en la biblioteca de este instituto. Instituto jalifiano de Muley el Hassan, Tetuan. Tetuan 1942. pp.66. 318. [2500.]

GUILLERMO GUASTAVINO GALLENT and CARLOS RODRÍGUEZ JOULIA SAINT-CYR, Catalogo de materias (obras relativas al Islam y Africa) de la Biblioteca general del Protectorado. Alta Comisaría de España en Marruecos: Delegación de educación y cultura: Dirección de archivos y bibliotecas del protectorado: Tetuán 1952. pp.611. [5810.]

MARIANO ARRIBAS PALAU, Catalogo de autores de la biblioteca, Sección europea. Alta Comisaria de España en Marruecos: Delegación de educación y cultura: Tetuán 1953. pp.[viii].160.[ii].

A[LEXANDER] G[EORGE] ELLIS, Catalogue of arabic books in the British museum. 1894-1901. pp.[iii].coll.986+pp.[iii].coll.864.[10,000.]
— — Indexes. By A[lexander] S. Fulton. 1935. pp.[iv].coll.454.
— — Supplementary catalogue ... By A. S. Fulton and A. G. Ellis. 1926. pp.[iv].coll.1188. [5000.]
— — Second supplementary catalogue. Compiled by Alexander S. Fulton and Martin Lings. 1959. pp.ix.cols.1131. [10,000.]

A LIST of books in the Central library as represented in the shelf list. 1959-1964 (1966). Baghdad 1965 (-1966?). pp.200 + 201-400 + 401-600 + 601-800 + 801-980 + 981-1160 + 1161-1320 + 1321-1480 + 1481-1640 + 1641-1800 + 1801 -1960. [15,680.]*

*UNION list of materials on islamic studies. Institute of asian economic affairs; Tokyo 1961. pp.ix.277. [4,000.]

CATALOGUE of books and periodicals in the Middle east research library of the American friends of the middle east, 8/A Habibullah road, off Davis road, Lahore 3, Pakistan. 1962. pp.5.268. [3000.]*
now in the library of the University of Peshawar.

BIBLIOTHÈQUE du Centre national pour l'étude des problèmes du monde musulman contemporain. (Acquisitions de l'année 1963.) Catalogue (no.4): Bruxelles 1963. pp.30. [282.]

ARABIC collection. Aziz S. Atiya library for middle east studies. University of Utah: Middle east library: Catalogue series: Salt Lake City 1968. pp.xv.841. [8407.]*
— Supplement one. 1971. pp.x.470. [3000.]

THE LIBRARY catalogs of the Hoover institution on war, revolution, and peace, Stanford university. Boston 1969.
Catalog of the arabic collection. pp.xiii.902. [18,914 cards.]
Catalogs of the turkish and persian collections. pp.xiii.670. [14,055 cards.]

4. Periodicals
UNION list of periodicals in the Cairo libraries. United States offices of information and educational exchange: Cairo 1950. pp.112. [1000.]*

J[AMES] D[OUGLAS] PEARSON and JULIA F[RANCIS] ASHTON, Index islamicus 1906-1955; a catalogue of articles on islamic subjects in periodicals and other collective publications. Cambridge 1958. pp. xxxvi. 897. [26,076.]
reprinted Cambridge 1961 and London 1972.
— Supplement, 1956-1960. By J. D. Pearson. 1962. pp.xxviii.316. [7296.]
— Second supplement, 1961-1965. 1967. pp. xxx.342. [8135.]
— Third supplement, 1966-1970. By J. D. Pearson and Ann Walsh. London, 1972. [8000.]

THE ARAB world index. A list of articles published in learned journals. The American university at Cairo library. Cairo 1960 &c.
in progress.

GUIDE to periodicals at the A.U.C. library. American university in Cairo library: Cairo 1965. pp.[vii].66.10. [1000.]*

M. AHMED BIOUD, 2,300 revues arabes. Titres translittérés et titres arabes. Paris 1965. pp.vi. [281]. [2264.]*

MUHAMMAD EL-MAHDI, Directory of current periodicals published in the arab world. Cairo 1965. pp.108.24. [863.]

MOHAMED M. EL-HADI, Union list of arabic serials in the United States. The arabic serial holdings of seventeen libraries. University of Illinois graduate school of library science: Occasional papers (no.75): [Urbana, Ill.] pp.1965. pp.61. [863.]*
also in an arabic edition.

J[OHN] F[RANCIS] P[RICE] HOPKINS, ed. Arabic periodical literature 1961. Cambridge 1966. pp.xi.104. [1874.]

A CATALOG of periodicals holdings at Central library, University of Baghdad, 1967. pp.ii.270. [1500.]*

FLORENCE LJUNGGREN, The Arab world index. An international guide to periodical literature in the social sciences and humanities in the contemporary Arab world 1960-1964. Cairo 1967. pp.xv.549. [5500.]

LOUIS E. FARES, Répertoire général des publications périodiques, mis-a-jour en avril/mai 1968 avec une documentation complète concernant les moyens de publicité en Syrie. Damas 1968. pp.101. [83.]*

ABDELGHANI AHMED-BIOUD, HASSAN HANAFI and HABIB FEKI, 3200 revues et journaux arabes de 1800 à 1965. Titres arabes et titres translittérés. Maison des Sciences de l'homme: Paris 1969. pp.xviii.256. [3258.]*

DEREK HOPWOOD, Arabic periodicals in Oxford; a union list. Oxford [c.1970]. pp.19+addendum slip. [138.]*

GENERAL directory of the press and periodicals in Jordan and Kuwait. Syrian documentation papers: Damascus 1970 &c.
in progress.

WILLIAM R. ROFF, Bibliography of malay and arabic periodicals published in the Straits Settlements and peninsula Malay states 1876–1941, with an annotated union list of holdings in Malaysia, Singapore and the United Kingdom. London oriental bibliographies (vol.3): London 1972. pp.[vi].74. [197.]

MUZAFFAR ALI, Periodica islamica; a check-list of serials available at McGill islamics library. Institute of islamic studies: McGill university: Montreal 1973. pp.28. [900.]

5. Manuscripts

LIBRI mss. Arabici & alii, quos pro Academia ex oriente advexit Jacobus Golius. [Lugduni Batavorum 1640.] pp.23. [231.]

— Catalogus codicum arabicorum bibliothecae Academiae lugduno-batavae. Editio secunda, auctoribus M[ichael] J[an] de Goeje et M[artijn] Th[eodoor] Houtsma [vol.ii, pars prior: et Th(eodore) W(illem) Juynboll]. Lugduni Batavorum 1888–1907. pp.[iii].xxxiv.498+[iv].256. [929.]
no more published.

MIGUEL CASIRI, Bibliotheca arabico-hispana Escurialensis, sive librorum omnium mss. quos arabicè ab auctoribus magnam partem arabo-hispanis compositos bibliotheca coenobii Escurialeusis complectitur, recensio & explanatio. Matriti 1760–1770. pp.[xvi].xxiv.544+[viii].352. [ccxiii]. [5000.]
the preface alone was also issued in a smaller format in 1760, under the title Vestibulum sive aditus Bibliothecæ arabico-hispanæ.

JACOB GEORG CHRISTIAN ADLER, Descriptio codicvm qvorvndam cvficorvm partes Corani exhibentivm in Bibliotheca regia hafniensi. Altonae 1780. pp.34. [6.]

J. L. ROUSSEAU, Catalogue d'une collection de cinq cents manuscrits orientaux. Paris 1817. pp.53. [arabic: 265.]

JOSEPHUS DE HAMMER [BARON JOSEPH VON HAMMER-PURGSTALL], Codices arabicos, persicos, turcicos, Bibliothecae caesareo-regio-palatinae vindobonensis. Vindobonae 1820. pp.[ii].68. [618.]

ALEXANDER NICOLL, Bibliothecæ bodlianæ codicum manuscriptorum orientalium catalogi partis secundæ volumen primum [and second], arabicos complectens. . . . Editionem absolvit. . . E[dward] B[ouverie] Pusey. Oxonii 1821–1835. pp.[iv].143+[ii].viii.145–730. [2000.]

A CATALOGUE of arabic, turkish and persian manuscripts. The private collection of Wm. B. Hodgson. Washington 1830. ff.10. [150.]

ANGELO MAI, Scriptorum veterum nova collectio e vaticanis codicibus edita. . . . Tomus IV [Codices arabici vel a Christianis scripti vel ad religionem christianam spectantes]. Romae 1831. pp.xvi.96.719. [1000.]

HENRICUS ORTHOBIUS [HEINRICH LEBERECHT] FLEISCHER, Catalogus codicum manuscriptorum orientalium Bibliothecae regiae Dresdensis. Accedit Friderici Adolphi Eberti catalogus codicum manuscriptorum orientalium Bibliothecae ducalis Guelferbytanae. Lipsiae 1831. pp.xii.106. [596.]

CATALOGUS librorum manuscriptorum qui in bibliotheca senatoria civitalis Lipsiensis asservantur edidit Aemilius Guilelmus Robertus Naumann. Codices orientalium linguarum descripserunt Henricus Orthobius Fleischer et Franciscus Delitzsch. Grimae 1838. pp.xxiv.562.lvi. [424.]

ALBRECHT KRAFFT, Die arabischen, persischen und türkischen handschriften der K.k. orientalischen Akademie zu Wien. Wien 1842. pp.xx. 208. [1000.]

J. MOHL and P. LACROIX, Catalogue des livres et manuscrits orientaux provenant de la bibliothèque de feu m. J. St. Harriot. Paris 1843.

B[ERNHARD] DORN, Das asiatische museum der Kaiserlichen akademie der wissenschaften zu St. Petersburg. St. Petersburg 1846. pp.xii.776.

[WILLIAM CURETON and CHARLES RIEU], Catalogus codicum manuscriptorum orientalium qui in Museo britannico asservantur. Pars secunda, codices arabicos amplectens. 1846–1871. pp.[iii]. ix.352.[iii].882. [2500.]

—— Supplement to the catalogue of the arabic manuscripts. . . . By C. Rieu. 1894. pp.xv.935. [1500.]

—— A descriptive list of the arabic manuscripts acquired . . . since 1894. 1912. pp.vii.111. [1000.]

[CARL] J[OHANN] TORNBERG, Codices arabici, persici et turcici bibliothecæ regiæ universitatis Upsaliensis. [Upsal] 1849. pp.[ii].xxiv.355. [512.]

——Forsetzung. Die arabischen, persischen und türkischen handschriften der Universitätsbibliothek zu Uppsala. Verzeichnet... von K[arl] V[ilhelm] Zetterstéen. Uppsala 1930–1935. pp.xviii.498+x.180. [1500.]

also issued as vols.iii–iv of Acta bibliothecae R. universitatis upsaliensis *and as vols.xxii and xxviii of* Le monde oriental.

[M. H. HOHLENBERG, JUSTUS OLSHAUSEN and AUGUST FERDINAND MICHAEL MEHREN], Codices hebraici et arabici Bibliothecae regiæ hafniensis. Hafniae 1851. pp.xi.188. [arabic: 400.]

R[UDOLF H. TH.] FRIEDERICH, Codicum manuscriptorum arabicorum in bibliotheca Societatis artium et literarum quae Bataviae floret asservatorum Catalogi pars prima. Bataviaasch genootschap: Verhandelingen (vol.xxv, no.10): Batavia 1853. pp.iv.34. [200.]
no more published.
——[another edition]. Codicum arabicorum in bibliotheca Societatis artium et scientiarum... catalogus.... Absolvit... L[odewijk] W[illem] C[hristiaan] van den Berg. Bataviae &c. 1873. pp.[vii].154. [500.]
——Supplement to the Catalogue [&c.]. By Ph[ilippus] S[amuel] van Ronkel. Batavia &c. 1913. pp.[iii].ix.554. [1000.]

WILLIAM H[OOK] MORLEY, A descriptive catalogue of the historical manuscripts in the arabic and persian languages, preserved in the library of the Royal asiatic society. 1854. pp.viii.160. [arabic: 4.]

COLLECTION de manuscrits arabes, persans et turcs appartenant à mme. la comtesse Alix Des Granges. 1859. pp.12. [arabic: 44.]

EMILIO LAFUENTE Y ALCÁNTARA, Catálogo de los códices arábigos adquiridos en Tetúan por el gobierno de s.m. Madrid 1862. pp.80.viii.[viii]. [600.]

B[ERNHARD] DORN, Die sammlungen von morgenländischen handschriften, welche die Kaiserliche öffentliche bibliothek zu St. Petersburg im jahre 1864 von h[rn]. v. Chanykov erworben hat. St. Petersburg 1865. pp.[ii].93. [150.]
——Nachträge. Morgenländische handschriften. 1865. pp.[ii].43. [100.]

GUSTAV FLÜGEL, Die arabischen, persischen und türkischen handschriften der Kaiserlich-königlichen hof bibliothek zu Wien. Wien 1865–1867. pp.x.723+iv.614+lxviii.653. [3000.]

JOSEPH AUMER, Die arabischen handschriften der K. hof- und staatsbibliothek in Muenchen. Catalogus codicum manu scriptortum Bibliothecae regiae monacensis (vol.i, part 2): München 1866. pp.viii.502. [3000.]

MICHELE AMARI, Abbozzo di un catalogo de' manoscritti arabici della Lucchesiana. [Firenze 1869]. pp.[16]. [30.]
reproduced from handwriting.

E[DWARD] H[ENRY] PALMER, A descriptive catalogue of the arabic, persian, and turkish manuscripts in the library of Trinity college, Cambridge. With an appendix, containing a catalogue of the hebrew and samaritan mss. in the same library [by William Aldis Wright]. Cambridge, London 1870. pp.vii.235. [arabic: 60]

W[ILHELM] AHLWARDT, Verzeichnis arabischer handschriften der Königlichen bibliothek zu Berlin aus den gebieten der poesie, schönen litteratur, litteraturgeschichte und biographik. Greifswald 1871. pp.xii.305. [1237.]

L[ODEWIJK] W[ILLEM] C[HRISTIAAN] VAN DEN BERG, Verslag van eene verzameling maleische, arabische, javaansche en andere handschriften, door de regeering van nederlandsch Indie aan het Bataviaasch genootschap van kunsten en wetenschappen ter bewaring afgestaan. Batavia &c. 1877. pp.xii.62. [400.]

BARON VICTOR [ROMANOVICH] ROSEN, Les manuscrits arabes de l'Institut des langues orientales. Institut des langues orientales: Collections scientifiques (vol.i): Saint-Pétersbourg 1877. pp.[vii].ix.268. [300.]
——non compris dans le no.1.... Par [baron] D[avid] Günzburg. ... (vol.vi): 1891. pp.xxiii. 271. [250.]

A CATALOGUE of the arabic manuscripts in the library of the India office.
[i]. By Otto Loth. 1877. pp.viii.324. [2000.]
ii. I. Qur'ānic literature. By C[harles] A[mbrose] Storey. 1930. pp.[iii].95. [167.]
ii. II. Ṣūfism and ethics. By A. J. Arberry. 1936. pp.[ii].97–198. [250.]
ii. III. Fiqh. By Reuben Levy. 1937. pp.[ii]. 199–336. [500.]
ii. iv. Kalām, by Reuben Levy. 1940. pp.337–440. [340]

E. LEROUX, Catalogué de la bibliothèque orientale de feu m. Belin. Livres sur la Turquie. Textes et manuscrits arabes, turcs et persans. Paris 1878. pp.56.

WILHELM PERTSCH, Die arabischen handschriften der Herzoglichen bibliothek zu Gotha. Die orientalischen handschriften der Herzoglichen bibliothek (part 3): Gotha 1878–1892. pp.xv.492+viii.495+viii.488+viii.564+vii.562. [2891.]

M. F. DELONCLE, Catalogue des livres orientaux et autres composant la bibliothèque de feu m. Garcin de Tassy, suivi du catalogue des manuscrits hindustanis, persans, arabes, turcs. Paris 1879. pp.viii.272. [arabic: 16.]

BARON VICTOR [ROMANOVICH] ROSEN, Notices sommaires des manuscrits arabes du Musée asiatique. . . . Première livraison. St.-Pétersbourg 1881. pp.257. [300.]

S[AMUEL] LANDAUER, Katalog der hebräischen, arabischen, persischen und türkischen handschriften der Kaiserlichen universitäts- und landesbibliothek. Strassburg 1881. pp.[iv].75. [125.]

CATALOGUE of a magnificent collection of manuscripts from Hamilton palace. London 1882.

RENÉ BASSET, Les manuscrits arabes de deux bibliothèques de Fas. Alger [print.] 1883. pp.32. [240.]

[COUNT] CARLO LANDBERG, Catalogue de manuscrits arabes provenant d'une bibliothèque privée à El-Medîna et appartenant à la maison E. J. Brill. Leide 1833. pp.viii.184. [664.]
the collection is now in the library of the University of Leyden.

BARON [WILLIAM MACGUCKIN] DE SLANE, Catalogue des manuscrits arabes. Bibliothèque nationale: 1883–1895. pp.[iii].vi.820. [8000.]
— — Catalogue des manuscrits arabes des nouvelles acquisitions (1884–1924). . . . Par E[dgard] Blochet. 1925. pp.[iii].xi.424. [2500.]

O[CTAVE] HOUDAS and RENÉ BASSET, Mission scientifique en Tunisie (1882). Alger 1884. pp.163. [165.]
largely a catalogue of arabic mss. in the libraries of Tunis.

HARTWIG DERENBOURG, Les manuscrits arabes de l'Escurial. École des langues orientales vivantes: Publications (2nd ser., vols.x &c.).
  i. Grammaire, rhétorique, poésie, philologie et belles-lettres, lexicographie, philosophie. 1884. pp.xliii.527. [708.]
  ii. 1. Morale et politique. 1903. pp.xxvii.81. [80.]
  ii. 2. Revues et complétées par H. P. J. Renaud. Médecine et histoire naturelle. 1941. pp.xi.125. [118.]
  ii. 3. Sciences exactes et sciences occultes. 1941. pp.140. [79.]
  iii. Théologie, géographie, histoire . . . Revues . . . par E[variste] Lévi-Provençal. 1928. pp.xi.329. [597.]
in progress.

W[ILHELM] AHLWARDT, Kurzes verzeichniss der Landberg'schen sammlung arabischer handschriften, Königliche bibliothek: Berlin 1885. pp.viii.107. [1200.]

ALFRED, FREIHERR VON KREMER, Ueber meine sammlung orientalischer handschriften. Wien 1885. pp.78. [212.]

VICTOR ROSEN, Remarques sur les manuscrits orientaux de la collection Marsigli à Bologne, suivies de la liste complète des manuscrits arabes de la même collection. Roma 1885. pp.135. [459.]

M. TH. HOUTSMA, Catalogue d'une collection de manuscrits arabes et turcs appartenant à la maison E. J. Brill à Leide. Leide 1886. pp.158. [791.]

W[ILHELM] AHLWARDT, Kurzes verzeichniss der Glaser'schen sammlung arabischer handschriften. Königliche bibliothek: Berlin 1887. pp.x.47. [500.]

W[ILHELM] AHLWARDT, Verzeichniss der arabischen handschriften. Königliche bibliothek: Handschriften-verzeichnisse (vols.vii–ix, xvi–xxii): Berlin 1887–1899. pp.xviii.413 + [vi]. 686 + [viii].628 + [vi.]561 + [viii].646 + [viii]. 628 + [viii].806 + [x].462 + [viii].618 + [iii].ix. 595. [25,000.]

C[ARL] SALEMANN and [BARON] V[ICTOR ROMANOVICH] ROSEN, Indices alphabetici codicum manu scriptorum persicorum, turcicorum, arabicorum qui in Bibliotheca imperiali literarum universitatis Petropolitanae adservantur. Petropoli 1888. pp.50. [1500.]
— — Supplementum, confecit A. Romaskewicz. Leningrad 1925. pp.[ii].19. [300.]

[FRANCISCO GUILLÉN ROBLES], Catálogo de los manuscritos árabes existentes en la Biblioteca nacional. Madrid 1889. pp.xi.335. [750.]

E. KAL, Персидскія, арабскія и тюркскія рукописи Туркестанской публичной библіотеки. Ташкентъ 1889. pp.79. [100.]

ALPHABETICAL index of manuscripts in the Government oriental mss. library, Madras. Arabic. Madras 1893. pp.6. [100.]

E[DMOND] FAGNAN, Catalogue général des manuscrits des bibliothèques publiques de France—Départements, t. xviii: Alger. Paris 1893. pp. xxxii.680. [1987.]

RENÉ BASSET, Notice sommaire des manuscrits orientaux de deux bibliothèques de Lisbonne. Mémoire destiné à la 10ème session du Congrès international des orientalistes. Lisbonne 1894. pp.31. [25.]

MARGARET DUNLOP GIBSON, Catalogue of the arabic mss. in the convent of S. Catharine on mount Sinai. Studia sinaitica (no.iii): 1894. pp.viii.138. [628.]

[JAMES LUDOVIC LINDSAY, EARL OF CRAWFORD AND BALCARRES, and MICHAEL KERNEY], Hand-list of oriental manuscripts, arabic, persian, turkish. Bibliotheca lindesiana: 1898. pp.xliii.268. [2500.]
100 copies privately printed.

E[DGARD] BLOCHET, Catalogue de la collection de manuscrits orientaux arabes, persans et turcs formée par m. Charles Schefer et acquise par l'état. Bibliothèque nationale: 1900. pp.[iii].v.231. [1000.]

CARLO CRISPO-MONCADA, I codici arabi, nuovo fondo della Biblioteca vaticana. Palermo 1900. pp.vii.104. [145.]

N. F. KATANOV, Императорского Казанского университета почетный член, профессор и библиотекарь Иосиф Федорович Готвальд (13.x.1813–7.viii.1897). Казань 1900. pp.xi.240. [arabic: 44.]

B. ROY, Extrait du catalogue des manuscrits et des imprimés de la bibliothèque de la Grande mosquée de Tunis. Histoire, avec la collaboration de Mhammed [sic] bel Khodja et de Mohammed el Hachaichi. Secrétariat général du gouvernement tunisien: Tunis 1900. pp.iii.85. [1003.]

CARLO ALFONSO NALLINO, I manoscritti arabi, persiani, siriaci e turchi della Biblioteca nazionale e della r. accademia delle scienze di Torino. Accademia reale delle scienze di Torino: Torino 1900. pp.104. [123.]

EDWARD G[RANVILLE] BROWNE, A hand-list of the muhammadan manuscripts, including all those written in the arabic character, preserved in the library of the university. Cambridge 1900. pp.xviii.440. [1541.]
— — A supplementary hand-list. 1922. pp.xii. 348. [1250.]
— — A second supplementary handlist of the muhammadan manuscripts in the university & colleges of Cambridge. By A[rthur] J[ohn] Arberry. 1952. pp.82. [450.]

KLEOPAS M. KOIKULIDES, Καταλογος ἀραβικων χειρογραφων τῆς Ἱεροσολυμιτικῆς βιβλιοθηκης. Ιεροσολύμοις 1901. pp.[vii].168. [202.]

HARTWIG DERENBOURG, Les manuscrits arabes de la Collection Schefer à la Bibliothèque nationale. 1901. pp.76. [200.]

[SIR] E[DWARD] DENISON ROSS and EDWARD G[RANVILLE] BROWNE, Catalogue of two collections of persian and arabic manuscripts preserved in the India office library. 1902. pp.vii.189. [280.]

C[ARL] BROCKELMANN, Verzeichniss der arabischen, persischen, türkischen und hebräischen handschriften der Stadtbibliothek. Breslau 1903. pp.v.53. [92.]

HARTWIG DERENBOURG, Notes critiques sur les manuscrits arabes de la Bibliothèque nationale de Madrid. 1904. pp.[ii].52. [250.]

[LUDWIG] ENNO LITTMANN, A list of arabic manuscripts in Princeton university library. Princeton &c. 1904. pp.viii.84. [355.]

ADDAÏ SCHER, Catalogue des manuscrits syriaques et arabes conservés dans la Bibliothèque épiscopale de Séert (Kurdistan). Mossoul 1905. pp.102. [arabic: 13.]

KAMAL UD-DĪN AḤMAD and ʿABD UL-MUKTADIR, Catalogue of the arabic and persian manuscripts in the library of the Calcutta Madrasah. Calcutta 1905. pp.[ii].iv.38.115. [arabic: 103.]

E[DGARD] BLOCHET, Inventaire des manuscrits arabes de la collection Decourdemanche. Besançon [printed] 1906. pp.23. [76.]

M[ARTIN] HARTMANN, Die arabischen handschriften der sammlung Martin Hartmann. To be sold by Rudolf Haupt, Halle a S. [1906]. pp.30. [130.]

M[ARTIN] HARTMANN, Die arabischen handschriften der sammlung Haupt. Katalog 8 der buchhandlung Rudolf Haupt. Halle a S. 1906.

ADDAÏ SCHER, Notice sur les manuscrits syriaques et arabes conservés à l'Archevêché chaldéen de Diarbékir. 1907. pp.82. [arabic: 44.]

CATALOGUE des manuscrits arabes conservés dans les principales bibliothèque algériennes. Alger.
[i]. Auguste Cour, Médersa de Tlemcen. 1907. pp.72. [110.]
[ii]. Mohammed ben Cheneb [Muhammad ibn Abī Shanab], Grande mosquée d'Alger. 1909. pp.xix.109. [xxii]. [106.]

CHRISTIAN [FRIEDRICH] SEYBOLD, Verzeichnis der arabischen handschriften der Könglichen universitätsbibliothek zu Tübingen. Tübingen 1907. pp.viii.96. [100.]
— — [supplement]. II. Von Max Weisweiler. Leipzig 1930. pp.viii.228. [200.]

ADDAÏ SCHER, Notice sur les manuscrits syriaques et arabes conservés dans la bibliothèque de l'Évêché chaldéen de Mardin. 1908. pp.36. [arabic: 21.]

CATALOGUE of the arabic and persian manuscripts in the Oriental public library at Bankipore, prepared for the government of Bihar and Orissa under the supervision of Sir E. Denison Ross.
iv. Arabic medical works. Prepared by Maulavî ʿAzîmu ʾd-din Aḥmad. 1910. pp.vii.208. [1–120.]
v. Tradition. Prepared by Maulavi Abdul Hamîd. 1920. pp.viii.214+vii.231. [121–484.]
x. Theology. 1926. pp.vii.150. [485–645.]
xii. Biography. Prepared by Maulavi Muinuddin Nadwi. 1927. pp.vii.167. [646–819.]
xiii. Ṣûfism. 1928. pp.vii.185. [820–959.]
xv. History. Prepared by Maulavi Muinuddin Nadwi. 1929. pp.v.210. [960–1115.]

xviii. Quranic science, 1930. pp.vii.187+v.
181. [1116–1488.]

xix. Principles of jurisprudence and jurisprudence (part ii: jurisprudence and law of
inheritance). 1931–3. pp.vi.172+vii.169.
[1489–1961.]

xx. Philology. Prepared by Dr. Azimuddin
Ahmad and Maulavi Muinuddin Nadwî.
1936. pp.vii.229. [1962–2221.]

xxi. Encyclopaedias, logic, philosophy and
dialectics. 1936. pp.v.138. [2222–2412.]

xxii. Science. 1937. pp.vii.164. [2413–2503.]

xxiii. Poetry and elegant prose. 1939.
pp.v.151. [2504–2642.]

xxiv. Ethics and prayer. 1940. pp.vii.138.
[2643–2770.]

xxv. Miscellanies. Prepared by Maulavi
'Abdu'l Hamid and revised by Maulavi
Mas'ûd 'Alam Nadwî. 1942. pp.vii.191.
[2771–2787.]

The Arabic (2787) entries were catalogued in vols.
iv, v, x, xii, xiii, xv, xviii–xxv by Maulavis Abdul
Hamîd, Muinuddin Nadwî, and 'Azimuddin Ahmad.

[MUḤAMMAD HIDĀYAT ḤUSAIN], List of arabic
and persian mss. acquired on behalf of the
Government of India by the Asiatic society of
Bengal during 1903–1907. [Calcutta 1908].pp.[ii].
61. [1106.]

— — 1908–1910. [By Nazîr Aḥmad and Hazîr
Rażawi]. [1911]. pp.[ii].62. [540.]

E[DGARD] BLOCHET, Catalogue des manuscrits
arabes, persans et turcs offerts à la Bibliothèque
nationale par m. J.-A. Decourdemanche. 1909.
pp.[iii].90. [400.]

OSKAR RESCHER, Arabische handschriften der
Köprülü-bibliothek. Berlin 1911. pp.36. [66.]

— — Weitere arabische handschriften [&c.].
1912. pp.29. [56.]

A[LEXANDER] G[EORGE] ELLIS and EDWARD
EDWARDS, A descriptive list of the arabic manuscripts acquired by the trustees of the British
museum since 1894. London 1912. pp.viii.111.
[832.]

J[ULIÁN] RIBERA [TARRAGO] and M[IGUEL] ASÍN
[PALACIOS], Manuscritos árabes y aljamiados de la
bibliotheca de la Junta. Junta para ampliación de
estudios é investigaciones científicas: Centro de
estudios históricos: Madrid 1912. pp.xxxii.320.
[200.]

DUNCAN BLACK MACDONALD, The arabic and
turkish manuscripts in the Newberry library.
Newberry library: Publication (no.2): Chicago
1912. pp.vi.18 [22.]

ARTHUR CHRISTENSEN and J. ØSTRUP, Description
de quelques manuscrits orientaux appartenant à la
bibliothèque de l'université de Copenhague.

Oversigt over det Kgl. danske videnskabernes
selskabs forhandlinger (1915, 3–4): [Copenhagen]
1915. pp.30. [21.]

E[DGARD] BLOCHET, Inventaire de la collection
de manuscrits musulmans de m. Decourdemanche.
Extrait du Journal asiatique (septembre–décembre
1916). Paris 1916. pp.112. [254.]

V. A. IVANOV, Измаилитсия рукописи Азиац-
ского музея. Собрание И. Зарубина 1916 г.
[Petrograd] 1917.

HERMAN ETHÉ, Catalogue of oriental manuscripts, persian, arabic and hindūstānī. National
library of Wales: Aberystwyth 1916. pp.iv.31.
[50.]
250 copies printed.

EUGENIO GRIFFINI, Catalogo dei manoscritti
arabi di nuovo fondo della Biblioteca ambrosiana
di Milano. ... Vol.i. Roma 1910–1919 [1920].
pp.ix.425. [1500.]
no more published.

V[INCENT] C[LARENCE] SCOTT O'CONNOR, An
eastern library. ... With two catalogues of its
persian and arabic manuscripts, compiled by
khan sahib Abdul Muqtadir ['Abd ul-Muḳtadir]
and Abdul Hamid ['Abd ul-Ḥamīd]. Glasgow
1920. pp.[iii].107. [arabic: 300.]
on the Oriental public library, Patna.

LES MANUSCRITS arabes de Rabat (Bibliothèque
générale du protectorat français au Maroc). Institut des hautes-études marocaines: Publications
(vol.viii &c.).

i. Publié par E[variste] Lévi-Provençal. ...
(vol.viii): 1921. pp.[iii].xi.306.[lxxvi].
[750.]

ii. 1921–1953. Publié par I. S. Allouche et A.
Regragui ['Abd Allāh al-Rajrāji]. ... (vols.
lviii, lxiii): 1954–1958. pp.[iii].iii.473+.

— — Deuxième série. ... Publié par I. S.
Allouche [Y. S. 'Alūsh] and A. Regragui ['Abd
Allāh al-Rajrāji]. ... (vol.lviii): 1954. pp.[v].iii.
473. [1226.]

COLLECTION de m. le docteur Gachet. ...
Manuscrits arméniens, arabes, persans. Bordeaux
[printed] 1922. pp.12. [88.]

SHAMS AL-'ULAMĀ MUḤAMMAD HIDĀYAT ḤUSAIN,
Catalogue of the arabic manuscripts in the Būhār
library. Catalogue raisonné of the Būhār library
(vol.ii): Calcutta 1923. pp.xi.619. [500.]

LOUIS CHEIKHO, كتاب المخطوطات العربية
لكتبة النصرانية.جمعها ونظمها على ترتيب
اسماء مولفيها لويس شيخو Catalogue des
manuscrits des auteurs arabes chrétiens depuis
l'Islam. Beyrouth 1924. pp.[iv]. ٢٨٦ [1250.]

W. RIEDEL, Katalog över Kungl. bibliothekets orientaliska handskrifter. Kungliga biblioteket [Stockholm]: Handlingar: Bilagor (n.s. vol.iii): Uppsala 1923. pp.xi.68. [150.]

E[DGARD] BLOCHET, Notices sur les manuscrits persans et arabes de la collection Marteau. Paris 1923. pp.308. [62.]

A[LEKSANDR] A[LEKSANDROVICH] SEMENOV, Каталог рукописей исторического отдела Бухарской центральной библиотеки. Труды библиографической комиссии при СНК ТССР (вып. 2). Catalogue des manuscrits historiques de la Bibliothèque centrale de Boukhara. Ташкеит 1925. pp.32. [arabic: 9.]

MOHAMMED ASHRAFUL HUKK [MUḤAMMAD ASHRAF AL-ḤAKḰ], HERMANN ETHÉ and EDWARD ROBERTSON, A descriptive catalogue of the arabic and persian manuscripts in Edinburgh university library. Edinburgh 1925. pp.viii.454. [arabic: 150.]

GIUSEPE GABRIELI, La fondazione Caetani per gli studi musulmani. Notizia della sua instituzione e catalogo dei suoi mss. orientali. Roma 1926. pp. 96.6. [300.]

[P. SBATH], Bibliothèque des manuscrits Paul Sbath. Le Caire 1928–1934. pp.204+252+146. [1325.]

CATALOGUE of arabic, persian & urdoo manuscripts presented to the Dacca university library by khan bahadur ... Aḥmad Siddiqui [Ṣiddiḳi]. Dacca [printed] [1929]. pp.iv.24. [50.]
only a small selection is catalogued.

[K. I. CHAYKIN], Восточные рукописи. Персидские, арабские, турецкие. Москва 1931. [arabic: 50.]

V. I. BELYAEV, Арабские рукописи бухарской коллекции Азиатского музея Института востоковедения АН СССР. Труды Института востоковедения Академии наук СССР (ii): Ленинград 1932. pp.xvii.52. [1157.]

REYNOLD ALLEYNE NICHOLSON, A descriptive catalogue of the oriental manuscripts belonging to the late E. G. Browne. Cambridge 1932. pp.xxii.325. [453.]

D[AVID] S[AMUEL] MARGOLIOUTH, Catalogue of arabic papyri in the John Rylands library. Manchester 1933. pp.xxiii.243. [400.]

CATALOGUE of the Mingana collection of manuscripts now in the possession of the trustees of the Woodbrooke settlement, Selly Oak, Birmingham. Cambridge.
  i. Syriac and garshūni manuscripts. By [Alphonse] Mingana. 1933. pp.viii.coll. 1256. [2000.]

  ii. Christian arabic manuscripts and additional syriac manuscripts. 1936. pp.vii.208. [600.]
  iii. Additional christian arabic and syriac manuscripts. pp.xxvii.138. [191.]
  iv. Islamic arabic mss. by H. L. Gottschalk et al. Compiled and edited by Derek Hopwood. Birmingham (1948–) 1963. pp.x.415. [2016.]

A[LPHONSE] MINGANA, Catalogue of the arabic manuscripts in the John Rylands library. Manchester 1934. pp.xiii.coll.1180.pp.1181–1192. [1000.]

N. A. FARIS, A demonstration experiment with oriental manuscripts (Princeton university arabic manuscripts. Garrett manuscripts 1–383). Union world catalog of manuscript books. Preliminary studies in method (vol.iv): New York 1934. pp.x.74. [383.]*

GEORG GRAF, Catalogue de manuscrits arabes chrétiens conservés au Caire. Studi e testi (63). Città del Vaticano 1934. pp.xiii.319. [730.]

S. KUPPPUSWAMI SASTRI, An alphabetical index of arabic manuscripts in the Government oriental manuscripts library, Madras. Madras 1934. pp.13. [186.]

'ABDU'L-ḲĀDIR-E-SARFARĀZ, A descriptive catalogue of the arabic, persian and urdu manuscripts in the library of the university of Bombay. Bombay 1935. pp.lv.432. [2000.]

GIORGIO LEVI DELLA VIDA, Elenco dei manoscritti arabi islamici della Biblioteca vaticana: vaticani, barberiniani, borgiani, rossiani. Studi e testi (vol.lxvii): Città del Vaticano 1935. pp.iii–xxxix.347.41. [2500.]

ARN. VAN LANTSCHOOT, Inventaire sommaire des mss. arabes d'Égypte (bibliothèque de l'université de Louvain), fonds Lefort, série A: mss. chrétiens. Louvain 1935. pp.14. [25.]

A[LEKSANDR] A[LEKSANDROVICH] SEMENOV, Описание персидских, арабских и турецких рукописей Фундаментальной библиотеки Среднеазиатского государственного университета. A descriptive catalogue of the persian, arabic and turkish manuscripts preserved in the library of Middle asiatic state university. Acta Universitatis Asiae mediae (series ii. Orientalia, fasc.4): Ташкент 1935–56. pp.88+88. [339.]

OLGA PINTO, Manoscritti arabi delle biblioteche governative di Firenze non ancora catalogati. Firenze 1935. pp.15. [37.]
Estratto dal volume XXXVII, Dispensa 6ª. 7ª della Bibliofilia.

PHILIP K. HITTI, NABĪH AMĪN FĀRIS and BUṬRUS 'ABD-AL-MALIK, Descriptive catalog of the

[Robert] Garrett collection of arabic manuscripts in the Princeton university library. Princeton 1938. pp.[iv].xii.668.xxiii.56.iv. [2225.]

PAUL SBATH, Al-Fihris (catalogue de manuscrits arabes). Le Caire 1938–1939. pp.[i].viii.4–146. xiii+[i].x.206.xiii. [2506.]

MARCUS SIMAIKA [MARQUS SIMAYKAH] and YASSA 'ABD AL MASIḤ [YASĀ 'ABD AL-MASĪḤ], فهارس المخطوطات القبطية والعربية الموجودة بالمتحف القبطى والدار البطريركية واهم كنائس القاهرة والاسكندرية وادية القطر المصرى، تاليف مرقس سميكه، بمساعدة يس عبد المسيح. Catalogue of the coptic and arabic manuscripts in the Coptic museum, the patriarchate, the principal churches of Cairo and Alexandria and the monasteries of Egypt. Vol.I [–II, fasc.I]. Cairo 1939–1942. pp.lv.183+x.610. [1409.]
no more published.

WLADIMIR IVANOW and M. HIDAYAT HOSAIN (Vol.ii: M. HIDAYAT HOSAIN, M. MAHFUZUL HAQ and M. ISHAQUE), Catalogue of the arabic manuscripts in the collection of the Royal asiatic society of Bengal. Bibliotheca indica (no.250): Calcutta 1939–49. pp.xviii.694+xi.270. [1541.]

P. P. SUBRAHMANYA SASTRI, A descriptive catalogue of the islamic manuscripts in the Government oriental manuscripts library, Madras. Madras 1939–54. pp.xxix.546. xiv.+xxiii. 547–729+xxvii. 730–950. [1224.]

HANS WEHR, Verzeichnis der arabischen handschriften in der bibliothek der Deutschen morgenländischen gesellschaft. Abhandlungen für die kunde des morgenlandes (band 25, nr.3): Leipzig 1940. pp.ix.62. [136.]
nachdruck, Nendeln 1966.

R[OBERT] B[ERTRAM] SERJEANT, A handlist of the arabic, persian and hindustani mss. of New college. Edinburgh 1942. pp.16. [arabic: 17.]*

FEHIM SPAHO, Arapski, perzijski i turski rukopisi Hrvatskih zemaljskih muzeja u Sarajevu. Sarajevu 1942. pp.ix.107. [203.]

ION I. NISTOR, Manuscrisele orientale din Biblioteca Academiei române cu inventarul lor. Analele Academiei române: Memoriile secţiunii istorice (seria iii, tomul xxviii, mem.4): Bucareşti 1946. pp.50. [216.]

DOROTHY M[AY] SCHULLIAN and FRANCIS E[RICH] SOMMER, A catalogue of incunabula and manuscripts in the Army medical library. New York [1948]. pp.xiii.361. [manuscripts: 200.]
most of the manuscripts are oriental.

GURGIS AWAD [KŪRKĪS 'AWWĀD], المخطوطات العربية فى دور الكتب الامبركية. بقلم كوركيس عواد. Arabic manuscripts in the American libraries. [1951]. pp.[iii]. ٥٤. [500.]

IGNACE ABDO KHALIFÉ, Catalogue raisonné des manuscrits de la bibliothèque orientale de l'université Saint Joseph. Seconde série. Université Saint Joseph: Mélanges (vol.xxix, no.4; vol.xxxi, no.3; xxxiv, no.1; xxxix, no.1 &c.): Beyrouth 1951– . pp.184+163+200+144+
the first series forms part of the Mélanges for 1913–1929.

ALFRED SIGGEL, Katalog der arabischen alchemistischen handschriften Deutschlands. . . . Im aufrage der Deutschen akademie der wissenschaften zu Berlin bearbeitet. Union académique internationale: Paris 1949–1956. pp.144+118+60. [1000.]

FEHMI EDHEM KARATAY, Istanbul universitesi kütüphanesi arapça yazmalar katalogu. cilt 1, fasikül 1. Kuranlar ve Kurani ilimler. Istanbul 1951. pp.viii.136. [332.]

A[LEKSANDR] A[LEKSANDROVICH] SEMENOV [and others] edd. Собрание восточных рукописей академии наук Узбекской ССР. Акабемия наук Узбекской ССР: Институт востоковедения: Ташкент 1952–1971. pp.440+590+556+560+544+738+555+799+600. [6755.]

M[UḤAMMAD] A[S'AD] ṬALASS, الكشاف عن مخطوطات خزائن كتب الاوقاف، تاليف محمد اسعد طلس Catalogue général des manuscrits arabes de la Bibliothèque des wakfs de Bagdad. Bagdad 1953. [7500.]

GEORGES [GEORGEI] VAJDA, Index général des manuscrits arabes musulmans de la Bibliothèque nationale de Paris. Institut de recherche et d'histoire des testes: Publications (vol.iv): 1953. pp.ix.744. [6000.]

'AZĪZ SURYAL 'AṬĪYAH, The arabic manuscripts of Mount Sinai. A hand-list of the arabic manuscripts and scrolls microfilmed at the library of the monastery of st. Catherine, mount Sinai. American foundation for the study of man: Publications (vol.i): Baltimore [1955]. pp.xxxiv.97. [1067.]

W[ILLIAM] E[LLIOTT] N[ORWOOD] KENSDALE, A catalogue of the arabic manuscripts preserved in the university library, Ibadan, Nigeria. [Ibadan] 1955[–1958]. pp.[ii].38. [200.]

ARTHUR J[OHN] ARBERRY, The Chester Beatty library. A handlist of the arabic manuscripts.

Dublin 1955–1959. pp.x.127+[iv].128+[iv].104.
+164+168+[i].158. [2500.]
— Volume viii. Indexes, by Ursula Lyons. 1966.
pp.[iii]. 141.

GEORGES [GEORGEI] VAJDA, Les certificats de
lecture et de transmission dans les manuscrits
arabes de la Bibliothèque nationale de Paris. Institut de recherche et d'histoire des textes (vol.vi):
1956. pp.ix.83. [72.]

ZAGORKA JANC, Исламски рукописи из југословенских колекција. Музеј приме ьенеумет-
ности. Београд 1956. pp.50, pls.20 [68.]

LEON NEMOY, Arabic manuscripts in the Yale
university library. Transactions of the Connecticut
academy of arts and sciences (vol. 40): New Haven
1956. pp.273. [1682.]

AGÂH SIRRI LEVEND, Gazavāt-nāmeler ve
Mihaloğlu 'Ali Bey' in Gazavāt-nāmesi. Türk
tarih kurumu yayınlarından (xi. seri, no.8):
Ankara 1956. pp.viii.392, pls.117. [350.]

M. NIZAMUDDIN, A catalogue of the arabic
manuscripts in the Salar Jang collection. Vol.1.
Hyderabad 1957. pp.xxvii.256. [351.]

P[ETRUS] VOORHOEVE, Handlist of arabic
manuscripts in the library of the university of
Leiden and other collections in the Netherlands.
Bibliotheca universitatis Leidenensis: Codices
manuscripti (vii): Lugduni Batavorum 1957.
pp.xx.541. [Large number.]*

JOSEPH NASRALLAH, Catalogue des manuscrits
du Liban. Harissa [printed].
i. Bibliothèque des missionnaires de Saint
Paul (Harissa), bibliothèque de Séminaire
de l'annonciation ('Ain-Traz). 1958. pp.3–
243. [500.]
in progress.

JOHN MACDONALD, Catalogue of oriental
manuscripts. The university of Leeds: Department
of semitic languages and literatures. [Leeds] 1958
&c. ff.i–v, 1–62+iii.1–54+iii.62+iii.73+iii.77.
[250.]

CEVDET TÜRKAY, İstanbul kütübhanelerinde
osmanlılar devrinde aïd türkçe – arabca – farsça
yazma ve basma çoğrafya eserleri bibliyografyası.
Maarif vekâleti bilim eserleri serisi: İstanbul 1958.
pp.94. [2000.]

JUSSI ARO, Die arabischen, persischen und türkischen handschriften der universitätsbibliothek zu
Helsinki. Helsingin yliopiston kirjaston julkaisuja
(no.28): Helsinki 1959. pp.84. [400.]
*also issued as vol.xxiii, no.4, of Studia orientalia
Helsinki).*

'ABDURRAHMÂN BADAWÎ, Les manuscrits des
traductions arabes d'Aristote. Le Caire 1959.
pp.42. [27 works, many mss.]

MUZAFFER GÖKMAN, İstanbul kütüphaneleri ve
yazma tıp kitapları. Libraries of Istanbul and their
medical manuscripts. İstanbul üniversitesi tıp
tarihi enstitüsü neşriyatından (sayi: 56): İstanbul
1959. pp.39. [2796.]

ÖMER NASUHI BILMEN, Büyük tefsir tarihi II
(Tabakatül-mufessirîn.) Diyanet işleri reisliği
yayınları (sayı 39/2): Ankara 1960. pp.480. [335.]

LISTE de manuscrits arabes précieux, exposés à
la Bibliothèque de l'Université Quaraouyine à
Fès, à l'occasion du onzième centenaire de la
fondation de cette université. Rabat 1960. pp.82.
[350.]

Каталог арабских рукописей Института
народов Азии Академии наук СССР. Москва.
1. A. B. KHALIDOV, Художественная проза,
1960. pp.136. [155.]
2. A. I. MIKHAYLOVA, Географические сочинения. 1961. pp.78. [55.]
3. A. I. MIKHAYLOVA, История. 1965. pp.200.
[110.]

FEHMI EDHEM KARATAY, Topkapı Sarayı Müzesi
kütüphanesi arapça yazmalar kataloğu. Istanbul
1962–9. pp.[vii.]620+viii.776,+[vi].952+[iii.]
576. [9043.]

A. M. MIRZOEV and A[LEKSANDR] N[IKOLAEVICH]
BOLDYREV, Каталог восточных рукописей Академии наук Таджикской ССР.
i. Сталинабад 1960. pp.323. [288.]
ii. Под редакцией и при участии . . . А. М.
Мирзоева и М. И. Занда. Душанбе 1968.
pp.239. [339.]
iv. 1970. pp.279. [403.]

SALAHUDDIN EL-MUNAJJED, Catalogue des
manuscrits arabes de l'Ambrosienne de Milan,
2ème partie, D, no.220–440. Ligue des états
arabes: Institut des manuscrits: Le Caire 1960.
pp.8. 137. [200.]

GHULAM SARWAR, A descriptive catalogue of the
oriental manuscripts in the Durgah library, Uch
Sharif Gilani, Bahawalpur state. Part 1: Arabic
and Persian. Urdu academy: Bahawalpur [1960?].
pp.xiv. 219. [390.]

M[UHAMMED] T[AQI] DANECHE-PAJOUH, Catalogue méthodique descriptif, et raisonné des
manuscrits de la Bibliothèque de la Faculté
de droit et des sciences politiques et économiques
de l'université de Téhéran. Publications de
l'Université de Téhéran (652): Téhéran 1961.
pp.xii.602. [631.]

MIROSLAV KREK, A catalogue of arabic manuscripts in the Oriental institute of Chicago. American oriental series: New Haven 1961. pp.ix.46. [103.]

KAREL PETRÁČEK, JOZEF BLAŠKOVIĆ, RUDOLF VESELÝ, Arabische, türkische und persische handschriften der Universitätsbibliothek in Bratislava. Unter der redaktion Jozef Blaškovićs. Bratislava 1961. pp.551. [598.]

PROVISIONAL hand-list of arabic manuscripts and lithographs: Africa, Arabia. 2nd draft. School of oriental studies: University of Durham: Sudan archive: 1961.ff.35. [267.]*

SALAHUDDIN MUNAJJID, A dictionary of arabic manuscripts edited.

> 1954–1960. Beirut 1962. pp.144. [275.]
> 1961–1965. 1967. pp.139. [257.]

IVOR WILKS, The tradition of islamic learning. With check-list of arabic works from Ghana compiled by Al-Hajy Osumanu Eshaka Boyo, Thomas Hodgkin, Ivor Wilks. Legon 1962. ff. 7.12. [64.]*

KASIM DOBRAČA, Katalog arapskih, turskih i perzijskih rukopisa. Gazi Husrev-begova biblioteka: Sarajevo 1963– . pp.xxxii.607. + . *in progress.*

IMTIYĀZ ʿALĪ ʿARSHĪ, Catalogue of the arabic manuscripts in Raza library, Rampur. Rampur.

> 1. Quranic sciences & the science of traditions. 1963. pp.xii.657. [1240.]
> 2. Prayers, theology & polemics. 1966. pp.vi.489. [767.]
> 3. Principles of jurisprudence, dialectics, polemics, jurisprudence and law of inheritance. 1968. pp.vi.529. [889.]

M. A. RAWDATI, Bulletin de catalogue des manuscrits arabes et persans des bibliothèques de l'Ispahan. [Vol.1.] Ispahan 1341 sh. pp.399. [80.]

BIBLIOGRAPHICAL list of the mss. microfilmed from al-Azhar library and its branches. Photographed by the M.M. unit of the national commission of the UNESCO. The National library: Cairo 1964. ff.4.113. [921.]

WOJCIECH DEMBSKI, Katalog rękopisów arabskich. Catalogue des manuscrits arabes. Katalog rękopisów orientalnych ze zbiorów polskich (tom v, cz.1): Warszawa 1964. pp.234. [348.]

M. Ş. IPŞIROĞLU, Saray-alben. Diez'sche klebebände aus den Berliner sammlungen. Verzeichnis der orientalischen handschriften in Deutschland (band viii): Wiesbaden 1964. pp.xiii. 135. [426.]

S. DE LAUGIER DE BEAURECUEIL, Manuscrits d'Afghanistan. Institut français d'archéologie orientale du Caire: Recherches d'archéologie, de philologie et d'histoire (t.xxvi). Le Caire 1964. pp.xiii.420. [400.]

AIDA S. ARIF and AHMAD M. ABU HAKIMA, Descriptive catalogue of arabic manuscripts in Nigeria. Jos museum and Lugard hall library, Kaduna. London 1965. pp.viii.216. [1000.]*

GURGIS AWAD, Catalogue of the arabic manuscripts in the Qassim Mohammad ar-Rajab collection, Baghdad. Baghdad 1965–71. pp.29+ 31+30. [565.]

EXPOSITION de livres et de manuscrits d'auteurs arabes traduits en langues étrangères. Centre culturel arabe de Genève. Genève 1965. pp.40. [441.]

HENRY GEORGE FARMER. The sources of arabian music: an annotated bibliography of arabic manuscripts which deal with the theory, practice and history of arabian music from the eighth to the seventeenth century. Leiden 1965. pp.xxvi.71. [353.]

MU'IZZ GORIAWALA, A descriptive catalogue of the Fyzee collection of ismaili manuscripts. Bombay 1965. pp.xi.172. [209.]

GIORGIO LEVI DELLA VIDA, Secondo elenco dei manoscritti arabi islamici della biblioteca vaticana. Città del Vaticano 1965. pp.xx.238.26. [311.]

MOKHTAR OULD HAMIDOUN and ADAM HEY-MOWSKI, Catalogue provisoire des manuscrits mauritaniens en langue arabe préservés en Mauritanie. Nouakchott & Stockholm 1965–6. ff.274. [2200.]*

ABID RAZA BEDAR, Catalogue of persian & arabic manuscripts of Saulat public library. Rampur 1966. pp.261.xviii.5.3.16. [551.]

A. B. M. HABIBULLAH, Descriptive catalogue of the persian, urdu & arabic manuscripts in the Dacca university library, with a note on the history of the manuscript collection, by M. Siddiq Khan. Dacca university library publication (1): Dacca 1966. pp.xxi.406+vi.407–566.58. [526.]

ARTHUR J[OHN] ARBERRY, The Koran illuminated: a handlist of the Korans in the Chester Beatty library. Dublin 1967. pp.xxvii.83.70pls. [244.]

A[NDREY] BERTEL'S and M[AMADVAFO] BAKOEV, Алфавитный каталог рукописей, обнаруженных в Горно-Бадахшанской автономной области экспедиции 1959–1963 гг. Alphabetic catalogue of manuscripts found by 1959–1963 expedition in Gorno-Badakhshan autonomous region. Edited and prefaced by B. G. Gafurov and A. M. Mirzoev. Moscow 1967. pp.120. [253.]

ABDÜLBÂKI GÖLPINARLI, Mevlânâ Müzesi yazmalar kataloğu. Eski eserler ve müzeler genel müdürlüğü yayınları (seri. III, no: 6): Ankara 1967. pp.xv.301+xx.484. [670.]

ABDULLAH AL-GUBURI, Catalogue de manuscrits arabes de la bibliothèque al-Angourli. Nagav 1967. pp.343. [155.]

SAMI HAMARNEH, Index of arabic manuscripts on medicine and pharmacy at the National library of Cairo. History of arabic medicine and pharmacy, studies based on original manuscripts (no.1): Cairo.

    i. Tibb Khalîl Aghâ collection, with a brief history of the library and an introduction to arabic medicine. 1967. pp.72.48. [26.]

A. Z. ISKANDAR, A catalogue of arabic manuscripts on medicine and science in the Wellcome historical medical library. London 1967. pp.xvi. 256,pls.35. [188.]

RENATO TRAINI, I manoscritti arabi di recente accessione della fondazione Caetani. Accademia nazionale dei Lincei. Indici e sussidi bibliografici della biblioteca (6): Roma 1967. pp.xvi.6. [81.]

JAN BAUWENS, Maktūb bilyad. Manuscrits arabes à la bibliothèque Albert Ier, catalogue. Bruxelles 1968. pp.xv.67, pls.24. [121.]
— Supplément. pp.7. [91.]*

BULLETIN bibliographique. Service des manuscrits arabes: Damas 1968 &c.
in progress.

MOHAMMAD GHOUSE, *ed.*, A catalogue of arabic manuscripts. The Sayeedin library: Hyderabad, India.

    i. The Holy Quran, quranic sciences, hadith, sirat and islamic law. 1968. pp.xiii.384.v. [700.]

SAMI K[HALAF] HAMARNEH, Index of manuscripts on medicine, pharmacy and allied sciences in the Zâhirîyah library. Damascus 1968. pp.52. 600. [180.]

ANOUAR LOUCA, Catalogue des manuscrits arabes. Bibliothèque publique et universitaire de Genève: Genève 1968. pp.76. [83.]
extrait de Genava, n.s., t.xvi, 1968.

    TZ. A. ABULADZE, R. V. GRAMANIYA and M. G. MAMATZASHVILI, Каталог арабских, тюркских и персидских рукописей Института рукописей им. К. С. Кекелидзе (коллекция К). Catalogue of the arabic, turkish and persian manuscripts in the Kekelidze institute of the manuscripts, Georgian academy of sciences (the K collection):

Tbilisi 1969. pp.viii.202. [263.] [arabic: 34.]

ABDOL HOSSEIN HAERI, A catalogue of the manuscripts in the Parliament library (persian & arabic & turkish). Vol. 10, part 3. Teheran 1969. pp.2. 1081–1675. [19+3323–3583.]
up to 19 vols. in all, but not all have English title pages.

M[UHAMMAD] MAHDI NAJAF, Catalogue manuscripts al-Emam al-Hakim public library, Najaf, Iraq. Vol.1, pt.1. Najaf 1969. pp.275. [1000.]

AZIZ S. ATIYA, Catalogue raisonné of the Mount Sinai arabic manuscripts. Complete analytical listing of the arabic collection preserved in the monastery of St. Catherine on Mount Sinai. Translated into arabic by Joseph N. Youssef. Alexandria. f.p, i. 1970. pp.vii.602. [300.]

ROLF REICHERT, Os documentos árabes do Arquivo do estado da Bahia editados, transcritos e comentados. Universidade federal da Bahia: Centro de estudos afro-orientais: Série documentos (no.9). Bahia 1970. [30.]

RACHID HADDAD and FAÈZ FREIJATE, Manuscrits du couvent de Belmont (Balamand). Catalogues de manuscrits et bibliographies: Beyrouth 1970. pp.[iv].165. [192.]

GÉRARD TROUPEAU, Catalogue des manuscrits arabes. Bibliothèque nationale: Département des manuscrits: Paris.
I. Manuscrits chrétiens.

    i. Nos.1–323. 1972. pp.279. [323.]

HELENE LOEBENSTEIN, Katalog der arabischen handschriften der Osterreichischen nationalbibliothek, neuerwerbungen 1868–1968. Museion, veröffentlichungen der Österreichischen nationalbibliothek, neue folge (iv.reihe,iii.band). Wien.

    i. Codices mixti ab nr.744. 1970. pp.xix.343. [513.]

HAMEED MAJEED HADDAW, The manuscripts in the library of Jami'at al-'ilm of the imam al-Khalisy the Grand in Kazimiyya (Baghdad-Iraq): Baghdad 1972. pp.xxxi.348. [650.]

6. *Arab writers*

Averroes

M. BOUYGES, Notes sur les philosophes arabes connus des Latins au moyen âge. v. Inventaire des textes arabes d'Averroès. Mélanges de l'université saint-Joseph (vol.viii. no.1): Beyrouth 1922. pp.54. [84.]
additions and corrections by the author appear at ix. 43–48.

[GIORGIO E. FERRARI, LIA SBRIZIOLO and ELPIDIO MIONI], Manoscritti e stampe venete dell'Aristotelismo e Averroismo (secoli X–XVI). Catalogo di mostra presso la Biblioteca nazionale marciani. Venezia 1958. pp.x.206. [375.]

Avicenna

G. C. ANAWATI, مؤلفات ابن سينا، وضعه جورج شحاته قنواتی. Essai de bibliographie avicennienne. Le Caire 1950. pp.22. ٤٣٤ [1250.]

SAÏD NAFICY [SA'ĪD NAFĪSĪ], Bibliographie des principaux travaux européens sur Avicenne. Université de Téhéran: Publications (no.173): Téhéran 1953. pp.[iii].30. [295.]

OSMAN ERGIN, Ibni Sina bibliöğrafyası. Üniversite: Tıp tarihi enstitüsü: Yayınlar (no.51): Istanbul 1956. pp.xxxi.168.

YAHYA MAHDAVI, Bibliographie d'Ibn Sina. Teheran 1954. pp.20.413. xxxiii. [450.]

Bīrūnī

B[ALDASSARE] BONCOMPAGNI, Intorno all'opera d'Albiruni sull'India. Roma 1869. pp.[ii].54. [20.]

Fārābī, al-

NICHOLAS RESCHER, Al-Fārābī. An annotated bibliography. [Pittsburgh] 1962. pp.54. [350.]

MÜJGÂN CUNBUR, İSMET BİNARK and NEJAT SEFERCIOĞLU, Fârâbî bibliyografyası. Kitap—makale. Başbakanlık kültür müsteşarlığı: Cumhuriyet'in 50. yıldönümü yayınları (4): Ankara 1973. pp.xx.115. [535.]

Ghazālī, Muḥammad ibn Muḥammad abu Ḥāmid al-

MAURICE BOUYGES and MICHEL ALLARD, Essai de chronologie des oeuvres de Al-Ghazali (Algazel). Institut de lettres orientales: Recherches (vol.xiv): Beyrouth [1959]. pp.xxiii.207. [404.]

'ABDURRAḤMÂN BADAWI, Les oeuvres d'al-Ghazâlî; étude bibliographique. Le Caire 1961. pp.xlvii.572. [457.]

Ḥunain b. Isḥāq

G. BERGSTRÄSSER, Ḥunain ibn Isḥāq über die syrischen und arabischen Galen-übersetzungen. Zum ersten mal herausgegeben und übersetzt. Abhandlungen für die kunde des morgenlandes (xvii band, no.2). Leipzig 1925. pp.xv.53. [129.]

G. BERGSTRÄSSER, Neue materialien zu Hunain ibn Ishaq's Galenbibliographie. Abhandlungen für die kunde des Morgenlandes (xix band, nr.2): Leipzig 1932. pp.108. [130–179.]

Ibn Khaldūn

IBN KHALDUN. A bibliographical list. ابن خلدون، قائمة. القاهرة، ١٩٦٢ [1962]. pp.٣٦.22. [100].

Jamal al-dīn al-Afghānī

A. ALBERT KUDSI-ZADEH, Sayyid Jamāl al-dīn al-Afghānī; an annotated bibliography. Leiden 1970. pp.xxiii.118. [688.]

Kindī

NICHOLAS RESCHER, Al-Kindi, an annotated bibliography. Pittsburg 1964. pp.55. [300.]

Rāzī

BĪRŪNĪ, Epître de Bīrūnī contenant le répertoire des ouvrages de Muḥammad b. Zakarīyā ar-Rāzī, publiée par Paul Kraus. Paris 1936. pp.51. [321.]

HOMA FIROUZABADI, Bibliographie der medizinischen werke Rhazes (Abu Bakar Muhammad ibn Zakaryya); dissertation. Institut für geschichte der medizin: Universität Düsseldorf: 1969. ff.[v]. 42. [95.]*

M[AḤMŪD] NADJMABADI, Bibliographie de Rhazes. Université de Téhéran: Publications (no. 500): Téhéran 1960. pp.[ii].vi.442. [500.]

Rihani, Ameen Fares

D[ANIIL] I[VANOVICH] YUSUPOV and N. M. ZAND, Амин ар-Рейхани. Био-библиографический указатель. Всесоюзная государственная библиотека иностранной литературы: Писатели зарубежных стран: Москва 1959. pp.35. [109.]

7. Literary characters

Barlaam

ERNST [WILHELM ADALBERT] KUHN, Barlaam und Joasaph. Eine bibliographisch-literargeschichtliche studie. Kaiserliche bayerische akademie: Philosophisch-philologische classe: Abhandlungen (vol. xx, no.1): München 1894. pp.88. [250.]

VICTOR CHAUVIN, Bibliographie des ouvrages arabes ou relatifs aux Arabes publiés dans l'Europe chrétienne de 1810 à 1885. . . . III. Louqmâne. . . . Barlaam. Liége 1898. pp.[iii].151. [Barlaam: 50.]

Bidpāī

VICTOR CHAUVIN, Bibliographie des ouvrages arabes ou relatifs aux Arabes publiés dans l'Europe chrétienne de 1810 à 1885. . . . I. Kalîlah. Liège 1897. pp.vii.239. [1000.]

Lukmān

VICTOR CHAUVIN, Bibliographie des ouvrages arabes ou relatifs aux Arabes publiés dans l'Europe chrétienne de 1810 à 1885. . . . III. Louqmâne et les fabulistes. Liège 1898. pp.[iii].151. [100.]

Sindbad

VICTOR CHAUVIN, Bibliographie des ouvrages arabes ou relatifs aux Arabes publiés dans l'Europe chrétienne de 1810 à 1885. . . . VIII. Syntipas. Liège 1904. pp.[iii].219. [100.]

8. Subjects

Medicine

P[IERRE] J[OSEPH] AMOREUX, Essai historique et littéraire sur la médecine des Arabes. Montpellier [1805]. pp.xvi.266. [500.]

[HEINRICH] FERDINAND WÜSTENFELD, Geschichte der arabischen aerzte und naturforscher. Göttingen 1840. pp.xvi.168.[xvi]. [2000.]
the title is misleading; this is a bio-bibliography.

H. BRETSCHNEIDER, Wissenschaftliches verzeichniss der in der Herzogl. bibliothek zu Gotha enthaltenen ausgaben, uebersetzungen und erläuterungsschriften medicinisch-physikalischer werke der griechischen, arabischen und der lateinischen literatur bis zum dreizehnten jahrhundert. Gotha 1851. pp.40. [400.]

MAULAVÎ 'AẒĪMU'D-DĪN AḤMAD, Arabic medical works. Catalogue of the arabic and persian manuscripts in the Oriental public library at Bankipore (vol.iv): Calcutta 1910. pp.vii.208. [120.]

ḤUNAYN IBN ISḤĀQ, Hunain ibn Isḥāq über die syrischen und arabischen Galen-übersetzungen. Zum ersten mal herausgegeben und übersetzt von G. Bergstrasser. Abhandlungen für die kunde des Morgenlandes (xvii. band, no.2): Leipzig 1925. pp.xv.53.48. [129.]

HELMUT RITTER und RICHARD WALZER, Arabische übersetzungen griechischer ärzte in stambuler bibliotheken. Sonderausgabe aus den Sitzungsberichten der preussischen akademie der wissenschaften, phil.-hist.klasse, 1934, xxvi. Berlin, 1934. pp.48. [160.]

GURGIS AWAD [KŪRKĪS 'AWWĀD], المخطوطات العربية فى مكتبة المتحف العراقى ببغداد. القسم الثالث: الطب، الصيدلة، البيطرة. A cata- logue of the Arabic manuscripts in the Iraq museum library. Part three. Medicine, pharmacology, veterinary. [1959]. pp.۲۸. [100.]

R[IFAAT] Y. EBIED, Bibliography of mediaeval arabic and jewish medicine and allied sciences. Publications of the Wellcome institute of the history of medicine: London 1971. pp.150. [1972.]

Music

HENRY GEORGE FARMER, The arabic musical manuscripts in the Bodleian library. 1935. pp.18. [17.]

HENRY GEORGE FARMER. The sources of arabian music: a bibliography of arabic mss. which deal with the theory, practice and history of arabian

music. Glasgow bibliographical society: Records (vol.xiii): Glasgow 1939. pp.iii–xvi.99. [302.]
reissued independently in 1940 with a slightly different subtitle.

Papyrology

A BIBLIOGRAPHY of works about papyrology. National library [Dār al-kutub al-miṣrīyah]: Cairo 1960. pp.64. [175.]

Philosophy

P[IERRE] J[EAN] DE MENASCE, Arabische philosophie. Bibliographische einführungen in das studium der philosophie (vol.6): Bern 1948. pp.49. [500.]

9. Translations

[HEINRICH] F[ERDINAND] WÜSTENFELD, Die übersetzungen arabischer werke in das lateinische seit dem XI. jahrhundert. Göttingen 1877. pp.[ii]. 133. [250.]

M[ORITZ] STEINSCHNEIDER, Die arabischen übersetzungen aus dem griechischen.
   i. Philosophie. Beihefte zum Centralblatt für bibliothekswesen (5,12). Leipzig 1889, 1893. pp.34+111. [84.]
Parts 2 & 3 were published in *Zeitschrift der Deutschen morgenländischen gesellschaft* 50 (1896), pp.161–219,337–370, and in *Virchow's Archiv* 124(1891).
The whole was reprinted in Graz, 1960.

MORITZ STEINSCHNEIDER, Die europäischen übersetzungen aus dem arabischen bis mitte des 17. jahrhunderts. Kaiserliche akademie der wissenschaften: Philosophisch-historische klasse: Sitzungsberichte (vols.cxlix, no.4; cli, no.1): Wien 1905-1906. pp.84+108. [500.]
a facsimile was published Graz 1956.

AMERICAN books in arabic translation. Catalog. United States information service: [Beirut] 1958. pp.[ii].110. [300.]

RICHARD MÖNNIG, ed. Übersetzungen aus der deutschen sprache; eine bibliographie. Arabisch. Göttingen 1968. pp.30. [314.]

AFGHANISTAN. IRANIAN PEOPLES

   i. *Afghanistan*
   ii. *Pushtu literature*
   iii. *Kurds*
   iv. *Tajiks*

i. Afghanistan

WHAT to read about Iran, Iraq and Afghanistan. East and west association: [New York] 1942. pp.8. [33.]*

MOHAMMED AKRAM, Bibliographie [analytique] de l'Afghanistan. I. Ouvrages parus hors de l'Afghanistan. Centre de documentation universitaire: 1947. pp.[iii].6.504.iii. [1956.]*

DONALD N[EWTON] WILBER, Annotated bibliography of Afghanistan. Human relations area files; Behavior science bibliographies: New Haven 1956. pp.[ii].ix.220.[xii]. [1068.]*

—— Third edition. 1968. pp.ix.252. [1600.]*

BIBLIOGRAPHY of russian works on Afghanistan. Central asian research centre: 1956. pp.12. [150.]*

T[ATIANA] I[VANOVNA] KUKHTINA, Библиография Афганистана. Литература на русском языке. Москва 1965. pp. 272. [5680.]

SCHUYLER JONES, An annotated bibliography of Nuristan (Kafiristan) and the Kalash Kafirs of Chitral.
　　1. København 1966. pp.110. [300.]
　　2. Selected documents from the secret and political records. 1969. pp.274.

BIBLIOGRAPHIE der Afghanistan-literatur 1945–1967. Arbeitsgemeinschaft Afghanistan und Deutsches orient-institut (Deutsche orientstiftung). Hamburg 1968. pp.189+209. [2352+2146.]

LLOYD C. PICKETT, MOHAMMED QASEM MA-YAR, ZARGHUNA SALEH, Bibliography of materials dealing with agriculture in Afghanistan. Kabul university faculty of agriculture: Technical bulletin (8): Kabul 1968. pp.xxiv. 316. [1392.]*

ii. Pushtu literature

[CARL] ED[UARD] SACHAU and HERMANN ETHÉ, Catalogue of the persian, turkish, hindûstânî, and pushtû manuscripts. Catalogi codd. mss. Bibliothecae bodleianae pars XIII: Oxford 1889–1930. pp.xii.coll.1150+pp.[v].coll.1157–1766. [3000.]

J. F. BLUMHARDT, Catalogue of the hindi, panjabi, sindhi, and pushtu printed books in the library of the British museum. 1893. pp.[ix].coll.284.64.24.54. [pushtu: 350.]

[JAMES FULLER BLUMHARDT], Catalogue of pushtu books. [India office: Library: 1902]. pp.[ii].13. [250.]

JAMES FULLER BLUMHARDT and D[AVID] N[EIL] MACKENZIE, Catalogue of pushto manuscripts in the libraries of the british isles. 1965. pp.xii.147. [169.]

iii. Kurds

ZH. S. MUSAELYAN, Библиография по Курдоведению. Академия наук СССР. Институт народов Азий: Москва 1963. pp.184. [2690.]

M[ARGARITA] B[ORISOVNA] RUDENKO, Описание курдских рукописей ленинградских собраний. Академия наук СССР: Институт народов Азии: Москва 1961. pp.126 [84.]*

N. A. ALEK'SANYAN, Библиография к'тебед Кордиейэ советиэ (салед 1921–1960). Академиа Р'СС Эрманистанейэ ӧлма: Сектора р'оьблатзание: Еребан 1962. pp.124. [477.]

SILVIO VAN ROOY and KEES TAMBOER, edd. ISK's Kurdish bibliography no.1. International Society Kurdistan: Amsterdam 1968. pp.xxxiii.329+330-658. [9350.]*

WOLFGANG BEHN, The Kurds, a minority in Iran; an annotated bibliography. [Toronto] 1969. pp.28. [72.]

KAMAL FUAD, Kurdische handschriften. Verzeichnis der orientalischen handschriften in Deutschland (xxx): Wiesbaden 1970. pp.lv.158. [97.]

iv. Tajiks

Akademiya nauk Tadzhikskoi SSR. Библиография изданий академии. Сталинабад.
　　i. 1951–1954. Составители: З. М. Шевченко, А. Г. Сижук. pp.85. [591.]

Z[INAIDA] V[ASILEVNA] PONOMAREVA and Z. A. CHERNUIKH, Таджикская литература. Рекомендательный указатель. Государственная . . . библиотека СССР имени В. И. Ленина [&c.]: Москва 1961. pp.149. [300.]

A. T. TAGIRZHANOV, Описание таджикских и персидских рукописей Восточного отдела библиотека ЛГУ. [Leningrad].*
　　i. История, биографии, география. 1962. pp.iii. 515. [169.]

Z[INAIDA] M[ATVEEVNA] SHEVCHENKO, Библиография библиографий Таджикистана. Академия наук Таджикской ССР: Центральная научная библиотека: Душанбе 1966. pp.168.

MIKHAIL ISAAKOVICH ZAND, Писатели Таджикистана. Сталинабад 1957. pp.84.

V. BELAN, Таджикская советская литература в социалистических странах, 1948–1970. Государственная республиканская библиотека Таджикской ССР имени А. Фирдоуси: Отдел иностранной литературы: Душанбе 1971. pp. 84. [429.]*

IRAN

i. *General*
ii. *Pre-Islamic period*
iii. *Subjects*
iv. *Scholars, etc.*
v. *Persian language*
vi. *Persian literature*

i. *General*

[ALEKSANDER BOROJKO CHODZKO], Principaux ouvrages et articles publiés par A. Chodzko relativement à la Perse. [*c*.1870]. pp.3. [10.]
reproduced from handwriting.

MOÏSE SCHWAB, فهرست کتب فارسی. Bibliographie de la Perse. 1875. pp.152. [1332.]
a facsimile was published Amsterdam 1962.

Z[INAIDA] M[IKHAILOVNA] PENKINA, Закаспій-скій край. Систематическій сборникъ библіографическихъ указаній книгъ и статей о Закаспійскомъ краѣ и сопредѣльныхъ странахъ, 1865–1885. С.-Петербургъ 1888. pp.[ii].ii.iv.123. [2416.]

A. HOTZ, Perzië. Overzicht van in de neder-landsche taal uitgegeven werken, gevolgd door een opgave van de voornaamste buitenlandsche schrijvers. Leiden 1897. pp.48. [150.]

[IDA AUGUSTA PRATT], List of works in the New York public library relating to Persia. New York 1915. pp.vi.151. [2750.]

LIST of assurances and undertakings, etc. be-tween the british government and the chiefs of southern Persia, Najd and Qatar. Calcutta 1920. ff.[i].ii. [23.]

SIR ARNOLD T[ALBOT] WILSON, A bibliography of Persia. Oxford 1930. pp.x.254. [7500.]

OTOYA TANAKA, A catalogue of books relating to Persia collected by Shigeru Araki. The Keimei-kwai institute: Tokyo 1934. pp.xii.157. [936.]

[LACY BAGGALLAY], Catalogue of the library of his majesty's Legation at Teheran. 1935. ff.[i].227. [1250.]*

M. ṢABĀ, Bibliographie de l'Īrān. Bibliographie méthodique et raisonnée des ouvrages français parus depuis 1560. Université de Paris: Faculté des lettres: 1936. pp.[iii].xxxii.228. [1900.]
— BIBLIOGRAPHIE française de l'Írán. Deux-ième édition revue et augmenteé. Tehran 1966. pp. xxvi.297.7.[iv]. [3000.]

WHAT to read about Iran, Iraq and Afghanistan. East and west association: [New York] 1942. pp.8. [33.]*

HAFEZ F[ITZHUGH] FARMAN, Iran. A selected and annotated bibliography. Library of Congress:

General reference and bibliography division: Washington 1951. pp.ix.100. [412.]*
— — [another edition]. Bibliography on Iran. Embassy of Iran: Washington 1958. pp.xi.100.iii. 36. [750.]*
a reprint, with the addition of a supplement by Meer Nasser Sharify [Nāṣer Sharī fī].

L[AURENCE] P[AUL] ELWELL-SUTTON, A guide to iranian area study. American council of learned societies: Ann Arbor 1952. pp.iii.235. [818.]*

M[IKHAIL] P[LATONOVICH] PETROV, Библио-графия по георафии Ирана. Указатель литературы на русском языке (1720–1954). Академия наук Туркменской ССР *and* Ака-демия наук СССР: Ашхабад 1955. pp.238. [960.]

A[NDRÉ] GUILLOU, Essai bibliographique sur les dynasties musulmanes de l'Irân. Ministerio de educación nacional de Egipto: Dirección general de relaciones culturales: Instituto egipcio de estudios islámicos: Madrid 1957. pp.94. [1200.]

PLAN organisation of Iran. Socio-economic development plan for the south-eastern region. Annotated bibliography. Rome 1959. pp.[176]. [586.]

IRAJ AFSHAR, *ed.* Bibliographie de l'Iran.
  1. 1954–5. pp.vi.20. [300.]
  2. 1955–6. pp.vii.79. [600.]
       [*continued as:*]
Bibliography of Persia.
  3. 1956–7. cols.82. pp.83–105. [600.]
  4. 1957–8. cols.166. [600.]
  5. 1958–9. pp.xi.cols.154. [650.]
  6. Founded and edited by Iraj Afshar, with collaboration of G. R. Farzaneh-Poor. 1959. pp.xi.107. [485.]
  7. — and M. E. Zandi. 1960. pp.ix.162. [568.]
  8. 1961. pp.ix.133. [587.]
  9.
  10. 1963. with collaboration of H. Bani-Adam and A. A. Jana. pp.164. [751.]
  11. 1964. pp.220. [946.]
  12. 1965. pp.xi.344. [1435.]
  13. 1969. pp.xii.339. [1865.]
in progress.

IRAJ AFSHAR, Index iranicus. Répertoire méthodique des articles persans concernant les études iranologiques, publiés dans les périodiques et publications collectives. Groupe bibliographique national iranien (no.3): Publication de l'Univer-sité de Tehran (no.697): Tehran.
  i. 1910–1958. pp.xlvii.984. [5969.]
  ii. 1959–1966. pp.xiv.708. [4642.]

ALI AKBAR JANA, An annotated catalogue of publications 1946–1964. University of Tehran (no.687): Teheran 1342sh. pp.x.273. [1063.]

G[EORGE] M[ICHAEL] WICKENS and ROGER M.
SAVORY, Persia in islamic times; a practical bibliography of its history, culture and language.
Edited by William J. Watson. Institute of islamic
studies: McGill University: Montreal 1964.
ff.[vii].57. [701.]*

MOHSEN ṢABA, English bibliography of Iran.
Centre for the study and presentation of the
iranian culture. Publication (no.1): Tehran 1965.
pp.xlix.313. [4,059.]

GEOFFREY HANDLEY-TAYLOR, Bibliography of
Iran. Coronation edition. 1967. pp.xviii.34.
[400.]
— — 5th edition. 1969.

A[NTONINA] K[ARLOVNA] SVERCHEVSKAYA, Библиография Ирана. Литература на русском
языке (1917–1965 гг.). Под редакцией Н. А.
Кузнецовой. Академия наук СССР: Институт
народов Азии: Москва 1967. pp.392. [7959.]

CONTENTS pages, science and social science
journals. Iranian documentation centre: Tehran.
   i. 1969–70. pp.52.72.94.68.94.88.100. [350.]
   ii. 1970–1. pp.74.74.66.56.62.72.66.62.60.61.
    62.60. [350.]
   iii. 1971–2. pp.94.91.86.
in progress.

Y. M[ĀHIYAR] NAWABI, A bibliography of Iran:
a catalogue of books and articles on Iranian
subjects, mainly in european languages. Iranian
culture foundation: Tehran 1969–71. pp.xvi.256.
[iv].+xx.479. [10,800.]

THOMAS RICKS, THOMAS GOUTTIERE and DENIS
EGAN, Persian studies; a selected bibliography of
works in english. Indiana university: Bloomington 1969. ff.v.[iii].266. [2500.]*

POORI SOLTANI, A directory of iranian periodicals 1969. Iranian documentation centre
(IRANDOC): Tehran 1969. pp.vi.106. [244.]*

PARVIN ABOOZIA, A directory of iranian newspapers 1969. Iranian documentation centre
(IRANDOC): Tehran 1970. pp.vi.47. [112.]*

THE IRANIAN national bibliography. Monthly
issue. National library: [Tehran].
   1970–71. pp. . . . 45.40.40.48.56.
   1971–2. pp.132.131.120.134. [1961.]
   1970–3. pp.148.128.128.
   1973–4. pp.123.132.
in progress.

A[ṢGHAR] KAZIMI, Iran-bibliographie, 1. teil.
Deutsch-sprachige abhandlungen, beiträge, aufsätze, bücher, dissertationen. Teheran universität:
Publications (no.1303): Teheran 1960. pp.viii.ii.
164.ii. [1337.]

RODMAN E. SNEED, Bibliography on the Makran
regions of Iran and west Pakistan. Edited by
Henry Field. Coconut Grove, Fla. 1970. pp.iii.38.
[778.]

BOOKS catalogued by Tehran book processing
centre. Annual cumulation.
   1971. pp.[viii].321.44. [7362.]
   1972. pp.v.283.62. [4770.]
   1973. pp.v.247.140. [5148.]
*published also as a quarterly; a quinquennial
cumulation was due for publication in april, 1974.*

JAN W. WERYHO, A guide to persian reference
sources available at McGill islamics library. The
library: Institute of islamic studies: McGill
university: Montreal 1973. pp.20. [74.]*

CATALOGUE of the books and manuscripts
presented by professor Sir Granville Bantock . . .
to the A.P.O.C. library at Britannic house. n.p.
n.d. ff.19. [112.]*

ii. Pre-Islamic period

E[DGARD] BLOCHET, Catalogue des manuscrits
mazdéens (zends, pehlvis, parsis et persans) de la
Bibliothèque nationale. Besançon 1900. pp.[iii].
132. [500.]

[É. HAUG], Notice sur les travaux scientifiques
de m. Émile Haug. Lille 1903. pp.96. [60.]

CHRISTIAN BARTHOLOMAE, Die Zendhand-
schriften der K. hof- und staatsbibliothek in
München. Catalogus codicum manu scriptorum
Bibliothecae regiae monacensis (vol.i, part 7):
München 1915. pp.xx.70.383. [500.]

JAMSHEDJI K. SAKLATWALLA, A bibliography of
religion (mainly avestan and vedic). Dorab J.
Saklatwalla memorial series (no.3): Bombay 1922.
pp.[iii].3.142.xvii. [3000.]

ERVAD BOMANJI NUSSERWANJI DHABHAR
(BĀMANJĪ NASARVANJI DHABHAR], Descriptive
catalogue of some manuscripts bearing on
Zoroastrianism and pertaining to the different
collections in the Mulla Feroze library. Parsee
Punchayet funds and properties: Bombay 1923.
pp.[iii].vi.120. [200.]

OLAF HANSEN, Die mittelpersischen papyri der
papyrussammlung der staatlichen museen zu
Berlin. Preussische akademie der wissenschaften:
Abhandlungen: Philosophisch-historische klasse
(1937, no.9): Berlin 1938. pp.102. [200.]

JAMSHED CAWASJI [KĀVASJĪ] KĀTRAK, Oriental
treasures, being condensed tabular descriptive
statement of . . . manuscripts and of their colo-
phons written in indian & iranian languages and
lying in private libraries . . . of Gujarat. Bombay
1941. pp.xxii.295. [1250.]

W[ALTER] B[RUNO HERMANN] HENNING, Bibliography of important studies on old iranian subjects. Tehran 1950. pp.[ii].58. [575.]

MARY BOYCE, A catalogue of the iranian manuscripts in manichaean script in the german turfan collection. Deutsche akademie der wissenschaften zu Berlin: Institut für orientforschung: Veröffentlichung (no.45): Berlin 1960. pp.xl.151 [3000.]

iii. Subjects

Art

HENRY CORBIN [and others], Les arts de l'Iran, l'ancienne Perse et Bagdad. Bibliothèque nationale: 1938. pp.x.208. [569.]

Bahaism

WILLIAM KENNETH CHRISTIAN, Classification of Bahá'í study sources. Bahá'í publishing committee: Wilmette, Ill. [1941]. pp.7. [125.]

Economics

WILLIAM H. BARTSCH and JULIAN BHARIER, The economy of Iran 1940–1970, a bibliography. University of Durham: Centre for middle eastern and islamic studies: Publication (no.2): Durham 1971. pp.[vi].114. [1200.]*

Education

H[OSAIN] BANI-ADAM, Bibliography on education: Persian subject bibliography series (no.2): Tehran 1968. pp.viii.288. [1129.]

Geology

NORMAN C. ROSEN, Bibliography of the geology of Iran. Geological survey of Iran: special publication (no.2): Teheran 1969. pp.iii.78. [300.]*

Librarianship

SHIRIN TA'AVONI, An annotated bibliography of library science. Institute for research and planning in science and education: Tehran book processing centre (TEBROC): Tehran 1973. pp. vii.154. [317.]*

LIST of library and information science periodicals in Irandoc and Tebroc as of january 1973. Institute for research and planning in science and education: Tehran book processing centre (Tebroc): Tehran 1973. pp.[iii].70.[xi]. [243.]*

Medicine

ADOLF FONAHN, Zur quellenkunde der persischen medizin. Leipzig 1910. pp.v .152. [408.]

Science

IRANDOC science and social science abstract bulletin. Iranian documentation centre (IRANDOC): Tehran. 1970 &c.
in progress.

ROBERT L. BURGESS, AHMAD MOKHTARZADEH and LINDON CORNWALLIS, A preliminary bibliography of the natural history of Iran. Science bulletin (no.1): Pahlavi university: College of arts and sciences: Shiraz 1966. pp.220.140. [1719.]*
titles in western languages and in persian translation.

FEHREST: an index to science and social science articles of iranian journals. Institute for research and planning in science and education: Iranian documentation centre (IRANDOC): Teheran 1971 &c.
in progress.

iv. Scholars, etc.

Chodzko, Aleksandr Borejko

[A. B. CHODZKO], Principaux ouvrages et articles publiés par A. Chodzko relativement à la Perse. [c.1860]. pp.3. [10.]
reproduced from handwriting.

Eastwick, E. B.

[E. B. EASTWICK, Statement of the services and writings . . . of E. B. Eastwick. [c.1880]. pp.11. [25.]

Fitzgerald, Edward

W[ILLIAM] F[RANCIS] PRIDEAUX, Notes for a bibliography of Edward FitzGerald. 1901. pp.xi. 88. [75.]

EDWARD FITZGERALD, 1809–1883. A list of books, with references to periodicals, in the Brooklyn public library. Brooklyn 1909. pp.12. [150.]

JOANNA RICHARDSON, Edward Fitzgerald. British council: British book news: Bibliographical series of supplements (no.125): 1960. pp.42. [75].

Nyberg, Henryk Samuel

CHRISTOPHER TOLL, Professor H. S. Nybergs författarskap. Bibliografi. Stockholm 1959. pp.46. [255.]

Ouseley, sir Frederick Arthur Gore

JOHN S. BUMPUS, The compositions of the rev. sir Frederick A. Gore Ouseley. 1892. pp.34. [250.]
privately printed.

Rabino, Joseph and H. Louis

H. L. RABINO, Bibliographie. H. L. Rabino et Joseph Rabino. Le Caire 1937. pp.8. [109.]

v. Persian language

MAULAVI ABDUL MUQTADIR ['ABD UL-MUḰ-TADIR], Catalogue of the arabic and persian manuscripts in the Oriental public library at Bankipore.

Volume IX (persian mss.). Philology and sciences. Patna 1925. pp.xiii.211. [philology: 136.]

vi. Persian literature

1. *Bibliographies*
2. *General*
3. *Manuscripts*
4. *Writers*

1. Bibliographies

IRAJ AFSHĀR, Bibliographie des catalogues des manuscrits persans. Université de Tehran: Publications (no.485): Tehran 1958. pp.96. [219.]

2. General

CATALOGUS centuriae librorum rarissimorum manuscript. & partim impressorum, arabicorum, persicorum, turcicorum ... qua ... Bibliothecam publicam Academiæ upsalensis auxit ... Ioan. Gabr. Sparvenfeldius. Upsaliæ 1706. pp.[vi].74. [120.]

T[HOMAS] X[AVIER] BIANCHI, Notice sur le premier ouvrage d'anatomie ... suivi du catalogue des livres turcs, arabes et persans imprimés à Constantinople depuis l'introduction de l'imprimerie en 1726–27 jusqu'en 1820. 1821. pp.[ii].40. [68.]
one of the copies in the Bibliothèque nationale contains a ms. supplement.

[CHRISTIAN MARTIN FRÄHN], Хронологической списокъ ста сочиненій, преимущественно историческаго и географическаго содержанія – на арабскомъ, персидскомъ и турецкомъ языкахъ, недостающихъ большею частью въ европейскихъ библіотекахъ. С.-Петербургъ 1834. pp.[ii].24. [120.]
— — [another edition]. Казан 1834. pp.[viii]. 24. [120.]

T[HOMAS] X[AVIER] BIANCHI, Catalogue général et détaillé des livres arabes, persans et turcs imprimés á Boulac en Égypte depuis l'introduction de l'imprimerie dans ce pays, en 1822, jusqu'en 1842. 1843. pp.43. [243.]

[C. M. FRÄHN], Indications bibliographiques relatives pour la plupart à la littérature historico-géographique des Arabes, des Persans et des Turcs, spécialement destinés à nos employés et voyageurs en Asie. St. Pétersbourg 1845. pp.[iv].lv.87. [244.]

TÚSY's list of Shy'ah books and 'Alam al-Hodà's notes on Shy'ah biography. Edited by A. Sprenger, Mawlawy 'Abd al-Haqq and Mawlawy Gholam Qadir. Bibliotheca indica (nos.60,71,91, 107). Calcutta 1855, pp.4.383 [892.]

M. DORN, Catalogue des ouvrages arabes, persans et turcs, publiés à Constantinople, en Égypte et en Perse qui se trouvent au Musée asiatique de l'Académie. St.-Pétersbourg 1866. pp.[ii].64. [387.]

CLÉMENT [IMBAULT] HUART, Bibliographie ottomane. Notice des livres turcs, arabes et persans imprimés à Constantinople.
1294–1296 (1877–1879). pp.31. [191.]
1297–1298 (1880–1881). pp.48. [218.]
1299–1301 (1882–1884). pp.[iii].88. [432.]
1302–1303 (1885–1886). pp.69. [344.]
1304–1305 (1887–1888). pp.[iii].62. [300.]
1306–1307 (1889–1890). pp.[iii].54. [303.]

MIRZĀ ASHRAF ALĪ, A catalogue of the persian books and manuscripts in the library of the Asiatic society of Bengal. Calcutta [1890–]1895. pp.[iii].200. [2000.]

EUGENE WILHELM and BOMONJI BYRAMJI PATEL [BAHMANJĪ BAHRĀMJĪ PATEL], Catalogue of books on irânian literature published in Europe and India. Bombay 1901. pp.[v].ii.63.[74]. [2000.]
this list is in two parts, one in english by Wilhelm, the other in gujarati by Bahmanji.

AUTHOR-CATALOGUE of the Haiderabad collection of manuscripts and printed books. Asiatic society of Bengal: Calcutta 1913. pp.iv.62.

EDWARD G[RANVILLE] BROWNE, The press and poetry of modern Persia. Partly based on the manuscript work of Mírzá Muhammad 'Alí Khán "Tarbiyat" of Tabriz. Cambridge 1914. pp.xl.357.v. [372.]

EDWARD EDWARDS, A catalogue of the persian printed books in the British museum. 1922. pp. viii.coll.968. [6000.]

C[HARLES] A[MBROSE] STOREY, Persian literature. A bio-biographical survey.
[I]:
i. Qur'ānic literature. 1927. pp.xxiii.58. [750.]
ii. 1. A. General history. B. The prophets and early Islām. 1935. pp.xxv–xl.pp.61–235. [2000.]
ii. 2. C–L. Special histories of Persia, central Asia and the remaining parts of the world except India. 1936. pp.[iv].237–432. [2000.]
ii. 3. M. History of India. 1939. pp.xlv–xlviii. 433–780. [3000.]
reprinted 1970.
ii. 4. Biography. Additions and corrections. Indexes. 1953. pp.xlix–lx.781–1355. [300.]
II:
i. A. Mathematics. B. Weights and measures. C. Astronomy and astrology. D. Geography. 1958. pp.1.192. [1000.]
reprinted 1972.
ii. E. Medecine. 1971. pp.iv.193–346. [1000.]
— —Персидская литература: био-библиографический обзор. Перевел с английского,

переработал и дополнил Ю. Э. Брегель. Москва 1972. pp.1884. [10,000.]

I'JAZ HUSAIN AL-KANTŪRĪ, Kashf al-hujub wal'astār 'an 'asmā' al-kutub wal asfar, or The bibliography of Shī'a literature, of Mawlānā I'jāz Ḥusain al-Kantūrī. Edited by M. Hidayat Hosain. Calcutta 1935. pp.5.607.118. [3414.]

AGHÂ BOZORG TEHERANI, Bibliography of shi'ite's literary works (az-Zari'a ila tasânîf ash-shi'a). Refined by A. Monžavi. 1936 &c.
in progress. Only some volumes have an english title-page.

A. J. ARBERRY, Catalogue of the library of the India office. Vol.II. — Part VI. Persian books. 1937. pp.[iii].572. [6000.]

ETTORE ROSSI and ALESSIO BOMBACI, Elenco di drammi religiosi persiani (fondo mss. vaticani Cerulli). Biblioteca apostolica vaticana: Studi e testi (no.209): Città del Vaticano 1961. pp.[ii]. lx.416. [1200.]

KHÂN BÂBÂ MOSHÂR, A bibliography of books printed in persian. Vol.one, book titles arranged alphabetically with relevant details. Iran library: Teheran 1958. pp.iv.cols. 1687. [8,500.]
— Bibliography of persian printed books, the supplement of Moshâr's bibliography, by Karâmat-e R'anâ-Husayni. Persian and iranian bibliographies series (4). Tehran 1970. pp.67. [748.]

MAHMOUD NADJMABADI, A bibliography of printed books in persian on medicine and allied subjects. Vol.one: Titles of books. Tehran 1964. pp.922.vii.iv. [5,500.]

BIBLIOGRAPHY of articles in persian on economics 1340–1344. (mar. 1961–mar. 1966). Bank markazi Iran library 1967. pp.xxx.241. [iii]. [1847.]

LABIB ZUWIYYA-YAMAK, Harvard college library catalogue of persian books. Preliminary edition. Cambridge, Mass. 1964. pp.218. [3921 cards.]*

HOSAIN BANI-ADAM, A bibliography of persian books for children and youngsters. Persian subject bibliographies (3): The book society of Persia. Tehran 1968. pp.182. [800.]

D[AVID] I[VANOVICH] KOBIDZE, Иранская филология в Грузии. Тбилиси 1971. pp.82. [450.]

3. Manuscripts

OTHMAR FRANK, Ueber die morgenländischen handschriften der Königlichen hof- und central-bibliothek in München. München 1814. pp.82. lii. [14.]
limited to persian mss.

J. L. ROUSSEAU, Catalogue d'une collection de cinq cents manuscrits orientaux. Paris 1817. pp.53. [persian: 169].

JOSEPHUS DE HAMMER [BARON JOSEPH VON HAMMER-PURGSTALL], Codices arabicos, persicos, turcicos, Bibliothecae caesareo-regio-palatinae vindobonensis. Vindobonae 1820. pp.[ii].68. [618.]

A CATALOGUE of arabic, turkish and persian manuscripts. The private collection of Wm. B. Hodgson. Washington 1830. ff.10. [150.]

HENRICUS ORTHOBIUS [HEINRICH LEBERECHT] FLEISCHER, Catalogus codicum manuscriptorum orientalium Bibliothecae regiae Dresdensis. Accedit Friderici Adolphi Eberti catalogus codicum manuscriptorum orientalium Bibliothecae ducalis Guelferbytanae. Lipsiae 1831. pp.xii.106. [596.]

CATALOGUS librorum manuscriptorum qui in bibliotheca senatoria civitalis Lipsiensis asservantur edidit Aemilius Guilelmus Robertus Naumann. Codices orientalium linguarum descripserunt Henricus Orthobius Fleischer et Franciscus Delitzsch. Grimae 1838. pp.xxiv.562.lvi. [424.]

CODICES arabici (-persici — turcici) vel a christianis scripti vel ad religionem christianam spectantes. Scriptorum veterum nova collectio e vaticanis codicibus edita ab Angelo Maio, tomus IV. Romae 1841. pp.718. [persian: 65.]

ALBRECHT KRAFFT, Die arabischen, persischen und türkischen handschriften der K. k. orientalischen akademie zu Wien. Wien 1842. pp.xx.208. [1000.]

J. MOHL and P. LACROIX, Catalogue des livres et manuscrits orientaux provenant de la bibliothèque de feu m. J.St.Harriot. Paris 1843.

B[ERNHARD] DORN, Das asiatische museum der Kaiserlichen akademie der wissenschaften zu St. Petersburg. St. Petersburg 1846. pp.xii.776. [persian: 9.]

C[ARL] J[OHAN] TORNBERG, Codices arabici, persici et turcici bibliothecae regiae universitatis upsaliensis. [Uppsala] 1849. pp.[ii].xxiv.355. [512.]
— — Fortsetzung. Die arabischen, persischen und türkischen handschriften der Universitäts-bibliothek zu Uppsala. Verzeichnet ... von K[arl] V[ilhelm] Zetterstéen. Uppsala 1930–1935. pp.xviii.498+x.180. [1500.]
also issued as vols. iii–iv of Acta bibliothecae R. universitatis upsaliensis and as vols. xxii and xxviii of Le monde oriental.

WILLIAM H. MORLEY, A descriptive catalogue of the historical manuscripts in the arabic and persian languages, preserved in the library of the Royal asiatic society. 1854. pp.viii.160. [163.]

A[LOYS] SPRENGER, A catalogue of the arabic, persian and hindústány manuscripts of the libraries of the king of Oudh.... Vol.1. Containing persian and hindústány poetry. Calcutta 1854. pp.viii.648. [732.]

no more published.

A[UGUST] F[ERDINAND MICHAEL] MEHREN, Codices persici, turcici, hindustanici variique alii Bibliothecæ regiæ hafniensis. Hafniæ 1857. pp. v.92. [250.]

WILHELM PERTSCH, Die orientalischen handschriften der Herzoglichen bibliothek zu Gotha. ... Erster theil: die persischen handschriften. Wien 1859. pp.[ii].xi.943. [87.]

COLLECTION de manuscrits arabes, persans et turcs appartenant à m^me la comtesse Alix des Granges. 1859. pp.12. [persian: 43.]

B[ERNHARD] DORN, Die sammlung von morgenländischen handschriften, welche die Kaiserliche öffentliche bibliothek zu St. Petersburg in jahre 1864 von h^rn v. Chanykov erworben hat. St. Petersburg 1865. pp.[ii].93. [150.]
— — Nachträge. Morgenländische handschriften. 1865. pp.[ii].43. [100.]

GUSTAV FLÜGEL, Die arabischen, persischen und türkischen handschriften der Kaiserlich-königlichen hofbibliothek zu Wien. Wien 1865–1867. pp.x.723+iv.614+lxviii.653. [3000.]

JOSEPH AUMER, Die persischen handschriften der K. hof- und staatsbibliothek in Muenchen. Catalogus codicum manu scriptorum Bibliothecae regiae monacensis (vol.i, part 3): München 1866. pp.152. [1000.]

[D. FORBES], Catalogue of oriental manuscripts, chiefly persian, collected within the last five and thirty years by Duncan Forbes. 1866. pp.[iii].92. [291.]

J. A. GOBINEAU, Collection d'ouvrages recueillis en Perse sur l'histoire, la poésie, la philosophie, les sciences occultes etc. Paris 1870. pp.16. [persian: 64.]

E[DWARD] H[ENRY] PALMER, A descriptive catalogue of the arabic, persian and turkish manuscripts in the library of Trinity college, Cambridge. With an appendix, containing a catalogue of the hebrew and samaritan mss. in the same library [by William Aldis Wright]. Cambridge, London 1870. pp.vii.235. [persian: 27.]

EDWARD REHATSEK, Catalogue raisonné of the arabic, hindustani, persian and turkish mss. in the Mulla Firuz library. [Bombay] 1873. pp.[iv].ix.279. [550.]
— — Supplementary catalogue... and descriptive catalogue of the avesta, pahlavi, pazend and

persian mss. . . . By S. A. Brelvi and Ervad B. N. Dhabhar. 1917. pp.[ii].ix.[vii].v.xliv.v–xiv.3–79. [250.]

nearly all the mss. are in persian.

E. LEROUX, Catalogue de la bibliothèque orientale de feu m. Belin. Livres sur la Turquie. Textes et manuscrits arabes, turcs et persans. Paris 1878. pp.56.

M. F. DELONCLE, Catalogue des livres orientaux et autres composant la bibliothèque de feu m. Garcin de Tassy, suivi du catalogue des manuscrits hindustanis, persans, arabes, turcs. Paris 1879. pp.viii.272. [persian: 32.]

CHARLES RIEU, Catalogue of the persian manuscripts in the British museum. 1879–1883. pp.[iv]. 432+vii.433–878+xxviii.881–1229. [5000.]
— — Supplement. 1895. pp.xi.308. [500.]

S[AMUEL] LANDAUER, Katalog der hebräischen, arabischen, persischen und türkischen handschriften der Kaiserlichen universitäts- und landesbibliothek. Strassburg 1881. pp.[iv].75. [125.]

CATALOGUE of a magnificent collection of manuscripts from Hamilton palace. 1882.

A[LFRED], FREIHERR VON KREMER, Ueber meine sammlung orientalischer handschriften. Wien 1885. pp.78. [212.]

VICTOR ROSEN, Remarques sur les manuscrits orientaux de la collection Marsigli à Bologne, suivies de la liste complète des manuscrits arabes de la même collection. Rome 1885. pp.135. [459.]

BARON VICTOR [ROMANOVICH] ROSEN, Les manuscrits persans de l'Institut de langues orientales. Collections scientifiques (vol.iii): Saint-Pétersbourg 1886. pp.[v].iv.369. [200.]

WILHELM PERTSCH, Verzeichniss der persischen handschriften. Königliche bibliothek: Handschriften-verzeichnisse (vol.iv): Berlin 1888. pp. xvi.1283. [2000.]

C[ARL] SALEMANN and [BARON] V[ICTOR] ROMANOVICH] ROSEN, Indices alphabetici codicum manu scriptorum persicorum, turcicorum, arabicorum qui in Bibliotheca imperialis literarum universitatis petropolitanae adservantur. Petropoli 1888. pp.50. [1500.]
— — Supplementum, confecit A. Romaskewicz. Leningrad 1925. pp.[ii].19. [300.]

[CARL] ED[UARD] SACHAU and HERMANN ETHÉ, Catalogue of the persian, turkish, hindûstânî, and pushtû manuscripts in the Bodleian library. Catalogi codd. mss. Bibliothecae bodleianae pars XIII: Oxford 1889–1930. pp.xii.coll.1150+pp.[iv]. 1157–1766. [persian: 2500.]

— — Part III. Additional persian manuscripts. By A. F. L. Beeston. 1954. pp.viii.177. *this volume also contains an index to the whole work.*

[ROBERT HOE], Catalogue of an exhibition of illuminated ... manuscripts ... also some examples of persian manuscripts. Grolier club: New York 1892. pp.xxxiii.64. [persian: 14.] *350 copies printed.*

ALPHABETICAL index of manuscripts in the Governmental oriental mss. library, Madras. Persian. Madras 1893. pp.22. [350.]

EDWARD G[RANVILLE] BROWNE, A catalogue of the persian manuscripts in the library of the university. Cambridge 1896. pp.xl.472. [336.]

[JAMES LUDOVIC LINDSAY, EARL OF CRAWFORD AND BALCARRES and MICHAEL KERNEY], Hand-list of oriental manuscripts, arabic, persian, turkish. Bibliotheca lindesiana: 1898. pp.xliii.268. [2500.] *100 copies privately printed.*

E. KAL', Персидскія, арабскія и тюркскія рукописи Туркестанской публичной библиотеки. Ташкенть 1899. pp.[ii].79. [90.]

E[DGARD] BLOCHET, Catalogue de la collection d^e manuscrits arabes, persans et turcs formée pa^r m. Charles Shefer et acquise par l'État. Bibliothèque nationale: 1900. pp.[iii].v.231. [1000.]

E[DGARD] BLOCHET, Catalogue des manuscrits mazdéens (zends, pehlvis, parsis et persans) de la Bibliothèque nationale. Besançon 1900. pp.[iii]. 132. [500.]

EDWARD G[RANVILLE] BROWNE, A hand-list of the muhammadan manuscripts, including all those written in the arabic character, preserved in the library of the university. Cambridge 1900. pp.xviii.440. [1541.]
— — A supplementary hand-list. 1922. pp.xii. 348. [1250.]
— — A second supplementary hand-list of the muhammadan manuscripts in the university & colleges of Cambridge. By A[rthur] J[ohn] Arberry. 1952. pp.82. [450.]

N. F. KATANOV, Императорского Казанского университета почетный член, профессор и библиотекарь Иосиф Федорович Готвальд. (13.X.1813–7.viii.1897). Казань 1900. pp.xi.240. [persian: 25.]

CARLO ALFONSO NALLINO, I manoscritti arabi, persiani, siriaci e turchi della Biblioteca nazionale e della r. accademia delle scienze di Torino. Accademia reale delle scienze di Torino: Torino 1900. pp.104. [123.]

[SIR] E[DWARD] DENISON ROSS and EDWARD G[RANVILLE] BROWNE, Catalogue of two collections of persian and arabic manuscripts preserved in the India office library. 1902. pp.vii.189. [280.]

C[ARL] BROCKELMANN, Verzeichnis der arabischen, perischen, türkischen und hebräischen handschriften der Stadtbibliothek. Breslau 1903. pp.v.53. [92.]

H[ERMANN] ETHÉ [vol.ii: and EDWARD EDWARDS], Catalogue of persian manuscripts in the library of the India office. Oxford 1903–1937. pp.xxiii.coll.1632+pp.[v].coll.1376. [3076.]

KAMAL UD-DĪN AḤMAD and ʿABD UL-MUKTADIR, Catalogue of the arabic and persian manuscripts in the library of the Calcutta madrasah. Calcutta 1905. pp.[ii].iv.38.115. [persian: 79.]

E[DGARD] BLOCHET, Catalogue des manuscrits persans de la Bibliothèque nationale. 1905–1934. pp.vii.411 + vii.333 + [iii].iii.491 + [iii].iv.484. [3000.]

[MUḤAMMAD HIDĀYAT ḤUSAIN], List of arabic and persian mss. acquired on behalf of the government of India by the Asiatic society of Bengal during 1903–1907. [Calcutta 1908]. pp.[ii].61. [1106.]
— — 1908–1910. [By Nazir Ahmad and Hazīr Razawi]. [1911]. pp.[ii].62. [540.]

CATALOGUE of the arabic and persian manuscripts in the Oriental public library at Bankipore, prepared for the government of Bihar and Orissa under the supervision of Sir E. Denison Ross.

[i]. Persian poets, Firdawsi to Hafiz. Prepared by Maulavî Abdul Muqtadir. 1908. pp.x.274. [161.]

ii. Persian poets. Kamâl Khujandi to Faydi. 1910. pp.viii.222. [162–264.]

iii. Persian poetry. 17th, 18th and 19th centuries. 1912. pp.xi.276. [265–448.]

iv. Arabic medical works. Prepared by Maulavî ʿAzīmu 'd-din Aḥmad. 1910. pp.vii.208. [1–120.]

v. Tradition. Prepared by Maulavî Abdul Hamîd. 1920–5. pp.viii.214+vii.231. [121–484.]

vi. History. 1918. pp.xii.212. [449–534.]

vii. Indian history. 1921. pp.xii.211. [535–648.]

viii. Biography, romances, tales and anecdotes. 1925. pp.xi.196. [649–768.]

ix. Philology and sciences. 1925. pp.xiii.211. [769–960.]

x. Theology. 1926. pp.vii.150. [485–645.]

xi. Sciences (continued) and arts. 1927. pp.xi.147. [961–1110.]

xii. Biography. Prepared by Maulavî Muinuddin Nadwi. 1927. pp.vii.167. [646–819.]

xiii. Sûfism. 1928. pp.vii.185. [820–959.]

xiv. Commentaries on the Qurân, Hadîs, law, theology and controversial works. 1928. pp.xi.182. [1111–1344.]

xv. History. Prepared by Maulavî Muinud-din Nadwi. 1929. pp.v.210. [960–1115.]

xvi. Sufism, prayers, hinduism and history of creeds and sects. 1929. pp.vii.142. [1345–1459.]

xvii. Manuscripts of mixed contents. 1930. pp.iv.183. [1460–1743.]

xviii. Quranic science. 1930–2. pp.vii.187+v.181. [1116–1488.]

xix. Principles of jurisprudence and juris-prudence (part ii: jurisprudence and law of inheritance). 1931–3. pp.vi.172+vii.169. [1489–1961.]

xx. Philology. Prepared by Dr. Azimuddin Ahmad and Maulavi Muinuddin Nadwî. 1936. pp.vii.229. [1962–2221.]

xxi. Encyclopaedias, logic, philosophy and dialectics. 1936. pp.v.138. [2222–2412.]

xxii. Science. 1937. pp.vii.164. [2413–2503.]

xxiii. Poetry and elegant prose. 1939. pp.v.151. [2504–2642.]

xxiv. Ethics and prayer. 1940. pp.vii.138. [2643–2770.]

xxv. Miscellanies. Prepared by Maulavi 'Abdul Hamid and revised by Maulavi Mas'ûd 'Âlam Nadwî. 1942. pp.vii.191. [2771–2787.]

—— Supplement to the catalogue of the persian manuscripts in the Oriental public library at Bankipore. Calcutta 1932–3. pp.[iv].267+iv.238. [1744–2351.]

—— Index to the catalogue raisonné of the persian manuscripts in the Oriental public library at Bankipore. Calcutta 1939. pp.v.171.

The Persian mss. numbering 2351 entries, were all catalogued by Maulavi Abdul Muqtadir in vols.i–iii, vi–ix, xi, xiv, xvi–xvii, Supplementary vols.i–ii; he also prepared the index.

E[DGARD] BLOCHET, Catalogue des manuscrits arabes, persans et turcs offerts a la Bibliothèque nationale par m. J.-A. Decourdemanche. 1909. pp.[iii.]90. [400.]

MAHOMMED MUSHARRAF–UL–HUKK [MUḤAMMAD MUSHARRAF AL–ḤAḴḴ], Katalog der bibliothek der Deutschen morgenländischen gesellschaft. Zwei-ter band. Handschriften. Teil B: persische und hindustanische handschriften. Leipzig 1911. pp. viii.76. [persian: 70]

A. V. WILLIAMS JACKSON and ABRAHAM YOHAN-NAN, A catalogue of the collection of persian manuscripts, including also some turkish and arabic, presented to the Metropolitan museum of art, New York, by Alexander Smith Cochran. Columbia university: Indo-iranian series (vol. i): New York 1914. pp.xxv.187. [23.]

CHRISTIAN BARTHOLOMAE, Die Zendhand-schriften der K. hof- und staatsbibliothek in München. Catalogus codicum manu scriptorum

Bibliothecae regiae monacensis (vol.i, part 7): München 1915. pp.xx.70.383. [500.]

ARTHUR CHRISTIANSEN and J. ØSTRUP, Descrip-tion de quelques manuscrits orientaux apparte-nant à la bibliothèque de l'université de Copen-hague. Oversigt over det Kgl. danske videns-kabernes selskabs forhandlinger (1915, 3–4): [Copenhagen] 1915. pp.30. [21.]

E[DGARD] BLOCHET, Inventaire de la collec-tion de manuscrits musulmans de M. Decourde-manche. Extrait du Journal asiatique (septembre-décembre 1916). Paris 1916. pp.112. [254.]

HERMAN ETHÉ, Catalogue of oriental manu-scripts, persian, arabic, and hindūstānī. National library of Wales: Aberystwyth 1916. pp.iv.31. [50.]
250 copies printed.

V[INCENT] C[LARENCE] SCOTT O'CONNOR, An eastern library. . . . With two catalogues of its persian and arabic manuscripts, compiled by khan sahib Abdul Muqtadir ['Abd ul-Muktadir] and Abdul Hamid ['Abd ul-Ḥamid]. Glasgow 1920. pp.[vii].107. [persian: 124.]
on the Oriental public library, Patna.

QUÂSIM ḤAṢÎR RADAVÎ [ḴĀSIM ḤAṢĪR RAZAVĪ], Catalogue of the persian manuscripts in the Buhâr library. . . . Revised and completed by maulavi 'Abd-ul-Muqtadir ['Abd al-Muktadir]. Cata-logue raisonné of the Buhâr library (vol.i): Calcutta 1921. pp.xiii.383. [500.]

COLLECTION de m. le docteur Gachet. . . . Manuscrits arméniens, arabes, persans, Bordeaux [printed] 1922. pp.12. [88.]

ERVAD BOMANJI NUSSERWANJI DHABHAR [BĀMANJI NASARVĀNJI DHABHĀR], Descriptive catalogue of some manuscripts bearing on Zoroastrianism and pertaining to the different collections in the Mulla Feroze library. Parsee Punchayat funds and properties. Bombay 1923. pp.[iii].vi.120. [200.]

W. RIEDEL, Katalog över Kungl. bibliothekets orientaliska handskrifter. Kungliga biblioteket [Stockholm]: Handlingar: Bilagor (n.s., vol.iii): Uppsala 1923. pp.xi.68. [150.]

E[DGARD] BLOCHET, Notices sur les manuscrits persans et arabes de la collection Marteau. Paris 1923. pp.308. [62.]

WLADIMIR IVANOW [VLADIMIR ALEKSEEVICH IVANOV], Concise descriptive catalogue of the persian manuscripts in the collection of the Asiatic society of Bengal. Bibliotheca indica (no.240): Calcutta 1924. pp.xxxvii.934. [2500.]

—— First supplement. Bibliotheca indica (Work no.244, Issue no. 1493 N.S.). 1927.pp.xii.160. [757–924.]

—— Second supplement. Bibliotheca indica (Work no.248, Issue no.1502 N.S.). 1928. pp.xxii. 138. [925–1098.]

MOHAMMED ASHRAFUL HUKK [MUHAMMED ASHRAF AL-HAĶĶ], HERMANN ETHÉ and EDWARD ROBERTSON, A descriptive catalogue of the arabic and persian manuscripts in Edinburgh university library. Edinburgh 1925. pp.viii.454. [persian: 300.]

A[LEKSANDR] A[LEKSANDROVICH] SEMENOV, Каталог рукописей Исторического отдела Бухарской центральной библиотеки. Труды библиографической комиссии при СНК ТССР (вып. 2).
Catalogue des manuscrits historiques de la Bibliotheque centrale de Boukhara. Ташкент 1925. pp.32. [persian 99.]

WLADIMIR IVANOV [VLADIMIR ALEKSEEVICH IVA-NOV], Concise descriptive catalogue of the persian manuscripts in the Curzon collection, Asiatic society of Bengal. Bibliotheca indica (no.241): Calcutta 1926. pp.xxviii.582. [756.]

NICHOLAS N. MARTINOVITCH, A catalogue of turkish and persian manuscripts belonging to Robert Garrett and deposited in the Princeton university library. Princeton 1926. pp.[iv].46. [persian: 64.]

GIUSEPPE GABRIELI, La fondazione Caetani per gli studi musulmani. Nolizia della sua istituzione e catalogo dei suoi mss. orientali. Roma 1926. pp.96.6. [300.]

CATALOGUE of arabic, persian & urdoo manu-scripts presented to the Dacca university library ... by ... Ahmad Siddiqui [Şiddiķi]. Dacca [printed] [1929]. pp.vi.24. [50.]
only a small selection is catalogued.

[K. I. CHAYKIN], Восточные рукописи. Пер-сидские, арабские, турецкие. Москва 1931. [persian: 33]

EDWARD G[RANVILLE] BROWNE, A descriptive catalogue of the oriental Mss. belonging to the late E. G. Browne. Completed & edited ... by Reynold A. Nicholson. Cambridge 1932. pp.xxii. 325. [468.]

S. KUPPUSWAMI SASTRI, An alphabetical index of persian manuscripts in the Government oriental manuscripts library, Madras. Madras 1932. pp.38. [614.]

FEHMI EDHEM [KARATAY] and IVAN STCHOUKINE, Les manuscrits orientaux illustrés de la biblio-thèque de l'université de Stamboul. Mémoires de l'institut français d'archéologie de Stamboul (1): 1933. pp.68. [persian: 20.]

Y[ŪSUF] ETESSAMI [I'TIŞĀMĪ], Catalogue des manuscrits persans et arabes de la Bibliothèque du Madjless. Téhéran 1933. pp.[vi].539.

L. T. GYUZAL'YAN and M. M. DYAKONOV, Рукописи шах-намэ в ленинградских собраниах. Институт востоковедения Академии наук СССР and Государственный Эрмитаж: Денинград 1934. pp.xxiv.126. [29.]

'ABDU'L-ĶĀDIR-E-SARFARĀZ, A descriptive cata-logue of the arabic, persian and urdu manuscripts in the library of the university of Bombay. Bombay 1935. pp.lv.432. [2000.]

A[LEKSANDR] A[LEKSANDROVICH] SEMENOV, Описание персидских, арабских и турецких рукописей Фундаментальной библиотеки Сред-неазиатского государственного университета. A descriptive catalogue of the persian, arabic and turkish manuscripts preserved in the library of Middle asiatic state university. Acta Universitatis Asiae mediae (series ii. Orientalia, fasc.4): 1935–56. pp.88+88. [339.]

FIRDAWSI celebration, 935–1935. Addresses ... A bibliography of the principal manuscripts and printed editions of the Shah-namah in certain leading public libraries of the world. Edited by David Eugene Smith. New York 1936. pp.xiii. 138. [750.]

OLAF HANSEN, Die mittelperischen papyri der papyrussammlung der staatlichen museen zu Berlin. Preussiche akademie der wissenschaften: Abhandlungen: Philosophisch-historische klasse (1937, no.9): Berlin 1938. pp.102. [200.]

MOHAMMĀD E. MOGHADAM [MUHAMMAD I'TIMĀD MUĶADDAM] and YAHYA ARMAJĀNĪ, Descriptive catalog of the Garrett collection of persian, turkish and indic manuscripts, including some miniatures, in the Princeton university library.... Under the supervision of Philip K[hūrī] Ḥitti. Princeton oriental texts (vol.6): Princeton 1939. pp.94.x.

JAMSHED CAWASJI [KAVASJI] KATRAK, Oriental treasures being condensed tabular descriptive statement of ... manuscripts and of their colo-phons written in indian & iranian languages and lying in private libraries ... of Gujurat. Bombay 1941. pp.xxii.295. [1250.]

FEHIM SPAHO, Arapski, perzijski i turski rukopisi Hrvatskih zemaljskih muzeja u Sarajevu. Sara-jevu 1942. pp.ix.107. [203.]

R[OBERT] B[ERTRAM] SERJEANT, A handlist of the arabic, persian and hindustani mss. of New college. Edinburgh 1942. pp.16. [persian: 72].

ION I. NISTOR, Manuscrisele orientale din Biblioteca Academiei române cu inventarul lor.

Analele Academiei române: Memoriile secţiunii istorice (seria iii, tomul xxviii, mem.4): Bucaresti 1946. pp.50. [216.]

ETTORE ROSSI, Elenco dei manoscritti persiani della biblioteca Vaticana: vaticani, barberiniani, borgiani, rossiani. Biblioteca apostolica vaticana: Studi e testi (vol.136): Città del vaticano 1948. pp.3–200. [500.]

FEHMI EDHEM KARATAY, İstanbul üniversitesi kütüphanesi farsça basmalar kataloğu. İstanbul üniversitesi yayınlarından (no.414): Edebiyat fakültesi şarkiyat enstitüsü. İstanbul 1949. pp.vii. 200. [1000.]

ALEKSANDR ALEKSANDROVICH SEMENOV, ed. Собрание восточных рукописей Академии наук Узбекской ССР. Ташкент 1952–1967. pp.440+590+544+560+543+738+554+798. [6009.]

MAKAR KHUBUA, Персидские фирманы и указы Музея Грузии. I. Институт истории им. акад. И. А. Джавахишвили Академии наук Грузинской ССР: Тбилиси 1949. pp.185. [48.]
Text in georgian and persian, preface in georgian and russian.

N. D. MIKLUKHO-MAKLAI, Описание таджикских и персидских (vol. 2— персидских и таджикских) рукописей Института востоковедения Академия наук СССР: Москва &c.
  [i]. 1955. pp.107. [91.]
  ii. Биографические сочинения. 1961. pp. 168. [116.]
  iii.
  iv. Персидские толковые словари (фарханги). 1962. pp.80. [55.]
  v. Двуязычные словари. 1968. pp. 103. [90.]

ZAGORKA JANC, Исламски рукописи из југословенских колекција. Музеj примењене уметности. Београд 1956. pp.50,pls. 20. [68.]

AGAH SIRRI LEVEND, Ġazavāt-nāmeler ve Mihaloğlu 'Ali Bey' in Ġazavāt-nāmesi. Türk tarih kurumu yayınlarından (xi. seri, no.8): Ankara 1956. pp.viii.392.pls.117. [350.]

VIDYA SAGAR SURI, Some original sources of Punjab history. Analytical catalogues of some outstanding persian manuscripts and annotated translations into english of contemporary chronicles entitled Dewan Ajndhia Parshad's Wagai-i-jang-i-sikhan (Pheroshehr and Sorbaon, 1846) and Muhammad Naqis' Sher Singh nama (Tarikh-i-Punjab). [Lahore 1957?] pp.iii.121.104. [218.]

CEVDET TÜRKAY, İstanbul kütübhanelerinde osmanlılar devrinde aîd türkçe-arabça-farsça yazma ve basma coğrafya eserleri bibliyografyası. Maarif vekâleti-bilim eserleri serisi: Istanbul 1958. pp.94. [2000.]

A. D. PAPAZYAN, Персидские Документы Матенадарана. Государственное хранилище древних рукописей при совете министров Армянской ССР (Матенадаран): Ереван.
  i. Указы (xv–xvi вв.). 1956. pp.316. [23.]
  ii. — (1601–1650 гг). 1959. pp.594. [43.]

THE CHESTER BEATTY LIBRARY, a catalogue of the persian manuscripts and miniatures. Dublin.
  i. By A[rthur] J[ohn] Arberry, M[ojtaba] Minovi and E[dgard] Blochet. Edited by J[ames] V[ere] S[tewart] Wilkinson. 1959. pp.xii.87,pls.39. [50.]
  ii. By M[ojtaba] Minovi, B[asil] W. Robinson, J[ames] V[ere] S[tewart] Wilkinson and E[dgard] Blochet. Edited by A[rthur] J[ohn] Arberry, 1960. pp.xiv.89,pls.43. [70.]
  iii. By A[rthur] J[ohn] Arberry, B. W. Robinson, E. Blochet and J. V. S. Wilkinson. Edited by A. J. Arberry, 1962. pp.xv. 117,pls.43. [178.]

MUZAFFER GÖKMAN, İstanbul kütüphaneleri ve yazma tıp kitapları. Libraries of Istanbul and their medical manuscripts. Istanbul üniversitesi tıp tarihi enstitüsü neşriyatından (sayı: 56): İstanbul 1959. pp.39. [2796.]

JUSSI ARO, Die arabischen, persischen und türkischen handschriften der universitätsbibliothek zu Helsinki. Helsingin yliopiston kirjaston julkaisuja (no.28): Helsinki 1959. pp.24. [100.]
also issued as vol.xxiii, no.4, of Studia orientalia (*Helsinki*).

OMER NASUHI BILMEN, Büyük tefsir tarihi II (Tabakatül-mufessirîn.) Diyanet işleri reisliği yayınları (sayı 39/2): Ankara 1960. pp.480. [335.]

MARY BOYCE, A catalogue of the iranian manuscripts in manichean script in the german Turfan collection. Deutsche akademie der wissenschaften zu Berlin: Institut für orientforschung: Veröffentlichung (no.45): Berlin 1960. pp.xl.151. [3000.]

M[UHAMMAD] T[AQI] DANECHE-PAJOUH, Catalogue méthodique, descriptif et raisonné des manuscrits de la Bibliothèque de la Faculté des lettres. Tehran 1960. pp.682. [598.]

E. KAZHDAROVA, Описание рукописных списков Дивана Махтумкули, хранящихся в Ашхабаде. Труды Института литературы им. Махтумкули. Ашхабад 1960.

A. M. MIRZOEV and A[LEKSANDR] N[IKOLAEVICH] BOLDYREV, Каталог восточных рукописей Академии наук Таджикской ССР. Сталинабад (Душанбе)
  i. 1960. pp.324. [288.]
  ii.
  ii. Под редакцией и при участии . . . А. М.

Мирзоева и М. И. Занда, 1968. pp.239. [339.]

iv. 1970. pp.279. [403.]

A. H. M. MUHIUDDIN and JOHN MACDONALD, Catalogue of oriental manuscripts. IX. Persian mss. University of Leeds: Department of semitic languages & literatures: [Leeds 1960]. ff.ii.59. [50.]*

KAREL PETRÁČEK, JOZEF BLAŠKOVIĆ, RUDOLF VESELÝ, Arabische, türkische und persische handschriften der Universitätsbibliothek in Bratislava. Unter der redaktion Jozef Blaskovićs. Bratislava 1961. pp.551. [598.]

M[UHAMMAD] T[AQI] DANECHE-PAJOUH, Catalogue méthodique, descriptif, et raisonné des manuscrits de la Bibliothèque de la Faculté de droit et des sciences politiques et économiques de l'Université de Téhéran. Publications de l'Université de Téhéran (652): Téhéran 1961. pp.xii.602. [631.]

Персидские исторические документы в книгохранилищах Грузии. Академия наук Грузинской ССР. Тбилиси 1961 &c.
in progress.

V. S. PUTURIDZE, Персидские исторические документы в книгохранилищах Грузии.
Acta et diplomata historica persice scripta, ed. V. P'ut'uridze. Академия наук грузинской ССР: Комиссия по публикации иностранных источников о грузии.
Fontes peregrini ad Georgiam pertinentes: Tbilisiis 1961–2. pp.023.98.pls.34.+[vi].104.pls.35. [69.]
Text in georgian & persian, preface also in russian.

ETTORE ROSSI and ALESSIO BOMBACI, Elenco di drammi religiosi persiani (fondo mss. vaticani Cerulli). Studi e testi (209): Citta del Vaticano 1961. pp.lx.416. [1055.]

M[ARGARITA] B[ORISOVNA] RUDENKO, Описание курдских рукописей ленинградских собраний. Академия наук СССР: Институт народов Азии: Москва 1961. pp.126. [84.]

FEHMI EDHEM KARATAY, Topkapı Sarayi müzesi kütüphanesi farsça yazmalar kataloğu. Topkapı sarayı müzesi yayınları (no.12): İstanbul 1961. pp.vii.395. [940.]

A. T. TAGIRDZHANOV, Описание таджикских и персидских рукописей Восточного отдела библиотека ЛГУ. [Leningrad]
i. История, биографии, география. pp.iii.515. [169.]

KIRPAL SINGH, A catalogue of persian and sanskrit manuscripts in the Sikh history research department until March 31, 1962. Khalsa college: Amritsar 1962. pp.xiv.148. [249.]

VICAJI D. B. TARAPOREVALA and DANA N. MARSHALL, Mughal bibliography: select persian sources for the study of mughals in India. Bombay 1962. pp.viii.164. [437.]

KASIM DOBRAČA, Katalog arapskih, turskih i perzijskih rukopisa. Gazi Husrev-begova biblioteka: Sarajevo 1963– . pp.xxxii.607. ii +
in progress.

O[LEG] F. AKIMUSHKIN [*and others*], Персидске и таджикские рукописи Института народов Азии АН СССР (краткий алфавитный каталог). Под редакцией Н. Д. Миклухо-Маклая. Москва.
i. 1964. pp.635. [4790.]
ii. 1964. Указатели и приложения. pp.147.

M. A. RAWDATI, Bulletin de catalogue des manuscrits arabes et persans des bibliothèques de l'Ispahan [Vol.1]. Ispahan 1341 sh. pp.399. [80.]

ASCAR HOGHOUGHI, Catalogue critique des manuscrits persans de la Bibliothèque nationale et universitaire de Strasbourg. Publications (ii): Strasbourg 1964. pp.xxviii.110. [32.]

S. DE LAUGIER DE BEAURECUEIL, Manuscrits d'Afghanistan. Institut français d'archéologie orientale du Caire: Recherches d' archéologie, de philologie et d'histoire (t.xxvi). Le Caire 1964. pp.xiii.420. [perisan: 892.]

MUHAMMAD ASHRAF, A catalogue of the persian manuscripts in the Salar Jung museum & library. Hyderabad (Andhra Pradesh).
i. Concerning (453) mss. of history. 1965. pp.iii.xliii.611. [453.]

SEYYED ABDOLLAH ANVAR, A catalogue of the manuscripts in the National library. Persian manuscripts. Tehran 1965–8. pp.[ii].xvi.527+iv.600. [1000.]

ABID RAZA BEDAR, Catalogue of persian & arabic manuscripts of Saulat public library. Rampur 1966. pp.261.xviii.5.3.16. [551.]

A TITLE catalogue of persian manuscripts in the National library till 1963. Natonal library & archives: Cairo 1966–7. pp.viii.358+368. [2542.]

A[NDREY] BERTEL'S and M[AMADVAFO] BAKOEV, Алфавитный каталог рукописей, обнаруженных в Горно-Бадахшанской автономной области экспедицией 1959–1963 гг.
Alphabetic catalogue of manuscripts found by 1959–1963 expedition in Gorno-Badakhshan autonomous region. Edited and prepared by B. G. Gafurov and A. M. Mirzoev. Moscow 1967. pp.120. [263.]

ABDÜLBÂKI GÖLPINARLI, Mevlânâ Müzesi yaz-malar kataloğu. Eski eserler ve müzeler genel müdürlüğü yayınları (seri: III, no: 6): Ankara 1967. pp.xv.301+xx.484+viii.488.

TADEUSZ MAJDA, Katalog rekopisów tureckich i perskich. Catalogue des manuscrits turcs et persans. Catalogue des manuscrits orientaux des collections polonaises (V,2): Zakład orientalistyki: Polskiej akademii nauk: Warszawa 1967. pp.236. [221.]

A. T. TAGIRDZHANOV, Список таджикских, персидских и тюркских рукописей Восточного отдела Библиотеки ЛГУ (продолжение списков К. Г. Залемана и А. А. Ромаскевича). Москва 1967. pp.19. [253.]*

AHMED ATEŞ, İstanbul kütüphanelerinde farsça manzum eserler. İstanbul.
i. Üniversite ve Nuruosmaniye kütüphaneleri. 1968. pp.xvi.638. [803.]

WILHELM HEINZ, Persische handschriften (teil i). Herausgegeben von Wilhelm Eilers. Verzeichnis der orientalischen handschriften in Deutschland (band xiv): Wiesbaden 1968. pp.xviii.pls.xi. pp.345. [400.]

GLYN M. MEREDITH-OWENS, Handlist of persian manuscripts 1895–1966. British museum: [London] 1968. pp.x.126. [972.]

TZ. A. ABULADZE, R. V. GRAMANIYA and M. G. MAMATZASHVILI, Каталог арабских, тюркских и персидских рукописей Института рукописей им. К. С. Кекелидзе (коллекция К). Catalogue of the arabic, turkish and persian manuscripts in the Kekelidze institute of the manuscripts, Georgian academy of sciences (the K collection): Tbilisi 1969. pp.viii.202. [persian: 192.]

ABDOL HOSSEIN HAERI, A catalogue of the manuscripts in the Parliament library (persian & arabic & turkish). Vol. 10, part 3. Teheran 1969. pp.2. 1081–1675. [280.]
up to 19 volumes in all, but not all have english title-pages.

AHMAD MONZAVI, A catalogue of persian manuscripts. R.C.D. publication (no.14): Regional cultural institute. Tehran 1969–71. pp.11.718. [14–23].[iii] + [iv].722–1489.[ii] + [iii].1490–1841+[vi].1846–2615. [27,154.]
in progress.

EVE APOR, The persian manuscripts of the Vámbéry bequest. Publications Bibliothecae Academiae scientiarum hungaricae (62): Budapest 1971. pp.19. [11.]

A. YUNUSOV, Дастнависхои Хофиз дар китабхонаи Давлатии РСС Точикистон ба номи Абулкосим Фирдавси: Фехраст. Душанбе 1971. pp.33. [32.]*

A. YUNUSOV, Каталог таджиксо-персидских рукописи. Министерство культуры Таджикской СССР: Государственная республиканская библиотека имени Фирдоуси: Отдел восточных рукописей Душанбе. 1971. pp.296. [132.]*

MOHAMMAD HOSSEIN TASBIHI, Catalogue of the manuscripts in the Ganjbakhsh library of Iran Pakistan institute of persian studies. Rawalpindi.
i. 1972. pp.xvi.834.xxvii. [428.]

MOHAMMAD HOSSEIN TASBIHI, Catalogue of the manuscripts of Khwajah Sana' Allah Kharabati. Iran Pakistan institute of persian studies: Rawalpindi 1972. pp.12.[1].222.57. [52.]

G. I. KOSTUIGOVA, Персидские и таджикские рукописи "новой серии" Государственной публичной библиотеки им. М. Е. Салтыкова-Щедрина. Алфавитный каталог. Ленинград 1973. pp.xxv.350. [777.]*

4. Writers

Firdausi

FIRDAUSI celebration, 935–1935. Addresses. ... A bibliography of the principal manuscripts and printed editions of the Shāh-nāmah in certain leading public libraries of the world. Edited by David Eugene Smith. New York 1936. pp.xiii. 138. [750.]

IRAJ AFSHAR, Bibliography on Firdowsī. Publications of Anjuman-e athare melli. Tehran 1968. pp.231. [1258.]

Hafiz

HENRI BROMS, Towards a Ḥāfiz bibliography. Demavend: Publication of the Finland–Iran society (no.2): Helsinki [1969.] pp.42. [321.]*

Hidayat, Sadik

D. S. KOMISSAROV and A. Z. ROZENFELD, Садек Хедаят. Всесоюзная государственная библиотека иностранной литературы: Писатели зарубежных стран: Москва 1958. pp.44. [200.]

Hikmet, Nazuim

A. K. SVERCHEVSKAYA, Назым Хикмет. Всесоюзная государственная библиотека иностранной литературы: Писатели зарубежных стран: Москва 1962. pp. 120. [1069.]

Iqbal

ABDUL R. GHANI and KHWAJA NUR ILAHI, Bibliography of Iqbal. Lahore [1954?]. pp.vii.16. [300.]

Omar Khayyām

AMBROSE G[EORGE] POTTER, A bibliography of printed editions of the quatrains of Omar Khayyám in foreign languages. Omar Khayyám club of America: [s.l.] 1923. pp.[20]. [200.]
225 copies privately printed; interleaved.

AMBROSE GEORGE POTTER, A bibliography of the Rubáiyát of Omar Khayyám. 1929. pp.xv.314. [1400.]
300 copies printed.

Rudaki

R. O. TAL'MAN, A. YUNUSOV, Рудаки (указатель литературы). Душанбе 1965. pp.218. [1235.]

Sa'di

HENRI MASSÉ, Bibliographie de Saadi. Université d'Alger: Faculté des lettres: Paris 1919. pp.[iii].lx. [600.]

TURKEY. TURKS

i. *Bibliography*
ii. *General*
iii. *Topography*
iv. *Cyprus*
v. *Periodicals*
vi. *Academic writings*
vii. *Subjects*
viii. *Persons*
ix. *Turkish languages*
x. *Turkish literature*

i. Bibliography

JOHN KINGSLEY BIRGE, A guide to turkish area study. Committee on near eastern studies: American council of learned societies: Washington 1949. pp.xii.240. [587.]

FILIZ BAŞBUĞOĞLU, LÂMIA ACAR and NECDET OK, 1928–1965 yılları arasında Türkiye de basılmış bibliografyaların bibliyografyası. Unesco Türkiye millî komisyonu yayınları: Ankara 1966. pp.270. [482.]

JAN W. WERYHO, Guide to turkish sources. The library: Institute of islamic studies: McGill university: Montreal 1973. pp.24. [142.]*

ii. General

GEORGES BENGESCO, Essai d'une notice bibliographique sur la question d'orient. Orient européen, 1821–1897. Bruxelles &c. 1897. pp.xiii.329. [2150.]
limited to works published in France and Belgium.

N[IKOLAI] V. MIKHOV, Библиография на Турция, България и Македония (малка бѣлѣжка). София 1908. pp.22. [500.]
a preliminary list.

G[ASTON] AUBOYNEAU and A[NDRÉ] FEVRET, Essai de bibliographie pour servir à l'histoire de l'empire Ottoman. ... Fascicule 1. Religion.—Moeurs et coutumes. 1911. pp.[vi].85. [706.]
no more published.

N V. MIKHOV, Библиографски източници за историята на Турция и България. Българска академия на наукитѣ: София 1914–1934. pp. 119+133+viii.166+xv.224. [2500.]

FRITZ REGEL, Die deutsche forschung in türkisch Vorderasien. [Länder und völker der Türkei (no.7):] Leipzig 1915. pp.48. [500.]

N. V. MIKHOV, Населението на Турция и България прѣзъ XVIII и XIX в. Библиографско-статистични изслѣдвания. Българска академия на наукитѣ: София 1915–1935. pp. [iii].xviii.483+xv.382+xv.486+xv.557. [4000.]

FRANZ BABINGER, Die geschichtschreiber der Osmanen und ihre werke. Leipzig 1927. pp.viii. 477. [2500.]

J. DENY, Sommaire des archives turques du Caire. Société royale de géographie d'Égypte: Publications spéciales: [Cairo] 1930. pp.iii–viii. 638. [100,000.]

ROBERT JOSEPH KERNER, Social sciences in the Balkans and in Turkey. A survey of resources for study and research. Berkeley, Cal. 1930. pp.137. [500.]

THE TURKISH republic: a bibliographical list. Library of Congress: Washington 1931. pp.47. [664.]*

ERNEST E. HIRSCH, Turk hukuk nesriyati bibliyografyası 1934–1940. Istanbul 1931. pp.860–992. [1699.]

AKDES NIMET KURAT, Ortazaman tarihi için kısa bir bibliyografya. Istanbul 1934. pp.viii.72. [650.]

L[ÁSZLÓ] RÁSONYI, Ungarische bibliographie der Türkologie und der orientalisch-ungarischen beziehungen 1926–1934. Kőrösi Csoma archivum (no.1): Budapest 1935. pp.78. [750.]

A[LLEN] [BANKS] HINDS, Descriptive list of state papers, foreign: Turkey (S.P. 97). Public record office: 1937. ff.i.85. [2000.]*

NICOLAS V. MICHOFF [NICOLA V. MIKHOV], Bibliographie des articles allemands, anglais, français et italiens sur la Turquie et la Bulgarie. Académie bulgare des sciences: Sofia 1938. pp.xv.688. [10,044.]

A[KDES] N[IMET] KURAT and K[ARL] V[ILHELM] ZETTERSTEEN, Türkische urkunden herausgegeben und übersetzt. Monografier utgivna av k. humanistiska vetenskaps-samfundet i Uppsala (1): Uppsala, Leipzig 1938. pp.59. [13.]

TOPKAPI sarayi müzesi arşivi kilavuzu. Istanbul 1938–40. ff.[iii].pp.xi.96. [17]+97–192. [28]. [large number.]

GLISHA ELEZOVIĆ, Турски споменици. Српска крале вская академија. Зборник за источњачку историску и кюижевну грађу (1, 1): Београд 1940–52. pp.xxiv.1204+xi.515. [404.]

L. F. RUSHBROOK WILLIAMS, Turkey. National book council: Book list (no.174): 1941. pp.[2]. [40.]

SELÇUK [T.] TRAK, Türkiyeye ait coğrafi eserler genel bibliöğrafyası. Dil ve Tarih Coğrafya fakültesi: Coğrafya enstitüsü: Neşriyeti (no.1): Ankara 1942. pp.274. [2500.]

TURKEY: a selected list of recent references. Library of Congress: Washington 1943: ff.11. [120.]*

GRACE HADLEY FULLER, Turkey. A selected list of references. Compiled ... under the direction of Florence S[elma] Hellman. Library of Congress: Division of bibliography: Washington 1943. pp.[iv].114. [916.]*
reissued in 1944 by the renamed General reference and bibliography division, without Florence Hellman's name.

HERBERT MELZIG, Yeni Türkiyenin siyasî bibliöğrafyası. Bibliographie universelle de la Turquie nouvelle. Istanbul 1944. pp.223. [697.]

K[ARL] V[ILHELM] ZETTERSTÉEN, Türkische, tatarische und persische urkunden im Schwedischen reichsarchiv verzeichnet und beschrieben. Uppsala 1945. pp.xvi.132. [218.]

ADNAN ÖTÜKEN, Seçme eserler bibliografyası. (Radyoda kitap saati) 1942–1945. I. İstanbul 1946. pp.xxxvii.155. [200.]

ÖĞRETIM üyeleri ve yardımcılarının yayınları, 1933–1947. Istanbul üniversitesi: Yayınları (no. 354 = Hukuk fakültesi, no.82): İstanbul 1948. pp.viii.371. [1099.]

ZEKI VELIDI TOGAN, Tarihde usul. Tarih araştırmaları (no.1). Istanbul üniversitesi edebiyat fakültesi yayınlarından (no.499): Istanbul 1950. pp.xxxi.374. [653.]

GLIŠA ELEZOVIĆ, Iz carigradskih turskih arhiva mühimme defteri. Les archives turques de Constantinople mühimme defteri. Zbornik za istočnjačku istorisku i književnu grahtu: Recueil de matériaux d'histoire de littérature orientale. Istoriski institut (krjiga 1): Beograd 1951. pp.579. [1971.]

LAWRENCE S[IDNEY] THOMPSON, Basic turkish reference books. University of Kentucky: Margaret I. King library: Occasional contributions: [Lexington 1952]. ff.[12]. [75.]*

ENVER KORAY, Türkiye tarih yayınları bibliyoğrafyası, 1729–1950. Ankara 1952. pp.xii.548. [4123.]

— — 2. basım. ... 1729–1955. Istanbul 1959. pp.xv.680. [4791.]
— — ... 1955–1968. 1971. pp.570.ii. [2474.]

TÜRKER ACAROĞLU, Essai de documentation analytique ... de documents en langue française relatifs aux Turcs et à la Turquie surtout juridique, économique et sociale. Institut national des techniques de la documentation: [1952.] pp.x.234. [1923.]*

YASAR KARAYALÇIN, Borçlar-ticaret ve banka hukuku bibliyografyasi (1928–1955). Bibliographie concernant le droit des obligations, le droit commercial et le droit bancaire. Banka ve ticaret hukuku araştırma enstitüsü (yayin no.1): Ankara 1956. pp.xxxi.322. [4104.]

YASAR KARAYALÇIN, Hukuk ve ekonomi dergiler üzerine bir bibliyografya denemesi. Müşterek yayınlar serisi (no.2): Ankara 1956. pp.83. [157.]

MIDHAT SERTOĞLU, Muhteva bakımından Başvekâlet arşivi. Ankara üniversitesi dil ve tarih coğrafya fakültesi yayınları (no.103): Ankara 1955. pp.xv.90. [large number.]

MOSTRA firmani imperiali ottomani alla serenissima. Catalogo. Archivio di stato: Venezia 1956. pp.10. [43.]

ALEXANDER NOVOTNY, Österreich, die Turkei und das Balkanproblem im jahre des Berliner kongresses, Kommission für neuere geschichte Österreichs: Veröffentlichungen (no.44): 1957. pp.376. [2000.]

ALBERT LEE STURM [and others], Bibliography on public administration in Turkey, 1928–1957, selective and annotated. University of Ankara: Faculty of political sciences [&c.]: Ankara 1959. pp.x.224.

JAMES REYNOLD VON REINHOLD JAMESSON, A selected, annotated bibliography of basic books and monographs in english on modern Turkey. Revised edition. Türk-amerikan eğitim derneği: Ankara 1959. ff.9.*

RIDRAN BÜLENT ERCIYEŞ, Türk hukuk bibliografyası 1955–1957. Müşterek yayınlar serisi (no.10): Ankara 1959. pp.[vii].355. [4180.]

MUHARREM D. MERCANLIGIL, Eski harflerle basılmış türkçe tarih kitapları. Ankara 1959. pp.36. [207.]

İSMAİL ARAR, Atatürk, Kurtulus savaşı, devrimler ve cumhuriyet tarihi ile ilgili kitaplar. Istanbul 1960. pp.80. [1130.]

FERIT H. SAYMEN, Türk hukuk kroniği 1955–1958. Idaresinde hazırlayan Server Tanilli. Istanbul üniversitesi yayınlarından (no.870). Hukuk fakültesi (no.181): Istanbul 1960. pp.xv. 379. [5605.]

— — 1953–1954. Idaresinde hazırlayanlar: Server Tanilli and Necip Kocayusufpaşaoğlu. Istanbul üniversitesi yayınlarından (no.659): Hukuk fakültesi (no.135): Istanbul 1956. pp.xii. 147. [1772.]

[GYÖRGY] HAZAI, Sovietico-Turcica, Beiträge zur bibliographie der türkischen sprachwissenschaft in russischer sprache in der Sowjetunion, 1917–1957. [Translated by A. T. Varga]. Bibliotheca orientalis hungarica (vol.ix): Budapest 1960. pp.319. [2749.]

A. K. SVERCHEVSKAYA and T. P. CHERMAN, Библиография Турции. Академия наук СССР: Институт востоковедения: Москва.
1713–1917. 1961. pp.268. [5116.]
1917–1958. 1959. pp.191. [3362.]

CARL GÖLLNER, Turcica. Die europäischen Türkendrucke des xvi. jahrhunderts. Bibliotheca bibliographica aureliana (xxiii): Bucureşti, Berlin (Baden-Baden) 1961–8. pp.464+807. [2463.]

ROBERT MANTRAN, Inventaire des documents d'archives turcs du Dar el-bey (Tunis). Université de Tunis: Publications de la Faculté des lettres: 5e série, Sources de l'histoire tunisienne (vol. no.1), Paris 1961, pp.xliv.135 [1000.]

Турски извори за ајдутството и арамиството во македонија (1650–1700). Sources turques pour le mouvement des haïdouques en Macédoine (1650–1700). Institut de l'histoire nationale. Skopje 1961. pp.140. [130.]

YASAR KARAYALÇIN, Borçlar-ticaret ve banka hukuku bibliyografyası (1956–1960). Bibliographie concernant le droit des obligations, le droit commercial et le droit bancaire. Banka ve ticaret hukuku araştırma enstitüsü (yayın nu.38): Ankara 1962. pp.xxii.187. [2047.]

ESKİ harfli türkçe süreli yayınlar toplu kataloğu (muvakkat basım): Millî kütüphane ile Ankara ve İstanbul kütüphanelerinde bulunan eski harfli türkçe gazete ve dergilerin, ayrıca diğer periyodiklerin biblioyografik künyeler. Milli kütüphane yayınları: Ankara 1963. ff.[374]. [1807.]

METODIJA SOKOLOSKI [and others], edd. Турски документи за историјата македонскиот народ. Documents turcs sur l'histoire du peuple macédonien. Скопје 1963–9. pp.lv.167, facs. 1–231+ lxiii. 196, facs.287+lxxxix.244, facs. 283. [801.]

KĂNCHO VASILEV and KIRILA VĂZVĂZOVA-KARATEODOROVA, edd. Обзор на архивите фондов, колекции и единични постъпления, съхранявани в Български исторически архив. Народна библиотека "Васил Коларов". Български исторически архив. София 1963–70. pp.250+246+228. [177 fonds.]

BERNA MORAN, Türklerle ilgili ingilizce yayınlar bibliyografyası. Onbeşinci yüzyıldan onsekizinci yüzyıla kadar. İstanbul üniversitesi edebiyat fakültesi yayınlarından (no.1050). İstanbul 1964. pp.vi.176. [302.]

PAUL MORAUX, Catalogue des manuscrits grecs (fonds du Syllogos). Bibliothèque de la Société turque d'histoire: Türk tarih kurumu yayınlarından (xii. serie—no.4): Ankara 1964. pp.xxiv.267. [183.]

STANFORD J. SHAW, Bibliography of ottoman history [Cambridge, Mass.? 1964?] ff.96. [1192.]*

STANFORD J. SHAW, Materials for a bibliography of the Balkans from the ottoman conquest to the start of the nineteenth century. [Cambridge, Mass.? 1964] ff.[34.]

MUZAFFER GÖKMAN, Atatürk ve devrimleri bibliografyası. Ankara 1967. pp.144. [926.]

BIBLIOGRAPHIE d'études balkaniques 1966. Sous la direction de N. Todorov, K. Georgiev et V. Traikov. Académie bulgare des sciences: Institut d'études balkaniques: Centre international de recherches scientifiques et de documentation: Sofia 1968. pp.348. [1951.]

A. GÜNDÜZ ÖKÇÜN, A guide to turkish treaties (1920–1964). Publication of the Faculty of political science (no.201–183) and of the Institute of international relations (no.17), University of Ankara. Ankara 1966. pp.xii.248. [1250.]

A[KHMET] KH[ALILOVICH] RAFIKOV, Историческая литература на турецком языке, хранящаяся в библиотеках Ленинграда. Сводный аннотированный каталог 1729–1963. Академия наук СССР: Ленинград 1968. pp.266. [1396.]

A. RİZA ATAY and SAMİ N. ÖZERDİM, Varlık yayınları bibliyografyası. Büyük cep kitapları (268): İstanbul 1968. pp.155. [1346.]

METİN TAMKOÇ, A bibliography on the foreign relations of the republic of Turkey, 1919–1967, and brief biographies of turkish statesmen. Middle east technical university: Faculty of administrative sciences: Publication (no.11): Ankara 1968. pp.xviii.248. [3000.]

BRIAN W. BEELEY, Köysel Türkiye bibliyografyasi. Hacettepe üniversitesi nüfüs etütleri ensitüsü: 1969. pp.iii.120. [1250.]
— — Rural Turkey: a bibliographic introduction. Hacettepe university publications (no.10): Ankara 1969. pp.iii.120. [1300.]

İSMET BINARK, Türk-Islâm kültür ve medeniyeti tarihi konularında Millî kütüphane'de mevcut yabancı dil, eski harfli türkçe ve türkçe eserlere ait bir bibliyografya denemesi. Ankara 1969. pp.viii. 18. [100.]

İSMET BINARK, Türk sefer ve zaferleri bibli-yografyası (izahlı). Milli kütüphaneye yardım derneği yayımları (1): Ankara 1969. pp.xv.234. [585.]

BÜLENT HABORA, Yasak kitaplar. Habora kitavevi yayınları: İstanbul 1969. pp.129. [large number.]

PETER T. SUZUKI, Social change in Turkey since 1950; a bibliography of 866 publications. University of Maryland: European division: [College Park] 1969. pp.vi.108. [866.]*

TEOMAN AKÜNAL and KÖKSAL BAYRAKTAR, Türk hukuk bibliyografyası 1963-1964-1965. İstanbul üniversitesi yayınları (no.1518): Hukuk fakültesi yayınları (no.332): İstanbul 1970. pp.xi.299. [3239.]

ÖMER LUTFÎ BARKAN and EKREM HAKKI AYVERDİ, İstanbul vakıfları tahrîr defteri 953 (1546) târîhli. İstanbul Fetih cemiyeti: İstanbul enstitüsü: İstanbul 1970. pp.xxxix.504. [2515.]

KLAUS SCHWARZ, Osmanische sultansurkunden des Sinaiklosters in türkischer sprache. Islam-kundliche untersuchungen (band 7): Freiburg im Breisgau 1970. pp.[vi].218. [255.]

PETER SUZUKI, French, german and swiss university dissertations on twentieth century Turkey: a bibliography of 593 titles, with english translations. Wiesbaden 1970. pp.v.138. [593.]

MARIA JOVANIĆ, ed., Historiographie de Macé-donie (1945-1970). Institut de l'histoire nationale: Skopje 1970-2. pp.   +561. [3633.]

NELI IVANOVA BOSTASHVILI, Библиография Турции (история). Тбилиси 1971. pp.290. [2045.]

entries in russian and georgian.

[MÜJGÂN CUNBUR and İSMET BİNARK], Selçuklu tarihi, Alparslan ve Malazgirt bibliyografyası. Kültür bakanlığı: Millî kütüphane yayınları (1): Ankara 1971. pp.xix.178. [1426.]

TÜRKIYEDE basılmış farsça eserler, çerinler ve Iran'la ilgili yayınlar bibliyografyası. 1971. pp.108.

BASIN yayın bibliyografyası. Milli kütüphane: Ankara 1972. pp.99.

YAŞAR KARAYALCIN and A. MUMCU, Türk hukuk bibliyografyası. Türk harflerinin kabulüne kadar yayınlanmış kitap ve makaleler. Banka ve ticaret hukuku araştırma enstitüsü: Ankara 1972. pp.xii. 355. [4306.]

HANS-JÜRGEN KORNRUMPF, Osmanische biblio-graphie mit besonderer berücksichtigung der Türkei in Europa. Handbuch der orientalistik (l.abt.): Der nahe und mittlere Osten: Ergän-zungsband (viii): Leiden, Köln 1973. pp.xxiv. 1378. [7500.]

iii. Topography

Black sea

SAVA N. IVANOV, Библиографиа за Черно море и карйбрѣжията му. Черноморски научен институт: Варна 1940. pp.268. [3515.]

E[UGÈNE] BELIN DE BALLU, L'histoire des colonies grecques du littoral nord de la mer Noire. Biblio-graphie annotée des ouvrages et articles publiés en U. R. S. S. de 1940 à 1957. 1960. pp.[ii].vi.165. [656.]*

MIHAI BĂCESCU, Bibliographie roumaine de la Mer noire. Bucarest 1965. pp.122. [1200.]

P. N. LAKING, Bibliography of scientific litera-ture on the Black Sea. Technical report: Woods Hole oceanographic institution (70-32). 1970. pp.280.

Dardanelles

BRIEF list of references on the attitude of the United States toward the neutrality of the Dar-danelles. Library of Congress: Washington 1923. ff.2. [29.]*

Istambul

V. GRUMEL, Les regestes des actes du patriarcat de Constantinople. Institut d'études byzantines des Augustins de l'Assomption: Le patriarcat byzantin (ser.1): [Constantinople].
1. Les actes des patriarches.
    i. Les regestes de 381 à 715. 1932. pp.xxxv. 131. [324.]
    ii. Les regestes de 715 à 1043. 1936. pp.xxiii. 267. [531.]
    iii. Les registes de 1043 à 1206. 1947. pp.xxiv. 246. [359.]
no more published.

Konya

MUZAFFER ERDOĞAN, İzahli Konya bibliyo-grafyası. Istanbul 1952. pp.99.xvi. [1000.]

Trabzon

ÖMER AKBULUT, Trabzon meşhurları bibliyo-grafyası: edebiyatta, san'atta, ilimde, politikada ve her sahada yetişmis Trabzonluların hayatı ve eserleri. Ankara 1970. pp.96. [77 writers.]

iv. Cyprus

CLAUDE DELAVAL COBHAM, An attempt at a bibliography of Cyprus. Nicosia 1886. pp.12. [152.]
—— New [sixth] edition. 1929. pp.[vii].76. [1830.]

MEMORANDA of books printed and registered [printed or lithographed] in Cyprus. ... (Published under the provisions of clause 6 of law no.II. of 1887 [section 23 of law no.26 of 1934]). Nicosia.

    1891. single leaf. [6.]
    1892. ff.[4]. [31.]
    1893. ff.[4]. [21.]
    1894. pp.[4]. [16.]
    1895. pp.[5]. [23.]
    1896. pp.[4]. [23.]
    1897. pp.[4]. [16.]
    1898. pp.[4]. [24.]
    1899. pp.[3]. [21.]
    1900. pp.[4]. [22.]
    1901. pp.[3]. [15.]
    1902. pp.[5]. [31.]
    1903. pp.[4]. [24.]
    1904. pp.[4]. [27.]
    1905. pp.[4]. [19.]
    1906. pp.[4]. [24.]
    1907. pp.[4]. [33.]
    1908. pp.[13]. [49.]
    1909. pp.[4]. [37.]
    1910. pp.[3]. [23.]
    1911. pp.[4]. [27.]
    1912. pp.[4]. [37.]
    1913. pp.[3]. [25.]
    1914. pp.[3]. [26.]
    1915. pp.[3]. [16.]
    1916. pp.[3]. [15.]
    1917. pp.[3]. [21.]
    1918. pp.[3]. [36.]
    1919. pp.[3]. [19.]
    1920. single leaf. [15.]
    1921. pp.[3]. [26.]
    1922. pp.[3]. [29.]
    1923. pp.[3]. [24.]
    1924. pp.[3]. [16.]
    1925. pp.[3]. [16.]
    1926. pp.[3]. [19.]
    1927. pp.[3]. [19.]
    1928. pp.[3]. [16.]
    1929. ff.[12]. [120.]
    1930. ff.[8]. [90.]
    1931. ff.[11]. [123.]
    1932. ff.[5]. [72.]
    1933. pp.[28]. [140.]
    1934.
    1935. pp.[18]. [94.]
    1936. pp.[14]. [99.]
    1937. ff.[5]. [101.]
    1938. ff.[6]. [97.]
    1939. ff.[5]. [105.]

in progress; earlier issues(for 1887–1890, 13 titles) form part of the issues for 10 January 1890 and 6 February 1891 of The Cyprus gazette.

INDEX to the statute law of Cyprus since the english occupation, including all ordinances and laws and orders of the queen or king in council

passed or made since the 12th of July, 1878, which were in force on the 1st of January, 1903. 1903. pp.40. [2000.]

BENJAMIN DICKINSON, A list of the orders of his majesty in council, and the subsidiary legislation thereunder, the local orders of his excellency the Governor in council, the orders of his excellency the Governor made under powers conferred by local legislation, and notifications made with the authority of the government of Cyprus, which are of a non-recurring character. Nicosia 1929. pp.[ii]. 32. [1000.]

—— [another edition], A list of laws enacted between 1st January 1924, and 31st December 1932, and a list of the orders [&c.]. Compiled by M. Shemri. 1933. pp.[iii].46. [2500.]

——— 1924–1936. 1937. pp.[iii].74. [4000.]

K. P. CHATZEIONNES, Βιβλιογραφια της κυπριακης λαογραφιαςκαι γλωσσολογιας. Λευκωσια 1933.pp.[ii].37.[350.]

NEOCLES G. KURIAZES, Κυπριακη βιβλιογραφια. Λαρνακι 1935 [1936].pp.343.[5000.]

EXHIBITION of books from the Louki Pierides library donated by mr. Zeno D. Pierides. Government of Cyprus: Department of antiquities: [Nicosia 1946]. pp.8. [50.]

KOSTAS D. STEPHANOU, Κυπρίακη βιβλιογραφια. Βιβλιογραφικὸν δελτίον. Λευκωσια.

    1960–1961. pp.377–362. [500.]
    1962. pp.17. [340.]
    1963. pp.15. [300.]
    1964.
    1965. pp.13.
    1966. pp.18.

ISMET PARMAKSIZOĞLU, Kıbrıs sultan ikinci Mahmud kütüphanesi. Türk kütüphaneciler derneği yayınları: Ankara 1964. pp.42. [99.]

PRICE list of publications for sale at the Government printing office, Nicosia, Cyprus. January 1970 &c.
in progress.

v. *Periodicals*

BIBLIYOĞRAFYA. Türkiyede çıkan kitap gazete ve mecmualardan bahsetmek üzere Maarif vekâleti millî talim ve terbiye tarafından çıkarılır neşriyat bültenidir. nos.1–14. 1928–33.
no more published?

İSMAIL HAKKI TEVFIK, Ankara vilâyeti gazete ve mecmualari, 1-9-1933 e kadar çikanlar. Filibe 1935. pp.93. [110.]

BAŞVEKÂLET. Matbuat umum müdürlüğü. Basın ve yayın umum müdürlüğü yayınlarından (no.6): [Ankara].

i.

ii.

[continued as:]
Türkiyede çıkmakta bulunan gazete ve mecmualar.

iii. 1943. pp.[xi].302.viii. [302.]

iv. 1944. pp.[xii].336.xvi. [336.]

FERİDUN FAZIL TÜLBENTÇİ, Gazeteler ve mecmualar 29 ikteşrin 1923–31 ilkkânun 1940. Cumhuriyetten sonra çıkan: [Ankara?] 1941. pp.vii.132. [1558.]

TÜRKIYE makaleler bibliyografyasi. Bibliographie des articles parus dans les périodiques turcs. Millî kütüphane: Istanbul.

1952. pp.[ii].124.135.157.119.138.60. [4640.]

1953. pp.130.131.113.163.53. [3453.]

1954. pp.155.201.133.157.36. [4445.]

1955. pp.xvi.431. [4335.]

1956. pp.[i].xiv.192.108.26. [2023.]

1957. pp.xvi.126+xiv.74+xiv.98+xiv.94. 30. [4012.]

1958. pp.xiii.89+xiii.70+xiii.77+xiv.148. 31. [3987.]

1959. pp.xviii.162+xix.159+xvii.109+ xviii.131.42. [5996.]

1960. pp.xviii.164+xvii.114+xix.147+xvii. 109.39 [5658.]

1961. pp.xvii.99 + xvi.104 + xvi.101 + xvii.144.35. [4633.]

1962. pp.xvi.106+xvi.101+xv.104+xvi. 113.31. [4425.]

1963. pp.xv.80+xvi.101+xvi.87+xvii.134. 34. [4062.]

1964. pp.xviii.182+xvi.126+xvi.96+xvii. 121.46. [6769.]

1965. pp.xx.219.+xviii.103+xx.141+xx. 174.55. [7752.]

1966. pp.xxiii.332+xx.121+xx.148+xix. 139.61. [9147.]

1967. pp.xx.192+xix.184+xvii.136+xviii. 160.56. [8318.]

1968. pp.xxiii.390+xxi.212+xix.122+xxi. 211.77. [11,375.]

1969. pp.xx.197+xxiv.203+xxiii.280+ xxiv.237.72. [9932.]

1970. pp.xxiv.181+xxiv.164+xxii.248+ xx.194.61. [7788.]

1971. pp.xvi.205+xxiii.185+xx.207+xx. 161.58. [7251.]

1972. pp.xxiii.270+xxi.232+xxii.238+ xxiii.318. [9844.]

1973. pp.xvi.184+
in progress.

CAVIT ORHAN TÜTENGIL, Diyarbakır basın tarihi üzerine notlar. Gazetelerle dergiler (1869–

1953). Üniversite: Yayınlarından (no.596): İstambul 1954. pp.31. [39.]

1957 yılına kadar Millî kütüphane'ye girmiş arap harfli türkçe süreli yayınların kataloğu. Ankara 1957. ff.[ii].71. [700.]*

MEHMET ERÖZ, İktisat fakültesi mecmuası 1940–1960 içindeki araştırmaları, çevirmeler ve muhtelif yazılar bibliyografyası. Türkiye harsî ve içtimaî araştırmaları derneği (seri A, sayı 36.) İstanbul 1962. pp.22. [396.]

FÜRZAN HUSREV TÖKIN, Basın ansiklopedisi. İstanbul 1963. pp.140. [300.]

TÜRKIYEDE gazeteler—dergiler ve basimevleri. Newspapers—periodicals and printing presses in Turkey. Ministry of tourism and information, Department of archives: Ankara 1964. [1653.]

JALE BAYSAL, Osmanli turklerinin bastıkları kitaplar, Muteferrika'dan birinci meşrutıyete kadar. 1968. pp.88. [large number.]

vi. *Academic writings.*

ADNAN ÖTÜKEN and TÜRKER ACAROĞLU, Istanbul üniversitesi yayımları biblyografyası, 1933–1945. Ankara 1947. pp.446. [616.]

CAN OKTAY, Ankara üniversitesi dil ve tarih-coğrafya fakültesi yayınları bibliyografyası. 1935–1945. Kütüphane kursu çalışmaları (no.1). Ankara 1946. pp.96. [64.]

ISTANBUL universitesinin (üniversite) Edebiyat fakültesi yayınları katalogu. İstanbul 1950. pp.136.

— 1952. pp.155. [large number.]

EDEBIYAT fakültesi yayınları kataloğu. İstanbul 1952. pp.[iii].155. [1000.]

ANKARA üniversitesi fen fakültesi yayınları kataloğu. İstanbul 1952. pp.[iv].31. [100.]

TÜRKER ACAROGLU, Üniversitesi yayımları bibliyografyası, 1926–1951. Ankara 1952 &c. *in progress.*

ADNAN YEŞILOGLU, Ankara üniversitesi dil ve tarih-coğrafya fakültesi yayınları bibliyografyası 1935–1956. I. Ankara universitesi dil ve tarih-coğrafya fakültesi yayınları (no.123): Ankara 1958. pp.164. [2400.]

ANKARA üniversitesi tıp fakültesi öğretim üyelerinin kitap yayınları. Ankara 1960. pp.16. [125.]
the copy in the Library of Congress contains ms. additions and corrections.

LEMAN BAKLA-ŞENALP, İstanbul üniversitesi yayınları bibliyografyası. İstanbul üniversitesi

rektörlügü (yayın nu. 1156): İstanbul pp.xxi.
328. [1511.]

    1933-1963. 1966. pp.xxi.328. [1511.]
    1964-1965. 1967. pp.xiv.184. [741.]
    1966. 1968. pp.xii.131. [455.]
    1967. 1969. pp.xi.150. [514.]
    1968. 1969. pp.xv.145. [558.]
    1969. 1970. pp.xv.156. [557.]
    1970. 1972. pp.xii.154. [531.]
    1971. 1973. pp.164.

BENAL ACIR, Ankara üniversitesi dil ve tarih-coğrafya fakültesi yayınları bibliyografyası 1935-1966. Dil ve tarih-coğrafya fakültesi yayınları (sayı: 179). Ankara 1968. pp.163. [2500.]

PETER [T.] SUZUKI, French, german and swiss university dissertations on twentieth century Turkey: a bibliography of 593 titles, with english translations. Wiesbaden 1970. pp.v.138. [606]*

vii. Subjects.

Archaeology

HALİL ETEM [EDHEM], İstambulda iki irfan evi. Alman ve Fransız arkeologi enstitüieri ve bunların neşriyatı. İstanbul müzeleri neşriyatı (no.xiv): İstanbul 1937. pp.34. [22.]

ARIF MÜFID MANSEL, Türkiyenin arkeoloji, epi-grafi ve tarihi coğrafyası için bibliografya. Türk tarih kurumu: Yayınlari (12th ser., vol.i): Ankara 1948. pp.xvi.616. [7500.]

Art

FEHMI EDHEM and IVAN STCHOUKINE [IVAN VASILEVICH SHCHUKIN], Les manuscrits orientaux illustrés de la bibliothèque de l'université de Stamboul. Institut français d'archéologie de Stamboul: Mémoires (vol.i): Paris 1933. pp.[iv].68. [48.]

GUSTAV ADOLF DEISSMANN, Forschungen und funde im Serai. Mit einem verzeichnis der nicht-islamischen handschriften im Topkapu Serai zu Istambul. Berlin &c. 1933. pp.xi.144. [135.]
a few manuscripts are in other languages.

SANAT tarihi kürsü ve ensitüsünün öğretim ve araştırma çalışmaları 1943-1962. İstanbul üniversitesi edebiyat fakültesi: İstanbul 1962. pp.118. [672.]

Communism

SALIM ŞEHIDOĞLU, Komünizme ve komünistlere karşı türkçe neşriyat—bibliyografya. Ankara 1967. pp.148. [166.]

Economics

SELIM İLKİN [*and others*], Türkiye ekonomi bibliyografyasi (1950-1965). Orta doğu teknik üniversitesi: Idari ilimler fakültesi: Publication (no.13): Ankara 1969. pp.xxiii.302. [1940.]

FRANK A. STONE, Çağdaş türk eğitim düşüncesine bibliyografik giriş. Modern turkish educational thought; a bibliographic introduction. 1971. pp.51. [500.]

Folk-lore

VEYSEL ARSEVEN, Açıklamalı Türk halk müziği kitap ve makaleler bibliyografyası. Millî folklor enstitüsü yayınları (1): İstanbul 1969. pp.[ix].210. [796.]

TÜRK folklor ve etnografya bibliyografyası. Millî eğitim bakanlığı Millî folklor enstitüsü yayınları (5): Ankara 1971-3. pp.xxvi.521+xvi.124. [6323.]

TÜRKER ACAROĞLU and FITRAT OZAN, Türk halkbilgisi ve halk edebiyatı üzerine seçme yayınlar kaynakçası. Türk dil kurumu yayınları: Ankara 1972. pp.152. [1552.]

Librarianship

MUZAFFER GÖKMAN, Türk kütüphaneciliğinin bibliyografyası (Bir deneme). Türk kütüphaneciler derneği yayınları (4): Ankara 1964. pp.32. [141.]

Medicine

A[HMET] SÜHEYL ÜNVER, Türk tıb tarihi hakkında M. Cevdetin bibliyoğrafısı. [İstanbul] 1937. pp.36.4. [100.]

BEDI N. ŞEHSUVAROĞLU, Basın tarihimizde sihhî mevkuteler. Türkiye harsî ve içtimai araştırmaları derneği (seri A, sayi 39): İstanbul 1962. pp.24. [143.]

AYKUT KAZANCIGIL and S. VURAL, Türk tıp ve tabiî ilimler tarihi bibliyografyası 1923-1973. 1973. pp.169.

Military arts

ASKERÎ nesriyat kataloğu 1923-1939. Erkânı-harbiyei umuniye riyaseti: İstanbul 1939. pp.[ii]. 102.

Mining

MADEN tetkik ve arama enstitüsü dergisi makaleler bibliyografyası, 1936-1958. Ankara 1959. pp.vii.26. [340.]

Numismatics

E. BOSCH, Türkiyenin antik devirdeki meskûkâtına dair bibliografya. Türk tarih kurumu yayınlarından (12th ser., no.2): Ankara 1949. pp.xii.243. [12,500.]

"People's houses"

HASAN TANER, Halkevleri bibliografyası. Ankara 1944. pp.108. [1500.]

Planning

DEVLET plânlama teşkilatı yayınları indeksi. T. C. Başbakanlık devlet plânlama teşkilâtı. Ankara 1965. pp.32. [800.]

Population

BEHİRE BALKAN, Türkiye nüfus bibliyografyası. Kitaplâr: 1928–1967, makaleler 1952–1967. Hacettepe üniversitesi yayınları (no.6). pp.xiv. 245. 1970. [1071.]

BEHİRE BALKAN, Türkiye özetli nüfus bibliyografyası. Cilt: 2. Hacettepe universitesi yayınları (D/16): Hacettepe 1971. pp.vii.328. [182.]

Psychology

BEĞLÂN TOĞROL, Psikoloji bölümü ve tecrübî psikoloji enstitüsü calışmaları bibliyografyası. 1972. pp.112.

Public administration

ALBERT L. STURM and CEMAL MIHÇIOĞLU, Turk âmme idaresi bibliyografyası 1928–1957 seçme ve notlu. Ankara üniversitesi siyasal bilgiler fakültesi idarî ilimler enstitüsü (Fakülte yayın no.87.69, Enstitüsü yayın no.5): Graduate school of public administration and social service, New York university: Ankara 1959. pp.x.224. [1133.]

METİN HEPER, Kısa âmme idaresi bibliyografyası 1958–1966. Ankara üniversitesi siyasal bilgiler fakültesi yayınları (no.214–196): Ankara 1966. pp.xvi.111. [781.]

Religion

ENISE YENER, Türkiye dinler tarihi ve islâm dinine ait bir bibliyografya denemesi (1928–1960.) Ankara üniversitesi İlâhiyat fakültesi yayınlarından (xlvi): Ankara 1963. pp.32. [454.]

Social Sciences

BIBLIOGRAPHY of social science periodicals and monograph series: Turkey, 1950–1962, by Foreign demographic analysis division, Bureau of the census, Foreign social science bibliographies (series P-92, no.14). Washington [1964]. pp.iv.88. [200.]

BÜLENT DAVER and METİN KIRATLI, Siyaset biliminde temel referanslar bibliyoğrafyasi. Ankara üniversitesi Siyasal bilgiler fakültesi yayınları (no.189–171): İdari ilimler enstitüsü yayın (no.15): Ankara 1965. pp.25. [211.]

BÜLENT DÂVER, METİN KIRATLI, ALÂATTIN ŞENEL, Siyaset biliminde seçilmiş eserler bibliyografyası. Ankara üniversitesi siyasal bilgiler fakültesi yayınları (no.208–190). Ankara 1966. pp.iv.78. [1000.]

Sociology

MAHMUT TEZCAN, Türk sosyloji bibliyografyası 1928–1968. Ankara üniversitesi eğitim fakültesi yayınları (6): Eğitim ve toplum araştırmaları enstitüsü yayınları (1): Ankara 1969. pp.xxviii. 1153. [6255.]

Theatre

SEMAHAT TURAN and BEHİRE ABACIOĞLU, Tiyatro bibliyografyası (1928–1959). Ankara üniversitesi dil ve tarih-coğrafya fakültesi: Tiyatro enstitüsü yayınları (no.1): Ankara 1961. pp.v.177. [1271.]

TÜRKÂN POYRAZ and NURNİSA TUĞRUL, Tiyatro bibliyografyası (1859–1928). Millî kütüphane yayınlari: Ankara 1967. pp.xv.288. [2488.]

Trade

TURGUT VAR, Alfabetik işletmecilik bibliyografyası (1938–1968). Orta doğu teknik üniversitesi, Middle east technical university: Faculty of administrative sciences publication (no.15): Ankara 1970. pp.xxiii.471. [6571.]

Veterinary science

NIHAL ERK and FERRUH DİNÇER, Türkiye'de veteriner hekimlik öğretimi ve Ankara üniversitesi veteriner fakültesi tarihi. Ankara üniversitesi veteriner fakültesi yayınları (259): Ankara 1970. pp.xii.308. [4500.]

Women

MÜJGÂN CUNBUR, Türk kadın yazarların eserleri. 'Bibliyografya' (1928–1955). Kadının sosyal hayatını tetkık kurumu yayınları (sayı 3): Ankara 1955. pp.255. [2300.]

NERİMAN DURANOĞLU, Türkiye'de kadınlar hakkında yayınlanmış eserler. 'Bibliyografya'. Bibliographie sur la femme en Turquie. A bibliography of women and feminism in Turkey. Kadının sosyal hayatını tetkik kurumu yayınları (sayi 6): Ankara 1959. pp.142. [523.]

Zoology

WOLFGANG NEU and HANS KUMMER LÖWE, Bibliographie der zoologischen arbeiten über die Türkei und ihre grenzgebiete. Leipzig 1939, pp.xii.62. [1100.]

viii. Persons

Ali, Sabahattin

N. G. KIREEV, Сабахаттин Али. Био-библиографический указатель к 50-летию со дня рождения. Всесоюзная государственная библиотека иностранной литературы: Писатели зарубежных стран: Москва 1957. pp.22.

Kemal Atatürk

HERBERT MELZIG, Atatürk bibliyoğrafyası. 1941. pp.143. [227.]

MUHARREM DOĞDU MERCANLIGİL, Atatürk ve devrim kitapları kataloğu. Bitlis ili kültür ve eğitim derneği yayınlarından (no.1): Ankara 1953. pp.96. [433.]

ORHAN DURUSOY and MUZAFFER GÖKMAN, Atatürk ve devrimleri bibliyografyası. Türkiye iş bankası. Atatürk ve devrim serisi (no.4): Ankara 1957. pp.[iii].144. [926.]

SAMI N. ÖZERDIM, 10 kasım-31 aralık 1938 günlerinde türk basınında Atatürk için yazılmış yazıların bibliyoğrafyası. Türk tarih kurumu yayınlarından (xii seri, no.3): Ankara 1958. pp.xvi.239. [4000.]

MUZAFFER GÖKMAN, Atatürk ve devrimleri tarihi bibliyografyası. Atatürk serisi (no.2): İstanbul 1963. pp.vi.432. [2157.]

M. ORHAN DURUSOY and M. MUZAFFER GÖKMAN, Atatürk ve devrimleri bibliyografyası. Ankara 1967. pp.144. [926.]

ATSIZ, Istanbul kütüphanelerine göre Birgili Mehmed Efendi (929-981 = 1523-1573) bibliyoğrafyası. Süleymaniye kütüphanesi yayınları (1): Istanbul 1966. pp.vii.91. [1167.]

Babinger, Franz Carl Heinrich

[F. BABINGER], Franz Babinger schriftenverzeichnis. Würzburg 1938. pp.[ii].30. [368.] *privately printed.*

[F. BABINGER], Franz Babinger schriftenverzeichnis, 1952-1957. Würzburg 1957. pp.8. [100.] *500 copies printed.*

FRANZ BABINGER schriftenverzeichnis 1910 bis 1961. Südosteuropa (vol.3): München 1962. pp. 51. [500.]

Cevdet, M.

OSMAN ERGIN, Muallim M. Cevdetin hayatı, eserleri ve kütüphanesi. Istanbul 1937. pp.[iv]. 748. [large number.]

Farkas, Gyula

OMELJAN PRITSAK, Julius von Farkas bibliographie. Festgabe zum 60. geburtstag. Wiesbaden 1954. pp.27. [197.]

Fatih

ISTANBUL kütüphanelerinde Fatih'in hususi kütüphanesine ve Fatih çağı müelliflerine ait eserler. İstanbul üniversitesi yayınlarından (no. 549): [Istanbul] 1953. pp.74. [427.]

Findikoğlu

FINDIKOGLU bibliyoğrafyası 1918-1958. İstanbul üniversitesi iktisat fakültesi: İktisat ve içtimaiyat enstitüsü neşriyatından (27): İstanbul 1958. pp.95. [2014.]

Fuzuli, Mehmet

MÜJGÂN CUNBUR, Fuzûlî hakkında bir bibliyografya. Türk kültür eserlei: İstanbul 1956. pp.iv. 129. [250.]

Gökalp, Ziya

CAVIT ORHAN TÜTENGIL, Ziya Gökalp hakkında bir bibliyografya denemesi. Üniversite: İktisat fakültesi: İçtimaiyat enstitüsü neşrıyatından (no. 13): İstanbul [1949]. pp.55. [500.]

ISMET BINARK and NEJAT SEFERCIOGLU, Doğumunun 95. yıldönümü münasebetiyle Ziya Gökalp bibliyoğrafyası. Kitap-makale. Türk kültürünü araştırma enstitüsü, yayınları (38, seri: X, sayı: A1). Ankara 1971. pp.xxviii.200. [1233.]

Guntekin, Resat Nuri

TÜRKÂN POYRAZ and MUAZZEZ ALPBEK, Reşat Nuri Güntekin hayatı ve eserlerinin tam listesi. Ankara 1957. pp.23. [99.]

Gürpinar, Huseyin Rahmi

MUZAFFER GÖKMAN, Hüseyin Rahmi Gürpinar: açıklamalı bibliyografya. Büyük türk yazarları ve şairleri (1, bibliyografya, 1). İstanbul 1966. pp.xv. 249. [691.]

Iorga, Nicolas

VICTOR IANCOULESCO, Bibliographie des travaux de m. Nicolas Iorga. 1933. pp.3-78. [1500.]

Köprülü, Mehmet Fuat

SERIF HULUSI sayman, O. prof. dr. Fuad Köprülü'nün yazıları için bir bibliyografya 1913-1934. İstanbul 1935. pp.[iv].19. [289.]

SERIF HULÛSI, O. prof. dr. Fuat Köprülü'nün yazıları için bir bibliyografya 1912-1940. Istanbul 1940. pp.24. [325.]

SAMI N. ÖZERDİM, Ord. prof. dr. M. Fuad Köprülü bibliografyası 1908-1950. Ankara 1951. pp.[ii].159-250. [1000.]

Mordtman, J. H.

FRANZ BABINGER, J. H. Mordtman zum gedächtnis. Berlin 1933. pp.16. [216.] *largely a bibliography.*

Müftüoğlu, Ahmed Hikmet

ISMET BİNARK and NEJAT SEFERCİOĞLU, Doğumunun 100. cü yıldönümü munasebetiyle Ahmed Hikmet Müftüoğlu bibliyografyası. Millî kütüphane yayınları: Ankara 1970. ff.11. [100.]*

Ozansoy, Faik Ali

ISMET BİNARK and NEJAT SEFERCİOĞLU, Ölümünün 20. yıldönümü munasebetiyle Faik Ali Ozansoy bibliyografyası. Milli kütüphane yayınları: Ankara 1970. pp.11. [100.]*

Radlov, Vasily Vasilevich

[C. SALEMANN], Ко дню семидесятилѣтія Василія Васильевича Радлова. С.-Петербургъ 1907. pp.111. [99.]

Şehsuvaroğlu, Bedi N.

NAZMI ÇAĞAN, Dr. Bedi N. Şehsuvaroğlu biyografi ve bibliyografyası. I.U. Tıp tarihi enstitüsü yayınlarından (sayı: 59). İstanbul 1963. pp.78. [1000.]

Süheyl Unver, A.

OSMAN ERGIN, Professör dr. A. Suheyl Ünver bibliyografyası. Istanbul üniversitesi Tıb tarihi entitüsü (adet: 20). İstanbul 1941. pp.63. [526.]

Tarhan, Abdulhak Hâmid

İSMET BİNARK and NEJAT SEFERCİOĞLU, Ölümünün 34. yıldönümü münasebetiyle Abdulhak Hâmid Tarhan bibliyografyası. Millî kütüphane yayınları: Ankara 1971. ff.35. [225.]*

Vámbéry, Armin

GYÖRGY HAZAI, Ármin Vámbéry, 1831–1913; a biobibliography. Micropublications of the library of the Hungarian academy of sciences: Budapest 1963. pp.30.

Yunus Emre

İSMET BİNARK and NEJAT SEFERCİOĞLU, Yunus Emre hakkinda bir bibliyografya denemesi. Millı kütüphane yardım derneği yayınları (2): Ankara 1970. pp.ix.48. [479.]

ix. Turkish languages

TÜRK dili bibliyoğrafyası. Türk dil kurumu. Istanbul.

    1928–1940. 1941. pp.163. [997.]
    1941. 1942. pp.35. [200.]
    1942. 1943. pp.39. [250.]
    1943. 1945. pp.23. [170.]

DONALD C[ARL EUGENE] SWANSON, A select bibliography of the anatolian languages. Public library: New York 1948. pp.26. [500.]

TÜRK dil kurumu yayınları, 1932–1952. Ankara 1952. pp.87.ii. [750.]
— 1932–1957. 1957. pp.12. [164.]

RUDOLF LOEWENTHAL, The turkic languages and literatures of central Asia. A bibliography. Central asiatic studies (vol.i): 's-Gravenhage 1957. pp.212. [2093.]

a preliminary edition was issued, Washington [1956].

GEORG [GYÖRGY] HAZAI, Sovietico-turcica. Beiträge zur bibliographie der türkischen sprachwissenchaft in russischer sprache in der Sowjetunion 1917–1957. Übersetzt von A[nna] T[álasi]-Varga. Durchgesehen von Cl. [Miklós] Hutterer. Bibliotheca orientalis hungarica (vol.ix): Budapest 1960. pp.328. [2749.]

TÜRK dil kurumu kol çalışmaları (1932–1972). Türk dil kurumu yayınları. Ankara 1972. pp.100. [416.]

x. Turkish literature

1. *Manuscripts*
2. *General*
3. *Translations*

1. Manuscripts

U[LRICH] J[ASPER] SEETZEN, Verzeichniss der für die orientalische sammlung in Gotha zu Damask, Jerusalem u.s.w. angekauften orientalischen manuscripte und gedruckten werke. Leipzig 1810. pp.20.27.40.

J. L. ROUSSEAU, Catalogue d'une collection de cinq cents manuscrits orientaux. Paris 1817. pp.53. [turkish: 66.]

JOSEPHUS DE HAMMER [BARON JOSEPH VON HAMMER-PURGSTALL], Codices arabicos, persicos, turcicos, Bibliothecae caesareo-regio-palatinae vindobonensis. Vindobonae 1820. pp.[ii].68. [618.]

A CATALOGUE of arabic, turkish and persian manuscripts. The private collection of Wm. B. Hodgson. Washington 1830. ff.10. [150.]

[SIR WILLIAM OUSELEY], Catalogue of several hundred manuscript works in various oriental languages. 1831. pp.viii.24. [725.]

HENRICUS ORTHOBIUS [HEINRICH LEBERECHT] FLEISCHER, Catalogus codicum manuscriptorum orientalium Bibliothecae regiae Dresdensis. Accedit Friderici Adolphi Eberti catalogus codicum manuscriptorum orientalium Bibliothecae ducalis Guelferbytanae. Lipsiae 1831. pp.xii.106. [596.]

CATALOGUS librorum manuscriptorum qui in bibliotheca senatoria civitalis Lipsiensis asservantur edidit Aemilius Guilelmus Robertus Naumann. Codices orientalium linguarum descripserunt Henricus Orthobius Fleischer et Franciscus Delitzsch. Grimae 1838. pp.xxiv.562. lvi. [424.]

CODICES arabici (—persici—turcici) vel a christianis scripti vel ad religionem christianam spectantes. Scriptorum veterum nova collectio e vaticanis codicibus edita ab Angelo Maio, tomus IV. Romae 1841. pp.718. [turkish: 64.]

ALBRECHT KRAFFT, Die arabischen, persischen und türkischen handschriften der K. k. orientalischen akademie zu Wien. Wien 1842. pp.xx.208. [1000.]

J. MOHL and P. LACROIX, Catalogue des livres et manuscrits orientaux provenant de la bibliothèque de feu m. J. St. Harriot. Paris 1843.

B[ERNHARD] DORN, Das asiatische museum der Kaiserlichen akademie der wissenschaften zu St. Petersburg. St. Petersburg 1846. pp.xii.776. [large number.]

C. J. TORNBERG, Codices arabici, persici et turcici Bibliothecæ regiæ universitatis upsaliensis. [Upsala] 1849. pp.[ii].xxiv.355. [512.]
— — Fortsetzung. Die arabischen, persischen und türkischen handschriften der Universitätsbibliothek zu Uppsala. Verzeichnet ... von K. V. Zetterstéen. Uppsala 1930–1935. pp.xviii.498 + x.180. [1500.]
also issued as vols.iii–iv of Acta bibliothecae R. universitatis upsaliensis and as vols.xxii and xxviii of Le monde oriental.

A[UGUST] F[ERDINAND MICHAEL] MEHREN, Codices persici, turcici, hindustanici variique alii Bibliothecæ regiæ hafniensis. Hafniæ 1857. pp. v.92. [250.]

COLLECTION de manuscrits arabes, persans et turcs appartenant à m^me la contesse Alix des Granges. 1859. pp.12. [turkish: 76.]

WILHELM PERTSCH, Die orientalischen handschriften der Herzoglichen bibliothek zu Gotha. ... Zweither theil: die türkischen handschriften. Wien 1864. pp.viii.240. [276.]

B[ERNHARD] DORN, Die sammlung von morgenländischen handschriften, welche die Kaiserliche öffentliche bibliothek zu St. Petersburg im jahre 1864 von h^rn v. Chanykov erworben hat. St. Petersburg 1865. pp.[ii].93. [150.]
— — Nachträge. Morgenländische handschriften. 1865. pp.[ii].43. [100.]

GUSTAV FLÜGEL, Die arabischen, persischen und türkischen handschriften der Kaiserlich-königlichen hofbibliothek zu Wien. Wien 1865–1867. pp.x.273 + iv.614 + lxviii.653. [3000.]

J. A. GOBINEAU, Collection d' ouvrages recueillis en Perse sur l'histoire, la poésie, la philosophie,

les sciences occultes, etc. Paris 1870. pp.16. [turkish: 32.]

E[DWARD] H[ENRY] PALMER, A descriptive catalogue of the arabic, persian, and turkish manuscripts in the library of Trinity College, Cambridge. With an appendix containing a catalogue of the hebrew and samaritan mss. in the same library by William Aldis Wright. Cambridge, London 1870. pp.vii.235. [turkish: 15.]

EDWARD REHATSEK, Catalogue raisonné of the arabic, hindostani, persian, and turkish mss. in the Mulla Firuz library. [Bombay] 1873. pp.[iv.]ix. 279. [550.]

E. LEROUX, Catalogue de la bibliothèque orientale de feu m. Belin. Livres sur la Turquie. Textes et manuscrits arabes, turcs et persans. Paris 1878. pp.56.

M. F. DELONCLE, Catalogue des livres orientaux et autres composant la bibliothèque de feu m. Garcin de Tassy, suivi du catalogue des manuscrits hindustanis, persans, arabes, turcs. Paris 1879. pp.viii.272.

S[AMUEL] LANDAUER, Katalog der hebräischen, arabischen, persischen und türkischen handschriften der Kaiserlichen universitäts- und landesbibliothek. Strassburg 1881. pp.[iv].75. [125.]

CATALOGUE of a magnificent collection of manuscripts from Hamilton palace. London 1882.

ALFRED, FREIHERR VON KREMER, Ueber meine sammlung orientalischer handschriften. Wien 1885. pp.78. [212.]

VICTOR ROSEN, Remarques sur les manuscrits orientaux de la collection Marsigli à Bologne, suivies de la liste complète des manuscrits arabes de la même collection. Rome 1885. pp.135. [459.]

M. TH. HOUTSMA, Catalogue d'une collection de manuscrits arabes et turcs appartenant à la maison E. J. Brill à Leide. Leide 1886. pp.158. [791.]

CHARLES RIEU, Catalogue of the turkish manuscripts in the British museum. 1888. pp.xi.345. [750.]

C. SALEMANN and [BARON] V[ICTOR ROMANOVICH] ROSEN, Indices alphabetici codicum manu scriptorum persicorum, turcicorum, arabicorum qui in bibliotheca Imperialis literarum universitatis petropolitanae adservantur. Petropoli 1888. pp.50. [1500.]
— — Supplementum, confecit A. Romaskewicz. Leningrad 1925. pp.[ii].19. [300.]

WILHELM PERTSCH, Verzeichniss der türkischen handschriften. Königliche bibliothek: Handschriften-verzeichnisse (vol.vi): Berlin 1889. pp. xi.583. [1000.]

[CARL] ED[UARD] SACHAU and HERMANN ETHÉ, Catalogue of the persian, turkish, hindûstânî, and pushtû manuscripts. Catalogi codd. mss. Bibliothecae bodleianae pars XIII: Oxford 1889–1930. pp.xii.coll.1150+pp.[v].coll.1157–1766. [3000.]

E. KAL', Персидскія, арабскія и тюркскія рукописи Туркестанской публичной библіотеки. Ташкентъ 1889. pp.79. [100.]

E[DMOND] FAGNAN, Catalogue général des manuscrits des bibliothèques publiques de France—Départements, t.xviii: Alger. Paris 1893. pp.680. [1987.]

W. D. SMIRNOV [VASILY DMITRIEVICH SMIRNOV], Manuscrits turcs de l'Institut des langues orientales. Institut des langues orientales: Collections scientifiques (vol.viii): Saint-Pétersbourg 1897. pp.[x].216. [150.]

[JAMES LUDOVIC LINDSAY, EARL OF CRAWFORD AND BALCARRES and MICHAEL KERNEY], Handlist of oriental manuscripts, arabic, persian, turkish. Bibliotheca lindesiana: 1898. pp.xliii.268. [2500.] *100 copies privately printed.*

E[DGARD] BLOCHET, Catalogue de la collection de manuscrits orientaux arabes, persans et turcs formée par m. Charles Schefer et acquise par l'état. Bibliothèque nationale: 1900. pp.[iii].v.231. [1000.]

EDWARD G[RANVILLE] BROWNE, A hand-list of the muḥammadan manuscripts, including all those written in the arabic character, preserved in the library of the university. Cambridge 1900. pp.xviii.440. [1541.]
—— A supplementary hand-list. 1922. pp.xii. 348. [1250.]
—— A second supplementary hand-list of the muḥammadan manuscripts in the university & colleges of Cambridge. By A[rthur] J[ohn] Arberry. 1952. pp.82. [450.]

CARLO ALFONSO NALLINO, I manoscritti arabi, persiani, siriaci e turchi della Biblioteca nazionale e della r. accademia delle scienze di Torino. Accademia reale delle scienze di Torino: Torino 1900. pp.104. [123.]

C[ARL] BROCKELMANN, Verzeichnis der arabischen, persischen, türkischen und hebräischen handschriften der Stadtbibliothek. Breslau 1903. pp.v.53 [92.]

E[DGARD] BLOCHET, Catalogue des manuscrits arabes, persans et turcs offerts à la Bibliothèque nationale par m. J.-A. Decourdemanche. 1909. pp.[iii].90. [400.]

DUNCAN BLACK MACDONALD, The arabic and turkish manuscripts in the Newberry library. Newberry library: Publications (no.2): Chicago 1912. pp.vi.18. [22.]

A. V. WILLIAMS JACKSON and ABRAHAM YOHANNAN, A catalogue of the collection of persian manuscripts, including also some turkish and arabic, presented to the Metropolitan museum of art, New York, by Alexander Smith Cochran. Columbia university: Indo-iranian series (vol. i): New York 1914. pp.xxv.187. [23.]

ARTHUR CHRISTENSEN and J. ØSTRUP, Description de quelques manuscrits orientaux appartenant à la bibliothèque de l'université de Copenhague. Oversigt over det Kgl. danske vidensakabernes selskabs forhandlinger (1915, 3–4): [Copenhagen] 1915. pp.30. [21.]

E[DGARD] BLOCHET, Inventaire de la collection de manuscrits musulmans de M. Decourdemanche. Extrait du Journal asiatique (septembre–décembre 1916). Paris 1916. pp.112. [254.]

W. RIEDEL, Katalog över Kungl. bibliothekets orientaliska handskrifter. Kungliga biblioteket [Stockholm]: Handlingar: Bilagor (n.s., vol. iii): Uppsala 1923. pp.xi.68. [150.]

A[LEKSANDR] A[LEKSANDROVICH] SEMENOV, Каталог рукописей исторического отдела Бухарской центральной библиотеки. Трудн библиографической комиссии при СНК ТССЯ (вып.2): Ташкент 1925. pp.32. [turkish: 6].

NICHOLAS MARTINOVITCH, A catalogue of turkish and persian manuscripts belonging to Robert Garrett and deposited in the Princeton university library. Princeton 1926. pp.[iv].46. [turkish: 13].

GIUSEPPE GABRIELI, La fondazione Caetani per gli studi musulmani. Notizia della sua istituzione e catalogo dei suoi mss. orientali. Roma 1926. pp.96.6. [300.]

JOSEPH SCHACHT, Aus den bibliotheken von Konstantinopel und Kairo vol.ii: Aus kairiner bibliotheken; vol.iii: Aus orientalischen bibliotheken. Preussische akademie der wissenschaften: Abhandlungen: Philosophisch–historische klasse (1928, no.8; 1929, no.6; 1931, no.1): Berlin 1928–1931. pp.76+36+57. [1250.]

K. I. CHAYKIN, Восточные рукописи. Персидские, арабские, турецкие. Москва 1931. [turkish: 5]

EDWARD G[RANVILLE] BROWNE, A descriptive catalogue of the oriental manuscripts belonging to the late E. G. Browne. Completed and edited by Reynold A. Nicholson. Cambridge 1932. pp.xxii. 325. [453.]

E[DGARD] BLOCHET, Catalogue des manuscrits turcs. Bibliothèque nationale. Paris 1932–3. pp.viii.402+314. [1815.]

FEHMI EDHEM [KARATAY] and IVAN STCHOUKINE, Les manuscrits orientaux illustrés de la bibliothèque de l'université de Stamboul. Mémoires de l'Institut français d'archéologie de Stamboul (1): 1933. pp.68. [48.]

A[LEKSANDR] A[LEKSANDROVICH] SEMENOV, Описание персидских арабских и турецких рукописей фундаментальной библиотеки Среднеазиатского государственного университета. A descriptive catalogue of the persian, arabic and turkish manuscripts preserved in the library of Middle asiatic state university. Acta universitatatis Asiae mediae (series ii. Orientalia, fasc. 4):Ташкент 1935–56. pp.88+88. [339.]

MOHAMMAD E. MOGHADAM [MUḤAMAD I'TIMĀD MUḰADDAM] and YAḤYA ARMAJĀNĪ, Descriptive catalog of the Garrett collection of persian, turkish and indic manuscripts, including some miniatures, in the Princeton university library.... Under the direction of Philip K[hūrī] Hittī. Princeton oriental texts (vol.6): Princeton 1939. pp.94.x. [191.]

A[LEKSANDR] A[LEKSANDROVICH] SEMENOV, Описание рукописей произведений Навои, хранящихся в Государственной публичной библиотеке УзССР. Ташкент 1940. pp.45. [91.]

FEHIM SPAHO, Arapski, perzijski i turski rukopsi Hrvatskih zemaljskih muzeja u Sarajevu. Sarajevu 1942. pp.ix.107. [203.]

İSTANBUL kütüpaneleri (kitaplıkları) tarih-coğrafya yazmaları katalogları. İstanbul.
    i. Türkçe tarih yazmaları. İstanbul 1943–51. pp.vi.816. [527.]

ION I. NISTOR, Manuscrisele orientale din Biblioteca Academiei române cu inventarul lor. Analele Academiei române: Memoriile secţiunii istorice (seria iii, tomul xxviii, mem.4): Bucureşti 1946. pp.50. [216.]

ISTANBUL kitaplikları (kütüphaneleri) türkçe yazma divanlar kataloğu. Milli eğitim bakanlığı kütüphaneler genel müdürlüğü tasnif komisyonunca hazırlanmıştır. Kütüphaneler katalogları yayınlarından (seri 2, no.4): İstanbul.
    i. xii–xvi. asır.1947. pp.219.xiv. [101.]
    ii. xvii. asır. 1959. pp.220–552. [101.]
    iii. 1965–9. pp.553–1066. [277.]

ISMET PARMAKSIZOĞLU, Manisa genel kütüphanesi tarih-coğrafya yazmaları kataloğu. i. Türkçe yazma tarihler. Kütüphaneler katalogları yayımlarından (seri.3, no.1). İstanbul 1952. pp.48. [64.]

UNE LISTE des manuscrits choisis parmi les bibliothèques de Bursa. Istanbul 1951. pp.80. [816.]

UNE LISTE des manuscrits choisis parmi les bibliothèques de Kayseri, Akşehir, Bor, Gülşehri, Nevşehir, Niğde, Urgüp. İstanbul 1951. pp.25. [201.]

UNE LISTE des manuscrits choisis parmi les bibliothèques de Konya. İstanbul 1957. pp.37. [423.]

UNE LISTE des manuscrits choisis parmi les bibliothèques de Manisa, Akhisar. İstanbul 1951. pp.31. [352.]

ETTORE ROSSI, Elenco dei manoscritti turchi della Biblioteca vaticana: vaticani, barberiniani, borgiani, rossiani, chigiani. Biblioteca apostolica vaticana: Studi e testi (vol.clxxiv): [Rome] 1953. pp.xxii.415. [195.]

ALEKSANDR ALEKSANDROVICH SEMENOV, ed. Собрание восточных рукописей академии наук Узбекской ССР. Академия наук Узбекской ССР. Институт востоведения: Ташкент 1952–71. p.440+590+556+560+544+738+555+799 +600. [6755.]

ZAGORKA JANC, Исламски рукописи из југословенских колекција. Музеj примењене уметности. Београд 1956. pp.50, pls.20. [68.]

AGÂH SIRRI LEVEND, Ġazavāt-nāmeler ve Mihaloğlu 'Ali Bey' in Gazavāt-nāmesi. Türk tarih kurumu yayınlarından (xi. seri, no.8): Ankara 1956. pp.viii.392, pls.117. [350.]

V[LADIMIR FEDEROVICH] MINORSKY, The Chester Beatty library. A catalogue of the turkish manuscripts and miniatures. Dublin 1958. pp.xxxvii. 147. [93.]

CEVDET TÜRKAY, İstanbul kütübhanelerinde osmanlılar devrinde aïd türkçe-arabca-farsça yazma ve basma çoğrafya eserleri bibliyografyası. Maarif vekâleti-bilim eserleri serisi: İstanbul 1958. pp.94. [2000.]

JUSSI ARO, Die arabischen, persischen und türkischen handschriften der universitätsbibliothek. Helsingin Yliopiston kirjaston julkaisuja (vol.28): Helsinki 1959 pp.84. [400.]
    also issued as vol. xxiii, no.4, of Studia orientalia (*Helsinki*).

MUZAFFER GÖKMAN, Istanbul kütüphaneleri ve yazma tıp kitapları. Libraries of Istanbul and their medical manuscripts. İstanbul üniversitesı tıp tarihi enstitüsü neşriyatından (sayı: 56): İstanbul 1959. pp.39. [2796.]

ÖMER NASUHI BILMEN, Büyük tefsir tarihi II (Tabakatül-mufessirîn. Diyanet işleri reisliği yayınları (sayı 39/2): Ankara 1960. pp.480. [335.]

E. KAZHDAROVA, Описание рукописных списков дивана Махтумкули, хранящихся в Ашхабаде. Труды Института литературы им. Махтумкули: Ашхабад 1960.

A. M. MUGINOV [and others], Тюркские рукописи в собрании Института востоковедения АН СССР. Москва 1960. pp.27.

A. M. MUGINOV [and others], Turcic manuscripts in the collection of the Institute of oriental studies of the Academy of sciences of the U.S.S.R. Moscow 1960. pp.31.

KAREL PETRÁČEK, JOZEF BLAŠKOVIĆ, RUDOLF VESELÝ, Arabische, türkische und persische handshcriften der Universitätsbibliothek in Bratislava. Unter der redaktion Jozef Blaškovićs. Bratislava 1961. pp.51. [598.]

Описание рукописей научной библиотеки им. Н.И. Лобачевского. Казань
  i. С. Б. Радзиевская, Фольклор. 1958. pp. 35. [59.]
  iii. Мустафа Нугман, Рукописи Каюма Насыри. 1958. pp.48. [83.]
  v, x. Альберт Фатхи, Рукописи татарских писателей и ученых. 1959–62. pp.64+48. [223.]
  vi. А. Каримуллин, Татарское народное творчество. 1961. pp.35. [66.]
  ix. А. Каримуллин, Тюркское языкознание. 1962. pp.20. [37.]

İSTANBUL kütüphaneleri türkçe hamseler kataloğu. Kütüphaneler katalogları yayımlarından (seri.4, no.1). İstanbul 1961. pp.vii.196. [500.]

FEHMI EDHEM KARATAY, Topkapı saray¹ müzesi kütüphanesi türkçe yazmalar kataloğu. Topkapı sarayı müzesi yayınları (no.11): İstanbul 1961. pp.xv.644+[iv].527. [3088.]

KASIM DOBRAČA, Katalog arapskih, turskih i perzijskih rukopsia. Gazi Husrev-begova biblioteka: Sarajevo 1963– . pp.xxxii.607. ii + . in progress.

S. DE LAUGIER DE BEAURECUEIL, Manuscrits d'Afghanistan. Institut français d'archaéologie orientale du Caire: Recherches d'archéologie, de philologie et d'histoire. (t.xxvi). Le Caire 1964. pp.xxiii.420. [turkish: 5.]

LYUDMILA VASIL'EVNA DMITRIEVA, ABDULLADZHAN MUGINOVICH MUGINOV and SAYFI NIZAMOVICH MURATOV, Описание тюркских рукописей Института народов Азии.
  i. История. Под редакцией А. Н. Кононова. Москва 1965. pp.259. [189.]

ABDÜLBÂKİ GÖLPİNARLI, Mevlânâ Müzesi yazmalar kataloğu. Eski eserler ve müzeler genel müdürlüğü yayınları (seri. III, no.6): Ankara 1967. pp.xv.301+xx.484. [670.]

TADEUSZ MAJDA, Katalog rekopisów tureckich i perskich. Catalogue des manuscrits turcs et persans. Catalogue des manuscris orientaux des collections polonaises (V,2): Zakład orientalistyki: Polskiej akademii nauk: Warsawa 1967. pp.236. [221.]

A. T. TAGIRDZHANOV, Список таджиксих, персидских и тюркских рукописей Восточного отдела Библиотеки ЛГУ (продолжение списков К. Г. Залемана и А. А. Ромаскевича). Москва 1967. pp.19. [253.]

BARBARA FLEMMING (teil ii: MANFRED GÖTZ), Türkische handschriften. Verzeichnis der orientalischen handschriften in Deutschland (band xiii). Wiesbaden 1968. pp.xv.392+xix.484. [1101.]

TZ. A. ABULADZE, R. V. GRAMANIYA and M. G. MAMATZASHVILI, Каталог арабских, тюркских и персидских рукописей Института рукописей им. Кекелидзе (коллекция К).
Catalogue of the arabic, turkish and persian manuscripts in the Kekelidze institute of the manuscripts, Georgian academy of sciences (the K collection). Tbilisi 1969. pp.viii.202. [263.]

ABDOL HOSSEIN HAERI, A catalogue of the manuscripts in the Parliament library (persian & arabic & turkish). Vol.10. part 3. Teheran 1969. pp.2. 1081–1675. [19+3323–3583.]
up to 19 volumes in all, but not all have english title-pages.

2. *General*

CATALOGUS centuriae librorum rarissimorum manuscript. & partim impressorum, arabicorum, persicorum, turcicorum ... qua ... Bibliothecam publicam. Academiæ upsalensis auxit ... Ioan. Gabr. Sparvenfeldius. Upsaliae 1706. pp.[vi].74. [120.]

T[HOMAS] X[AVIER] BIANCHI, Notice sur le premier ouvrage d'anatomie ... suivi du catalogue des livres turcs, arabes et persans imprimés à Constantinople depuis l'introduction de l'imprimerie en 1726–1727 jusqu'en 1820. 1821. pp.[ii]. 40. [68.]
one of the copies in the Bibliothéçue nationale contains a ms. supplement.

MUSTAFA IBN 'ABD ALLAH (ḤĀJJI KHALĪFA or KĀTIB CHELEBĪ), Lexicon bibliographicum et encyclopaedicum ... Ad codicum vindobonensium, parisiensium et berolinensium fidem primum edidit, latine vertit et commentario indicibusque instruxit Gustavus Fluegel. Oriental translation fund: Leipzig 1833–1858. pp.[ii].xxiii.520+[ii]. xii.660+[ii].xx. 648 + [ii].xxvi. 591 + x.661 + viii.680+xiv.1258. [25,000.]

— [Another edition.] Elde mevcut yazma ve basma nushaları ve zeyilleri gözden geçirilerek,

müellifin elyazisiyle olan nüshaya göre fazlaları çıkarılmak, eksikleri tamamlanmak suretiyle Maarif vekilliğinin kararı uzerine ... Serefettin Yaltkaya ile Kilisli Rifat Bilge tarafından hazırlanmıştır. [İstanbul] 1941-3. cols.48.[v].940+941-2058. [35,0000.]
— [Another edition.] 1971-2.
— Kesf-el-zunun zeyli. İzāh al-maknūn fī al-zayli 'alā Kaşf al-ẓunūn 'an asāmī al-kutubī va'l-funūn. Bağdatlı Ismail Paşa. Müellif nüshası esas tutulmak suretiyle tashihleri Diyanet İşleri Baskani ord. prof. Şerefettin Yaltkaya ve muallim Kilisi Rifat Bilge tarafından yapılmıştır. İstanbul 1945. cols. [ii].624.pp.vi+cols.836. [12,000.]
— [Second edition.] 1972. pp.622+732.

[CHRISTIAN MARTIN FRÄHN], Хронологическiй снисокъ ста сочиненiй, преимущественно историческаго и географическаго содержанiя, на арабскомъ, персидскомъ и турецкомъ языкахъ, недостающихъ большею частью въ европейскихъ библiотекахъ. С.-Петербургъ 1834. pp.[ii].24. [120.]
— — [another edition]. Казанъ 1834. pp.[viii]. 24. [120.]

T[HOMAS] X[AVIER] BIANCHI, Catalogue général et détaillé des livres arabes, persans et turcs imprimés à Boulac en Égypte depuis l'introduction de l'imprimerie dans ce pays, en 1822, jusqu'en 1842. 1843. pp.43. [243.]

[C. M. FRÄHN], Indications bibliographiques relatives pour la plupart a la littérature historico-géographique des Arabes, des Persans et des Turcs, spécialement destinées a nos employés et voyageurs en Asie. St. Pétersbourg 1845. pp.[iv].lv.87. [244.]

[THOMAS XAVIER] BIANCHI, Bibliographie ottomane, ou notice des ouvrages publiés dans les imprimeries turques de Constantinople, et en partie dans celles de Boulac, en Égypte, depuis les derniers mois de 1856 jusqu'à ce moment. ... No.1. 1863. pp.125. [146.]

[FRANÇOIS ALPHONSE] BELIN, Bibliographie ottomane, ou notice des livres turcs imprimés a Constantinople durant les années 1281 [&c.] del'Hégire.
  1281-1283 (1864-1866). pp.31. [100.]
  1284-1285 (1867-1868). pp.35. [107.]
  1286-1287 (1869-1870). pp.37. [97.]
  1288-1289 (1871-1872). pp.46. [171.]
  1290-1293 (1873-1876). pp.27. [132.]
    [continued as:]
Bibliographie ottomane. Notice des livres turcs, arabes et persans imprimés à Constantinople. ... Par Clément [Imbault] Huart.
  1294-1296 (1877-1879). pp.31. [191.]
  1297-1298 (1880-1881). pp.48. [218.]
  1299-1301 (1882-1884). pp.[iii].88. [432.]
  1302-1303 (1885-1886). pp.69. [344.]

  1304-1305 (1887-1888). pp.[iii].62. [300.]
  1306-1307 (1889-1890). pp.[iii].54. [303.]

EDWARD G[RANVILLE] BROWNE, A hand-list ... of the turkish and other printed and lithographed books presented by mrs. E. J. W. Gibb to the Cambridge university library. Cambridge 1906. pp.viii.87. [297.]

TÜRKİYE bibliyoğrafyası. Türkiye cümhuriyeti maarif vekaleti: İstanbul.
  1928-1933. pp.v.359.ii. [3000.]
  1934. pp.211. [1468.]
  1935. pp.168+143. [1618.]
  1936. pp.153+161. [1972.]
  1937. pp.180+194. [2123.]
  1938. pp.226+207. [2520.]
  1928-1938. pp.xv.704+xv.916. [15,000.]
  1939. pp.99.111.95.87. [4000.]
  1940. pp.99.101.83. [3000.]
  1941. pp.94.92.88.39. [3000.]
  1942. pp.83.80.90.88. [3000.]
  1943. pp.92.111.97.128. [4000.]
  1944. pp.600. [4000.]
  1945. pp.664. [4000.]
  1946. pp.680. [4000.]
  1947. pp.710. [4000.]
  1948. pp.690. [4000.]
  1939-1948. 1957-1962. pp.xviii.888+xvii.889-2014. [20,000.]
  1949. pp.564. [3000.]
  1950. pp.560. [3000.]
  1951. pp.516. [3000.]
  1952. pp.531. [3000.]
  1953. pp.976.220. [4392.]
  1954. pp.vii.496. [2915.]
  1955. pp.v.325.125.121. [3863.]
  1956. pp.103.127.51.181.128. [2886.]
  1957. pp.124.119.79.107.122. [2689.]
  1958. pp.96.127.131.130.124. [2888.]
  1959. pp.180.121.160.204.143. [3921.]
  1960. pp.134.130.163.226.137. [3958.]
  1961. pp.97.171.145.264.159. [4079.]
  1962. pp.143.111.149.215.122. [3640.]
  1963. pp.188.169.215.331.185. [5483.]
  1964. pp.183.159.297.271.184. [5612.]
  1965. pp.123.152.194.261.170. [4352.]
  1966. pp.208.196.252.254.196. [4967.]
  1967. pp.218.221.264.407.224. [6220.]
  1968. pp.169.298.210.287.276. [5421.]
  1969. pp.184.268.223.281.284. [5618.]
  1970. pp.260.321.154.347.272. [5470.]
  1971. pp.308.282.241.349.301. [6160.]
  1972. pp.423.288.321.360.353. [7767.]
  1973. pp.298.266.

HARRY W. CHAPMAN, 1939-1948. Türkiye bibliografyası özad indeksi. A first-name index to the Türkiye bibliyografyasi 1939-1948. Robert college research center: Bulletin series (no.501): Istanbul 1968.

BIBLIYOĞRAFYA. [An official journal, issued monthly, of books published in Turkey.] Vol.1, no.1–vol.3, no.15. Ankara 1928–33.
no more published?

KÜLTÜR bakanliği yayınları. İstanbul 1936. pp.15. [250.]

ÂDEM RUHI KARAGÖZ, Bulgaristan türk basını 1879–1945. Bulgaristan türklerinin kültür hayatına dair incelemeler (n: 1): [İstanbul] 1945. pp.66. [98.]

BİBLİYOGRAFYA, Cilt 1, sayı 1 [–3]. [Ankara] 1946. pp.130+168. [646.]
no more published.

HEINZ GRIESBACH-TUGAN, Новітне турецьке красне письменство. Український морський інститут (ио.63): Чужині 1948. pp.34. [500.]

TRANSLATIONS from world literature published by the turkish Ministry of education. Ankara 1950. pp.16. [300.]

ISTANBUL belediye kütüphanesi alfabetik kataloğu.
i. Osman Ergin kitapları, arapça ve farsça basma eserler. Tertipliyen M. Orhan Durusoy. Istanbul 1953. pp.xvi.298. [1958.]
ii. Belediye ve M. Cevdet kitapları, arapça ve farsça basma eserler. 1954. pp.[ii.]155. [1959–3046.]
iii. Osman Ergin kitapları, türkçe ve yavancı dil basma eserler. 1954. pp.[ii].508. [3047–7007.]

1953 denberi yayınlanan çocuk kitapları broşürü. [Millî eğitim vekâleti:] Ankara 1955. pp.20. [302.]

FEHMI EDHEM KARATAY, İstanbul üniversitesi kütüphanesi türkçe basmalar alfabe kataloğu . . . (1729–1928). İstanbul üniversitesi yayınlarından (no.658): İstanbul 1956. pp.vii.1295. [12,000.]

MİLLÎ kütüphanede mevcut arap harfli türkçe kitaplarin muvakkat kataloğu. Ankara 1956–1957. ff.[i].3.377+[ii].xxiii.378–774. [12,000.]*
— Genişletilmis ikinci basım . . . –1968. pp. 1735. [15,600.]*

YENİ yayınlar. Aylık bibliyografya dergisi. Revue mensuelle de bibliographie renfermant toutes les publications turques. Ankara.
i. 1956. pp.32.32. [500.]
ii. 1956. pp.368. [3500.]
iii. 1957. pp.384. [4000.]
iv.
v.
vi.
vii.
viii. 1963. pp.396. [4000.]

ix. 1964. pp.432. [4300.]
x. 1965. pp.432. [4300.]
xi. 1966. pp.432. [4300.]
xii. 1967. pp.432. [4300.]
xiii. 1968. pp.432. [4300.]
xiv. 1969. pp.432. [4300.]
xv. 1970. pp.432. [4300.]
xvi. 1971. pp.432. [4300.]
xvii. 1972. pp.436. [6000.]
in progress.

SÉVÉRIEN SALAVILLE and EUGÈNE DALLEGIO D'ALLESSIO, Karamlidika. Bibliographie analytique d'ouvrages en langue turque imprimés en caractères grecs. Centre d'études d'Asie Mineure: Archives musicales de folklore: Collection (no.11 = Institut français d'Athènes: Collection, no.47): Athènes.
i. 1584–1850. 1958. pp.xi.327. [113.]
no more published.

[STANFORD J. SHAW], The Harvard college library collection of books on ottoman history and literature. [Cambridge Mass. 1959.] [ff.140] [1665.]
also in a xerox copy with title:
Catalogue of turkish publications in Harvard university library.

İSMAIL ARAR, İsmail Arar kütüphanesi kataloğu.
i. Atatürk, Kurtuluş Savaşı devrimler ve Cumhuriyet Türkiyesi ile ilgili kitaplar. İstanbul 1960. pp.80. [1130.]
ii. Millî eğitim bakanlığınca yayımlanan ve 1962 yılı başında mevcudu bulunan kitapları gösterir taksitli satış kataloğu. İstanbul 1962. pp.iii.53. [1000.]

AHMET OKUTAN, Kayseri umumi kütüphanesi Raşit Efendi kısmı usul-i hadis ve hadis ilmine ait arapça elyazma eserler kataloğu. İstanbul 1964. pp.vi.100. [87.]

CATALOGUE of arabic, persian and ottoman turkish books. Harvard university library: Cambridge, Mass. 1968. pp.xiv.539+672+583+697+554 [63, 891 cards.]
1–3. Authors, titles and personal subjects: Arabic.
4. Authors, titles and personal subjects: Persian, Ottoman Turkish.
5. Topical subjects.

H. F. HOFMAN, Turkish literature, a bio-bibliographical survey. Section III, Moslim central asian turkish literature . . . Utrecht 1969 &c. pp. cl+265+348+293+305+312.
in progress.

BEHÇET NECATIGIL, Edebiyatımızda eserler sözlüğü. İstanbul 1971. pp.368. [400.]

BIBLIYOGRAFYA. Kitap haberleri bülteni. Book news bulletin. Bibliographia.

i. 1972.pp.308. [500.]

in progress.

FAHRI Bilge kütüphanesi basma eserler bölümü, np. n.d. ff.219.120 [12,055.]*

M. SEYFETTİN ÖZEGE, Eski harflerle basılmış türkçe eserler kataloğu.

in progress.

BURSALI MEHMED TÂHIR, Osmanlı müellifleri. I.cild. Hazırlayanlar A. Fikri Yavuz, İsmail Özen. İstanbul [   ] pp.xxxi.480. [large number.]

— — [Another edition.] A bio-bibliographical dictionary of the ottoman literature. 1334/1915–16 — 1343/1924–25. Farnborough 1970. pp.408.vi. vii+510+328.12.177. [large number.]

earlier editions in ottoman characters.

3. *Translations*

ADNAN [CAHIT] ÖTÜKEN, Dünya edebiyatından tercümeler, klâsikler bibliyografyası, 1940–1948. Ankara 1949. pp.xv.248. [536.]

DÜNYA edebiyatından tercümeler listesi. Klâsikler — klâsikler için yardımcı eserler — modern edebiyatlar — modern tiyatro eserleri — tiyatro sanatı üzerine eserler — bilim eserleri. Ankara 1959. pp.165. [2000.]

ADNAN [CAHIT] ÖTÜKEN [*and others*], Dünya edebiyatından tercümeler klâsikler bibliyografyası 1940–1966. Ankara 1967. pp.xv.421. [1117.]

CENTRAL ASIA. SIBERIA
U.S.S.R. IN ASIA

i. *Bibliographies*
ii. *General*
iii. *Peoples, places, languages*

i. *Bibliographies*

A. G. BISNEK and K. I. SHAFRANOVSKY, Библиография библиографии средней Азии. Академия наук СССР: Институт востоковедения: Москва &c. 1936. pp.48. [289.]

Z. D. TITOVA, Этнография. Библиография русских библиографий по этнографии народов СССР (1851–1969). Государственная библиотека им. М. Е. Салтыков-Щедрина: Москва 1970. pp.144. [734.]

ii. *General*

O. V. MASLOVA, Обзор русских путешествии и экспедиций в Среднюю Азию. Материалы к истории изучения Средней Азии. Среднеазиатский государственный университет им.

В. И. Ленина: Материалы к библиографии (vii).

i.

ii. 1856–1869. pp.102. [255.]

MIKHAIL PAVLOVICH PUTSILLO, Указатель дѣламъ и рукописямъ, относящимся по Сибири и принадлежащихъ Московскому главному архиву Министерства иностранныхъ дѣлъ. Москва 1879. pp.iii.123. [750.]

V[LADIMIR] I[ZMAILOVICH] MEZHOV, Recueil du Turkestan, comprenant des livres et des articles sur l'Asie centrale en général et le [*sic*] province du Turkestan en particulier. St. Pétersbourg 1878–1884. pp.[ii].iii.viii.184+viii.167. [3404.]

also published in two other issues entitled respectively Туркестанскій сборникъ *and* Систематический и азбучный указатели.

V[LADIMIR] I[ZMAILOVICH] MEZHOV, Туркестанскій сборникъ сочиненій и статей относящихся до Средней Азіи вообще и Туркестанскаго края въ особенности ... Систематическій и азбучные указатели сочиненій и статей на русскомъ и иностранныхъ языкахъ. Санкт-петербургъ.

Томы 151–300. 1884. pp.viii.184. [1397.]
Томы 300–416. 1888. pp.vi.105. [1309.]

V[LADIMIR] I[ZMAILOVICH] MEZHOV, Сибирская библіографія. Указатель книгъ и статей о Сибири на русскомъ языкѣ и однѣхъ только книгъ на иностранныхъ языкахъ за весь періодъ книгопечатанія. С.-Петербургъ 1891–1892. pp.xii.485+x.470+x.303+[iii].188. [12,250.]

reprinted in 1903 with the omission of some preliminary pages.

A[LEKSIEI] A[RSENIEVICH] IVANOVSKY, Періодическія изданія Сибири и средней Азіи 1789–1801 гг. Указатель статей по этнографии. Библіографическія зачиски: Москва 1892. pp.[i].14. [480.]

S[TEPAN] N[IKOLAEVICH] MAMEEV, Матеріалы для библіографіи Сибири. Тобольскъ 1892–1896.

A[NATOLY] A[LEKSANDROVICH] TERNOVSKY, Матеріалы для библіографіи Сибири. Тобольскъ [printed] [1893]. pp. 52. [818.]

N. N. OGLOBLIN, Обзрѣніе столбцовъ и книгъ сибирскаго приказа (1592–1768 гг.). Москва 1895–1901. pp.422.viii+162+[ii].iii. 394+288. [12,500.]

I[VAN] K[ALLINIKOVICH] GOLUBEV, Сибирская періодическая печать. Москва 1895. pp.12. [40.]

SELECT list of references on Russia in the East. Library of Congress: Washington 1904. ff.2. [9.]*

LIST of references on the natural resources and industries of Siberia and the possibilities of future development. Library of Congress: Washington 1918. ff.5. [50.]*

E[DUARD] E[DUARDOVICH] AHNERT, Bibliography of the mines and minerals of asiatic Russia. Chinese institution of mining and metallurgy: Peking 1926. pp.[ii].34.[ii]. [400.]

E. A. VOZNESENSKAYA and A. B. PIOTROVSKY, Материалы для библиографии по антропологии и этнографии Казахстана и Среднеазиатских республик. Академия наук: Труды Комиссии по изучению племенного состава населения СССР и сопредельных стран (vol.xiv): Ленинград 1927. pp.[iii].ix. 249. [2780.]

P. R. KONOGOROV, Картография северной Азии (1917–1927 г.г.). Библиографический указатель. Общество изучения Урала, Сибири и Дальнего востока: Москва 1928. pp.78. [296.]

M[IKHAIL] G[EORGIEVICH] KURLOV, Библиографический справочник по сибирской бальнеологии. Томский государственный физиотерапевтический институт: Томск 1929. pp.[ii].ii.[ii].165. [3000.]

N. YA. VITKIND, Библиография по Средней Азии. Указатель литературы по колониальной политике царизма в Средней Азии. Труды Научно-исследовательской ассоциации при коммунистическом университете трудящихся востока имени И. В. Сталина (выпуск 4): Москва 1929. pp. 166. [1271.]

указатель изданий Средне-азиатскаго государственного университета. 1.[1922–1929]. Ташкент 1930. pp.[iv].31. [112.]

A. M. BELOV, Материалы к указателю литературы о Сибири на европейских языках с 1917 г. по 1930 г. Академия наук СССР. Труды Совета по изучению производительных сил: Ленинград 1931. pp.35. [494.]

RICHARD A. PIERCE, Russian central Asia, 1867–1917. A selected bibliography. Berkeley, Cal. 1953. ff.ii.28. [483.]

O. V. MASLOVA, Систематический указатель к изданиям . . . с 1922–1950 гг. Среднеазиатский государственный университет: Материалы к библиографии (vol.ii): Ташкент 1952. pp.119. [1500.]

— — Издание 2-е. И Составители . . . О. В. Маслова, В. А. Вяткина, А. И. Кормилицин . . . (vol.viii): 1958. pp.192. [2026.]

A. V. PAEVSKAYA and V. N. STEFANOVICH, Зарубежная художественная литература в советских изданиях на иностранных языках. Библиографический список в СССР в 1945–1953 гг. Всесоюзная государственная библиотека иностранной литературы: Москва 1954. pp.72. [600.]

Азий. Среднеазиатский государственный университет им. В. И. Ленина: Материалы к библиографии (vol. v): Ташкент.

    i. 1715–1856. 1955. pp.85. [300.]
    ii. 1856–1869. 1956. pp.102. [400.]

G[ALINA] P[ETROVNA] BOGATOVA, Освоим природные богатства Сибири и дальнего востока. Беседа о книгах. Государственная . . . библиотека ССР имени В. И. Ленина: Москва 1956. pp.31. [100.]

N. A. KOZICHEVA, Что читать о Сибири и Дальнем Востоке. Указатель литературы. Государственная публичная историческая библиотека: Москва 1956. pp.36. [200.]

ОБЗОР русских путешествий и экспедиций в Среднюю Азию. Материалы истории изучения Средней Азия. Университет: Материалы к библиографии (ло. 7): Ташкент.

    i.
    ii. 1856–1869. Составитель . . . О. В. Маслова. 1956. pp. 107. [300.]

ЗАРУБЕЖНАЯ ЛИТЕРАТУРА. Библиотека СССР им. В. И. Ленина: Новинки художественной литературы: Москва.

    [1956. By] A[rnold] M[atveevich] Gorbunov. pp.154. [300.]
    1957. [By] A. M. Gorbunov, M[ilitrisa] I[vanovna] Davuidova. pp.135. [250.]
    1958. pp.204. [400.]
    1959. pp.196. [375.]
    1960. [By] A. M. Gorbunov, M. I. Davuidova, Z[oya] P[etrovna] Shalashova. pp. 191. [350.]

I[VAN] I[VANOVICH] STARTSEV, Художественная литература народов СССР в переводах на русский язык. Библиография, 1934–1954. Москва 1957. pp.752. [10,000.]

BIBLIOGRAPHY of recent soviet source material on soviet central Asia and the borderlands. Central asian research centre.

    1957. pp.ii.27. [200.]
    1958. pp.ii.47+ii.49. [900.]
    1959. pp.i.53+ii.59. [1000.]
    1960. pp.ii.64+ii.84. [1300.]
    1961. pp.ii.56+ii.72. [1200.]
    1962. pp.ii.64+ii.61. [1200.]
no more published?

ROMAN [O.] YAKOBSON, GERTA HÜTTL-WORTH and JOHN FRED BEEBE, Paleosiberian peoples and languages. A bibliographical guide. Human relations area files: Behavior science bibliographies. New Haven 1957. pp.vii.222. [2000.]

V. V. TOMASHEVSKY, Материалы к библиографии Сибири и Дальнего Востока. Академия наук Союза ССР: Дальневосточный филиал имени В. Л. Комарова: Владивосток 1957. pp.215. [3500.]

R. K. AGISHEV, Советский дальний восток в художественной литературе. 2-ое издание. Библиографический указатель. Хабаровская краевая библиотека: Хабаровск 1957. pp.206. [500.]

R[OZA] B[ORISOVNA] MILKINA, Библиография литературы народов СССР в переводах на русский язык. Управление учебных заведений: Москва 1958. pp.71. [500.]

ПРОИЗВЕДЕНИЯ советских писателей в переводах на иностранные языки . . . 1945–1953. Библиографический указатель. Союз советских писателей СССР and Всесоюзная государственная библиотека иностранной литературы: Москва.
    1945–1953. 1954. pp.322.
    1954–1957. 1959. pp.280. [5314.]

M[ARIYA] P[ETROVNA] AVSHAROVA, Русская периодическая печать в Туркестане (1870–1917). Библиографический указатель литературы. Государственная публичная библиотека им. А. Навои: Ташкент 1960. pp.198. [200.]

I. M. AKSELROD and E. R. BOCHKAREVA, Художественная литература зарубежного востока. Библиография переводов на языки народов СССР, 1918–1960. Академия наук СССР. Институт народов Азии: Москва 1963. pp.129.

DENIS SINOR, Introduction à l'étude de l'Eurasie centrale. Wiesbaden 1963. pp.xxiv.371. [4403.]

CENTRAL Asia and Transcaucasia, minority problems and general conditions; a selected bibliography. External research paper (158): External research staff: Department of state: Washington 1964. pp.[ii].14. [204.]*

EDWARD ALLWORTH, Central asian publishing and the rise of nationalism; an essay and a list of publications in the New York public library. New York public library: New York 1965. pp.100. [834.]

N. N. AKSENOVA, Флора западной Сибири. Библиографический указатель. Научная библиотека: Томский государственный университет им. В. В. Куйбышева: Томск 1966. pp.105. [1228.]

История Сибири. Текущий указатель литературы. Академия наук СССР: Сибирское отделение; Государственная научно-техническая библиотека: Новосибирск 1966 &c.
in progress.

A[NDREY] BERTHELS and M. BAQOEV, Alphabetic catalogue of manuscripts found by 1959–1963 expedition in Gorno-Badakhshan autonomous region. Edited and prefaced by B. G. Gafurov and A. M. Mirzoev. USSR academy of sciences: Institute of the peoples of Asia. Tadjik SSR academy of sciences: Department of oriental studies and written sources: Moscow 1967. pp.119. [253.]
in Russian, with English summary.

ANNEMARIE VON GABAIN, Die drucke der Turfansammlung. Sitzungsberichte der Deutschen akademie der wissenschaften zu Berlin: Klasse für sprachen, literatur und kunst (jhg. 1967, no.1): Berlin 1967. pp.40. [50.]

M[IKHAIL] N[IKOLAEVICH] TIKHOMIROV, Описание Тихомирского собрания рукописей. Академия наук СССР: Сибрское отделение: Институт истории, филологии и философии: Москва 1968. pp.194. [500.]

D. Y. STAVISKY [and others], Советская археология Средней Азии и кушанская проблема. Аннотированная библиография.
Soviet central asian archaeology and the Kushan problem. An annotated bibliography. International conference on the history, archaeology and culture of Central Asia in the Kushan period (Dushanbe 1968): Moscow 1968. pp.164+195. [720.]*

E. I. DUBROVINA, R. I. NIYAZOVA and N. S. KHABIROVA, Геология Средней Азии. Указатель литературы за 1917–1960 гг. Академия наук Узбекской ССР: Фундаментальная библиотека. Министерство высшего и среднего специального образования: Фундаментальная библиотека ТашГу, Ташкент,
    v. Полезные ископаемые, 1969. pp.598. [4578.]

Проблемы Севера. Текущий указатель литературы. Академия наук СССР: Сибирское отделение. Государственная публичная научно-техническая библиотека: Новосибирск 1968 &c.
in progress.

N. S. ROMANOV, Annotated bibliography on fisheries of the southern basins of the U.S.S.R. (1918–1953): fish resources and replenishment of commercial fish stocks. Translated from the russian. Israel program for scientific translations: Jerusalem 1968. pp.400. [3906.]*

original title: Указатель литературы по хозяйству южных бассейнов СССР за 1918–1953 гг. (Москва 1955).

V. V. VOROB'EV, География населения Сибири и Дальнего Востока. Библиографический указатель. Институт географии Сибри и Дальнего Востока: Иркутск 1968. pp. 323. [2212.]

JOHN R. KRUEGER, The uralic and altaic series: an analytical index including a complete index to Keleti szemle. Indiana university, Bloomington: Uralic and altaic series (vol.100): The Hague 1970. pp.[iv]. 81. [700.]*

Народное хозяйство Сибири и Дальнего Востока. Информационно-библиографический бюллетень. Государственная публичная научно-техническая библиотека Сибирского отделения Академии наук СССР: Отдел научной библиографии: Новосибирск 1970 &c.
in progress.

EDWARD ALLWORTH, Nationalities of the soviet east; publications and writing systems. A bibliographical directory and transliteration tables for iranian- and turkic-language publications, 1818–1945, located in U.S. libraries. The modern middle east series (no.3): New York and London 1971. pp.xi.440. [3341.]

O. E. AGAHANJANC and A. S. SINKOVSKAYA, Библиография Памира.
  i. Природа.

iii. *Peoples, places, languages*

Altai

V. I. RUIBACHENKO [*and others*], Алтайский край. Библиографический указатель. Алтайская краевая библиотека: Барнаул 1957. pp.128. [500.]

Altaic

JOHN R. KRUEGER, The Uralic and altaic series; an analytical index, including a complete index to *Keleti Szemle*. Indiana university publications: Uralic and altaic series (vol.100): Bloomington 1970. pp.iv.81. [798.]

Astrakhan

FR[ANTS FEDOROVICH] SPERK, Опытъ хронологическаго указателя литературы объ Астраханскомъ краѣ съ 1473 по 1887 г. включительно. Астраханский губернскій статистическій комитетъ: С.-Петербуръ 1892. pp.[ii]. vii.249. [5848.]

Bashkiria

M[IDKHAT FAZLYEVICH] GAYNULLIN and G[AYSA BATYRGALEEVICH] KHUSAYNOV, Писатели советской Башкирии, библиографический справочник. Уфа 1969. pp.408 [large number]

Chuvash

V. P. KLIMOVA [*and others*], Чувашия в годы гражданской войны. Образование Чувашкой автономной области. Сборник документов. Чувашский научно-исследовательскйи институт языка, литературы, истории и экономики: Центральный государственный архив ЧАССР: Партийный архив Чувашского обкома КПСС. Чевосксары 1960. pp. 718. [449.]

Crimea

G[RIGORY NIKOLAEVICH] GENNADI, Списокъ сочиненій о Крымѣ. [*s.l.* 1856]. pp.8. [100.] *no more published.*

E. E. GOPSHTEIN, Библиография библиографических указателей литературы о Крыме. Общество по изучению Крыма: Симферополь 1930. pp.15. [28.]

A. D. BELIKOVA and A. A. STEPANOVA, *edd.* Крымский областной государственный архив. Путеводитель. Симферополь 1961. pp.327. [large number.]

Kabardia

D. A. SARAKHAN, Библиография Кабарды и Балкарии. Ленинский учебный городок: Кабинет краеведения (vol.i): Нальчик 1930. pp.iii. 113.[1140.]

Karakalpaks

ALEKSYEI [NIKOLAEVICH] KHARUZIN, Библіографическій указатель статей, касающихся этнографій киргизовъ и каракиргизовъ съ 1734 по 1891 г. Москва 1891. pp.68. [800.]

Katanov, Nikolai Fedorovich

S[ERGEI] N[IKOLAEVICH] IVANOV, Николай Федорович Катанов (1862–1922). Очерк жизни и деятельности. Хакасский научно-исследовательский институт языка, литературы и истории: Научно-популярная серия: Москва &c. 1962. pp.107. [227.]

Kazakhs

ПОЛЕЗНЫЕ ископаемые Казакстана. Материалы по библиографии за 1752–1929. Всесоюзное геолого-разведочное объединение: Москва &c. 1931. pp.[iii].240. [1804.]

БИБЛИОГРАФИЯ изданий Академии наук Казахской ССР. Академия наук Казахской ССР: Центральная научная библиотека: Алма-Ата.
  1946–1950. Составители Б. М. Яхнович и С. Н. Беккулова. pp.148. [1733.]
  1951–1955. Составители Э. И. Инанчинова и М. З. Цинман. pp.212. [1900.]
  1932–1959. Составители Э. И. Иванчикова [*and others*]. pp.1108. [12,500.]

A. N. SAMOILOVICH, *ed.* Казахстан в изданиях Академии наук, 1734–1935. Академия наук СССР: Казахстанский филиал: Труды (vol.9): Москва &c. 1936. pp.72. [654.]

книжная летопись. Орган государственной библиографии Казахской ССР. Алма-Ата 1937 &c.

VIKTOR M. SPELNIKOV, Библиографический указатель по казахскому творчеству. Академия наук Казахской ССР: Алма-Ата 1951 &c.
in progress.

КАЗАХСТАН. Библиография. Государственная публичная библиотека [республиканская библиотека Казахской ССР] им. А. С. Пушкина: Алма-Ата.
    1952. 1953. pp.108. [1328.]
    1953.
    1954.
    1955. 1960. pp.343. [4000.]
    1956. 1960. pp.276. [3500.]
    1957. 1962. pp.340. [5000.]

LAWRENCE KRADER, Bibliography of Kazakhstan. American university: Bureau of social science research: Washington 1954. ff.[i].40. [350.]★

БЛАНК пля заказов. Академия наук КССР: Алма-Ата.
    1955. pp.99. [400.]
            [continued as:]
    Тематический план изданий.
    1956. pp.82. [250.]
    1957. pp.60. [150.]
    1958. pp.84. [250.]

KITAП летописі. Казак ССР-ы мемлекеттік библиография органы 1954 жыл. Алматы 1955. pp.135. [1176.]

F. V. ZHIZNEVSKY, Опыт передовиков сельского хозяйства Казахской ССР. Аннотированный указатель литературы. Академия наук Казахской ССР: Центральная научная библиотека: Алма-Ата 1955. pp. 291. [750.]

S[HORA] S[HAMGALIEVICH] SARUIBAEV, Казак тіл білімініц библлиографиялык корсеткіщі. Казак ССР тыым академиясы: Тіл жане адебиет институты: Алматы 1956. pp.98. [1500.]

КАЗАХСКАЯ ССР к 40-летню великой октябрьской социалистической революции. Краткие справочные сведения и указатель литературы. Государственная республиканская публичная библиотека Казахской ССР им. А. С. Пушкина: Алма-Ата 1957. pp.235. [250.]

R. F. VASILENKO and V. N. PAZDMIKOV, Библиографический сборник Казахского государственного университета им. С. М. Кирова. Алма-Ата 1957. pp.178. [2273.]
  — — [second edition].

БИБЛИОТЕЧНО-БИБЛИОГРАФИЧЕСКИЙ бюллетень. Академия наук Казахской ССР: Центральная научная библиотека: Алма-Ата.
    i. 1958. pp.187. [1500.]
  in progress.

Художественная литература Казахстана 1946–1957 (библиографический указатель). Государственная республиканская библиотека Казахской ССР имени А. С. Пушкина: Алма-Ата 1958. pp.688.

V[ASILY] O[RESTOVICH] GREBENSHCHIKOV, Здравоохранение и медицина в дореволюционном Казахстане. Библиографический указатель литературы (1731–1917 гг.). Государственная научная медицинская библиотека Казахстана: Alma-Ata 1960. pp.291. [2415.]

Библиографический указатель трудов сотрудников Казахского государственного университета им. С. М. Кирова. [&c.] [By E. E. Trunova, U. Kudekova and N. P. Nesterova]. 1961. pp.375. [3781.]

YA. SUBKHANBERDINA, Казактан революциядан бурынгы мерзімді дастнасозинден материалар. Мазмундалган библиотекафиялик, керсетким. Алматы 1963. pp.292. [2500.]

M. MYRZAKHMETOV, B. K. KOYCHUBAEVA and F. I. EL'KONINA, Абай Кунанбаев; библиографический указатель. Государственная республиканская библиотека Казахской ССР им. А. С. Пушкина. Алма-Ата 1965. pp.292. [1123.]
  in kazakh and russian.

LEILYA MUKHTAROVNA AUEZOVA, Библиографический указатель по творчеству М. О. Ауэзова. Академия наук Казахской ССР: Институт литературы и искусства им. М. О. Ауэзова. Алма-Ата 1972. pp.254. [2200.]

[E. KAZBEKOVA and E. SKURISHINA, Летопись периодических изданий Казахской ССР 1917–1959 гг. Сводный библиографический указатель. Книжная палата Казахской ССР: Алма-Ата 1963. pp. 191. [1555.]

Khazars

THE KHAZARS, A bibliography. Compiled by the Slavonic division. Public library: New York 1939. pp.20. [350.]

Kirghiz

ALEKSYEI [NIKOLAEVICH] KHARUZIN, Библиографическій указатель статей, касающихся этнографій киргизовъ и каракиргизовъ съ 1734 по 1891 г. Москва 1891. pp.68. [800.]

A. E. ALEKTOROV, Указатель книгъ, журнальныхъ и газетныхъ статей и замѣтокъ о Кургизахъ. Казань 1900. pp.970.15.vi. [4000.]

DZH[ENBAI] SAMAGANOV, Писатели советского Киргизстана. Фрунзе 1958. pp.3–275. [1000.]

ПЕЧАТЬ советского Киргизстана. [Путеводитель по выставке]. Государственная республиканская библиотека Киргизской ССР им. Н. Г. Чернышевского: Фрунзе 1958. pp.100. [250.]

D[AVYD] S[EMENOVICH] LOSEV and O[LEG] D[MITRIEVICH] MOROZOV, Киргизская литература. Рекомендательный указатель. Государственная ... библиотека СССР имени В. И. Ленина and Государственная публичная библиотека Киргизской ССР имени Н. Г. Чернышевского: Москва 1958. pp.79. [200.]

Z. L. AMITIN-SHAPIRO, Аннотированный указатель лиературы по истории, археологии и этнографии Киргизии, 1750–1917. Академия наук Киргизской СССР: Институт истории: Фрунзе 1958. pp.353. [2168.]

L. M. ERMAN and M. M. GERASIMOV, Библиография изданий Академии наук Киргизской ССР, 1943–1956 гг. Фрунзе 1957. pp.152. [1181.]
— — 1957–1959. 1961. pp.147. [934.]

N[AMASBEK] BEISHEKEEV, Кыргыз тили (адабияттардын библиографиялых корсоткучу) 1929–1959 жж. Кыргыз ССР илимлер академиясы: Фрунзе 1961. pp.152. [900.]

L. M. ERMAN [and others], Экономика сельского хозяйства Киргизии. Библиографическийи указатель (1956–1964). Академия наук Киргизской ССР: Институт экономики. Центральная библиотека: Фрунзе 1968. pp.276. [1811.]

Kokand Khans

A[NNA] L[EONIDOVNA] TROITZKAYA, Каталог архива кокандских ханов XIX века. Академия наук СССР: Институт народов Азии. Государственная публичная библиотека им. М. Е. Салтыкова-Щедрина: Москва 1968. pp.583. [3800.]

Komi

ЛИТЕРАТУРА о Коми АССР за 1956 год. Республиканская библиотека Коми АССР: Сыктывкар 1958. pp.140. [2000.]

MARIYA GRIGOREVNA KARAKCHIEVA, Библиографический указатель литературы о Коми АССР. Сыктывкар 1963. pp.234.

Navā'i

A[LEKSANDR] A[LEKSANDROVICH] SEMENOV, Материалы к библиографическому указателю печатных произведений Алишера Навои и литературы о нем. Труды Среднеазиатского университета (2nd ser., no.5): Ташкент 1940. pp.[ii].38. [134.]

KHAMID SULEYMAN, Рукописи произведений Алишера Навои, хранящихся в фондах Советского союза ...   [938.]

Tatars

LEON NAJMAN MIRZA KRYCZYŃSKI, Bibljografja do historji Tatarów polskich. Zamość 1935. pp. xv.69.[iii]. [2000.]

G. A. SKOPIN, Gosudarstvennyi muzei Tatarskoi ASSR. Издания музея 1894–1956.pp.36. [216.]

E. G. BUSHKANETS, Казань в воспоминаниях современников. Аннотированный указатель. Государственный музей Татарской АССР: Казань.
  i. 1800–1850. 1955. pp.18. [56.]
  ii. 1850–1880. 1956. pp.24. [70.]

I. A. GEORGIEVSKAYA [and others], Центральный государственный архив ТАССР; путеводитель. Архивный отдел при совете министров Татарской АССР. Казань 1967. pp.278. [600.]

A. K. GINIYATULLINA, Писатели советского Татарстана. Био-библиографический справочник. Казань 1957. pp.488. [127 writers.]

S. B. RADZHIEVSKAYA [and others], Описание рукописей научной библиотеки им. Н. И. Лобачевского. Казанский ордена трудового красного знамени государственный университет им. В. И. Ульянова-Ленина. Казань.
  i. Фольклор. 1958. pp.35. [55.]
  ii. Лингвистика. 1958. pp.35. [112.]
  iii. Mustafa Nogman, Рукописы Канома Насыры. 1958. pp.48. [85.]
  iv. S. B. Radzhievskaya, Археология, этнография и нумизматика. 1959. pp.42. [150.]
  v. Al'bert Fetkhi, Рукописи татарских писателей и ученых. 1960. pp.63. [98.]
  vi. A[brar] Karimullin, Татарское народное творчество, 1961. pp.35. [67.]
  vii. V. V. Aristov, Материали цензурного комитета при Казанском университете. 1961. pp.47. [57.]
  viii.
  ix. Abrar Karimullin, Тюркское языкознание. 1962. pp.20. [37.]

x. Al'bert Fatkhi, Рукописи татарских писателей и ученых. 1962. pp. 48. [129.]

xi.

xii.

xii. Е. М. Il'enko, Художественные произведоения. 1963. pp.48. [62.]

A[BRAR] G[UBADULLOVICH] KARIMULLIN, Библиография литературы по татарскому языкознанию. Татар тел белеме библиографиясе. Казанский ... универеитет имени В. И. Ульянова-Ленина. Научная библиотека имени Н. И. Лобачевского: Казань 1958. pp.115. [1088.]

Е. М. MISHINA, Систематический указатель статей к периодическим изданиям Казанского ... государственного университета нм. В. И. Ульянова-Ленина, 1815–1947 гг. Казань 1960. pp.280. [4659.]

A. G. KARIMULLIN, Муса Джалиль (библиография, 1919–1961). Казанский ... университет им. В. И. Ульянова-Ленина and Научная библиотека им. Н. И. Лобачевского: Казань 1961. pp.77. [1000.]

ABRAR KARIMULLIN, Татарская литература (фопгклор, литературоведение и история литературы); библиография 1917–1959. Казанский университет ... научная библиотека им. Н. И. Лобачевского: Казан 1961. pp.216. [2445.]

A[BRAR] G[UBADULLOVICH] KARIMULLIN, Татарская литература в переводах на русский язык. (Библиографический указатель 1917–1960): Казан 1962. pp.92. [818.]

СССР ђэм чит ил халыклары адабияты, фолыклоры ђэм сэнгате. Татар теленэ таржемэлэр, Библиография 1917–1962. Казан деулет университеты ... Н. И. Лобачевский исемендэге фэнни китабханэ: Казан 1963. pp.337. [4906.]

ABRAR G[UBADULLOVICH] KARIMULLIN, Татар матур эдэбияты библиографиясе (1917–1960). Н. И. Лобачевский исемендэге фэнни китабханэ: Казан 1964. pp.156. [1500.]

Е. М. MISHINA [and others], История Татарской АССР. (С древцейших времен до наших дней.) Указатель советской литературы (1960–1967). Казанский ... университет ... Научная библиотека им. Н. И. Лобачевского: Казань 1970. pp.160. [2172.]

Tokharian language

ERNST SCHWENTNER, Tocharische bibliographie 1890–1958. Deutsche akademie der wissenschaften zu Berlin: Institut für orientforschung: Veröfftenlichung (no.47): Berlin 1959. pp.47. [526.]

Turkestan

V[LADIMIR] I[ZMAILOVICH] MEZHOV, Recueil du Turkestan, comprenant des livres et des articles sur l'Asie centrale en général et le [sic] province du Turkestan en particulier. St. Pétersbourg 1878–1884. pp.[ii].iii.viii.184+viii.167. [3404.]

also published in two other issues entitled respectively, Туркестанскій сборникъ *and* Систематическій и азбучный указатели.

Turkmen

Летопись пепати Туркменистана. Туркменские книги на старом алфавите поступившие в Книжную палату. Ашхабад.

i. до 30. xii. 1928. 1930. pp.iv.176. [313.]

ii. 1930. pp.38. [162.]

iii. до 30. xii. 1930. 1931. pp.[v].54. [224.]

Е. А. KNYAZHETSKAYA, Литература о Западном Узбое 1714–1950. Библиографический указатель. Академия наук Туркменской ССР and Академия наук СССР: Библиотека: Ашхабад 1956. pp.136. [551.]

ZH. SEITNUIYAZOV, Аман Кекилов. Доглан гунунун 50. йыллылына. Библиографиаи горкезижи. ТССР медениет министрлиги: Карл Маркс адындакы туркмен девлет китапханасы: Ашгабат 1962. pp.20. [220.]

М. KUVALOVA, V. PANOVA and A. PIRLIEV, Книга советского Туркменистана. Сводная библиография 1926–1960. Книга первая. Государственный комитет совета министров Туркменской ССР по печати. Государственная книжная палата Туркменской ССР. Ашхабод 1965. pp.708. [7020.]

М. Е. MASSON, *ed.*, Перечень опубликованнух работ и материалов по тематики Южнотуркменистанской археологической комплексной экспедиции. К xxv-летию её деятельности 1946–1970. Ашхабад 1970. pp. [527.]

O. NURUIEV and A. YA. STEPANOV, Библиография изданий Академин наук Туркменской ССР 1941–1961 гг. Академия наук Туркменской ССР: Центральная научная библиотека: Ашхабад 1971. pp. 414. [3576.]

Uigur

A[BDULLADZHAN] M[UGINOVICH] MUGINOV, Описание уйгурских рукописей Института народов Азии. Академия наук СССР: Институт народов Азии: Москва 1962. pp.208. [359.]

A[BDU-ALI TUGANBAEVICH] KAIDAROV, Уигурский язык и литература. Аннотированный библиографический указатель Акаде-

мия наук Казахской ССР: Институт языко-
знания: Алма-Ата.

    i. 1962. pp.140. [824.]

Ural region

O[LGA] M[IKHAILOVNA] SHUBNIKOVA, Литература о минералах южного Урала. Академия
наук СССР: Минералогический институт:
Минералогия СССР (ser. B, part 1): Ленинград 1933. pp.160. [2000.]

L. YA. ZHUCHKOVA [and others], Урал. Аннотированный указатель литературы. Сверд-
ловская государственная публичная библиотека им. В. Г. Белинского: Свердловск
1963. pp.241. [1713.]

JOHN R. KRUEGER, The uralic and altaic series; an
analytical index, including a complete index to
Keleti szemle. Indiana university publications:
Uralic and altaic series (vol.100): Bloomington
1970. pp.[iv].81. [798.]

Uzbek

УЗБЕКИСТАН. Библиографический указатель
литературы. Государственная публичная библиотека УзССР им. Навои: Ташкент.

    1953–1955. Составитель: Н. М. Культиа-
    зова. 1958. pp.384. [3000.]

    1956. Составитель: С. И. Кайзер. 1960.
    pp.280. [2082.]

    1957. Составитель: Н. М. Культиазава.
    pp.468. [3089.]

    1958.

    1959. Составитель: Евгения Дмитриевна
    Свидина. 1961. pp.624. [4304.]

in progress.

УКАЗАТЕЛЬ докторских и кандидатских дис-
сертаций защищенных в Узбекистане в 1936–
1951 гг. Общественные науки, естественные
науки, математика. Среднеазиатскнй государственный университет им. Ленина [&c.]:
Материалы к библиографии (vol.iv): Ташкент
1954. pp.175. [595.]

M[ARIYA] P[ETROVNA] AVSHAROVA and E[VGE-
NIYA] D[MITRIEVNA] SVIDINA, Узбекская литература. Рекомендательный указатель. Государственная ордена Ленина библиотека
СССР имени В. И. Ленина and Государственная публичная библиотека УзССР пме-
ни Алишера Навои: Москва 1959. pp.135.
[300.]

M. P. AVSHAROVA, Узбекская женщина
в прошлом и настоящем. Библиографический указатель литературы. Государственная публичная библиотека УзССР: Ташкент 1958. pp.176. [1000.]

БИБЛИОГРАФИЯ изданий Академии наук Узбекской ССР. Ташкент.

    1943–1952. Составители: Ф. А. Шнай-
    дерман и В. Г. Бек-Назарова. 1956.
    pp.258. [2896.]

    1953–1957. 1959. pp.332. [3318.]

    1958–1960. 1963. pp.370. [3500.]

    1961–1963. 1967. 1967. pp.543. [3979.]

    [continued as:]

Ежегодник изданий. Сталинабад [1959–
: Душанбе].

    1955. 1956. pp.64. [223.]

    1956. 1959. pp.42. [328.]

    1957. 1959. pp.58. [413.]

    1958. 1959. pp.49. [348.]

    1959. 1961. pp.103. [397.]

    1960. 1962. pp.68. [452.]

in progress.

V. I. BEK–NAZAROVA, История Узбекистана.
Библиографический указатель книг и статей
в изданиях Комитета наук при совете народных
комиссаров УзССР Узбекистанского филиала.
Академии наук УзССР (1938–1957 гг.). Ташкент 1960. pp.120. [1122.]

N. G. UMAROV, *ed.*, Библиография изданий
Академии наук Узбекской ССР. Системати-
уеский указатель книг и статей (1961–1963 гг.).
Академия наук Узбекской ССР. Фулдамен-
тальная библиотека: Ташкент 1967. pp.544.
[3979.]

Yakut

N[IKOLAI] E[GOROVICH] PETROV, Якутский
язык. (Указатель литературы.) Якутский
филиал Академии наук СССР [&c.]: Якутск
1958. pp.96. [891.]

[N. M. ALEKSEEV *and others*], Библиография Якутской АССР, 1931–1955 [–1959] . . .
История изучения, история народов, социа-
листическое строительство. Академия наук
СССР: Совет по изучению производительных сил: Сектор сети специальных библио-
тек and Якутская республиканская библиотека им. А. С. Пушкина: Москва 1958–1962.
pp.168+256. [5000.]

CAUCASUS

    i. *Languages and literatures*
    ii. *General*
    iii. *Azerbaijan*
    iv. *Armenia*
    v. *Georgia*

i. Languages and literatures

G. N. KACHARAVA and G. V. TOPURIA,
Библиография языковедческой литературы иб-
рийско-кавказких языках. Университет: Ка-
федра кавказских языков: Тбилиси 1958 &c.
in progress.

DAVID MARSHALL LANG, Catalogue of georgian
and other caucasian printed books in the British
museum. 1962. pp.xi.coll.430. [2000.]

ii. *General*

M [M.] MIANSAROV [MIANSAREANTS], Bibliographia caucasica et transcaucasica. Опытъ
справочнаго систематическаго каталога пе-
чатнымъ сочиненіямъ о Кавказѣ, Закавказьи
и племенахъ, эти края населяющихъ ...
Томѣ 1, Отдѣлы i и п. С.-Петербургъ 1874–
1876. pp.[v].xlii.804. [4840.]
no more published, reprint Amsterdam 1967.

N. I. VOROBEV, Указатель сочиненій о
Черноморскомъ Побережьѣ Кавказа ... выпускъ 1. Petrograd 1915. pp.xiv.245. [2267.]

A. V. BAGRY, Народная словесность Кавказа. Материалы для библиографическаго
указателя. Баку 1926. pp.131. [1439.]

A. P. SUTUGIN, Бпблиография бассейна
озера Гокчи (Севана). Академия наук: Материалы Комиссии экспедиционных иссле-
дованнй (vol.iii): Ленинград 1928. pp.80.[v].
[577.]

NINA A[LEKSEEVNA] STEPANOVA, Annotated bibliography of the climate of the Caucasus. Weather
bureau: Washington 1960. pp.[v].43. [134.]★

CENTRAL Asia and Transcaucasia, minority
problems and general conditions; a selected
bibliography. External research paper (158):
External research staff: Department of state:
Washington 1964. pp.[ii].14. [204.]★

E. V. SKAZIN, Дагестан в советской истори-
ческой литературе. Дагестанский филиал АН
СССР: Институт истории, языка и литературы:
Махачкала 1963. pp.195. [1400.]

iii. *Azerbaijan. Azerbaijani literature*

A. V. BAGRY, Материалы для библиографии
Азербайджана. Дома работников просвеще-
ния: Библиографическая секция. Баку 1924–
1925. pp.87+74+92. [4956.]

A. A. Ибрагимов, Описание архива М. Ф.
Ахундова. Составлено на основе материалов
Республиканского рукописного фонда Академия наук Азербайджанской ССР. Институт
литературы и языка им. Низами. Баку 1955.
pp.294. [618.]
— [Another edition.] Баку 1962. pp.274. [500.

M[ARIYA] N[AUMOVNA] MEILMAN. Азербайджанская литература. Рекомендательный
указатель. Государственная ... библиотека
СССР имени В. И. Ленина and Азербайджанская республиканская библиотека имени М. Ф. Ахунова: Москва 1958. pp.119.
[500.]

книги издательства академии ... (1948–
1958). Каталог. Баку 1959. pp.48. [500.]

M. PASHAEVA, Описание архива Джалил
Мамедкулизаде (Молла Насреддин). Академия
наук Азербайджанской ССР. Рукописный фонд:
Баку 1961. pp.156. [417.]

G. A. GULIEV, Библиография этнографии
Азербайджана (изданной на русском языке
до 1917 года). Баку 1962– . pp.128+ .
in progrcss.

A[RON] N[ATANOVICH] LERMAN, Мирза Фа-
тали Ахундов в русской печати 1837–1962 гг.
Биобиблиография. Азербайджакская республиканская библиотека имени М. Ф.
Ахундова: Баку 1962. pp.235. [1724.]

T. D. GADZHEVA [*and others*], Библиография изданий Академии наук Азербайдхан-
ской ССР 1945–1959 гг. Баку 1962. pp.676.
[7500.]

DZH. M. NAGIEVA, С. С. Ахундов архивинин
тасвири. Азербајчан ССР елимләр академи-
јасы: Республика әлјазмалары фонду: Бакы
1962. pp.90. [210.]

M. S. SULTANOV, Әлјазмалары каталогу чилд.
(Тарих, чографија, адабијјат назаријјаси, таз-
киралар, бодии әдәбијјат ва муәшәат). Азнр-
байчан ССР елимлер академиласы: Респлика
әлјазмалары фонду: Бакы 1963. pp.514. [1281.]

A. O. Маковельский библиография. Деятели
науки и культуры Азербайджана: Академия
наук Азербайджанской ССР: Фундаментальная
библиотека: Баку 1964. pp.68. [175.]

H. Z. MAHMUDOV, Гейдар Гусейнов 1908–
1950. Библиография. Деятели наук и культуры
Азербайджана: Академия наук Азербайджанской ССР. Фундаментальная библиотека: Баку
1965. pp.48. [263.]

Летопись печати Азербайджана. Орган государственной библиографии Азербайджанской
ССР. Государственный комитет совета министров Азербайджанской ССР по печати.
Републиканская книжная палата: Баку 1965
&c?
in progress?

Мамед Ариф Дадашзаде. Библиография.
Академия наук Азербайджанской ССР: Фундаментальная библиотека: Баку 1965. pp.84.
[630.]

Самед Вургун 1906–1956. Библиография.
Академия наук Азербайджанской ССР: Фундаментальная библиотека: Баку 1965. pp.192.
[1434.]

Ежегодник книги Азербайджана. 1965. Комитет по печати при совете министров: Азербайджанская государственная книжная палата: Баку 1966. pp.148. [1863.]

Китаблар алеминдә. [Баки.] 1966. &c?
in progress?

Летопись печати Азербайджана. Орган государственной библиографии Азербайджанской ССР. Азербайджанская государственная книжная палата: Комитет при печати совете министров Азербайджанской ССР: Баку 1966.
in progress?

A. M. GAMIDOVA, А. Ю. Гусейнов; библиография. Деятели науки и культуры Азербайджана: Академия наук Азербайджанской ССР: Фундаментальная библиотека: Баку 1966. pp.88. [309.]

N. M GULIJEV [*and others*], Великий октабрь и Азербайджан. Библиография. Академия наук Азербайджанской ССР: Фундаментальная библиотека. Баку 1967. pp.172. [1800.]

ISMET SAFAROV, Мир-Али Кашкай. Библиография. Деятели наук и культуры Азербайджана: Академия наук Азербайджанской ССР: Фундаментальная библиотека: Баку 1967. pp.161. [671.]

L. E. AGADZHANOVA [*and others*], Ученые Азербайджана в мировой печати. Библиография. Академия наук Азербайджанской ССР: Фундаментальная библиотека: Баку 1970. pp.112. [515.]

T. D. HAJIYEVA [*and others*], Развитие науки в советском Азербайджане (1920–1970); библиография. Академия наук Азербайджанской ССР: Фундаментальная библиотека: Баку 1970. pp.145. [1700.]

N. M. KULIEV, История Азербайджна (1920–1961). Библиография. Академия наук Азербайджанской ССР: Фундаментальная библиотека: Баку 1970. pp.288. [3500.]

iv. *Armenia*

1. *Bibliographies*
2. *General*
3. *Armenian literature*

1. *Bibliographies*

P. ISHKANIAN, *ed.* Մատենագիտություն Հայկական Մատենագիտության. (Ուրվագիծ) [Erevan] 1963. pp.344. [1324.]

2. *General*

CARL HEINRICH TROMLER, Bibliothecae armenicae specimen. Plaviae 1759. pp.lvi. [150.]

K. P. PARKANOV [KEROVPE PETROVICH BADGANIAN], Библіографическій очеркъ армянской исторической литературы. С.-Петербургъ 1879. pp.57. [250.]

ARSEN GHAZAROS GHAZIKEAN, Nouvelle bibliographie arménienne et encyclopédie de la vie arménienne, 1512–1905. Venise 1909–1912. coll. xxx.2079. [5000.]
incomplete; no more published.

WILLIAM WALKER ROCKWELL, Armenia. A list of books and articles. American committee for armenian and syrian relief: New York [1916]. pp.8. [75.]

IDA A[UGUSTA] PRATT, Armenia and the Armenians. A list of references in the New York public library. New York 1919. pp.[iii].96. [2000.]

BRIEF list of references on the United States as a mandatory for Armenia. Library of Congress: [Washington] 1920. ff.3. [27.]*

A. SALMASLIAN, Bibliographie de l'Arménie. 1946. pp.196. [1750.]

ARTHUR HAMPARIAN, A selective check-list of books in print relating to Armenia and of armenian interest. [New York] 1956. ff.6. [40.]*

E. S. VLASYAN and A. S. MANASERYAN, Библиография изданий АрмФАНа и Академин наук Армянской ССР 1936–1956 г.г. Ереван 1957. pp.536. [5179.]

G. M. DAVTYAI [*and others*], Հայ Հնատիպ գրքեր Մատենագիտական ցուցակ 1512–1800. [Erevan] 1963. pp.xviii.308. [1041.]

V. N. KARMENYAN, E. S. VLASYAN, A. E. KHACHATRYAN, Библиография изданий Академии наук Армянской ССР. Книги и стати 1935–1949. Академия наук Армянской ССР: Центральная библиотека: Ереван 1950. pp.240. [1955.]

3. *Armenian literature*

[SUKIAS SOMALEAN], Quadro delle opere di vari autori anticamente tradotte in armeno. Venezia 1825. pp.46. [200.]

CATALOGO dei libri stampati nella tipografia armena dell'isola di S. Lazzaro presso Venezia. [San Lazzaro degli Armeni] 1833. pp.12. [300.]

[TH. KHORGANEANTS and YÔHANNĒS SHAHKHATHOUNEANTS, Каталогъ кнжгамъ Эчмядзинской. Изданный Г. Броссе [Marie Félicité Brosset]. ... Catalogue de la bibliothèque d'Edchmiadzin. Санктпетербургъ 1840. pp. [iv]. 121. [481.]

the text including the titles, is in russian and french throughout.

CATALOGUE des livres de l'imprimerie armé-nienne de Saint-Lazare. Institut des mekhitharistes: Venise 1876. pp.37. [1000.]

N. KARAMIANZ, Verzeichniss der armenischen handschriften. Königliche bibliothek: Hand-schriften-verzeichnisse (vol.x): Berlin 1883. pp.viii.88. [250.]

BIBLIOGRAPHIE arménienne 1565–1883. Venetik 1883. pp.xxxii. 754. [6000.]
All in Armenian except for above title on title-page and wrapper.

CATALOGUE des anciennes traductions arméni-ennes (siècles IV–XIII): Venetik [Venice] 1889. pp.[xxxi]. 783. [large number.]

Ս՛այր Յուցցակ Հայերէ Ջեռագրաց.
. . . Haupt-catalog [katalog] der armenischen handschriften. Wiener Mechitharisten-congre-gation: Wien.

I. Die armenischen handschriften in Öster-reich.
  i. Catalog der armenischen handschriften in der K.k. hofbibliothek zu Wien. Von Jacobus Dashian [Yakôbos Tašean]. 1891. pp.[viii].49. [50.]
  ii. Catalog der armenischen handschriften in der Mechitharisten-bibliothek zu Wien. Von J. Dashian [Y. Tašean]. 1895. pp. xviii.277.[64].164. [1000.]
  Bd.ii. Von Hamasp Oskian. Calouste Gulbenkian foundation armenian library: 1963. pp.vi.1154. [731.]
II. Die armenischen handschriften in Deutsch-land.
  i. Catalog der armenschen handschriften in der K. hof- und staatsbibliothek zu Mün-chen. Von Gregoris Kalemkiar[ian]. 1892. pp.viii.37. [150.]
IV. Die armenischen handschriften in Russland.
  i.
  ii. Katalog der armenischen handschriften in Novo-Bayazet. Von H. Adjarian. Wien 1924. pp.xi.61. [51.]
VI. Die armenischen handschriften in der Türkei [und Persien].
  i. Catalog der armenischen handschriften in der bibliothek des Sanassarian-institutes zu Erzerum. Von H. Adjarian. 1900. pp.xv.37. [200.]
  ii. Katalog der armenischen handschriften in Täbris. Von Hratchia Adjarian. 1910. pp.xxxii.155. [1000.]
  Katalog der armenischen handschriften in Teheran. von Hratchia Adjarian. 1936. pp.vi.[iv].17. [9.]

iii. Katalog der armenischen handschriften in Nikosia auf Cyprus, von Nerses Akinian. pp.[xv]. 140.
iv. Katalog der armenischen handschriften des klosters Sourb Neschan in Sebaste. Von Thorgom, erzbischof Gouschakian. 1961. pp.[xv].140.
  Katalog der armenischen handschriften des armenischen hospizes zum hl. Blasius in Rom und des pont. Leoniano collegio armeno, Roma, von Nerses Akinian. 1961. pp.[xv].76.
  Katalog der armenischen handschriften in den bibliotheken zu Lewow und Stanislawow, von Nerses Akinian. 1961. pp.[xii].60.
  Katalog der armenischen handschriften der klöster zum hl. Karapet und zum hl. Daniel, von Trdat, bischof von Balian. 1963. pp.[x].88. [48.]
  Katalog der armenischen handschriften der Arznian-schule und der dörfer von Erzerum, von Jakob Kossian [K'ōsean]. 1964. pp.[xi].131.
  Katalog der armenischen handschriften in der bibliothek des klosters Bzommar, von Mesrop Keschischian (band ii. N. Akinian and H. Oskian). Calouste Gul-benkian foundation armenian library: 1964–1971. pp.v.809+322. [682.]

CATALOGUE des livres de l'imprimerie arméni-enne de Saint-Lazare. Venise 1894. pp.112. [1300.]

GREGORIS KALEMKIAR [KALEMKIARIAN], Eine skizze der literarisch-typographischen thätigkeit der Mechitharisten-congregation in Wien. Wien 1898. pp.[iii].99. [1950.]

FRIEDRICH MÜLLER, Die armenischen hand-schriften des klosters von Aryni (Arghana). Kaiserliche akademie der wissenschaften: Philo-sophisch-historische classe: Sitzungsberichte (vol. cxxxiv, no.4): Wien 1896. pp.14. [142.]

FRIEDRICH MÜLLER, Die armenischen hand-schriften von Sewast (Siwas) und Šenquš. Kaiser-liche akademie der wissenschaften: Philosophisch-historische classe: Sitzungsberichte (vol.cxxxv, no.6): Wien 1897. pp.13. [128.]

FRANZ NIKOLAUS FINCK, Յուցցակ Տփիսսնից Ս՛գար ՅովՀաննէսեանի Հայերէն Ջեռագրերի Երկասիրեց Ցիրանց Ս՛իկոլաուս Ֆինկ. Leipzig &c. 1903. pp. xxiii.260. [300.]

FRANZ NIKOLAUS FINCK and LEVON GJAND-SCHEZIAN, Verzeichnis der armenischen hand-schriften. Königliche universitätsbibliothek:

Systematisch-alphabetischer haupt-katalog (M.a. xiii): Tübingen 1907. pp.vii.276+iii.43. [1500.]

FRÉDÉRIC MACLER, Catalogue des manuscrits arméniens et géorgiens de la Bibliothèque nationale. 1908. pp.xxx.205. [armenian: 500.]

FREDERICK CORNWALLIS CONYBEARE, A catalogue of the armenian manuscripts in the British museum. 1913. pp.xii.411. [500.]

FRÉDÉRIC MACLER, Notices de quelques manuscrits arméniens vus dans quelques bibliothèques de l'Europe centrale. 1914. pp.184. [52.]

BASILE SARGHISSIAN, Grand catalogue des manuscrits arméniens de la bibliothèque des pp. mekhitharistes de Saint-Lazare. Venise 1914–1924. pp.xviii. cols.838+cols.1312. [319.]

SUKIAS BARONIAN and F. C. CONYBEARE, Catalogue of the armenian manuscripts in the Bodleian library. Catalogi codd. mss. Bibliothecae bodleianae pars xiv: Oxford 1918. pp.viii.coll.254. pp.[xiii]. [124.]

COLLECTION de m. le docteur Gachet. ... Manuscrits arméniens, arabes, persans. Bordeaux [printed] 1922. pp.12. [88.]

FRÉDÉRIC MACLER, Notices de manuscrits arméniens ou relatifs aux Arméniens vus dans quelques bibliothèques de la péninsule ibérique et du sud-est de la France. 1923. pp.[v].204. [50.]

EUGENIUS [EUGÈNE] TISSERANT, Codices armeni Bibliothecae vaticanae, borgiani, vaticani, barberiniani, chisiani. Romae 1927. pp.xix.395. [500.]

OV. PETROSYAN, Հայ Գրականութեան Թիւլիւղղաբիա. Երեվան 1953. pp.xxxii.402. [7680.]

L. V. MIRZOYAN, E. S. VLASYAN and S. S. YAZUICHYAN, Виктор Амазаспович Амбарцумян. Академия наук СССР: Материалы и библиографии ученых АССР: Ереван 1954. pp.75. [300.]

T. E. ERIKSSON, Die armenische büchersammlung der universitätsbibliothek zu Helsinki. Helsingin yliopiston kirjaston julkaisuja (no.xxiv): Helsinki 1955. pp.[i].85. [400.]
also issued as vol.xviii, no.2, of Studia orientalia (Helsinki).

ARMENIAN manuscripts. An exhibition at the university of Kansas library. [Lawrence] 1955. pp.16. [21.]
the manuscripts form part of the Harry Kurdian collection.

N. S. VLASYAN, A. S. MANASERYAN and M. A. BARTIKAYAN, Иосиф Абгарович Орбели. Академия наук Армянской ССР: Материалы к биобиблиографии ученых СССР: Ереань 1957. pp.77. [200.]

SIRARPIE DER NERSESSIAN, A catalogue of the armenian manuscripts, with an introduction on the history of armenian art. The Chester Beatty library: Dublin 1958. pp.xliv.216+vii.pls.66. [60.]

KAZIMIERZ ROSZKO and JAN BRAUN, Katalog rękopisów ormiańskich i gruzińskich. Catalogue des manuscrits arméniens et géorgiens. Manuscrits arméniens décrits par Kazimierz Roszko sous le direction de Eugeniusz Słuszkiewicz, manuscrits géorgiens décrits par Jan Braun. Catalogue des manuscrits orientaux des collections polonaises (tome iii): Warszawa 1958. [armenian: 49].

ERROLL F. RHODES, An annotated list of armenian New Testament manuscripts. Annual report of theology: Monograph series (vol.i): Department of christian studies: Rikkyo (St. Paul's) university: Ikebukuro, Tokyo 1959. pp.xiv.192. [1244.]

Список издании, выпущенных в свет. Академия наук Армянской ССР: Ереван 1960 &c. in progress?

JULIUS ASSFALG and JOSEPH MOLITOR, Armenische handschriften. Verzeichnis der orientalischen handschriften in Deutschland (band iv): Wiesbaden 1962. pp.xvi.158. [38.]

H. TOPDJIAN, Catalogue des manuscrits d'Armache. Bibliothèque arménienne de la Fondation Calouste Culbenkian. Venice 1962. pp.543. [223.]

SIRARPIE DER NERSESSIAN, Armenian manuscripts in the Freer gallery of art. Freer gallery of art: Oriental studies (no.6): Washington 1963. pp.xix.146. [11.]

UNIVERSITY of California, Los Angeles. Dictionary catalog of the university library 1919–1962. Vol.129: Japanese collection A–Z. Armenian collection A–Z. Boston 1963. pp.606. [armenian: 1288 cards.]

Каталог рукописей Матенадарана имени Маштоца. Институт древных рукописей имени Маштоца: Ереван.
   i. Составили О. Еганян, А. Зейтунян, П. Антабян. 1965. pp.1634. [5000.]
   ii. 1970. pp.1549. [5001–10408.]

NORAIR BOGHARIAN, Grand catalogue of St. James manuscripts. Calouste Gulbenkian foundation armenian library: Jerusalem 1966–71.pp. [xii]. 675+[xii]. 670+[xii].647+xx.696+xii. 606. [1700.]

SAHAG A. MOURADIAN and NAZARETH B. MARDI-ROSSIAN, Catalogue of armenian manuscripts of St. Arakelotz-Tarkmanchatz monastery (Moush) and the environs. Edited by Ara Kalaydjian. Calouste Gulbenkian foundation armenian library: Jerusalem 1967. pp.220.[12]. [285.]

STEPANOS HOVAGUIMIAN, Catalogue des manuscrits de Nicomédie et des environs. Bibliothèque arménienne de la Fondation Calouste Gulbenkian: Venise 1969. pp.91. [87.]

SMBAT TER-AVETISSIAN, Katalog der armenischen handschriften in der bibliothek des klosters in Neu-Djoulfa. Calouste Gulbenkian foundation armenian library: Wien 1970. pp.vi.926. [587.]
— band ii, bearbeitet von L. G. Minassian, redigiert von O. S. Eganian. Wien 1972. pp.xvi.293. [229.]

EDWARD GULBEKIAN, Armenian press directory. London 1971. pp.76. [429.]

K. N. GRIGORYAN, Армянская литература в русских переводах. Ереванский Государственный университет: Кабинет литературных связей. Ериван.
  i. 1786–1917. 1969. pp.164. [1523.]

iv. Georgia

1. General
2. Georgian literature

1. General

Грузинская библиографія. I. Указатель къ статьямъ и матеріаламъ въ грузинской периодической печати (1852–1910). Петроградъ 1916. pp.viii.160. [2462.]

CHALVA BÉRIDZÉ, Bibliographie française de la Géorgie. 1932. pp.193–229. [400.]

БИБЛИОГРАФИЯ русской периодики Грузии. Тбилиси.
  i. 1828–1920. 1941. pp.vi.195. [463.]

L[YUDMILA] E[RASTOVNA] TSKHOVREBOVA, Коста Хетагуров (1859–1906). Библиография. Сталинир 1959. pp.98. [1300.]

Библиография изданий Академин наук Грузинской ССР 1937–1956 гг. Академия наук Грузинской ССР: Центральная библиотека: Тбилиси 1959. pp. 945.
— 1957–1960 гг. 1963. pp.580. [4381.]

B. E. KURASHVILI, N. G. KAMALOV, and I. YA. ELIAVA, Библиография по гельминтам и гелминтозам человека, животных и сельскохозяйственных растений в Грузии (за период с 1865 года до 1967 год). Bibliography of the helminths and helminthoses of man, of animals and of agricultural plants in Georgia (1865–1967). Тбилиси 1968. pp.100. [1200.]

2. Georgian literature

[LAURENT BROSSET and ARIST ARISTOVICH KUNIK], Liste des travaux de m. Brosset. Académie impériale des sciences: [St. Petersburg] 1880. pp.19. [237.]
also issued in smaller format, pp.53.

N[IKOLAI] YA[KOVLEVICH] MARR, Краткій каталогъ собранія грузинскихъ рукописей пріобрѣтеннаго Императорскою публичною библіотекою въ 1896 году. С.-Петербургъ 1900. pp.13. [26.]

T. ZHORDANYA and (vol.iii) M. DZHANASHVILI, Описание рукописей Тифлискаго церковнаго музея.
  i, ii. 1903.
  iii. 1908.
  iv. 1954.
  v. 1955.

[ALEKSANDR SOLOMONOVICH KHAKHANOV], Les manuscrits géorgiens de la Bibliothèque nationale à Paris. [*s.l. c.*1900]. pp.20. [25.]
the text is in georgian.

FRÉDÉRIC MACLER, Catalogue des manuscrits arméniens et géorgiens de la Bibliothèque nationale. 1908. pp.xxx.205. [Georgian: 30.]

FREDERICK CORNWALLIS CONYBEARE, A catalogue of the armenian manuscripts in the British museum . . . to which is appended a catalogue of georgian manuscripts . . . by J. Oliver Wardrop. 1913. pp.xii.411. [Georgian: 6.]

BIBLIOGRAPHIA georgica, 1928. Систематический указатель научной литературы Грузии. Книжная палата Грузии. Тифлис 1930. pp.ix.136. [1004.]

E. TAKAÏCHVILI, Les manuscrits géorgiens de la Bibliothèque national de Paris et les vingt alphabets secrets géorgiens. [Paris] 1933.

N[IKOLAI] YA[KOVLEVICH] MARR, Описание грузкнских рукописей синайского монастыра. Академия наук СССР: Москва 1940. pp.xii.276. [65.]

TS. KALANDADZE and O. SOSELIYA, საქართველოს ისტორიის ლიტერატურული წყაროები·Литературные источники истории Грузии. Научносправочное пособие. Академия наук Грузинской ССР: Тбилиси 1955. pp.viii.384. [5252.]

R. R. ORBELI, Грузинские рукописи института. Академия наук СССР: Институт востоковедения: Москва.
  i. история, география, путешествия, археология, законодательство, философия, языкознание, библиография. 1956. pp.187. [161.]
no more published.

KATALOG rękopisów ormiańskich i gruzińskich. Catalogue des manuscrits arméniens décrits par Kasimierz Roszko sous la direction de Eugeniusz Słuszkiewicz, manuscrits géorgiens décrits par Jan Braun. Catalogue des manuscrits orientaux des collections polonaises (tome iii). Warszawa 1958. [georgian: 11.]

DAVID MARSHALL LANG, Catalogue of georgian and other caucasian printed books in the British museum. 1962. pp.xi.coll.430. [2000.]

JULIUS ASSFALG, Georgische handschriften. Verzeichnis der orientalischen handschriften in Deutschland (vol.iii): Wiesbaden 1963. pp.xxi.87. [250.]

TZ. P. CHUKASHVILI, Каталог рукописей и архивных материалов, хранящисхя в Государственной республиканской библиотеке Грузинской ССР им. К. Маркса. Тбилиси 1964. pp.134. [246.]

in georgian and russian.

Грузинская книга. Библиография. Das georgische buch; vollständige bibliographie. Государственная книжная палата Грузинской ССР: Тбилиси.

    i. 1629–1920. 1941. pp.xl.560. [5833.]
    ii. 1921–1945. 1950. pp.xiv.815+   +161. [9452 in part 1.]
    iii. 1946–1950. 1964. pp.viii.498. [4704.]
in georgian.

N. AKKERMAN, Шота Руставели (800 лет со дня рождения). Рекомендательний указател литературы. Тбилиси 1966. pp.24. [227.]

E. M. TUMALISHVILI and T. K. BURKADZE, Библиография изданий Кавказского музея и Государственная музея Грузии имени С. Н. Джанашина. Тбилиси 1966. pp.163. [927.]

georgian titles provided with russian translation.

"Витязь в тигровой шкуре". Библиографический указатель изданий. Государственная республиканская библиотека Грузинской ССР им. К. Маркса. Тбилиси 1966. pp.44. [239.]

S[AURMAG] S[ARKISOVICH] KAKABADZE, Грузинские документы института народов Азии АН СССР. Академия наук СССР: Институт народов Азии: Москва 1967. pp. 512. [612.]

E. B. ZHUZHUNADZE, Библиография произведений Николая Николаевича Кецховели. Тбилиси 1970. pp.140. [657.]

in georgian and russian.

DAVID BARRETT, Catalogue of the Wardrop collection and of other georgian books and manuscripts in the Bodleian library. 1973. pp.xvii.354. [3696.]

Библиография литературы и трудов в области филологических наук —72. Академия наук Грузинской ССР: Сектор научной информации по общественным наукам: Серия филологических наук. Тбилиси.

    i.
    ii. Составители: Г.Г. Тевазде, М.А. Гачечиладзе и Н. Г. Окруашвили. 1973. pp.170. [620.]*

SOUTH ASIA

i. *Bibliography*
ii. *Periodicals*
iii. *General*
iv. *Subjects*

i. *Bibliography*

G. RAYMOND NUNN, South and southeast Asia; a bibliography of bibliographies. Occasional paper (no.4): East west center library [Honolulu] 1966. ff.v, 59. [350.]*

HENRY SHOLBERG, Bibliography of south asian bibliographies in the Ames library of south Asia; with a special section on southeast Asia. [Minnesota, 1970.] ff.ii.22. [320.]*

ii. *Periodicals*

S[ĪGĀRI] R[ĀMĀRITA] RANGANATHAN [RAṄGĀNATHAN] [*and others*]. Union catalogue of learned periodical publications in south Asia. Volume I. Physcial and biological sciences. India library association: English series (no.7): [Delhi] &c. 1953. pp.391. [6000.]

INDEX indo-asiaticus. Edited by S. Chaudhuri, Calcutta, New Delhi.
  i. 1968. pp.[vi]. 24.16.8.
  ii. 1968. pp.[xviii].48.
  iii. 1968. pp.[viii].80.
  iv. 1968. pp.44.
  v. 1969. pp.104.
  vi. 1969. pp.28. viii.
  vii. 1969. pp.iv.76.
  viii. 1969. pp.48.
  ix. 1970. pp.[x].48.36.
  x.
  xi.
  xii. 1970. pp.84.
  xiii–xiv. 1971. pp.112.
each issue contains contents lists of a varying number of orientalist journals, with other bibliographical material.
in progress.

SOUTHERN Asia publications in western languages. A quarterly accessions list. Library of Congress: Division of orientalia [*afterwards:* Orientalia division]: Washington.*
  i. 1952. pp.226. [3500.]
  ii. 1953. pp.190. [3000.]
  iii. 1954. pp.218. [3500.]
  iv. 1955. pp.253. [4000.]
  v. 1956. pp.324. [4500.]
        [*continued as:*]
Southern Asia accessions list.
  vi. 1957. pp.466. [5000.]
  vii. 1958. pp.564. [6000.]
  viii. 1959. pp.760. [8000.]
  ix. 1960. pp.689. [7500.]
no more published.

iii. *General*

SOUTHERN Asia publications in western languages. A quarterly accessions list. Library of Congress: Division of orientalia [*afterwards:* Orientalia division]: Washington.*
  i. 1952. pp.iv.226. [4000.]
  ii. 1953. pp.vi.190. [3000.]
  iii. 1954. pp.vi.218. [3500.]
  iv. 1955. pp.vii.253. [4500.]
  v. 1956. pp.vii.324. [4500.]
        [*continued as:*]
Southern Asia accessions list.
  vi. 1957. pp.ix.466. [4000.]
  vii. 1958. pp.x.564. [5500.]
  viii. 1959. pp.x.760. [7500.]
  ix. 1960. pp.xi.689. [6500.]
no more published.

PATRICK WILSON, South Asia. A selected bibliography of India, Pakistan, Ceylon. American institute of Pacific relations: New York 1957. pp.[v].iii.41. [600].*

ADELA R. FREEBURGER, South Asia. Office of education: International education relations: Keep tab on the lab (vol.ii, no.4): Washington 1960. pp.10. [125.]*

EARL R. SCHMIDT, Preliminary list of Ph.D. dissertations on south Asia 1933–1960 (unedited). Madison, Wis. [1960?]. pp.27. [500.]*

MAUREEN L. P. PATTERSON and RONALD B. INDEN, South Asia: an introductory bibliography. University of Chicago: Introduction to the civilization of India: Chicago 1962. pp.xxxvi.412. [4369.]*

CATALOGUE of european printed books. India office library: Commonwealth relations office. Boston 1964. [90,000.]*
  i, ii. Sheaf catalogue. pp.948+1010.
  iii–vi. Author catalogue. pp.767+740+789+713.
  vii–ix. Subject catalogue. pp.630+635+850.
  x. Catalogue of periodicals. pp.143.

INDEX of post-1937 european manuscript accessions. India office library: Commonwealth relations office: Boston 1964. pp.iii.156. [3264.]*

M. D[OREEN] WAINWRIGHT and NOEL MATTHEWS, A guide to Western manuscripts and documents in the British Isles relating to south and south east Asia. London, 1965. pp.xix.532. [20,000.]

M. M. EVANS, Catalogue of papers relating to: South Asia, 1792–1914 ... Baptist missionary society: 1964. pp.179.

STEPHEN N. HAY, EDITH EHRMAN, WARD MOREHOUSE, Preliminary bibliography on South Asia for undergraduate libraries. University of the state of New York: The State education department: Center for international programs and services: Foreign area materials center: New York 1967. pp.ix.393. [2687.]*

MARGARET H. CASE, South asian history 1750–1950; a guide to periodicals, dissertations and newspapers. Princeton 1968. pp.xiii.561. [6750.]

SOUTHERN ASIA. Afghanistan, Bhutan, Burma, Cambodia, Ceylon, India, Laos. Malaya, Nepal, Pakistan, Sikkim, Singapore, Thailand, Vietnam. Harvard university library: Widener library shelflist (19). Cambridge, Mass. 1968. [10,292.]

THE COMMONWEALTH in south and south east Asia. National book league and the Commonwealth institute: [London] 1969. pp.32. [172.]

RICHARD J. KOZICKI and PETER ANANDA, South and southeast Asia: doctoral dissertations and masters' theses completed at the university of California at Berkeley 1906–1968. Occasional papers of the Center for south and southeast Asia studies, University of California (no.1): Berkeley 1969. ff.viii.49. [307.]*

D. A[NTHONY] LOW, J. C. ILTIS and M. D[OREEN] WAINWRIGHT, edd. Government archives in South Asia; Pakistan. Cambridge 1969. pp.xii.355. [Large number.]

LOUIS A. JACOB [and others], South Asia; a bibliography for undergraduate libraries. Williamsport, Pa. 1970. pp.xvi.103. [1610.]

MILTON W[ALTER] MEYER, South Asia: an introductory bibliography. Department of history; California state university: Los Angeles 1972. pp.14.

FRANK J. SHULMAN, Doctoral dissertations on south Asia 1966–1970; an annotated bibliography covering north America, Europe and Australia. Michigan papers on south and southeast Asia (4): Center for south and southeast asian studies: University of Michigan: Ann Arbor 1971. pp.xvii.228. [1305.]*

MARY THATCHER, Cambridge south asian archive. Records of the British period in south Asia relating to India, Pakistan, Ceylon, Burma, Nepal and Afghanistan held in the Centre of south asian studies, University of Cambridge. 1973. pp.xi.346. [large number.]

iv. Subjects

Anthropology

CUMULATIVE index to current literature on anthropology & allied subjects. Department of anthropology: Calcutta*
  i. 1955. pp.viii.171. [1500.]
  ii. 1956. pp.iv.144. [1250.]

ELIZABETH VON FÜRER-HAIMENDORF, An anthropological bibliography of south Asia, together with a directory of recent anthropological field work. École pratique des hautes études: Le monde d'outre-mer passé et présent (4th ser., vol.iii):
  i. 1958. pp.748. [5316.]
  ii. 1955–9. pp.459. [2762.]
  iii. 1960–1964. Bibliographies (vol.8). 1970. pp.562. [4525.]

Archaeology

SOUTHERN ASIA. Council for old world archaeology: COWA surveys bibliographies: Cambridge, Mass.
  i. 1958. pp.8. [118.]
  ii. 1960. pp.138. [121.]
  iii. 1964. pp.199. [139.]
  iv. 1970. pp.823. [379.]

Economics

EUGENE DE BENKO and V. N. KRISHNAN, Research sources for south asian studies in economic development; a select bibliography of serial publications. Asian studies center: Michigan state university, East Lansing. 1966. pp.xi.97. [918.]

Folk-lore

EDWIN CAPERS KIRKLAND, A bibliography of south asian folklore. Indiana university folklore series (no.21): Asian folklore studies monographs (no.4): Indiana university research center in anthropology, folklore, and linguistics. [Bloomington 1966.] pp.xxiv.291. [6852.]

Land tenure

NEAR east and south Asia: a bibliography. A bibliography of materials dealing with the near east and south Asia in the Land tenure center library . . . University of Wisconsin . . . Madison 1971. pp.74. [1000.]*
— Supplement 1972.

Missions

ROBERT STREIT and JOHANNES DINDINGER, Bibliotheca missionum. Fortgesetzt von Johannes Rommerskirchen und Josef Metzler. xxviii. Missionsliteratur Südasiens (Indien, Pakistan, Birma, Ceylon), 1947–1968. 1971. pp.xix.579. [1734.]

Public administration

PAUL E. MENGE, Government administration in south Asia: a bibliography. Papers in comparative public administration: Special series (no.9): Comparative administration group: American society for public administration: Washington [1968]. pp.iii.100. [1025.]*

Religion

HARRY DANIEL SMITH, Profile of a library in transition. A bibliographical survey of history of religious resources. Syracuse university: Program of south Asia studies: Syracuse. 1966.★
i. History of religions in south Asia. pp.205. [2800.]

Science

BIBLIOGRAPHY of scientific publications of south Asia (India, Burma, Ceylon). Unesco: Science co-operation office for south Asia [iv–xi: South Asia science co-operation office; xii: Indian national scientific documentation centre]: New Delhi &c.
i–ii. 1949. pp.[vi].107+[ii].88. [4305.]
iii–iv. 1950. pp.[iv].xiii.84+[v].86. [4245.]
— Name index to . . . 1–4. [1952]. pp.[ii].48.
v–vi. 1951. pp.[iii].ii.97.v+[v].viii.ii.124. [5321.]
vii–viii. 1952. pp. [vii].178+[v].157. [6679.]
ix–x. 1953. pp.[v].174+[v].158. [6912.]
xi–xii. 1954. pp.[v].212+[v].129. [7796.]
[continued as:]
Bibliography of scientific publications of south & south east Asia. 1955–64.
no more published.

★S[ĪGĀRI] R[ĀMĀRITA] RANGANATHAN [RAṄGA-NATHAN] [and others], Union catalogue of learned periodical publications in south Asia. Volume 1. Physical and biological sciences. India library association: English series (no.7): [Delhi] &c. 1953. pp.391. [6000.]

PATRICK WILSON, Science in South Asia, past and present. A preliminary bibliography of writings on science in India, Pakistan, and Ceylon. Occasional publication (no.3): Foreign area materials center: University of the State of New York: State education department: New York, 1966. pp.xii. 100. [1500.]★

Social sciences

SOUTH Asia social science abstracts. South Asia science co-operation office. New Delhi.
1952. 1954. ff.iii.pp.86. [363.]★
1953. 1955. pp.vi.136. [390.]
1954. Research centre on the social implications of industrialization in southern Asia: Calcutta 1956. pp.v.123. [327.]
1955. 1956. pp.v.169. [385.]
1956. 1958. pp.vi.157. [334.]
1957. 1958. pp.v.147. [334.]
1958. 1959. pp.v.150. [316.]
merged with South Asia social science bibliography.

SOCIAL science bibliography: India. South Asia science co-operation office: New Delhi.
i. 1952. 1954. pp.v.176.xiv. [1677.]★

ii. 1953. 1955. pp.vi.123. [1905.]
iii. 1954. Research centre on the social implications of industrialization in southern Asia.
iv. 1955. 1957. pp.iv.101. [1672.]
v. 1956. 1958. pp.v.135. [2347.]
[continued as:]
SOCIAL science bibliography. India. Pakistan.
vi. 1957. pp.[v].159. [2801.]
[continued as:]
SOUTH Asia social science bibliography.
vii. 1958. pp.[v].141. [2402.]
viii. (with annotations and abstracts) 1959. pp.[v]. 230. [1413.]
ix. Research centre on social and economic development in southern Asia. 1960. pp. [ix]. 190. [1196.]
x. 1961. pp.ix.124.xxxxv [sic]. [1034.]
xi. 1962. pp.ix.204. [1098.]
xii. 1963. pp.ix.254. [1519.]
xiii. 1964. pp.viii.206. [1294.]
xiv. 1965. pp.vi.193.xlvi. [1137.]★
[continued as:]
NAND KISHORE GOIL, Asian social science bibliography, with annotations and abstracts, 1966. Institute of economic growth: Delhi, Dobbs Ferry [1970.] pp.xxiii.490. [1968.]

Zoology

D. B. JAMES and R. S. LAL MOHAN, Bibliography of the echinoderms of the Indian ocean. Bulletin of the Central marine fisheries research institute (no.15): Mandapam camp 1969. pp.[i].44. [650.]

INDIA

i. *Bibliographies*
ii. *Periodicals*
iii. *General*
iv. *Cartography*
v. *Constitution and government*
vi. *History*
vii. *Law*
viii. *Academic writings*
ix. *Official publications*
x. *Topography. Provinces, &c.*
xi. *Central India.*
xii. *French India*
xiii. *Portuguese India*
xiv. *South India*
xv. *Subjects*
xvi. *Persons.*

i. *Bibliographies*

FRANK [FRANCIS BUNBURY FITZ-GERALD] CAMPBELL, An index-catalogue of bibliographical works (chiefly in the english language) relating to India. 1897. pp.99. [1000.]

BENOYENDRA SENGUPTA. Indiaana: a select list of reference & representative books on all aspects of indian life & culture. Calcutta 1966. pp.xiv.125. [550.]

H. D. SHARMA, S. P. MUKHERJI and L. M. P. SINGH, Indian reference sources; an annotated guide to indian reference books. Indian bibliographic center: Varanasi, Jullundur 1972. pp.vii. 313. [2076.]

A. K. MUKHERJEE, Annotated guide to reference materials in the human sciences. Bombay &c. 1962. pp.xv.267. [1164.]

ii. *Periodicals*

[THOMAS] LUKER, Indian press guide. Madras 1885. pp.38. [500.]

LIST of periodicals received in the Imperial library. Calcutta 1913. pp.[iii].12. [225.]
— Second edition. 1933. pp.[v].17. [281.]

*STANLEY KEMP, Catalogue of the scientific serial publications in the principal libraries of Calcutta. Asiatic society of Bengal: Calcutta 1918. pp.xii.292. [1607.]

[BANKATALĀLA OJHA], Bibliography of hindi newspapers (1826–1925). Vol.I. [Hyderabad 1925]. pp.[iv].2.6.8.8.80. [750.]

INDIANA. An index to articles in indian periodicals. Benares 1936–8. 1950.
no more published.

J. N. GANDHI, The all-India press annual. 3rd edition. Lahore 1935. pp.[iv].ii.176. [750.]

PAMPHLET showing publications ... the supply of which is undertaken by the Central publication branch on payment of an annual subscription. Delhi 1935. pp.8. [34.]

PÉRIODIQUES reçus à la bibliothèque. ... Inde. Bureau international du travail: List de références bibliographiques (no.20): Genève 1951. pp.4. [92.]*
— [another edition]. ... (no.53): 1952. pp.5. [99.]*

LIST of scientific periodicals published in India. Unesco: Paris 1952. pp.18.

CURRENT periodicals. India office: Library: 1953. pp.11. (300.]
— [another edition]. 1958. ff.15. [400.]

NIFOR guide to indian periodicals 1955–1956. National information service: Poona [1955]. pp.xxii.386. [2000.]

CATALOGUE of periodicals available in CSIR organisations: Council of scientific & industrial research: New Delhi 1955. pp.[iii].108. [1500.]

[BENOY SEN GUPTA], Catalogue of periodicals, newspapers & gazettes. National library: Calcutta 1956. pp.[ii].vi.285. [1697.]
limited to periodicals in european languages.

ANNUAL report of the registrar of newspapers for India. [New Delhi].
    1956. pp.510. [6570.]
    1957. pp.313. [5932.]
    1958. pp.vi.604. [6918.]
    1959.
    1960. pp.[ii].vii.308+[iii].696. [7651.]
    1961. pp.iv.330+[iii].707. [6435.]
    1962. pp.iv.343+714. [6623.]
    1963. pp.[ii].iii.329. [7397.]
    1964. pp.iv.306+[iii].793. [7790.]
        [*continued as:*]
PRESS in India. Annual report on the press compiled by the Registrar of newspapers for India under the PRB act. Ministry of information and broadcasting, Government of India: New Delhi Part II.
    1965. pp.vi.259+ii.801.[8161.]
    1966. pp.vi.272+801. [7906.]
    1967. pp.x.368+vi.1243. [8640.]

*J[IBANANDA] SAHA, Union list of learned periodicals. . . . A selection from the periodicals being currently received in certain libraries in Calcutta and neighbourhood. Indian statistical institute: Library: Bibliographical series (no.1): Calcutta [1959]. pp.[viii].55. [2500.]

PRĀCĪ-JYOTI: digest of indological studies. Institute of indic studies: Kurukshetra university 1963 &c. includes: Titles of doctoral theses submitted to indian universities up-to-date.
    i. 1963. Editors: D. N. Shastri, Buddha Prakash. pp.xiv.296. [223].
    ii. 1964. pp.xvi.309+xvi. 323. [856.]
    iii. 1965. Editor: Buddha Prakash. pp.xxx. 361+xxxi.362–698. [1151.]
    iv. 1966. pp.xxxii.372+xvi.373–660. [916.]
    v. 1967. joint editor (part ii): V. C. Pandey, xxiv.295+xv.602. [779.]
    vi. 1968. Editor: Sūrya Kānta. pp.xiii.249. [362.]
    vii. 1971. Editor: Gopikamohan Bhattacharya. pp.l.280. [1332.]
    viii. 1972. pp.l.324. [1207.]
in progress.

CATALOGUE of european printed books, India office library, Commonwealth relations office, London. Vol.IX. Periodical publications. Boston 1964. pp.[ii].143. [3003.]

GUIDE to indian periodical literature (social sciences and humanities).
    i. 1964. Editor, Vijay Kumar Jain. Compilers, Syed Mohammed Ali, Krishan Gopal Tyagi, pp.xv.437. [14,000.]

ii. 1965. pp.xv.454. [14,500.]
iii. 1966. pp.xvi.419. [13,500.]
iv. 1967. pp.xvi.518. [16,500.]
v. 1968. pp.xvi.868. [26,000.]
H. S. Sharma added to names of compilers.
vi. 1969. pp.xvi.244+xvi.170+xvi.339+
xvi.267. [32,000.]
vii. 1970. pp.xvi.208+xvi.130+xvi.242+
xvi. 144. [23,000.]
viii. 1971. pp.xvi.136+xvi.164+xvi.277+
xvi.330. [29,000.]
ix. 1972. pp.xvi.151+xvi.230+xvi.216+
xvi.202. [25,000.]
K. G. Tyagi no longer a compiler.
x. 1973. pp.xv.154.
in progress. annual volumes set out when available.

A. K. MUKERJEE, Bibliography of periodicals.
Central institute of education: Delhi 1964. pp.118.

KRISHNA KANTA SUD, *ed.* Indian periodicals
directory. Calcutta [1964]. pp.[vi].188. [1600.]

INDEX India: a quarterly documentation list
of selected articles, editorials, notes and letters
etc. from periodicals and newspapers published in
english language all over the world (a quarterly
documentation list on India of materials in english).
Edited by N. N. Gidwani. Rajasthan university
library: Jaipur.
i. 1967. pp.1141.ccv. [35,363.]*
ii. 1968. pp.[x].ix.360.xcix.xxxviii.xv.
[44,702.]
iii. 1969. pp.xviii.xi.859.cxc.xcviii. [51,049.]
iv. 1970. pp.xxi.929.ccxxi.cx. [54,222.]
v. 1971. [47,212.]
vi. 1972.
annual cumulations only entered.
in progress.

THE CATALOGUE of periodicals. Mysore university library: Mysore 1970. pp.[iii].pp.172.
[1784.]

INDIAN periodicals and newspapers: National
library of Australia. Canberra 1970. pp.211.
[1250.]*

N. N. GIDWANI and K. NAVLANI, Indian periodicals: an annotated guide. pp.viii.191. [5121.]

ABSTRACTS and index of reports and articles.
Lok sabha secretariat: New Delhi.
i. 1963. pp.229. [1227.]
ii. 1964. pp.285. [1434.]
iii. 1965. pp.257. [1589.]
iv. 1966.
v. 1967. pp.327. [2285.]
vi. 1968. pp.369. [2564.]
vii. 1969.
in progress?

INDIAN news index; a (quarterly) subject guide
to selected english newspapers of India. Punjab

university extension library, Ludhiana (Punjab
university library, Chandigarh).
i. 1965. pp.[viii].132+[iv].158+[iv].165+
[iv].142. [20,000.]
vi. 1970. pp.[viii].521. [20,000.]
volumes two to five were not published.

iii. *General*

A CATALOGUE of the library of the Hon. East-
India company. 1845. pp.viii.325. [4250.]
— A supplement. 1851. pp.viii.240. [3000.]
— [supplement]. List of references on the
East India company. Library of Congress:
Washington 1916. ff.9. [91.]*

CATALOGUE of books belonging to the library
of the government of India. Part II. Calcutta 1861.
pp.220. [1500.]

CATALOGUE of books belonging to the library
of the Home department, government of India.
Calcutta 1867. pp.[ii].474. [8000.]
— Part II. 1870. pp.[ii].157. [3000.]
a supplement.

CATALOGUE of the library. Colombo museum:
Colombo 1877. pp.22. [450.]

GUSTAV OPPERT, Index to sixty-two ms. volumes
deposited in the Government oriental manuscripts library, containing references to archæological, historical, geographical, and other subjects.
Madras 1878. pp.5.xlvii. [5000.]

REPORTS on publications issued and registered in
the several provinces of british India. Selections
from the records of the government of India,
Home department. Calcutta.

1877. pp.[i].138. [4890.]
1878.
1879.
1880. pp.[i].155. [5370.]
1881. pp.[i].147. [5534.]
1882. pp.[i].218. [6199.]
1883. pp.[i].134. [7530.]
1884. pp.[i].84. [7501.]
1885. pp.[i].73. [8708.]
1886. pp.[i].80. [8950.]
1887. pp.[i].81. [8243.]
1888. pp.[i].89. [9712.]
1889.
1890. pp.[i].76. [7884.]
1891. pp.[i].104. [7041.]
1892. pp.[i].105. [6713.]
1893.
1894. pp.[i].105. [7179.]
1895. pp.[i].125. [8015.]
1896. pp.[i].119. [7181.]
1897. pp.[i].109. [7055.]
1898. pp.[i].133. [7323.]

KAVI RAJA SHAMAL DAS JI's private library. [*s.l. c.*1885]. pp.14. [82.]

LIBRARY catalogue of the Historical department of Meywar. Oodeypore 1886. pp.22. [130.]

CATALOGUE of the library of the India office. Vol.I. 1883. pp.[iii].567+[iii].228. [15,000.]
— Supplement. 1885. pp.[ii].384. [7500.]
— Supplement 2. 1909. pp.[iii].616. [9000.]
— Accessions.
    i. 1911. pp.[ii].56. [750.]
    ii. 1911. pp.59. [750.]
    iii. 1912. pp.[ii].122. [1500.]
    iv. 1912. pp.90. [1000.]
    v. 1913. pp.69. [750.]
    vi. 1913. pp.68. [750.]
    vii. 1918. pp.68. [750.]
    viii. 1919. pp.72. [750.]
    ix. 1920. pp.58. [750.]
    x. 1921. pp.110. [1500.]
    xi. 1923. pp.192. [3000.]
    xii. 1924. pp.105. [1500.]
    xiii. 1926. pp.171. [3000.]
    xiv. 1928. pp.213. [4000.]
    xv. 1931. pp.206. [4000.]
    xvi. 1934. pp.108. [2000.]
    xvii. 1936. pp.374. [6000.]
    xviii. 1936. pp.55. [1000.]
vol.ii of the main work sets out books in various oriental languages.

CATALOGUE of the library of the Madras government museum. Madras 1894. pp.243. [10,000.]

[GERARD A. JOSEPH], A catalogue of the library of the Ceylon branch of the Royal asiatic society. Colombo 1895. pp.[iii].98. [1000.]

AUTHOR – catalogue of printed books in european languages. With a supplementary list of newspapers. Imperial library: Catalogue: Calcutta 1904. pp.xii.903+904–1643. [50,000.]
— First supplement, 1917. pp.739+740–1335. 94. [40,000.]
— Part II. Subject-index to the author catalogue, 1908–10. pp.547+315.
— — First supplement, 1929. pp.iii. 575.
— — Second supplement, 1939. pp.ii. 360.
— Part IV, Catalogue of indian official publication. Vol.I, A–L, 1909. pp.iii, cols.543. [15,000.]

STEN KONOW, Classified catalogue of the library of the Director general of archaeology. Calcutta 1908. pp.[iii].xi.246. [2500.]
— — Supplement I. 1911. pp.[ii].54. [500.]
— — Supplement II. 1912. pp.[ii].32. [300.]
— — Supplement III. 1916. pp.[ii].viii.88. [800.]

CATALOGUE of the Nizam college library' english section. Madras 1909. pp.ix.127. [4500.]

CATALOGUE OF THE State library, Hyderabad, Deccan. English section. Madras 1910. pp.ix.90. [2500.]

CATALOGUE of books in the Secretariat library, Fort St. George. Madras 1913. pp.[iii].viii.449. [8000.]
— Supplement. No.2. [1916]. pp.32. [500.]
— — No.3. 1920. pp.35. [600.]
supplement no.1 forms part of the main work.

CATALOGUE of manuscripts in european languages belonging to the library of the India office.
    ii. I. The Orme collection. By S. C. Hill. 1916. pp.xxxv.421. [5000.]
    ii. II. Minor collections and miscellaneous manuscripts. By George Rusby Kaye and Edward Hamilton Johnston. 1937 &c.
in progress; vol.i is entered under Java, below.

BRIEF list of references on India. Chiefly economic, political and social. Library of Congress: [Washington] 1920. ff.3. [34.]*

INDIA. Far eastern books and journal lists (nos. 21–26): Public library: Newark, N.J. [1922]. ff.[6]. [130.]

SIR J[OHN] G[HEST] CUMMING, Bibliography relating to India (1900–1926). [National book council: Book lists] (no.62): 1927. pp.16. [500.]
the title is misleading; limited to works published in 1900–1926.
— — [supplement]. India ... compiled by Evans Lewin ... (no.62a): 1935. pp.12. [400.]
— — India and Burma. Compiled by sir Frank Brown. Third edition. 1942. pp.8. [250.]

SAMUEL CHARLES HILL, Catalogue of the home miscellaneous series of the India office records. India office: 1927. pp.vii.682. [100,000.]

CLASSIFIED CATALOGUE of the Dyal Singh library, Lahore. Published by the Board of trustees. Lahore 1933. pp.xiv.822. [10,000.]

A SHORT catalogue. Office of the High commissioner for India: India house library: 1933. pp.ix. 534. [5500.]

DOUGLAS C[RAWFORD] MCMURTRIE, Early mission printing presses in India. Rajkot 1933. pp.[i].3. [15.]
100 copies printed.

DOUGLAS C. MCMURTRIE, The beginning of printing in India. Rajkot 1933. pp.[i].3. [20.]
100 copies printed.

CATALOGUE of books of the Secretariat library of the government of Bombay. Bombay 1938. pp.[iii].viii.503. [10,000.]

ANNUAL bibliography of indian history and indology . . . to which are added publications of islamic world. Bombay historical society: Bombay.

    i. 1938. By Braz A. Fernandes. pp.viii.80. [1500.]

    ii. 1939. 1941. pp.viii.191. [1401.]

    iii. 1940. 1944. pp.li.378. [2177.]

    iv. 1941. 1946. pp.xxxi.337. [1713.]

    v. 1942. 1949. pp.xxviii.343. [1582.]

INDIC studies in America. American council of learned societies: Bulletin (no.28): Washington 1939. pp.vi.242. [755.]
consists of a guide to collections, of 'A basic bibliography for indic studies' by Elmer H. Cutts, and of other select bibliographies.

GIULIA PORRU, Studi d'indianistica in Italia dal 1911 al 1938. Publicazioni della r. università degli studi di Firenze: Facultâ di lettere e filosofia (iii.serie, vol.x): Firenze 1940. pp.viii.257. [972.]

AUTHOR catalogue of printed books in european languages. Imperial library: Calcutta 1941 &c. pp.vii.519+520–1036+1037–1543+1544–1958+1959–2583 + 2584–3115 + 3116–3432 + 3433–4039+4040–4374.
   — Supplement (1951–1961). Vol.1.A.1964, pp. [vi].380. [4500.]

WHAT to read about India. East and west association: [New York] 1942.*

    i. General bibliography. pp.15. [60.]

    ii. A list for the armed forces. pp.5. [12.]

    iii. A list for women's clubs. pp.4. [12.]

    iv. A list for business men. pp.5. [12.]

    v. A list for high school students. pp.6. [19.]

    vi. A list for college students. pp.9. [28.]

    vii. A list for labor unions. pp.5. [12.]

    viii. A popular list. pp.4. [12.]

R. N. DANDEKAR, *ed.* Progress of indic studies 1917–1942. Government oriental series (class B no.8): Bhandarkar oriental research institute: Poona 1942. pp.2. ii.406. [large number.]
a series of bibliographical essays.
   — Second volume. Poona 1961. pp.xxiii.760. [6000.]

GEORGE M[ARK] MORAES, Bibliography of indological studies, 1942. Konkan institute of arts and sciences: Bombay 1945. pp.xxxviii.188[sic, 190]. [1974.]

K. NAGARAJA RAO, Bibliography of indian culture and its preparation. Library in India series (vol.ii): Lahore 1945. pp.[vi].35. [100.]

SELECTED list of recent books on India. Corporation public libraries: Glasgow 1948. pp.11. [100.]

CATALOGUE of books added to the library, Bombay branch of the Royal asiatic society. Bombay 1946 &c. 1948 &c.

INDIA. A general reading list. Department of state: Division of library and reference services: BL [Bibliographic list] (no.32): [Washington] 1950. ff.4. [38.]*

A CLASSIFIED catalogue of books on the section XII. India in the Toyo Bunko acquired during the years 1917–1950. Toyo Bunko: Tokyo 1950. pp. x.288.xi–xviii. [4500.]
   — Author catalogue. 1952. pp.[iv]. 116.

SOCIAL science bibliography. India. (Pakistan). Unesco: South Asia science cooperation office [iii–v: Research center on the social implications of industrialization in southern Asia]: New Delhi. [Calcutta].
for details see under South Asia, social sciences, *above.*

[CARROL HUNTER QUENZEL], India. Bibliography of books in the library of Mary Washington college of the university of Virginia. [Fredericksburg 1953]. ff.16. [250.]*

THE INDIAN national bibliography. Central reference library, Calcutta. General editor: B. S. Kesavan.

    Oct.–Dec. 1957. pp.xiii.273. [2700.]

   — Annual volume.

    1958. pp.xvi.840.241. [10,000.]

    1959. pp.xvi.791.283. [10,000.]

    1960. pp.xvi.774.279. [9,500.]

    1961. pp.xvi.897.357. [12,000.]

    1962. pp.xvi.905.301. [11,500.]

   — Cumulated index 1958–1962, 1970.

    pp.[v].1384.338. [95,000.]

    1963. pp.xvi.1008.393. [12,500.]

    1964. General editor: D. R. Kalia, pp.xvi.922. 353. [11,000.]

    1965. General editor: C. R. Banerji, pp.xvi. 802.321. [9,500.]

    1966. [*monthly parts.*]

    1967. [*monthly parts.*]

    1968.

    1969.

    1970.

    1971. pp.xvi.520.436.159.302. [11,000.]

    1972. [*monthly parts.*]

    1973. [*monthly parts.*]
in progress; annual volumes only set out; the bibliography for 1968–70 will be published as annual volumes only. Separate bibliographies are also published for Sanskrit and the major vernaculars.

SIBADAS CHAUDHURI, Index to the publications of the Asiatic society 1788–1953. Calcutta.

    I, i. 1956. pp.xiii.336. [5139.]

    ii. 1959. [ff.iii].pp.[337]–472. [2022.]

CATALOGUE and index of the Allahabad public library. Allahabad 1954. pp.v.573+v.379+v.298 +v.507. [15,000.]

BIBLIOGRAPHY on India and short note on foods available in north India. University of Delhi: Delhi school of economics: Training and orientation centre for foreign technicians in India: Delhi [?1954]. ff.[i].13.[vii]. [100.]*

L[IDIYA] I[VANOVNA] STEPANOVA, Республика Индия. Краткий рекомендательный указатель литературы. Государственная ... публичная библиотека СССР имени В. И. Ленина: Москва 1955. pp.40. [50.]

L[IDIYA] I[VANOVNA] STEPANOVA, Что читать об Индин, Бурме и Афганистане. Беседа о книгах. Государственная ... публичная библиотека СССР имени В. И. Ленина. За новые ухпехи в шестой пятилетке. Москва 1956. pp 19. [15.]

IRENA BAROWA, Indie wczoraj i dzis'. Katalog wystawy. Biblioteka jagiellońska: Kraków 1956. pp.40. [209.]*

MIROSLAV KAFTAN, Indie-Barma-Indonesie. Výběrový seznam literatury. Universita: Knihovna: Čteme a studujeme (1956, no.3): Praha 1956. pp. 16. [100.]

S[IBADAS] CHAUDHURI, Bibliography of indological studies in 1953. (A survey of periodical publications). Asiatic society: Calcutta 1958. pp. [viii].54. [984.]
an earlier edition appears in the Journal of the Asiatic society (*1956*), *xxii*.
— — 1954. [1958.]

EXTERNAL research: a listing (list) of recently completed studies. South Asia, Iran, Iraq (South Asia). External research staff: Office (Bureau) of intelligence research: [Washington] 1957–64. pp.12+10+13+13+16+15+19. [1200.]*

DOUG KELLEY, Seventy-seven paperbound books on India in print, October 1959.
[East Lansing? 1959?] ff.8. [77.]

A SELECTED bibliography of works about the republic of India. قائمة بيليوجرافية مختارة عن جمهورية الهند. [1959] ١٩٥٩ pp.١٨.60. [400.]

G. G. KOTOVSKY [*and others*], Библиография Нндии. Дореволюционная и советская литература на русском языке и языках народов СССР, оригинальная и переводная. Академия наук СССР: Институт востоковедения [&c]: Москва 1959. pp.220. [3858.]

GILBERT ÉTIENNE, L'inde contemporaine. Fondation nationale des sciences politiques: Centre d'étude des relations internationales: États des travaux (ser. B, no.21): 1960. pp.36. [258.]

IMPEX reference catalogue of indian books. The list of all important indian books (in english) in print. New Delhi 1960. pp.[xxiv].468. [10,000.]

A BIBLIOGRAPHY of indology (enumerating basic publications on all aspects of indian culture). National library: Calcutta.
   i. Indian anthropology. Compiled by J. M. Kanitkar. Edited, revised and enlarged by D. L. Banerjee and A. K. Ohdedar. 1960. pp.xi.290. [2067.]
   ii. Indian botany. Compiled by V. Narayanaswami. Part 1, A–J, 1961. pp.xlii.370. [5374.]
   iii. Bengali language and literature. Compiled by S. C. Dasgupta. Part 1 (early period). 1964. pp.xii.390. [1769.]

BRITISH books on India. A selection written between the eighteenth century and the present day showing something of the contributions made by british scholars to indian studies. An exhibition arranged by the British council — India 1961. 1961. pp.xvi.17–142. [1500.]

KLAUS LUDWIG JANERT, Verzeichnis indienkundlicher hochschulschriften. Deutschland, Österreich, Schweiz. Wiesbaden 1961. pp.ix.80. [931.]

AN UP-TO-DATE encyclopaedia of all indological publications published in India and other countries relating to ancient indian learning, classified and arranged subjectwise in alphabetical order. Delhi 1962. pp.2.385.39. [14,464.]

D. L. BANERJEE, Index translationum indicarum. A cumulation of entries for India in 'Index translationum', Unesco, Paris, vols. 2–11, Calcutta 1963. pp.x.450. [2870.]

SAILEN GHOSE, Archives in India: history and assets. Calcutta 1963. pp.xii. 358. [large number.]

INDEX to papers in commemoration volumes. Bhandarkar oriental research institute: Postgraduate and research department series (no.5): Poona 1963. pp. vii.647. [4644.]

CATALOGUE of european printed books, India office library, Commonwealth relations office, London. Boston 1964.
   i. Sheaf catalogue, A–Z.
   ii. Author catalogue, A–Dij. pp.[ii].767. [15,246.]
   iii. –Dik–J. pp.[ii].740. [15,540.]
   iv. –K–Ram. pp.[ii].789. [15,009.]
   v. –Ran–Z. pp.[ii].713. [14,973.]
   vi. Subject catalogue, A–to English (fiction). pp.[ii].630. [13,230.]
   vii. –English (language: land). pp.[ii].635. [13,335.]
   viii. –Landlord–Z. pp.[ii].850. [17,850.]

ix. Periodical publications, A–Z. pp.[ii].143. [3003.]

this is a photographic reproduction of catalogue cards; the numbers in square brackets refer to these cards.

KATHARINE SMITH DIEHL, Early indian imprints. New York &c. 1964. pp.533. [1038.]★

J. MICHAEL MAHAR, India; a critical bibliography. Tucson [1964]. pp.[x].119. [2023.]

ACCESSIONS list: India. The library of congress: Public law 480 project: American libraries book procurement center: New Delhi.
    i. 1962. pp.[iv].311.liv. [3000.]
    ii. 1963. pp.[iv].695.lxviii. [7000.]
    iii. 1964. ff.[ii].pp.520.lix. [5000.]
    iv. 1965. ff.[ii].pp.715.lxix. [7000.]
    v. 1966. ff.[ii]. pp.948.lxxxix. [9500.]
    vi. 1967. ff.[ii].pp.1150.cxvi. [11,500.]
    vii. 1968. pp.[iii].997.cl.[10,000.]
    viii. 1969. pp.[vii].797.clxiii. [8,000.]
    ix. 1970. pp.[vii].840.cxcvi. [8,500.]
    x. 1971. ff.[ii].pp.770.clxxxv. [7,500.]
    xi. 1972. ff.[ii].pp.970.cclxiv. [10,000.]
    xii. 1973.
in progress.

UNION catalogue of documentary materials on southeast Asia. Institute of asian economic affairs: Tokyo 1964.
    i. General and southeast Asia in general. pp.x.172. [2406.]★
    ii. India (i): the social sciences. pp.ix.317. [4437.]★
    iii. India (ii): the humanities and natural sciences. pp.x.288. [4032.]★
    iv. Other countries in Asia. pp.x.489. [5838.]★
    v. Index. pp.ix.237.

D. A. BIRMAN, G. G. KOTOVSKIY [*and others*], Библиография Индии: дореволюционная и советская литература на русском языке и языках народов СССР, оригинальная и переводная. Академия наук СССР: Институт народов Азии: Москва 1965. pp. 608. [9073.]

INDIAN book reporter, Author, Subject, title index to new publications. Prabhu book service: Gurgaon, Haryana, 1965 &c.
    i. 1965.
    ii. 1966.
    iii. 1967.
    iv. 1968.
    v. 1969.
    vi. 1970.
in progress. Published on the 15th of every month and replaced by an annual volume.

P. J. CHINMULGUND, V. V. MIRASHI, Review of indological research in the last 75 years. M. M. Chitraoshastri felicitation volume: Poona [1967]. pp.xxxix.849. [large number.]

K. KAPADIA and K. WORSFOLD, India: a select list of books in the State library of South Australia. Research service bibliographies (series 4, no.87): Adelaide 1967. ff.[ii].pp.8.[96.]★

KATHARINE SMITH DIEHL, Carey library pamphlets (secular series); a catalogue. Serampore college: Serampore 1968. pp.xiii.107. [1364.]

EARLY writings on India. A catalogue of books on India in english language published before 1900. An exhibition arranged by the India international centre, New Delhi, december 19–25, 1968. pp.vi.124.xxxiii. [643.]

BOOKS on India: A select bibliography of titles on India published in english during 1969 from all parts of the world. Rajasthan university library: Jaipur 1970. pp.ii.251.lxii. [3207.]

H. D. SHARMA, L. M. P. SINGH and RANJEE SINGH, Indian books 1969: a bibliography of indian books published or reprinted in 1969 in the english language. Varanasi 1970. pp.[vi].297. [5750.]
— 1970. Compiled by H. D. Sharma, L. M. P. Singh and S. P. Mukherji. 1971. pp.ix.365. [2750.]
— 1971. Compiled by L. M. P. Singh, S. P. Mukherji, H. D. Sharma. 1972. pp.[x.] 101.96.114. 34. [2500.]

SHER SINGH, S. N. SADHU and VIMLA SADHU, Indian books in print 1955–67: a select bibliography of english books published in India. Delhi [1969]. pp.vi.1116. [40,000.]

MASOODUL HASAN, Rare english books in India; a select bibliography. Aligarh [1970]. pp.vi.216. [2672.]

NIRMAL SINGLE, Bibliography of selected indian books 1970–1971. New Delhi 1971. pp.xxxvi.143. [700.]

NATIONAL catalogue of university level books 1971. National book trust: New Delhi 1972. pp.xi.659. [6656.]

iv. *Cartography*

A CATALOGUE of maps of the british possessions in India and other parts of Asia published by order of her majesty's Secretary of state for India in council. 1870. pp.60.[400.]
— [another edition]. A catalogue of maps, plans, &c., of India and Burma and other parts [&c.]. 1891. pp.[iii].154. [6000.]
there are several intermediate editions.

LIST of maps and publications relating to forest administration in the provinces under the government of India, sent to the Paris exhibition of 1878. Simla 1878. pp.[ii].12. [75.]

A CATALOGUE of manuscripts and printed reports, field books, memoirs, maps &c., of the indian surveys, deposited in the map room of the India office. 1878. pp.xxi.672. [10,000.]
— [supplement]. The following maps and plans have been received in the Map room [afterwards: The following maps have been received from India for official record]. India office.
 i–iv. 1878. pp.
 v–xii. 1879. pp.2+1+4+2+1+1+2+1. [125.]
 xiii–xviii. 1880. pp.1+2+3+3+2+2. [150.]
 xix–xxi. 1881. pp.3+4+2. [100.]
 xxii–xxvii. 1882. pp.3+3+3+3+3+2. [200.]
 xxviii–xxxi. 1883. pp.2+2+3+3. [125.]
 xxxii–xxxiv. 1884. pp.2+2+4. [100.]
 xxxv–xxxvi. 1885. pp.3+2. [75.]
 xxxvii–xl. 1886. pp.4+2+2+4. [150.]
 xli–xliii. 1887. pp.3+2+3. [100.]
 xliv–xlvii. 1888. pp.6+2+2+1. [175.]
 xlviii–li. 1889. pp.2+2+2+2. [100.]
 lii–liii. 1890. pp.2+2. [50.]
 liv–lv. 1891. pp.5+2. [150.]
parts i–xxxv are by Trelawney Saunders and xxxvi–lv by Charles E. D. Black; part xli is wrongly dated 1886 instead of 1887 and parts lii–liii 1889 instead of 1890.

LIST of publications and maps relating to forest administration in India sent to the Edinburgh international forestry exhibition. Calcutta 1884. pp.[ii].28. [186.]

CATALOGUE of maps and plans in the Imperial library. Calcutta 1910. pp.[ii].72. [700.]

LIST of maps, published by the Survey of India during the quarter ending 31st March 1911 [&c.]. Survey of India: Map record and issue office: Calcutta 1911 [&c.].
in progress; since 1927 reproduced from typewriting.

CECIL L. BURNS, Catalogue of the collection of maps, prints and photographs illustrating the history of the island and city of Bombay. Municipality of Bombay: Victoria and Albert museum, Bombay: Bombay 1918. pp.[vi.]92. [175.]

CATALOGUE of maps published by the Survey of India. Calcutta 1924. pp.[v].61. [1250.]
— [another edition]. 1931. pp.[iii].35. [2000.]

v. *Constitution and government*

SIR JOHN [GHEST] CUMMING, Indian constitutional reform. A selection of books. National book council: Book list (no.127): 1930. pp.[4]. [125.]

INDIA, its government and politics. A list of books. Library of Congress: [Washington] 1930. ff.5. [45.]*
— Supplement. 1930. ff.16. [230.]*

INDIA — constitutional reform. House of commons: Library: Bibliography (no.24): [1947]. ff.12. [78.]*

PATRICK WILSON, Government and politics of India and Pakistan, 1885–1955: a bibliography of works in western languages. University of California: Institute of east asiatic studies: Modern India project: Bibliographical study (no.2): Berkeley [1956]. pp.[ii].viii.357. [5294.]*

OLIVE I[RENE] REDDICK, BIDUYUT KUMAR SARKAR and LAURA KENT, A selected and annotated bibliography of the government, politics and foreign relations of India. Human relations area files: Berkeley 1956. ff.65. [256.]*

BERNARD S. COHN, The development and impact of british administration in India; a bibliographic essay. Indian institute of public administration: New Delhi 1961. pp.viii.88. [500.]

ANNUAL lists and general index of the parliamentary papers relating to the east Indies 1801–1907. Irish university press series of british parliamentary papers: Special index (1): Shannon 1968. pp.xlvii.194. [7000.]

vi. *History*

[SIR] H[ENRY] M[IERS] ELLIOT, Bibliographical index to the historians of muhammedan India.... Vol. I. General histories. Calcutta 1849. pp.[ii]. xxxi.8.394.[xcvi]. [67.]
no more published.

PRESS list of India office records, 1700–1750. [1860]. pp.25. [5000.]

M[ANUEL] BELLETTY, An index to [C. U.] Aitchison's Collection (revised edition) of treaties, engagements, and sunnuds relating to India and neighbouring countries. Compiled ... alphabetically and chronologically. Calcutta 1878. pp. [ii].743.cxx. [2000.]

[SIR GEORGE CHRISTOPHER MOLESWORTH BIRDWOOD], Report on the miscellaneous old records of the India office. 1879. pp.92. [5000.]
— — Report on the old records of the India office. Second report. 1891. pp.xii.316. [5000.]

PRESS list of India office records from the earliest date to 1630, including also notices of all documents extant in India for the same period. 1891. pp.54. [2655.]

A CLASSIFIED list, in alphabetical order, of reports and other publications in the Record branch of the India office. 1894. pp.viii.230. [4500.]

[FREDERICK CHARLES DANVERS], List of marine records of the late East India company, and of subsequent date, preserved in the Record department of the India office. 1896. pp.xxi.160. [5000.]

[FREDERICK CHARLES DANVERS], List of factory records of the late East India company, preserved in the Record department of the India office. 1897. pp.xxviii.91. [50,000.]

LIST of proceedings, &c.: India. 1834–1858. Preserved in the Record department of the India office. 1900. pp.[xi].59. [large number.]
— 1859–1898. 1900. pp.129. [very large number.]

S. CHARLES HILL, An abstract of the early records of the foreign department. Part i. 1756–1762. Calcutta 1901. pp.103. [1000.]

LIST of general records. 1599–1879. Preserved in the Record department of the India office. 1902. pp.xxviii.303. [very large number.]

[MARQUIS DU CAUZÉ DE NAZELLE], Catalogue des manuscrits concernant Joseph-François marquis Dupleix ... appartenant à m. le m^{is} de Nazelle. Laon 1903. pp.215. [1500.]

L. P. TESSITORI, Bardic and historical survey of Rajputana. A descriptive catalogue of bardic and historical manuscripts. Asiatic society of Bengal: Biblioteca indica (n.s. 1409, 1412, 1413): Calcutta 1917–1918. pp.[ii].69+[ii].94+[iii].87. [1000.]
limited to Jodhpur and Bikaner; no more published.

[SIR] WILLIAM FOSTER, A guide to the India office records, 1600–1858. 1919. pp.[ii].xii.130. [very large number.]

[J. M. MITRA], Press list of 'mutiny papers', 1857. Imperial record department: Calcutta 1921. pp.v. 424. [8500.]

LIST of muhammadan histories of India, excluding those of independent provincial monarchies. [*s.l.* (India) 1921]. pp.15. [316.]

MAULAVI ABDUL MUQTADIR ['ABDUL-MUQTADIR], Catalogue of the arabic and persian manuscripts in the Oriental public library at Bankipore. Volume VII. Indian history. Patna 1921. pp.iii–xii. 212. [114.]

A HAND-BOOK to the records of the government of India in the Imperial record department, 1748 to 1859. Calcutta 1925. pp.[iii].ii.158. [1,000,000.]

J[OSEPH] VAN KAMP, Compagniebescheiden en aanverwante archivalia in britisch-Indië en op Ceylon. Verslag van een onderzook in 1929–1930. Batavia 1931. pp.vi.253. [very large number.]

ROB[ERT] STREIT and JOHANNES DINDINGER, Bibliotheca missionum. Sechster band. Missionsliteratur Indiens, der Philippinen, Japans und Indochinas 1700–1799. Internationales institut für missionswissenschaftliche forschung: Aachen 1931. pp.32.616. [2005.]

— — Achter band. Missionsliteratur Indiens u. Indonesiens 1800–1909. 1934. pp.35.1028. [3201.]
— — Fortgesetzt von Johannes Rommerskirchen und Josef Metzler. Siebenundzwanzigster band. Missionsliteratur Indiens 1910–1946 und Nachtrag zu B.M.iv bis viii. 1970. pp.xv.613. [2260.]

KHĀN BAHĀDUR MAULVI ẒAFAR ḤASAN, Bibliography of indo-moslem history, excluding provincial monarchies. Archæological survey of India: Memoirs (no.45): Calcutta 1932. pp.[iii]. v.42. [307.]

J. VAN KAN, Lijst der oude boeken van de voormalige nederlandsche oostindische compagnie ter Kuste Coromandel. List of records of the Dutch india company settlement on the Coromandel coast 1702–1795. Verhandelingen van het Koninglijk bataviaasch genootschap van kunsten en wetenschappen (deel lxxii, eerste stuk). Bandoeng 1932. pp.62. [1250.]

BRAZ. A. FERNANDES, Bibliography of indian history and oriental research. Bombay historical society.
[1]. 1938. pp.viii.80. [600.]
2. 1939. 1941. pp.xxxiii.191. [1401.]
3. 1940. 1944. pp.li.374. [2177.]
4. 1941. 1946. pp.xxxi.337. [1713.]
5. 1942. 1949. pp.xxviii.343. [1582.]

SRI RAM SHARMA [SRĪ-RĀMA ṢARMĀ], A bibliography of mughal India (1526–1707 A.D.). Bombay [1939]. pp.xi.206. [1000.]

C[HARLES] A[MBROSE] STOREY, Persian literature. A bio-bibliographical survey. ... Section II. Fasciculus 3. M. History of India. 1939. pp.xlv–xlviii.433–780. [3000.]

R. N. DANDEKAR, Vedic bibliography ... since 1930 in the field of the Veda, and allied antiquities, including Indus valley civilization. New Indian antiquity (extra ser., vol.iii): Bombay 1946. pp. xx.398. [3500.]
— Second volume. University of Poona: 1961. pp.xxiii.760. [6000.]
— Third volume. 1973.

INDEX to papers read at the Indian historical records commission sessions, 1920–1956. National archives of India: New Delhi [1956]. pp.[v].97. [500.]

FRANK M. GARDNER, The indian mutiny. Library association: Special subject list (no.18): 1957. pp.4. [30.]★

INDEX to the foreign & political department records. National archives of India: Delhi.
i. 1756–1780. 1957. pp.xii.548. [large number.]

ii. 1781–1783. 1968. pp.ix.414. [large number.]

K. K. DATTA, A survey of recent studies on modern indian history. Patna [1957]. pp.152. [1000.]
—— [Another edition.] Calcutta 1963. pp. [vii].115. [large number.]

K. D. BHARGAVA, Guide to the records in the National archives of India. Part I (introductory). New Delhi 1959. ff.[iii].pp.73. [large number.]

JAGDISH SARAN SHARMA, Indian national congress. A descriptive bibliography of India's struggle for freedom. Delhi 1959. pp.xxxix.816. [9135.]

K. D. BHARGAVA, Descriptive list of Mutiny papers in the National archives of India, Bhopal. New Delhi 1960–63. pp.v.67+v.92. [1000.]

A. K. OHDEDAR, The Sapru correspondence; a check-list (first series). National library: Calcutta 1961. pp.vi.394. [3052.]

VICAJI D. B. TARAPOREVALA and D. N. MARSHALL. Mughal bibliography. Select Persian sources for the study of Mughals in India. Bombay, 1962. pp.viii.164. [437.]

MOLLY C. POULTER, A catalogue of the Morley collection (MSS. Eur.D.573), the private papers of John viscount Morley of Blackburn (1838–1923), Secretary of state for India in council 1905–1910 and march–may 1911. India office library: Commonwealth relations office. 1965. ff.158+ 159–301. [large number.]*

P. SARAN, Descriptive catalogue of non-persian sources of medieval indian history (covering Rajasthan and adjacent regions). [1965]. pp.xi.234. [205.]

JANICE M. LADENDORF, The revolt in India 1857–58; an annotated bibliography of english language materials. Bibliotheca indica (I). Zug, Switzerland 1966. pp.v.165. [990.]

JOAN C[ADOGAN] LANCASTER, A guide to lists and catalogues of the India office records. Commonwealth office. 1966. pp.iii.26. [30.]

DARA NUSSERWANJI MARSHALL, Mughals in India; a bibliographical survey. Vol.I — Manuscripts. New York [1967]. pp.xix.634. [2204.]

GANDHI and the british raj. An exhibition of documents, photographs, and other material to illustrate the relations between Mahatma and the british authorities. (—Mohandas Karamchand Gandhi 1869–1948: a reading list.) India office library: India office records. 1969. pp.23.4. [72]*

NATIONAL register of private records. National archives of India.
I.i. Descriptive list of documents in the Kapad Divara collection, Jaipur (based on the information received from Rajasthan in 1959–60). 1971. pp.xiv.202. [1592.]*
ii. Descriptive list of documents available in Rajasthan (based on the information received in 1959–60). 1972. pp.vi.113. [839.]*
iii. Descriptive lists of documents available in Mysore, Orissa, Punjab, Rajasthan, Tamil Nadu and National archives of India, New Delhi (based on the information received in 1959–60). 1972. pp.vi.192. [417.]*
[II.?.] Descriptive lists of documents available in Bihar, Kerala, Madhya Pradesh, Orissa, Punjab, Rajasthan, Tamil Nadu and Uttar Pradesh (based on the information received in 1961–62). pp.xviii.290. [2570.]*

H. S. PATIL and BINA RANI, edd., History and culture (select bibliographies). Aspects of indian culture (ii): Indian council for cultural relations: Delhi 1971. pp.[vi]. 216. [947.]

T. V. MAHALINGAM, Mackenzie manuscripts. Summaries of the historical manuscripts in the Mackenzie collection. Madras university historical series (no.25): Madras 1972. pp.lxxiv.342. [86.]

LUDWIK STERNBACH, Bibliography on *dharma* and *artha* in ancient and medieval India. Wiesbaden 1973. pp.xiv.152. [2230.]

vii. *Law*

1. *General*

A[RTHUR] C[OKE] BURNELL, A classified index to the sanskrit mss. in the palace at Tanjore. . . .
Part II. Philosophy and law. Madras government: Madras 1879. pp.[iii].81–151. [1000.]

[J. B. W.], Catalogue of books in the library of the Legislative department of the government of Bengal. Calcutta 1900. pp.[iii].26.v. [250.]
—— Revised edition. 1905. pp.[iii].42.viii. [400.]

CHIEF COURT library catalogue. Rangoon 1903. ff.58. [1000.]

CHARLES HENRY ALEXANDROWICZ, A bibliography of indian law. Madras 1958. pp.ix.69. [750.]

INDEX to Indian legal periodicals. Indian law institute: New Delhi 1963 &c.
in progress.

H. C. JAIN, Indian legal materials: a bibliographical guide. Bombay, Dobbs Ferry 1970. pp.xiii.123. [1500.]

2. *Statute law*

JAMES SMALL, Index to the acts passed by the Legislative council of India, from their commencement in 1834 to the end of the year 1849. Calcutta 1851. pp.[iv].525. [14,235.]

C. D. FIELD, Chronological table of, and index to, the indian statute-book from the year 1834. [1873]. pp.vi.278. [1250.]
— — A supplement. . . . Second edition. [1873]. pp.34. [250.]

R. A. MANUEL, A comprehensive, alphabetical and analytical index, to all the acts . . . of the Governor general of India, the governors of Bombay and Madras, and the Lieutenant-governor of Bengal. Calcutta 1874. pp.[v].660.17. [24,000.]

STEPHEN JACOB, Index to the enactments relating to India. Calcutta 1880. pp.[iii].iv.2.757. [27,500.]
— — Second edition. By William Fischer Agnew. 1883. pp.xi.910. [32,500.]

J. M. MACPHERSON, Lists of british enactments in force in native states. . . . Western India, comprising the native states under the political control of the government of Bombay and the Baroda agency together with a supplement relating to the Persian coast and islands, Maskat, the Somali coast and Zanzibar. Calcutta 1894. pp.xx.424. [5000.]

[FREDERICK GEORGE WIGLEY], Chronological tables of enactments of british indian legislatures. Calcutta 1895–1896. pp.[ii].iv.170+[iii].166. [4000.]
— — [third edition]. Chronological tables [vol.ii: and index] of the indian statutes. 1909–1911.pp.xii.549. [6000.]
[—] — [fourth edition]. Chronological tables and index of the indian statutes. Vol.I. [By Satiṣa-Chandra-Gupta]. 1917. pp.xii.544. [6000.]
no more published.

JNANENDRA NATH BAKSI, Index and chronological table of central acts and ordinances (repealed and unrepealed) from 1834 to June 1951. Calcutta [1951]. pp.xvi.200.76. [3000.]
— Supplement . . . to December 1952. 1953. pp.21. [125.]

INDEX to unrepealed central acts. Ministry of law: Delhi.
    1954. pp.[ii].46. [500.]
    1955. pp.[ii].48. [500.]

BIBLIOGRAPHY on the Code of civil procedure (amendment) bill, 1954. Bibliography (No.27). Lok Sabha secretariat: New Delhi 1954. pp.13. [243.]

BIBLIOGRAPHY on Indian company law. With reference to the Companies (amendment) bill,

1959. Bibliography (no.43). Lok Sabha secretariat: New Delhi 1959. ff.[ii].55. [388.]*

3. *Case law*

a. *Digests*

α. *General*

WILLIAM H. MORLEY, An analytical digest of all the reported cases decided in the supreme courts of judicature in India, in the courts of the hon. East-India company, and on appeal from India, by her majesty in Council. 1830–1849. pp.[iv].4.8.cccxxiii.740+[ii].xxi.689. [6000.]
— — New series. Vol.I. Containing the cases to the end of the year 1850. 1852. pp.[v].xviii.467. [3500.]
no more published.

HERBERT COWELL and JOSEPH VERE WOODMAN, The indian digest, being a complete index to the reported cases of the high courts established in India. Calcutta 1870. pp.[v].898. [15,000.]
— — Second edition. By H. Cowell. 1873. pp.xvi.1057. [20,000.]

S. DEVARAJA AIYAR [DEVA-RĀJA AIYAR], Digest of cases decided in the High court of Bombay. Bombay 1879. pp.[v].xxxiii.xxiv.v.coll.728. [2500.]

DAMODAR DAS[A], A digest of the cases, civil and criminal, reported in the North-Western high court reports . . . and in the Indian law reports, 1876–1878 . . . of Calcutta, Madras, Bombay and Allahabad high courts and of the Privy council. Agra 1879. pp.[iv].14.355.xli. [1500.]

R. B. MICHELL, Digest of the Indian law reports for the year 1876. . . . Second edition. Madras 1879. pp.x.coll.108. [1000.]
— — 1877. 1879. pp.xi.coll.142. [1500.]

GOVINDRA ROW [RAO], A digest of the Indian law reports . . . for 1879. Madras 1880. pp.[ii].130. [500.]

REGINALD M. A. BRANSON, Digest of cases reported in the Indian law reports, Calcutta . . . Bombay . . . Allahabad . . . Madras series . . . and . . . indian appeals [up to December 1881]. Bombay 1884–1886. pp.xlix.coll.1518+pp.lxx.coll.1468. [6000.]

D. E. CRANENBURGH, A digest of civil cases reported in the Indian law reports from 1876 to 1885. Calcutta 1886. pp.[iii].iii.lvii.coll.1718. [5000.]
— — 1876 to 1894, and in the Calcutta law reports, 1878 to 1883. Vol.I. 1895. pp.[ii].ii.coll.2420. [6000.]
A–L only; no more published.

A DIGEST of indian law cases, containing high court reports ... and Privy council reports of appeals from India. Calcutta.

1836–1886. By Joseph Vere Woodman. 1887–1888. pp.xxi.coll.1562+pp.xiii.coll. 1565–2940 + pp.xv.coll.2941–4230 + pp. xvii.coll.4231–5986 + pp.xvi.coll.5987– 6290.pp.6291–6781. [30,000.]

1887–1889. pp.xlvii.coll.1084. [2500.]

1890–1893. pp.lvi.coll.1150. [2500.]

1894–1897. pp.lvi.coll.1348. [3000.]

1836–1900. 1901–1902. pp.xxii.coll.2054+ pp.xiii.coll.2057–4170 + pp.xii.coll.4173– 6216 + pp.xiii.coll.6217–8078 + pp.xii. coll.8081–9604 + pp.xiv.9605–10257. [40,000.]

1901–1903. By F. G. Wigley. 1906. pp.lxxx. coll.1216. [2500.]

1904. By C. E. Grey. 1907. pp.xxxiii.coll.362. [750.]

1905. 1907. pp.[ii].xxviii.coll.364. [750.]

1906. 1908. pp.xxxvi.384. [750.]

1907. By B. D. Bose [Varada-dāsa Vasu], 1908. pp.[ii].xxxvi.coll.420. [750.]

1908. By C. E. Grey. 1910. pp.xxxvii.386. [750.]

1836–1909. 1912–1913. pp.xxi.coll.3068+ pp.xvii.coll.3067–5890 + pp.xi.coll.5889– 8712 + pp.xv.coll.8713–11,144 + pp. xiii coll.11,143–13,203+pp.xv.13,203–14,066. [50,000.]

1910. pp.xxxvii.coll.388. [750.]

1911. pp.xxxviii.coll.376. [750.]

1912. pp.xxxviii.coll.364. [750.]

1913. pp.xxxix.coll.398. [750.]

1914. pp.xxxvii.coll.396. [750.]

1915. pp.xlii.coll.476. [1000.]

1916. pp.xli.coll.436. [1000.]

1917. pp.xxx.coll.308. [500.]

1918. pp.xxxiv.coll.308. [500.]

1919. pp.xxxiii.coll.304. [500.]

1910–1921. By S. Webb-Johnson. pp.xxix. coll.2192 + pp.[ii].xxxi–li.coll.2193–4296 +pp.[iii].clxxxiv.ii. [10,000.]

1922. pp.xli.coll.420. [750.]

1923. pp.xliv. coll.480. [1000.]

1924. pp.xliii.coll.408. [750.]

1925. pp.xliv.coll.440. [750.]

1926. pp.xliii.coll.450. [1000.]

1927. pp.xlvi.coll.464. [1000.]

1928. pp.xlviii.coll.528. [1000.]

1929. pp.xlvi.coll.470. [1000.]

1930. pp.xlviii.coll.552. [1000.]

1931. pp.xlvi.coll.476. [1000.]

1932. pp.xlvi.coll.520. [1000.]

J. B. WORGAN, Consecutive tables, civil cases; being an annotation, up to June 1900, of the civil cases in the Indian law reports from their commencement, in 1876, to December 1893, for the Allahabad, Bombay, and Madras series, and to June 1894 for the Calcutta law reports, and of those in the Calcutta law reports that are not reported in the I.L.R. Calcutta 1901. pp.xxvii.622. [7509.]

S. SRINIVASA AIYAR, The digest of indian cases. Madras.

1901–1903. pp.[iii].xviii.68.coll.1866. [7500.]

1903–1904. pp.[iii].xxxii.29.coll.828. [2500.]

1905. pp.[iii].xix.21.xoll.452. [1250.]

1906.

1907. pp.[iii]. xvii.26.coll.462. [1250.]

1908.

1909. pp.[ii].xvi.20.12.coll.436. [1250.]

THE INDIAN digest, civil, criminal and revenue Triplicane [afterwards: Mylapore, Lahore].

1909–1920. By V. V. Chitale. [Vāmana Vāsudeva Chitale]. pp.[iii].iii.coll.1824+ pp.[v].coll.20.1825–3788 + pp.[v].coll.30. 2128. [20,000.]

1921. pp.[iii].27.coll.750. [4000.]

1911–1923. By V. V. Chitale and R. Narayanaswami Iyer [R. Nārāyaṇasvāmi Aiyar]. pp.vii.coll.1140 + pp.v–xiv.coll.1141– 1992. [10,000.]

1921–1925. The quinquennial digest. pp.[v]. xii.coll.2540+pp.xxiii.coll.2868. [25,000.]

1921–1930. The decennial index. pp.xix. coll.2038 + pp.xxii.coll.3150 + pp.xxviii. coll.2918+pp.xxix.coll.3460. [60,000.]

1916–1931. The fifteen years' digest. pp.[iv]. 7.coll.1900 + pp.xii.coll.2240 + pp.xv. coll.2241–4584. [80,000.]

the numbering of the columns is very inaccurate.

V. V. CHITALE [VĀMANA VĀSUDEVA CHITALE] and R. NARAYANASWAMI IYER [R. NĀRĀYAṆASVĀMI AIYAR], The civil digest (1911–1923). Mylapore 1924–1925. pp.xi.1672 + pp.[ii].xv.coll.1966 + pp.xx.coll.2482+pp.[ii].xvi.coll.2294. [40,000.]

A. S. SRINIVASA AIYAR, The all-India law digest (1921–1930) and century referencer (1821–1920). Mylapore 1931. pp.[vii]. coll.1988+pp.[v].coll. 2264. [9000.]

THE "YEARLY DIGEST" of indian & select english cases. Madras law journal: Mylapore 1934 &c.

DAYARAM GANESHJI, Fifteen years digest of western India states agency law reports [civil, criminal, giras, & political cases], 1926–40. Limbdi 1940. pp.8.76.coll.632. [3000.]

R. NARAYANASWAMI IYER [NĀRĀYAṆASVĀMI AIYAR], The quinquennnial digest, 1936–1940. Madras 1941. pp.viii.coll.3352+pp.xi.coll.4184. [35,000.]

V. M. KULKARNI, Kulkarni's digest of indian case law for fourteen years, 1931–1944. Lahore 1944 &c.

in progress.

B. P. VARMA, All India full bench digest, civil — criminal — revenue. Lucknow &c.

1901–1954. pp.[v].coll.xvi.pp.iv.1332 + pp.[v].coll.xvi.1333–2372 + pp.[iii].coll.xvi.2373–3284.pp.3285–3370. [15,000.]
1955–1957. pp.xiv.16.coll.17–496. [1500.]

JURIDICAL digest. (Abstracts of cases involving articles [provisions] of the constitution of India). Part I: Supreme court [II: High court]. Lok Sabha secretariat: New Delhi 1955 &c.
in progress.

D. V. CHITALEY [CHITALE] and N. RAMARATNAM, The fifty years' digest, 1901–1950 (civil, criminal & revenue). Nagpur [1957].

   i. Abadi to Boilers act. pp.[xix].coll.2248 [*sic*]. [10,000.]
   ii. Bombay abkari act to C.P. code, s.48. pp.[xiv].coll.2948. [15,000.]
   iii. C.P.c., s.49 to 0.6, R.18. pp.[xx].coll.2424. [10,000.]
   iv. C.P. code 0.7 to 0.34 rule 5. pp.[iii].xvi.coll.2578. [12,500.]
   v. C.P.c., 0.34, R.6 to Crown lands act (1884) of New Youth Wales [*sic*]. pp.[xxvi].coll.2856. [15,000.]
   vi. Contradictory statement to Criminal procedure code, s.344. pp.[iv].xvi.coll.2842. [15,000.]
   vii. Cr.P.C., s.345 to Easements act (5 of 1882), s.14. pp.xxiv.2708.pp.[vi]. [15,000.]
   viii. Easements act s.15 to Hindu law-debts. pp.[x].coll.3200. [17,500.]
   ix. Hindu law-debts to landlord and tenant. pp.[xxiv].3296. [17,500.]
   x. Land tenure to Madras city civil court act (7 of 1892). pp.[viii].coll.2670. [15,000.]
   xi. Madras city municipal act (5 of 1873) to Penal code s.160. pp.[xxxii].coll.2702. [15,000.]
   xii. Penal code (XLV of 1860) s.161 to Public gambling act (III of 1867). pp.[viii].coll.3152. [17,500.]
   xiii. Public health . . . to Transfer of property act (1882), s.52. pp.28.[viii].coll.2824. [15,000.]
   xiv. Transfer of property act (IV of 1882), s.53 to Zur-i-peshgi lease. pp.[iv].v.coll.2796.pp.lxxiv. [15,000.]
the numbering of the columns is extremely erratic in vol.i.

OM PRAKASH AGGARAWALA [OM-PRAKĀSA AGAR-VĀLĀ], The Indian supreme court digests (1950–1957) annotated. . . . Second edition. Delhi 1958. pp.lxviii.1388.cvii. [2000.]

β. *Privy council*

HERBERT COWELL, Digest of cases decided in the Privy council and reported in Indian appeals . . .

1874–1893 . . . and . . . 1872–3. Law reports: 1894. pp.xli.coll.228. [2500.]

T. V. SANJIVA ROW [RAO], A digest of Privy council rulings. . . . Second edition. Trichinopoly 1903. pp.xi.lxxxviii. 1311. [2500.]

A. S. VISWANATHA AIYAR, The Privy council digest (1836–1930). Mylapore 1930. pp.viii. xlviii.coll.4272. [10,000.]
limited to indian cases.

b. *Indexes*

RASHBEHARY GHOSE [RĀSAVIHĀRĪ GHOSHA], Indexes of cases judicially noticed (1875–1894), being a list of all cases cited in judgments reported in the Indian law reports — Calcutta, Allahabad, Bombay and Madras series, — Calcutta law reports, and law reports, Indian appeals (1872–1894). Calcutta 1895. pp.vii.604. [30,000.]

NRISIMHA-DĀSA VASU, A subject-noted index of cases judicially noticed (1809–1913). Calcutta 1914. pp.320. [7500.]

A. S. SRINIVASA AIYAR, The point-noted index of cases overruled and reversed (1809–1929). Mylapore 1929. pp.viii.167. [2500.]

N. SIVASWAMI [ŚIVA-SVĀMĪ] and S. K. L. RATAN, The index of foreign cases overruled, followed, etc. Madras 1943. pp.[v].554. [20,000.]

viii. *Academic writings*

ABSTRACTS of publications by members of the university. University of Lucknow: Lucknow.
   1921–1927. 1928. pp.[v].156. [500.]
   1928–1932. 1933. pp.[vii].244. [1000.]
   1933–1937. 1938. pp.[vii].352. [1500.]

DESCRIPTIVE catalogue of university publications. University of Calcutta: Calcutta.
   1930. pp.[ii].92.7. [500.]
   1931. pp.[ii].177. [600.]
   1932. pp.[ii].133. [750.]

BIBLIOGRAPHY of doctorate theses in science and arts accepted by indian universities. Inter-university board of India: Mitijhil [&c.] 1930–1934.

BIBLIOGRAPHY of doctorate theses in science and arts accepted by indian universities from 1939. Inter-university board, India: [Lucknow] 1941. pp.15. [131.]

RESEARCH work of the university teachers. [Madras 1946]. pp.75. [1250.]
— Supplement. Choolai 1949. pp.43. [750.]

LIST of research papers published from affiliated colleges during 1947–52. Agra 1952. pp.30. [500.]

RESEARCH in the Annamalai university. [Chidambaram] 1955. pp.36. [50.]

G[IRIRAJ] P[RASAD] GUPTA, Economic investigations in India. (A bibliography of researches in commerce and economics approved by indian universities). Agra [1961]. pp.[iii].v.81. [750.]

[MUHAMMAD AZAM SIDDIQI], Bibliography of theses, dissertations & research reports, university of the Panjab. West Pakistan bureau of education: Bibliographical [sic] series (no.ii): Lahore 1961. pp.[iii].v.212. [2086.]

KLAUS LUDWIG JANERT, Verzeichnis indienkundlicher hochschulschriften. Deutschland, Österreich, Schweiz. Wiesbaden 1961. pp.ix.80. [931.]

ABSTRACTS of the theses accepted for the doctorate degrees of Banaras hindu university.
  i.
  ii.
  iii.
  iv. 1965. pp.iv.159. [53.]
  v. 1964. pp.vi.234. [64.]

WRITINGS of members of department of history. 1960–70: a guide. Patna university: Patna 1970, pp.iv.32. [324.]

ix. *Official publications*

PUBLICATIONS received in the Record department [India office]. [Official publications received in the Publications branch. Office of the High commissioner for India].
  1880. pp.[71]. [1500.]
  1881. pp.[65]. [1500.]
  1882. pp.[62]. [1250.]
  1883. pp.[56]. [1250.]
  1884. pp.[52]. [1250.]
  1885. pp.[53]. [1250.]
  1886. pp.[51]. [1250.]
  1887. pp.[46]. [1250.]
  1888. pp.[43]. [1000.]
  1889. pp.[44]. [1000.]
  1890. pp.[38]. [750.]
  1891. pp.[40]. [750.]
  1892. pp.[43]. [750.]
  1893. pp.[42]. [750.]
  1894. pp.[44]. [750.]
  1895. pp.[46]. [750.]
  1896. pp.[46]. [750.]
  1897. pp.[46]. [750.]
  1898. pp.[40]. [750.]
  1899. pp.[28]. [750.]
  1900. pp.[32]. [750.]
  1901. pp.[32]. [750.]
  1902. pp.[33]. [750.]
  1903. pp.[36]. [750.]
  1904. pp.[32]. [750.]
  1905. pp.[32]. [750.]
  1906. pp.[30]. [750.]
  1907. pp.[38]. [750.]
  1908. pp.[44]. [750.]
  1909. pp.[42]. [750.]
  1910. pp.[47]. [1000.]
  1911. pp.[49]. [1000.]
  1912. pp.[52]. [1250.]
  1913. pp.[51]. [1250.]
  1914. pp.[55]. [1500.]
  1915. pp.[52]. [1250.]
  1916. pp.[48]. [1250.]
  1917. pp.[47]. [1250.]
  1918. pp.[35]. [750.]
  1919. pp.[41]. [1000.]
  1920. pp.[41]. [1000.]
  1921. pp.[41]. [1000.]
  1922. pp.[11].ff.[30]. [1000.]
  1923. ff.[38]. [1000.]
  1924. ff.[54]. [1500.]
  1925. ff.[62]. [1750.]
  1926. ff.[55]. [1500.]
  1927. ff.[57]. [1500.]
  1928. ff.[70]. [2500.]
  1929. ff.[70]. [2500.]
  1930. ff.[84]. [3000.]
  1931. ff.[78]. [3000.]
  1932. ff.[88]. [3500.]
  1933. ff.[90]. [3500.]
  1934. ff.[78]. [3000.]
  1935. ff.[82]. [3000.]
  1936. ff.[81]. [3000.]
  1937. ff.[84]. [3000.]
  1938. ff.[89]. [3000.]
  1939. ff.[92]. [3000.]
  1940. ff.[20].pp.[67]. [2500.]
  1941. pp.[76]. [2500.]
  1942. pp.[58]. [1500.]
  1943. pp.[48]. [1500.]
  1944. pp.[48]. [1500.]
  1945. pp.[60]. [2000.]
  1946. ff.[39]. [2000.]
  1947. ff.[43]. [2000.]
  1948. ff.[49]. [2500.]
  1949. ff.[81]. [3500.]
  1950. ff.[53]. [2500.]
published at first irregularly, then monthly; the issues for 1880–1887 are not limited to indian official publications; the title first appears in 1908; before that date there is only the heading: 'The undermentioned documents have been received [are available for official use . . .] in the Record department'; the issues for April 1922 &c. are reproduced from typewriting.

A CLASSIFIED list of reports and other publications in the Record branch of the India office. 1883. pp.200. [3500.]
— [another edition]. A classified list, in alphabetical order, of reports [&c.]. . . . December 1892. 1894. pp.viii.230. [4000.]

FRANK [FRANCIS BUNBURY FITZ-GERALD] CAMPBELL, Catalogue of official reports relating to India . . . 1892. 1893. pp19. [50.]

LIST of official publications (other than confidential) issued by local governments and administrations and departments of the government of India during the quarter ... which are exempted from registration. [Calcutta].

    1892. pp.37.25. [487.]
    1893. pp.31.39.51.37. [1031.]
    1894. pp.37.47.53.55. [1262.]
    1895. pp.47.43.55.49. [1211.]
            [continued as:]

List of non-confidential publications exempted from registration, which were issued by the departments of the government of India and by local governments and administrations.

    1896. pp.47.45.67.51. [1233.]
    1897. pp.45.47.53.47. [1186.]
    1898. pp.43.43.53.45. [1166.]
    1899. pp.43.43.57.51. [1201.]
    1900 (January–March). pp.47. [281.]
    1900–1901. pp.143. [1065.]
    1901 (April–December). pp.113. [883.]
    1902. pp.147. [1134.]
    1903. pp.151. [1168.]
    1904. pp.151. [1200.]
    1905. pp.147. [1160.]
    1906. pp.169. [1266.]
    1907. pp.171. [3094 (*sic*, 1294).]
  the change of title took place after the second issue for 1895; continued by separate lists for the several governments and departments.

FRANK CAMPBELL, Index-catalogue of indian official publications in the library. British museum. [1900]. pp.7.193.314.72.[ii].coll.16. [15,000.]
  —— Accessions. No.1.1899.f.[i].coll.16. [150.]

LIST of non-confidential publications [publications (other than confidential)] exempted from registration, which were issued by the government of India in the Home department and offices subordinate to it, during the year. [Calcutta].

    1908. pp.11. [56.]
    1909. pp.9. [50.]
    1910. pp.9. [30.]
    1911. pp.5. [20.]
    1912. pp.9. [25.]
    1913. pp.9. [25.]
    1914. pp.7. [30.]
    1915. pp.7. [30.]
    1916. pp.7. [25.]
    1917. pp.4. [27.]
    1918. pp.4. [27.]
    1919. pp.4. [27.]
    1920. pp.4. [22.]
    1921. pp.[ii].2. [21.]
    1922. pp.[ii].2. [21.]
    1923. pp.3. [22.]
    1924. pp.3. [21.]
    1925. pp.4. [27.]
    1926. pp.3. [23.]
no more published.

LIST of official publications [of publications] (other than confidential) issued by the [government of India in the] Foreign [and political] department [and the offices subordinate to it] during the year ... [which are exempted from registration]. [Simla].

    1908. single leaf. [4.]
    1909. pp.2. [20.]
    1910. pp.3. [10.]
    1911. pp.[3]. [9.]
    1912. pp.[3]. [9.]
    1913. pp.[3]. [4.]
    1914. pp.6. [12.]
    1915. pp.7. [47.]
    1916. pp.9. [49.]
    1917. pp.7. [44.]
    1918. pp.7. [43.]
    1919. pp.6. [36.]
    1920. pp.6. [36.]
    1921. pp.8. [44.]
    1922. pp.7. [42.]
    1923. pp.8. [38.]
    1924. pp.9. [43.]
    1925. pp.10. [52.]
    1926. pp.8. [53.]
no more published.

LIST of non-confidential publications exempted from registration, which were issued by the Legislative department of the government of India, during the year. [Calcutta].

    1908. pp.11. [76.]
    1909. pp.15. [121.]
    1910. pp.15. [104.]
    1911. pp.
    1912. pp.10. [57.]
    1913. pp.7. [33.]
    1914. pp.16. [75.]
    1915. pp.10. [50.]
    1916. pp.10. [54.]
    1917. pp.[ii].8. [68.]
    1918. pp.[ii].8. [66.]
    1919. pp.[ii].12. [110.]
    1920. pp.[ii].12. [118.]
    1921. pp.[ii].12. [107.]
    1922. pp.[ii].12. [110.]
    1923. pp.[ii].11. [109.]
    1924. pp.[ii].11. [48.]
    1925. pp.[ii].10. [105.]
    1926. pp.[ii].12. [114.]
no more published.

CATALOGUE of indian official publications. Vol.1., A–L. Imperial library: Catalogue (part iv): Calcutta 1909. pp.[v].coll.544. [6000.]
  no more published.

LIST of parliamentary collections, with index. Third edition, revised, enlarged, and corrected to date. Record department (Parliamentary branch): India office. 1913. pp.61. [376.]

CATALOGUE of publications . . . by the government of India. Calcutta [1926]. pp.[ii].x.232. [5000.]

— [another edition]. Catalogue of civil publications [&c.]. New Delhi 1950. pp.274. [2000.]

there are numerous intermediate editions; supplements are issued in various forms.

LIST of non-confidential [of official] publications not included in the General catalogue of government of India publications. Calcutta [New Delhi].

    1927. pp.[ii].32. [450.]
    1928. pp.36. [500.]
    1929. pp.39. [550.]
    1930. pp.43. [600.]
    1931. pp.42. [600.]
    1932. pp.37. [500.]
    1933. pp.42. [600.]
    1934. pp.38. [500.]
    1935. pp.44. [600.]
    1936. pp.42. [600.]
    1937. pp.31. [450.]
    1938. pp.35. [500.]
    1939. pp.32. [450.]

PAMPHLET showing publications . . . the supply of which is undertaken by the Central publication branch on payment of an annual subscription. Delhi 1935. pp.8. [34.]

CATALOGUE of civil publications relating to agriculture, forestry, civic, commerce, finance, legislation, industry, public health, railways, science, trade . . . up to 31 December, 1948. New Delhi 1950. pp.274. [2000.]
    — Supplement for the year.
    1949. pp.40. [300.]
    1950. pp.72. [500.]
    1951. pp.64. [400.]
in progress.

LIST of publications (periodical or *ad hoc*) issued by various ministries of the government of India. (Second edition). New Delhi 1952. pp.[ii].155. [1500.]
    — Third edition. 1958. ff.iii.pp.292. [2975.]

CATALOGUE of government of India civil publications (subject-wise arranged). Government of India publication branch. Delhi 1966 &c.
    in progress.
    — Supplement for the years 1960–1964. Delhi [1968]. pp.xv.713. [2636.]
    — Supplement for the year 1965. Delhi 1967, pp.xv.217. [636.]
    — — 1966. 1969. ff.[iii]. pp.288. [838.]

MOHINDER SINGH and J. F. PANDYA, Government publications of India, a survey of their nature, bibliographical control and distribution system (including over 1500 titles). Delhi 1967. ff.[iii]. pp.ii.ii.271. [1500.]

RAJESHWARI DATTA, Union catalogue of the central government of India publications held by libraries in London, Oxford and Cambridge. Centre of south asian studies: University of Cambridge. 1970. pp.[vi]. cols.471. [4700.]

TERESA MACDONALD, Union catalogue of the serial publications of the indian government 1858–1947 held in libraries in Britain. Centre of south asian studies. 1973. pp.[xi]. 154. [2500.]

LIST of publications received in India house library . . . Office of the High Commissioner of India.
in progress.

x. *Topography*

GEORGE BUIST, Index to books and papers on the physical geography, antiquities, and statistics of India. Bombay 1852. pp.5–103. [4000.]

A CATALOGUE of manuscript and printed reports, field books, memoirs, maps, etc., of the indian surveys, deposited in the Map room of the India office. 1878. pp.xxi.672. [10,000.]

T. H. D. LA TOUCHE, A bibliography of indian geology and physical geography. Calcutta 1917–1918. pp.[iii].xxviii.572+[iii].ii.490. [6000.]

ABULHASAN MANSUR, Arabische schriftsteller über die geographie Indiens. [Berlin] 1919. pp. [ii].74. [500.]

HENRY SCHOLBERG, The district gazetteers of british India; a bibliography. Bibliotheca asiatica (no.3): Zug, Switzerland [1970]. [1344.]*

Ajmer-Merwara

CATALOGUE of books and periodicals published in Ajmer-Merwara and registered under act xxxv of 1867 (as amended by act x of 1902) during the quarter. 1886–1955. [large number.]

Andhra

CATALOGUE of books and periodicals registered in the Andhra state. The Andhra gazette: [Supplement]: Kurnool 1953 &c.*
in progress.

Assam

CATALOGUE of books (and pamphlets) registered [in Assam] during [books and pamphlets for] the quarter [registered in eastern Bengal and Assam for the quarter]. [Shillong].
    1875. ff.[4]. [9.]
    1876. ff.
    1877. ff.[4]. [17.]
    1878. ff.[4]. [23.]
    1879. ff.[4]. [12.]
    1880. ff.[4]. [10.]

1881. ff.[4]. [12.]
1882. ff.[4]. [21.]
1883. ff. ... [5].
1884. ff.[4]. [16.]
1885. ff.[4]. [12.]
1886. ff.[4].
1887. ff.[3]. [12.]
1888. ff.[4]. [25.]
1889. ff.[4]. [20.]
1890. ff.[4]. [25.]
1891. ff.[7]. [31.]
1892. ff.[4]. [17.]
1893. ff.[4]. [11.]
1894. ff.[4]. [11.]
1895. ff.[4]. [18.]
1896. ff.[4]. [20.]
1897. ff.[4]. [6.]
1898. ff.[7]. [32.]
1899. ff.[6]. [47.]
1900. ff.[4]. [28.]
1901. ff.[4]. [24.]
1902. ff.[5]. [37.]
1903. ff.[2]. [6.]
1904. ff.[4]. [21.]
1905. ff.[4]. [45.]
1906. ff.1.3.6.6. [123.]
1907. ff.5.8.6.7. [247.]
1908. ff.10.5.5.7. [250.]
1909. ff.6.6.6.8. [250.]
1910. ff.6.10.18.21. [500.]
1911. ff.8.25.13.5. [500.]
1912. ff.14.2.2.2. [200.]
1913. ff.[9]. [75.]
1914. ff.[9]. [75.]
1915. ff.3.4.2.2. [100.]
1916. ff.4.3.2.2. [100.]
1917. ff.[7]. [50.]
1918. ff.[7]. [50.]
1919. ff.[4]. [25.]
1920. ff.[6]. [50.]
1921. ff.[8]. [60.]
1922. ff.[9]. [75.]
1923. ff.[8]. [60.]
1924. pp.[7]. [50.]
1925. pp.[9]. [61.]
1926. pp.[6]. [63.]
1927. pp.2.2.2.
1928. pp.[7]. [52.]
1929. pp.[8]. [68.]
1930. pp.[9]. [68.]
1931. pp.[10]. [70.]
1932. pp.[9]. [72.]
1933. pp.[10]. [76.]
1934. pp.2 ... 2.
1935. pp.[7]. [54.]
1936. pp.1 .. 1.1.
1937. pp. ... 1 ... 1.
1938. pp.. 1.1.1.
1939. pp.2. [30.]
1940. pp.3. [33.]

eastern Bengal is included during the quarters ending 31 March 1906–31 March 1912; for the continuation see Bengal.

HENRI CORDIER, Biblioteca indo-sinica. Essai d'une bibliographie des ouvrages relatifs à la presqu'île Indo-Chinoise. ... Première partie: Birmanie et Assam. Leide. 1908. pp.269. [Assam: 563.]

100 copies printed; no more published.

LIST of non-confidential publications exempted from registration, which were issued by the government of eastern Bengal and Assam [1912 &c.: by the Assam administration] during the year.

    1908. pp.5. [29.]
    1909. pp.5. [32.]
    1910. pp.5. [33.]
    1911. pp.5. [28.]
    1912. pp.5. [16.]
    1913. pp.5. [25.]
    1914. pp.5. [30.]
    1915. pp.5. [24.]
    1916. pp.5. [33.]
    1917. pp.5. [27.]
  — [another edition]. pp.[iii].3. [27.]
    1918. pp.[iii].3. [25.]
    1919. pp.[iii].3. [23.]
    1920. pp.[iii].4. [32.]
    1921. pp.[iii].3. [29.]
    1922. pp.[iii].3. [30.]
    1923. pp.[iii].3. [29.]
    1924. pp.[iii].3. [28.]
    1925. pp.3. [27.]
    1926. pp.3. [27.]
the title varies.

CATALOGUE of books and publications of the Assam government which are intended for sale during the half-year [of the Assam government book depot]. Shillong.

    1924. pp.[ii].94. [1000.]
    1935. pp.[ii].91 + [ii].93. [2000.]
    1942. pp.[iii].51. [1500.]
a selection only of the editions is set out.

CATALOGUE of books and articles relating to the tribes of Assam and North east frontier available in the State central library, Assam, Shillong. [Shillong *n.d.*] ff.[ii].24. [508.]*

Bangalore

A CATALOGUE of books printed in the civil & military station of Bangalore (and registered under the provisions of act xxv of 1867] during the ... quarter. Bangalore.

    1884. pp.3.3. [20.]
    1885. pp.3.3.1.1. [16.]
    1886. pp.1. ...

1887. List of works on science and practical indian botany, and of all other works of scientific, historical, or antiquarian interest published in the state of Mysore and the civil and military station of Bangalore. p.1. [4.]

1888.

1889–1922 [each year]. ff.[4]. [10–15.]

1923. pp.[8]. [55.]

1924. pp.[5]. [38.]

1925. pp.2.3.5.4. [83.]

1926. pp.3.2.2.2. [57.]

1927. pp.4.5.4.6. [124.]

1928. pp.5.6.6.5. [150.]

1929. pp.5.5.6.6. [144.]

1930. pp.6.7.7.7. [200.]

1931. pp.7.5.6.7. [183.]

1932. pp.7.7.6.6. [165.]

1933. pp.8.3.3.2. [194.]

1934. pp.3.3.2.3. [273.]

1935. pp.3.3.3.3. [163.]

1936. pp.3.3.3.3. [255.]

1937. pp.3.3.3.2. [212.]

1938. pp.3.3.5.7. [241.]

1939. pp.4.4.5.6. [214.]

1940. pp.6.6.6.4. [253.]

1941. pp.6.6.8.7. [337.]

1942. pp.5.6.

typed lists for the quarter ending september 1943 to the first quarter of 1947 are to be found in the India Office library.

Baroda

M. F. LOKHANDWALA, A. G. KELKAR and AMIR-ALI HUSEN-ALI, Persian catalogue, being a list of the persian documents in the archives of the Baroda government. 1945. pp.139. [417.]

Bengal

[M. H. TURNBULL], Index to the circular ordres, passed by the Sudder dewanny adawlut. [Calcutta c.1818]. pp.7. [100.]

D. DALE, Alphabetical index to the regulations of government for the whole of the territories under the presidency of Fort William in Bengal. Calcutta 1830. pp.vi.509. [16,365.]

INDEX to the circular ordres of the courts of Sudder dewanny adawlut, for the lower and western provinces, to the end of 1845. Calcutta 1847. pp.[ii].iii.79.19. [500.]

J[AMES] LONG, Returns relating to native printing presses and publications in Bengal . . . and a catalogue of bengali newspapers and periodicals which have issued from the press from the year 1818 to 1855. Calcutta. pp.66.

J. CARRAU, Index to the decisions of the Sudder dewanny adawlut, from 1792 to 1855. Calcutta 1856. pp.10.ccccxxxii.

INDEX excerpta of selected precedents of the Suddur dewanny court, from 1849 to 1858. Calcutta [1859]. pp.[iii].204. [1500.]

BENGAL library catalogue of books for [registered in the presidency of Bengal during] the quarter. Calcutta gazette: Appendix: [Calcutta].

1867. pp. . . 31. .

1868. pp.65.47.85.54. [1284.]

1869. pp.84.74. .68. [968.]

1870. pp.68.90.58.50. [898.]

1871. pp.70.42.55.43. [2000.]

1872. pp.62.23.37.50. [1700.]

1873. pp.44.24.38. .

1874. pp.83.140.76.57. [1823.]

1875. pp.37.65.53.47. [1528.]

1876. pp.53.41.57.43. [1498.]

1877. pp.53.53.59.47. [1515.]

1878. pp.49.51.67.47.12. [1487.]

1879. pp.73.83.74.45. [1391.]

1880. pp.92.63.73.65.4. [1772.]

1881. pp.72.55.59.41. [1476.]

1882. pp.59.59.68.60. [1568.]

1883. pp.85.93.74.91. [2218.]

1884. pp.60.113.83.69. [2389.]

1885. pp.102.90.113.75. [2731.]

1886. pp.80.105.88.80. [2571.]

1887. pp.100.73.56.81. [2255.]

1888. pp.96.81.86.86. [2693.]

1889. pp.111.99.69.64. [2603.]

1890. pp.77.79.57.22. [1731.]

1891. pp.85.94.68.58. [2177.]

1892. pp.52.64.52.72. [1675.]

1893. pp.72.74.65.76. [2067.]

1894. pp.54.55.92.52. [1898.]

1895. pp.92.104.107.77. [2628.]

1896. pp.100.80.99.85. [2346.]

1897. pp.76.111.65.85. [2282.]

1898. pp.81.83.40.80. [2174.]

1899. pp.81.84.105.81. [2177.]

1900. pp.114.94.115.83. [2590.]

1901. pp.116.100.115.77. [3069.]

1902. pp.47.45.67.43. [3366.]

1903. pp.53.51.49.39. [2887.]

1904. pp.53.49.51.47. [3054.]

1905. pp.55.45.ff.51.47. [2799.]

1906. ff.71.65.92.71. [3434.]

1907. ff.83.79.84.92. [2995.]

1908. ff.126.103.134.117. [3417.]

1909. ff.154.146.152.118. [3837.]

1910. ff.176.165.174.136. [3300.]

1911. ff.172.157.188.149. [4500.]

1912. ff.164.139.158.160. [3733.]

1913. ff.197.195.172.147. [4083.]

1914. ff.204.160.206.156. [4092.]

1915. ff.191.190.159.115. [3910.]

1916. ff.200.120.147.90. [3500.]

1917. ff.168.133.123.119. [3658.]

1918. ff.182.124.128.108. [3691.]

1919. ff.168.127.152.102. [3903.]

1920. ff.113.125.115.180. [3500.]
1921. ff.139.198.141.138. [4229.]
1922. ff.182.134.174.139. [4382.]
1923. ff.200.172.160.70. [4681.]
1924. ff.106.88.97.81. [5028.]
1925. ff.101.94.76.82. [4623.]
1926. ff.100.83.93.87. [4683.]
1927. ff.116.90.98.77. [4722.]
1928. ff.101.103.84.71. [4651.]
1929. ff.122.94.91.92. [4940.]
1930. ff.132.127.107.85. [5324.]
1931. ff.131.104.84.77. [4607.]
1932. ff.111.105.94.75. [4478.]
1933. ff.114.122.96.98. [4671.]
1934. ff.135.131.126.94. [5189.]
1935. ff.156.93.175.89. [5750.]
1936. ff.137.95.114.106. [4811.]
1937. ff.138.133.106.103. [5061.]
1938. ff.144.119.145.111. [5419.]
1939. ff.148.121.181.
1940. ff.177.139.131.100. [5823.]
1941. ff. . . 98.94.
1942. ff.76.48.38.43. [3114.]
1943. ff.48.41.50.44. [2884.]
1944. ff.64.49.47.51. [3193.]
1945. ff.70.53.50.50.52. [3282.]
1946. ff.64.54.39.37. [2754.]
1947. pp.58.42.33.38. [2464.]
1948. pp.44.44.52.51. [2671.]
1949. pp.64.34.56.46. [2688.]
1950. pp.45.43.46.54. [2545.]
1951. pp.54.40.37.37. [2276.]
1952. ff.41.39.47.49. [2252.]
1953. ff.47.48.54.52. [2492.]
1954. ff.60.63.62.53. [3113.]
title varies.

J. V. WOODMAN, A digest of the cases reported in the Bengal law reports, vols. I to XV, and in the supplement volume of full bench rulings. Calcutta 1878. pp.liii.coll.658. [3000.]

A. C. MITRA [AVINĀṢACHANDRA MITRA], A digest of the Indian law reports (Calcutta series . . .), being a complete index to cases determined by the High court, Calcutta, and by the Judicial committee of the Privy council, from 1876 to 1883. Monghyr 1884. pp.[iii].324.x. [1000.]

WALTER K. FIRMINGER, *ed.* Bengal district records, Dinajpur. Assam secretariat printing office: Shillong.
   [i]. 1787–1789. 1914. pp.iii.340. [504.]
   ii. 1786–88. Letters issued. 1924. pp.[v].362. [449.]

WALTER K. FIRMINGER, *ed.* Bengal historical records. Proceedings of the select committee at Fort William in Bengal, 1758. Calcutta 1914. pp.xiii.61. [large number.]

WALTER K. FIRMINGER, *ed.* Bengal district records Rangpur. Bengal secretariat record room: Calcutta.
   i. 1770–1779. 1914. pp.ix.110. [147.]
   ii. 1779–1782. Letters received. 1920. pp.vii. 330. [453.]
   iii. 1783–1785. Letters received. 1920. pp. [vii].406. [612.]
   iv. 1779–1785. Letters issued. 1921. pp.[iii.] 252. [291.]
   v. 1786–1787. Letters received. 1927. pp.[iv]. 323. [425.]
   vi. 1786–1787. Letters issued. 1928. ff.[ii]. pp.288. [297.]
   Supplement, i. 1770, 1777–1779. 1923. pp.9. [147.]

WALTER K. FIRMINGER, *ed.* Bengal district records, Midnapur. Bengal secretariat record room: Calcutta 1915.
   ii. 1768–1770. pp.vi.206. [579.]
   iii. 1771–1774. Letters received. 1925. pp.296. [342.]
   iv. 1770–1774. Letters issued. 1926. ff.[iii]. pp.203. [264.]

CALENDAR of records of the select committee at Fort William in Bengal. Preserved in the Bengal secretariat room. Calcutta 1915–1916. pp. [v].212+xvii. [521.]

PRESS list of ancient documents preserved in the secretariat record-room of the government of Bengal. Series ii: Intermediate revenue authorities. Calcutta.
   i. Comptrolling council of revenue, Patna 1st March 1765 to 23rd December 1773. 1917. pp.422.xiv. [4200.]
   ii. Comptrolling council of revenue, Murshidabad, etc. 1769–74. 1918. pp.459.xxv. [4600.]
   Supplementary volume. General letters to and from the court of directors. 1771–1775. 1918. pp. ii.iii. [33.]

PRESS-LIST of ancient documents preserved in the secretariat record-room of the government of Bengal. Calcutta.
   i. Controlling committee of commerce. 28th March 1771 to 20th November 1773. 1919. pp.48.iv. [500.]
   ii. Board of trade. 24th November 1774 to 17th December 1776. 1921. pp.429.xv. [4500.]
   iii. Revenue board of the whole council. 13th October 1772 to 30th December 1774. 1915. pp.622.xxviii. [6200.]
   iv. Governor general of Bengal in council. 6th January to 29th December, 1775. 1917. pp.367.xvii. [3600.]
   v. 2nd January to 31st December 1776. 1918. pp.348.xxii. [3500.]

i. Controlling committee of revenue. April, 1771 to 10th October, 1772. 1915. pp.112. viii. [1000.]

ii. Committee of circuit, 10th June, 1772 to 18th February, 1773. 1916. pp.94.ix. [900.]

W. SUTTON PAGE, A bibliography for missionaries and others living in Bengal. Calcutta 1920. ff.[ii].pp.48. [774.]

CATALOGUE of the english records, 1758–1858, preserved in the historical record room of the Government of Bengal. Calcutta 1922. pp.[iv].v.123. [250,000.]
— Correction slip no.1. [1925]. ff.4.
— — no.2.[1925]. ff.4.

BENGAL district records, Chittagong. Bengal secretariat book depot: Calcutta.

i. 1760–1773. Letters received and issued. 1923. pp.[vii]. 327. [406.]

SELECT index to the general letters from the Court of directors in the Judicial department 1795–1854. Preserved in the Bengal secretariat record room. Calcutta 1924. pp.58. [1000.]

RECORDS of the government of Bengal. Proceedings of the Committee of circuit, vols.i–iii in 1, iv, v–viii in 1. 1926–7.

SELECT index to general letters to and from the court of directors in the revenue, territorial revenue, territorial financial and miscellaneous revenue departments of the Government of Bengal. Preserved in the Bengal secretariat record room. Calcutta 1926–1927.

i. 1771–1858. pp.iii.235. [2300.]

ii. (separate revenue, commercial, commercial financial and territorial financial departments) 1765–1954. pp.ii.103. [1000.]

iii. (to the court of directors for 1793–1858 and from the court of directors for 1827–1829 in the judicial department). pp.178. [1800.]

iv. (public or general, ecclesiastical public works, railway, public works revenue, legislative and financial departments) 1834–1856. pp.154. [1500.]

PRESS list of ancient documents relating to the governor-general of Bengal in council preserved in the secretariat record-room of the government of Bengal. Calcutta.
Series i — Revenue department. 1931–1937.

i. 2 January to 29 December 1778. pp.363. [3600.]

ii. 5 January 1779 to 20 February 1781. pp. 480. [4400.]
Series ii — Intermediate revenue authorities. 1930–1939.

i. 6 December 1773 to 28 December 1775. pp.325. [3000.]

ii. 2 January 1776 to 29 December 1777. pp. 593. [5500.]

iii. 5 January to 30 December 1778. pp.285. [2600.]

EDMOND GAUDART, Catalogue des manuscrits des anciennes archives de l'Inde française. Tome III. Chandernagor et les loges du Bengale, 1730–1815. Société de l'histoire de l'Inde française: Pondichéry &c. 1933. pp.[iii].423.xxvii. [893.]

BIBLIOGRAPHY of Bengal records, 1756–1858. List of records of the Government of Bengal printed and published by the Bengal record room or otherwise with official sanction. Record room: [Calcutta] 1924. pp.[ii].9. [88.]
— Second edition. Bibliography of Bengal records, 1632–1858. List of english records relating to the Company's administration in Bengal which can be consulted in print. 1925. pp.[v].15. [184.]

MANIBHŪSHAN MAJIRMDĀR, Index to the imperial and Bengal council acts and the ordinances. [Calcutta] 1933. pp.[iv].156. [4500.]

DESCRIPTIVE catalogue of books and publications registered in West Bengal during the quarter. Calcutta gazette: Appendix: [Calcutta] 1950 &c. *in progress?*

INDIRA SARKAR, Social thought in Bengal (1757–1947): a bibliography of bengali men and women of letters. Calcutta 1949. pp.xv.109.ix. [1200.]

SIR WILLIAM WILSON HUNTER, Bengal ms. records. A selected list of 14,136 letters in the Board of revenue, Calcutta, 1782–1807. 1894. pp.336+15–324+15–320+15–388. [14,136.]

D. E. CRANENBURGH, A digest of civil cases reported in the Indian law reports, 1876 to 1894, and in the Calcutta law reports, 1878 to 1883. [Second edition]. Vol.1. Calcutta 1895. pp.[ii].ii.coll.2420. [5000.]
a–l only; no more published.

C. S. MCLEAN, Catalogue of the Bengal secretariat library. Calcutta 1895. pp.v.516.cii.xlvii. [7500.]
— — [Eighth edition]. By Kali Prosunno Banerjea [Kāli-Prasanna Vandyopādhyāya]. 1901. pp.[ii].iii.718.cci. [12,500.]

THE ALPHABETICAL index to circulars and circular memos. From 1890 to 1897. [Calcutta 1898]. pp.[ii].xxv. [400.]

LIST of consultations, proceedings, &c.: Bengal, 1704–1858. Preserved in the Record department of the India office. 1899. pp.[ii].iii.3.516. [very large number.]
— 1859–1897. 1899. pp.[iii].iii.40. [large number.]

BIBLIOGRAPHY of Bengal. (Being part of the medico-topographical history of the province). (Issued for the guidance of medical officers who are preparing the district histories). Calcutta [1900]. pp.[ii].27. [500.]

THE DISTRICT officers' handy reference book, being a general index to acts and regulations and to important rules, notifications and orders in force in Bengal, with a list of useful books of reference. Second edition. General department: Calcutta 1908. pp.[ii].ix.377. [6000.]

this is an adaptation rather than a second edition of W. C. Macpherson, Aid to revenue and magisterial duties in the lower provinces of Bengal (1891).

LIST of non-confidential publications exempted from registration, which were issued by the Government of Eastern Bengal and Assam during the year.

    1908. pp.5. [29.]
    1909. pp.5. [32.]
    1910. pp.5. [33.]
    1911. pp.5. [28.]
    the continuation is entered under Assam, above.

LIST of official publications [of publications] (other than confidential) issued by the government of Bengal [from the Bengal secretariat book depôt] during the year ... which are exempted from registration. [Calcutta.]

    1908. pp.17. [122.]
    1909. pp.29. [196.]
    1910. pp.31. [183.]
    1911. pp.33. [189.]
    1912. pp.25. [155.]
    1913. pp.27. [154.]
    1914. pp.25. [137.]
    1915. pp.
    1916. pp.39. [184.]
    1917. pp.[ii].25. [234.]
    1918. pp.35. [325.]
    1919. pp.40. [313.]
    1920. pp.30. [207.]
    1921. pp.39. [271.]
    1922. 1926. pp.[ii].24. [300.]
    1923.
    1924. 1927. pp.25. [300.]
    1925. pp.27. [300.]
    1926. pp.19. [300.]

CATALOGUE of books and pamphlets registered in eastern Bengal for the quarter. The Calcutta gazette: Appendix: [Calcutta] 1912. ff.38. [400.]
no more published.

[MAULAVĪ ẒARĪF MUḤAMMAD *and others*], Calendar of persian correspondence. Being letters, referring mainly to affairs in Bengal, which passed between some of the Company's servants and indian rulers and notables. Imperial record department: Calcutta.

    i. 1759–1767. 1911. pp.xxviii.509. [2815.]
    ii. 1767–1769. 1914. pp.xxiii.470.[v].23. [1780.]
    iii. 1769–1772. 1919. pp.[v].xxxiii.285.xx. [1050.]
    iv. 1772–1775. 1925. pp.xviii.365.xxvi. [2087.]
    v. 1776–1780. 1930. pp.xxiv.507.xxxi. [2075.]
    vi. 1781–1785. 1938. pp.xvii.441.xxvii. [1623.]
    vii. 1785–1787. 1940. pp.xv.463. xxxvii. [1935.]

CATALOGUE of the publications of the government of Bengal. Calcutta 1912. pp.58. [600.]

    Berar. [see also *Central Provinces.*]

MEMORANDUM of books registered in the Hyderabad assigned districts. Akola 1867–1903.

MEMORANDUM of books registered during the quarter ending on 30th June 1880 [–31st December 1902]. Akola 1880–1903.

LIST of publications (other than confidential) issued during the quarter ending 30th June 1897 [–31st December 1902] which are exempted from registration. [Hyderabad 1897–1903]. pp.[88]. [600.]

VAMAN VASUDEO CHITALE [VĀMANA VĀSUDEVA CHITALE] and MAHADEO SITARAM MUNDLE [MAHĀDEVA SĪTĀRĀMA MUNDLE], Chitale and Mundle's Digest of C. P. & Berar case-law, 1862–1920 March. Triplicane [printed] 1920. pp.[ii].4. coll.1148.118. [4641.]

    Bihar and Orissa [see also *Orissa*]

LIST of official publications [*afterwards:* of publications] (other than confidential) issued from the office of the Superintendent, Government press, Bihar and Orissa [*afterwards:* Bihar and Orissa book depôt; Bihar book depot] during the year ... which are exempted from registration. [Patna].

    1912. pp.[2]. [18.]
    1913. pp.2. [34.]
    1914. pp.11. [68.]
    1915. pp.9. [47.]
    1916. pp.11. [69.]
    1917. pp.[iii].12. [79.]
    1918. pp.[iii].13. [98.]
    1919. pp.[iii].13. [93.]
    1920. pp.[iii].24. [130.]
    1921. pp.[iii].23. [125.]
    1922. pp.[iii].26. [150.]
    1923. pp.[iii].20. [125.]
    1924. pp.[iii].22. [150.]
    1925. pp.[iii].20. [125.]
    1926. pp.[ii].20. [125.]
    1927. pp.17. [200.]
    1928. pp.25. [250.]

1929–1930. pp.51. [500.]
1931. pp.34. [300.]
1932. pp.31. [300.]
1933. pp.27. [250.]
1934. pp.
1935–1936. pp.48. [500.]
1937. pp.27. [300.]
1938. pp.33. [500.]

CATALOGUE of books registered [Statement of particulars regarding (Catalogue of) books and periodicals published] in the province of Bihar and Orissa [registered under act XXV of 1867] during the quarter. [Bihar & Orissa gazette: Appendix:] [Ranchi] Patna.

1912. pp.24.34.29. [495.]
1913. ff.36.40.35.13. [661.]
1914. ff.47.30.32.31. [899.]
1915. ff.38.36.57.26. [882.]
1916. ff.42.28.37.46. [814.]
1917. ff.35.52.63.33. [1091.]
1918. ff.44.31.31.31. [837.]
1919. ff.35.29.32.23. [709.]
1920. ff.31.37.42.28. [836.]
1921. ff.33.32.39.35. [807.]
1922. ff.45.38.43.38. [1027.]
1923. ff.64.39.73.15. [1254.]
1924. ff.33.34.32.44. [1540.]
1925. ff.22.32.20.16. [859.]
1926. ff.34.21.74.40. [1843.]
1927. ff.40.36.33.31. [1500.]
1928. ff.18.24.15.16. [765.]
1929. ff.34.26.19.16. [1029.]
1930. ff.23.22.20.15. [822.]
1931. ff.31.21.21.18. [849.]
1932. ff.18.23.20.26. [764.]
1933. ff.20.16.18.18. [680.]
1934. ff.15.16.22.16. [607.]
1935. ff.28.22.21.18. [803.]
1936. ff.23.12.10.12. [483.]
1937. ff.14.13.14.9. [515.]
1938. ff.10.6.6.6. [176.]
1939. ff. .5.10.5.
1940. ff.6.6.7.4. [168.]
1941. pp.4. . . 4.
1942. pp.1.3.3. .
1943. pp.3.3.2.3. [115.]
1944. pp.4.3.3. .
1945. pp.3.3.2.3. [99.]
1946. pp.3.3.3.3. [98.]
1947. pp.3.3.2.3. [99.]
1948. pp.4.3.3.2. [72.]
1949. pp.7.3.6.4. [205.]
1950. pp.5.5.2.2. [122.]

viii. 1956–xii.1957. pp.9. [121.]
1965. pp.2. [24.]
the issues from the 2nd quarter of 1936 inclusive register publications in Bihar only.

BIHAR DIGEST. Civil, criminal & revenue. 1934–

1940. Bihar reports: [Lahore 1940]. pp.[ii].xxvi. coll.866. [5000.]

HARISHCHANDRA PRASAD and GITA SEN GUPTA, A bibliography of folklore of Bihar; books, articles, reports and monographs in english and hindi. Indian publications folklore series (no.17): Calcutta 1971. pp.96. [2000.]

Bombay

SIR A[LEXANDER] GRANT, Catalogue of native publications in the Bombay presidency up to 31st December 1864. . . . Second edition. Bombay 1867. pp.[iii].35.239. [1679.]
—— [Supplement]. 1865–1867. . . . By J. B. Peile [or rather, by Krishṇa Ṣāstri Chiplonkar]. 1869. pp.[iii].120. [1250.]

CATALOGUE of books printed in the Bombay presidency [*afterwards:* state] during the quarter. [Poona; Bombay].

1867. pp.7.8. [136.]
1868. pp.18.17.19.5. [516.]
1869. pp.19.17.17.15. [658.]
1870. pp.14.15.23.21.112.116.120.173. [611.]
1869–1870. Supplementary catalogue. pp.15. [106.]
1871. pp.13.15.25.41. [750.]
1872. pp.15.17.15.24. [680.]
1873. pp.21.20.19.19. [800.]
1867–1873. Supplementary catalogue. pp.15. [380.]
1874. pp.19.23.23.21. [870.]
1875. pp.21.19.23.29. [920.]
1876. pp. . .33.37.
1877. pp. .29.35.31.
1878. pp.31.25.41.37. [750.]
1879. pp.31.33.39.43. [750.]
1880. pp.37.27.33.33. [750.]
1881. pp.27.33.39.43. [750.]
1882. pp.41.51.39.49. [1000.]
1883. pp.43.50.65.73. [1250.]
1884. pp.51.65.83.75. [1500.]
1885. pp.81.73.117.83. [1750.]
1886. pp.87.91.77.67. [1500.]
1887. pp.85.97.75.59. [1500.]
1888. pp.63.89.89.77. [1500.]
1889. pp.57.99.79.103. [1750.]
1890. pp.93.93.97.57. [1750.]
1891. pp.51.63.69.64. [1250.]
1892. pp.62.51.60.69. [1000.]
1893. pp.81.65.71.77. [1250.]
1894. pp.63.87.53.61. [1250.]
1895. pp.65.53.57.61. [1000.]
1896. pp.63.47.47.59. [1000.]
1897. pp.37.35.37.43. [750.]
1898. pp.31.55.51.45. [750.]
1899. pp.39.43.43.61. [750.]
1900. pp.45.42.59.55. [1000.]
1901. pp.49.45.45.41. [750.]

1902. pp.37.47.37.49. [750.]
1903. pp.41.33.41.47. [750.]
1904. pp.39.45.39.43. [750.]
1905. pp.43.33.47.ff.47. [750.]
1906. pp.51.55.71.50. [1000.]
1907. ff.47.48.61.48. [750.]
1908. ff.48.44.46.54. [1250.]
1909. ff.64.52.56.48. [1250.]
1910. ff.57.75.57.62. [1250.]
1911. ff.55.64.63.61. [1250.]
1912. ff.65.69.74.72. [1500.]
1913. ff.89.78.77.72. [1750.]
1914. ff.63.75.95.93. [1750.]
1915. ff.88.83.94.90. [2000.]
1916. ff.121.71.116.88. [2500.]
1917. ff.92.90.91.86. [2000.]
1918. ff.102.74.77.90. [2000.]
1919. ff.84.84.92.87. [2000.]
1920. ff.88.59.87.83. [2000.]
1921. ff.78.98.68.85. [2000.]
1922. ff.84.88.81.75. [2000.]
1923. ff.94.104.102.43. [2500.]
1924. ff.42.51.48.56. [2500.]
1925. ff.52.42.44.44. [2500.]
1926. ff.65.49.50.47. [2500.]
1927. ff.45.37.37.pp.37. [2611.]
1928. pp.26.36.52.45. [2399.]
1929. pp.34.83.40.32. [2131.]
1930. pp.34.36.63. .
1931. pp. .41.36.49.
1932. pp.41.41.ff.44.38. [2389.]
1933. ff.50.39.47.46. [2187.]
1934. ff.37.52.51.31. [2484.]
1935. ff.49.40.56.57. [2500.]
1936. ff.59.53.55.50. [2500.]
1937. ff.46. .60.
1938. ff.49.50.51.41. [3460.]
1939. ff.46.47.58.60. [3894.]
1940. ff.54.pp.53. .ff.49.
1941. pp.53.ff.61. .60.
1942. ff.65.63.56.pp.35. [4368.]
1943. pp.30.ff.40.pp.34.
1944. pp.34.37.41.ff.34. [3638.]
1945. ff.38.31.pp.37.37. [3635.]
1946. pp.34.ff.30.pp.26.38. [3145.]
1947. pp.33.36.41.
1948. pp.40.43.40.52. [4330.]
1949. pp.40.48.44.44. [4181.]
1950. pp.58.44.61.49. [5546.]
1951. ff.49.pp.64.54.54. [5779.]
1952. ff.65.pp.68.ff.55.pp.67. [5832.]
1953. pp.61.65.74.71. [6517.]
1954. pp.63.69. .69.
1955. pp.84.70. . .
1956.
1957. pp. .112.73.91.
1958. pp.61.43.69.55. [5000.]
1959. pp.54.46.98.31. [4500.]

REGINALD M. A. BRANSON, Digest of the printed

but unreported judgements of the High court of Bombay, from 1869 to 1884. Bombay 1886. pp. xxxiii.coll.412. [1250.]

[SIR] GEORGE W[ILLIAM] FORREST, Alphabetical catalogue of the contents of the Bombay secretariat records (1630–1780). Bombay 1887. pp. 1750. [1000.]

LIST of official publications printed in the Bombay presidency during the quarter [year; &c.]. Bombay.

    1892. pp.5.5. [58.]
    1893. pp.3.5.7.5. [105.]
    1894. pp.5.9.11.9. [192.]
    1895. pp.7.7.11.7. [168.]
    1896. pp.7.7.11.7. [166.]
    1897. pp.5.5.5.8. [127.]
    1898. pp.5.5.7.7. [116.]
    1899. pp.7.5.7.7. [125.]
    1900–1901. pp.5.15.11. [216.]
    1902. pp.13. [102.]
    1903. pp.17. [119.]
    1904. pp.17. [120.]
    1905. pp.15. [107.]
    1906. pp.19. [148.]
    1907. pp.26. [166.]
        [continued as:]
List of non-confidential publications exempted from registration, which were issued by the departments of the government of Bombay, during the year [exclusive of publications appearing in general catalogue].
    1908. pp.19. [117.]
    1909. pp.21. [130.]
    1910. pp.19. [122.]
    1911. pp.23. [139.]
    1912. pp.21. [131.]
    1913. pp.19. [117.]
    1914. pp.25. [163.]
    1915. pp.39. [273.]
    1916. pp.31. [280.]
    1917. pp.35. [324.]
    — [another edition]. pp.[ii].30. [324.]
    1918. pp.[ii].37. [398.]
    1919. pp.[ii].42. [414.]
    1920. pp.[ii].53. [529.]
    1921. pp.[ii].46. [442.]
    1922. pp.[ii].54. [529.]
    1923. pp.[ii].48. [571.]
    1924. pp.[ii].53. [604.]
    1925. pp.[ii].51. [627.]
    1926. pp.[ii].79. [919.]
    1927. pp.36. [412.]
    1928. pp.44. [478.]
    1929. pp.47. [513.]
    1930. pp.55. [637.]
    1931. pp.40. [438.]
    1932. pp.51. [571.]
    1933.
    1934. pp.47. [529.]

1935. pp.14. [136.]
1936. pp.15. [143.]
1937. pp.30. [321.]
1938. pp.
1939. pp.
1940. pp.
1941. pp.13. [133.]
in progress.

CALENDAR of land revenue settlements for the districts comprised in the Bombay presidency, including Sind. [Bombay 1899–1906.] pp.83+iii. 95. [3000.]

LIST of proceedings, &c.: Bombay, 1702–1900, preserved in the Record department of the India office. 1902. pp.v.166. [very large number.]

PRESS list of ancient documents preserved in the Bombay record office. [Bombay].
1646–1700. [1904.] pp.[ii].172. [3000.]
1700–1719. [1907]. pp.[ii].101. [2000.]
1719–1740. [1917]. pp.189. [4000.]
1740–1760. [1922]. pp.[ii].677. [15,000.]

THE BLUE book quarterly. .... A review of the publications of the government of Bombay.
i. 1914. pp.v.353.iii. [250.]
ii. 1915. pp.256.iii. [250.]
iii. 1916. (1st–3rd quarters). pp.172. [200.]

A. F. KINDERSLEY, A handbook of the Bombay government records. Bombay 1921. pp.[iii].vi. 1000. [very large number.]

RATANLAL RANCHHODDAS [RATANLĀLA RAÑ-CHHODDĀSA] and DHIRAJLAL KESHAVLAL THAKORE [DHĪRAJLĀLA KEṢAVLĀLA ṬHĀKURA], The twenty years' digest of the Bombay law reporter . . . 1899–1918. Bombay 1921. pp.[iii].lxxxvi.coll.1952.pp. 1953–1957. [5000.]

GENERAL catalogue of all publications of the Government of Bombay [including Sind]. No.4. [that is, 4th edition]. Bombay [1928]. pp.102. [2000.]
— No.13. Catalogue of publications. [1940]. pp.118. [2000.]
— [Another edition]. Catalogue of government publications. 1952. pp.63. [1500.]
— [another edition]. 1958. pp.[ii].91. [2000.]
supplementary leaflets are issued, under the title of Government publications for sale, *in various forms and at irregular intervals.*

LIST showing newspapers published in the province of Bombay. [Bombay] 1943. pp.15.
— Additions and alterations. 1943 &c.

V. G. DIGHE, Descriptive catalogue of the secret and political department series 1755–1820. Bombay records series: Descriptive catalogue (vol.1): Bombay 1954. pp.viii. 652. xl.2. [496.]

Central Provinces

CATALOGUE of books &c. issued from the presses in the Central Provinces and registered under act xxv. of 1867 [books registered in the Central Provinces; registered in the Central Provinces (and Berar) under act xxv. of 1867, as amended by act x of 1890 (as amended by act x of 1913)] during the quarter. Nagpur 1867–1922.
brief and irregular lists; continued as:

Catalogue of books and pamphlets registered in Central Provinces and Berar [*afterwards:* in the Madhya Pradesh]. [Central Provinces gazette].
1923. ff.9. [64.]
1924. ff.9.8.7.6. [186.]
1925. ff.8.5.10.7. [187.]
1926. ff.8.8.6.8. [173.]
1927. ff.9.8.11.6. [217.]
1928. ff.9.6.8.6. [172.]
1929. ff.6.5.7.6. [132.]
1930. ff.6.10.10.6. [190.]
1931. ff.6.6.7.5. [128.]
1932. ff.6.5.7.5. [121.]
1933. ff.6.8.6.7. [162.]
1934. ff.7.7.8.8. [154.]
1935. ff.9.14.17.12. [201.]
1936. ff.11.10.14.7. [158.]
1937. ff.9.15.16.9. [172.]
1938. ff.14.17.17.7. [199.]
1939. ff.18.23.18.16. [305.]
1940. ff.11.11.11.13. [206.]
1941. ff.12.8.16.
1942. ff.7.10.6.6. [126.]
1943. ff.4.8.8.6. [104.]
1944. ff.8.16.16.10. [236.]
1945. ff.10.7.12.8. [156.]
1946. ff.5.6.8.6. [110.]
1947. ff.5.8.3.5. [85.]
1948. ff.4.5.12.9. [119.]
1949. ff.6.9.8.11. [141.]
1950. ff.6.6.8.7. [166.]
1951. ff.6.   .5.2.
1952. ff.6.4.5.   .
in progress?

LIST of official publications (other than confidential) issued in the Central Provinces (including Berar) during the year ... which are exempted from registration. [Nagpur].
1908. pp.8. [41.]
1909. pp.7. [39.]
1910. pp.7. [38.]
1911. pp.9. [42.]
1912. pp.9. [41.]
1913. pp.9. [44.]
1914. pp.9. [46.]
1915. pp.7. [48.]
1916. pp.9. [42.]
1917. pp.[ii].10. [76.]
1918. pp.[ii].7. [42.]

1919. pp.[ii].8. [49.]
1920. pp.[ii].6. [40.]
1921. pp.[iii].7. [50.]
1922. pp.[iii].8. [61.]
1923. pp.[iii].8. [70.]
1924. pp.[ii].7. [60.]
1925. pp.[ii].8. [70.]
1926. pp.[ii].8. [60.]
no more published.

VAMAN VASUDEO CHITALE [VĀMANA VĀSUDEVA CHIṬALE] and MAHADEO SITARAM MUNDLE [MAHĀDEVA SĪTĀRĀMA MUNDLE], Chitale and Mundle's digest of C. P. & Berar case-law, 1862–1920 March. Triplicane [printed] 1920. pp.[ii].4.coll. 1148.118. [4641.]

LIST of publications for sale at the Central Provinces government press book depot. Nagpur 1933. pp.[iv].44. [1000.]
— [another edition]. 1938. pp.[ii].53. [1250 *issued annually, with quarterly, later monthly, supplements entitled* List of publications. Supplement to the Catalogue, *&c.*

N. B. CHANDURKAR [CHANDRA-KARA], The Triennial digest of Central Provinces & Berar case law & Privy council & federal court cases 1936. 1937 & 1938. Nagpur 1939. pp.xxvii.coll.622. [2000.]

Cochin

STATEMENT of important publications published from the presses in the Cochin state during the fourth quarter of 1113 [1938] [&c.] [Trichur].
    [1938]. pp.3. [69.]
    [1939]. pp.4.4.4. .[.]
fragments of issues for 1940–1946 have also been seen.

Coorg

CATALOGUE of books published in Coorg under the provisions of the Press and registration of books act, 1867 (xxv of 1867). Bangalore 1867 &c. *occasional slips and leaflets.*

LIST of non-confidential [official (other than confidential)] publications exempted from registration which were issued by the administration of Coorg during the year.
    1908. pp.[3]. [7.]
    1909. pp.[3]. [7.]
    1910. pp.[3]. [7.]
    1911. pp.[3]. [6.]
    1912. pp.[3]. [3.]
    1913. pp.[3]. [3.]
    1914. pp.[3]. [3.]
    1915. pp.[3]. [3.]
    1916. pp.[3]. [3.]
    1917. pp.[3]. [4.]
    1918. pp.[3]. [3.]
    1919. pp.[3]. [3.]

1920. pp.[3]. [3.]
1921. pp.[3]. [3.]
later issues are in the form of typewritten sheets and official letters.

Delhi province

LIST of official publications (other than confidential) issued by the chief commissioner, Delhi, during the year ending 31st December 1914 [&c.] which are exempted from registration. Delhi.
leaflets in various forms; since 1919 typewritten.

CATALOGUE of books registered [in the Delhi province] during the quarter ... Chief commissioner: Delhi.
    1913. pp.2.4.11.10. [157.]
    1914. pp.10.3.6.17. [158.]
    1915. pp.9.4.6.8. [179.]
    1916. pp.13.5.9.12. [204.]
    1917. pp.10.8.8.8. [210.]
    1918. pp.8.2.3.3. [157.]
    1919. pp.3.2.3.3. [148.]
    1920. pp.2.3.2.3. [171.]
    1921. pp.4.3.2.3. [205.]
    1922. pp.8.4.3.4. [336.]
    1923. pp.3.2.2.3. [165.]
    1924. pp.5.3.2.2. [227.]
    1925. pp.3.3.3.2. [211.]
    1926. pp.4.3.3.4. [274.]
    1927. pp.6.7.4.2. [414.]
    1928. pp.6.4.5.3. [394.]
    1929. pp.3.5.3.4. [308.]
    1930. pp.5.2.3.2. [193.]
    1931. pp.2.3.3.4. [181.]
    1932. pp.4.3.3.4. [217.]
    1933. pp.5.5.5.5. [304.]
    1934. pp.3.3.5.5. [242.]
    1935. pp.4.4.4.3. [240.]
    1936. pp.6.4.3.4. [261.]
    1937. pp.4.5.5.2. [242.]
    1938. pp.9.3.7.3. [357.]
    1939. pp. .8.9. .
    1940. pp.7.3.3.4. [266.]
    1941. pp.5.5.3. .
    1942. pp.4.3.3.2. [181.]
    1943. pp.3.6. . . [382.]*
    1944. ff. .6.6. . [367.[*
    1945. ff.[20]. [255.]*
    1946. ff.[10]. .6.4.
    1947.
    1948.
    1947.
    1949. pp. .6. . .
    1950.
    1951. pp.8. . . .
    1952. pp.7.9.16.26.[1152.]
    1953. pp.[31.] [1200.]
    1954. pp.[28.] [1000.]
    1955. pp.[24.] [1000.]
    1956. pp.[31.] [1200.]

1957. pp.[34.] [1300.]
1958. pp.[8]. .7.10.
1959. pp.[9]. .7.9.
1960. pp. .9. .11.
1961. pp.[10].[9]. . .
1962. pp. .8. . .

Himalayas

HIMALAJA-BIBLIOGRAPHIE (1801–1933). Deutsche Himalaja-expedition: München 1934. pp.48. [750.]

Hyderabad

MEMORANDUM of books registered in the Hyderabad assigned districts during the quarter. Akola 1867–1903.
occasional leaflets.

Indian ocean

[ANNE E. YENTSCH], A partial bibliography of the Indian ocean. Oceanographic institution: Contribution (no.1286): Woods Hole, Mass. 1962. pp.[iii].395.iii. [5750.]*

Madhya-bhārata

H. V. TRIVEDI, The bibliography of Madhya-Bhàrata archaeology, part 1. Department of archaeology: Government of Madhya Bharat: Gwalior 1953. pp.viii. 51. [450.]

Madras

J. TALBOYS WHEELER, Handbook to the Madras records. Being a report on the public records preserved in the Madras government office, previous to 1834. Madras 1861. pp.xx.48. [very large number.]
reprinted in 1907.

MEMORANDUM of books registered in the Madras presidency.
    1867. ff.[6]. [116.]
    1868. ff.[32]. [418.]
         [continued as:]
A CATALOGUE of books printed [registered] in the Madras presidency during the ... quarter. Fort St. George gazette: Supplement: Madras.
    1869. pp.46. [422.]
    1870. pp.56. [496.]
    1871. pp.50. [476.]
    1872. pp.44. [252.]
    1873. pp.62. [605.]
    1874. pp.64. [756.]
    1875. pp.58. [749.]
    1876. pp.76. [900.]
    1877. pp.61. [750.]
    1878. pp.73. [900.]
    1879. pp.15.55. [800.]

1880. pp.81. [1000.]
1881. pp.79. [1000.]
1882. pp.69. [900.]
1883. pp.93. [1100.]
1884. pp.93. [1100.]
1885. pp.101. [1250.]
1886. pp.103. [1250.]
1887. pp.105. [1250.]
1888. pp.113. [1250.]
1889. pp.133. [1500.]
1890. pp.111. [1250.]
1891. pp.95. [1100.]
1892. pp.107. [1250.]
1893. pp.99. [1100.]
1894. pp.111. [1250.]
1895. pp.117. [1250.]
1896. pp.119. [1250.]
1897. pp.123. [1250.]
1898. pp.143. [1500.]
1899. pp.153. [1750.]
1900. pp.165. [2000.]
1901. pp.151. [1750.]
1902. pp.135. [1500.]
1903. pp.143. [1500.]
1904. pp.137. [1500.]
1905. ff.126. [1500.]
1906. ff.109. [1250.]
1907. ff.140. [1500.]
1908. ff.257. [2000.]
1909. ff.296. [2500.]
1910. ff.375. [3000.]
1911. ff.395. [3500.]
1912. ff.428. [3500.]
1913. ff.427. [3500.]
1914. ff.428. [3500.]
1915. ff.366. [3000.]
1916. ff.366. [3000.]
1917. ff.362. [3000.]
1918. ff.333. [3000.]
1919. ff.344. [3500.]
1920. ff.316. [3500.]
1921. ff.398. [4500.]
1922. ff.426. [5000.]
1923. ff.396. [6000.]
1924. ff.310. [5000.]
1925. ff.268. [6275.]
1926. ff.258. [6000.]
1927. ff.284. [5000.]
1928. ff.274. [5000.]
1929. ff.257. [4500.]
1930. ff.256. [4500.]
1931. ff.248. [4500.]
1932. ff.198. [4000.]
1933. ff.198. [4000.]
1934. ff.184. [4000.]
1935. ff.186. [4000.]
1936. ff.164. [3500.]
1937. ff.166. [3500.]
1938. ff.167–338. [3500.]
1939. ff.170. [3500.]

1940. ff.148. [5652.]
1941. ff.152.
1942. ff.40.22.pp.28. ff.30. [4632.]
1943. ff.28.61.56.68. [3903.]
1944. ff.66.63.63.59. [3979.]
1945. ff.59.52.63.71. [4398.]
1946. ff.82.50.

1953. . . . pp.40.
1954. pp.41.38.52.72 [7348.]
1955. pp.76.72.78. .
1956. pp.69. . . 74.
1957. pp.64.60.74.62. [8293.]
1958. pp. . . 60. .
1959.
1960.
1961. pp.56. . . .
1962. pp. .56. . .

PRESS list of ancient records in Fort St. George.
[Madras].
    i. 1670–1674. 1891. pp.5. [55.]
    ii. 1675–1679. 1891. pp.93. [834.]
    iii. 1680–1684. [c.1892]. pp.199. [1834.]
    iv. 1685–1689. [c.1893]. pp.300. [2107.]
    v. 1690–1694. [c.1894]. pp.145. [1091.]
    vi. 1695–1699. [c.1894.] pp.221. [1430.]
    vii. 1700–1704. [c.1892]. pp.233. [1748.]
    viii. 1705–1709. [c.1893]. pp.127. [1075.]
    ix. 1710–1714. [c.1893]. pp.281. [1864.]
    x. 1715–1719. [c.1894]. pp.190. [1327.]
    xi. 1720–1724. [c.1894]. pp.124. [960.]
    xii. 1725–1729. [c.1894]. pp.166. [1202.]
    xiii. 1730–1734. [c.1894]. pp.141. [1018.]
    xiv. 1735–1739. [c.1895]. pp.215. [1646.]
    xv. 1740–1744. [c.1895]. pp.432. [3399.]
    xvi. 1745–1749. [1896]. pp.546. [3720.]
    xvii. 1750–1754. [1896.] pp.961. [6202.]
    xviii. 1755–1759. [1897]. pp.1105. [7279.]
    xix. 1760–1764. [1898]. pp.1181. [6949.]
    xx. 1765–1769. 1899. pp.[ii].1252. [8510.]
    xxi. 1770–1774. 1900. pp.[ii].1286. [10,256.]
    xxii. 1775. 1900. pp.[ii].267. [1603.]
    xxiii. 1776. 1900. pp.[ii].231. [1243.]
    xxiv. 1777. 1900. pp.[ii].306. [1598.]
    xxv. 1778. 1901. pp.[ii].400. [2111.]
    xxvi. 1779. 1900. pp.[ii].355. [1953.]
    xxvii. 1780. 1901. pp.[ii].382. [2896.]
    xxviii. 1781. 1901. pp.[ii].339. [2497.]
    xxix. 1782. 1901. pp.[ii].506. [3996.]
    xxx. 1783. 1902. pp.[ii].606. [3956.]
    xxxi. 1784. 1902. pp.[ii].571. [3619.]
    xxxii. 1785. 1902. pp.[ii].532. [3245.]
    xxxiii. 1786. 1902. pp.[ii].476. [2345.]
    xxxiv. 1787. 1902. pp.[ii].462. [2432.]
    xxxv. 1788. 1902. pp.[ii].562. [2484.]
    xxxvi. 1789. 1902. pp.[ii].540. [5000.]
    xxxvii. 1790. 1902. pp.[ii].583. [5000.]
    xxxviii. 1791. 1903. pp.[ii].737. [6000.]
    xxxix. 1792. 1905. pp.[ii].965. [8000.]
    xl. 1793. 1907. pp.[ii].1012. [9000.]

    xli. 1794. 1907. pp.[ii].740. [6000.]
    xlii. 1795. 1907. pp.[ii].823. [7000.]
    xliii. 1796. 1908. pp.[ii].985. [8000.]
    xliv. 1797. 1908. pp.[ii].936. [8000.]
    xlv. 1798. 1909. pp.[ii].780. [7000.]
    xlvi. 1799. 1910. pp.[ii].793. [7000.]
    xlvii. 1800. 1910. pp.[ii].666. [6000.]
privately printed.

CLASSIFIED catalogue of the Public Reference library, consisting of books registered from 1867 to 1889 at the office of the Registrar of books, ... Madras. 1894. pp.[iii].466. [9000.]

[A. J. M. HEYLINGERS], Press list of ancient dutch records, from 1657 to 1825. Presidency of Madras: [1897]. pp.137. [1750.]

LIST of proceedings, &c.: Madras. 1702–1900. Preserved in the Record department of the India office. 1904. pp.iv.252. [very large number.]

J. TALBOYS WHEELER, Hand-book to the Madras records, being a report on the public records preserved in the Madras government office, previous to 1834, with chronological annals of the Madras presidency. Madras 1907. pp.xx.48. [208.]

LIST of [official] publications (other than confidential) issued by the government of Madras during the year ... which are exempted from registration [including those printed by the Superintendent, Government press, Madras, and published by the government of India Central publication branch, Calcutta (Publication branch ... Delhi)]. [Madras].
    1908. pp.31. [248.]
    1909. pp.43. [317.]
    1910. pp.39. [291.]
    1911. pp.59. [399.]
    1912. pp.55. [391.]
    1913. pp.29. [346.]
    1914. pp.25. [308.]
    1915. pp.41. [500.]
    1916. pp.45. [550.]
    1917. pp.[ii].44. [650.]
    1918. pp.[ii].46. [650.]
    1919. pp.[ii].46. [650.]
    1920. pp.[ii].44. [650.]
    1921. pp.[ii].58. [750.]
    1922. pp.[ii].55. [700.]
    1923. pp.[ii].56. [700.]
    1924. pp.[ii].57. [700.]
    1925. pp.[ii]. 58. [750.]
    1926. pp.[ii].60. [750.]
    1927. pp.[ii].62. [750.]
    1928. pp.[ii].70. [850.]
    1929. pp.[ii].83. [1000.]
    1930. pp.[ii].77. [900.]
    1931. pp.[ii].78. [900.]
    1932. pp.[ii].73. [850.]
    1933. pp.[ii].69. [800.]

1934. pp.[ii].75. [850.]
1935. pp.[ii].70. [800.]
quarterly supplements, under the title of List of
acts and publications placed on sale at the Madras
government publication depot, *are also issued.*

LIST of dutch manuscripts, letters, and official
documents copied by the rev. P. Groot. Selections
from the records of the Madras government:
Dutch records (no.6): Madras 1909. pp.[iii].35.
[large number.]

THE CALENDAR of the Madras records for 1748.
Provisional issue. Madras 1912. [714.]

H[ENRY] DODWELL, A calendar of the Madras
records, 1740–1744. Madras 1917. pp.[ii].xxi.550.
[1871.]

HENRY DODWELL, Calendar of the Madras
despatches. Madras.

1744–1755. 1920. pp.xxi.289. [200.]
1754–1765. 1930. pp.[v].468. [250.]

GUIDE to the records of the Chingleput district
from 1763 to 1835. Madras 1934. pp.193. [197.]

GUIDE to the records of the Coimbatore
district, 1799 to 1835. Madras 1934. pp.280.
[105.]

GUIDE to the records of the Ganjam district,
from 1744 to 1835. Madras 1934. pp.614. [179.]

GUIDE to the records of the Guntur district,
1795 to 1835. Madras 1934. pp.257. [68.]

GUIDE to the records of the Nellore district,
1801 to 1835. Madras 1934. pp.298. [142.]

A GUIDE to the records preserved in the Madras
record office. Madras 1936. pp.44. [very large
number.]

A CATALOGUE of presidency maps, district
maps, taluk maps, town maps, road maps, etc.
Survey department: Madras 1938. pp.[iii].vi.
ff.v–xxix.pp.30. [800.]

GUIDE to the records of the South Arcot district
1708 to 1835. Madras 1934. pp.312. [411.]

GUIDE to the records of the Vizagapatam
district, 1769 to 1835. Madras 1934. pp.381. [169.]

LIST of newspapers and periodicals published in
the Madras state for the year 1955. [Madras 1956].
pp.23. [888.]

PAUL HOCKINGS, A bibliography of studies on
the Nilgiri hills of Madras. Bulletin of the
Deccan college research institute (vol.26, part i
and ii): Poona 1968. pp.[vi].116. [1222.]

Mahabalipuram

WILLIAM Y. WILLETTS, An illustrated annotated
annual bibliogrpahy of Mahabalipuram on the
Coromandel coast of India, 1582–1962. Department of indian studies: University of Malaya:
Kuala Lumpur 1966. pp.69. [155.]

Malabar

MĀDHAVAN NAIR [NĀYAR], The Malabar law
digest (1862–1941). Calicut 1941. pp.[v].xix.336.
[1000.]

Maharashtra

DATTA SHANKARRAO KHARBAS, Maharashtra and
the Marathas, their history and culture. A bibliographical guide to western language materials.
South Asia center: University of Rochester:
Rochester, N.Y. 1973. pp.xii.326. [5535.]*

Mysore

A CATALOGUE of books printed in the Mysore
province [registered under the government of
Mysore] [registered in accordance with the provisions of act xxv of 1867]. Mysore government
library: Bangalore.

1878. pp.[15]. [30.]
1879. pp.[15]. [30.]
1880. pp.[15]. [30.]
1881. pp.[15]. [30.]
1882. pp.7.5.[5].5. [100.]
1883. pp.7.5.7.5. [100.]
1884. pp.15.7.7.9. [175.]
1885. pp.9.7.7.5. [150.]
1886. pp.9.
1887. pp.
1888. pp.
1889. pp.7.7.5.5. [125.]
1890. pp.7.7.11.9. [175.]
1891. pp.9.7.9.7. [150.]
1892. pp.9.11.5.7. [150.]
1893. pp.9.7.9.11. [175.]
1894. pp.9.3.5.5. [100.]
1895. pp.3.3.5.7. [100.]
1896. pp.7.7.5.5. [125.]
1897. pp.5.5.5.3. [100.]
1898. pp.3.5.5.5. [100.]
1899. pp.5.3.5.5. [100.]
1900. pp.3.3.5.3. [50.]
1901. pp.3.3.3.5. [50.]
1902. pp.3.3.3.3. [30.]
1903. pp.5.3.5.3. [50.]
1904. pp.3.3.3.3. [50.]
1905. pp.5.5.3.7. [100.]
1906. pp.7.3.3.3. [66.]
1907. pp.3.3.3.3. [58.]
1908. pp.5.2.4.2. [60.]
1909. pp.3.3.3.8. [100.]
1910. pp.5.3.9.7. [125.]

1911. pp.7.7.8.5. [125.]
1912. pp.7.6.9.5. [125.]
1913. pp.7.6.6.6. [125.]
1914. pp.7.7.8.7. [150.]
1915. pp.7.5.8.6. [125.]
1916. pp.7.8.7.6. [150.]
1917. pp.9.12.9.6. [175.]
1918. pp.9.13.11.10. [225.]
1919. pp.11.8.9.9. [200.]
1920. pp.3.8.10.6. [150.]
1921. pp.3.11.8.6. [150.]
1922. pp.7.7.3.12. [150.]
1923. pp.9.8.11.12. [225.]
1924. pp.9.7.3.7. [150.]
1925. pp.10.8.6.4. [150.]
1926. pp.9.9.10.11. [200.]
1927. pp.7.9.11.10. [200.]
1928. pp.6.8.17.14. [250.]
1929. pp.16.13.4.19. [300.]
1930. pp.9.16.11.9. [250.]
1931. pp.11.13.14.7. [250.]
1932. pp.18.12.15.10. [300.]
1933. pp.9.13.17.14. [300.]
1934. pp.13.15.16.16. [273.]
1935. pp.22.16.14.16. [316.]
1936. pp.11.17.15.15. [253.]
1937. pp.21.17.21. .
1938. pp.19.18.18.28. [363.]
1939. pp.13.16.28.15. [300.]
1940. pp.15.15. . .
1941.
1942.

[N. T. GOPALIENGAR (GOPĀLA AIYANGĀR)], A consolidated digest of the cases decided by the Chief court of Mysore (1878–1916). Madras 1917. pp.[iii].5.122.coll.1550. [7500.]

CATALOGUE of books in oriental languages published by the Oriental library, Mysore during the months of ... or the ... quarter of 1909 [–1940?].

North-west frontier [see also Pakistan]

R[OGER EDWARD FRANCIS GUILFORD] NORTH. The literature of the north-west frontier of India; a select bibliography. [Peshawar 1946]. pp.66. [600.]

Orissa [see also Bihar]

CATALOGUE of books and periodicals published in the province [afterwards: state] of Orissa, and registered under act xxv of 1867, during the second quarter ... 1936 [&c.]. Orissa gazette: Appendix: Cuttack.
1936. ff.15.12.9. .
1937. ff.18.17.11.14. [584.]
1938. ff.12.13.13.14. [473.]
1939. ff.12.12.19.13. [523.]
1940. ff.13.19.16.24. [709.]

1941. ff.12. . .24.
1942. pp. . .5.4.
1943. pp.2
1944.
1945.
1946.
1947. pp.8.5.5.
1948. pp.6.6.7.
1949. pp.6.
1950. pp. . . .9.
1951. pp.12.9.11.12. [555.]
1952. pp.9.
1953.
1954.
1955.
1956. ff. . .9. .
1957.
1958. ff. .9. . .
for earlier issues see Bihar and Orissa.

CATALOGUE of publications. Government of Orissa. Cuttack.
1938. pp.41. [1000.]
1940. pp.[ii].53. [1250.]

Oudh [see also United Provinces]

GOKARAN NATH MISRA [GOKARṆA-NĀTHA MIṢRA], The Oudh digest, being a digest of all the reported decisions relating to Oudh (from 1859 to 1905). Lucknow 1906. pp.[vii].lxv.xxiii.coll.1776. [10,000.]
—— 1906–1915–. 1917. pp.[iii].2.civ.[viii]. coll.2652. [20,000.]

MUḤAMMAD NŪR AL-ḤASAN, A digest and easy reference of Oudh case law ... (1874–1913). Lucknow 1914. pp.[vii].553.lxvii. [2000.]

MOHAN-LĀL KHARBANDA, Oudh digest, civil, criminal & revenue, 1859–1940. Allahabad 1941 &c.

CATALOGUE of books printed in Oudh ...
1868. pp.[4].4.4. [267.]
1869. pp.4.4. [101.]
1870. pp.4. [97.]
1871. pp.5.5. [99.]
1872. pp.5.1. [111.]
1873. pp.1.11.13.11. [284.]
1874. pp.15.5.17.21. [381.]
1875. pp.17.19.13. [363.]
1876. pp.21.15.13.11. [501.]

Panjab

CATALOGUE of books (and periodicals) registered in the Punjab [under act xxv of 1867 (and act x of 1890)] during the quarter. Lahore.
1867–1868. pp. . . . 21. [273.]
1868–1869. pp.32.14.12.29. [571.]
1869–1870. pp.12.23.14.13. [425.]
1870. pp.13.23.9. [304.]

1871. pp.17.21.17.7. [438.]
1872. pp.5.11.15.9. [273.]
1873. pp.13.25.31.19. [641.]
1874. pp.23.29.31.25. [728.]
1875. pp.25.49.31.39.[1018.]
1876. pp.   .40.34.32.
1877. pp.29.   .25.22.
1878. pp.38.44.54.26. [915.]
1879. pp.50.52.42.38. [926.]
1880. pp.44.   .71.50.
1881. pp.43.55.48.49. [1090.]
1882. pp.38.73.62.34. [1198.]
1883. pp.64.83.57.68. [1786.]
1884. pp.69.68.62.51. [1535.]
1885. pp.63.67.103.52. [1566.]
1886. pp.100.69.63.68. [1857.]
1887. pp.65.93.55.93. [1760.]
1888. pp.115.88.95.100. [2301.]
1889. pp.87.122.92.85. [2206.]
1890. pp.108.74.65.49. [1577.]
1891. pp.61.79.55.76. [1286.]
1892. pp.133.59.53.50. [1483.]
1893. pp.70.112.89.61. [1452.]
1894. pp.63.41.37.21. [967.]
1895. pp.45.37.37.45. [1492.]
1896. pp.27.56.31.29. [1162.]
1897. pp.46.33.31.40. [1275.]
1898. pp.54.40.45.37. [1859.]
1899. pp.48.30.42.54. [1455.]
1900. pp.44.50.53.35. [1729.]
1901. pp.40.43.51.41. [1446.]
1902. pp.43.39.47.29. [1236.]
1903. pp.27.45.56.42. [1479.]
1904. pp.40.54.43.40. [1486.]
1905. pp.68.56.52.44. [2059.]
1906. ff.71.117.22.94. [1778.]
1907. ff.43.68.60.48. [1204.]
1908. ff.35.22.78.43. [1100.]
1909. ff.28.59.30.48. [1000.]
1910. ff.51.43.57.38. [1200.]
1911. ff.44.61.54.48. [1300.]
1912. ff.50.50.50.53. [1300.]
1913. ff.59.54.60.41. [1400.]
1914. ff.95.74.67.49. [1800.]
1915. ff.57.62.46.47. [1400.]
1916. ff.67.42.51.58. [1400.]
1917. ff.56.52.58.42. [1400.]
1918. ff.52.65.53.44. [1400.]
1919. ff.45.45.60.29. [1500.]
1920. ff.79.58.43.52. [1900.]
1921. ff.49.84.56.48. [1900.]
1922. ff.81.75.48.61. [2200.]
1923. ff.74.72.24.32. [2400.]
1924. ff.26.25.32.36. [2214.]
1925. ff.28.37.32.25. [2208.]
1926. ff.43.47.30.28. [2694.]
1927. ff.28.45.35.31. [2537.]
1928. ff.18.31.58.23. [2324.]
1929. ff.44.37.28.34. [2569.]
1930. ff.24.27.42.18. [1859.]

1931. ff.25.15.27.29. [1609.]
1932. ff.16.28.35.36. [1978.]
1933. ff.30.32.31.24. [1942.]
1934. ff.33.24.24.26. [1762.]
1935. ff.34.31.31.27. [1764.]
1936. ff.31.30.30.28. [1736.]
1937. ff.30.34.41.35. [2079.]
1938. ff.36.43.43.33. [2366.]
1939. ff.41.46.42.42. [3061.]
1940. ff.28.43.38.32. [2602.]
1941. ff.28.29.42.21. [2267.]
1942. ff.24.34. [1947.]
1943. ff.16.16.19.10. [1253.]
1944. ff.18.18.26.18. [1742.]
1945. ff.21.22.19.18. [1698.]
1946. ff.23.23.20.   .
1947.

[*continued as:*]

MEMORANDA of books (and periodicals) registered in (east) Punjab (India) under act xxv of 1867 and act x of 1890 during the quarter.
1948. pp.2.2.2.   .
1949. pp.6.6.4.6. [345.]
1950. pp.6.6.8.2.2. [482.]
1951. pp.6.2.8.5.2.6. [603.]
1952. pp.10.12.2.9.2.7.3. [881.]
1953. pp.24.3.15.3.14.3.4.4. [1580.]
1954. pp.9.4.7.11.17. [1171.]
1955. pp.11.7.8.13. [1002.]
1956. pp.9.14.9.9. [967.]
1957. pp.10.14.6.10. [1022.]
1958. pp.9.8.14.11. [1045.]
1959. pp.12.13.13.7. [1200.]
1960. pp.12.12.10.13. [1290.]
1961. pp.   .   .   .   .14.
1962. pp.13.14.   .7.
1963.
1964.
1965. pp.29.[24].[31].44. [1604.]
1966. pp.17.16.26.10. [1092.]

brief annual typewritten lists, entitled Catalogue of books worthy of notice published in the native states of the Punjab, *have also been issued.*

E. REYNOLDS, A digest of the civil, criminal and revenue cases, published in the Punjab record during the years 1866–1875. Lahore 1876. pp.[v]. vii.247. [1500.]

A DIGEST of the cases reported in the Punjab record. Lahore.
1890. By Madan Gopal. pp.[ii].v.coll.68. [200.]
1891. By J. A. Sinclair. pp.[ii].v.coll.88. [200.]
1892. pp.[ii].v.coll.110. [200.]
1893. By H. A. B. Rattigan. pp.[ii].v.coll.140. [200.]
1894. pp.[ii].vi.coll.260. [250.]
1895. pp.[ii].iv.coll.168. [200.]
1896. pp.[ii].iv.coll.90. [150.]

1897. pp.[ii].iii.coll.128. [150.]
1898. pp.[ii].iv.coll.114. [150.]
1899. pp.[ii].iii.coll.76. [150.]
1900. By Alweyne Turner. pp.[ii].iv.coll.80. [200.]
1901. pp.
1902. pp.
1903. pp.[ii].iv.coll.96. [150.]
1904. pp.[ii].iv.coll.110. [150.]
1905. pp.[ii].iv.coll.104. [200.]
1906. pp.
1907. pp.[ii].iv.coll.92. [150.]
1908. pp.[ii].iv.coll.106. [200.]
1909. By C. H. Oertel. pp.[ii].iv.coll.70. [150.]
1910. pp.
1911. pp.[ii].iv.coll.72. [150.]
1912. pp.[ii].v.coll.90. [250.]
1913. pp.
1914. pp.[ii].coll.84. [200.]
1915. pp.[ii].coll.90. [200.]
1916. pp.
1917. pp.[ii].coll.98. [250.]
1918. pp.[ii].coll.92. [200.]
1919. pp.[ii].coll.122. [250.]

LIST of publications (other than confidential) issued by departments of the government of India [sic, Punjab] and local governments and administrations during the year ... which are exempted from registration. Lahore.

1908. pp.2. [30.]
1909. pp.3. [35.]
1910. pp.4. [45.]
1911. pp.3. [34.]
1912. pp.4. [45.]
1913. pp.4. [44.]
1914. pp.4. [45.]
1915. pp.6. [73.]
1916. pp.5. [65.]
1917. pp.7. [73.]
1918. pp.10. [75.]
1919. pp.10. [75.]
1920. pp.18. [125.]
1921. pp.13. [100.]
1922. pp.12. [100.]
1923. pp.13. [100.]
1924. pp.16. [125.]
1925. pp.13. [100.]
1926. pp.18. [150.]
　　　　　　　[continued as:]
Punjab government publications. General catalogue.

1941. pp.92.xi. [2000.]
1949. pp.[ii].94. [2000.]
1952. pp.[v].86. [2000.]
　　　　　　　[continued as:]
General catalogue of the Punjab government publications.

1959. pp.44. [1000.]

the name of the Punjab appears in the titles of the 1909–1910 issues, but that of India reappears in those for 1911–1917.

DĪWĀN-CHAND OBRĀI, The Punjab referencer, being a digest and analytical summary ... of cases reported ... (civil, criminal and revenue). Madras 1914. pp.[ii].11.167.lv. [500.]

A. B. BROADWAY and A. L. DANSON, Consolidated digest of the civil and revenue cases reported in the Punjab record, 1866 to 1911. Lahore 1914. pp. lxiii.coll.2880. [7500.]

DĪWĀN-CHAND OBHRĀI, The Punjab ready referencer, 1866–1915, or the consolidated subject-index of the cases reported. ... B–civil portion. Madras 1918. pp.[ii].2.1192+[ii].1193–2254. [50,000.]
— — C–revenue portion. 1918. pp.[ii].60. [1250.]
section A is entered under India, above.

SITA-RAM KOHLI, Catalogue of Khalsa darbar records. Lahore 1919–1927. pp.[v].158+[v].315. [20,000.]

A. N. KHANNA and VEDA VYĀSA, A complete digest of the Punjab case-law. (1866–1930[1931]). Lahore 1931– . pp.[iii].coll.1056.388+pp.[ii].coll.460.xliv.461–1488+
— — Continuation. Octavinial Punjab digest (civil, criminal & revenue), 1931–1938. ... By A. N. Khanna. Lahore 1939. pp.[ii].coll.807+pp.[iii].coll.801–1630+pp.[ii].coll.400.118. [10,000.]

CYRIL P. K. FAZAL, A guide to Punjab government reports and statistics. Board of economic inquiry, Punjab : Publication (no.10) : Lahore 1939. pp.[ii].xii.256. [7500.]

ĀNANDA-MOHANA SŪRI and HARIDĀSA SŪRI, An exhaustive & up-to-date Punjab digest, civil, criminal & revenue, 1931 to 1938. Lahore [1939–1940]. pp.[vi].xii.iii.coll.748 + pp.[ii].coll.749–1718+pp.[iii].v.coll.1717–3230. [10,000.]

MUḤAMMAD SADULLAH [SAʿD ALLĀH], A catalogue of the Punjab government record office publications. Lahore 1942. pp.[ii].xi. [85.]

GANDA SINGH, A bibliography of the Punjab. Patiala 1966. pp.xv.246. [4000.]

IKRAM ALI MALIK, A bibliography of the Punjab and its dependencies (1849–1910). Research society of Pakistan. Lahore 1968. pp.iv.310. [2259.]

N[ORMAN] GERALD BARRIER, The Punjab in nineteenth century tracts: an introduction to the pamphlet collections in the British museum and India office. Research series on the Punjab (no.1): East Lansing 1969. ff.[iv].pp.76. [286.]*

Patna

ADITYA NARAYANLAL [ĀDITYA-NĀRAYAṆA LĀLA], The Patna digest, criminal & revenue, with decisions of the Privy council, 1926–1935. Gaya 1936. pp.[vii].xxvi.coll.694. [1500.]

Pondichéry

EDMOND GAUDART, Catalogue des manuscrits des anciennes archives de l'Inde française. Tome 1 [II, VII]. Pondichéry, 1690–1789 [–1855]. Société de l'histoire de l'Inde française: 1922–1934. pp. [iii].xvii.410.xvi + [iii].xi.487.xviii + xii.384. xliv. [9681.]

Rajasthan

G. N. SHARMA, A bibliography of mediaeval Rajasthan (social & cultural). Agra [1965]. pp.vii. 96. [702.]

Rangpur

SUPPLEMENT to the Bengal district records, Rangpur, vol.I, 1770, 1777–1779, containing a list of the letters received and issued. Calcutta 1923. pp.[ii].9. [150.]

Surat

RÉSUMÉ of the contents of the dutch diaries in the agency records of the Surat district, Bombay. [s.l. (India) 1898]. pp.28. [400.]

Travancore

THE FOLLOWING government publications are held for sale at the Government press, Trivandrum. [1939]. pp.15. [500.]

United Provinces

STATEMENT of particulars regarding books' maps, &c. [books and periodicals] published in the North-Western Provinces [and Oudh; in the United Provinces; in Uttar Pradesh] and registered under act xxv. of 1867. Allahabad.

  1867. pp.19.49. [250.]
  1868.
  1869.
  1870.
  1871.
  1872.
  1873.
  1874.
  1875.
  1876. pp.12.11.12.11. c400.]
  1877. pp.7. .45.34.
  1878. pp.25.25.16.26. [900.]
  1879. pp.18.25.15.19. [700.]
  1880. pp.17.15.20.6.9.1. [600.]
  1881. pp.27.40.4.42.22. [1250.]
  1882. pp.30.41.49.40. [1500.]
  1883. pp.30.29.43.29. [1250.]

  1884. pp.27.28.29.31. [1000.]
  1885. pp.25.58.49.36. [1500.]
  1886. pp.40.41.64.41. [1750.]
  1887. pp.33.11.44.47. [1250.]
  1888. pp.36.41.46.48. [1500.]
  1889. pp.38.42.41.75. [1750.]
  1890. pp.36.36.35.
  1891. pp.29.47.37.41. [1500.]
  1892. pp.37.26.11.66. [1250.]
  1893. pp.
  1894. pp.46.43.48.48. [1750.]
  1895. pp.43.41.44.45. [1500.]
  1896. pp.20.42.42.46. [1250.]
  1897. pp.35.49.48.47. [1750.]
  1898. pp.35.46.39.38. [1500.]
  1899. pp.52.52.55.43. [1500.]
  1900. pp.39.53.55.38. [1750.]
  1901. pp.34.40.35.39. [1250.]
  1902. pp.50.42.45.39. [1500.]
  1903. pp.35.41.38.43. [1500.]
  1904. pp.41.52.34.47. [1500.]
  1905. pp.44.34.ff.57.51. [1750.]
  1906. ff.51.65.64.64. [1700.]
  1907. ff.34.36.72.40. [1500.]
  1908. ff.63.48.36.47. [1500.]
  1909. ff.79.55.75.120. [2500.]
  1910. ff.88.75.80.42. [2000.]
  1911. ff.80.44.44.58. [1750.]
  1912. ff.62.61.57.47. [1750.]
  1913. ff.59.49.50.64. [1750.]
  1914. ff.75.59.58.63. [2000.]
  1915. ff.75.52.50.83. [900.]
  1916. ff.77.75.89.54. [2250.]
  1917. ff.74.74.55.83. [2250.]
  1918. ff.84.83.39.56. [2000.]
  1919. ff.61.55.44.58. [1750.]
  1920. ff.55.75.55.59. [1750.]
  1921. ff.72.61.71.59. [2000.]
  1922. ff.119.80.76.98. [2750.]
  1923. ff.93.116.79.40. [2530.]
  1924. ff.61.50.54.60. [2727.]
  1925. ff.63.46.51.36. [2653.]
  1926. ff.48.28.37.40. [2886.]
  1927. ff.43.50.46.40. [3381.]
  1928. ff.41.35.52.41. [3194.]
  1929. ff.52.42.48.43. [3424.]
  1930. ff.50.44.42.57. [3565.]
  1931. ff.43.31.49.44. [3115.]
  1932. ff.43.37.48.50. [3350.]
  1933. ff.47.46.54.46. [3612.]
  1934. ff.48.42.44.51. [3448.]
  1935. ff.43.40.38.54. [3412.]
  1936. ff.49.41.48.44. [3425.]
  1937. ff.32.37.46.45. [3162].
  1938. ff.38.40.34.39. [2708.]
  1939. ff.38.34.48.38. [2742.]
  1940. ff.38.33.[38].30. [2372.]
  1941. ff.36.38.28.26. [2153.]
  1942. ff.30.26.29.17. [1714.]
  1943. ff.16.12.12.13. [1024.]

1944. ff.16.18.23.21. [1480.]
1945. ff.18.21.21.21. [1568.]
1946. ff.17.17.12.13. [1115.]
1947. ff.17.17.12.13. [1115.]
1947. ff.9.13.   .17. [1020.]
1948. ff.13.10.7.12. [873.]
1949. ff.9.13.19.10. [1000.]
1950. ff.19.7.10.15. [1028.]
1951. ff.17.19.17.11. [1326.]
1952. pp.14.10.13.13. [1163.]
1953. pp.13.14.36.19. [1635.]
1954. ff.257. [1953.]
1955. ff.70.ii.274. [2197.]
1956. pp.ii.311. [2578.]
1957. .   .61.57.
1958–64. [Title in Hindi.]

LIST of non-confidential publications exempted from registration, which were issued in the United Provinces of Agra and Oudh during the year. [Allahabad].

1908. pp.13. [92.]
1909. pp.13. [96.]
1910. pp.17. [118.]
1911. pp.19. [132.]
1912. pp.17. [101.]
1913. pp.17. [125.]
1914. pp.19. [125.]
1915. pp.17. [125.]
1916. pp.15. [100.]
[continued as:]

List of publications (other than confidential) issued by the government of the United Provinces and officers subordinate to it during the year . . . which are exempted from registration.

1917. pp.[ii].14. [102.]
1918. pp.[ii].9. [63.]
1919. pp.[ii].16. [117.]
1920. pp.[ii].16. [125.]
1921. pp.[ii].21. [160.]
1922. pp.[ii].22. [200.]
1923. pp.[ii].28. [250.]
1924. pp.[ii].23. [200.]
1925. pp.[ii].24. [200.]
1926. pp.[ii].21. [200.]
1927. pp.20. [200.]
1928. pp.28. [250.]
1929. pp.27. [250.]
1930. pp.26. [250.]
1931. pp.23. [200.]
1932. pp.26. [250.]
1933. pp.32. [200.]
1934. pp.26. [250.]
1935. pp.28. [250.]
1936.
1937. pp.20. [200.]
1938. pp.24. [250.]
1939. pp.23. [250.]
1940. pp.33. [350.]
1941. pp.28. [300.]

1942. pp.18. [200.]
1943. pp.9. [100.]
1944. pp.7. [100.]
1945. ff.18. .21.21. [1568.]
1946. ff.16.17.12.13. [1115.]
1947. pp.9.13.11.17. [1020.]
1948. ff.13.10.7. .
1949. ff.9.13.19.10. [1000.]
1950. ff.19.7.10.15. [1028.]

Uttar Pradesh [see also *United Provinces*]

CATALOGUE of publications issued by the government of Uttar Pradesh. Allahabad 1955. pp.x.215. [4500.]
— [another edition]. 1956. pp.[xiv].211. [4500.]

Quarterly catalogues of books registered were issued, sometimes in typescript (or even manusctipt) form, for many other states than are listed here. Copies of these lists, often incomplete, may be found in the Catalogue hall of the India office library for the following:

Afghanistan. 1917.
Ajaigarh. 1932–1933.
Alwar. 1938–1940.
Baluchistan. 1939–1940.
Baroda. 1867–1909; 1913.
Baghelkand.
Bangalore. 1884–1921.
Bhopal. 1876–1906; 1924–1944.
Bundelkhand. 1867–1906; 1943; 1945.
Bundi. 1925–1944.
Central India. 1908–1946.
Gohilwad. 1951.
Gwalior. 1921–1945.
Hyderabad. 1909–1943; 1951–1952; 1956.
Hyderabad city. 1938–1946.
Indore. 1920–1942.
Jaipur. 1924–1946.
Jammu & Kashmir. 1909–1947.
Jaora. 1943–1944.
Jhalawar. 1925–1945.
Jodhpur. 1924–1945.
Kishangarh. 1924–1938.
Kotah. 1924–1947.
Madhya Pradesh. 1949–1954; 1953–1962.
Nagod. 1867–1906; 1928.
North-west frontier. 1867–1893; 1933–1945.
Palanpur. 1937; 1939.
Panna. 1933–1944.
Patiala. 1953–1955.
Sailana. 1930; 1937; 1946.
Shahpura. 1946.
Sind. 1936–1947.
Southern central India states agency. 1924.
Travancore. 1940–1941.
Travancore-Cochin. 1951–1954.
Udaipur. 1914?; 1928–1947.

xi. *Central India*

C[HARLES] ECKFORD LUARD, A bibliography of

the literature dealing with the Central india agency. 1908. pp.118. [750.]

xii. *French India*

ALFRED MARTINEAU, Inventaire des anciennes archives de l'Inde française. Société de l'histoire de l'Inde française: Archives de l'Inde française: Pondichéry 1914. pp.[ii].38. [25,000.]

EDMOND GAUDART, Catalogue des manuscrits des anciennes archives de l'Inde française. Société de l'histoire de l'Inde française.
 i. Pondichéry, 1690–1789. 1922. pp.[iii].xxii. 410.xvi. [1121.]
 ii. Pondichéry, 1789–1815. 1924. pp.[iii].xi. 487.xviii. [1168.]
 iii. Chandernagor et les loges du Bengale, 1730–1815. 1933. pp.[i].423.xxviii. [893.]
 iv. Karikal, 1736–1815. 1933. pp.xvi.352. xxix. [1243.]
 v. Mahé et les loges de Calicut et de Surate, 1739–1808. 1934. pp.xviii.343.xxxiii. [672.]
 vi. Yanaon, Mazulipatam et diverse localités, 1669–1793. 1935. pp.x.203.xxxiv. [285.]
 vii. Pondichéry, 1816–1855. 1936. pp.[iii]. xii.384.xliv. [889.]
 viii. Établissements secondaires et loges 1816–1855. 1936. pp.[iii].xii.286.xvi. [596.]

H. G. TRANCHELL, Catalogue des cartes, plans et projets d'études du dépôt des anciennes archives de Pondichéry. 1930. pp.viii.55. [250.]

xiii. *Portuguese India*

FRANCISCO JOÃO XAVIER, Breve noticia da imprensa nacional de Goa, seguida de um catalogo das obras e escriptos publicados pela mesma imprensa desde a sua fundação. Nova-Goa 1876. pp.[vi].195. [752.]

A[RTHUR] C[OKE] BURNELL, A tentative list of books and some mss. relating to the history of the Portuguese in India proper. Mangalore 1880. pp. vi.133. [500.]
15 copies privately printed.

[—] SILVA LEAL, Jornaes indo-portuguezes. Lisboa 1898. pp.44. [138.]

JOSÉ MARIA BARROS DE VALLADARES, Repertorio bibliographico dás obras que tratam da India e possue a Bibliotheca nacional de Nova Goa. Nova-Goa 1905. pp.x.37. [500.]

[PANDURONGA S. S. PISSURLENCAR, *ed.*], Roteiro dos arquivos da índia portuguesa. Arquivo histórico do Estado da índia: Bastorá 1955. pp.xxi.163. [large number.]

JOSÉ ANTONIO ISMAEL GRACIAS, A imprensa em Goa nos séculas XVI, XVII e XVIII. Apontamentos historico-bibliographicos. Nova-Goa 1880. pp. [vii].112. [100.]

MARY C. SCHLOEDER, Salazar's Portugal (Angola, Goa, Macao, Mozambique, Portugal and Timor.) ATMC monthly memo: [Washington?] 1968. ff.9*. [250.]
—— Addendum. 1968. ff.4. [100.]

xiv. *South India*

H. H. WILSON, Mackenzie collection. A descriptive catalogue of the oriental manuscripts and other articles ... illustrative of the ... south of India; collected by the late lieut.-col. Colin Mackenzie. Calcutta 1928. pp.[ii].clvii.357+[iv]. 149.cclxx.[xiv]. [6000.]
—— Second edition. Madras 1882. pp.xviii. 636. [7500.]

WILLIAM TAYLOR, Examinations and analysis of the Mackenzie manuscripts deposited in the Madras college library. Calcutta 1838. pp.[ii].144. [100.]

xv. *Subjects*

Agriculture

CATALOGUE of books in the library of the Board of revenue (revenue settlement, land records and agriculture), Madras. Madras 1898. pp.180. [4000.]

LIST of references on agricultural machinery in India. Library of Congress: Division of bibliography: [Washington] 1922. pp.6. [75.]*

DRY farming in India, Egypt and South Africa. Science library: Bibliographical series (no.287): 1935 [1937]. single sheet. [22.]*

A BIBLIOGRAPHY of indian agricultural economics. Directorate of economics and statistics: Ministry of food and agriculture: Government of India: Delhi [1952]. pp.[v].194. [1500.]
— Agricultural economics in India; a bibliography. Second edition. [1960.] pp.v.342. [3500.]

[N. N. CHATTERJI *and others*], Bibliography of IARI publications 1905 to 1963; scientific contributions from IARI. Indian agricultural research institute: New Delhi [1965]. pp.[iv].204. [3532.]*

Anthropology. See also *Caste*

DAVID G[OODMAN] MANDELBAUM, Materials for a bibliography of the ethnology of India. [Berkeley, Cal. 1949]. ff.[iii].220. [2300.]*

A TENTATIVE bibliography of basic publications on all aspects of indian culture. Section I— Indian anthropology. Government of India: The national library: Calcutta 1951. ff.viii.177. [1487.]*
— Author index, and an appendix on geographical divisions.

A BIBLIOGRAPHY of indology ... National library: Calcutta.
  i. Indian anthropology. Compiled by J. M. Kanitkar. Edited, revised and enlarged by D. L. Banerjee and A. K. Ohdedar. 1960. pp.xi.290. [2067.]

HENRY FIELD and EDITH M. LAIRD, Bibliography on the physical anthropology of the peoples of India. Field research projects: Coconut Grove, Florida.
  [i]. 1968. pp.vi.82. [800.]*
  ii. Supplement. [1970?] Field research projects: Study (no.23). [2000.]
  — Author index (i). (no.24).
  iii. By Russell M. Reid. 1973. (no.67).

Archaeology

GEORGE BUIST, Index to books and papers on the physical geography, antiquities, and statistics of India. Bombay 1852. pp.5–103. [4000.]

A LIST of archaeological reports, published under the authority of the Secretary of state, government of India, local governments, etc., which are not included in the imperial series of such reports. Calcutta 1900. pp.13. [175.]

M. N. BASU, An alphabetical index to the classified catalogue of the library of the Director general of archaeology. Calcutta 1917. pp.[iii].162 +[iii].302. [2500.]
the library covers asiatic archaeology in general.

ANNUAL bibliography of indian archæology. Kern institute: Leyden.
  [i]. 1926. pp.x.107. [540.]
  [ii]. 1927. pp.x.143. [721.]
  [iii]. 1928. pp.xi.141. [721.]
  [iv]. 1929. pp.xi.141. [731.]
  [v]. 1930. pp.xi.149. [929.]
  [vi]. 1931. pp.xi.211. [982.]
  vii. 1932. pp.xi.179. [752.]
  viii. 1933. pp.xii.133. [706.]
  ix. 1934. pp.xi.167. [847.]
  x. 1935. pp.xii.163. [832.]
  xi. 1936. pp.vi.125. [807.]
  xii. 1937. pp.x.136. [697.]
  xiii. 1938. pp.xi.109. [787.]
  xiv. 1939. pp.xi. 69. [428.]
  xv. 1940–1947. pp.lxxii.221. [2462.]
  xvi. 1948–1953. pp.cviii.368. [4192.]
  xvii. 1954–1957. pp.xvi.245. [2368.]
  xviii. 1958–1960. pp.xiii.168. [1644.]
  xix. 1961. pp.xii.59. [528.]
  xx. 1962–1963. pp.xiii.119. [1022.]
  xxi. 1964–6. pp.xiii.175. [1583.]

B. M. PANDE and K. S. RAMACHANDRAN, Bibliography of the harappan culture. Field research projects: Study (no.56).

Art

ANANDA K. COOMARASWAMY [KUMĀRASVĀMI], Bibliographies of indian art. Museum of fine art: Boston 1925. pp.v.54. [1250.]

INDIAN art. Third edition. [National book council]: Book list (no.45): 1931. pp.[4]. [125.]
  — Fourth edition. 1941. pp.[2]. [65.]

HARIDAS [HARI-DĀSA] MITRA, Contribution to a bibliography of indian art and aesthetics. Santiniketan 1951. pp.[v].240. [500.]
limited to sanskrit writings on architecture, sculpture and painting.

HENRI DEYDIER, Contribution à l'étude de l'art du Gandhâra: essai de bibliographie analytique et critique des ouvrages parus de 1922 à 1949. Paris 1950. pp.xxviii. 327. [431.]

SUMAN CHANDRA and MRINAL KANTI PAL, Bibliography of indian arts and crafts (with particular reference to ancient period). Census of India 1961 (vol.I, part xi(ii)): New Delhi [1961]. pp.viii.71. [1408.]

H. S. PATIL and R. N. SAR, The arts. Aspects of indian culture: Select bibliography (i). Delhi 1966. pp.ix.227. [1389.]

Astronomy

[J. M. F.] GUÉRIN, Catalogue de manuscrits orientaux en langue sancrite sur l'astronomie ... recueillis dans les Indes orientales. 1855. pp.20. [63.]

HRISHÍKEŚA ŚÁSTRÍ and ŚIVA CHANDRA GUI, A descriptive catalogue of sanksrit manuscripts in the library of the Calcutta sanskrit college. Volume ix. Astrology and astronomy manuscripts. Calcutta [1904–] 1906. pp.[ii].180.ii. [193.]

Banking

LIST of references on money and banking in India, with a section on agricultural credit. Library of Congress: [Washington] 1921.ff.16.[18]. [200.]*

Behavioural science

UDAI NARAIN PAREEK, Behavioural science in India; a directory, 1925–65. Behavioural science centre: Delhi 1966. pp.xi.575. [16,729.]

UDAI [NARAIN] PAREEK, Foreign behavioural research on India. Delhi 1970. pp.ix.159. [1598.]

Bhoodan

JAGDISH SARAN SHARMA, Vinoba and bhoodan. A selected descriptive bibliography of bhoodan in hindi, english and other indian languages. National bibliographies (no.3): New Delhi [1956]. pp.ix.vi.92. [927.]

SELECT bibliography on Bhoodan. Bibliography (no.33): Lok sabha secretariat: New Delhi 1957. pp.ii.26. [278.]

Botany

LIST of publications on the botany of indian crops.

    [i].   –1927. Imperial institute of agricultural research: Bulletin (no.202): Pusa 1930.

    ii. 1928–1932. By R. D. Bose [Rāhhāldās Vasu]. Imperial council of agricultural research: Miscellaneous bulletin (no.12): 1936. pp.[v]. 198. [3000.]

A BIBLIOGRAPHY of indology ... National library: Calcutta.

    ii. Indian botany. Compiled by V. Narayanaswami.

    i. A–J. 1961. pp.xlii.370. [5374.]

*A. R. DAS [and others], Union catalogue of the books in the libraries of the Botanical survey of India. Calcutta 1967–   ff.[vii].205+[iii].206–388+iii.389–588. [7000.]

Caste

WILLIAM H. GILBERT, Caste in India; a bibliography. Library of congress: Washington.*

    i. 1948. pp.174. [1970.]

Y. B. DAMLE, Caste—a review of the literature on caste. Center for international studies: Massachusetts institute of technology: Cambridge Mass. 1961. ff.125. [272.]*

Censuses

HENRY J. DUBESTER, Census and vital statistics of India and Pakistan, contained in official documents and famine documents; an annotated bibliography. Library of congress: Census Library project: Washington 1950. pp.118.

CENSUS of India. Price list of publications. Office of the Registrar general: New Delhi 1957. pp.15, [150.]

INDIA census 1872–1951: a check list and index. Basic collections in microedition: Inter documentation company AG: Zug 1966. pp.x.18. [100.]*

C. G. JADHAV, CHARAN SINGH and ANAND PRAKASH, Bibliography of census publications in India. Edited by B. K. Roy Burman. Census centenary publication (no.5): Census of India 1971: New Delhi 1972. pp.vii.520. [2771.]

Children's books

BOOKS on India for children. Government of India information service: New York [?1952]. ff.6. [50.]*

Communications

K. E. EAPEN, Mass communications in India: an annotated bibliography of journal articles. [Madison] 1966. ff.26. [217.]*

Community development

BIBLIOGRAPHY on community development. Bibliographical series (no.1): Clearing house: National institute of community development: Mussoorie.

    i. 1962. pp.iii.265. [1949.]

    ii. October–December 1961. 1963. pp.v.85. [630.]

    iii. January–March 1962. 1963. pp.v.71. [495.]

    iv. April–June 1962. 1963. pp.v.95. [553.]

    v. July–September 1962. 1964. pp.v.76. [416.]

    vi. October–December 1962. 1964. pp.v.70. [473.]

    vii. January–March 1963. 1965. pp.v.78. [417.]

Cottage industries

C. K. CHATTERJEE, Bibliography of small scale and cottage industries and handicrafts. Census of India 1961 (vol. 1, part XI (i)). New Delhi [1967]. pp.v.111. [1729.]

Crime, criminal law

D. E. CRANENBURGH, A digest of criminal cases reported in the Indian law reports from 1876 to 1885. Second edition. Calcutta 1886. pp.[v].coll. 262.pp.ix. [750.]

S. RAGHAVA AIENGAR [SRINIVASA RAGHAVAIYANGAR], A digest or index to the criminal cases decided by the High courts of Calcutta, Madras, Bombay, and Allahabad and by the Privy council ... 1885–1890. Kumbakonam 1891. pp.[iii].132. [750.]

J. B. WORGAN, Consecutive tables, criminal cases, being an annotation of the criminal cases in the Indian law reports from their commencement to the end of 1897, and of those in the Calcutta law reports that are not reported in the I.l.r. Calcutta 1898. pp.ix.111. [2500.]

D. E. CRANENBURGH. The general digest of criminal rulings, being a compendium of all criminal rulings of the several high courts in India from 1862 to 1899. [Second edition]. Calcutta 1901. pp.xxii.1973. [4000.]

NRISIMHA-DĀSA VASU, A subject-noted index of criminal cases judically noticed (1809–1913). Calcutta 1914. pp.154. [3500.]

C. H. OERTEL, A digest of the criminal rulings of the Chief court of the Punjab and High court at Lahore ... 1866 to 1920. Lahore 1922. pp.[iii].2. coll.1000.pp.xxi. [7500.]

DIWAN-CHAND OBHRĀI, The Punjab ready referencer, 1866–1923 (June), or the consolidated subject index to the Punjab criminal references. . . . A-criminal portion. Second edition. Madras 1923. pp.vi.438. [7500.]

V. V. CHIATLE [VĀMANA VĀSUDEVA CHITALE] and R. NARAYANASWAMI IYER [R. NĀRĀYAṆASVĀMI AIYAR], The criminal and revenue digest, 1911–1923. Mylapore 1924. pp.vii.coll.1140+pp.v.–xiv.195.coll.1141–1992. [10,000.]

A FULL digest of the Madras criminal cases, 1924 to 1936. Madras [1937]. pp.[iv].282. [2500.]

MOHAN-LĀL KHARBANDA, The Allahabad criminal digest. Being a digest of criminal cases decided by the Allahabad High court and the Privy council, 1811–1938. Allahabad 1938. pp.viii.coll.840+pp.[iv].coll.841–1548. [6500.]

B. K. PAL [VASANTA-KUMĀRA PĀLA], 8 Years criminal digest, 1931–1938. Calcutta 1939. pp.[ii]. ii.496.4. [3000.]

S. K. IYER [S. KRISHNAMŪRTI AIYAR], The all India criminal digest 1904–1940. Lahore 1941. pp.viii. coll.1816 + pp.[iv].coll.1817–3968 + pp.vi.coll. 3969–6104. [100,000.]

Development

STANLEY SPARKS, ARUN SHOURIE, JAY B. WESTCOTT, Bibliography on development administration, India and Pakistan. Publication (no.11): Center for overseas operations and research: Maxwell graduate school of citizenship and public affairs: Syracuse university: [Syracuse] 1964. ff.[iv].pp.51. [300.]★

Economics

LIST of non-confidential publications [publications (other than confidential)] exempted from registration, which were issued by the Department of revenue and agriculture [*1923–1926: of revenue*] and the departments subordinate to it during the year. [Calcutta]:

    1908. pp.17. [93.]
    1909. pp.17. [82.]
    1910. pp.17. [71.[
    1911. pp.17. [95.]
    1912. pp.15. [106.]
    1913. pp.17. [125.]
    1914. pp.15. [107.]
    1915. pp.17. [128.]
    1916. pp.21. [210.]
    1917. pp.11. [92.]
    1918. pp.12. [80.]
    1919. pp.11. [85.]
    1920. pp.10. [71.]
    1921. pp.20. [133.]
    1922. pp.18. [124.]

    1923. pp.
    1924. pp.6. [26.]
    1925. pp.17. [55.]
    1926. pp.19. [52.]
no more published.

LIST of references on the early economic and industrial history of India. Library of Congress: [Washington] 1921. ff.12. [97.]★

SHIB CHANDRA DUTT, Thirty-five years of indian economic thought, 1898–1932. [Calcutta 1933]. pp.20. [600.]

CYRIL P. K. FAZAL, A bibliography of economic literature relating to the Punjab. Board of economic inquiry: Publication (no.73): [Lahore] 1941. pp.viii.116. [2000.]

GIRIRAJ PRASAD GUPTA, Economic investigations in India. (A bibliography of researches in commerce and economics approved by India Universities.) With supplement, 1962 (1966). Department of commerce: Madhar college (Vikram university), Ujjain: Agra 1961. pp.vii.170. [3,500.]

VIMAL RATH, Index of indian economic journals 1916–1965. Gokhale institute of politics and economics: Poona 1971. pp.liv.302. [6500.]

NIKKI R. KEDDIE and ELIZABETH K. BAUER, *edd.* Annotated bibliography on the economy of India. Annotations by Ravi S. Sharma [*and others*]. Human relations area files: Berkeley, Cal. 1956. ff.[ii].37. [174.]★

Education

LIST of non-confidential publications exempted from registration which were issued by the government of India in the Department of education [and health] and offices subordinate to it, during the year. [Calcutta].

    1910. pp.7. [30.]
    1911. pp.9. [40.]
    1912. pp.9. [40.]
    1913. pp.9. [30.]
    1914. pp.9. [40.]
    1915. pp.9. [30.]
    1916. pp.
    1917. pp.[ii].6. [45.]
    1918. pp.[ii].8. [50.]
    1919. pp.[ii].8. [50.]
    1920. pp.[ii].6. [40.]
    1921. pp.[ii].6. [40.]
    1922. pp.[ii].6. [30.]
    [*continued as:*]
List of publications (other than confidential) exempted from registration, which were issued by the Department of education, health and lands and offices subordinate to it, during the year.
    1923. pp.[ii].17. [100.]
    1924. pp.[ii].15. [75.]

1925. pp.[ii].21. [150.]
1926. pp.[ii].17. [100.]
no more published.

PUBLICATIONS of the Department of education, 1911–1914. Government of India: Department of education: Calcutta 1915. pp.[vii].18. [40.]
— 1911–1915. 1916. pp.[vii].18. [50.]

CATALOGUE of publications. Ministry of educations: Publication (no.198): Delhi 1956. pp.[iii].22. [400.]

BASIC education bibliography. Government of India: National institute of basic education: New Delhi [1960]. pp.iii.52. [1233.]

COLE S. BREMBECK, EDWARD W. WEIDNER, Education and development in India and Pakistan; a select and annotated bibliography. Michigan state university education in Asia series (1): [East Lansing 1962.] pp.viii.221. [500.]*

EDUCATIONAL investigations in indian universities (1939–1961). A list of theses and dissertations approved for doctorate and master's degrees in education. National council of educational research and training: New Delhi 1966. pp.[v]. 286. [2941.]

EDUCATION in India; keyword in context index and bibliography. University of Michigan: Comparative education program: [Ann Arbor] 1966. pp.[106]. [500.]*

MONICA ALICE GREAVES, Education in british India 1698–1947; a bibliography and guide to the sources of information in London. University of London: Institute of education: Education libraries bulletin, supplement (vol.13). [London] 1967. pp.xx.182. [1379.]

VIDYUT K. KHANDWALA, *ed.* Education of women in India, 1850–1967; a bibliography. Golden jubilee commemoration volume (part iv): Bombay 1968. pp.[x].115. [976.]

JUDITH C. ELKIN, Books for the multi racial classroom: a select list of children's books, showing the backgrounds of India, Pakistan and the West Indies. Pamphlets (no.10): The library association youth libraries group: Birmingham 1971. pp.67. [199.]

English language and literature

DOROTHY M[ARY] SPENCER, Indian fiction in english. An annotated bibliography. Philadelphia [1960]. pp.98. [200.]

SUSHIL KUMAR JAIN, Indian literature in english; a bibliography, being a check-list of works of poetry, drama, fiction, autobiography and letters, written by indians in english, or translated from

modern indian languages into english. Regina campus library: University of Saskatchewan: Regina, Sask. 1965. ff. iv.60+31+xi.42. [1000.]*

A BIBLIOGRAPHY of indian english. Prepared by Central institute of english and foreign languages: Hyderabad, India 1972. ff.[v].219.vi.23. [2001.]*

SUSHIL KUMAR JAIN, India in english fiction; a bibliography. 1972.

SUSHIL KUMAR JAIN, A bibliography of indian autobiographies, including journals, diaries, reminiscences, and letters, etc. University of Saskatchewan: Regina campus library: Regina 1965. ff.39. [265.]*

Entomology

LIST of publications on indian entomology. Agricultural research institute, Pusa: Bulletin (no.139 &c.): Bombay [1930 &c.: Imperial council of agricultural research: Miscellaneous bulletin (no.1, &c.): Delhi].

1920–1921. [By T. B. Fletcher] ... (no.139): 1922. pp.[ii].67. [750.]
1922 ... (no.147): 1923. pp.[ii].42. [500.]
1923 ... (no.155): 1924. pp.[ii].59. [750.]
1924 ... (no.161): 1925. pp.[ii].41. [500.]
1925 ... (no.165): 1926. pp.[ii].62.x. [750.]
1926 ... (no.168): 1927. pp.[ii].48. [500.]
1927 ... (no.184): 1928. pp.[ii].33. [400.]
1928 ... (no.200): 1929. pp.[ii].33. [400.]
1929 ... (no.207): 1931. pp.[ii].36. [400.]
1930 ... (no.1): 1934. pp.[ii].45. [500.]
1931 ... (no.2): 1934. pp.[ii].27. [300.]
1932. [By T. B. Fletcher and P. V. Isaac]. ... (no.3): 1934. pp.[ii].36. [400.]
1933. [By P. V. Isaac] ... (no.5): 1935. pp.[ii]. 29. [300.]
1934 ... (no.7): 1935. pp.[ii].38. [400.]
1935. [By H. S. Pruthi] ... (no.14): 1937. pp.[ii].40. [400.]

Films

FIROZE RANGOONWALLA, Indian filmography: silent & hindi films (1897–1969). Bombay 1970. pp.xx.471. [5383.]

Finance

LIST of official publications (other than confidential) issued by the government of India in the Finance department and the offices subordinate to it during the calendar year ..., which are exempted from registration. [Simla].

1908. pp.[3]. [131.]
1909. pp.5. [14.]
1910. pp.3. [10.]
1911. pp.2. [9.]
1911. pp.2. [9.]
1912. pp.[3]. [8.]

1913. pp.[2]. [9.]
1914. pp.3. [14.]
1915. pp.[3]. [15.]
1916. pp.5. [13.]
1917. pp.[ii].2. [13.]
1918. pp.[ii].2. [12.]
1919. pp.[ii].3. [15.]
1920. pp.[ii].3. [14.]
1921. pp.[ii].3. [15.]
1922. pp.[ii].4. [20.]
1923. pp.[ii].6. [33.]
1924. pp.2. [8].
1925. pp.2. [8.]
1926. pp.3. [9.]
no more published.

Folklore

STITH THOMPSON and WARREN E. ROBERTS, Types of indic oral tales, India, Pakistan, and Ceylon. Folklore fellows: FF communications (vol.lxxiii, no.180): Helsinki 1960. pp.181. [3500.]

SUSHIL KUMAR JAIN, Folklore of India and Pakistan: a complete catalogue of publications in english language. Compiled from up-to-date sources with short notes and annotations. Regina Campus library: University of Saskatchewan Regina, Sask. 1965. ff.36. [209.]*

SANKAR SEN GUPTA and SHYAM PARMA, A bibliography of indian folklore and related subjects. Indian folklore series (no.11): Calcutta 1967. pp.196. [3,700.]

Forestry

LIST of maps and publications relating to forest administration in the provinces under the government of India, sent to the Paris exhibition of 1878. Simla 1878. pp.[ii].12. [75.]

LIST of publications and maps relating to forest administration in India sent to the Edinburgh international forestry exhibition. Calcutta 1884. pp.[ii].26. [186.]

Freemasonry

J. H. LESLIE, A catalogue of the library belonging to 'Steward' lodge, no.1960, E.C., holding at Rawal Pindi & Murree, in the Punjab. Calcutta 1894. pp.35.iii. [200.]
—— Additions. 1902. ff.[i].5. [100.]

Geology

R[ICHARD] D[IXON] OLDHAM, A bibliography of indian geology, being a list of books and papers relating to the geology of british India and adjoining countries. Calcutta 1888. pp.xiii.145. [2500.]

T[HOMAS] H[ENRY] D[IGGES] LA TOUCHE, A bibliography of indian geology and physical geography, with an annotated index of minerals of economic value. Geological survey of India: Calcutta 1917–1926. pp.[iii].xxviii.572+[iii].ii.490+[ii].xiii.143+[iii].348+[v].414. [5500.]

LIST of publications. Geological survey of India: Calcutta 1947. pp.40. [600.]

CATALOGUE of publications of the Geological survey of India and index of geological maps. Geological survey of India: Memoirs (vol.lxxvii): Calcutta &c. 1947 [*on cover:* 1948]. pp.[iii].129. [2000.]

UNION catalogue of serials in the Geological survey of Indian libraries. Union catalogue series (11): Indian national scientific documentation centre: Delhi 1969. pp.x.536. [4033.]*

Hinduism

P. C. SEN [PRASANNKUMARA SENA], Digest of recent rulings on hindu law. Konnagar [1898]. pp.16. [50.]

LIST of references on the origin and early migration of the Hindus. Library of Congress: Washington 1921. ff.5. [43.]*

LOUIS RENOU, Bibliographie védique. 1931. pp.[iv].v.339. [6750.]
the text is reproduced from typewriting.

R. N. DANDEKAR [RĀMA-CHANDRA NĀRĀYANA DANDEKAR], Vedic bibliography ... of all important work done since 1930 in the field of the Veda and allied antiquities, including Indus valley civilisation. New indian antiquary (extra ser. vol.iii): Bombay 1946. pp.xx.398. [3500.]
—— Second volume. University of Poona: 1961. pp.xxiii.760. [6000.]
—— Third volume. 1961–1972. Poona 1963. pp.xxiv. 1082.

BIBLIOGRAPHY on the hindu succession bill 1954. Lok Sabha secretariat: Bibliography (no.28): New Delhi 1955. pp.17. [150.]

Hydrology

BIBLIOGRAPHY of hydrology in India. Association internationale d'hydrologie scientifique [Louvain printed].
1936–1952. 1955. pp.162. [800.]

Indians abroad

G[ILBERT] R. MORRIS, A bibliography of the indian question in south Africa. University of Cape Town: School of librarianship: Bibliographical series: Cape Town 1946 [1950]. ff.17. [200.]

J. CLARE CURRIE, A bibliography of material published during the period 1946–56 on the indian question in South Africa. University of Capetown: School of librarianship: Bibliographical series: [Capetown] 1957. pp.[vii].ii.28. [204.]*

SUSHIL KUMAR JAIN, East indians in Canada; an essay with a bibliography. Unexplored fields of canadiana (vol.3): Minorities in Canada series (no.2): Windsor, Ont. 1970. ff.25. [99.]*
— — [Another edition.] Research group for european migration problems: Bulletin: Supplement(9): The Hague 1971. [105.]

Inventions

LIST of patents granted in India during the years 1856 to 1879 (both inclusive) under acts VI of 1856 and XV of 1859. [s.l. 1885]. pp.72. [1200.]
continued to date by quarterly and annual lists and indexes, which have been consolidated as shown in the next entry.

INVENTIONS. Subject-matter index, 1901–1907. Government of India: Department of commerce and industry: Calcutta. 1908. pp.[ii].21. [2500.]
— Subject-matter index. 1900–1908. Chronological list, 1900–1904. 1909. pp.[ii].ii.43.[236]. [5000.]
— Chronological list (1900–1904) and name index (1900–1911). 1923. pp.[236]+129–280. Patent office: Calcutta 1923. [6000.]
— Subject-matter index, 1900–1911. Chronological list, 1905–1911. 1915. pp.250. [7500.]
— Chronological list, subject-matter index, name index, 1913–1920. 1923. pp.v.356. [6480.]
— Name index to applicants for patents from 1921–1931. Patent office: Delhi 1933. pp.[ii].ii.97. [7600.]
— Consolidated subject-matter index (1912 to 1932). 1937. pp.[ii].ii.143. [15,000.]

PATENT office journal. Calcutta [Delhi].
1932. pp.2.viii.104. [940.]
1933. pp.2.x.109. [928.]
1934. pp.2.xii.113. [954.]
1935. pp.2.vii.112. [1007.]
1936. pp.2.viii.119. [980.]
1937. pp.2.x.128. [1068.]
1937–1938. pp.2.x.149. [1246.]
1938–1939. pp.2.x.145. [1243.]
1939–1940. pp.2.x.122. [1060.]
1940–1943. pp.2.x.417. [3274.]
1944–1946. pp.xvi.576. [6126.]
1947–1950. pp.vii.275. [2370.]
1948–1951. pp.ix.243. [1921.]
1949–1952. pp.viii.230. [1725.]
1950. pp.x.239. [1849.]
1951. pp.xii.258. [2107.]
1952–1955. pp.x.722. [7003.]
1955. pp.x.414. [2735.]
1956. pp.x.433. [3067.]

1957. pp.x.493. [3456.]
1958. pp.ix.478. [3572.]
in progress.

Jains. See also *Sanskrit: manuscripts*

JOH[ANNES] KLATT, Specimen of a literary-bibliographical jaina-onomasticon. Leipzig 1892. pp.iv.55. [500.]

FRANCESCO L[ORENZO] PULLÈ, Catalogo dei manoscritti giainici della Biblioteca nazionale centrale.... Num. 1–4. Firenze 1894. pp.40. [3.]
no more published.

LIST of sanskrit, jaina and hindi manuscripts purchased by order of government and deposited in the Sanskrit college, Benares ... 1897[-1918]. Allahabad.
details of this work are entered under Sanskrit literature, below.

A[RMAND ALBERT] GUÉRINOT, Essai de bibliographie jaina. Répertoire analytique et méthodique des travaux relatifs au Jainisme. Musée Guimet: Annales: Bibliothèque d'études (vol. XXII): 1906. pp.[v].xxxvii.568. [852.]
a supplement by the author appears in the Journal asiatique (*1909*), *10th ser. xiv. 46–148.*

HRISHÍKESA SÁSTRÍ and NÍLAMANI CAKRAVARTTI, A descriptive catalogue of sanskrit manuscripts in the library of the Calcutta sanskrit college. Volume X [*sic*, XII]. Jaina manuscripts. Calcutta 1909[-1915]. pp.[ii].594.ii.7. [202.]

H. D. VELANKAR [HARIDĀSA VELANKAR]. A descriptive catalogue of sānskṛta and prākṛta manuscripts in the library of the Bombay branch of the Royal asiatic society. ... Vols.III–IV. Jain and vernacular literature. Bombay 1930. pp.[ii]. 381–500. [750.]

CHAMPAT RĀI JAIN, A complete digest of cases. S. B. Jaina academy: Delhi 1941. pp.[iv].80. [200.]

HARI DAMODAR VELANKAR, Jinaratnakosa, an alphabetical register of jain works and authors. Governmental oriental series (class C, no.4): Poona 1944, pp.xi.466. [very large number.]

CHHOTE LAL JAIN, Jaina bibliography. Jaina bibliography series (no.1): Calcutta 1945. pp.xii 380. [509.]

Labour

LIST of non-confidential publications exempted from registration which were issued by the government of India in the Department of industries [and labour] during the year ... 1921[-1926]. Simla.
details of this publication are entered under Trade, below.

LIBRARY catalogue. Government of India: Ministry of labour: Delhi 1949. pp.50.214.215.3. [4000.]

P. N. KAULA, *ed.* A bibliography on labour relations in India. Bibliographical series (6): Ministry of labour and employment [library]: Government of India: NewDelhi[1958?]. pp.viii. 44. [345.]

AN ANNOTATED bibliography of labour research in India 1956–62. Labour bureau: Governmentof India ministry of labour and employment. [Simla 1963]. ff.[iv],pp.140. [350.]

Librarianship

RAM GOPAL PRASHER, Indian library literature; an annotated bibliography. New Delhi 1971. pp.xliii.504. [3550.]

Management

NARENDRA K. SETHI, A bibliography of Indian management, with reference to the economic, industrial, international, labor, marketing, organizational, productivity, and the public administration perspectives. Bombay [1967]. pp.xvi.116. [1080.]

Marketing

[R. M. BHATNAGAR], Bibliography on overseas market surveys of indian products. (Fourth edition.) Marketing research division: Indian institute of foreign trade: New Delhi [1971]. pp.ii.85. [1000.]*
first published in 1966.

Medicine

[J. M. F.] GUÉRIN, Catalogue de manuscrits orientaux en langue sancrite sur l'astronomie, la médecine, etc., recuellis dans les Indes orientales. 1855. pp.20. [medicine: 56.]

HRISHÍKEŚA SASTRA and ŚIVA CHANDRA GUI, A descriptive catalogue of sanksrit manuscripts in the library of the Calcutta sanskrit college. Volume x. Medicine manuscripts. Calcutta 1906. pp.[ii].86.ii. [105.]

J. A. SINTON, A bibliography of malaria in India. Malaria survey of India: Records (vol.i, no.1): Calcutta 1929. pp.[ii].200. [2500.]

INDEX to indian medical periodicals. Central medical library: New Delhi 1959 &c.
in progress.

Meteorology

PUBLICATIONS of the India meteorological department. Complete list. [Delhi 1944]. pp.12. [300.]

Military arts

MAURICE J. D. COCKLE, A catalogue of books relating to the military history of India. Simla 1901. pp.[v].101. [750.]

LIST of non-confidential publications [publications (other than confidential)] exempted from registration, which were issued by the Finance department [Office of the Financial adviser] (Military finance) and offices subordinate thereto during the year. [Simla].

    1908. pp.5. [17.]
    1909. pp.3. [20.]
    1910. pp.3. [30.]
    1911. pp.3. [27.]
    1912. pp.5. [31.]
    1913. pp.5. [30.]
    1914. pp.5. [36.]
    1915. pp.3. [4.]
    1916. pp.3. [3.]
    1917. pp.[3]. [3.]
    1918. p.[1]. [2.]
    1919. p.[1]. [2.]
    1920.
    1921.
    1922.
    1923. pp.[ii].4. [26.]
    1924. pp.[ii].6. [43.]
    1925. pp.[ii].7. [43.]
    1926. pp.[ii].7. [39.]
no more published.

LIST of non-confidential publications exempt from registration, issued by the late Department of military supply, and offices subordinate to that department during the year ending 31st December 1908. [Simla 1909]. pp.4. [34.]
no more published.

LIST of non-confidential publications exempt from registration, issued by the Army department, and offices subordinate thereto during the year ending 31st December 1908. [Simla 1909]. pp.3. [34.]
    [continued as:]
List of official publications (other than confidential) issued by the Army department of the government of India, during the year . . ., which are exempted from registration.

    1909. pp.5. [30.]
    1910. pp.5. [20.]
    1911. pp.5. [30.]
    1912. pp.5. [30.]
    1913. pp.5. [40.]
    1914. pp.7. [50.]
    1915. pp.5. [30.]
    1916. pp.7. [75.]
    1917. pp.6. [59.]
    — [another edition]. pp.[ii].8. [60.]
    1918. pp.[ii].10. [65.]

1919. pp.[ii].10. [75.]
1920. pp.[iii].12. [85.]
1921. pp.[iii].7. [50.]
1922. pp.6. [60.]
1923. pp.[ii].6. [40.]
1924. pp.[ii].6. [40.]
1925. pp.[ii].7. [50.]
1926. pp.[ii].8. [70.]
no more published.

LIST of publications (other than confidential) [non-confidential publications] issued by the government of India in the Indian munitions board [Board of industries and munitions] during the year . . ., which are exempted from registration.

1917. single leaf. [1.]
1918. single leaf. [3.]
1919. single leaf. [3.]
1920. pp.[ii].5. [22.]
no more published.

LIST of certain ancient documents received from Madras in connection with the class composition of the coast and bay army. Calcutta 1912. pp.[ii]. 143. [1500.]

LIST of certain ancient documents received from Madras, comprising regimental returns, registers or long rolls, and memoirs of services of certain regiments of the army, including some miscellaneous documents. Calcutta 1913. pp.160. [3000.]

Miniature painting

O. C. GANGOLY, Critical catalogue of miniature paintings in the Baroda museum. Baroda 1961. pp.vii.192. pls.A–E. i–lix. [1000.]

Minerals

P. K. CHATTERJEE, Annotated index of indian mineral occurrences (as in april, 1960). Based on *A bibliography of indian geology and physical geography, with an annotated index of minerals of economic value*, by T. H. D. la Touche, 1918. Geological survey of India: Calcutta 1963–4.

Missions

BIBLIOTHECA missionum. Internationales institut für missionswissenschaftliche forschung.
vi. Missionsliteratur Indians, der Philippinen, Japans and Indochinas 1700–1799. Fortigeführt und ergänzt von Johannes Dindinger. 1931. pp.32.616. [2005.]
— Zweite, unveränderte auflage. Rom, Freiburg, Wien 1964. pp.xx.[21]–616. [2005.]
— Achtundzwanzigster band: Missionsliteratur Südasiens (Indien, Pakistan, Birma, Ceylon) 1947–1968. 1971. pp.xix.579. [2261–3994.]

Music

BIBLIOGRAPHY of writings and publications on subjects of music, dance and drama by dr. V. Raghavan. [Madras] 1964. pp.20. [200.]

Natural history

THE EAST INDIA company and natural history. An exhibition of water-colours, manuscripts, rare books and other material illustrating the interest of the East India company and its servants in the natural history of India and the east Indies. India office library: India office records: [London] 1970. pp.22. [53.]*

Naval and maritime arts

[FREDERICK CHARLES DANVERS]. List of marine records of the late East India company, and of subsequent date, preserved in the Record department of the India office. 1896. pp.xxi.160. [5000.]

Non-violence

HIRA RAI, Bibliography on non-violence and satyagraha. Rajghat, Varanasi 1971. pp.xv.109. [859.]

Numismatics

C. R. SINGHAL, Bibliography of indian coins. . . . Edited by A. S. Altekar. Numismatic society of India: Bombay 1950–1952. pp.viii.163 + [iv].vi. 220. [2000.]

Nutrition

N. GANGULEE [NAGENDRA-NĀTHA GANGOPĀDHYĀYA], Bibliography of nutrition in India. 1940. pp.[ii].viii.79. [1000.]

Parsees

EBERHARD KULKE, Die Parsen/The Parsees. Bibliographie über eine indische minorität, zusammengestellt und mit einer einführung versehen. A bibliography of an indian minority, compiled and introduced. Materialien des Arnold-Bergestraesser-instituts für kulturwissenschaftliche forschung. Freiburg i.Br. 1968. pp.xxiv.52. [930.]

Philosophy

FITZEDWARD HALL, A contribution towards an index to the bibliography of the indian philosophical systems. Calcutta 1859. pp.[iv].xxii.237. [748.]

A[RTHUR] C[OKE] BURNELL, A classified index to the sanskrit mss. in the palace at Tanjore. . . . Part II. Philosophy and law. Madras government: Madras 1879. pp.[iii].81–151. [1000.]

HRISHÍKEŚA ŚÁSTRÍ and ŚIVA CHANDRA GUI, A descriptive catalogue of sanskrit manuscripts in the library of the Calcutta sanskrit college. Volume III. Philosophy manuscripts. Calcutta [1899–]1900. pp.[ii].v.327. [583.]

[G-KRṢNA SĀSTRĪ and] OTTO SCHRÂDER [sic], Bibliography of sakhya-yoga-samuĆĆaya works. Adyar 1906. pp.[ii].18. [152.]

BRIEF list of references on hindu philosophy. Library of Congress: Washington 1923. ff.5.[53.]*

JEAN HERBERT, Wat kan het westen van het oosten leren? Deventer &c. 1949. pp.34. [150.]

A BIBLIOGRAPHY of indian philosophy. C. P. Ramaswami Aiyar research endowment committee: Madras 1963–8. pp.v.46.18.17.6.10.18.58. 14.11+viii.10.49.19.13.8.3.23.8.85.vii. [4000.]

KARL H. POTTER, Bibliography of indian philosophies. Encyclopedia of indian philosophies (vol.1). Delhi, etc. [1970]. pp.xxxv.811. [9222.]

Planning

H. N. PATHAK, Select bibliography of articles on India's five year plans. Ahmedabad [1962]. pp.iv. 50. [850.]

Political science

BRIJENDRA PRATAP GAUTAM, Researches in political-science in India (a detailed bibliography). Kanpur [1965]. pp.v.116. [1500.]

Public enterprises

L. VENKATESAN, A bibliography on public enterprises in India. The indian institute of public administration: New Delhi 1961. ff.[iii].pp.106. [742.]*

Railways

CATALOGUE of technical papers issued by the technical section of Railway board of India. Railway Department: Delhi 1925. pp.[v].53. [600.]
— [another edition]. Lucknow [1954]. pp.44. [333.]
there are numerous intermediate editions.

Saivism

S. KUPPUSWAMI SASTRI [SRI KUPPU-SVĀMI ṢĀSTRI], A descriptive catalogue of the tamil manuscripts in the Government oriental manuscripts library. Vol.III[–IV]. Religion and philosophy (Saivism). Madras 1927–1937. pp.[ii].vi.999–1420.xxi+[iii]. v.v.1421–1608.viii. [745.]

Science

[J. M. F. GUÉRIN], Catalogue de manuscrits orientaux en langue sanscrite sur l'astronomie,

la médecine, etc., recueillis dans les Indes orientales. 1855. pp.20. [medecine: 56].

STANLEY KEMP, Catalogue of the scientific serial publications in the principal libraries of Calcutta. Asiatic society of Bengal: Calcutta 1918. pp.xii. 292. [1607.]

[MANOHAR BHASKAR ARTE], List of scientific periodicals in the Bombay presidency. Bombay 1931. pp.[vi].ii.107.

INDIAN science abstracts. (Being an annotated bibliography of science in India). National institute of sciences of India: Calcutta.
[i]. 1935. pp.[ii].5.10.48.81.37.72.77.32. [2000.]
[ii]. 1936. pp.18.59.33.66.34.61.67.35.45. [2000.]
[iii]. 1937. pp.18.38.46.63.39.43.61.69.64. [2000.]
[iv]. 1938. pp.22.50.73.76.69. [1500.]
[v]. 1939. pp.21.46.48.59.92.59. [2000.]
no more published.

LIST of scientific periodicals published in India. Unescoe: Paris 1952. pp.18.

INDIAN scientific & technical publications exhibition. Council of scientific & industrial research: New Delhi 1960. pp.198.195. [12,000.]

[G. K. ARORA and others], DIRECTORY of indian scientific periodicals. Indian national science documentation centre: Delhi 1964. pp.[ix].133. [725.]*

CATALOGUE of serials in the National science library. Union catalogue division: Indian national science documentation centre: New Delhi 1965. pp.407.

VINOD K. SAXENA and A. S. SIDHU, Indian scientific and technical publications 1960–1965; a bibliography. Council of scientific & industrial research: New Delhi 1966. pp.xii.284. [4492.]

INDIAN science abstracts. Indian national scientific documentation centre: Delhi.
i. 1965. pp.1400. [12,128.]
ii. 1966. pp.1394. [12,027.]
iii. 1967. pp.1153. [9195.]
iv. 1968. pp.1308.204. [11,269.]
v. 1969. pp.1736.252. [13,863.]
vi. 1970. pp.1777.260. [14,156.]
vii. 1971. pp.
viii. 1972. pp.1638.253. [13,404.]
in progress.

Sikhs

N[ORMAN] GERALD BARRIER, The Sikhs and their literature. A guide to tracts, books and periodicals, 1849–1919. Delhi [1970.]. pp.xlv.153. [1240.]

Social sciences

C. G. JADHAV [and others], Census of India 1961. Bibliography of social studies in India. [New Delhi 1968.] pp.vii.402+x.955. [20,000.]

MOHINDER SINGH, J. F. PANDYA and M. C. SHAH, Facets of social control and nationalisation in India; a selected annotated bibliography. Ahmedabad 1970. pp.136. [459.]

DURGAPRASAD BHATTACHARYA, A guide to a socio-economic bibliography of India, 1870–1970. Tech. report (no. Econ./1/71): Research and training school: Indian statistical institute: Calcutta 1971. pp.31.

Sociology

ELIZABETH E. BACON, MORRIS E. OPLER and EDWARD E. LECLAIR, A selected and annotated bibliography of the sociology of India. Prepared by India project, Cornell university. Human relations area files: New Haven 1957. ff.[ii].pp.iii. 112. [569.]

Soil

K. K. GUHA ROY, Bibliography of soil science and fertilizers with reference to India. Indian council of agricultural research: Bulletin (no.74): Delhi 1954. pp.iv.131. [2156.]

I. C. GUPTA, Bibliography of characteristics & management of salt affected soils in India (1893–1972). Agricultural research communication centre: Sadar, Karnal 1972. pp.[iv].92. [681.]

Statistics

GEORGE BUIST, Index to books and papers on the physical geography, antiquities, and statistics of India. Bombay 1852. pp.5–103. [4000.]

Trade and manufactures

SIR WILLIAM FOSTER, The english factories in India. . . . A calendar of documents in the India office, British museum and Public record office. Oxford.

1618–1621. 1906. pp.xlviii.380. [460.]
1622–1623. 1908. pp.xl.391. [376.]
1624–1629. 1909. pp.xlviii.388. [366.]
1630–1633. 1910. pp.xl.354. [320.]
1634–1636. 1911. pp.xl.356. [320.]
1637–1641. 1912. pp.xlvii.340. [185.]
1642–1645. 1913. pp.xxxvii.340. [157.]
1646–1650. 1914. pp.xxxii.362. [257.]
1651–1654. 1915. pp.xxxix.324. [250.]

the subtitle varies from volume to volume; four further volumes, covering 1655–1669, were published in 1921–1927, in the form of a continuous narrative.

LIST of non-confidential publications exempted from registration, which were issued by the government of India in the Department of commerce and industry and the departments subordinate to it. [Calcutta].

1908. pp.25. [133.]
1909. pp.27. [148.]
1910. pp.27. [132.]
1911. pp.27. [152.]
1912. pp.25. [150.]
1913. pp.27. [148.]
1914. pp.37. [201.]
1915. pp.33. [229.]
1916. pp.26. [326.]

[*continued as:*]
List of publications (other than confidential) issued by the government of India in the Department of commerce and industry [1920–1926: of commerce] and the departments subordinate to it during the year . . ., which are exempted from registration.

1917. pp.[ii].44. [350.]
1918. pp.42. [350.]
1919. pp.43. [350.]
1920. pp.32. [246.]
1921. pp.27. [250.]
1922. pp.21. [200.]
1923. pp.11. [100.]
1924. pp.12. [125.]
1925. pp.13. [125.]
1926. pp.11. [100.]

no more published.

LIST of non-confidential publications exempted from registration which were issued by the government of India in the Department of industries [and labour] during the year. [Simla.]

1921. pp.[ii].11. [54.]
1922. pp.[ii].7. [34.]
1923. pp.[ii].11. [85.]
1924. pp.[ii].10. [74.]
1925. pp.[ii].11. [93.]
1926. pp.[ii].13. [89.]

no more published.

BIBLIOGRAPHY of industrial publications published in India from 1921. Industrial research bureau: Bulletins (no.1): Delhi 1936. pp.[v].257. [1250.]

Urbanization

ASHISH BOSE. Urbanization in India; an inventory of source materials. Bombay [1970]. pp.xx.389. [1529.]

xvi. Persons

Aurobindi, Sri

H. K. KAUL, Sri Aurobindo; a descriptive bibliography. New Delhi 1972. pp.xxxv.222. [1950.]

Bhave, Vinova

JAGDISH SARAN SHARMA, Vinova and Bhoodan; a selected descriptive bibliography of Bhoodan in hindi, english and other indian languages. National bibliographies (no.3): Indian national congress: New Delhi [1956]. pp.vii.92.[927.]

Bhuyan S. K.

BIBLIOGRAPHY of the works of dr. S. K. Bhuyan. Gauhati 1951. pp.21. [123.]

Carey, William

[JOHN TAYLOR], Biographical and literary notices of William Carey ... with bibliographical list of works relating to, or written by Carey; and pertaining to baptist missions in the east, etc. Northampton 1866. pp.x.113. [350.]

Demiéville, Paul

[P. DEMIÉVILLE], Titres et travaux de Paul Demiéville, 1948. pp.5. [30.]

Emerit, Marcel

[M. EMERIT], Travaux d'histoire de Marcel Emerit [1953]. ff.7. [100.]

Gandhi, Mahatma Karamchand

LIST of references on the Gandhi movement in India. Library of Congress: [Washington] 1921. ff.5.[56.]*

P. G. DESHPANDE, गांधी साहित्य सूचि Gandhiana. (A bibliography of gandhian literature). Ahmedabad [1948]. pp.[ii].xiii.239. [2500.]

JAGDISH SARAN SHARMA [JAGADĪSA-SARANA SARMA], Mahatma Gandhi. A descriptive bibliography. National bibliographies (no.1): Delhi &c. 1955. pp.xxi.565. [3671.]

DHARMA VIR, Gandhi bibliography. Chandigarh 1967. pp.xxiv.575. [3485.]

Glasenapp, Helmuth von

ZOLTÁN KÁROLYI, Helmuth von Glasenapp bibliographie. pp.xiii.100. [758.]

Gobind Singh

JAGINDAR SINGH RAMDEV, Guru Gobind Singh; a descriptive bibliography. Chandigarh [1967]. pp.xvi.260. [1367.]

Gode, Parasu-Rāma-Krishan

BIBLIOGRAPHY of the published writings of P. K. Gode ... (from 1916 to 1939). Poona 1939. pp.20.
privately printed.

Jones, sir William

GARLAND H[AMPTON] CANNON, Sir William

377

Jones, orientalist. An annotated bibliography of his works. Honolulu [1952]. pp.xvi.88. [46.]

Müller, Friedrich Max

[F. M. MÜLLER], An offering of sincere gratitude to my many friends ... on the ... fifteenth anniversary of my ... doctor's degree. Oxford [printed] [1893]. pp.23. [150.]
consists of 'Catalogue of principal works published by ... F. Max Müller. Compiled by M.W.'

Nehru, Jawāhir-Lāl

JAGDISH SARAN SHARMA. Jawahrlal Nehru. A descriptive bibliography. Delhi &c. 1955. pp. xvi.421. [3710.]

Neog, Maheswar

A SHORT bibliography of the works of dr. Maheswar Neog. Gauhati 1964. pp.[ii].14. [102.]

Raghavan, V.

BIBLIOGRAPHY of the books, papers & other contributions of dr. V. Raghavan. Ahmedabad [1968]. pp.x.370. [755.]

Roy, Manabendra Nath

PATRICK [GARLAND] WILSON, A preliminary checklist of the writings of M. N. Roy. University of California: Institute of International studies: Modern indian projects: Bibliographical study (no.1): Berkeley [1955]. pp.12. [150.]*
— — [another edition]. A checklist [&c.]. 1957. ff.14. [150.]*

Roy, Rammohun

ADRIENNE MOORE, Rammohun Roy and America. (Part ii: The works of Rammohun Roy and periodicals containing articles dealing with him; a bibliography.) Calcutta 1942. pp.xii.190. [650.]

Sankalia, H. D.

BIBLIOGRAPHY of books, articles and reports of excavations as a joint author of H. D. Sankalia from the year 1930–1967. ff.17. [152.]*

Upadhye, A. N.

A. N. UPADHYE, Books and papers. Kolhapur 1967. pp.xi.67. [194.]

Vivekānanda, Svāmi, pseud.

JEAN HERBERT, Swâmi Vivekânada. Bibliographie des œuvres parues dans des langues européennes. Grands maîtres spirituels dans l'Inde contemporaine: 1938. pp.3–16. [100.]

378

INDIAN LANGUAGES AND LITERATURES

i. *Manuscripts*

[J. PHILIPPE WERDIN, *in religion*] PAULINUS A SANCTO BARTHOLOMAEO, Examen historico-criticum codicum indicorum bibliothecae Sacrae congregationis de propaganda fide. Romae 1792. pp. 80. [36.]

N[IELS] L[UDWIG] WESTERGAARD, Codices indici Bibliothecæ regiæ havniensis. Havniæ 1847. pp.x. 122. [350.]

[RUDOLF VON ROTH], Systematisch-alphabetischer hauptkatalog der Königlichen universitätsbibliothek ... M. Handschriften. a Orientalische. 1. Indische handschriften. Tübingen 1865. pp.[v]. 24. [600.]
the indian manuscripts of the Köngliche öffentliche bibliothek of Stuttgart are set out in an appendix.
—— Verzeichniss der indischen handschriften. ... [Zuwachs der jahre 1865–1899). Von Richard Garbe. Verzeichniss der doktoren welche die Philosophische fakultät ... im dekanatsjahre 1898–1899 ernannt hat: 1899. pp.[iii].114. [250.]

E[UGEN] HULTZSCH, Ueber eine sammlung indischer handschriften und inschriften. Separatabdruck aus der Zeitschrift der Deutschen morgenländischen gesellschaft (bd.xl.). Leipzig 1886. pp.80. [637.]

ALPHABETICAL index of manuscripts in the Government oriental mss. library, Madras. Madras 1893. pp.[ii].140.92.30.48.5.16.2.6.22.3. [5000.]

J[AMES] F[ULLER] BLUMHARDT, Catalogue of the marathi, gujarati, bengali, assamese, oriya, pushtu, and sindhi manuscripts in the library of the British museum. 1905. pp.xi.48.[iii].34.[v].51. [250.]

P[AOLO] E[MILIO] PAVOLINI, I manoscritti indiani della Biblioteca nazionale centrale di Firenze (non compresi nel catalogo dell'Aufrecht). Società asiatica italiana: Giornale (vol.xx): Firenze 1908. pp. 65. [382.]
Aufrecht's Florentine sanskrit manuscripts *is entered under Sanskrit literature, below.*

J. PH. VOGEL, Catalogue of the Bhuri Singh museum at Chambā (Chambā state, Panjab). Calcutta 1909. pp.[vii].81. [681.]

A[NTOINE] CABATON, Catalogue sommaire des manuscrits indiens, indo-chinois & malayo-polynésiens. Bibliothèque nationale: 1912. pp.[vi].320. [indian: 936.]

A TRIENNIAL catalogue of manuscripts collected ... for the Government oriental manuscripts library ... Part 4.—Miscellaneous. Madras.
   i. 1910–1913. By M. Rangacharya and S. Kuppuswami Sastri. 1913. pp.6. [43.]
   ii. 1913–1916. By S. Kuppuswami Sastri. 1917. pp.6. [51.]
   iii. 1916–1919. 1922. pp.7. [106.]
   iv. 1919–1922. 1927. pp.10. [121.]

N[IKOLAI] D. MIRONOV, Каталогъ индійскихъ рукописей. Каталоги Азіатскаго музея Императорской академіи наукъ (vol.1): Петроградъ 1914. pp.5.360. [466.]

N[IKOLAI] D. MIRONOV, Каталогъ индійскихъ рукописей россійской публичной библіотеки. ... Выпускъ 1. Петроградъ 1918. pp.[ii].ii.288. [350.]
no more published.

H[ORACE] I. POLEMAN, A census of indic manuscripts in the United States and Canada. American oriental society: American oriental series (vol.xii): New Haven 1938. pp.xxix.542. [7300.]*

MOHAMMAD E. MOGHADAM [MUḤAMMAD I'TIMĀD MUḰADDAM] and YAḤYA ARMAJĀNĪ, Descriptive catalog of the Garrett collection of persian, turkish and indic manuscripts, including some miniatures, in the Princeton university library. ... Under the supervision of Philip K[hūri] Hitti. Princeton oriental texts (vol.6): Princeton 1939. pp.94.x. [191.]

[HORACE I. POLEMAN], Indic manuscripts and paintings. Library of Congress: Washington 1939. pp.iv.16. [82.]
an exhibition catalogue.

HARAPRASĀDA SHĀSTRI, A descriptive catalogue of the vernacular manuscripts in the collections of the Royal asiatic society of Bengal. Revised and edited by Jogendra Nath Gupta. Calcutta 1941. pp.xi.433. [445.]

KALI PRASAD, Catalogue of oriental manuscripts in the Lucknow university library, Lucknow (India). [Lucknow] 1951. ff.[iii].pp.75. [1164.]

WALTHER SCHUBRING, (vol.1), KLAUS L. JANERT) und N. NARASIMHAN POTI (vol.2), and (vol.3, E. R. SREEKRISHNA SARMA, Indische (und nepalische) handschriften. Verzeichnis der orientalischen handschriften in Deutschland (band II, 1–3): Wiesbaden, 1962–70. pp.xiii.293+359+ix.48. [1113.]
the third volume lists mss. in tamil.

MANUSCRIPTS from indian collections. Descriptive catalogue. National museum: New Delhi 1964. pp.viii.113. [152.]

KLAUS LUDWIG JANERT, An annotated bibliography of the catalogues of indian manuscripts, part I. Verzeichnis der orientalischen handschriften in Deutschland (Supplementband 1): Wiesbaden 1965. pp.175. [375.]

AKIRA YUYAMA, Indic manuscripts and chinese blockprints (non-chinese texts) of the oriental collection of the Australian national university library, Canberra. Centre of oriental studies: the Australian national university: Canberra 1967. pp.viii.124. [large number.]

C. REGAMEY, Manuscrits sur feuilles de palmier. Les manuscrits indiens et indochinois de la section ethnographique du Musée historique de Berne; catalogue descriptif. Sonderdruck aus dem Jahrbuch des Bernischen historischen museums in Bern (xxviii.jhg.) [Bern] 1968. pp.23. [51.]

ii. General.

[JOSEPH HÉLIODORE] GARCIN DE TASSY, Les auteurs hindoustanis et leurs ouvrages. 1855. pp. [ii].47. [100.]
—— Seconde édition. 1868. pp.[iii].111. [200.]

JOHN MURDOCH, Catalogue of the christian vernacular literature of India. Madras 1870. pp.ix.xiii. 313. [2000.]

[JOSEPH HÉLIODORE] GARCIN DE TASSY, La langue et la littérature hindoustanies de 1850 à 1869. . . . Seconde édition. 1874. pp.[v].488. [2000.]
first published in various forms in annual parts.
—— La lange [&c.]. . . . Revue annuelle.
1870. pp.48. [100.]
1871. pp.83. [250.]
1872. pp.109. [250.]
1873. pp.86. [200.]
1874. pp.116. [250.]
1875. pp.128. [250.]
1876. pp.178. [250.]
1877. pp.104. [250.]
no more published.

H. U. WEITBRECHT, A descriptive catalogue of urdu christian literature . . . and a supplementary catalogue of christian publications in the other languages of the Panjáb. Lahore 1886. pp.[v].4. li.86. [1000.]

INTERESTING & important donation from the Indian government. Shakespeare memorial library: [Stratford-upon-Avon 1890]. single sheet. [59.]
the donation consists of translations of Shakespeare's works into indian languages.

E[MIL] SIEG, Verzeichnis der Bibliotheca indica und verwandter indischer serien nach werken und nummern. Leipzig 1908. pp.24. [230.]

M[URRAY] B[ARNSON] EMENEAU, A union list of printed indic texts and translations in american libraries. American oriental society: American oriental series (vol.vii): New Haven 1935. pp.xv. 540. [4500.]

CATALOGUE of the publications of the Government oriental manuscripts library, Madras. Corrected up to 1st august 1950. Madras 1950. pp.8. [35.]

INDIA office library, Commonwealth relations office, *later* Foreign and commonwealth office. Accessions in modern indian languages (Accessions in the modern languages of India and Pakistan).
Assamese. 1963. &c.
Bengali. 1955 &c.
Gujarati. 1951 &c.
Hindi. 1952 &c.
Kannada (Kanarese). 1954 &c.
Malayalam. 1964 &c.
Marathi. 1954 (?) &c.
Oriya. 1967.
Panjabi. 1953 (?) &c.
Sanskrit, Pali and Prakrit (Select accessions). 1963 &c.
Tamil. 1963 &c.
Urdu. 1957 &c.
in progress.

INDIAN national bibliography. General editor: B. S. Kesavan. Central reference [National] library: Calcutta.
1957. pp.xii.273. [2700.]
i. 1958. pp.xvi. 840.241. [10,000.]
ii. 1959. pp.xvi.791+283. [10,000.]
iii. 1960. pp.xvi.774+279. [10,000.]
iv. 1961. pp.xvi.897+357. [12,000.]
v. 1962. pp.xvi.902+361. [12,000.]
— Cumulated index 1958–1962. 1970. pp.[v]. 1384.338. [95,000.]
vi. 1963. pp.xvi.1008.373. [12,500.]
vii. 1964. General editor: D. R. Kalia. pp.xvi.922.353. [11,000.]
viii. 1965. General editor: C. R. Banerji. pp.xvi.802.321. [9500.]
ix. 1966. [*monthly parts.*]
x. 1967. [*monthly parts.*]
xi. 1968.
xii. 1969.
xiii. 1970.
xiv. 1971. pp.xvi.520.436.159.302. [11,000.]
xv. 1972. [*monthly parts.*]
xvii. 1973. [*monthly parts.*]
in progress; annual volumes only set out; the bibliography for 1968–70 will be published as

annual volumes only. Separate bibliographies are also published for Sanksrit and the major vernaculars.

ACCESSIONS list, India. Library of Congress: American libraries book procurement center: New Delhi.★

    i. 1962. pp.[iv].311.liv. [3000.]
    ii. 1963. pp.[iv].695.lxviii. [7000.]
in progress.

B[ELLARY] S[HAMANNA] KESAVAN and V. Y. KUL-KARNI, *edd.* The national bibliography of indian literature, 1901–1953. Sahitya akademi: New Delhi.

    i. Assamese, bengali, english, gujarati. 1962. pp.xi.797. [15,000.]
    ii. Hindi, kannada, kashmiri, malayalam. [1966.] pp.[xvi].632. [10,000.]
    iii. Marathi, oriya, panjabi, sanskrit. 1970. pp.xv.646. [10,000.]
in progress.

A LIST of linguistic materials for the most part unpublished, bequeathed to S. O. A. S. by ... D[avid] L[ockhart] R[obertson] Lorimer. University of London: School of oriental and african studies: [1962]. pp.viii. [150.]★

C. C. MEHTA, Bibliography of stageable plays in indian languages. New Delhi 1963–5. pp.viii.292. +viii.228. [5350.]

A BIBLIOGRAPHY of dictionaries and encyclo-paedias in indian languages. National library: Calcutta 1964. pp.x.165. [2190.]

M[IKHAIL SERGEEVICH] ANDRONOV, Materials for a bibliography of dravidian linguistics. Inter-national association of tamil research series: Department of indian studies: University of Malaya: Kuala Lumpur [1966]. pp.52 [45–52 blank]. [877.]

D. P. PATTANAYAK, Indian languages biblio-graphy. Educational resources center: New Delhi 1967. pp.84.

H. S. PATIL and S. MASIHUL HASSAN, *edd.*, Indian literature; select bibliographies. Aspects of Indian culture (iii): Delhi 1972. pp.ix.262. [1243.]

iii. Sanskrit

1. Manuscripts

JAMES FRASER, The history of Nadir Shah, formerly called Thamas Kuli Khan, the present emperor of Persia. To which is prefix'd A short history of the Moghol emperors. At the end is inserted, A catalogue of about two hundred manuscripts in the persic and other oriental languages, collected in the east. The second edi-tion. London 1742. pp.vi.234.[vi].40. [sanskrit: 35.]

CHARLES WILKINS, A catalogue of sanscrita manuscripts presented to the Royal society by sir William and Lady Jones. [1798]. pp.14. [60.]

ALEXANDER HAMILTON and L[OUIS MATHIEU] LANGLÈS, Catalogue des manuscrits samskrits de la Bibliothèque impériale. 1807. pp.118. [400.]

[FRIEDRICH AUGUST ROSEN], Catalogue of the sanskrit manuscripts, collected during his residence in India, by the late sir Robert Chambers. 1838. pp.[iv].36. [750.]

PROFESSOR [Horace Hayman] Wilson's sanskrit manuscripts, now deposited in the Bodleian library. [Oxford] 1842. pp.20. [627.]
copies in the Bodleian library and the Library of Congress contain ms. notes and additions.

[ALBRECHT] WEBER, Verzeichniss der sanskrit-[vol.ii: and prâkrit-] handschriften. Königliche bibliothek: Handschriften-verzeichnisse (vols.i, v): Berlin 1853–1892. pp.xxiv.481+viii.352+ v–x.353–828+[ii].xxvii.829–1364. [7500.]

[J. M. F.] GUÉRIN, Catalogue des manuscrits orientaux en langue sanscrite sur l'astronomie, la médecine, etc., recueillis dans les Indes orientales. 1855. pp.20. [119.]

TH[EODOR] AUFRECHT [vol.ii: MORIZ WINTER-NITZ and A. B. KEITH], Catalogi codicum manu-scriptorum Bibliothecae bodleianae pars octava, codices sanscriticos complectens. Oxonii [1859–] 1864–1905. pp.vii.578.[854]+xxvi.350. [1621.]
  — — Appendix to vol I ... by Arthur Berrie-dale Keith. 1909. pp.xi.124.

F[RANZ] KIELHORN, A classified alphabetical catalogue of sanskrit mss. in the southern division of the Bombay presidency.... Fascicle I. Bombay 1869. pp.[iii].95. [1250.]
no more published.

TH[EODOR] AUFRECHT, A catalogue of sanskrit manuscripts in the library of Trinity college. Cambridge 1869. [94.]

A[RTHUR] C[OKE] BURNELL, Catalogue of col-lection of sanskrit manuscripts. ... Part 1. 1869 pp.[ii].65. [230.]
of the author's own collection, which he presented to the India office.

RĀJENDRALĀLA MITRA [vol.x: HARAPRASĀDA ŚĀSTRĪ], Notices of sanskrit mss. Calcutta [1870–] 1871–1892. pp.[ii].15.[ii].2.5.337+iv.12.401+ v.12.366+[ii].15.319+xv.317.xxxi+[ii].13.316. 11+xvi.321+xvii.336+xvi.13.xxvii.316+ [ii].8.[xvi].367. [4265.]
  — An alphabetical list of mss. noticed by the late Rājā Rājendratala Mitra (from 1870–1891) by Haraprasada Shastra. 1895.

—— Second series. By mahāmahopādhyāya Haraprasāda Cāstri [Sāstri]. 1900–1911. pp.[ii]. xl.432 + [ii].xxii.238 + [ii].xxvi.13.253 + [ii]. xxxvi.11.265. [1413.]

CATALOGUE of sanskrit mss. existing in Oudh. Calcutta [Lucknow, Allahabad].
  i.
  ii.
  iii. 1873. By Colin [Arrott Robertson] Browning. pp.[iii].23. [150.]
  iv. 1874. By John Nerfield [sic, Nesfield]. pp.[iii].20. [150.]
  v.1875. pp.[iii].31. [250.]
  vi. 1875. pp.[iii].15. [100.]
  vii. 1875. pp.[iii].9. [50.]
  viii. 1876. pp.[iii].37. [250.]
  ix. 1877. pp.[iii].29. [200.]
  x. 1878. pp.[iii].27. [200.]
  xi. 1878. pp.[iii].39. [250.]
  xii. 1880. By pandit Deví Prasada. pp.[iii].55. [150.]
  xiii. 1881. pp.119. [211.]
  [xiv]. 1882. pp.[ii].v.117. [202.]
  xv. 1883. pp.[iii].145. [300.]
  [xvi]. 1884. pp.[iii].149. [300.]
  [xvii]. 1885. pp.[iii].115. [300.]
  [xviii]. 1886. pp.[iii].95. [200.]
  [xix]. 1887. pp.[iii].139. [400.]
  [xx]. 1888. pp.[iii].259. [600.]
  [xxi]. 1889. pp.[iii].179. [400.]
  [xxii]. 1890. 1893. pp.[iii].131. [400.]
no more published; the issues for 1874–1879 were also published in another form, under the title List of sanskrit manuscripts discovered in Oudh.

[JOHANN] G[EORG] BÜHLER, ed. A catalogue of sanskrit manuscripts contained in the private libraries of Gujarât, Kâthiâvâd, Kachchh, Sind and Khândes. Bombay 1871–1873. pp.ix.245+ viii.135+141+277. [5450.]

REPORT on [the search for] sanskrit mss. [Presidency of Bombay: Department of education: Bombay].
  1872–1873. [By Johann Georg Bühler]. pp.7.17. [200.]
  1874–1875. pp.21. [54.]
  1875–1876. pp.90.clxxi. [838.]
  1877–1880. [By Franz Kielhorn] pp.26. [500.]
  1879–1882. pp.13. [618.]
  1880. By R. G. Bhandarkar. pp.37. [122.]
with an appendix covering 1873–1874.
  1881–1882. pp.39.41. [467.]
  1882–1883. pp.229. [772.]
  1883–1884. pp.479. viii. [737.]
  1884–1887. pp.138. [1406.]
  1887–1891. pp.114.xci. [1502.]
  1891–1895. By Abaji Vishnu Katharate. pp.21.121. [1675.]

[RĀMANĀTHA SUKULA; parts vii–xi: DHUṆḌHIRĀJA DHARMĀDHIKĀRI; SUDHĀKARA DVIVEDĪ], A catalogue of sanskrit manuscripts in private libraries of the North-West Provinces. Benares [parts ii–x: Allahabad] 1874–1886. pp.[iii].627+[iii].165+ [iii].151 + [iii].123 + [ii].53 + [ii].207 + [iii].71+ [v.]75+[iii].67+[vii].65+[iii].65. [4000.]

ED[WARD] B[YLES] COWELL and J[ULIUS] EGGELING, Catalogue of buddhist sanskrit manuscripts in the possession of the Royal asiatic society (Hodgson collection). Hertford [printed] 1875. pp.56. [79.]

[L. DE ZOYSA], Catalogue of pali, sinhalese, & sanskrit manuscripts, in the Ceylon government oriental library. Colombo 1876. pp.26. [209.]

RĀJENDRALĀLA MITRA, A descriptive catalogue of sanskrit mss. in the library of the Asiatic society of Bengal. Part first. Grammar. Calcutta 1877. pp.ix.171.lvii. [321.]
no more published.

G[EORG] BÜHLER, Detailed report of a tour in search of sanskrit mss. made in Kaśmîr, Rajputana, and Central India. Extra number of the Journal of the Bombay branch of the Royal asiatic society. Bombay 1877. pp.90.clxxi. [823.]

A[RTHUR] C[OKE] BURNELL, A classified index to the sanskrit mss. in the palace at Tanjore. . . . Madras government: Madras 1880. pp.xii.239. [12,376.]

R. G. BHANDARKAR, [Report on the search for sanskrit manuscripts.] Bombay 1880.pp.37. [122.]

RĀJENDRALĀLA MITRA, A catalogue of sanskrit manuscripts in the library of h.h. the mahárájá of Bikáner. Calcutta 1880. pp.xii.745. [1794.]

GUSTAV OPPERT, Lists of sanskrit manuscripts in private libraries of southern India. Madras 1880–1885. pp.vii.620+ix.694. [18,797.]

CATALOGUE of newly discovered, rare and old sanskrit manuscripts in the Lahore division. [Lahore 1881]. pp.23. [190.]

[KĀṢĪNĀTHA KUNTE], Report on sanskrit manuscripts for [July 1880–June 1881]. [Lahore 1881]. pp.[ii].3.9.13.55. [500.]
  —— 1881–1882. [1883]. pp.[ii].7.12. [200.]

PETER PETERSON, Report of operations in search of sanskrit mss. in the Bombay circle. Royal asiatic society: Bombay branch: Journal (vol.xvi, extra no.xli [&c.]): Bombay.
  i. 1882–1883 . . . (vol.xvi, extra no.xli): 1883. pp.[iv].132.129. [367.]
  ii. 1883–1884 . . . (vol.xviii, extra no.xliv): 1884. pp.[iii].183.29. [301.]

iii. 1884–1886 ... (vol.xviii, extra no.xlv): 1887. pp.[iv].xxx.407. [657.]

iv. 1886–1892 ... (vol.xviii, extra no.xlix A): 1894. pp.[v].cxlii.177.58. [1500.]

v. 1892–1895. 1896. pp.[iii].lxxxviii.317. [800.]

vi. 1895–1898. 1899. pp.[iii].xxviii.144. [100.]

[SIR] W[ILLIAM] W[ILSON] HUNTER, Catalogue of sanskrit manuscripts collected in Nepal and presented to various libraries ... by Brian Houghton Hodgson. 1881. pp.27.

CECIL BENDALL, Catalogue of the buddhist sanskrit manuscripts in the University library Cambridge 1883. pp.lvi.225. [500.]

LISTS of sanskrit manuscripts collected for the government of Bombay in 1879–1880 and 1881–1882. [Bombay 1883]. pp.13. [618.]

[B.] LEWIS RICE, Catalogue of sanskrit manuscripts in Mysore and Coorg. Bangalore 1884. pp.[ii].2.2.327. [2944.]

F[RANZ] KIELHORN and [SIR] R[ĀMAKRISHNA] G[OPĀLA] BHĀNDĀRKAR, A catalogue of sanskrit manuscripts in the library of the Deccan college. [?Poona] 1884. pp.[61]. [1000.]

JULIUS EGGELING [vol.ii: ARTHUR BERRIEDALE KEITH], Catalogue of the sanskrit [vol.ii: and prakrit] manuscripts in the library of the India office. 1887–1935. pp.vii.1628+xii.920+[ii].921–1851. [8220.]

SHRIDHAR R. BHANDARKAR [SRĪDHARA RĀMA-KRISHNA BHĀNDĀRKAR], A catalogue of the collection of manuscripts deposited in the Deccan college. Bombay 1888. pp.[iii].3.539. [7000.]

CATALOGUE of sanskrit manuscripts in the Sanskrit college library. Benares. Allahabad 1888. pp.[539.]. [760.]

THEODOR AUFRECHT, Catalogus catalogorum. An alphabetical register of sanskrit works and authors. Leipzig 1891. pp.viii.795.iv.239+iv.161. [40,000.]

reprinted Wiesbaden 1962.

PETER PETERSON, Catalogue of the sanskrit manuscripts in the library of his highness the maharaja of Ulwar. Bombay 1892. pp.[ii].3.101.ᴣ̣˙[261]. [2500.]

THEODOR AUFRECHT, Florentine sanskrit manuscripts. Leipzig 1892. pp.iv.181. [503.]

[A. HALLY], Catalogue of the Colombo museum library. Part I. Páli, sinhalese, and sanscrit manuscripts. Colombo 1892. pp.[ii].18. [250.]

—— [second edition. By Henry M. Gunasekera]. 1901. pp.xiv.47. [500.]

HRISHIKEŚA ŚĀSTRĪ and ŚIVA CHANDRA GUI [vol.x (*sic*, xii): and NĪLAMANI CAKRAVARTTI], A descriptive catalogue of sanskrit manuscripts in the library of the Calcutta sanskrit college. Calcutta.

i. Vedic manuscripts. [1892–]1895. pp.[ii]. v.392. [643.]

ii. Smriti and Níti manuscripts. [1896–]1898. pp.[ii].518.v. [637.]

iii. Philosophy manuscripts. [1899–]1900. pp.[ii].v.327. [583.]

iv. Purāna manuscripts. [1901–]1902. pp.[ii]. 192.iii. [314.]

v. Tantra manuscripts. [1902–]1903. pp.[ii]. 136.ii. [135.]

vi. Kāvya manuscripts. 1903. pp.[ii].164.ii. [281.]

vii. Alankārah, Chandah, political science & lexicography manuscripts. 1904. pp.[ii].39. 15.3.31. [100.]

viii. Grammar manuscripts. 1904. pp.[ii]. 147.ii. [193.]

ix. Astrology & astronomy manuscripts. [1904–]1906. pp.[ii].180.ii. [193.]

x. Medicine manuscripts. 1906. pp.[ii].86.ii. [105.]

x [*sic*, xi]. Vaisnava literatures manuscripts. 1907[–1910]. pp.[ii].164.ii. [138.]

x [*sic*, xii]. Jaina manuscripts. 1909[–1915]. pp.[ii].594.ii.v. [202.]

the last volume also contains a supplement to the whole work.

ALPHABETICAL index of manuscripts in the government oriental mss. library, Madras. Sanskrit. Madras 1893. pp.[ii].140. [2500.]

R. G. BHANDARKAR [SIR RĀMAKRISHNA GOPĀLA BHĀNDĀRKAR], List of sanskrit manuscripts in private libraries in the Bombay presidency. ... Part I. Bombay 1893. pp.[167]. [337.]

no more published.

[SIR] M[ARK] A[UREL] STEIN, Catalogue of the sanskrit manuscripts in the Raghunatha temple library of his highness the maharaja of Jammu and Kashmir. Bombay &c. 1894. pp.xvi.li.423. [4500.]

E[UGEN] HULTZSCH, Reports on sanskrit manuscripts in southern India. ... No.I[–III]. Madras 1895–1905. pp.xi.98+xviii.161+xii.148. [2250.]

no more published.

SESAGIRI SĀSTRĪ, Report on a search for sanskrit and tamil manuscripts. Madras.

i. 1896–1897. 1898. pp.xxxii.281. [309.]

ii. 1893–1894. 1899. pp.xxxi.3.59. [358.]

LIST of sanskrit, jaina and hindi [sanksrit and hindi] manuscripts purchased by order of government and deposited in the Sanskrit college [A catalogue of sanskrit manuscripts acquired for the Government sanskrit library, Sarasvati Bhavana], Benares, Allahabad.

1897–1901. pp.[ii]. 80 [40].x.2 [2].241. [1005.]

1902. pp.[ii].19. [29.]

1903. pp.[ii].57. [195.]

1904. pp.[ii].27. [83.]

1905. pp.[ii].39. [135.]

1906. pp.[ii].22. [66.]

1907. pp. } *not published?*
1908. pp. }

1909. pp.[ii]. [25]. [96.]

1909–1910. pp. [20.] [118.]

1910–1911. pp. [ii]. [26]. [25.]

1911–1912. pp.[ii]. [28]. [90.]

1912–1913. pp.[ii]. [20]. [106.]

1913–1914. pp.[ii]. [23.] [152.]

1914–1915. pp.[ii]. [18]. [85.]

1915–1916. pp.[ii]. [20]. [113.]

1916–1917. pp.[ii]. [21]. [136.]

1917–1918. pp.[ii]. [25]. [77.]

1918–1919. By Gopinath Kaviraj. pp.[ii].30. [23.]

THEODOR AUFRECHT, Katalog der sanskrithandschriften der universitäts-bibliothek. Katalog der handschriften der universitäts-bibliothek (vol. i): Leipzig 1901. pp.vi.494. [1400.]

A PARTIAL list of rare mss. belonging to the Adyar library. [Madras 1901]. pp.4. [60.]

MAHĀMAHOPĀDHYĀYA HARAPRASĀDA ŚĀSTRĪ, Report on the search of sanskrit manuscripts (1895 to 1900). Asiatic society of Bengal: Calcutta 1901. pp.25. [300.]
the British museum copy contains a ms. index.

— — (1901–1902 to 1905–1906). 1906. pp.18. [200.]

— — (1906–1907 to 1910–1911). 1911. pp.10.

A DESCRIPTIVE catalogue of the sanskrit manuscripts of the Government oriental manuscripts library. Madras.

 i–ii. Vedic literature. By M. Śeṣa Giri Śāstri and Malūr Raṅgāchārya. 1901–1905. pp. [v].110 + iv.105–278 + vii.267–590.xvi. +viii.591–906.xi. [1245.]

 iii. Grammar, lexicography and prosody. By M. Raṅgāchārya. 1906. pp.viii.907–1244. x. [560.]

 iv.1. Itihāsa and Purāṇa. 1907. pp.vi.1245–1598.x. [532.]

 iv.2. Upapurāṇas and Sthalamāhātmyas. 1908. pp.vi.509–1917.x. [273.]

 v–vii. Dharma-śāstra. 1909. pp.vii.1919–2270.xvii + ix.2271–2754.x + xi.2575–2920.x. [1262.]

 viii–xi. Arthaśāstra, Kamaśāstra, and systems of indian philosophy. 1910–1911. pp.vii. 2921–3214.x + viii.3215–3570.x. + viii. 3571–3926.xiii+x.3927–4329.xv. [1686.]

 xii–xvi. Religion. By M. Raṅgāchārya and S[rī] Kuppu-Svāmi Śāstri. 1912–1913. pp.

xi.4329–4748.xxii + xii.4749–5148.x. + x.5149–5550.xi + x.5551–5907.ix + ix. 5909–6378.xiii. [3222.]

xvii–xix. Stōtras. 1914–1915. pp.viii.6379–6690.viii + xv.6691–7238.xviii + xii.7239–7686.xv. [2670.]

xx–xxi. Kāvyas. By S. Kuppu-Svāmi. 1918. pp.viii.7687–8118.x + viii.8119–8597.xiv. [1333.]

xxi. Rhetoric and poetics, music and dancing, and śilpaśāstra. 1918. pp.vii. 8599–8786.vi. [285.]

xxiii. Medicine. 1918. pp.viii.8787–9010.v. [313.]

xxiv. Jyautisa. 1918. pp.xiii.9011–9490.viii. [695.]

xxv–xxvi. Supplemental. 1924–1927. pp.[ii]. 10.3.9491–9744.v + [ii].ix.9745–9948.v. [924.]

xxvii. 1937. By S. Kuppu-Svāmi and P. P. Subrahmanya Sastri. pp.vii.xv.xix. 9949–10532.xiv. [692.]

xxvii.1939. [580.]

xxix. 1942. By P. P. Subrahmanya Sastri and A. Sankaran. [500.]

xxx. 1947. By A. Sankaran and Syed Muhammad Fazlullah. [200.]

xxxi. 1951. By T. Chandrasekharan. [500.]

xxxii. 1958. Supplemental (C). [500.]

xxxiii. 1961. D. [500.]

xxxiv. 1961. D. pp.li.11720–11908. [500.]

CECIL BENDALL, Catalogue of the sanskrit manuscripts in the British museum. 1902. pp.vii. 262. [559.]

A[RTHUR] BERRIEDALE KEITH, A catalogue of the sanskrit and prakrit mss. in the Indian institute library. Oxford 1903. pp.[iv].100. [162.]

CHARLES H[ENRY] TAWNEY and F[REDERICK] W[ILLIAM] THOMAS, Catalogue of two collections of sanskrit manuscripts preserved in the India office library. 1903. pp.[iv].60. [86.]

A CLASSIFIED list of sanskrit manuscripts in the library, with an index of works. . . . (The Pandit Bhagvanlal Indraji collection). Royal asiatic society: Bombay branch: Bombay 1903. pp.[ii]. 36. [211.]

[ŚRĪDHARA RĀMAKRISHNA BHĀṆḌĀRKAR], [Report of a tour in search of sanskrit manuscripts]. [Poona 1904]. pp.19. [100.]

— — Report of a second tour in search of sanskrit manuscripts made in Rajputana and central India in 1904–1905 and 1905–1906. Bombay 1907. pp.[ii.]100. [500.]

HRISHIKEŚA ŚĀSTRĪ and ŚIVA CHANDRA GUI, A descriptive catalogue of sanskrit manuscripts in the library of the Calcutta sanskrit college. . . .

Lexicography manuscripts. Calcutta 1904. pp.31.
[43.]

also issued as part of vol.viii of the authors' A descriptive catalogue of sanskrit manuscripts in the library of the Calcutta sanskrit college, *1904.*

MAHĀMAHOPĀDHYĀYA HARAPRASĀDA ṢĀSTRĪ, A catalogue of palm-leaf & selected paper mss. belonging to the Durbar library, Nepal. [Notices of sanskrit mss. (extra number):] Calcutta 1905–1915. pp.[iii].xxxii[*sic*, lxxxii].32.[273].20.23 + [iii].xxxv.[293]. [1000.]

ALPHABETICAL list of palm-leaf manuscripts, paper manuscripts and parabaiks (pali, burmese and sanskrit) preserved in the Manuscript department of the Bernard Free library, Rangoon. [Rangoon] 1906. ff.60. [1333.]

A[NTOINE] CABATON, Catalogue sommaire des manuscrits sanscrits et pālis. . . . 1er fascicule.— Manuscrits sanscrits. 1907. pp.[v].189. [1102.]

F. OTTO SCHRADER, A descriptive catalogue of the sanskrit manuscripts in the Adyar library (Theosophical society). Vol.1. — Upaniṣads. Madras 1908. pp.xiii.316. [500.]

THEODOR AUFRECHT [vol.ii: JULIUS JOLLY], Die sanskrit-handschriften der K. hof- und staatsbibliothek in München. Catalogus codicum manuscriptorum Bibliothecae regiae monacensis (vol.i, parts 5, 6): München 1909, 1912. pp.viii.228+ xii.85. [800.]

[FRIEDRICH OTTO SCHRADER, *ed.*], A preliminary list of the saṃskrt and prākrt manuscripts in the Adyar library (Theosophical society). Madras 1910. pp.viii.279. [5270.]
—— [another edition]. A catalogue of the sanskrit manuscripts in the Adyar library. [Edited by Alladi Mahadeva Ṣāstri]. 1926–1928. pp.[xii]. 257+xv.[242].xiv. [3825.]

A TRIENNIAL catalogue of manuscripts collected . . . for the Government oriental manuscripts library. . . . Part 1. Sanskrit Madras.
  i. 1910–1913. By M. Raṅgāchārya and S[ri] Kuppuswami [Kuppu-Svāmi] Ṣāstri. 1913. pp.[iv].4.8.xxxix.464 + [ii].465–789 + [ii].791–1705.xviii.44. [810.]
  ii. 1913–1916. By S. Kuppuswami Ṣāstri. 1917. pp.xxv.lxxxiv.1077–1682 + [ii]. 1684–2056 + [ii].2057–2702.lxxxv–clxvi. [1150.]
  iii. 1916–1919. 1922. pp.lxxviii.2704–3234+ [ii].3235–3814 + [ii].3815–4173.xxxix. [960.]
  iv. 1919–1922. 1927. pp.[ii].3.ix.lxxxix.4175– 4755 + [ii].4757–5375 + [ii].5377–6116. xl. [1261.]
  v. 1922–1925. 1931–1932. pp.[iii].2.7.xliv. 6117–6326 + [ii].6327–6475 + [ii].6477– 6910.xxiii. [886.]

  vi. 1925–1928. 1935. pp.[ii].iii.xx.6911–7414. xi. [339.]
  vii. 1928–1931. By S. Kuppuswami Sāstri and P. P. Subrahmanya Sāstri. 1937. pp.[iii].iii.vii.iii.7415–7599.vi. [152.]
  viii. 1931–1934. By P. P. Subrahmanya Sastri 1939. pp.xxiv.7601–7658. [168.]
  ix. 1934–1937. By P. P. Subrahmanya Sastri and A. Sankaran. 1943. pp.xliv.7659–7684. [296.]
  x. 1937–1940. By T. Chandrasekharan. 1950. pp.xxx.7865–8139 + xxxiii.8140–8142 + xxx.8143–8730. [1500.]
  xi. 1940–1943. 1958. pp.xx.8731–8837. [221.]
no more published?

N. D. MIRONOV, Каталогъ индійскихъ рукописей. Выпускъ i. Академия наук СССР: Азіатскій музей: Каталоги (vol.i): Петроградъ 1914. pp.vi.360. [466.]
no more published.

DESCRIPTIVE catalogue of the government collections of manuscripts deposited at the Deccan college, Poona (Bhandarkar oriental research institute).
  i. Compiled by the assistant to the professor of sanskrit. Vedic literature. 1. Saṃhitās and Brāhmaṇas. 1916. pp.xlvi.420. [566.]
  ii. Compiled by Shripad Krishna Belvalkar. Grammar. 1. Vedic and Pāṇinīya. Poona 1938. pp.xvi.348. [435.]
  iii. Dharmasastra. Edited by Madhukar Mangesh Patkar. 1966. pp.viii.137. [515.]
  ix. Compiled by Sumitra Mangesh Katre. Vedānta. 1949–55. pp.xix.478+xix.420. [822.]
  xii. Compiled by Parashuram Krishna Gode. Alaṁkāra, saṁgita and nātya. 1936. pp.xxi. 486. [347.]
  xiii.1,2. Kāvya. 1940–42. pp.xxiii. 490+xxi. 523. [794.]
  xiii,3. Stotras, etc. 1950. pp.xxiii.515. [795– 1313.]
  xiv. Nātaka. 1937. pp.xix.303. [240.]
  xvi,1. Compiled by Har Dutt Sharma. 1939. pp.xxiii.418. [320.]
  xvii. Compiled by Hiralal Rasikdas Kapadia. Jaina literature and philosophy. (Agamika literature.) 1935–54. pp.xxiii. 390+xxv. 363.24+xxxv.530+xxiii.280+6.xxii. 298. [1463.]
  xviii,1. Jaina literature and philosophy. Logic, metaphysics, etc. 1952. pp.xxvii. 498. [305.]
  xix,1. Jaina literature and philosophy. 1957. pp.xxvii.367. [354.]

A DESCRIPTIVE catalogue of sanskrit manuscripts in the government collection under the care of the Asiatic society of Bengal (—in the collection of the

Asiatic society). By Haraprasāda Shāstrī). Calcutta.

    i. Buddhist mss. 1917. pp.ix.199. [119.]

    ii. Vedic. 1923. pp.x.222–1455. [1726.]

    iii. Smṛti. 1925. pp.lxxiv.1066. [1232.]

    iv. History and geography. 1923. pp.vi.123. [65.]

    v. Purāṇa. 1928. pp.ccxvii.897. [1080.]

    vi. Vyākaraṇa. 1931. pp.cccxxxix.521. [732.]

    vii. Kāvya. 1934. pp.xx.653. [869.]

    viii. Tantra. 1939–46. pp.iii.892. [1022.]

    ix. Bengali (and assamese mss.). 1941. pp.xi. 433+x.116. [553.]

    x. Astronomy. 1945–8. pp.614. [596.]

    xi. Philosophy. 1957. pp.xlix.998. [1471.]

    xiv. Kāma-śāstra [etc.]. 1955. pp.ix.62. [89.]

L. P. TESSITORI, Bardic and historical survey of Rajputana. A descriptive catalogue of bardic and historical manuscripts. Asiatic society of Bengal: Bibliotheca indica (n.s.1409, 1412, 1413): Calcutta 1917–18. pp.[ii].69+[ii].94+[iii].87. [77.]
Limited to Jodhpur and Bikaner; no more published.

R. ANANTA KRISHNA SASTRY, Kavindracharya list, edited with introduction. Gaekwad's oriental series (no.xvii): Baroda 1921. pp.xv.3.2.34. [2192.]

T. R. GAMBIER-PARRY, A catalogue of the sanskrit manuscripts purchased for the administrators of the Max Müller memorial fund. Oxford 1922. pp.iv.62. [100.]

GOPI NATH KAVIRAJ, A descriptive catalogue of sanskrit manuscripts deposited in the Government sanskrit library, Sarasvati Bhavana, Benares. Allahabad.

    i. Pūrva-Mimāmsa. 1923.
no more published?

C[HIMANLĀL] D[ĀHYĀBHĀĪ] DALĀL, A catalogue of manuscripts in the jain bhandars at Jesalmere. ... Edited ... by Lālchandra Bhagawāndās Gāndhi. Gaekwad's oriental series (vol.xxi): Baroda 1923. pp.[ii].70.101. [2200.]

THE BUDDHA-GAYA library. Calcutta &c. 1925. pp.[ii].47. [500.]

H. D. VELANKAR [HARIDĀSA VELANKAR], A descriptive catalogue of sānskṛta and prākṛta manuscripts in the library of the Bombay branch of the Royal asiatic society. Bombay 1925–1930. pp.4.147+149-379+[ii].381-500. [2100.]

GAJANAN K. SHRIGONDEKAR and K. S. RAMAS-WAMI SHASTRI SIROMANI, A descriptive catalogue of manuscripts in the Central library (*vol. ii:* Oriental institute), Baroda. Gaekwad's oriental series (nos.xxvii, xcvi): Baroda 1925–42. pp.xxviii. 264+xviii.396. [929.]

RĀI BAHĀDUR HĪRĀ-LĀL, Catalogue of sanskrit & prakrit manuscripts in the Central Provinces and Berar. Nagpur 1926.pp.[v].5.lv.808.8. [8185.]

A CATALOGUE of the sanskrit manuscripts in the Adyar library. By the pandits of the library. [Madras] 1926–8. pp.ix.252.v.+xv.242.iii. [17,529.]

KASHIPRASAD [KĀṢĪ-PRASĀDA] JĀYASWĀL and ANANTAPRASAD [ANANTA-PRASĀDA] ṢĀSTRĪ, A descriptive catalogue of manuscripts in Mithila. Bihar and Orissa research society: Patna.

    i. Smṛti manuscripts 1927. pp.[v].xv.[536]. xv.xvii. [455.]

    ii. Literature, prosody & rhetoric manuscripts. 1933. pp.[ii].19.34.82.185. [300.]

    iii. Jyotiḥsāstra. Astronomy, mathematics, & astrology manuscripts. 1937. pp.[vi].xiv. [iv].526.xxxii. [437.]

    iv. Vedic mss. 1940. pp.[vi].2.5.viii.[iii]. 353.7. [211.]
no more published.

P. P. S. SASTRI [P. P. SUBRAHAMANYA ṢĀSTRĪ], A descriptive catalogue of the sanskrit manuscripts in the Tanjore mahāraja Serfoji's Sarasvatī Mahāl library. Srirangam.

    i-ii. Vedas. 1928. pp.[ii].xi.476.3 + [ii].ix.v. 477–929.8. [1426.]

    iii. Vedas-Vedāṅgas. 1929. pp.[xii].xl.921– 1470.37. [516.]

    iv. Vedāṅgas – Kalpa-Śrauta. 1929. pp.[iii]. xxvi.1471–1940.10. [414.]

    v. Kalpa-Śrauta. 1929. pp.[iii].xxxiv.1941– 2403.20. [420.]

    vi-vii. Kāvyas. 1929–1930. pp.[iii].xxii.2403– 2859.8+[vi].xlvii.2861–3300.24. [1470.]

    viii. Natakas. 1930. pp.[vi].xxxviii.3301– 3715.18. [465.]

    ix. Kośa, Chandas & Alaṅkāra. 1930. pp.[vi]. xxxvi.3717–4113.17. [614.]

    x. Vyākaraṇa. 1930. pp.[iii].xxvii.4115–4438. 18. [646.]

    xi. Vaiśesika, Nyāya, Sāṅkhya & Yoga. 1931. pp.[iii].xxxiv.4439–4985.24. [783.]

    xii. Pūrva-Mīmāmsā and Uttara-Mīmāmsā (Advaita). 1931. pp.[iii].xxii.4987–5488.18. [658.]

    xiii. Uttramīmāmsā (Advaita). 1931. pp. [iii].xxvii.5489–5938.6.15. [360.]

    xiv. Uttramīmāmsā (Viśiṣṭādvaita, Dvaita, Śaiva, Caitanya) & Avaidika. 1932. pp. [iii].xxii.5939–6412.16. [472.]

    xv. Mahābhārata, Gītā, Rāmāyāna, Sivara-hasya, Mahāpurāṇas & Upapurāṇas. 1932. pp.[iii].xxxvii.6413–7220.37. [2405.]

    xvi. Nātya Saṅgīta, Kāmāśāstra, Vaidya & Jyotisa. 1933. pp.[iii].xxxi.7221–7812.26. [1088.]

    xvii. Gṛhyasūtras, Bhāṣyas and Prayogas. 1933. pp.[iii].xxvii.7813–8356.24. [2442.]

    xviii. Vrāta, Āgana & Tantra, Dharma-Sūtra, Bhāṣya & Prayoga. 1934. pp.[iii]. xxii.8357–8755.30. [2632.]

xix. General introduction. Mantra, Stotra & supplement. Indices. 1934. pp.[iii].lviii.254. [7621.]

xx. Supplemental. Mantra Śāstra. 1952. pp.ii.6.9.iii.853.58. [1320.]

HEMCHANDRA GOSWAMI, Descriptive catalogue of assamese manuscripts. [Calcutta] 1930. pp. xxxvi.274. [sanskrit: 77.]

T. R. GAMBIER-PARRY, A catalogue of photographs of sanskrit mss. purchased for the administrators of the Max Müller memorial fund. Oxford 1930. pp.59. [60.]

RICHARD FICK, Keilhorns handschriftensammlung. Verzeichnis der aus Franz Kielhorns nachlass 1908 der Göttinger üniversitätsbibliothek überwiesenen sanskrit-handschriften. Nachrichten von der Gesellschaft der wissenschaften zu Göttingen: Philosophisch-historische klasse: Göttingen 1930. pp.65–94. [91.]
A 'Nachtrag' was published in the 'Nachrichten', 1941.

CATALOGUE of sanskrit manuscripts in the Panjab university library. [Lahore] 1932–1941. pp.xiii.ff.138+pp.xvii.292.65. [7972.]

JEAN FILLIOZAT, État des manuscrits sanscrits, bengalis et tibétains de la Collection Palmyr [Uldéric Alexis] Cordier. Bibliothèque nationale: 1934. pp.19. [350.]

A CATALOGUE of sanskrit manuscripts acquired for and deposited in the Government sanskrit college library, Sarasvati Bhavana, Benares (1918–1930). Prepared under the supervision of Gopi Nath Kaviraj. Vol.1. Allahabad 1934. pp.[iv].132. [1021.]
no more published.

HĪRĀLĀL RASIKDĀS KAPADA [KĀPADIYĀ], Descriptive catalogue of the government collections of manuscripts deposited at the Bhandarkar oriental research institute. . . . Volume XVII. Jaina literature and philosophy. Poona 1935–1936. pp. xxii.390+xxiii.363.24.[643.]

CHINTAHARAN CHAKRAVARTI, A descriptive catalogue of the sanskrit manuscripts in the Vangiya Sahitya Parishat. Sahitya Parishat series (no.85): Calcutta 1935. pp.xlv.270. [1652.]

C[HIMANLĀL] D[ĀHYĀBHĀI] DALĀL, A descriptive catalogue of manuscripts in the jain bhandars at Pattan. Compiled from the notes . . . by Lālchandra Bhagawāndās Gāndhi. Vol. 1. Gaekwad's oriental series (vol.lxxvi): Baroda 1937. pp.72.498.10. [600.]
no more published.

M. S. BASAVALINGAYYA and T. T. ŚRĪNIVĀSAGOPĀLĀCHĀR[YA], A descriptive catalogue of the sans-

krit manuscripts in the Government oriental library. Mysore 1937–44. pp.xxviii.784+ix.216. [816.]

THE SAYEEDIA library, Hyderabad Deccan 1937. (Appendix ii: Short notes on some of the manuscripts in the library, arranged according to the subject). pp.16. [69.]

S. KUPPUSWAMI SASTRI and P. P. SUBRAHMANYA SASTRI. An alphabetical index of sanskrit manuscripts in the Government oriental manuscripts library, Madras. Madras 1938–42. pp.11.609+16. 610–944.+ix.290. [31,412.]

P. P. SUBRAHMANYA SASTRI, Author index of sanskrit manuscripts in the Government oriental manuscripts library, Madras. Madras 1940. pp.x. 127. [5000.]

JEAN FILLIOZAT, Catalogue du fonds sanscrit. Bibliothèque nationale: Département des manuscrits.

i. Nos.1–165.1941. pp.xviii.103.v.

ii. Paris 1970. pp.271.vii. [287.]

CATALOGUE of the sanskrit manuscripts in the Panjab university library. Lahore.

i. 1932. pp.xiv.276. [3000.]

ii. 1941. pp.xvii.292.65. [6169.]

DESCRIPTIVE catalogue of sanskrit manuscripts in the Adyar library. . . . Under the supervision of C. Kunhan Raja [Kuññan Rājā]. Madras.

i. Vedic. By K. Mādhava-Krishṇa Śarmā and C. Kunhan Raja. 1942. pp.xxxvi.415. [1103.]

ii.

iii.

iv. Stotra-s. Parts 1–2. By Pandit K. Parameswara Aithal. [Madras 1968]. pp.xxxv.623+ 404. [3244.] [*Part 2 gives extracts from some of the MSS.*]

v. Kāvya, Nātaka and Alaṅkāra. By H. G. Narahari and C. Kunhan Raja. 1951. pp.xxix.604. [1848.]

vi. Grammar, prosody and lexicography. By V. Krishnamacharya and C. Kunhan Raja. 1947. pp.xxxii.451. [1037.]

ix. Mīmāṁsā and Advaita Vedānta. 1952. pp.xxviii.529. [1360.]

x. Viśiṣṭādvaita and other vedāntas. By Pandit V. Krishnamacharya. Madras 1966. pp.xx.596. [978.]

R. G. HARSHE, A descriptive catalogue of sanskrit mss. of the Vinayak Mahader Gorhe collection. Deccan college postgraduate & research institute: Poona 1942. pp.49. [124.]

G[OVIND] V[ĪNAYAK] DEVASTHALI, A descriptive catalogue of the saṃskṛta and prākṛta manuscripts (Bhagvatsinghji collection & H. M. Bhadkamkar collection) in the library of the university of Bombay. Bombay 1944. pp.10.496+[iv].497–877. [2408.]

WALTER SCHUBRING and GÜNTHER WEIBGEN, Die jaina-handschriften der Preussischen staatsbibliothek. Neuerwerbungen seit 1891. Preussische staatsbibliothek: Verzeichnis der handschriften im Deutschen reich (III.i.1): Leipzig 1944. pp.xiii.647. [1127.]

C. KUNHAN RAJA and K. MADHAVA KRISHNA SARMA, Catalogue of the Anup sanskrit library. Bikaner 1944–8. Fasc.1–5. pp.iv.500. [6682.]
no more published?

V. KRISHNAMACHARYA, Alphabetical index of sanskrit manuscripts in the Adyar library. [Madras]. 1944. pp.vii.210. [7864.]

V. RAGHAVAN, New catalogus catalogorum. An alphabetical register of sanskrit and allied works and authors. Madras university sanskrit series: Madras.

 i. A. 1949. pp.[vii].xxxvi.380. [10,000.]
 —Revised edition. 1958. pp.xliv.505. [15,000.]
 ii. –ĀU. 1966. pp.xl.415. [10,500.]
 iii. Ū–Kartavīrya. 1967. pp.iv.398. [10,000.]
 iv. Kartavīryārjuna–Kṛṣṇasarasvati. 1968. pp.iv.374. [9500.]
 v. Kṛṣṇasahasranāma–Gāyatrīkalpalatā. 1969. pp.iv.359. [9000.]
 vi. Gāyatrikavaca–Cahāgitā 1971. pp.ii.472. [10,500.]
in progress; a preliminary part was issued in 1937.

AMARENDA MOHAN TARKATIRTHA, A brief catalogue of Sanskrit manuscripts in the Postgraduate department of sanskrit. University of Calcutta 1954. pp.vi.147. [1054.]

H. D. VELANKAR, A descriptive catalogue of the sanskrit manuscripts in "the Itchharam Suryaram Desai collection" in the library of the university of Bombay. Bombay 1953. pp.[vi].340. [1756.]

SURANAD KUNJAN PILLAI, Alphabetical index of the sanskrit manuscripts in the university manuscripts library, Trivandrum. Trivandrum.

 i. A to NA. 1957. pp.[vi].241. [6079.]

V. W. KARAMBELKAR, Catalogue of sanskrit manuscripts in the Nagpur university library. Nagpur 1958. pp.ii.519.12. [2500.]

KEDARNATH MAHAPATRA, A descriptive catalogue of sanskrit manuscripts of Orissa in the collection of the Orissa state museum, Bhubaneswar. Bhubaneswar.

 i. Smṛti manuscripts. 1958. pp.viii.xliv.141. xvii. [257.]
no more published.

VISHVA BANDHU and others. Catalogue of VVRI manuscript collection. V.I. publications (159): V.I. series (10): Hoshiarpur 1959. pp.xxvii. 436+481. [8360.]

CATALOGUE & index of manuscripts Shri Bhu vaneshwari Pith, Gondal, Saurashtra, India. 1960. pp.120. [8000.]

P. C. CHOUDHURY, A catalogue of sanskrit manuscripts at the D[epartment of] H[istorical and] A[ntiquarian] S[tudies in Assam]. Gauhati 1961. pp.xxiii.177. [443.]

DESCRIPTIVE catalogue of ancient manuscripts. Vol. 1: Dharmashastra—Smriti—Purana. State Chandradhari museum: Darbhanga 1961. pp.[vi]. 193. [154.]

MUNI PUNYAVIJAYA, Catalogue of palm-leaf manuscripts in the Śāntinātha jain bhaṇḍāra, Cambay. Gaekwad's oriental series (nos.135, 149): Oriental institute: Baroda 1961–6. pp.6. 200+xiii.201–497. [290.]

M. N. BOPARDIKAR, Catalogue of old manuscripts in sanskrit in the collection of the Sanatan Dharma Sabha, Ahmednagar. Ahmednagar 1962. pp.48. [322.]

A DESCRIPTIVE catalogue of the sanskrit manuscripts, acquired for and deposited in the Sanskrit university library (Sarasvati Bhavana), Varanasi, during the years 1791–1950. Compiled by the staff of the manuscripts section. Benares 1953–65. pp.601 + 457 + 231 + 303 + 575 + 255 + 321 + 2.367.28.6 + [i].337.36.4 + [i].241.18.2 + [i].361. 31.5 + ii.293.48. [43,911.]

KIRPAL SINGH, "Akāl Sahāi". A catalogue of persian and sanskrit manuscripts in the Sikh history research department uptil March 31, 1962. Khalsa college: Amritsar 1963. pp.xiii.148. [Sanskrit: 1]

MUNIRĀJA ŚRĪ PUNYAVIJAYAJI, Catalogue of sanskrit and prakrit manuscripts, Muniraja Śrī Puṇavijayaji's collection. Lalbhai Dalpatbhai series (nos.2,5): Ahmedabad 1963–5. pp.12.481. 210+12.482–849.211–424. [6645.]

BIRAJMOHAN TARKA-VEDĀNTATĪRTHA and JAGADISH CHANDRA TARKATĪRTHA, A descriptive catalogue of sanskrit manuscripts in the collections of the Sanskrit college. Calcutta sanskrit college research series (nos.xx,xxxvi): Sanskrit college: Calcutta 1963. pp.ii.144.iv+145–512. [600.]

PRIYABALA SHAH, A descriptive catalogue of sanskrit manuscripts (Gujarat vidya sabha collection). Ahmedabad. 1964. pp.6.505+7.506–968.72. [3000.]

CATALOGUE of sanskrit manuscripts in Deccan college postgraduate and research institute, Poona. Deccan college monograph series (28–30): Poona 1964–6.

    i. Veda manuscripts, ed. by Madhukar Anant Mehendale. pp.viii.70. [280.]

    ii. Kāvya manuscripts, ed. by Narayan Govind Kalelkar. pp.vii.91. [422.]

    iii. Dharmaśāstra, ed. by Madhukar Mangesh Patkar. pp.viii.137. [595.]

WALTER CLAWITER and LORE [SANDER-] HOLZMANN, hrsg. [Zusammengestellt von] ERNST WALDSCHMIDT, Sanskrithandschriften aus den Turfanfunden. Verzeichnis der orientalischen handschriften Deutschlands (band X, 1–3). Wiesbaden, 1965–71. pp.xxxv.368+x.87+x.286. [1014.]

PADMASHRI MUNI JINAVIJAYA, A catalogue of sanskrit and prakrit manuscripts in the Rajasthan oriental research institute (Jodhpur collection). Rajasthan puratana granthamala (nos.71 etc.): Jodhpur 1963–8. pp.16.86.373.159+16.70.321.99 + 14.72.349.202 + 14.39.203.116. + 16.84.429. 98+8.99.533.175. [8486.]

DAULAT RAM JUYAL, A catalogue of manuscripts in the Akhila bharatiya sanskrit parishad, Lucknow. Edited by a board of editors. Lucknow [1963]. pp.xxiv.543. [1304.]

    — — Second series. 1970. pp.xv.275+xii.527. [1698.]

SEIREN MATSUNAMI, A catalogue of the sanskrit manuscripts in the Tokyo university library. Suzuki research foundation: Tokyo 1965. pp.ix. 387. [518.]

UMESHA MISHRA, Descriptive catalogue of sanskrit manuscripts in Ganganatha Jha research institute, Allahabad. Allahabad 1967. pp.x.387+ 388–929. [4593.]

A DESCRIPTIVE catalogue of sanskrit manuscripts in the library of the Asiatic society (the Indian museum and the Asiatic society collections). Calcutta.

    iv. Philosophy. Part ii. Pūrva-mimaṁsa. Compiled by Pulinbihari Chakravarti, revised by Narendra Chandra Vedantatirtha. 1969. pp.[viii].92. [148.]

in progress?

MUNI SHRI PUNYAVIJAYAJI, New catalogue of sanskrit and prakrit manuscripts, Jesalmer collection. L. D. Institute of indology: Ahmedabad 1972. pp.vi.471. [2697.]

B. RAMA RAO, A check-list of sanskrit medical manuscripts in India. Central council for research in indian medicine and homoeopathy: New Delhi 1972. pp.viii.102. [1082.]

2. General

ERASMUS [RASMUS] NYERUP, Catalogus librorum sanskritanorum, qvos bibliothecæ Universitatis havniensis vel dedit vel paravit Nathanael Wallich. Hafniæ 1821. pp.vi.53. [100.]

FRIEDRICH [VON] ADELUNG, Versuch einer literatur der sanskrit-sprache. St. Petersburg 1830. pp. xv.259. [350.]

    — — An historical sketch of sancrit literature. From the german . . . [by D. A. Talboys]. Oxford 1832. pp.xviii.234. [400.]

    — — Zweite . . . ausgabe. Bibliotheca sanscrita. Literature der sanskrit-sprache. 1837. pp.xxii.431. [1650.]

JOHANN GILDEMEISTER, Bibliothecae sanskritae sive recensvs librorvm sanskritorvm hvcvsqve typis vel lapide exscriptorvm critici specimen. Bonnae ad Rhenvm 1847. pp.xiv.192. [603.]
a copy in the Bodleian library contains ms. notes by Franz Kielhorn and H. G. C.

J. WENGER, A catalogue of sanskrit and bengalee publications printed in Bengal. Selections from the records of the Bengal government (no.xli): Calcutta 1865. pp.[iii].iii.60. [1500.]

JAMES D'ALWIS, A descriptive catalogue of sanskrit, pali, & sinhalese literary works of Ceylon. . . . Vol.1. Colombo 1870. pp.xxxi.244. [23.]
no more published.

A CLASSIFIED catalogue of sanskrit works in the Saraswati bhandaram library of his highness the maha raja of Mysore. Bangalore 1870. pp.[iii].23. [608.]

    — A supplementary catalogue. Bombay 1874. pp.[ii].9.
a revised version of certain entries which appear in the earlier catalogue.

[JOHN ROBINSON], Catalogue of sanskrit and bengali books procured under the dispatch of the Secretary of state, no55, dated the 24th July 1863. [Calcutta 1871]. pp.43. [300.]

CATALOGUE of sanskrit and pali books in the British museum. By Ernst Haas. 1876. pp.viii. 188. [4000.]

    — Catalogue of sanskrit, pali, and prakrit books . . . acquired during the years 1876–1892. By Cecil Bendall. 1893. pp.x.coll.624. [4000.]

    — A supplementary catalogue . . . 1892–1906. By L[ionel] D[avid] Barnett. 1908. pp.vii.coll. 1096. [7500.]

    — A supplementary catalogue . . . 1906–1928. 1928. pp.vi.coll.1694. [7500.]

VISHVANÁTH NÁRÁYAN MANDLIK [VIṢVANĀTHA NĀRĀYAṆA MAṆḌALIKA] and ARDASEER FRAMJEE MOOS [ARDESHER FRĀMJĪ MŪS], Catalogue of manuscripts and books belonging to the Bhau Daji

memorial. Bombay 1882. pp.[iii].147.clx. [1500.]
this collection is now in the library of the Royal asiatic society, Bombay branch.

THEODOR AUFRECHT, Catalogus catalogorum. An alphabetical register of sanskrit works and authors. German oriental society [Deutsche morgenländische gesellschaft]: Leipzig 1891–1903. pp.viii.795+iv.239+iv.62. [40,000.]
reprinted Wiesbaden, 1962.
— — New catalogus catalogorum. Prepared by V. Raghavan. Editor-in-chief C. Kunhan Raja. Madras university: Sanskrit series (no.18 &c.): [Madras].

  i. A. 1949. pp.[vii].xxxvi.380. [10,000.]
  —Revised edition. 1968. pp.xliv. 505. [15,000.]
  ii. Ā–U. 1966. pp.xl.415. [10,500.]
  iii. Ū–Kartavīrya. 1967. pp.iv. 398. [10,000.]
  iv. Kartavīryārjuna–Kṛṣṇasarasvatī. 1968. pp. iv.374. [9500.]
  v. Kṛṣṇasahasranāma–Gāyatrīkalpalatā. 1969 pp.iv.359. [9000.]
  vi. Gāyatrikavaca–Cahāgītā. 1971. pp.ii. 412. [10,500.]
in progress; a preliminary part was issued in 1937.

CECIL BENDALL, Catalogue of sanskrit, pali, and prakrit books . . . acquired during the years 1876–1892. British museum: 1893. pp.x.coll.624. [5000.]

[REINHOLD ROST], Catalogue of the library of the India office. Vol.II.—Part I. Sanskrit books. 1897. pp.[iv].294. [4500.]
[—] — Revised edition. . . . By Prāṇā-Natha . . . and Jitendra-Bimala [Vimala] Chaudhurī.
  i. A–G. 1938. pp.xxiv.990. [10,000.]
  ii. H–K. 1951. pp.[iii].991–1374. [3500.]
  iii. K–R. 1953. pp.viii.1375–2220. [8000.]
  iv. S–Z. 1957. pp.[iii].2221–3149. [8000.]

KUNJA VIHARI KĀVYATĪRTHA, Catalogue of printed books and manuscripts in Sanskrit belonging to the oriental library of the Asiatic society of Bengal. Calcutta [1899–]1904. pp.[vi].320.25. [5000.]

MONTGOMERY SCHUYLER, A bibliography of the sanskrit drama. Columbia university: Indo-iranian series (vol.iii): New York 1906. pp.xi.105. [750.]

CATALOGUE of sanskrit, pali and prakrit books. Volume I. A–G. National library: Calcutta 1951. pp.[ii].vi.333. [4000.]
  Volume II. H–Q. 1956. ff.ii. pp.427. [5000.]
  in progress?

A DESCRIPTIVE analysis of the Kashmir series of texts & studies. Research and publications department: Jammu & Kashmir govt.: Srinagar [1952?]. pp.60. [87.]

GOPINATH KAVIRAJ, Gleanings from the history and bibliography of the Nyaya-Vaisesika literature. Calcutta [1961]. pp.[iii].85. [65.]

S. N. SEN, A bibliography of sanskrit works on astronomy and mathematics. Part I: Manuscripts, texts, translations & studies. National commission for the compilation of history of sciences in India: Source materials series: National institute of sciences of India: New Delhi 1966. pp.xxiii.258. [1500.]

DAVID PINGREE, Census of the exact sciences in Sanskrit. Series A, volume I. American philosophical society (Memoirs, vol.81): Philadelphia 1970. pp.vii.60. [3100.]

3. Individual writers or works

Appayadīkṣitācārya

[KRISHNA ŚĀSTRI], Bibliography of Sankya-yoga-samuććaya works. [Adyar library:] Madras 1906. pp.[ii].18. [152.]

Guṇāḍhya

[S. OLDENBURG], Матеріалы для изслѣдованія индійскаго сказочнаго сборника Bṛhatkathā. [St. Petersburg 1888]. pp.10. [35.]

Kālidāsa

[NATALYA MIKHAILOVNA IVANOVA], Калидаса. Био-библиографический указатель. Всесоюзная государственная библиотека иностранной литературы: Писатели зарубежных стран: Москва 1957. pp.31. [200.]

Saddharmapuṇḍarīkasūtra

AKIRA YUYAMA, A bibliography of the sanskrit texts of the Saddharmapuṇḍarīka-sūtra. Oriental monograph series (no.5): Faculty of asian studies: Australian national university: Canberra 1970. pp.xxxv.115. [175.]

iv. Pali literature

JAMES D'ALWIS, A descriptive catalogue of sanskrit, pali, & sinhalese literary works of Ceylon. . . . Vol.I. Colombo 1870. pp.xxxi.244. [23.]
no more published.

CATALOGUE of sanskrit and pali books in the British museum. By Ernst Haas. 1876. pp.viii.188. [4000.]
— Catalogue of sanskrit, pali, and prakrit books . . . acquired during the years 1876–1892. By Cecil Bendall. 1893. pp.x.coll.624. [4000.]
— A supplementary catalogue . . . 1872–1906. By L[ionel] D[avid] Barnett. 1908. pp.vii.coll. 1096. [7500.]

— A supplementary catalogue ... 1906–1928. 1928. pp.vii.coll.1694. [7500.]

CATALOGUE of sanskrit, pali and prakrit books. Volume I. A–G National library: Calcutta 1951. pp.[ii].vi.333. [4000.]
Volume II. H–Q.1956.ff.ii.pp.427. [5000.]

Pali manuscripts

[LOUIS DE ZOYSA], Catalogue of pali, sinhalese' & sanskrit manuscripts, in the Ceylon government oriental library. Colombo 1876. pp.26. [209.]

E. FORCHHAMMER, Report on the literary work performed on behalf of government during the year 1879–1880. Rangoon 1882. pp.[ii].14.xl. [1250.]
— — [Another edition.] pp.8.xx.
an account of the discovery and transcription of Pali, Burmese, Sanskrit and Mon mss.

HERMANN OLDENBERG, Catalogue of pali mss. in the India office library, being appendix to the Journal of the Pali text society for 1882. London 1882. pp.59–128. [110.]

LOUIS DE ZOYSA, A catalogue of páli, sinhalese, and sanskrit manuscripts in the temple libraries of Ceylon. Colombo 1885. pp.iv.31. [750.]
limited to pali writings.

[A. HALY], Catalogue of the Colombo museum library. Part I. Páli, sinhalese, and sanscrit manuscripts. Colombo 1892. pp.[ii].18. [250.]
— — Catalogue of pali ... manuscripts in the Colombo museum library. 2nd edition, revised and enlarged. [By Henry M. Gunasekara]. pp.xiv. 47. [500.]

V. FAUSBÖLL, Catalogue of the Mandalay mss. in the India office library. Reprinted from the Journal of the Pali text society. Woking, London 1897. pp.52. [176.]

ALPHABETICAL list of palm-leaf manuscripts, paper manuscripts and parabaiks (pali, burmese and sanskrit) preserved in the Manuscript department of the Bernard Free library, Rangoon. [Rangoon] 1906. ff.60. [1333.]

A[NTOINE] CABATON, Catalogue sommaire des manuscrits sanscrits et pālis. ... 2e fascicule. Manuscrits pālis. 1908. pp.[iii].195. [863.]

CATALOGUE of pâli and burmese books and manuscripts belonging to the library of the late king of Burma and found in the palace at Mandalay in 1886. Rangoon 1910. pp.[115]. [1000.]

LIST of the pâli and sanskrit books and manuscripts in the Vajirañāna national library. With a preface by H.R.H. Prince Damrong Rajanubhab. [1921].

E. W. ADIKARAM, Descriptive catalogue of the pāli manuscripts in the Adyar library. The Adyar library series (no.62): [Madras 1947].pp.xxxi.111. [47.]

GEORGE COEDÈS, Catalogue des manuscrits en pāli, laotien et siamois provenant de la Thailande. Catalogue of oriental manuscripts, xylographs etc. in danish collections (vol.2, part 2): Bibliothèque royale de Copenhague 1966. pp.x.116. [115.]

ALAKA CHATTOPADHYAYA, MRINALKANTI GANGOPADHYAYA, DEBIPRASAD CHATTOPADH-YAYA, Catalogue of indian (buddhist) texts in tibetan translation. Kanjur and Tanjur (alphabetically arranged). Indo–tibetan studies: Calcutta 1972. pp.xv.535. [3000.]

Prakrit literature

[bibliographies dealing with both sanskrit and prakrit literature are entered only under Sanskrit.]

ARTHUR BERRIEDALE KEITH, Catalogue of prākrit manuscripts in the Bodleian library. Oxford 1911. pp.viii.coll.50. pp.51–53. [68.]

Saurāshtran literature

L[IONEL] D[AVID] BARNETT, Catalogue of saurāshtra books in the library of the British museum. 1960. pp.12. [19.]

v. Modern languages

Assamese

[JAMES FULLER BLUMHARDT], Catalogue of assamese books. [British museum: 1894]. coll.10. [75.]
reissued in 1906.

J[AMES] F[ULLER] BLUMHARDT, Catalogue of the library of the India office. Vol.II.—Part IV. Bengali, oriya, and assamese books. 1905. pp.viii.354. [Assamese: 125.]
the supplement of 1923 contains no assamese books.

JAMES FULLER BLUMHARDT, Catalogue of the bengali and assamese manuscripts in the library of the india office. 1924. pp.[iii].21. [assamese: 3].

HEMCHANDRA GOSWAMI, Descriptive catalogue of assamese manuscripts. [Calcutta] 1930. pp. xxxvi.274. [assamese: 156.]
also includes sanskrit manuscripts.

Badaga

L[IONEL] D[AVID] BARNETT, A catalogue of the kannada, badaga, and kurg books. British museum: 1910. pp.iv.coll.278. [Badaga: 5.]

Bengali

i. *Manuscripts*
ii. *General*
iii. *Individual writers*

i. *Manuscripts*

JAMES FULLER BLUMHARDT, Catalogue of the bengali and assamese manuscripts in the library of the India office. 1924. pp.[vii].21. [bengali: 27.]

BASANTARANJAN RAY, BASANTAKUMAR CHATTERJEE and (*vols. ii, iii:* Manindra Mohan Bose). Descriptive catalogue of bengali manuscripts. University: Calcutta 1926–30. pp.xxxvii.252+xxvi.253–491+x.492–791. [1150.]

JEAN FILLIOZAT, État des manuscrits sanscrits, bengalis et tibétains de la collection Palmyr [Uldéric Alexis] Cordier. Bibliothèque nationale: 1934. pp.19. [350.]

MANINDRAMOHAN BOSE [MANĪNDRA-MOHANA VASU], A general catalogue of bengali manuscripts in the library of the university of Calcutta. Calcutta.
    i. 1940. pp.vii.180. [2111.]

ABDUL KARIM ['ABD AL-KARIM] and AHMAD SHARIF, A descriptive catalogue of bengali manuscripts in Munshi Abdul Karim's collection. Asiatic society of Pakistan: Publication (no.3): Dacca 1960. pp.xxviii.589.xxix. [584.]

ii. *General*

J[AMES] LONG, Returns relating to native printing presses and publications in Bengal. A return of the names and writings of 515 persons connected with bengal literature ... chiefly during the last fifty years. Calcutta 1855. pp.66. [1300.]

J[AMES] LONG, A descriptive catalogue of bengali works, ... which have issued from the press, during the last sixty years. Calcutta 1855. pp.[vi].108. [1400.]

a reprint was published as an appendix, with a separate titlepage, to Dīneśachandra Sena, বঙ্গভাষা ও সাহিত্য, *Calcutta 1928.*

J[AMES] LONG, Returns relating to publications in the bengali language, in 1857. Selections from the records of the Bengal government (no.xxxii): Calcutta 1859. pp.[iii].xiv.83. [322.]

also contains A. J. Arbuthnot, 'Books and pamphlets printed and published in the town of Madras, during the year 1855' [188].

J. WENGER, A catalogue of sanscrit and bengalee publications printed in Bengal. Selections from the records of the Bengal government (no.xli): Calcutta 1865. pp.[iii].iii.60. [1500.]

[JOHN ROBINSON], Catalogue of sanskrit and bengal books procured under the despatch of the Secretary of state, no.55, dated the 24th July 1863. [Calcutta 1871]. pp.43. [300.]

J. F. BLUMHARDT, Catalogue of bengali printed books in the library of the British museum. 1886. pp.xi.151. [2500.]
    — — A supplementary catalogue. 1910. pp.[v]. coll.470. [3000.]
    — — Second supplementary catalogue. By J. F. Blumhardt and J. V. S. Wilkinson. 1939. pp.[iv].coll.680. [4000.]

J. F. BLUMHARDT, Catalogue of the library of the India office. Vol.II—part IV. Bengali, oriya, and assamese books. 1905. pp.viii.354. [bengali: 5000.]
    — — Supplement, 1906–1920. Bengali books. 1923. pp.[iii].523. [6000.]

AUTHOR catalogue of printed books in bengali language. Imperial library: Calcutta.
    i. A–F. [By Nanda Lal Dutt]. 1941. pp.[ii].v.282. [2500.]
    ii. G–L. 1943. pp.[ii].321. [3000.]
    iii. M–R. [By K. B. Roy Choudhury]. 1959. pp.[iii].491. [4000.]
    iv. S–Z. 1941. pp.[ii].445. [13,000.]

INDIRA SARKAR, Social thought in Bengal [1757–1947). A bibliography of bengali men and women of letters. Calcutta 1949. pp.xv.109.ix. [1000.]

A BIBLIOGRAPHY of indology ... National library: Calcutta.
    iii. Bengali language and literature. Compiled by S. C. Dasgupta.
    i. Early period. 1964. pp.xii.390. [1769.]

SIBADAS CHAUDHURI, Catalogue of bengali printed books in the library of the Asiatic society. Calcutta 1968. pp.[iv].318]. [large number.]

iii. *Individual writers*

Ravīndra Nātha Thākura

LIST of references on Rabindranath Tagore (Ravindranatha Thakura). Library of Congress: Washington 1915. ff.2. [27]★

ETHEL M. KITCH, Rabindranath Tagore. ... A bibliography. Oberlin college: Library bulletin (no.6): Oberlin 1922. pp.14. [250.]

L. A. STRIZHEVSKAYA, Рабиндранат Тагор. Всесоюзная государственная библиотека иностранной литературы: Писатели зарубежных стран: Москва 1961. pp.175. [1162.]

VIRGIL CÂNDEA, Tagore en Roumanie. Bibliographie sélective. [Comisia naționalā a Republicii Populare Romîne pentro Unesco. Bucharest 1961]. pp.39. [300.]

[MARIE ROBERTE GUIGNARD *and others*], Rabindranath Tagore, 1861–1941. Bibliothèque nationale: 1961. pp.xii.152. [510.]
an exhibition catalogue.

RABINDRANATH TAGORE. A bibliographical list issued on the occasion of his centenary celebration. رابندرانات طاغور، قائمة القاهرة، ١٩٦١ pp.١٦.20.[75.] [1961].

Sourīndramohana Thākura, sir

LIST of titles, distinctions and works of raja sir Sourindro Mohun Tagore. Calcutta 1895. pp.[ii].xi.36.iii. [60.]

Vinaya-Kumāra Sarkār

[VINAYA-KUMĀRA SARKĀR], Ouvrages en anglais par m. Benoy Kumar Sarkar. Ouvrages en bengali . . . par le même auteur. [*c.*1921]. pp.8. [43.]

BANESVAR DASS [BANĀSVARA DASA], The works of Benoy Sarkar. A chronological statement. Calcutta 1938. pp.[ii].14. [151.]

DILIP MALAKAR, The political and sociological publications and lectures of Bemoy Sarkar, 1926–49. Calcutta 1949. pp.[iv].46. [600.]

Gujarati

J[AMES] F[ULLER] BLUMHARDT, Catalogue of the gujarati & rajasthani manuscripts in the India office library. . . . Revised and enlarged by Alfred Master. Commonwealth relations office: 1954. pp.xi.168. [gujarati: 741.]

J[AMES] F[ULLER] BLUMHARDT, Catalogue of marathi and gujarati printed books in the library of the British museum. 1892. pp.[viii].coll.232. pp.[ii].coll.196. [gujarati: 1500.]
— — A supplementary catalogue. 1915. pp.[v]. coll.256.336. [2500.]

J. F. BLUMHARDT, Catalogue of the library of the India office. Vol.II — Part V. Marathi and gujarati books. 1908. pp.ix.320. [gujarati: 2000.]

Hindi

i. *Manuscripts*
ii. *General*

i. *Manuscripts*

LIST of sanskrit, jaina and hindi manuscripts purchased by order of government and deposited in the Sanskrit college. Benares, . . . 1897[–1918]. Allahabad.
details of this work are entered under Sanskrit literature above.

J. F. BLUMHARDT, Catalogue of the hindi, panjabi and hindustani manuscripts in the library of the British museum. 1899. pp.xii.85.91. [250.]

SYAMSUNDAR DAS [ṢYĀMASUNDARA DĀSA], Annual [Triennial] report on the search for hindi manuscripts. Government of the United Provinces: Allahabad.

1900. 1903. pp.[vii].138. [156.]
1901. 1904. pp.[v].104. [136.]
1902. 1906. pp.[v].95. [302.]
1903. 1905. pp.[v].96. [186.]
1904. 1907. pp.[v].78.7.2.
1905. 1908. pp.[iii].97. [98.]
1906. 1908. pp.[ii].4.xv. [250.]
1906–1908. 1912. pp.[vii].383. [1000.]
1909–1911. By Shyam Behari Misra [Syām Binārī Misra]. 1914.
1912–1914. 1924. pp.[i].279. [482.]
xi.
xii. 1923–5. By Hiralal. 1944. pp.976+977–1600.176.xix. [1111.]
xiii. 1926–8. [*In hindi.*]
xiv. 1929–31. [*In hindi.*]
xv. 1932–4. [*In hindi.*]

G[EORGY] A[LEKSANDROVICH] ZOGRAF, Описание рукописей хинди и панджаби Института востоковедения. Академия наук СССР: Институт востоковедения: Москва 1960. pp.100. [106.]

ii. *General*

[JOSEPH HÉLIODORE] GARCIN DE TASSY, Histoire de la littérature hindoui et hindoustani. . . . Tome I. Biographie et bibliographie. Oriental translation committee [London]: Paris 1839. pp.[iii].xvi.630. [2000.]
— — Seconde édition. 1870–1871. pp.[iii].iv.624 + [iii].608 + [iii].viii.603. [5000.]

J[AMES] F[ULLER] BLUMHARDT, Catalogues of the hindi, panjabi, sindhi, and pushtu printed books in the library of the British museum. 1893. pp.[ix].coll.284.64.24.54. [Hindi: 2000.]
— — A supplementary catalogue of hindi books in the library of the British museum acquired during the years 1893–1912. 1913. pp.[v].coll.472. [3500.]
[—] — L[ionel] D[avid] Barnett, J. F. Blumhardt and J[ames] V[ere] S[tewart] Wilkinson, A second supplementary catalogue of printed books in hindi, bihari (including bhojpuria, kaurmali and maithili), and pahari (including nepali or khaskura, jaunsari, mandali, &c.) in the library of the British museum. 1957. pp.viii.coll.1676. pp.1677–1678. [6000.]

[J. F. BLUMHARDT], Catalogue of hindi books. [India office: Library: 1902]. pp.[ii].ii.151. [2500.]

LIST of hindi accessions. India office: Library: 1951 &c.★
in progress.

GIRIJANATH BHATTACHARYA, A catalogue of printed hindi books in the library of the Asiatic society. Calcutta 1967. pp.[viii].xvii.50. [350.]

GORDON C. ROADARMEL, A bibliography of english source materials for the study of 19th and 20th century hindi literature. New York 1968. ff.[iii].68. [1148.]

PITAMBAR NARAIN and S. BHASKARAN NAIR, Hindī-sāhitya-sārinī or Hindi bibliography, being a universal, classified and scientifically arranged record of hindi books published up to the end of 1964. Vishveshvaranand institute: Hoshiarpur 1971. pp.xiv.908. [3000.]

Kanarese

i. *Manuscripts*
ii. *General*

i. *Manuscripts*

ALPHABETICAL index of manuscripts in the Government oriental mss. library, Madras. Kanarese. Madras 1893. pp.[ii].48. [750.]
— [another edition]. An alphabetical index of kanarese manuscripts in the Government [&c.]. By ... Kuppuswāmi Śāstri and (vol.ii) T. Chandrasekharan and the staff of the library. 1929–52. pp.[ii].79+ii.51. [3369.]

S. KUPPUSWAMI SASTRI and (vols. ii,iii, P. P. SUBRAHMANYA ŚĀSTRI; vol.iv, A. SANKARAN; vols. v,vi,vii, T. CHANDRASEKHARAN), A descriptive catalogue of the kanarese (–kannada) manuscripts in the Government oriental manuscripts library, Madras. Madras 1934. pp.vi.262.5+iv.2.3.263–506.9 + ii.xviii.507–794 + xxiv.795–1154 + xii. 1155–1632+xvi.1364–1632+viii.226. [1405.]

ii. *General*

L. D. BARNETT, A catalogue of the kannada, badaga, and kurg books. British museum: 191. pp.iv.coll.278. [kanada: 2000.]

A CATALOGUE of printed kannada works in the Oriental research institute, Mysore. Mysore 1951. pp.137. [3395.]

A SELECT list of kanada books 1824–1956. Karnatak university: Library: [Dharwar 1956]. ff.77. [1500.]*

Kurg

L[IONEL] D[AVID] BARNETT. A catalogue of the kannada, badaga, and kurg books. British museum: 1910. pp.iv.coll.278. [kurg: 4.]

Malayalam

i. *Manuscripts*
ii. *General*

i. *Manuscripts*

ALPHABETICAL index of manuscripts in the Government mss. library, Madras. Malayalam. Madras 1893. pp.5. [75.]

S. KUPPUSWAMI SASTRI, An alphabetical list of malayalam manuscripts in the Government oriental manuscripts library, Madras. Madras 1930. pp.22. [344.]

P. K. NARAYANA PILLAI, Index of malayalam manuscripts. University of Travancore: Trivandrum malayalam series (no.77): Trivandrum 1951. pp.[ii].ii.163. [4374.]

CHELNAT ACHYUTA MENON, Catalogue of the malayalam manuscripts in the India office library. 1954. pp.26. [107.]

P. P. SUBRAHMANYA SASTRI and (vol.ii) T. CHANDRASEKHARAN, A descriptive catalogue of the malayalam manuscripts in the Government oriental manuscripts library, Madras. Madras 1940–50. pp.xvi.322+iv.323–339. [368.]

T. CHANDRASEKHARAN, A triennial catalogue of malayalam manuscripts collected (from 1946 to 1957) for the Government oriental manuscripts library, Madras.
i. pp.x.176. 1959. [215.]
no more published?

ii. *General*

ALBERTINE GAUR, Catalogue of malayalam books in the British museum, with an appendix listing the books in brahui, gondi, kui, malto, oraon (kuru*kh*), toda and tulu. London 1971. pp.xxvii.587. [5000.]

Marathi

i. *Manuscripts*
ii. *General*

i. *Manuscripts*

ALPHABETICAL index of manuscripts in the Government oriental mss. library, Madras. Mahráthi. Madras 1893. pp.16. [250.]

T. B. RAMACHANDRA RAO, A descriptive catalogue of the marathi manuscripts and books in the Tanjore Maharaja Sarfoji's Sarasvati Mahal library, Tanjore. Tanjore 1929–63. pp.10.2.393.18 +3.396–833.45+3.289.47+227. [2677.]

R. S. SHELVANKAR, A report on the modi manuscripts in the Saraswati Mahal library, Tanjore. Madras 1933. pp.vii.59. [27 bundles.]

T. CHANDRASEKHARAN, An alphabetical index of marathi manuscripts in the Government oriental manuscripts library, Madras. Madras 1949. pp.3. 42.20. [922.]

J. F. BLUMHARDT and SADASHIV GOVIND KANHERE [SADĀṢIVA GOVINDA KĀNHERE], Catalogue of the marathi manuscripts in the India office library. Oxford 1950 [1951]. pp.viii.125. [251.]

T. CHANDRASEKHARAN, A descriptive catalogue of the marathi manuscripts in the Government oriental manuscripts library, Madras. Madras 1953–8. pp.ix.289+ii.291–389. [444.]

ii. General

J[AMES] F[ULLER] BLUMHARDT, Catalogue of marathi and gujarati printed books in the library of the British museum. 1892. pp.[viii].coll.322. pp.[ii].coll.196. [marathi: 2000.]
— — A supplementary catalogue. 1915. pp.[v]. coll.256.336. [2000.]

J. F. BLUMHARDT, Catalogue of the library of the India office. Vol.II.—Part v. Marathi and gujarati books.1908. pp.ix.320. [marathi: 2500.]

Oriya

ALPHABETICAL index of manuscripts in the Government oriental mss. library, Madras. Uriya. Madras 1893. pp.[ii].2. [25.]

[J. F. BLUMHARDT], Catalogue of oriya books. [British museum: 1894]. coll.34. [250.]

J. F. BLUMHARDT, Catalogue of the library of the India office. Vol.II.—Part IV. Bengali, oriya, and assamese books. 1905. pp.viii.354. [oriya: 500.]
the supplement of 1923 contains no oriya books.

JAMES FULLER BLUMHARDT, Catalogue of the oriya manuscripts in the library of the India office. 1924. pp.[vii].24. [50.]

Punjabi

i. *Manuscripts*
ii. *General*

i. *Manuscripts*

KIRPAL SINGH, "Akāl Sahāi". A catalogue of punjabi and urdu manuscripts in the Sikh history research department uptil March 31, 1963. Khalsa college: Amritsar 1963. pp.x.251. [punjabi: 287.]

AGHA IFTIKHAR HUSAIN, A catalogue of manuscripts in Paris—urdu, punjabi and sindhi. Urdu development board: Karachi 1967. pp.vi.35.30. [55.]

G[EORGY] A[LEKSANDROVICH] ZOGRAF, Описание рукописей хинди и панджаби Института востоковедения. Академия наук СССР: Институт востоковедения. Москва 1960. pp.100. [106.]

ii. *General*

[see also *Hindi*]

[JAMES FULLER BLUMHARDT], Catalogue of panjabi books. [India office: Library: 1902]. pp. [iii].54. [1000.]

LIONEL DAVID BARNETT, Panjabi printed books in the British Museum; a supplementary catalogue. British Museum: 1961. pp.vi.cols.121. [1500.]

Rajasthani

J[AMES] F[ULLER] BLUMHARDT, Catalogue of the gujarati & rajasthani manuscripts in the India office library. . . . Revised and enlarged by Alfred Master. Commonwealth relations office: 1954. pp.x.167. [rajasthani: 14.]

[RAWATMAL SARASWAT and DINA NATH KHATRI]. Catalogue of the rajasthani manuscripts in the Anup sanskrit library. Bikaner 1947. pp.v.218. [359.]

Sindhi

J. F. BLUMHARDT, Catalogue of the hindi, panjabi, sindhi, and pushtu printed books in the library of the British museum. 1893. pp.[ix].coll. 284.64.24.54. [sindhi: 150.]

[JAMES FULLER BLUMHARDT], Catalogue of sindhi books. [India office: Library: 1902]. pp.[ii].14. [300.]

Tamil

i. *Manuscripts*
ii. *General*

i. *Manuscripts*

[E. H. J. VINSON], Manuscrits tamouls. [Bibliothèque nationale: c.1880]. ff.49. [250.]
proofs of a catalogue; not published?

ALPHABETICAL index of manuscripts in the Government oriental mss. library, Madras. Tamil. Madras 1893. pp.[ii].30. [500.]

ṢEṢAGIRI ṢĀSTRI, Report on a search for sanskrit and tamil manuscripts. Madras.
    i. 1896–1897. 1898. pp.xxxii.281. [309.]
    ii. 1893–1894. 1899. pp.xxxi.359. [338.]

A TRIENNIAL catalogue of manuscripts collected . . . for the Government oriental manuscripts library. . . . Part 2.—Tamil. Madras.
    [i]. 1910–1913. By M. Raṅgāchārya and S[ri] Kuppuswami [Kuppu-Svāmi] Ṣāstri 1913. pp.x.v.3.258.19. [117.]
    ii. 1913–1916. By S. Kuppuswami Ṣāstri. 1917. pp.xv.259–827.liii. [200.]
    iii. 1916–1919. 1923. pp.[iv].xii.2.829–1074. xxii.4. [100.]
    iv. 1919–1922. 1930. pp.[iv].xvii.1075–1369. [ii].xiii.4. [132.]
    v. 1922–1925. 1936. pp.[iv].viii.v.vii.1371–1641.9. [325.]
    vi. 1925–1928. By P. P. Subrahmanya Sastri. 1937. pp.vi.vii.iii.1643–1862.8. [93.]

vii. 1928–1934. 1939. pp.xvii.1863–1938. [103.]

viii. 1935–1943. by Syed Muhammad Fazlullah Sahib Bahadur and T. Chandrasekharan. 1949. pp.xl.1939–2294. [416.]

ix. 1943–1947. 1949. pp.xvi.2295–2430. [132.]

x. 1947–1950. By T. Chandrasekharan. 1960.
pp.lxvii.2432–2908. [732.]

xi.

xii. 1953–1956. 1961. pp.xcv.4032–4858. [1590.]

xiii. 1956–1959. 1961. pp.lxi.684. [2367.]

A DESCRIPTIVE catalogue of the tamil manuscripts in the Government oriental manuscripts
library. Madras.

i. Alphabet-primer, lexicography, grammar and literature. By M. Rangacharya.
1912. pp.xiv.486.xxxi. [511.]

ii. Itihāsa and Purānā, and religion and philosophy (Vaisnavism). By M. Rangacharya
and S. Kuppuswami Sastri. 1916. pp.x.487–
997.xxx. [611.]

iii–iv. Religion and philosophy (Saivism).
By S. Kuppuswami Sastri and P. P.
Subrahmanya. 1927–1937. pp.[ii].vi.999–
1420.xxi+[iii].v.v.1421–1608. viii. [745.]

v. Alchemy, medicine, magic, witchcraft and
supplemental. By P. P. Subrahmanya.
1939. pp.xix.1609–1888. [306.]

vi. 1948. By Syed Muhammad Fazlullah and
T. Chandrasekharan. pp.xxvi.1889–2372.
[552.]

vi. 1948. pp.xxxiv.2373–2553. [225.]

viii. 1953. By T Chandrasekharan. pp.xxi.
2554–2830. [219.]

ix. 1954. pp.xvi.2831–3030. [465.]

x. 1955. pp.xvii.3031–3156. [257.]

xi. 1960. pp.xxix.234. [430.]

no more published?

L. OLGANATHA PILLAY, A descriptive catalogue of
the tamil manuscripts in the Tanjore Maharaja
Sarfoji's Saraswathi Mahal library, Tanjore.
Srirangam 1925–7. pp.xvi.531+xii.326+vii.251.
124. [1292.]

S. KUPPŪ SVĀMI ŚĀSTRI, An alphabetical index
of tamil manuscripts in the Government oriental
manuscripts library. Madras [i].1932. pp.[ii].212.
[4337.]

ii. By T. Chandrasekharan. 1951. pp.vi.
68. [2177.]

iii. 1951. pp.45. [1379.]

T. CHANDRASEKHARAN, Author index of tamil
manuscripts in the Government oriental manuscripts library, Madras (corrected up to 31st
march 1947). Madras 1950. pp.[iii].36. [1000.]

A DESCRIPTIVE catalogue of tamil manuscripts in
mahāmahōpadhyāya dr. V. Swāminathaiyar
library. Adyar, Madras 1956–62. pp.iv.398+iv.
664+iv.712+iv.531. [2326.]

ii. *General*

JOHN MURDOCH, Classified catalogue of tamil
printed books. Christian vernacular education
society: Madras 1865. pp.ci.287. [1750.]

JOHN MURDOCH, Classified catalogue of tamil
christian literature at the close of the nineteenth
century. Christian literature society for India:
1901. pp.iv.46. [750.]

L[IONEL] D[AVID] BARNETT and G[EORGE]
U[GLOW] POPE, A catalogue of the tamil books in
the library of the British museum. 1909. pp.viii.
coll.592. [4000.]

—— Supplementary catalogue ... by L. D.
Barnett. 1931. pp.iii–viii.coll.696. [2500.]

THE MADRAS state tamil bibliography 1867–
1900. Madras 1961–3. pp.xxi.383+xv.384–858+
v.288. [3718.]

A. THIRUMALAIMUTHUSWAMI, A bibliography
on Thirukkural. Madurai 1962. pp.50. [150.]

XAVIER S. THANI NAYAGAM, A reference guide to
tamil studies: *books*. Kuala Lumpur: 1966. pp.viii.
122. [1355.]

RAMA SUBBIAH, Tamil malaysiana: a check list
of tamil books and periodicals published in
Malaysia and Singapore. University of Malaysia
library: Kuala Lumpur 1969. pp.78. [900.]

Telugu

i. *Manuscripts*
ii. *General*

i. *Manuscripts*

ALPHABETICAL index of manuscripts in the
Government oriental mss. library, Madras.
Telugu. Madras 1893. pp.[ii].92. [1500.]

A TRIENNIAL catalogue of manuscripts collected
... for the Government oriental manuscripts
library. ... Part 3.—Telugu. Madras.

[i]. 1910–1913. By M. Rańgāchārya and
S[ri] Kuppuswami [Kuppu-Svāmi] Śāstri.
1913. pp.[ii].xiv.438.xxxii. [140.]

ii. 1913–1916. By S. Kuppuswami Śāstri.
1917. pp.xi.439–830.xiv.xxvii. [160.]

iii. 1916–1919. 1925. pp.[ii].ii.x.vii.831–
1402.25.3.3. [275.]

iv. 1919–1922. 1934. pp.[ii].ii.viii.vi.1403–
1771.23. [155.]

v. 1922–1925 & 1925–1928. By P. P.
Subrahmanya Sastri and A. Sankaran.
1942. pp.xxii. 1773–1931. [97.]

vi. 1928–1941. By Syed Muhammad Fazlullah Sahib Bahadur and T. Chandrasekharan. 1949. pp.xxiii. 1934–2276. [252.]

A DESCRIPTIVE catalogue of the telugu manuscripts in the Government oriental manuscripts
library. Madras.
  i. Prabandha, Itihāsa, Purāṇa, Mahātmaya.
  By M. Rangacharya and S. Kuppuswami
  Sastri. 1915. pp.[iii].415.xxv. [369.]
  ii. Prabandha, Sṛingāraprabandha. By S.
  Kuppuswami Sastri. 1921–7. pp.[iv].417–
  795+iv.797–1064.xvi. [429.]
  iii. 1934. pp.[ii].1065–1240.9. [135.]
  iv. 1936. pp.iv.1241–1542.14. [280.]
  v. Grammar, prosody and lexicography.
  1935. pp.iv.1543–1717.6. [174.]
  vi. Vacanakāvya. By S. Kuppuswami Sastri
  and P. P. Subrahmanya Sastri. 1937. pp.ii.
  1720–1780.3. [71.]
  vii. Śatakas. 1939. pp.xviii. 1782–2051. [367.]
  viii. Yakṣagānam and Dandakam. By P. P.
  Subrahmanya Sastri. 1940. pp.iv.xv.2054–
  2280. [207.]
  ix. Viśiṣṭādvaita, Advaita, Saiva, and Christianity. By A. Sankaran and Syed Muhammad Fazlullah. 1947. pp.xv.2282–2562.
  [233.]
  x. Graṇita and Jyotiṣa. By Syed Muhammad
  Fazullah and T. Chandrasekharan. 1949.
  pp.x.2562–2678. [126.]
  xi. Medicine. 1948. pp.v.2680–2746. [82.]
  xii. Samgita. By T. Chandrasekharan. 1949.
  pp.vi.2748–2850. [111.]
  xiii. History. 1951. pp.iii.2582–2911. [65.]
  xiv. Mackenzie local tracts volumes. 1952.
  pp.xxxvi. 299. [150.]
  xv. 1958. pp.viii. 302–534. [100.]

S. KUPPUSWAMI SASTRI, An alphabetical index
of telugu manuscripts in the Government oriental
manuscripts library, Madras. Madras 1932. pp.177.
[3870.]

[PALAMADAI PICHUMONI SUBRAHMANYAM
SASTRI and (vol.ii) V. SUNDARA SARMA, A descriptive
catalogue of the telugu manuscripts in the Tanjore
Māharāja Serfoji's Saṛasvatī mahāl library.
Andhra university series (no.11): Waltair 1933–
59. pp.[vi].xiii.14.362.xxi.+2.31.20.463.xxviii.2.
[1042.]

ii. *General*

L[IONEL] D[AVID] BARNETT, A catalogue of the
telegu books in the library of the British museum.
1912. pp.vii.coll.446. [2750.]

Urdu

i. *Manuscripts*
ii. *General*

i. *Manuscripts*

PAULINUS a S. BARTHOLOMAEO, Musei Borgiani

Velitris codices manuscripti avenses peguani
siamici malabarici indostani animadversionibus
historico-criticis castigati et illustrati. Accedunt
monumenta inedita, et cosmogonia indico-tibe-
tana. Romae 1793. pp.xii.266. [17.]

A[LOYS] SPRENGER, A catalogue of the arabic,
persian and hindústány manuscripts, of the
libraries of the king of Oudh.... Vol. 1. Containing persian and hindústány poetry. Calcutta 1854.
pp.viii.648. [732.]
no more published.

A[UGUST] F[ERDINAND MICHAEL] MEHREN, Codices persici, turcici, hindustanici variique alii
Bibliothecæ regiæ hafniensis. Hafniæ 1857. pp.
v.92. [250.]

ED[UARD] SACHAU and HERMANN ETHÉ, Catalogue of the persian, turkish, hindûstânî, and
pushtû manuscripts. Catalogi codd. mss. Bibliothecae bodleianae pars XIII: Oxford 1889–1930.
pp.xiii.coll.1150+pp.[v].coll.1157–1766. [3000.]

ALPHABETICAL index of manuscripts in the
Government oriental mss. library, Madras.
Hindustani. Madras 1893. pp.3. [40.]

J. F. BLUMHARDT, Catalogue of the hindi,
panjabi and hindustani manuscripts in the library
of the British museum. 1899. pp.xii.85.91. [250.]

MAHOMMED MUSHARRAF-UL-HUKK [MUḤAMMAD
MUSHARRAF AL-ḤAḰḰ], Katalog der bibliothek der
Deutschen morgenländischen gesellschaft. Zwei-
ter band. Handschriften. Teil B: persische und
hindustanische handschriften. Leipzig 1911. pp.
viii.76. [hindustani: 2].

AUTHOR-CATALOGUE of Haidarābād collection of manuscripts and printed books: Asiatic
society of Bengal: Calcutta 1913. pp.iv.62. [700.]

HERMANN ETHÉ, Catalogue of oriental manuscripts, persian, arabic, and hindūstānī. National
library of Wales: Aberystwyth 1916. pp.iv.31.
[50.]
250 copies printed.

JAMES FULLER BLUMHARDT, Catalogue of the
hindustani manuscripts in the library of the India
office. 1926. pp.xii.171. [269.]

CATALOGUE of arabic, persian & urdoo manuscripts presented to the Dacca university library
by Khan Bahadur ... Ahmad Siddiqui [Ṣiddiḳi].
Dacca [printed] [1929]. pp.iv.24. [50.]
only a small selection is catalogued.

S. KUPPUSWAMI SASTRI, An alphabetical index of
urdu manuscripts in the Government oriental
manuscripts library, Madras. Madras 1931. pp.4.
[35.]

'ABDU'L-ḲĀDIR-E-SARFARĀZ, A descriptive catalogue of the arabic, persian and urdu manuscripts in the library of the university of Bombay. Bombay 1935. pp.lv.432. [2000.]

P. P. SUBRAHMANYA SASTRI, A descriptive catalogue of the islamic manuscirpts in the Government oriental manuscripts library, Madras. Madras 1939. pp.xxix.546.xiv. [733.]

R[OBERT] B[ERTRAM] SERJEANT, A handlist of the arabic, persian and hindustani mss. of New college. Edinburgh 1942. pp.16. [hindustani: 15.]*

S. MOHIUDDIN QADRI ZORE, Tazkirah-e-makhtutat. A descriptive catalogue of urdu, persian, arabic and hindi manuscripts preserved in the library of the Idara-e-adabiyat-e-urdu. Hyderabad-Dn 1943–57. pp.   +176.9+384. 8. [975.]

C. H. SHAIKH, A descriptive handlist of arabic, persian and hindusthani mss belonging to the Satara historical museum at present lodged at the Deccan college research institute, Poona. Reprinted from Bulletin of the Deccan college research institute (vol.iv, no.3): Poona [1943]. pp.17. [18.]

GHULAM SARWAR, A descriptive catalogue of the oriental manuscripts in the Durgah library, Uch Sharif Gilani, Bahawalpur state. Urdu academy: Bahawalpur [1960?]. pp.xv.219. [390.]

KIRPAL SINGH, A catalogue of punjabi and urdu manuscripts in the Sikh history research department uptil march 31, 1963. Khalsa college: Amritsar 1963. pp.x.251. [urdu: 42.]

[QAZI MAHMUD UL HAQ], The British museum, London. A descriptive catalogue of the un-catalogued arabic, persian and urdu manuscripts, relevant to the history and culture of the Muslims in India, acquired by the British museum since the publication of its last printed catalogues ... [London 1965]. ff.50. [124.]*

[QAZI MAHMUD UL HAQ], The Royal asiatic society, London. A descriptive catalogue of the uncatalogued oriental manuscripts, relevant to the history and culture of the Muslims in India, acquired by the Royal asiatic society since the publication of its last printed catalogue ... [London 1965]. ff.10. [16.]*

A. B. M. HABIBULLAH, Descriptive catalogue of the persian, urdu & arabic manuscripts in the Dacca university library. With (vol.1) a note on the history of the manuscript collection by M. Siddiq Khan. Dacca university library publication (1): Dacca 1966–8. pp.xxi.406+vi.407–566. 58. [526.]

S. MUJAHID HUSAIN ZAIDI, Urdu-handschriften. Verzeichnis der orientalischen handschriften in Deutschland (band xxv): Wiesbaden 1973. pp.xviii.104. [70.]

ii. General

[JOSEPH HÉLIODORE] GARCIN DE TASSY, Histoire de la littérature hindoui et hindoustani. ... Tome 1. Biographie et bibliographie. Oriental translation committee [London]: Paris 1939. pp.[iii]. xvi.630. [2000.]
— — Seconde édition. 1870–1871. pp.[iii].iv. 634+[iii].608+[iii].viii.603. [5000.]

H. U. WEITBRECHT, A descriptive catalogue of urdu christian literature ... and a supplementary catalogue of christian publications in the other languages of the Panjáb. Lahore 1886. pp.[v].4. li.86. [urdu: 750.]

J[AMES] F[ULLER] BLUMHARDT, Catalogue of hindustani printed books in the library of the British museum. 1889. pp.viii.coll.458. [3500.]

J[AMES] F[ULLER] BLUMHARDT, Catalogue of the library of the India office. Vol.ii—Part ii. Hindustani books. 1900. pp.viii.380. [6500.]

AUTHOR-CATALOGUE of the Haidarābād collection of manuscripts and printed books: Asiatic society of Bengal: Calcutta 1913. pp.iv.62. [700.]

M. H. LANGLEY, Annotated urdu bibliography. U[nited] P[rovinces] c[ongress] c[ommittee]: Committee on adult literacy: Landaur printed 1944. pp.24. [385.]

PAKISTAN

i. Bibliographies

AKHTAR H. SIDDIQUI, A guide to reference books published in Pakistan. Pakistan reference publications: Karachi 1966. pp.41.

AKHTAR H. SIDDIQUI, Reference sources on Pakistan; a bibliography. National book centre of Pakistan: Karachi 1968. pp.32. [99.]

M. ADIL USMANI, Status of bibliography in Pakistan. Library promotion bureau publication (no.4): Karachi 1968. pp.viii.91. [xv]. [421.]

ii. General

A. R. GHANI, Pakistan; a select bibliography. Pakistan association for the advancement of science: University institute of chemistry: Lahore 1951. pp.xxii.339. [9000.]

SELECTED bibliography on Pakistan. FAO 52/4/2179. pp.4. [57.]*

JAMES G[OODWIN] HODGSON and IRENE COONS REESE, Pakistan. A bibliography prepared to furnish a background for the advisory project with the university of Peshawar. Colorado A & M college library: Library bulletin (no.24): Fort Collins 1955. pp.32. [600.]*

STANLEY MARON [and others], Annotated bibliography for Pakistan: sociology, economics, and politics. University of California: South Asia project: Human relations area files: Berkeley 1956. ff.[ii].64. [500.]*

GEORGE L. ABERNETHY, Pakistan. A selected, annotated bibliography. American institute of Pacific relations: New York 1957. ff.[ii].ii.30. [250.]*
— — Third edition, revised and enlarged. University of British Columbia: Vancouver [1968]. ff.iii.56. [450.]*

GEORGE B. MORELAND and AKHTAR H. SIDDIQUI, Publications of the government of Pakistan, 1947–1957. University of Karachi: Institute of public and business administration: Karachi 1958. pp.[ii].iv.187. [1578.]

A SELECT Pakistan bibliography: Department of advertising, films and publication: [Karachi 1958]. pp.[ii].46. [650.]

GEORGE B. MORELAND and AKHTAR H. SIDDIQUI, Star and crescent. A selected and annotated bibliography of Pakistan 1947–1957. University of Karachi: Institute of public and business administration: Karachi 1958. pp.[vi].36. [200.]

Z. A. TAMMANNAI, Bibliography of reading materials for new literates in Urdu. Anjuman taraqqi urdu Pakistan: Karachi [1959]. [589.]

ACCESSIONS list, Pakistan. Library of Congress: American libraries book procurement center: Karachi.*
   i. 1962. pp.[ii].26.v. [300.]
   ii. 1963. pp.[ii].179.xx. [2000.]
   iii. 1964. pp.[ii].155.xvi. [1600.]
   iv. 1965. pp.[ii].145.xvi. [1500.]
   v. 1966. pp.[ii].95.xv. [1000.]
— Annual list of serials 1966. pp.[ii].145. [1500.]
— Quinquennial index 1962–1966. 1968. pp.64.
   vi. 1967. pp.xix.236. [2500.]
   vii. 1968. pp.xxiii.226. [2400.]
   viii. 1969. pp.xxv.212. [2200.]
   ix. 1970. pp.xxviii.229.102. [3500.]
   x. 1971. pp.xxix.108. [1200.]
— Quinquennial index 1967–1971. 1972. pp.98.
   xi. 1972. pp.xxxviii.125.107. [2500.]
   xiv. 1973. pp.[ii].128.xxxvi. [1500.]
in progress.

PAKISTAN index translations (translation). Directorate of archives and libraries: National bibliographical unit: Karachi.
   1963 to 1965. pp.vi.302.vi. [804.]
   1966. pp.iii.103. [168.]

SUGGESTED reading list on Pakistan. Military assistance institute: Library: Arlington, Va. 1963. pp.38. [300.]*

STANLEY SPARKS, ARUN SHOURIE and JAY B. WESTCOTT, Bibliography on development administration, India and Pakistan. Syracuse university: Maxwell graduate school: Publication (no 11): [Syracuse] 1964. pp.[ix].51. [275.]*

PAKISTAN book trade directory, by M. Adil Usmani, Ghaniul Akram Sabzwari. Karachi 1966. *includes 'Books published in Pakistan 1948–1964.'*

BOOKS on Pakistan; a bibliography. National book centre of Pakistan: Karachi. [2nd edition. July 1965.] pp.71. [450.]

THE PAKISTAN national bibliography. Annual volume 1962. Government of Pakistan; Directorate of archives and libraries: National bibliographical unit: Karachi 1966. pp.ix.335. [2500.]
— 1963 and 1964. 1973. pp.iv.738. [4700.]
— 1968. 1969. pp.iv.144. [750.]

SHAUKAT ALI and RICHARD W. GABLE, Pakistan: a selected bibliography. International public administration series (7): International public administration center: School of public administration: University of Southern California: Los Angeles, California, 1966. ff.iv.44. [700.]*

ENGLISH language publications from Pakistan; a guidelist. National book centre of Pakistan: Karachi 1967. pp.xii.242. [1800.]

BOOKS from Pakistan published during the decade of reforms 1958–1968. National Book Centre of Pakistan: Karachi, August 1968. Second edition. pp.xi.159. [1050.]
— — 1969; the first annual supplement. [1969.]

MUSHTAQUR RAHMAN, Bibliography of Pakistan geography 1947–1967. Department of geography: University of Karachi: Karachi 1968. pp.v.89.xii. [1151.]

MUMTAZ A. ANWAR and BASHIR ALI TIWANA, Pakistan: a bibliography of books and articles published in the United Kingdom from 1947–64. Research society of Pakistan: Lahore 1969.pp.102. [1000.]

D. A. BIRMAN and M. H. KAFITINA, Библиография Пакистана. Академия наук СССР. Институт востоковедеиия. Институт научной информации по общественным наукам. Москва 1973. pp.55. [804.]

iii. Topography. Provinces

Baluchistan

N. M. BILLIMORIA, Biblography [*sic*] of publications on Sind & Baluchistan. Karachi 1929. pp.53.xv. [600.]

— — 2nd edition. 1930. pp.136. [872.]

North-West Provinces, Pakistan. [see also *India: United Provinces*]

INDEX to the leading decisions of the Sudder dewanny adawlut, North western provinces. Roorkee 1859. pp.[ii].ciii. [750.]
interleaved.

LIST of proceedings, &c.: North-West Provinces and other minor administrations. 1834–1899. Preserved in the Record department of the India office. 1902. pp.vi.126. [very large number.]

LIST of non-confidential publications [of publications (other than confidential)] exempted from registration, which were issued by the Chief commissioner, North-West Frontier Province, and officers subordinate to him, during the year. [Peshawar].

    1910. pp.6. [29.]
    1911. pp.6. [30.]
    1912. pp.6. [30.]
    1913. pp.6. [30.]
    1914. pp.6. [35.]
    1915. pp.6. [34.]
    1916. pp.6. [32.]
    1917.
    1918.
    1919. pp.5. [29.]
    1920. pp.5. [30.]
    1921. pp.6. [39.]
    1922.
    1923.
    1924.
    1925.
    1926. pp.10. [50.]
    1927.
    1928. pp.10. [50.]

S. M. JAFFAR, Guide to the archives of the Central record office N.W.F.P. Peshawar 1948. pp.x.50. [large number.]

Sind [see also *Bombay*]

N. M. BILLIMORIA [BILIMORIYA], Bibl[i]ography of publications on Sind & Baluchistan. Karachi 1929. pp.53.xv. [600.]

— — 2nd edition. 1930. pp.136. [872.]

CATALOGUE of books printed in the province of Sind during the quarter. [Karachi].

    1936. pp. .12.9.8.
    1937. pp.9.13.8.8. [496.]
    1938. pp.10.8.5.7. [452.]

    1939. pp.6.10.9.6. [435.]
    1940. pp.10.13.7.7. [490.]
    1941. pp.8.8.9.5. [363.]
    1942. pp.5.3.2.3. [143.]
in progress?

M[ĀNEKJI] B[EJANJĪ] PITHAWALLA [PĪṬHĀVĀLĀ], A bibliography of Sind (publications of geographical value). Karachi 1939. pp.17. [151.]

CATALOGUE of publications. Sind government: Karachi 1939. pp.197. [2000.]
various supplements have been issued.

GEOLOGICAL bibliography of the former province of Sind. Department of geology: University of Sind: Jamshoro 1968. ff.17. [450.]*

iv. History

K[HURSEED] K[AMAL] AZIZ, The historical background of Pakistan 1857–1947; an annotated digest of source material. Pakistan institute of international affairs: Karachi 1970. pp.xi.626. [9244.]

MUHAMMAD ANWAR, Quaid-e-azam Jinnah; a selected bibliography. [Karachi 1970.] pp.[viii]. 110. [1625.]

v. Official publications

CATALOGUE of the government of Pakistan publications. Karachi 1952. pp.77. [1000.]

GEORGE B. MORELAND and AKHTAR H. SIDDIQUI, Publications of the government of Pakistan, 1947–1957. University of Karachi: Institute of public and business administration: Karachi 1958. pp. [ii].iv.187. [1578.]

CATALOGUE of the government of Pakistan publications, Karachi 1962. pp.iii.168. [4500.]

CATALOGUE of publications. Government of East Pakistan: Tejgaon 1963. pp.[ii].ii.78. [1000.]

CATALOGUE of publications. East Pakistan government press: Publication branch: Tejgaon, Dacca 1966. pp.ii.90. [1300.]

ALPHABETICO-classed catalogue of government reports, pamphlets, and miscellaneous publications corrected up to 30th June, 1963. Pakistan administrative staff college: Lahore 1963. pp.122.

RAJESHWARI DATTA, Union catalogue of the government of Pakistan publications held by libraries in London, Oxford and Cambridge. Centre of south asian studies: Cambridge 1967. [pp.5].cols.116. [880.]*

vi. Periodicals

A. R. GHANI, A guide to the current scientific

journals received in various libraries of west Pakistan. Pakistan association for the advancement of science: Lahore 1950. pp.[ii].ii.26. [750.]

[A. MOID and AKHTAR H. SIDDIQUI], A guide to periodical publications and newspapers of Pakistan. Pakistan bibliographical working group: Publication (no.2): Karachi [1953]. pp.iv.60. [750.]

GENERAL list of newspapers published in Pakistan. Press information department: Karachi 1954. pp.[ii].vii.47. [800.]
— [another edition]. General list of newspapers and periodicals [&c]. 1959. pp.[ii].xi.57. [1250.]
— [another edition.]
GENERAL list of newspapers and periodicals published in Pakistan. January 1960. Press information department: Ministry of information and broadcasting: Karachi 1960. pp.xi.59. [1374.]

FAZAL ELAHI and AKHTAR H. SIDDIQUI, Union catalogue of periodicals in social sciences held by the libraries of Pakistan. Pakistan bibliographical working group: Publication (no.5): Karachi 1961. pp.v.92. [1000.]*

SCIENTIFIC & technical periodicals of Pakistan. Pakistan national scientific and technical documentation centre: Pansdoc bibliography (no.303): Karachi [1961]. ff.[ii].12. [70.]*

[AKHTAR H. SIDDIQUI], Scientific & technical periodicals of Pakistan. Pakistan national scientific & technical documentation centre: Pansdoc bibliography (no.303). Karachi [1962]. ff.ii.12. [70.]*

KARACHI university library periodical holdings. Karachi 1963. pp.[vi].2–118. [1031.]

LIST of newspapers and periodicals published in Karachi. [Karachi? 1966].pp.20. [277.]*

LIST of newspapers and periodicals published in West Pakistan excluding Karachi. [Karachi? 1966]. pp.65. [859.]*

PAKISTAN press index (a monthly index to newspapers of Pakistan—a monthly news and views digest). Documentation and information bureau: Karachi 1966–1969.
no more published?

ENGLISH language periodicals from Pakistan; a guidelist. National book centre of Pakistan: Karachi 1967. pp.55.

LIST of newspapers and periodicals printed or published in East Pakistan corrected up to 19.8.67. [Dacca?] 1967. ff.18. [417.]*

vii. Academic writings

BIBLIOGRAPHY of these, dissertations & research reports, university of Sind. West Pakistan bureau of education: Bibliographical series (no.iv): Lahore [1961]. ff.[ii].10. [75.]*

[MUSSAWIR ALI HAMIDI], Bibliography of theses dissertations & research reports, university of Karachi. West Pakistan bureau of education: Bibliographical series (no.iii): Lahore [1962]. ff. [ii].16. [161.]*

[MUSSAWIR ALI HAMIDI], Bibliography of theses, dissertations & research reports, university of Peshawar. West Pakistan bureau of education: Bibliographical series (no.iii): Lahore [1961]. ff.[ii].6. [15.]*

BIBLIOGRAPHY of theses, dissertations & research reports, university of Rajshahi. West Pakistan bureau of education: Bibliographical series (no. vi): Lahore [1962]. ff.[iii].9. [36.]*

viii. Subjects

agriculture

AKHTAR H. SIDDIQUI, Agriculture in Pakistan; a selected bibliography 1947–1969. [Karachi] 1969. pp.iv.88. [825.]*

botany

BIBLIOGRAPHY on the botany of west Pakistan and Kashmir and adjacent regions. Coconut Grove, Miami, Fla.
i. Taxonomy, by S. M. A. Kazmi. Edited by Henry Field and Edith M. Laird. 1970. pp.vii.136. [2500.]

censuses

HENRY J. DUBESTER, Census and vital statistics of India and Pakistan, contained in official publications and famine documents; an annotated bibliography. Library of congress: Census library project: Washington 1950. pp.118.

civil service

RALPH BRAIBANTI, Research on the bureaucracy of Pakistan; a critique of sources, conditions, and issues, with appended documents. Program in comparative studies on southern Asia: Duke university commonwealth-studies center: Durham 1966, pp.xxv. 569. [large number.]

economics

PAKISTAN. A basic list of annotated references to evaluate programs for economic development. Department of state: Library division: Bibliography (no.65): Washington 1952. pp.[ii].80. [634.]

NIKKI R. KEDDIE and ELIZABETH K. BAUER, Annotated bibliography for Pakistan sociology, economics and politics. University of California: Human relations area files south Asia project: Berkeley 1956. pp.64.

WOLFRAM EBERHARD, Studies on Pakistan's social and economic conditioner; a bibliographical note. Working bibliography prepared for the South Asia colloquium may 1958. Center for South Asia Studies: Institute of international studies: University of California [1958]. pp.47. [500.]*

ABDUL HAFEEZ AKHTAR, Small and medium industries of Pakistan, 1948–1962; a select bibliography. Pakistan institute of development economics: Karachi 1963. ff.ii.51. [407.]*

AKHTAR H. SIDDIQUI, The economy of Pakistan; a select bibliography 1947–1962. The Pakistan institute of development economics: Karachi 1963. pp.iv.162. [4248.]
—— 1963–1965. 1967. pp.iv.42. [1127.]

STANLEY SPARKS, ARUN SHOURIE and JAY B. WESTCOTT, Bibliography on development administration, India and Pakistan. Syracuse university: Maxwell graduate school: Publication (no. 11): [Syracuse] 1964. pp.[ix].51. [275.]*

EDGAR A. SCHULER and RAGHU SINGH, The Pakistan academies for rural development, Comilla and Peshawar 1959–1964. Asian studies center: Michigan state university: East Lansing 1965. pp.ix.116. [972.]

AKHTAR H. SIDDIQUI, Industrial Pakistan; a select bibliography. 1948–1966. Karachi 1968. pp.vii.131. [1500.]

ALAUDDIN TALUKDER, Cumulative index of PIDE publications 1961–1968. Pakistan institute of development economics: Karachi 1969. pp.iv.75. [400.]*

M. AZIM, Bibliography of Academy publications 1959–69. Pakistan academy for rural development, Peshawar 1970. pp.ii.48. [100.]

education

BIBLIOGRAPHY of books, pamphlets on education (english & urdu) in Pakistan. West Pakistan bureau of education: Bibliographical series (no.1): Lahore [1961]. ff.[ii].10. [129.]*

BIBLIOGRAPHY on education in Pakistan. West Pakistan bureau of education: Education department 1970. pp.viii.112.

geology

M. W. A. IQBAL, Bibliography of tertiary pelecypod and gastropod species of west Pakistan. Records of the Geological survey of Pakistan (vol.18): Quetta 1969. pp.iii.63. [1000..]

government

GARTH N. JONES, Pakistan government and administration; a comprehensive bibliography. Colorado state university: Fort Collins 1972.

inventions

THE GAZETTE of Pakistan. Part iv: Notifications and notices issued by the Patent office. Karachi.
  1955. [463.]
  1956. [1049.]
  1957. [1129.]
  1958. [895.]
  1959. [1926.]
  1960. pp.278. [964.]
  1961. pp.266. [883.]
  1962. pp.320. [1099.]
  1963. pp.278. [965.]
in progress.

Iqbal

ABDUL R. GHANI and KHWAJA NUR ILAHI, Bibliography of Iqbal. Bazm-i-Iqbal: Lahore [1954]. pp.vii.16. [267.]

MUHAMMAD BAQIR, A catalogue of the Iqbal exhibition 1963 arranged by the Panjabi Adabi academy. Lahore 1963. pp.24. [151.]

K. A. WAHEED, A bibliography of Iqbal. Iqbal academy, Pakistan: Karachi 1965. pp.iii.224. [2500.]

population

A[LLAH] D[ITTA] BHATTI, A bibliography of Pakistan demography. Pakistan institute of development economics: Karachi 1965. pp.vii.59. [356.]

public administration

MOHAMMAD ASLAM NIAZ and AYYAZ MAHMOOD QURESHI, Public administration in Pakistan; a select bibliography. National institute of public administration: Karachi 1966. pp.ii.75. [1000.]

M. A. RAHMAN, Administrative reforms in Pakistan, an annotated bibliography. Pakistan administrative staff college: Lahore 1969. pp.ix.124. [600.]

science

*A. R. GHANI, A guide to the current scientific journals received in various libraries of west Pakistan. Pakistan association for the advancement of science: Lahore 1950. pp.[ii].iii.26. [750.]

SCIENTIFIC & technical periodicals of Pakistan. Pakistan national scientific and technical documentation centre: Pansdoc bibliography (no.303): Karachi [1961]. ff.[ii].12. [70.]*

PAKISTAN scientific literature. Current bibliography. Pakistan national scientific and technical documentation centre: Karachi.*
  i. 1961. pp.[iii].ii.34+[iii].iii.50+[iii].91. [1432.]

[continued as:]

PAKISTAN science abstracts. Pakistan national scientific & technical documentation centre: Karachi.

    ii. 1962. pp.viii.iv.114. [318.]
    iii. 1963. pp.63. [298.]
    iv. 1964. pp.iv. 100. [508.]
    v. 1965. pp.xii.121. [550.]
    vi. 1966.
    vii. 1967.
    viii. 1968. pp.xi.138.xix. [846.]
in progress?

A. R. GHANI and A. GHANI, Scientific & technical periodicals of Pakistan: a preliminary survey of holdings in foreign libraries. Pakistan national scientific and technical documentation centre: Karachi 1963. pp.[ii].4.xc. [50.]*

[AKHTAR H. SIDDIQUI], Scientific & technical periodicals of Pakistan. Pakistan national scientific & technical documentation centre: Pansdoc bibliography (no.303): Karachi [1962]. ff.ii.12. [70.]*

LIST of bibliographies compiled by Pansdoc. [Pakistan national scientific & technical documentation centre: Karachi] 1963. pp.[ii].16. [369.]*

DIRECTORY of current scientific research projects in Pakistan. National science council: Karachi 1968. pp.viii.162. [2926.]

social sciences

NIKKI R. KEDDIE and ELIZABETH K. BAUER, Annotated bibliography for Pakistan sociology, economics and politics. University of California: Human relations area files south Asia project: Berkeley 1956. pp.64.

WOLFRAM EBERHARD, Studies on Pakistan's social and economic conditioner; a bibliographical note. Working bibliography prepared for the South Asia colloquium, May 1958. Center for South Asia studies: Institute of international studies: University of California [1958]. pp.47. [500.]*

FAZAL ELAHI and AKHTAR H. SIDDIQUI, Union catalogue of periodicals in social sciences held by the libraries in Pakistan. Pakistan bibliographical working group: Publication (no.5): Karachi 1961. pp.v.92. [1000.]

trade

AKHTAR H. SIDDIQUI, Tariffs in Pakistan; a select bibliography. Tariff commission: Government of Pakistan: [Karachi] 1954. pp.iv.27. [430.]

AKHTAR H. SIDDIQUI, Foreign trade of Pakistan; a select bibliography. Karachi 1968. ff.[iii].57. [755.]

BANGLADESH

ACCESSIONS list: Bangladesh. Library of congress: American libraries book procurement center: New Delhi.*

    i. 1972. pp.[iii].35.i. [350.]
    ii. 1973. pp.[iii].26.ii.+
in progress.

SRI LANKA (CEYLON)

i. *General*
ii. *Periodicals*
iii. *Subjects*
iv. *Sinhalese literature*

i. *General*

CEYLON. [Colonial office (no.18 of a series of lists of works in the library): 1860]. pp.8. [125.]

TH. CH. L. WIJNMALEN, De drukpers te Colombo. Proeve eener singaleesche biliographie. [c.1880]. pp.23. [40.]

[W. and D. W. FERGUSON], List of writers on Ceylon. [1885]. pp.24. [1000.]

STATEMENT of books printed in Ceylon, and registered under ordinance no.1 of 1885. Ceylon government gazette: Supplement: Colombo.

    1885. pp.7.9. [96.]
    1886. pp.5.9.9.7. [177.]
    1887. pp.9.7.12.8. [221.]
    1888. pp.10.10.8.10. [219.]
    1889. pp.10.12.8.10. [260.]
    1890. pp.10.10.10.12. [270.]
    1891. pp.12.10.12.12. [336.]
    1892. pp.12.12.14.12. [391.]
    1893. pp.12.14.12.16. [421.]
    1894. pp.14.16.12.8. [386.]
    1895. pp.14.18.8.12. [381.]
    1896. pp.12.12.14.12. [358.]
    1897. pp.14.12.8.8. [278.]
    1898. pp.
    1899. pp.
    1900. pp.
    1901. pp.
    1902. pp.
    1903. pp.14.10.22. [412.]
    1904. pp.
    1905. pp.
    1906. pp.
    1907. pp.
    1908. pp.
    1909. pp.12.18.14.32. [2000.]
    1910. pp.36. [1000.]
    1911. pp.14.8.14.10. [1250.]
    1912. pp.12.12.10.10. [1250.]
    1913. pp.10.12.14.12. [1250.]
    1914. pp.14.12.12.10. [1250.]
    1915. pp.
    1916–1917. pp.12.10.34.8. [2000.]

1918. pp.14.16. [1000.]
1919. pp.8.8.8.10. [1000.]
1920. pp.12.10.10.10. [1000.]
1921. pp.10.10.12.12. [1000.]
1922. pp.10.12.12.12. [1000.]
1923. pp.12.12.12.12. [1250.]
1924. pp.14.14.14.14. [1500.]
1925. pp.14.14.12.12. [1250.]
1926. pp.16.12.14.12. [1500.]
1927. pp.14.14.14.14. [1500.]
1928. pp.14.12.14.16. [1500.]
1929. pp.14.14.18.28. [2000.]
1930. pp.26.9.10.8. [1500.]
1931. pp.9.9.9.9. [1000.]
1932. pp.10.10.11.10. [1250.]
1933. pp.10.10.11.10. [1250.]
1934. pp.11.12.12.10. [1250.]
1935. pp.11.11.11.12. [1250.]
1936. pp.13.11.11.13. [1500.]
1937. pp.14.16.15.15. [2000.]
1938. pp.17.16.16.15. [2000.]
1939. pp.12.14.14.14. [1750.]
in progress; the first issue (2nd quarter of 1885, four titles) formed p.1000 of the Ceylon government gazette *for 10 July 1885.*

JOSEPH MARTINUS PERERA, A collection of select decisions of the Supreme court on points of kandyan law. ... Vol.II [of Perera's edition of J. Armour's translation of Nīti-nighaṇḍuva]. Colombo 1892. pp.xviii.338. [1500.]

B. P. DE S. BASNAYEKE SAMARASINHA, A numerical and an alphabetical list of the legislative enactments of Ceylon. Colombo 1893. pp.[iii].v.111. [1000.]
interleaved.

R[ICHARD] G[ERALD] ANTHONISZ, Report on the dutch records in the government archives at Colombo. Colombo 1907. pp.[v].138. [large number.]

[EDWARD BEAUMONT FRASER SUETER], Index and epitome of government minutes and circulars issued from 1896 to 1905. Colombo 1907. pp.[ii].58. [1500.]

E. B. F. SUETER, Index to proclamations and notifications under ordinances, published in the "Ceylon government gazette" from 1860 to 1908. Colombo 1909. pp.[iii].76. [3500.]

A DIGEST of Ceylon cases reported. Jaffna [Colombo].
     1820–1914. By S. Rajaratnam. [1919]. pp.[vi]. 1901. [12,500.]
     1914–1936.
     1936–1940. By V. S. Sivagurunathan. pp.[ii]. coll.2417–2624. [1000.]

CATALOGUE of government publications dealing with Ceylon. Colombo.

1926. pp.16. [300.]
1930. pp.30. [750.]
1934. pp.32. [750.]

[ERHARDUS CORNELIS GODÉE MOLSBERGEN], Report on the dutch records in the government archives at Colombo. [Papers laid before the legislative council of Ceylon:] Sessional paper [1929, no.ix]: Colombo 1929. pp.6. [large number.]

J[OSEPH] VAN KAMP, Compagniebescheiden en aanverwante archivalia in britische-Indië en op Ceylon. Verslag van een onderzooks in 1929–1930. Batavia 1931. pp.vi.253. [very large number.]

DOUGLAS C. MCMURTRIE, Memorandum on the first printing in Ceylon. With a bibliography of ceylonese imprints of 1737–1760. Chicago 1931. pp.10. [35.]
250 copies privately printed.

S. GUNAWARDANA, Index to papers and sessional papers laid before the Legislative council of Ceylon from 1855 to July 1931, and before the State council of Ceylon from July 1931, to end of 1933. Colombo 1934. pp.53. [2500.]
— Index to sessional papers, 1934–1950. 1951. pp.15.
— — 1951–1955. 1956. pp.7.
— — 1951–1959. 1960. pp.11.

EXHIBITION of historical manuscripts ... at the Colombo museum. Catalogue. Historical manuscripts commission: Colombo [printed] 1937. pp. [v].6. [100.]

M[ARIA] W[ILHELMINA] JURRIAANSE, Catalogue of the archives of the dutch central government of coastal Ceylon, 1640–1796. Colombo 1943. pp. [xiv].354. [very large number.]

K. BALASINGHAM, Corpus juris. A digest of statute law, common law and case law of Ceylon. Colombo [printed] [1947]. pp.iii.coll.320. [500.]

J. H. O. PAULUSZ, The Ferguson section of Mr. D. R. Wijewardene's library. [Colombo 1948]. pp.75. [196.]

THE GOVERNMENT archives department and its contents in brief. Department of the government archivist: Nugegoda 1962. pp.35. [600.]*

EDITH M. WARE, Bibliography on Ceylon. Coral Gables, Florida 1962. pp.xxiv. 181. [9000.]

The CEYLON national bibliography. National bibliography branch: Department of the govt. archivist: Nugegoda 1963 &c.
in progress.

E. D. T. KULARATNE and MANIL SILVA. A select list of books and other publications on Ceylon. Ceylon library association: Colombo 1965. pp.56. [500.]

ACCESSIONS list: Ceylon. Library of congress: Public law 480 project: New Delhi.*
    i. 1967. pp.[ii].31.iii. [300.]
    ii. 1968. pp.94.ix. [1000.]
    iii. 1969. pp.115.xiii. [1200.]
    iv. 1970. pp.101.xvii. [1000.]
    v. 1971. pp.135.xxiv. [1350.]
    vi. 1972. pp.109.xx. [1100.]
        [continued as:]
Accessions list: Sri Lanka
vii. 1973.
in progress.

H[ENRY] A[LFRED] I[AN] GOONETILEKE, A bibliography of Ceylon. A systematic guide to the literature on the land, people, history and culture published in western languages from the sixteenth century to the present day. Bibliotheca asiatica (5): Zug, Switzerland 1970. pp.lxxx.408+ix.409–865. [9948.]

TERESA MACDONALD, Union catalogue of the government of Ceylon publications held by libraries in London, Oxford and Cambridge. Centre of south asian studies: University of Cambridge: London 1970. pp.vi.cols.75. [750.]*

N. AMARASINGHE, Theses presented for higher degrees of the university of Ceylon (1942–1971) deposited in the library of the university of Ceylon: a classified list with author and title index. University of Ceylon library publications (1): Peradeniya 1971, ff.vi.pp.35. [157.]*

H[ENRY] A[LFRED] I[AN] GOONETILEKE, The april 1971 insurrection in Ceylon; a select bibliography (July 1973). C[entre] de R[echerches] S[ocio-] R[eligieuses]: Louvain [1973] ff.[iii].vii.89. [346.]*

ii. *Periodicals*

CATALOGUE of newspapers. Newspapers printed in Ceylon and registered under the newspapers ordinance (cap.180). Office of registrar, books and newspapers: Nuwara Eliya.
    1961. pp.iv.11. [90.]
in progress?

CEYLON periodicals index. National museum library: Colombo.*
    i. 1969–70.
    ii. 1970. pp.iv.109.xx.124.xxxviii. [1219.]
    iii. 1971. pp.[viii].32.xix.[vi].71.xxxv. [1217.]
in progress.

CEYLON periodicals directory. National museum library: Colombo 1971 &c.*
    i. Sinhala publications.
    ii. Tamil publications.
    iii. English publications.
annual supplements?

iii. *Subjects*

agriculture

T[OM] PETCH, Bibliography of books and papers relating to agriculture and botany to the end of the year 1915. Peradeniya manuals (vol.iii): Colombo 1925. pp.[iii].256. [5059.]

botany

T[OM] PETCH, Bibliography of books and papers relating to agriculture and botany to the end of the year 1915. Peradeniya manuals (vol.iii): Colombo 1925. pp.[iii].256. [5059.]

crime, criminal law

E. P. WIJETUNGE [EDMUND P. VIJĒTUṄGE], A complete digest of case law on the penal code 1820 to 1955, illustrated with references to english and indian cases. [Colombo 1955]. pp.[vi].xxxvii.616. [1750.]

education

H. D. EVERS, S. VON SCHWERIN, H. WEILER, Erziehungswesen in Ceylon, Israel und Nigeria; eine bibliographie. Arbeitsstelle für kulturwissenschaftliche forschung: Freiburg i. Br.1962. pp.45. [Ceylon: 109.]

science

M[OHAMED] U[VAIS] S[IDDEEK] SULTANBAWA, List of the scientific periodicals in the libraries of Ceylon. Ceylon association for the advancement of science: [Colombo] 1953. pp.143. [3000.]

Sinhalese literature

MAT. P. J. ONDAATJE, A tabular list of original works and translations, published by the late dutch government at their printing press at Colombo. Royal asiatic society: [1867]. pp.4. [52.]

JOHN MURDOCH and JAMES NICHOLSON, Classified catalogue of printed tracts and books in singhalese. Madras 1868. pp.vii.70. [2000.]
the titles are given in english.

JAMES D'ALWIS, A descriptive catalogue of sanskrit, pali, & sinhalese literary works of Ceylon. ... Vol.1. Colombo 1870. pp.xxxi.244. [23.]

[L. DE ZOYSA], Catalogue of pali, sinhalese, & sanskrit manuscripts, in the Ceylon government oriental library. Colombo 1876. pp.26. [209.]
— — [another edition. By Henry M. Gunasekera]. 1901. pp.xiv.47. [500.]

TH. CH. L. WIJNMALEN, De drukpers te Colombo. Proeve eener singaleesche bibliographie. [s.l. c.1880]. pp.23. [40.]

MARTINO DE ZILVA WICKREMASINGHE, Catalogue of the sinhalese manuscripts in the British museum. 1900. pp.xxiii.200. [250.]

M. DE ZILVA WICKREMASINGHE, Catalogue of the sinhalese printed books in the library of the British museum. 1901. pp.vii.coll.308. [2000.]

W. A. DE SILVA, Catalogue of the palm leaf manuscripts in the library of the Colombo museum. Colombo museum: Memoirs (ser. A, nos.4–   ): Colombo 1938–   . pp.[ii].xxxiv. 472+   . [2456.]

HEINZ BECHERT and MARIA BIDOLI. Singhalesische handschriften, teil 1. Verzeichnis der orientalischen handschriften in Deutschland (vol.xxii,1). Wiesbaden 1969. pp.xix.146. [198.]

NEPAL

HUGH B[ERNARD] WOOD, Nepal bibliography. American-Nepal education foundation: Eugene, Or. 1959. pp.[ii].108. [1000.]

T[ATSU] KAMBARA, Nepal bibliography. Tokyo 1959. pp.121.

ACCESSIONS list: Nepal. Library of congress: Public Law 480 project. New Delhi.*
    i. 1966. pp.25.iv. [250.]
    ii. 1967. pp.44.vi. [450.]
    iii. 1968. pp.30.iii. [300.]
    iv. 1969. pp.34.iv. [350.]
    v. 1970. pp.58.ix. [600.]
    vi. 1971. pp.88.xvi. [900.]
    vii. 1972. pp.82.xiv. [850.]
in progress.

MARGARET W. FISHER, A selected bibliography of source materials for Nepal. Institute of international studies: University of California: Berkeley 1966. ff.ii.54. [315.]*
Second edition, revised, but not brought up-to-date, with an index by Carolyn Heffer. Originally issued in 1956.

ASAD HUSAIN, Bibliography on Nepal, i: Historical and political. Kathmandu 1966. pp.iv. 30. [244.]

L. BOULNOIS and H. MILLOT, Bibliographie du Népal.
    1. Sciences humaines. Références en langues européennes. Cahiers népalais: Paris 1969. pp.289. [4515.]

BHARAT M. GYAWALI, GARLAND L. STANDROD, Nepal documentation. Documentation centre: Centre for economic development and administration: Occasional bibliography (no.1): Kirtipur 1972. pp.100. [607.]*

JOURNALS in the english language available in the university of Michigan library containing articles on Nepal. [Ann Arbor? 1972?] ff.26. [400.]*

SIKKIM

LINDA G. SCHAPPERT, Sikkim, 1800–1968: an annotated bibliography. Occasional papers of East-west center library (no.10). East-west center: University of Hawaii: Honolulu 1968. ff.iii.69. [342.]*

SOUTH-EAST ASIA

i. *Bibliography*
ii. *General*
iii. *Periodicals*
iv. *Academic writings*
v. *Subjects*

i. *Bibliography*

ERNEST J. FREI, Bibliographies of southeast Asia and the Pacific area. Bibliographical society of the Philippines: Occasional papers (no.1): Quezon City 1958. pp.34. [300.]

G[ODFREY] RAYMOND NUNN, South and southeast Asia; a bibliography of bibliographies. Occasional paper (no.4): East west center library: [Honolulu] 1966. ff.v.59. [350.]★

[TOKIHITO TANAKA], A survey of bibliographies in western languages concerning east and southeast asian studies. Editor: Kazuo Enoki. Centre for east asian cultural studies: Bibliography (no.4): Tokyo 1966. pp.iv.227. [1251.]

DONALD CLAY JOHNSON, A guide to reference materials on southeast Asia. Based on the collections in the Yale and Cornell university libraries. Yale southeast asia studies (6): New Haven, London 1970. pp.xi.160. [2500.]★

ii. *General*

NAMPO bunken mokuroku. Bibliography of studies of Southeast Asia and Oceania. Kyoto imperial university.
i. Thailand, Indo-China, Dutch East Indies. pp.28.
ii. Malaya, Burma, the Philippines. pp.18.
iii. Borneo, Micronesia, New Guinea. pp.23.
iv. Australia, South Asia in general, supplm. pp.30.
Reprinted from Toa Keizai Ronso, 1–1/4, 1942.

SELECTED bibliographies, nos. 1–3. Southeast Asia Institute: New York 1946.
i. A selected list of books and articles on the religions of Southeast Asia.
ii. A selected list of books and articles on further India (Burma, Siam, French Indo-China, Malaya).
iii. A selected list of books and articles in english on government, economy, sociology, education and political movement in Southeast Asia.

CECIL [CARLTON] HOBBS, Southeast Asia, 1935–1945. A selected list of reference books. Library of Congress: Orientalia division: Washington 1946. pp.86. [750.]
— — [another edition]. Southeast Asia. An annotated bibliography of selected reference sources. 1952. pp.ix.163. [345.]★

— Southeast Asia: an annotated bibliography of selected reference sources in western languages. Revised and enlarged. New York 1968. pp.v.180. [535.]

EXTERNAL research: a listing of recently completed studies. Southeast Asia (and Southwest Pacific). External research staff: Office of intelligence research (and analysis): Department of state: [Washington]★
3.5. Oct. 1954–Oct. 1955. pp.6. [112.]
3.7. Oct. 1956. pp.8. [109.]
3.9. Oct. 1957. pp.9. [130.]
3.11. Oct. 1958. pp.10. [125.]
3.13. Oct. 1959. pp.12. [145.]
3.15. Oct. 1960. pp.12. [128.]
3.17. Fall 1961. pp.17. [215.]
3.19. Fall 1962. pp.15. [207.]
3.21. Fall 1963–Winter 1964. pp.19. [244.]
no more published.

SOUTHERN Asia publications in western languages. A quarterly accessions list. Library of Congress: Division of Orientalia: Washington★
i. 1952. pp.iv.226. [4000.]
ii. 1953. pp.vi.190. [3000.]
iii. 1954. pp.vi.218. [3500.]
iv. 1955. pp.vii.253. [4000.]
v. 1956. pp.vii.324. [4500.]
[*continued as:*]
Southern Asia accessions list.
vi. 1957. pp.ix.466. [4000.]
vii. 1958. pp.x.564. [5500.]
viii. 1959. pp.x.760. [7500.]
ix. 1960. pp.xi.689. [6500.]
no more published.

KARL J[OSEF] PELZER, Selected bibliography on the geography of southeast Asia. Part I. Southeast Asia—general. Yale university: Southeast Asia studies: New Haven 1949. ff.[i].ix.45. [700.]★

JOHN F[EE] EMBREE and LILLIAN O[TA] DOTSON, Bibliography of the peoples and cultures of mainland southeast Asia. Yale university southeast Asia studies: New Haven 1950. pp.xxix.822.xii. [12,000.]

SOUTHEAST Asia and the Philippines. A selected list of political, economic and cultural sources. Department of state: Division of library and reference services: Bibliographic list (no.33): [Washington] 1950. ff.9. [100.]★

JOHN F[EE] EMBREE, A selected bibliography of southeast Asia. Institute of Pacific relations: New York 1950. ff.15. [150.]★
— — [Fifth edition]. Book on southeast Asia: a select bibliography. 1959. pp.62. [900.]★
— — [Revised edition to April 1960]. pp.70. [1300.]
From fourth edition the work was revised by Bruno Lasker.

GIOK PO OEY, Survey of chinese language materials on southeast Asia in the Hoover institute and library. Cornell university: Department of far eastern studies: Southeast Asia program: Data paper (no.8): Ithaca 1953. ff.[v].73. [262.]★

[R. PAMUNTJAK], Social science bibliography for south east Asia. Ministry of education and culture: National bibliographic centre: [Djakarta 1955]. pp.ii.65. [594.]

RECENT studies and materials on southeast Asia: 1950–1955. Cornell university: Department of far eastern studies: Southeast Asia program: [Ithaca 1955]. ff.11. [125.]★

JAMES K. IRIKURA, Southeast Asia: selected annotated bibliography of japanese publications. Human relations area files: Behavior science bibliographies: New Haven 1957. pp.[ii].544. [xiv]. [965.]★

RUTH T[HOMAS] MCVEY, Bibliography of soviet publications on southeast Asia as listed in the Library of Congress Monthly index of russian acquisitions. Cornell university: Department of far eastern studies: Southeast Asia program: Data paper (no.34): Ithaca 1959. pp.[ii].v.109. [1600.]★

GIOK PO OEY, Southeast Asia accessions list. Cornell university library: Wason collection: Ithaca 1959 &c.

in progress.

A. M. GRISHINA [*and others*], Библиография Юго-Восточной Азии. Дореволюционная и советская литература на русском языке, оригинальная и переводная. Академия наук СССР: Институт народов Азии: Фундаментальная библиотека общественных наук: Москва, 1960. pp.256. [3752.]

YU. YA. PLAM and YU. H. SIRK, Fifty years of soviet oriental studies. The languages of Southeast Asia. [Moscow 1960?]

NORMAN P. HORNE, A guide to published United States government documents pertaining to southeast Asia, 1893–1941. Catholic university of America: Washington 1961. ff.iii.147. [1500.]★

STEPHEN N. HAY and MARGARET H. CASE, Southeast asian history. A bibliographic guide. New York [1962]. pp.xi.138. [1250.]★

BIBLIOGRAPHY of southeast Asia studies, being a classified list of books wholly or partly in english relating to the countries in the region of Southeast Asia. Nanyang university library: Singapore 1962. ff.[iii].47. [1250.]

CHAN THYE SENG, Southeast Asia: history and politics, with emphasis on Burma, Indonesia, Malaya and Vietnam. A selected, annotated

bibliography. Library school: Wellington 1962. ff.v.27. [143.]★

YUVA newsletter; a quarterly (bi-monthly) review of Soviet writing on South-East Asia. Central Asian research centre in association with St. Anthony's college (Oxford): Soviet affairs study group: 1962–4.★
    i. 1962. pp.36+49+43+36.xx. [1608.]
    ii. 1963. pp.37.viii+39+23+20+16.xxv. [1350.]
    iii. 1964. pp.22+25+27+32+57+35.x. [2000.]
    iv. 1964. pp.24+20+17+22+23+19.vii. [1200.]
merged with Mizan *in 1966.*

M. M. EVANS, Catalogue of papers relating to: South Asia, 1792–1914; South east Asia, 1813–1914 [from the Baptist missionary society archives]. Baptist missionary society: London 1964. pp.179.

ROBERT HACKENBERG, Southeast Asia. Tucson 1964.

UNION catalogue of documentary materials on Southeast Asia. Institute of asian economic affairs: Tokyo 1964. pp.x.172+x.137+x.288+x.489+ix.237. [20,248.]

KENJIRO ICHIKAWA, Southeast Asia viewed from Japan: a bibliography of japanese works on Southeast asian societies, 1940–1963. Data paper (no.56): Southeast Asia program: Department of asian studies: Cornell university: Ithaca 1965. pp.[vi].112. [1500.]

KENNETH G. ORR, A working bibliography [*sic*] of selected reference sources in western languages on the societies and cultures of southeast Asia. USAID/OP Laos: Vientiane 1965. ff.7. [200.]★

SEATO publications. South-east Asia treaty organisation: Bangkok 1965 etc. pp.13. [160.]★

M. D[OREEN] WAINWRIGHT and NOEL MATTHEWS, A guide to western manuscripts and documents in the British Isles relating to south and southeast Asia. 1965. pp.xix.532. [20,000.]

PAUL BIXLER [*and others*], materials for college libraries on southeast Asia. [New Brunswick 1966.] ff.24+5+2+3+2. [400.]★

BONEW (Mme), Premiers éléments bibliographiques relatifs aux problêmes actuels du sud-est de l'Asie. Centre d'étude du sud-est asiatique: Bruxelles 1966. ff.[iii]. pp.515. [5000.]

OLE KARUP PEDERSEN, Litteratur om Sudøstasien; historie og moderne samfundsforhold. 2. rev. udg. Mellemfolkeligt samvirke (Danish association for international co-operation): København: 1966. pp.14. [116.]★

PETER BERTON and ALVIN Z. RUBINSTEIN, Soviet works on southeast Asia: a bibliography of non-periodical literature, 1946–1965. School of politics and international relations: University of Southern California: Far eastern and russian research series (no.3): Los Angeles 1967. pp.201. [401.]*

INDIA and south-east Asia; a bibliography. Department of indian studies: University of Malaya: Kuala Lumpur 1967.

LARRY STERNSTEIN and CARL SPRINGER, An annotated bibliography of material concerning southeast Asia from Petermann's geographische mitteilungen: 1885–1966. Siam society: [Bangkok] 1967. pp.[v].389. [3200.]

[W. DE BEL], Éléments bibliographiques du sud-est asiatique et de l'extrême-orient (problèmes actuels). II. Centre d'étude du sud-est asiatique et de l'extrême-orient: Bruxelles 1968. ff.[ii].pp.98. [1000.]

REVISED list of southeast Asia holdings in the Swen Franklin Parson library. Compiled by Southeast Asia library & Center for southeast asian studies: Northern Illinois university: De Kalb 1968. ff.[iii]. 284. [5600.]

LIST of recent southeast Asia acquisitions. 1968. ff.[iii]. 65. [1300.]
— 1969. ff.[iii].58. [1100.]
— 1970. ff.[iii].85. [1700.]

THE COMMONWEALTH in south and southeast Asia. National book league and the Commonwealth institute: [London] 1969. pp.32. [172.]

CONRAD P. COTTER, Information on japanese monographs in the files of the office of the Chief of military history and information relating to the access thereto. [Ithaca 195–?]. ff.12. [37.]

CECIL HOBBS, Understanding the people of southern Asia: a bibliographical essay. University of Illinois Graduate school of library science: Occasional papers (no.8): 1967. pp.58. [300.]

AUSTIN C. W. SHU and WILLIAM W. L. WAN, Twentieth century chinese works on southeast Asia; a bibliography. East–West center [Honolulu]: Annotated bibliography series (no.3) ff.iii.201. [758.]*

SOUTHERN Asia: Afghanistan, Bhutan, Burma, Cambodia, Ceylon, India, Laos, Malaya, Nepal, Sikkim, Singapore, Thailand, Vietnam. Harvard university library: Widener library shelflist (19): Cambridge, Mass. 1968. pp.v.543. [10,292.]*

GAYLE MORRISON, A guide to books on southeast asian history, 1961–1966. Stephen Hay, editor. Bibliography and reference series (no.8): Santa Barbara, Calif. 1969. pp.viii.105.

KENNEDY G. TREGONNING, Southeast Asia; a critical bibliography. Tucson 1969. pp.[ix].103. [2058.]

DONALD CLAY JOHNSON [and others], Southeast Asia: a bibliography for undergraduate libraries. Occasional publication (no.13): Foreign area materials center: University of the state of New York, State education department and National council of associations for international studies: Williamsport 1970. pp.xviii.59. [771.]*

THE EAST India company in south east Asia. An exhibition of documents, maps, drawings, prints and rare books illustrating the relations of the East India company with southeast Asia. India office library: India office records: [London] 1971. pp.41. [47.]*

INSULAR southeast Asia; a bibliographic survey. Department of the army: Washington [1971]. pp.xi.411. [large number.]

MILTON W[ALTER] MEYER, Southeast Asia; an introductory bibliography. Department of history: California state college: Los Angeles 1971. pp.36. [700.]*

R[ALPH] B. SMITH, South east Asia: bibliography. Prepared by the Centre of Southeast asian studies, School of oriental and african studies, August 1971. pp.70. [1300.]*

SOUTHEAST Asia subject catalog, Library of congress: Orientalia division: Boston 1972. pp.ix.429 + vi.917 + vi.361 + vi.845 + ix.795 +viii.585. [82,495 cards.]

iii. Periodicals

LIST of scientific and technical journals published in southeast Asia (Philippines, Indonesia, Malaya, Thailand, Indo-China). [United nations educational, scientific and cultural organization:] East Asia scientific cooperation office: Manila 1950. ff.[i].28. [125.]*
— [revised edition]. 1951. ff.xii.32. [142.]*
— — Supplement ... (China). 1951. ff.[i]. xiii.28. [120.]*

— Second [sic] edition. Scientific and technical journals of east and south east Asia (Hong Kong, Japan, Indonesia, Macao, Malaya, north Borneo, the Philippines, Sarawak, Thailand, Vietnam). 1953. pp.[v].233. [800.]*

LIST of scientific & other periodicals published in the indo–pacific area. 2nd edition. Indo–pacific fisheries council: Bangkok 1953. pp.50. [400.]

LIST of periodicals published in south-east Asia. ... National diet library: General reference division, and Economic counsel board: Library: [Tokyo 1954]. pp.117. [1100.]

LIST of classified journals. Unesco research centre on the social implications of industrialization in southern Asia. Calcutta 1960. pp.27.

CHECKLIST of southeast asian serials, Southeast Asia collection. Yale University library. Boston 1968. pp.xxiv.320. [3748.]

[GEORGE MILLER], Southeast asian newspapers. National library of Australia: Canberra 1969. pp.24. [222.]

SOUTHEAST asian periodicals & official publications. National library of Australia: Canberra 1970. pp.50+16+28+29+17 [1400.]

INDEX to Chinese periodical literature on Southeast Asia, 1905–1966. Institute of southeast Asia: Nanyang university: Singapore 1968. pp.[ix].365. [10,000.]

iv. *Academic writings*

JAMES C. JACKSON, Recent higher degree theses on social, political and economic aspects of southeast Asia presented in the universities of the United Kingdom and in the universities of Malaya and Singapore. Miscellaneous series (no.6): Department of geography: University of Hull [1966]. pp.iii.[14]. [143.]*

RICHARD J. KOZICKI and PETER ANANDA, South and southeast Asia: doctoral dissertations and masters' theses completed at the university of California at Berkeley 1906–1968. Occasional papers of the Center for south and southeast Asia studies, University of California (no.1): Berkeley 1969. pp.viii.49. [307.]*

LIAN THE and PAUL W. VAN DER VEUR, Treasures and trivia: doctoral dissertations on southeast Asia accepted by universities in the United States. Ohio university: Center for international studies: Papers in international studies: Southeast Asia series (no.1): 1968. pp.xiv.141. [958.]*

D. R. SAR DESAI and BHANU D. SAR DESAI, Theses and dissertations on southeast Asia: an international bibliography in social sciences, education and fine arts. Bibliotheca asiatica (6): Zug 1970. pp.iv.176. [2814.]

THESES on southeast Asia presented at Northern Illinois university 1960–1971; an annotated bibliography. The Center for southeast asian studies: Northern Illinois university: DeKalb, Illinois 1972. pp.iii.13. [21.]*

v. *Subjects*

archaeology

ANNUAL bibliography of indian archaeology. Kern institute: Leyden.

[i]. 1926. pp.x.107. [540.]
[ii]. 1927. pp.x.143. [721.]
[iii]. 1928. pp.xi.141. [721.]
[iv.] 1929. pp.xi.141. [731.]
[v.] 1930. pp.xi.149. [929.]
[vi]. 1931. pp.xi.211. [982.]
vii. 1932. pp.xi.179. [752.]
viii. 1933. pp.xiii.133. [706.]
ix. 1934. pp.xi.167. [847.]
x. 1935. pp.xii.163. [832.]
xi. 1936. pp.vi.125. [807.]
xii. 1937. pp.x.136. [697.]
xiii. 1938.pp.xi.109. [787.]
xiv. 1939. pp.xi.69. [428.]
xv. 1940–1947. pp.lxxii.221. [2462.]
xvi. 1948–1953. pp.cviii.368. [4192.]
xvii. 1954–1957. pp.xvi.245. [2368.]
xviii. 1958–1960. pp.xii.168. [1644.]
xix. 1961. pp.xii.59. [528.]
xx. 1962–1963. pp.xiii.119. [1022.]
xxi. 1964–1966. pp.xiii.175. [1583.]

COWA bibliography. Current publications in old world archaeology. Area 19—Southeast Asia.*
    i. 1959. pp.y. [75.]
        [*continued as:*]
COWA surveys and bibliographies.
    ii. 1963. pp.9. [106.]
    iii. 1966. pp.7. [113.]

COWA bibliography. Current work in old world archaeology. Area 20—Indonesia (Republic of Indonesia, Portugese Timor, Philippines, Sarawak, North Borneo and Madagascar.)*
    1. 1957. pp.3.11. [138.]
        [*continued as:*]
COWA surveys and bibliographies.
    2. 1960. pp.3.6. [77.]
    3. 1964. pp.5.5. [81.]
    4. 1969. pp.7.10. [147.]

H. H. E. LOOFS, Elements of the megalithic complex in Southeast Asia; an annotated bibliography. Oriental monograph series (no.3): Canberra 1967. pp.x.114. [559.]

botany

CLYDE F[RANKLIN] REED, Bibliography to floras of southeast Asia: Burma, Laos, Thailand, Cambodai, Vietnam ... Malay peninsula, and Singapore. Baltimore 1969. pp.191. [4000.]*

chinese

JOSEPH-JOHN NEVADOMSKY and ALICE LI, The Chinese in Southeast Asia: a selected and annotated bibliography of publications in western languages, 1960–1970. Center for south and southeast Asia studies: University of California Occasional paper (no.6): Berkeley 1970. pp.xvi. 119. [662.]

christianity

GERALD H. ANDERSON, *ed.* Christianity in Southeast Asia: a bibliographical guide. An annotated bibliography of selected references in western languages. Missionary research library: New York and Yale university, Southeast Asia studies. New Haven 1966. pp.ix.69. [1100.]

education

KENNETH L[EE] NEFF, Selected bibliography on education in southeast Asia. U.S. Department of health, education and welfare: Office of education: Studies in comparative education (OE–14071): [Washington] 1963. pp.iii.16. [167.]

forestry

DONN V. HART, A selective bibliography of the State university college of forestry, Syracuse, New York, related to Burma, Thailand, Malaya, Indochina, Indonesia and the Philippines. Syracuse 1961. ff.[i].14. [126.]*

labour

SELECTED bibliographies on labor and industrial relations in Burma, Indonesia, Korea, Malaya, Singapore, Thailand. Industrial relations center: University of Hawaii: Honolulu 1962. pp.ii.64. [660.]*

land tenure

AN ANNOTATED bibliography on land tenure in the british and british protected territories in South east Asia and the Pacific. Colonial office [London] 1952. [1600.]

languages

H[ARRY] L. SHORTO, JUDITH M. JACOB and E. H. S[TUART] SIMMONDS, Bibliographies of mon-khmer and tai linguistics. London oriental bibliographies (vol.2): London 1963. pp.x.87. [931.]

leaders

ALICE SIOW, Leaders of southeast Asia; a selective bibliography. Library School: Wellington 1966.

literature

PHILIP N. JENNER, Southeast asian literatures in translation: a preliminary bibliography. Asian studies at Hawaii (no.9): [Honolulu] 1973. pp.xvii. 198. [3690.]

music

WALTER GERBOTH, Music of east and southeast Asia: a selected bibliography of books, pamphlets, articles and recordings. University of the state of New York: Albany 1963. pp.v.23. [303.]*

oil

QUAH SWEE LAN, Oil discovery and technical change in southeast Asia; a preliminary biblio-

graphy. Library bulletin (no.2): Institute of southeast asian studies: Singapore 1971. pp.[ii].23. [157.]*

population

KAN SIEW MEE, Population of southeast Asia; a selected, annotated bibliography. Library school: Wellington 1964.

science

LIST of scientific and technical journals published in southeast Asia (Philippines, Indonesia, Malaya, Thailand, Indo-China). [United nations educational, scientific and cultural organization:] East Asia scientific cooperation office: Manila 1950. ff.[i].28. [125.]*
— [revised edition]. 1951. ff.xiii.32. [142.]*
— — Supplement . . . (China). 1951. ff.[i].xiii. 28. [120.]*
— Second [*sic*] edition. Scientific and technical journals of east and south east Asia (Hong Kong, Japan, Indonesia, Macao, Malaya, north Borneo, the Philippines, Sarawak, Thailand, Vietnam). 1953. pp.[v].ii.233. [800.]*

BIBLIOGRAPHY of scientific publications of south Asia (India, Burma, Ceylon). Unesco: Science co-operation office for south Asia [iv–xi: South Asia science co-operation office; xii: Indian national scientific documentation centre]: New Delhi &c.
  i–ii. 1949. pp.[vi].107+[ii].88. [4305.]
  iii–iv. 1950. pp.[iv].xxii.84+[v].86. [4245.]
  — — Name index to . . . 1–4. [1952.] pp.[ii]. 48.
  v–vi. 1951. pp.[iii].ii.97.v+[v].viii.ii.124. [5321.]
  vii–viii. 1952. pp.[vii].178+[v].157. [6679.]
  ix–x. 1953. pp.[v].174+[v].158. [6912.]
  xi–xii. 1954. pp.[v].212+[v].129. [7796.]
      [*continued as:*]
Bibliography of scientific publications of south & south east Asia. 1955–64.
[*no more published.*]

PRELIMINARY list of scientific journals in southeast Asia: survey of scientific journals in Southeast Asia by the Unesco field science office, Djakarta, compiled by the Indonesian national scientific documentation center, Indonesian institute of sciences. Djakarta 1971. pp.105.

statistics

BIBLIOGRAPHY of the statistical materials on Southeast Asia. Institute of Asian economic affairs: [Tokyo] 1960. pp.ix.66. [750.]

youth

PAUL PEDERSEN and JOSEPH B. TAMNEY, Youth in Southeast Asia; a bibliography. Occasional paper (no.6): Institute of southeast asian studies: Singapore 1971. pp.v.69. [667.]★

BURMA

i. *General*
ii. *Manuscripts*
iii. *Catalogues of printed books*
iv. *Subjects*

i. *General*

List of non-confidential publications exempted from registration which were issued in Burma during the year. [Rangoon].

    1908. pp.17. [93.]
    1909. pp.21. [125.]
    1910. pp.27. [162.]
    1911. pp.23. [126.]
            [*continued as:*]

List of official publications (other than confidential) issued in Burma during the year . . . which are exempted from registration.

    1912. pp.27. [151.]
    1913. pp.23. [177.]
    1914. pp.25. [137.]
    1915. pp.27. [157.]
    1916. pp.25. [160.]
    1917. pp.15. [144.]
  — [another edition]. pp.[ii].19. [143.]
    1918. pp.[ii].17. [125.]
    1919. pp.[ii].21. [151.]
    1920. pp.[ii].19. [128.]
    1921. pp.[ii].21. [144.]
    1922. pp.[ii].20. [150.]
    1923. pp.[ii].23. [188.]
    1924. pp.[ii].30. [262.]
    1925. pp.[ii].25. [218.]
    1926. pp.[ii].24. [198.]
    1927. pp.[ii].29. [234.]
    1928.
    1929.
    1930.
    1931.
    1932.
    1933.
    1934.
    1935.
    1936.
            [*continued as:*]

List of publications (for official use only) issued during the year.

    1937. pp.[ii].5. [48.]
    1938. pp.[ii].5. [45.]

CATALOGUE of books and pamphlets published in british Burma during the . . . quarter [books printed in lower Burma (Burma)]. Rangoon.

    1868. ff. .1.1.1.
    1869. ff.1.1.1. .
    1870. ff.[4]. [32.]

    1871. ff.[4]. [10.]
    1872. ff.1.1. .1.
    1873. ff.[4]. [41.]
    1874. ff.[2]. [25.]
    1875. ff.[4]. [50.]
    1876. pp.[5]. [50.]
    1877. pp.[8]. [100.]
    1878. pp.[6]. [100.]
    1879. ff.[4]. [100.]
    1880. ff.[4]. [125.]
    1881. ff.[4]. [125.]
    1882. pp.3.3.3.3 [201.]
    1883. pp.3.3.5.6. [170.]
    1884. pp.2.1.4.4. [200.]
    1885. ff.[4]. [75.]
    1886. pp.2.1.2.3. [150.]
    1887. pp.5.4.3.3. [70.]
    1888. pp.[7]. [75.]
    1889. pp.[8]. [100.]
    1890. pp.[8]. [125.]
    1891. pp.1.2.3.4. [200.]
    1892. pp.[6]. [75.]
    1893. pp.[6]. [52.]
    1894. ff.[4]. [35.]
    1895. ff.[4]. [68.]
    1896. ff.[4]. [73.]
    1897. ff.[4]. [49.]
    1898. pp.[5]. [102.]
    1899. pp.2.2.9.9 [119.]
    1900. pp.5.11.7.7. [115.]
    1901. pp.7.5.5.5. [134.]
    1902. pp.5.5.5.7. [123.]
    1903. pp.7.5.5.5. [146.]
    1904. pp.7.3.5.7. [146.]
    1905. pp.7.5.7.4. [140.]
    1906. ff.8.13.12.10. [263.]
    1907. ff.8.6.6.10. [171.]
    1908. ff.15.6.5.8. [200.]
    1909. ff.7.6.9.8. [200.]
    1910. ff.7.12.14.9. [250.]
    1911. ff.15.9.9.12. [300.]
    1912. ff.12.11.13.9. [300.]
    1913. ff.10.8.13.10. [300.]
    1914. ff.10.9.10.6. [300.]
    1915. ff.8.8.8.7. [250.]
    1916. ff.6.8.8.7. [250.]
    1917. ff.6.8.5.5. [200.]
    1918. ff.4.5.7.4. [175.]
    1919. ff.6.5.6.5. [175.]
    1920. ff.8.8.11.6. [200.]
    1921. ff.7.10.7.6. [200.]
    1922. ff.5.6.6.4. [175.]
    1923. ff.7.3.7.7. [175.]
    1924. ff.3.2.2.3. [156.]
    1925. ff.3.2.4.3. [177.]
    1926. ff.4.3.2.3. [167.]
    1927. ff.3.2.4.2. [142.]
    1928. ff.1.2.3.3. [72.]
    1929. ff.4.2. [90.]
    1930. ff.3.4.2.2. [192.]

1931. ff.1.2.5.2. [172.]
1932. ff.2.2.4.2. [202.]
1933. ff.3.2.3.1. [164.]
1934. ff.2.2.2.2. [155.]
1935. ff.2.2.8.2. [217.]
1936. ff. .3.2.3. [185.]
1937. ff.2.2.4.2. [191.]
1938. ff.2.2.3.4. [211.]
1939. ff.6.6.12. [562.]
1940. ff.6.7.9. [531.]
1941. ff.6. [140.]
the title varies.

CATALOGUE of books published in Burma, 1868–1941. Extracted from the Government gazette, Rangoon, 1868–1941.
reproduced in microfiche form by Inter-documentation company, Zug.
— From 4th quarter 1962. 1963 &c.
in progress?

THE BURMA laws list: a list of unrepealed statutes, acts, and regulations and rules and notifications thereunder in force in Burma. Fourth edition. Rangoon 1892. pp.[ii].vii.503.xxix.7. [2500.]
— Fifth edition. 1897. pp.viii.336.64.xxiv. [2500.]
many pages are blank.

HENRI CORDIER, Bibliotheca indo-sinica. Essai d'une bibliographie des ouvrages relatifs à la presqu'île Indo-Chinoise. ... Première partie: Birmanie et Assam. Leide 1908. pp.269. [Burma: 1700.]
100 copies printed; no more published.

N. C. DATTA [NAGENDRA-CHANDRA DATTA]' Index of Burma cases judicially noticed. Rangoon 1909. pp.[xi].151.23. [1500.]

T. Z. OUNG [AUNG], A digest of Burma rulings of the courts of the Judicial commissioners, upper and lower Burma, and the Chief court, lower Burma, from 1872–1908. Rangoon 1912. ff.viii. pp.ix.xxiv.coll.662. [2000.]

CATALOGUE of books [and maps] at the government book depot. Rangoon 1917. pp.61.ix. [1250.]
— [another edition]. 1962. pp.86. [2000.]
now published annually.

S. S. HALKAR [SUBBARĀU ṢESHAGIRI HĀLKAR], A digest of civil rulings of Burma, including cases reported in ... reports ... 1872 ... to 1917 ... Second edition. Rangoon [printed] 1918.

WORLD of books. Burma books club: Rangoon 1925 &c.
ceased publication.

S. S. HALKAR [SUBBARĀU ṢESHAGIRI HĀLKAR], A digest of criminal rulings of Burma, including cases reported in all official and non-official re-

ports (1872 to 1925). ... Second edition. Mylapore [printed] 1926. pp.[iii].32.coll.588.v. [3000.]

SIR FRANK BROWN, India and Burma. Third edition. National book council: Book list (no.62): 1942. pp.8. [240.]
— 4th edition. 1946. pp.12.

NOTES of foreign publications. Department of state: Washington 1950.
List of newspapers & periodicals published in Burma in the english, burmese, chinese, urdu, hindi, tamil and telegu languages.

JOSEPH FISHER, Research bibliography of books, documents and pamphlets on Burma. Rangoon-Hopkins center for southeast asian studies: University of Rangoon: Rangoon 1953.*

FRANK N. TRAGER, JOHN N. MUSGRAVE and JANET WELSH, Annotated bibliography of Burma. Human relations area files: Behavior science bibliographies: New Haven 1956. pp.[ii].viii.230. [1018.]*

MIROSLAV KAFTAN, Indie-Barma-Indonesie. Výběravy seznam literatury. Universita: Knihovna: Cteme a studujeme (1956, no.3): Praha 1956. pp.16. [5100.]

FRANK N. TRAGER, A bibliography, chinese language materials relating to Burma, 1931–1953. New York university: Burma research project: New York [1956]. ff.[i].v.32. [52.]*

HYMAN KUBLIN and LU-YU KIANG, Japanese and chinese language sources on Burma. An annotated bibliography. Human relations area files: Behavior science bibliographies: New Haven 1957. pp.x. 122.[xii]. [229.]*

A CATALOGUE of books, pamphlets, papers, etc. on Burma in the library of mr. & mrs. G. Kirkham. Rangoon 1959. ff.21. [275.]*

CATALOGUE of publications in stock at the Book depot, Rangoon, 1960. Rangoon 1961.
issued under various titles since 1919.

SUGGESTED reading list on Burma. Military assistance institute: Library: Arlington, Va. 1963. pp.22. [750.]

DENISE BERNOT, Bibliographie birmane, années 1950–1960. Atlas ethno-linguistique: Recherche coopérative sur programme no.61: troisième série: bibliographies: Paris 1968. pp.229. [3000.]

CATALOGUE of books published in Burma, 1941–1962. Compiled in 1969 by students of the Department of burmese in the Arts and science university, Rangoon.
MS. in the British museum.

FRANK N. TRAGER [*and others*], Burma; a selected and annotated bibliography. Behavior science bibliographies: Human relations area files: New Haven 1973. pp.xii.356. [2086.]*

TAN SOK JOO, Library resources on Burma in Singapore. Library bulletin (no.5): Institute of southeast asian studies: Singapore 1972. ff. vii.35. [700.]*

ROBERT STREIT and JOHANNES DINDINGER, Bibliotheca missionum. Fortgesetzt von Johannes Rommerskirchen and Joseph Metzler. Achtundzwanzigster band. Missionsliteratur Südasiens (Indien, Pakistan, Birma, Ceylon) 1947–1968. Aachen 1971. pp.xix.517. [1734.]

ii. Manuscripts

LIST of palm leaf manuscripts, paper manuscripts and parabaiks in the mon language preserved in the Manuscript department. Bernard Free library: Rangoon n.d. ff.60.

VIGGO M. FAUSBÖLL, Catalogue of the Mandalay manuscripts in the India office library. London and Woking 1897. pp.52. [176.]
reprinted from Journal of the Pali text society 1896.

TAW SEIN KO, *ed.* Catalogue of the Hlutdaw records. Rangoon 1901–9.

ALPHABETICAL list of palm-leaf manuscripts, paper manuscripts and parabaiks (pali, burmese and sanskrit) preserved in the manuscript department of the Bernard Free library, Rangoon. 1906. ff.60. [2624.]

CATALOGUE of pâli and burmese books and manuscripts belonging to the library of the late king of Burma [Thibaw] and found in the palace at Mandalay in 1886. Rangoon 1910. pp.[115]. [1000.]

iii. Catalogues of printed books

ALPHABETICAL LIST of books in the library of the Burma public works secretariat. Rangoon 1893. pp.71.8.13.
Catalogue of books, periodicals, reports &c. 1909. pp.ii.233.
Catalogue of books. 1924.

LIST of books and reports in library, Intelligence branch, Burma, Mandalay, the 1st December 1892. Rangoon 1893. pp.8.

REVISED catalogue of books in the Burma secretariat library. Rangoon 1896.
Catalogue of books. 1913.

THE BERNARD Free library catalogue, i. General Department. Rangoon 1903.

L[IONEL] D[AVID] BARNETT, A catalogue of the burmese books in the British museum. 1913. pp.iii–vii.coll.348. [2500.]

CATALOGUE of the Central settlement library in the office of the Commissioner of settlements and land records, Burma. Rangoon 1924. pp.62. [1500.]

A CATALOGUE of periodicals in the university & other libraries of Rangoon.... Compiled under the direction of the Library committee, university of Rangoon. Rangoon 1937. pp.[ii].ii.56. [400.]

CATALOGUE of books, pamphlets, papers &c. on Burma in the library of mr. & mrs. G. Kirkham. Rangoon 1959. ff.21. [275.]*

A CATALOGUE of chinese books in the library of the Burma historical commission. Rangoon 1961. pp.119.

KENNETH WHITBREAD, Catalogue of burmese printed books in the India office library. Foreign and commonwealth office: London 1969. pp.xiii. 231. [2800.]

iv. Subjects

agriculture

JOHN HENRY DAVIS, Selected bibliography, Burma and adjacent region: agriculture. University of Florida, Gainesville 1961. ff.80.

MICHAEL Y. NUTTONSON, Climate, soils and rice culture of Burma: supplementary information and a bibliography of the physical environment and agriculture of Burma; a study based on field survey and pertinent records, material and reports. American institute of crop ecology: Washington 1963.

biology

JOHN HENRY DAVIS, Selected bibliography, Burma and adjacent regions: biology, natural history. University of Florida, Gainesville 1961. [*various pagings.*]

buddhism

RICHARD A[BBOTT] GARD, A select bibliography for the study of buddhism in Burma in western languages. Tokyo 1957. pp.iii.40. [500.]*

catholics

H. HOSTEN and E. LUCE, Bibliotheca catholica birmana. Rangoon 1915. pp.122. [658.]

crime, criminal law

S. S. HALKAR [SUBBARĀU ṢESHAGIRI HĀLKAR], A digest of criminal rulings of Burma, including cases reported in all official and non-official reports (1872 to 1925). ... Second edition. Mylapore [printed] 1926. pp.[iii].32.coll.588.v. [3000.]

Furnivall, John S.

FRANK N. TRAGER, Furnivall of Burma: an annotated bibliography of the works of John S. Furnivall. Bibliography series (no.8): Yale university in co-operation with University of British Columbia: Detroit 1963. pp.ii.51. [220.]*

Mon-khmer languages

H. L. SHORTO, JUDITH M. JACOB and E. H. S. SIMMONDS, Bibliographies of mon-khmer and tai linguistics. London oriental bibliographies (vol. 2): 1963. pp.x.88. [931.]

world war II

BURMA campaign 1941–1945. Imperial war museum: Library: [1952]. pp.8. [125.]*
— 2nd edition. [1954]. pp.6. [75.]*

THE SECOND world war. The Burma campaign. Imperial war museum: Library: [1955–1958]. pp. 11+11. [400.]*

INDOCHINA

    i. *General*
    ii. *Subjects*

i. *General*

REVUE bibliographique de l'Indo-Chine. [Rochefort].
    1881. [By Louis Delavaud]. pp.7. [50.]
        [*continued as:*]
    Bibliographie indo-chinoise.
        1881–1882. pp.8. [79.]

MARQUIS [EDMÉ CASIMIR] DE CROIZIER, Contributions a la bibliographie indo-chinoise pour l'année 1883. 1884. pp.60. [50.]

A. LANDES and A. FOLLIOT, Bibliographie de l'Indo-Chine orientale depuis 1880. Bulletin de la Société des études indo-chinoises de Saïgon (année 1889, 1er semestre): Saïgon 1889. pp.87. [1250.]

E. AYMONIER, Sommaire des travaux relatifs a l'Indo-Chine pendant la période 1886–1891. Woking 1893. pp.7.

[L. PÉRALLE], Catalogue de la bibliothèque de la Société des études indochinoises. Saïgon 1897. pp.87. [2000.]

HENRI CORDIER, Bibliotheca indo-sinica. Essai d'une bibliographie des ouvrages relatifs à la presqu'île Indo-Chinoise. ... Première partie: Birmanie et Assam. Leide 1908. pp.269. [2250.]
100 copies printed; no more published.

ANTOINE BRÉBION, Bibliographie des voyages dans l'Indochine française du IXe au XIXe siècle. Saïgon 1910. pp.vi.300.xliv. [300.]

CHARLES B. MAYBON. Note sur les travaux bibliographiques concernant l'Indochine française. Hanoi 1910. pp.13.

A[NTOINE] CABATON, Catalogue sommaire des manuscrits indiens, indo-chinois & malayo-polynésiens. Bibliothèque nationale: 1912. pp.[vi].320. [Indochinese: 350.]

HENRI CORDIER, Bibliotheca indosinica. Dictionnaire bibliographique des ouvrages relatifs à la péninsule indochinoise. École française d'extrême-orient: Publications (vol.xv–xviii bis): 1912–1932. pp.vii.coll.1104 + pp.[iii].coll.1105–1510 + pp.[iii].coll.1511–2280 + pp.[iii].coll.2281–3030 + pp.[iii].coll.311.[20,000.]
the last volume is an index by mme M. A. Roland-Cabaton.

H. PETITJEAN, Répertoire chronologique et alphabétique des lois, décrets, ordonnances, etc. promulgués ou appliqués en Indochine depuis l'occupation de la Cochinchine (1861) jusqu'au 31 décembre 1917. Saïgon 1918. pp.[iii].xi.193. [2500.]
the list actually goes back to 1776.

LIST of references of French Indo-China. Library of Congress: [Washington] 1921. ff.19. [206.]*

PAUL BOUDET and REMY BOURGEOIS, Bibliographie de l'Indochine française, 1913–1926. Hanoi 1929. pp.[iii].vii.271.75. [4000.]
— — 1927–1929. École française d'extrême-orient: 1931. pp.vii.240. [2500.]
— — 1930–1935. 1943. pp.viii.496. [5000.]

P[AUL] B[OUDET], Pour mieux connaître l'Indochine. Essai d'une bibliographie. Hanoi-Haiphong 1922. pp.92. [480.]

ROB[ERT] STREIT and JOHANNES DINDINGER, Bibliotheca missionum. Sechster band. Missionsliteratur Indiens, der Philippinen, Japans und Indochinas 1700–1799. Internationales institut für missionswissenschaftliche forschung: Aachen 1931. pp.32.616. [2005.]
reprint 1964.
— — Elfter band. Missionsliteratur Indochinas 1800–1909. 1939.

ANTOINE BRÉBION, Dictionnaire de bio-bibliographie général ancienne et moderne de l'Indochine française. Publié ... par Antoine Cabaton Académie des sciences coloniales: Annales (vol. viii): 1935. pp.iv.446. [5000.]

TRAN-VÂN-GIÁP, Les chapitres bibliographiques de Lê-quí-Don et de Phan-huy-Chú. Société des études indochinoises: Bulletin (new ser., vol.xiii, no.1): Saïgon 1938. pp.5–217. [329.]
with another titlepage, dated 1937.

BIBLIOGRAPHIE analytique des travaux scientifiques en Indo-Chine 1939–1940–1941. Hanoi 1943.

INDOCHINA. Selected list of references. Widener library: Cambridge, Mass. 1944. pp.108. [550.]

CECIL C[ARLTON] HOBBS [and others], Indochina. A bibliography of the land and people. Library of Congress: Reference department: Washington 1950. pp.xii.367. [1850.]*

ROBERT AUVADE. Bibliographie critique des oeuvres parues sur l'Indochine française. Un siècle d'histoire et d'enseignement. Paris 1965. pp.153. [230.]

ii. Subjects

agriculture

PIERRE CARTON, Catalogue de la bibliothèque. Institut scientifique de l'Indochine: Hanoï 1922. pp.xi.433. [5000.]

botany

A. PÉTELOT, Analyse des travaux de zoologie et de botanique concernant l'Indochine publiés en 1929. Direction générale de l'instruction publique: Hanoï 1930. pp.[i].22. [60.]

geology

PUBLICATIONS du service géologique de l'Indochine. Catalogue et prix-courant. Hanoï 1931. pp.16. [100.]
— [another printed]. 1937. pp.27. [200.]

medicine

B[ORIS] NOYER, Bibliographie analytique des travaux scientifiques en Indochine, 1939–1941. Sciences médicales et vétérinaires. Hanoï 1943. pp.48. [569.]

zoology

A. PÉTELOT, Analyse des travaux de zoologie et de botanique concernant l'Indochine publiés en 1929. Direction générale de l'instruction publique: Hanoi 1930. pp.22. [100.]

CAMBODIA

G[EORGE] COEDÈS, Bibliographie raisonnée des travaux relatifs a l'archéologie du Cambodge et du Champa. 1909. pp.47. [368.]

CATALOGUE de la bibliothèque populaire de Takhmau. Service del 'I. P. P. [Institut de Phnom-Pen]: [Takhmau 1944]. pp.9. [cambodian: 100.]
250 copies printed.

[LOUIS FINOT], Liste des manuscrits khmères de l'École française d'extrême orient. Hanoi 1902. pp.14. [165.]

BIBLIOGRAPHY of Cambodia. Behavior science bibliographies: Human relations area files: New Haven 1951.

LISTE des journaux, des bulletins, des revues et des livres en dépôt légal aux Archives nationales a Phnom Penh et qui ont été partagés pour remettre au Gouvernement fédéral par Pach Choeun. Phnom-Penh 1951.

DIK KEAM, Catalogue des auteurs et des livres publiés au Cambodge. Association des écrivains khmers: Phnom Penh 1966. ff.24. [684.]*

CAMBODIA: a select bibliography. Mekong documentation centre of the Committee for co-ordination of investigations of the lower Mekong basin: Economic commission for Asia and the Far east: Bankgok 1967. pp.iv.101. [1013.]*

MARY L. FISHER, Cambodia: an annotated bibliography of its history, geography, politics and economy since 1954. Center for international studies: Massachusetts institute of technology: [Cambridge, Mass.] 1967. pp.v.66. [359.]*

JACQUES BARUCH, Bibliographie des traductions françaises des littératures du Viet-Nam et du Cambodge. Etudes orientales (no.3): Bruxelles 1968. ff.63. [308.]*

SENG PHAN, Catalogue des ouvrages en langue européenne classés par matière. Bibliothèque de l'Institut buddhique. Revue et corrigé par Tan-Kim-Huon. Mis en page par Dik Keam. Edité sur l'initiative de Leang-Hap-An. Phnom Penh.
    i. A–AR. 1966. ff.[ii].ii.76. [1209.]
    ii. AR–CON. 1967. ff.ii.77–152. [1340.]
    iii. CON–FIN. 1969. ff.153–232. [1416.]

DONN V. HART, Cambodia bibliography: preliminary draft. Department of anthropology: Syracuse 1970. ff.v.5. [28.]*

G[ODFREY] RAYMOND NUNN, and DO VAN ANH, Vietnamese, Cambodian & Laotian newspapers; an international union list. [Taipei]. 1972. pp.xiii.104. [948.]

JOEL M. HALPERN and JAMES A. HAFNER, A preliminary and partial bibliography of miscellaneous research materials on Laos, with special reference to the Mekong development scheme, plus selected items on Cambodia, Thailand and Vietnam. Courrier de l'extrême-orient (iii): Centre d'étude du sud-est asiatique et de l'extrême-orient: Bruxelles 1971. ff.vii.113. [1200.]*

LAOS

M. MEILLIER, Bibliothèque royale de Luang-Prabang. Catalogue. Hanoi-Haiphong 1918. pp.42. [1173.]

GERALD C. HICKEY, *ed.*, Area handbook on Laos. Human relations area files: Subcontractor's monograph no.23: University of Chicago. Chicago 1955.★

BIBLIOGRAPHY of Laos. Behavior science bibliographies: Human relations area files: Chicago university, Laos research project: New Haven 1956.

[THAO KÉNE], Bibliographie du Laos. Comité littéraire lao: [Vientiane] 1958. ff.[iii].68.[vii]. [750.]★

THAO KÉNE, Catalogue des manuscrits de la littérature du Laos. Ministère de l'éducation nationale: Comité littéraire Lao: [Vientiane?] 1958. ff.43. [1163.]★

JOEL HALPERN, An annotated bibliography on the peoples of Laos and northern Thailand. Selected sources in english, french and japanese published since 1945. Laos project paper (no.5): Los Angeles 1961. ff.6. [84.]★

JOHN MCKINSTRY, Bibliography of Laos and ethnically related areas. Laos project paper (no. 22): Los Angeles [1962?]. ff.91. [1000.]★

SUGGESTED reading list on Laos Military assistance institute: Library. Arlington, Va. 1963. pp. 20. [200.]★

PIERRE BARNARD LAFONT, Bibliographie du Laos. Publications de l'École française d'extrême-orient (vol. L): Paris 1964. pp.269. [2116.]

BIBLIOGRAPHIE nationale. Bibliothèque nationale: Vientiane [1969?]. pp.97.

DONN V. HART, Laos bibliography: preliminary draft. Department of anthropology: Syracuse [1970?]. ff.iv.12. [100.]★

G[ODFREY] RAYMOND NUNN and DO VAN ANH' Vietnamese, cambodian and laotian newapapers' An international union list. Taipei 1972. pp.xiii' 104. [948.]

JOEL M. HALPERN and JAMES A. HAFNER, A preliminary and partial bibliography of miscellaneous research materials on Laos, with special reference to the Mekong development scheme, plus selected items on Cambodia, Thailand and Vietnam. Courrier de l'extrême-orient (iii): Centre d'étude du sud-est asiatique et de l'extrême-orient: Bruxelles 1971. ff.vii.113. [1200.]★

DAVID K. WYATT, Preliminary checklist of Laos serials. Second edition. Southeast Asia program: Cornell university: Ithaca 1973. pp.20. [131.]★

ANNAM

V. A. BARBIÉ DU BOCAGE, Bibliographie annamite. Livres, recueils périodiques, manuscrits, plans. 1867. pp.[iii].107. [1250.]

continued in the Bulletin du Comité agricole cochinchine *and the* Bulletin de la Société académique indo-chinoise.

LA COCHINCHINE intellectuelle. Catalogue des ouvrages d'auteurs, français ou annamites, habitant la Cochinchine. Exposition nationale intercoloniale de Marseille en 1906: Saïgon [printed] 1906. pp.16.iii. [150.]

G. COEDÈS, Bibliographie raisonnée des travaux relatifs a l'archéologie du Cambodge et du Champa. 1909. pp.47. [368.]

L. CADIÈRE, Listes des publications de L. Cadière sur l'Annam, 1901-1920. Hanoi 1920. pp.10.

ÉM. GASPARDONE, Bibliographie annamite. Hanoï 1935. pp.173.

TRAN-VĂN-GIÁP, Les chapitres bibliographiques de Lê-quí-Dôn et de Phan-huy-Chú. Société des études indochinoises: Bulletin (new ser., vol.xiii, no.1): Saigon 1938. pp.5-217. [329.] *with another titlepage, dated 1937.*

CATALOGUE de la bibliothèque populaire de Takhmau. Service de l'I.P.P. [Institut de Phnom-Penh]: [Takhmau 1944]. pp.9. [annamite: 64.] *250 copies printed.*

PAUL K. BENEDICT, Selected list of materials for the study of the annamese language. Language series (no.3): Southeast Asia institute: New York 1947. pp.7.

VIETNAM

MIROSLAV KAFTAN, Lidově demokratické země Asie: Korea-Vietnam-Mongolsko. Výberovy seznam literatury. Universita: Knihovna: Čteme a studujeme (1956, no.2): Praha 1956. pp.16. [100.]★

C. G. AMBEKAR, Viet-Nam. A reading li*l*.]st. [*s*. 1958. pp.[iii].42. [800.]★

ORAL E. PARKS and MILAN JAN REBAN, Recent articles on Vietnam. An annotated bibliography. Michigan state university: Vietnam project: [East Lansing] 1958. ff.25.5.★

NGUYEN XUAN DAO and RICHARD K. GARDNER, Bibliography of periodicals published in Viet Nam. Michigan state university: Vietnam project: East Lansing 1958. ff.[8]. [150.]★

— — [another edition]. Saigon 1962. ff.[ii].26. [250.]★

DOAN THI DO, Le journalisme au Viêt-Nam et les périodiques vietnamiens de 1865 a 1944 conservés a la bibliothèque nationale. [1958]. pp.8. [100.]

WHAT to read on Vietnam. A selected annotated bibliography. Institute of Pacific relations. New York 1959. pp.[v].67. [400.]★

— Second edition. 1960. ff.[iv].73. [500.]★

NGUYEN DINH HOA, Reading list on Vietnamese language and writing. Saigon 1960. pp.13. *reprinted from* Van-hoá Nguyet-san, XI-6, 685–697, 1962.

LOUIS ANDREATTA, Education in Vietnam; a selected bibliography. American friends of Vietnam: New York 1966. pp.4. [29.]★

LOUIS ANDREATTA, Vietnam 1961; a checklist. American friends of Vietnam: New York 1962. pp.6.
— 1962. ff.2.
— 1963.

QUYNH BUI and NGUYEN HUNG-CUONG, Elenchus bibliographicus scientiarum socialium in Viet-Nam. Saigon 1962.

ROY JUMPER [*and others*], Bibliography on the political and administrative history of Vietnam, 1802–1962. Michigan state university: Vietnam advisory group: [Saigon] 1962. ff.vi.179. [964.]★

JANE GODFREY KEYES, A bibliography of vietnamese publications in the Cornell university library. Cornell university: Department of asian studies: Southeast Asia program: Data paper (no.47): Ithaca 1962. pp.[x].116.[x]. [1100].
limited to publications on North Vietnam.
— Supplement. A bibliography of western language publications concerning north Viet Nam in the Cornell university library. Data paper (no.63): Ithaca 1966. pp.xi.280. [1750.]★

DONALDA FAZAKAS, Vietnamese art and archaeology: a selected bibliography. American friends of Vietnam: New York 1962. ff.[ii].9. [77.]★

NOUVELLES acquisitions. [Directorate of national archives and libraries.] Saigon 1962–8.

BULLETIN analytique des travaux scientifiques publiés au Viet-Nam, volume 1 (1942–1962). Section 1, Médecine et sciences affiliées par Nguyen-huu et Vu-van-nguyen. Service de documentation: Saigon [1963]. pp.[xxi].160. [1494.]

NGUYEN-KHAC-KHAM, A bibliography on vietnamese buddhism. Directorate of national archives and libraries: Saigon 1963. ff.[ii].32. [250.]★

THE REPUBLIC of Vietnam (south Vietnam); a bibliography. External research paper (143): External research staff: Department of state: Washington 1963. pp.22.

SUGGESTED reading list on Vietnam. Military assistance institute: Library: Arlington, Va. 1963. pp.36. [350.]★

JOSEPH COATES, Bibliography of Vietnam. Institute for defense analysis: Research and

engineering support division: International development agency: Washington 1964. ff.vi.52. [709.]★

THE DEMOCRATIC republic of Viet-nam (north Viet-nam); a bibliography. External research paper (142, reprint). External research staff: Department of state: Washington 1964. ff.ii.pp. 21. [230.]★

TRAN THI-KIMSA, Bibliography on Vietnam, 1954–1964. National institute of administration: Saigon 1965. pp.xi.255. [3500.]

PETER BERTON, Bibliography of soviet writings on Vietnam; books and pamphlets, book reviews, and periodical & newspapers. First quarter 1966. School of international relations: University of California: Los Angeles 1966. pp.47.

BIBLIOGRAPHIE commentée sur la culture vietnamienne. Commented bibliography on Vietnamese culture. Vietnam national commission for UNESCO: Saigon 1966. pp.[i].226.

A BIBLIOGRAPHY on Christianity in Vietnam. Directorate of national archives and libraries: [Saigon] 1966. ff.81. [634.]★

A BIBLIOGRAPHY on confucianism in Vietnam. Directorate of national archives and libraries: [Saigon] 1966. ff.41. [253.]★

RENNIE C. JONES, Vietnam: historical background, the 1954 Geneva conference, the International commission for control. Research service bibliographies (1966 no.5): State library of Victoria: Melbourne 1966. pp.iv.ff.10. [72.]★

NGUYÊN KHÁC-KHAM [*and others*], A bibliography on the acceptance of western cultures in Vietnam from the XVIth century to the XXth century. Directorate of national archives and libraries: Saigon 1966. ff.35. [294].★

NHA VĂN-KHÔ and THU-VIÊN QUÔC-GIA, Reading list on vietnamese language. Directorate of national archives and libraries: [Saigon] 1966. ff.29. [243.]★

VIET-NAM; a reading list. Mekong documentation centre of the Committee for co-ordination of investigations of the lower Mekong basin: Economic commission for Asia and the Far east: Bangkok 1966. pp.iv.119. [1251.]★

P. F. COX, Vietnam; a critical booklist. Hertfordshire county library: [Hertford 1967?] [62.]★

NATIONAL bibliography of Vietnam. Thu-tich quoc-gia Viet-nam. Directorate of national archives and libraries: Saigon.★
1967-8. pp.36.51.36. [498.]
1969. ff.66.60. [522.]
1970. ff.72.
in progress?

NGYUEN-THE-ANH, Bibliographie critique sur les relations entre le Viêt-Nam et l'Occident (ouvrages et articles en langues occidentales). Paris 1967. pp.310. [1627.]

JACQUES BARUCH, Bibliographie des traductions françaises des littératures du Viêt-Nam et du Cambodge. Etudes orientales (no.3): Bruxelles 1968. ff.[iv].65. [308.]*

P. A. O'BRIEN, Vietnam. Research service bibliographies (series 4, no.113): State library of South Australia: Adelaide 1968. pp.50. [660.]*

ANNIE E. GRIMES, An annotated bibliography of climatic maps of north Vietnam. U.S. Department of commerce: Environmental science services administration: Environmental data service: Silver Spring, Md. 1968. ff.x.43. [125.]*

RUSSELL W. RAMSEY, Some keys to the Vietnam puzzle. Bibliographic series (no.7): Department of reference and bibliography: University of Florida libraries: Gainesville 1968. pp.55. [174.]*

UNIVERSITY of California library holdings on Vietnam. 1968. ff.54. [1000.]*

HARRISON YOUNGREN [and others], Bibliography. Center for vietnamese studies and programs: Southern Illinois university: Carbondale 1969. pp.vii.43. [1600.]

GORDON O. ALLEN and MICHAEL J. KOLL, edd., Vietnam subject index catalog. Research files of the Engineer agency for resources inventories and Vietnam research and evaluation information center, Bureau for Vietnam. 1970. ff.vii.pp.288. [4600.]*

JANET G. GEE and MARY ANGLEMYER, edd., Vietnam agriculture; a select annotated bibliography, prepared by Engineer agency for resources inventories in co-operation with Vietnam research and evaluation information center, Bureau for Vietnam, Agency for international development: Washington 1970.

G[ODFREY] RAYMOND NUNN and DO VAN ANH, Vietnamese, cambodian & laotian newspapers; an international union list. Taipei 1970. pp.xiii.104. [948.]

VIETNAM, a selected annotated bibliography: agriculture. U.S. Department of the army: Engineer agency for resources inventory: Washington 1970. pp.58.

VIETNAM subject index; catalog. Research files of the Engineer agency for resources inventories and Vietnam research and evaluation information center: Bureau for Vietnam: [Washington 1970]. pp.vii.288. [4000.]*

VIETNAM, subject index: maps. Research files of the Engineer agency for resources inventories and Vietnam research and evaluation information center: Bureau for Vietnam: [Washington] 1970. ff.xviii.182. [182.]*

NGUYEN HUNG CUONG, Bibliographie des sciences sociales au Vietnam. A bibliography of social science materials published in Vietnam (1947–1967). Saigon 1970. pp.246. [1247.]

JOEL M. HALPERN and JAMES A. HAFNER, A preliminary and partial bibliography of miscellaneous research materials on Laos, with special reference to the Mekong development scheme plus selected items on Cambodia, Thailand and Vietnam. Centre d'étude du sud-est asiatique et de l'extrême-orient: Bruxelles 1971. ff.vii.113. [1200.]
Constitutes nos. 45–47 (1972) of Courrier de l'extrême-orient.

GIOK PO OEY and NGUYEN HOA, A checklist of the vietnamese holdings of the Wason collection, Cornell university libraries, as of June 1971. Data paper (no.84): Southeast Asia program: Department of asian studies: Cornell university: Ithaca 1971. pp.vii.377. [6199.]*

MILTON LEITENBERG, Bibliography: Vietnam. Stockholm 1971. ff.18. [421.]*

[FRANÇOISE DIRER and EDITH BOUCHÉ], Vietnam 1954–1971: essai d'une bibliographie pratique. Association d'amitié franco-vietnamienne: [1972]. pp.[35]. [800.]*

BRUNO CARUSO, DANIELA VIGLIONE and SILVIA DE BENEDETTO, Vietnam, Bibliografia e documenti sull' aggressione imperialista contro il popolo vietnamita. Roma 1972. pp.90. [2000.]

JOHN H. M. CHEN, Vietnam; a comprehensive bibliography. Metuchen, N.J. 1973. pp.ix.314. [2331.]*

MARION W[RIGHT] ROSS, Bibliography of vietnamese literature in the Wason collection at Cornell university. Data paper (no.90): Southeast Asia program: Cornell university: Ithaca 1973. pp.vii.178. [2841.]*

EAST INDIES

i. *General*
ii. *Periodicals*
iii. *Subjects*

i. *General*

[GEORG] M[ICHAEL] ASHER, A bibliographical and historical essay on the dutch books and pamphlets relating to New-Netherland, and to the Dutch west-India company and to its possessions in

Brazil, Angola, etc. Amsterdam 1854–1867. pp.
lii.234. [369.]

a photographic reprint was issued, Amsterdam 1960.

LABUAN and the Indian archipelago. [Colonial
office (no.28 of a series of lists of works in the
library): 1860]. pp.4. [60.]

NUMERICAL list and index to the East India
papers presented by the East India company to
the library of the House of commons, and continued by order of the Secretary of state for India.
1861. pp.xxvi.189. [3000.]

W. NOEL SAINSBURY, Calendar of state papers,
colonial series, East Indies ... preserved in her
majesty's Public record office.

> 1513–1616. 1862. pp.lxxvii.556. [1250.]
> 1617–1621. 1870. pp.lxxxi.597. [2000.]
> 1622–1624. 1878. pp.lxxii.600. [2000.]
> 1625–1629. 1884. pp.xxiii.804. [2000.]
> 1630–1634. 1892. pp.xlix.720. [1500.]
> *[continued as:]*

Ethel Bruce Sainsbury, A calendar of the court
minutes, etc. of the East India company. Oxford.

> 1635–1639. 1907. pp.xxxvi.396. [500.]
> 1640–1643. 1909. pp.xxx.408. [400.]
> 1644–1649. 1912. pp.xxviii.424. [500.]
> 1650–1654. 1913. pp.xxxii.404. [500.]
> 1655–1659. 1916. pp.xxxiv.388. [750.]
> 1660–1663. 1922. pp.xlvi.402. [750.]
> 1664–1667. 1925. pp.xxix.467. [1000.]
> 1668–1670. 1929. pp.xx.444. [1000.]
> 1671–1673. 1932. pp.xxvii.356. [1000.]
> 1674–1676. 1935. pp.xl.444. [1000.]
> 1677–1679. 1938. pp.xxix.376. [750.]

— — A supplementary calendar of documents
in the India office relating to India or to the home
affairs of the East India company, 1600–1640. By
sir William Foster. India office: 1928. pp.[iii].viii.
181. [512.]

W. N. VERLEGH, Algemeen alphabetisch register
op de verzameling der algemeene orders voor het
leger in nederlandsch Indie ... 1830–1868. Zalt-
bommel 1869. pp.[iv].107. [2000.]
interleaved.

J. BOUDEWIJNSE, Catalogus der bibliotheek van
het Indisch genootschap, te s' Gravenhage. 1869.
pp.8.180. [2000.]
— — Supplement. 1874. pp.[iii].37. [450.]
— — 2e Supplement. 1877. pp.34. [450.]

J[ACOBUS] A[NNE] VAN DER CHIJS, Proeve eener
ned. indische bibliographie (1659–1870). Bataviaasch genootschap van kunsten en wetenschappen: Verhandelingen (vol.xxxvii). Batavia &c.
1875. pp.[vi].325. [4000.]
— — Vermeerderdeen verbeterdeherdruk voor
de jaren 1659–1720, supplement en verbeteringen
voor de jaren 1721–1870. ... (vol.xxxix): 1880.
pp.[ii].iv.95. [1000.]

— — Supplement II. ... (vol.lv, no.3): 1903.
pp.64. [500.]

J. C. HOOYKAAS, Repertorium op de koloniale
litteratuur, of systematische inhoudsopgaaf van
hetgeen voorkomt over de koloniën, (beoosten
de Kaap) in mengelwerken en tijdschriften, van
1595 tot 1865 uitgegeven in Nederland en zijne
overzeesche bezittingen. ... Ter perse bezorgd
door W[illem] N[ikolaas] Du Rieu. Amsterdam
1877–1880. pp.xiv.31.652+xvi.752. [21,373.]

C[ORNELIUS] M[ARIUS] KAN, Proeve eener geographische bibliographie van nederlandsch Oost-
Indië voor de jaren 1865–1880. Utrecht 1881.
pp.xvi.128. [2000.]

J[ACOBUS] A[NNE] VAN DER CHIJS, Inventaris van
'slands archief te Batavia (1602–1816). Batavia
1882. pp.xix.477. [100,000.]

REALIA. Register op de generale resolutiën van
het kasteel Batavia, 1632–1805. Bataviaasch genootschap van kunsten en wetenschappen: Leiden
[vols.ii–iii: 's-Hage] 1882–1886. pp.[iii].ii.504+
[iii].285+[iii].406. [50,000.]

FREDERICK CHARLES DANVERS, Report to the
Secretary of state for India in council on the
records of the India office.... Vol.I. Part I. Records
relating to agencies, factories, and settlements not
now under the administration of the government
of India. 1887. pp.[iii].189.xxxviii. [large number.]

NEDERLANDSCH koloniaal centraalblad. Maan-
delijksch overzicht betreffende de litteratuur van
nederlandsch Oost- en West-Indië. ... Geredi-
geerd door C. M. Pleyte, 1ste jaargang ... no.1
[–10]. Leiden 1894. pp.124. [1000.]
no more published.

A. HARTMANN, Reportorium op de literatuur
betreffende de nederlandsche koloniën in Oost-
en West-Indie voor zoover zij verspreid is in
tijdschriften en mengelwerken. 1895. pp.xviii.455.
[15,000.]
covers the years 1840–1893.

> — Eerste vervolg (1894–1900). 1901. pp.xvi.
>   225. [7000.]
> — Tweede vervolg (1901–1905.) 1906. pp.
>   xvi. 235. [7000.]
> — Derde vervolg (1906–1910). By W. J. P. J.
>   Schalker and W. C. Muller. 1912. pp.xiii.
>   271. [800.]
> — Vierde vervolg (1911–1915). 1917. pp.xv.
>   378. [10,000.]
> — Vijfde vervolg (1916–1920). 1923. pp.xii.
>   509. [13,000.]
> — Zesde vervolg (1921–1925). 1928. pp.xii.
>   523. [14,000.]
> — Zevende vervolg (1926–1930). By D.
>   Sepp. 1935. pp.xxiv.712. [17,500.]

— Achtste vervolg (1931–1932). 1934. pp.xx. 189. [5000.]
no more published.

LIST of marine records of the late East India company, and of subsequent date, preserved in the record department of the India office, London. 1896. pp.xxi.160. [5250.]

[FREDERICK CHARLES DANVERS], List of factory records of the late East India company, preserved in the record department of the India office. 1897. pp.xxviii.91. [50,000.]

PRESS list of ancient dutch records, from 1657 to 1825. Presidency of Madras: [1897]. pp.137. [1750.]

[G. P. ROUFFAER], Catalogus der land- en zeekaarten toebehoorende aan het Koninklijk instituut voor de taal-, land- en volkenkunde van nederlandsch-Indie. 's-Gravenhage 1898. pp.85. [600.]
[—] — [another edition]. Door W. C. Muller. 1913. pp.viii.151. [1500.]

ANNWINSTEN betreffende de kolonien gedeeltelijk behoorende tot de koloniale boekerij van wijlen jhr. mr. J. K. W. Quarles van Ufford. Met eene lijst der koloniale tijdschriften. Universiteit: Bibliotheek: Amsterdam 1904. pp.viii.42. [750.]

CATALOGUS der boekverzameling. Nieuwe uitgaave. Koloniaal museum: Haarlem. 1908. pp. viii.208. [4000.]

JOHAN DUPARC, Verzameling van nederlandsch-indische rechtspraak en rechtsliteratuur, 1898–1907. 's-Gravenhage 1909. pp.779.
— — [supplements.]
    i. 1908–1909. pp.169.
    ii. 1909–1919. Door A. S. Hirsch.
    iii. 1920–1924. Door Joh. Paulus.
    iv. 1925–1929. pp.176.

FLORIS PRIMS, Inventaris op het archief der Generale indische compagnie (Compagnie d'Ostende) 1723–1777, omvattende het archief van het Comptoir generaal te Antwerpen, de scheepskapiteins, de indische fatorijen. Stadsarchief: Antwerpen 1925. pp.48. [large number.]

J. C. VAN SLEE, Catalogus van de chineesch-indische boekverzameling. Athenaeum-bibliotheek: Deventer 1925. pp.40. [East Indies: 150.]

RAADGEVER voor koloniale jeugdlectuur. Kon. vereeniging "Koloniaal instituut": Amsterdam 1935. pp.32. [75.]

LITERATUUR-OVERZICHT voor de taal-, land- en volkenkunde en geschiedenis van nederlandsch-Indië. Koninklijk instituut voor de taal-, land- en volkenkunde von nederlandsch Indië: 's-Gravenhage.
    i. 1937. Samengesteld door F. H. van Naerssen. pp.37. [600.]
    ii. 1938.
    [iii]. 1939. Door H. van Meurs. pp.104. [1080.]
    iv. 1940.

GERONEOGRAFEERDE catalogus der werken betreffende land en volk van Nederlandsch-Indië (afzonderlijke eilanden). K. Bataviaasch genootschap van kunsten en wetenschappen: Bibliotheek: Batavia 1938. pp.278.

CATALOGUS der boekwerken betreffende Nederlandsch-Indië aanwezig in de bibliotheek van het Central kantoor voor de statistiek. Batavia 1938. pp.309.

CATALOGUS dari boekoe-boekoe [buku-buku] dan madjallah-madjallah. Batavia [Bandung].
    1870–1937. [By] G. Ockeloen. [1940]. pp. [viii].612. [6000.]
    1937–1949. 1950. pp.140.115. [5000.]
    1950–1951. 1952. pp.312. [4000.]
    1952–1953. 1954. pp.276. [3000.]

G. OCKELOEN, Catalogus van boeken en tijdschrifien uitgegeven in Ned. Oost-Indië van 1870–1937. Batavia &c. [1940]. pp.[vii].1016.25. [10,000.]*
— — Catalogus van in Nederlandsch-Indië verschenen boeken in den jaren 1938–1941 en enkele aanvullingen. . . . Nederlandsche uitgaven. 1942. pp.322. [2500.]
limited to publications in dutch.

[A. J. BERNET KEMPERS], Register op de uitgaven van het Konninklijk bataviaasch genootschap van kunsten en wetenschappen, 1920–1940. Bandoeng 1942. pp.[vii].90. [1000.]

HELEN F[IELD] CONOVER, The Netherlands East Indies. A selected list of references. Compiled . . . under the direction of Florence S[elma] Hellman. Library of Congress: [Washington] 1942. pp.46. [446.]*

MATERIALS in the National archives relating to the Netherlands East Indies. National archives. Reference information circular (no.12): [Washington] 1942. pp.10. [large number.]

NETHERLANDS East Indies. A bibliography of books published after 1930, and periodical articles after 1932, available in U.S. libraries. Library of Congress. Reference department: Washington 1945. pp.[ii].v.208. [7000.]

VOORLOOPIGE catalogus. Opgave van kaarten. Topografische dienst in Nederlandsch Indië: [s.l.] 1947. pp.21. [300.]

w. ph. coolhaas, A critical survey of studies on dutch colonial history. Bibliographical series (4): Koninklijk instituut voor taal-, land- en volkenkunde: 's-Gravenhage 1960. pp.lvi.154. [1500.]

H. DE BUCK and E. M. SMIT, Bibliografie der geschiedenis van Nederland. Samengesteld in opdracht van het Nederlands comité voor geschiedkundige wetenschappen. Leiden 1968. pp.xx.712. [colonial history: 448.]

ii. *Periodicals*

AANWINSTEN betreffende de kolonien gedeeltelijk behoorende tot de Koloniale boekerij van wijlen jhr. mr. J. K. W. Quarles van Ufford. Met eene lijst der koloniale tijdschriften. Universiteit: Bibliotheek: Amsterdam 1904. pp.viii.42. [periodicals: 150.]

SYSTEMATISCHE katalogus van tijdschrift- en dagbladartikelen. Bureau voor ekonomische en sociale dokumentatie: Koloniale studien (bijlage): Weltevreden 1926. pp.238.
only parts 1–8 were published.

iii. *Subjects*

customary law

LITERATUURLIJST voor het adatrecht van Indonesië. Uitgeveven door de Adatrechtstichting te Leiden. 's-Gravenhage 1920. pp.ix: 192. [3000.]
— Tweede druk. 1929. pp.[viii]. 455. [7250.]

ADATRECHTBUNDELS. Aanvullende literatuurlijst voor het adatrecht van Indonesïe. 1927–1937. Den Haag 1938. pp.xl. 297–451.
[*continued as:*]
LITERATUUROPGAVE voor het adatrecht. (Leiden? 1940 &c.?]

economics

LIST of references on the commerce, resources, and economic conditions of the Dutch East Indies. Library of Congress: Washington 1918.ff.6. [70.]*

education

CATALOGUS van leermiddelen en gedrukten ten behoeve van de scholen van westersch lager onderwijs. Departement van onderwijs en eeredienst: Batavia 1940. pp.71.

forestry

CATALOGUS van de bibliotheek van het boschwezen in Nederlandsch-Indië. 3de druk. Weltevreden 1910. pp.[iii].104. [1000.]
— Supplement. 1911. pp.[iii].62. [600.]

geology

OPGAVE van geschriften over geologie en mijnbouw van Nederlandsch oost-Indie. Geologisch mijnbouwkundig genootschap voor

Nederland en koloniën: Verhandelingen (vols.i &c): 's-Gravenhage.
i. Door R[ogier] D[iederik] M[arius] Verbeek. 1912–1915.
ii. 1913–1922.
[*continued as:*]
Geologisch mijnbouwkundige bibliographie van Nederlandsch-Indië.
iii. 1923–1932. Door R. D. M. Verbeek [parts 13–20: Nicolas Wing Easton].
iv. 1933–1936.

medicine

C[ORNELIS] L[EENDERT] VAN DER BURG, Proeve van een overzicht der in nederlandsch Indië gepubliceerde geneeskundige boeken en der verhandelingen over geneeskundige onderwerpen voorkomende in de tijdschriften in nederlandsch Indië uitgegeven. Batavia 1877. pp.46.

mining

UITGAVEN van den Dienst van den mijnbouw in Nederlandsch-Indië, 1900–1939. Batavia 1939. pp.39. [300.]

science

H[ENRI] C[ONSTANTINOS] A[LEXANDROS] MULLER, Catalogue of manuscripts, old curious and more recent and richly illustrated books concerning the study of science in the Dutch East Indies exhibited in the Technical high school at Bandoeng. [Bandoeng 1929]. pp.38. [136.]

world war II

A. G. VROMANS, De indische collectie van het Rijksinstituut voor oorlogsdocumentatie te Amsterdam. Stichting "Indie in de tweede wereldoorlag": Amsterdam 1954. pp.38. [large number.]*

INDONESIA [see also EAST INDIES]

i. *General*
ii. *Periodicals*
iii. *Academic writings*
iv. *Subjects*
v. *Topography*
vi. *Indonesian languages and literatures*

i. *General*

[W. J. MULLER], Literatuurlijst voor het adatrecht van Indonesië. Adratrechstichting te Leiden: 's-Gravenhage 1920. pp.[viii].193. [3500.]
— — Tweede druk. [By Johannis Anthonie Quist]. 1927. pp.[viii].455. [9120.]
— — — Aanvullende literatuurlijst ... (1927–1 september 1937). 1938. pp.159. [2500.]

ROB[ERT] STREIT and JOHANNES DINDINGER, Bibliotheca missionum. Achter band. Missionsliteratur Indiens u. Indonesiens 1800–1909. Internationales institut für missionswissenschaftliche forschung: Aachen 1934. pp.35.1028. [3201.]

RADEN M. NG[ABEI] POERBATJARAKA [PŪRVACHARAKA], P. VOORHOEVE and C. HOOYKAAS, Indonesische handschriften. Koninklijk bataviaasch genootschap van kunsten en wetenschappen: Bandung 1950. pp.210. [500.]

HEDWIG SCHLEIFFER, Bibliography [Selective bibliography] on the economic and political development of Indonesia. Edited by Douglas S. Paauw. Massachusetts institute of technology: Center for international studies: Cambridge 1953–1955. ff.iv.27+[ii].28–78+[ii].79–110+[ii].111–142+[ii].143–169+[i].61. [2999.]*

W[ILLEM] A[LEXANDER] BRAASEM, Moderne indonesische literatuur. Doorbraak uit oude bedding. Met een bio-bibliografie van indonesische letterkindigen. Amsterdam 1954. pp.99. [250.]

INDONESIA. Commonwealth national library, Canberra: Select bibliographies: General series (no.3): Canberra 1954. ff.[iv].2.14.8.6.10.19.17.9.5.21. [800.]*

R. PAMUNTJAK, A regional bibliography of social science publications: Indonesia. National bibliographic centre: [Djakarta 1955]. pp.[ii].ii.65. [594.]

MIROSLAV KAFTAN, Indie-Barma-Indonesie. Výběravy seznam literatury. Universita: Knihovna: Čteme a studujeme (1956, no.3): Praha 1956. pp. 16. [100.]

DANIEL S. LEV, A bibliography of indonesian government documents and selected indonesian writings on government in the Cornell university library. Cornell university: Department of far eastern studies: Southeast Asia program: Data paper (no.31): Ithaca 1958. ff.[iii].58. [450.]*
—— [another edition]. Editors ... Thomas W[alter] Maretzki and H[enri] Th[éodore] Fischer. Human relations area files: Behavior science bibliographies: 1955. pp.[ii].xxviii.320+[ii].321–663. [12,500.]*

ドネシア軍政に関する資料目録
[List of japanese documents for a 日本のイン study of the impact of the japanese military government to the indonesian independence]. [Tokyo] 1958. ff.10.15. [350.]*

PHILIPPE DEVILLERS, L'Indonésie depuis 1942. Fondation nationale des sciences politiques: Centre d'étude des relations internationales: États des travaux (ser. B, no.15): 1958. pp.878–908. [177.]

M. A. JASPAN, Social stratification and social mobility in Indonesia. A trend report and annotated bibliography. Seri ilmu dan masjarakat. [Djakarta 1959]. pp.76. [129.]

CATALOGUS der bibliotheek. Koninklijk bataviaasch genootschap van kunsten en wetenschappen. Bandoeng.
    D. Godsdienstwetenschap. 1948. pp.viii. cols.160. [3000.]
    F–G. Geschiedenis. 1940. pp.xvi. cols.474. [8000.]

BIBLIOGRAFIE overzeese gebeidsdelen vanaf 1945. Nederlandse Regeeringsvoorlichtingsdienst. 's Gravenhage, 1949.
— Supplement: 1950.

GARTH N. JONES, Bibliography. Publications in English: Indonesian social-political-economic life and institutions. Jogjakarta, Public Administration center, University of Gadjah Mada: Jogjakarta 1960. pp.23.17.14. [500.]*

RAYMOND KENNEDY, Bibliography of indonesian peoples and cultures. Revised and edited by Thomas W. Maretzki and H. Th. Fischer. Second revised edition. Behavior science bibliographies: New Haven 1962. pp.xxii.207. [12,500.]*

THEODORE E. KYRIAK, Indonesia 1957–1961. A bibliography and guide to contents of a collection of United States joint publications research service translations on microfilm. Annapolis [1962]. pp.vi.34. [178.]

H. J. DE GRAAF, Catalogus van de handschriften in westerse talen toebehorende aan het Koninklijk instituut voor taal-, land- en volkenkunde. s' Gravenhage 1963. pp.xi.172. [850.]

SOEDJATMOKO [and others, edd.], An introduction to indonesian historiography. Prepared under the auspices of the Modern Indonesia project, Southeast Asia program, Cornell university: Ithaca 1965. pp.xxix. 427. [large number.]

ACCESSIONS list: Indonesia. The library of congress: Public law 480 project. American libraries book procurement center: Djakarta.*
    i. 1964–66. pp.[ii].554.xxix. [6500.]
— Cumulative list of serials (january 1964 through september 1966). 1967. pp.[ii].63. [600.]
—— (1964 through 1968). pp.[ii].106. [1200.]
—— Cumulative serial additions and changes 1969. pp.[ii].22. [250.]
    ii.
    iii.
    iv. 1969. pp.105.viii. [1200.]
        [continued as;]
Accessions list: Indonesia, Singapore and Brunei. The library of congress: National program for acquisitions and cataloging.

v. 1970. pp.[ii].149.xii. [1800.]
in progress.

UNIVERSITY of California library holdings on Indonesia in english. 1968. ff.37. [700.]*

INDONESIA, Catalogue of an important collection of old and new books, periodicals and pamphlets about the indonesian archipelago. Offered for sale by Gé Nabrink, bookseller, Amsterdam [1970?]. pp.160. [3300.]

EXCERPTA indonesica. Centre for documentation on modern Indonesia: Royal institute of linguistics and anthropology: Leiden.*
[i]. 1970. pp.79.88.80.61. [1500.]
[ii]. 1972–   pp.83.80.86.
in progress.

INDONESIAN acquisitions list: National library of Australia: Canberra.*
1971. pp.ff.10. [26]. [444.]
1972. pp.[82].ff.41.51.48.27.50.38.20.51.57. 40. [5866.]
1973. pp.   58.49.
in progress.

F. G. P. JAQUET, Gids van in Nederland aanwezige bronnen betreffende de geschiedenis van Nederlands-Indonesie 1816–1942. Koninklijk instituut voor taal-, land- en volkenkunde: [Leiden].*
i. Lijst van bibliografische werken. 1968. ff.24. [148.]
ii. Algemeen rijksarchief met supplement op aflevering 1. 1970. pp.ix.93.3. [82.]
iii. Koninklijk instituut voor taal-, land-, en volkenkunde. International instituut voor sociale geschiedenis. Doctor Abraham Kuyperstitchting. Rijksmuseum "Bronbeek". Nederlandsch Bijbelgenootschap. Zendingsbureau der Nederlands hervormde kerk. Missiehuis Tilburg. Met supplement op aflevering ii. 1970. pp. [x].86.3. [97.]
[*continued as:*]
Gids van in Nederland aanwezige bronnen betreffende de geschiedenis van Azie en Oceanie 1796–1949.
iv. Koninklijke bibliotheek. Universiteits-bibliotheek Leiden. 1971. pp.[ix].49. [36.]
v. Algemeen rijksarchief. Ministerie van binnenlandsche zaken (supplement af aflevering ii). 1971. pp.[ix].94. [83.]
vi. Eerste kamer der Staaten-generaal. Tweede kamer der Staaten-generaal. Ministerie van buitenlandsche zaken. Stichting Oosters instituut. 1972. pp. [vi].56. [61.]
vii. Ministerie van defensie. Adatrechtstichting. 1973. pp.[iv].52. [57.]
the figures for contents refer to collections or deposits, not to individual items.

I. W. L. A. CAMINADA and F. J. M. OTTEN, Inventaris van de papieren van dr. J. W. Meyer Ranneft. Algemeen rijksarchief: 's-Gravenhage 1971. pp.128. [873.]*

F. J. M. OTTEN, Inventaris van de papieren van jhr. B. C. De Jonge. 's-Gravenhage 1971. pp.[iv]. 40. [180.]*

SOEDARMINTO MARTODIREDJO, Bibliography on the struggle for the indonesian independence. Koninklijk instituut voor de tropen: Amsterdam 1972. ff.8. [56.]*

ENDANG SETIASIH, G-30-S: September 30 movement in Indonesia; its sources and analysis. A bibliography. Koninklijk instituut voor de tropen: Amsterdam 1972. ff.17. [106.]*

DOROTHÉE BUUR, Persoonlijke documenten. Nederlands Indië/Indonesië. Keuze-bibliografie. Koninklijk instituut voor taal-, land- en volkenkunde: [Leiden] 1973. ff.xi.pp.241. [2067.]*

MARIËTTE HOENDERKAMP, De Verenigde naties en de indonesische kwestie 1947–1963. Koninklijk instituut voor de tropen: Literatuurlijsten (no.6): Amsterdam 1973. ff.ii.8. [59.]*

F. G. P. JAQUET, Lijst van stukken deel uitmakend van de collectie Korn (Or. 435). Koninklijk instituut voor taal-, land- en volkenkunde: [Leiden] 1973. ff.[ii]. pp.56. [large number.]

F. G. P. JAQUET, Overzicht van het archief van de Adatrechtstichting. Koninklijk instituut voor taal-, land- en volkenkunde: [Leiden] 1973. pp.21. [120.]

ii. *Periodicals*

LIJST van periodieken. Bataviaasch genootschap van kunsten en wetenschappen: Bibliotheek: [Batavia 1949]. pp.[ii].38. [450.]*

PERSLIJST Indonesië. Een nominatieve opgave van in Indonesië verschijnende periodieken. Regeringsvoorlichtingsdienst: Afdeeling documentatie: Batavia 1949. pp.[xi].58. [750.]
— [another edition]. 1954–1955. ff.[ii].97. [400.]*

UNION catalogue of periodical holdings in the main science libraries of Indonesia. Pilot edition. Unesco science co-operation office for south east Asia: Djakarta 1953. pp.[v].302. [3000.]*

INDEX of indonesian learned periodicals (indeks madjalah ilmia). Indonesian institute of sciences: Bulletin: Indonesian national scientific documentation center: Djakarta.
iii. 1960. pp.89.4. [1075.]
iv. 1961. pp.127. [1051.]
v. 1962. pp.100. [788.]
vi. 1963. pp.74. [509.]

vii. 1964. pp.95. [792.]
viii. 1965. pp.ix.134. [717.]*
ix. 1966. pp.xii.170. [401.]*
x. 1967. pp.viii.204. [454.]*
xi. 1968. pp.v.167. [813].*
xii. 1969. pp.[ix].167. [853.]*
xiii. 1970. pp.[xi].183. [952.]*
xiv. 1971. pp.[ix].228. [1261.]*
the numbers are those of the Bulletin; i and ii were not abstracts.

BENEDICT R. ANDERSON, Bibliography of indonesian publications: newspapers, non-government periodicals and bulletins 1945–1958 at Cornell university. Cornell university: Department of far eastern studies: Southeast Asia program: Data paper (no.33): Ithaca 1959. pp.[vii].69. [275.]*

JOHN M. ECHOLS, Preliminary checklist of indonesian imprints, 1945–1949, with Cornell university holdings. Southeast Asia program: Modern Indonesian project: Bibliography series: Ithaca 1965. pp.vi.186. [1782.]*

YVONNE THUNG and JOHN M. ECHOLS, A guide to indonesian serials, 1945–1965, in the Cornell university library. Southeast Asia program: Modern Indonesia project: Bibliography series: Ithaca 1966. pp.iv.151. [1102.]*

INDEKS selektif artikel² harian Bandung & Djakarta (dari tahun 1965 s/d 1968) jang ada dalam clippings file biro Perpustakaan I.K.I.P.-Bandung. Bandung 1969. ff.[iv].57. [1500.]*

CATALOGUE of newspapers in the collection of the Central museum library, Djakarta. 1970. pp.[146.] [1200.]*

HERNANDO, Katalog induk madjalah pada perpustakaan-chusus di Indonesia. Union catalogue of serials in special libraries in Indonesia. Pusat dokumentasi ilmiah nasional: Lembaga ilmu pengetahuan Indonesia: Indonesian national scientific documentation centre: Indonesian institute of sciences: Djakarta 1971. ff.ix.[299]. ix. [311]. [5000.]*

G[ODFREY] RAYMOND NUNN, Indonesian newspapers; an international union list. Chinese materials and research aids: Occasional series (no.14): [Taipei] 1971. pp.xv.131. [1008.]*

LIAN THE and PAUL W. VAN DER VEUR, The Verhandelingen van het bataviaasch genootschap: an annotated content analysis. Center for international studies: Ohio university: Papers in international studies: Southeast Asia series (26): Athens, Ohio 1973. pp.vii.143. [403.]*

YVONNE THUNG and JOHN ECHOLS, A checklist of indonesian serials in the Cornell university library (1945–1970). Data paper (no.89): South-east Asia program: Department of asian studies: Cornell university: Ithaca 1973. pp.[iv].225. [2269.]*

iii. *Academic writings*

PUBLICATIES, Technische hoogeschool, Bandoeng, in de periode 1920–1936. Bandoeng [1936]. pp.25. [250.]

SARDJANA skripsi titles, Universitas Indonesia, Fakultas Ekonomi. 1956–January 1962. Djakarta 1962. pp.16.

ABSTRAK skripsi dan laporan. Departemen Ilmu Sosial Ekonomi Pertanian, Fakultas Pertanian, I.P.B. Bogor 1965. pp.76.*

M. MAKAGIANSAR, Research di Indonesia 1945–1965, Departemen urusan research nasional: Djakarta.
   1. Bidang kesehatan. Editor: Poorwo Soedarmo. 1965. pp.xiv.748. [large number.]
   2. Bidang teknologi dan industri. Editor: R. M. Soemantri. 1965. pp.xi.312. [large number.]
   3. Bidang pertanian. Editor: Sadikin Soeintawikarta. 1965. pp.vii.285. [large number.]
   4. Bidang ekonomi, sosial dan budaja. Editor: Widjojo Nitisastro. pp.378. [large number.]

DAFTAR kepustakaan. Departemen ilmu sosial ekonomi pertanian, Fakultan pertanian, I.P.B.: Bogor 1965. pp.132.

W. H. MAKALIWE [ed.], List of doctoral dissertations and sarjana skripsis (theses), Universitas Hasanuddin 1960–1972. Faculty of economics: Hasanuddin university: Institute of economic and social research: Ujung Pandang 1972. ff.ii.46. [750.]

BASJRAL HAMIDY HARAHAP, Bibliografi skripsi Fakultas ekonomi Universitas Indonesia. *n.d.*, *n.p.*

iv. *Subjects*
anthropology

JOHANNES P[IETER] KLEIWEG DE ZWAAN, Anthropologische bibliographie van den Indischen archipel en van Nederlandsch West-Indië. Bureau voor de bestuurzaken der buitengewesten: Mededeelingen (vol.xxx). Batavia 1923. pp.473.

RAYMOND KENNEDY, Bibliography of indonesian peoples and cultures. Yale university: Department of anthropology: Yale anthropological studies (vol.iv): New Haven 1945. pp.212. [10,000.]*
—— Revised edition. Editors ... Thomas W. Maretzki and H. Th. Fischer. Human relations

area files: Behavior science bibliographies: 1955. pp.[ii].xxviii.320+[ii].321-663. [12,500.]*
reprinted in 1962 in a different format.

archaeology

COWA survey (-COWA bibliography.). Current work in old world archaeology. Area 20— Indonesia (republic of Indonesia, portuguese Timor, Philippines, Sarawak, north Borneo and Madagascar). Cambridge, Mass.*
    i. 1957. pp.3.11. [138.]
    [*continued as:*]
COWA surveys and bibliographies.
    ii. 1960. pp.3.6. [77.]
    iii. 1964. pp.5.5. [81.]
    iv. 1969. pp.7.10. [147.]

economics

GEORGE L. HICKS and GEOFFREY MCNICOLL, The indonesian economy, 1950–1965: a bibliography. Bibliography series (no.9): Southeast Asia studies: Yale university: Detroit 1967. ff.iii. pp.248. [1270.]

PAUL W. VAN DER VEUR, The Eurasians of Indonesia: a political-historical bibliography. Bibliography series: Modern Indonesia project: Southeast Asia program: Cornell university: Ithaca 1971. pp.viii.115. [1503.]*

education

R. MURRAY THOMAS, SUTAN ZANTI ARBI and SOEDIJARTO, Indonesian education: an annotated bibliography. Indonesian bibliography project: University of California *and* Educational development center, Republic of Indonesia: Santa Barbara, Djakarta 1973. pp.v.239. [2000.]*

folklore

GABRIEL ADRIANO BERNARDO, A critical and annotated bibliography of philippine, indonesian and other malayan folklore. Edited by Francisco Demetrio y Radaza. Xavier university: Cagayan de Oro city 1972. pp.xviii.150. [417.]

islam

HEDWIG SCHLEIFFER, Islam in Indonesia. 1955.

nutrition

S[IMON] POSTMUS, R. LUYKEN and P. J. VAN DER RIJST, Nutrition bibliography of Indonesia. Honolulu 1955. pp.ix.135. [400.]*

population

MASRI SINGARIMBUN, The population of Indonesia, 1930–1968: a bibliography. Family planning and national development: Bandung 1969. pp.vii. 56. [850.]*

rubber

CATALOGUS van de bibliotheek van het algemeen proefstation der A. V. R. O. S. [Algemeene vereeniging van rubberplanters ter costkust van Sumatra] te Medan. Kampong Baru 1957-1958. pp.[ii].259+[ii].615. [4000.]*
— Eerste aanvulling. 1958. pp.63.45. [750.]*

science

UNION catalogue of periodical holdings in the main science libraries of Indonesia. Pilot edition. Unesco science co-operation office for south east Asia: Djakarta 1953. pp.[v].302. [3000.]

INDONESIAN abstracts. Abstracts on current scientific indonesian literature. Madjelis ilmu pengetuhuan Indonesia: Djakarta.
    i. 1958–1959. pp.129. [400.]
    ii. 1960. pp.74. [200.]
    iii. 1961. pp.62. [150.]
    iv. 1962. pp.v.83. [240.]
    v. 1963. pp.xii.175. [500.]
    vi. 1964. pp.ix.78. [220.]
    vii. 1965. pp.44. [132.]
    viii. 1966. pp.48. [138.]
    ix. 1967. pp.53. [151.]
    x. 1968. pp.53. [176.]
    xi. 1969.
    xii. 1970.
    xiii. 1971.
    xiv. 1972.
    xv. 1973. pp.53+.
in progress?

DOKUMENTASI guntingan surat kabar mengenai biologi dan pertanian di Indonesia. Departemen pertanian: Lembaga perpustakaan biologi dan pertanian "Bibliotheca bogoriensis". Bogor 1969 &c.
in progress.

BIBLIOGRAFI KESEDJAHTERAAN sosial Indonesia. Departemen sosial R.I. penerbitan: Djakarta 1971 &c.

MAS'UDI, Books on sociology of Indonesia at the Central library of the Royal tropical institute, Amsterdam. Bibliography 1951–1968. International centre: Amsterdam 1969. ff.18. [35.]*

ANNE HARPER, Soybean processing and utilization: a partially annotated bibliography. Lembaga ilmu pengetahuan Indonesia: Jakarta 1973. ff.vi. 56.

v. Topography

Bali

CORNELIS LIEKKERKERKER, Bali en Lombok. Overzicht der literatuur omtrent deze eilanden. Bali institute: Rijswijk 1920. pp.456. [925.]

Batak

M[EINT] JOUSTRA, Litteratuuroverzicht der Bataklanden. Leyden 1907. pp.[iii].vii.180. [1000.]
— — [supplement]. 1910.

Java

RADEN POERWA SOEWIGNJA. Inhoudsopgave der javaansche couranten in de bibliotheek van het Bataviaasch genootschap van kunsten en wetenschappen. Batavia 1911. pp.157. [1000.]

C[HARLES] O[TTO] BLAGDEN, Catalogue of manuscripts in european languages belonging to the library of the India office. Volume 1. The Mackenzie collection. Part 1: the 1822 collection & the private collection. 1916. pp.xxxii.302. [2500.]
no more published.

RADEN POERWA SOEWIGNJA and R. WIRAWANGSA, Javaansche bibliographie, gegrond op de boekwerken in die taal aanwezig in de boekerij. Bataviaasch genootschap van kunsten en wetenschappen: Batavia 1920–1921.

FORMOSA and Java. Public library: Far eastern book and journal lists (no.15): Newark, N.J. [1921]. single leaf. [Java: 10.]

LIJST van publicaties van het proefstation midden- en oost-Java ... 1911 tot 1936. De Bergcultures (vol.x, no.26: supplement): Batavia 1936. coll.16.

JAMES DANANDJAJA, An annotated bibliography of javanese folklore. University of California: Center for south and southeast Asia studies: Occasional paper series (no.9): Berkeley 1972. pp.xxx.162. [873.]*

Jakjakarta

KADARSIH TIRTO OETOMO, Djokjakarta before the second world war; 1900–1942; a bibliography. International centre: Royal tropical institute: Amsterdam 1972. ff.[13]. [94.]*

Lombok

CORNELIS LEKKERKERKER, Bali en Lombok. Overzicht der litteratuur omtrent deze eilanden. Bali instituut: Rijkswijk 1920. pp.456. [925.]

Menado

CATALOGUS van literatuur en ambtelijke gegevens betreffende de residentie Menado. Adriani-Kruyt instituut: Menado 1939. pp.33.

Minangkabau

MEINT JOUSTRA, Overzicht der literatuur betreffende Minangkabau. Minangkabau instituut: Uitgaaf (no.2): Amsterdam 1924. pp.162.

— — 1923–1936. . . . (no.3): 1936. pp.77. [335.]
[by J. Tideman.]

A. M. and M. NAIM, Bibliografi Minangkabau; skripsi, tesis dan disertasi. Center for Minangkabau studies: Padang 1973.

Moluccas

OVERZICHT van de literatuur betreffende de Molukken. Molukken instituut: Amsterdam.
    i. 1550–1921. Door W. Ruinen 1928..
    ii. 1922–1933. Door A.B. Tutein Nolthenius.

Roti, Savu, Sumba

JAMES and IRMGARD FOX, A working bibliography on the islands of Roti, Savu and Sumba in eastern Indonesia. ff.39. n.p. [600.]*

Sumatra

ZUID-SUMATRA, Overzicht van de literatuur der gewesten Bengkoelen, Djambi, de Lampongsche districten en Palembang. Zuid-Sumatra instituut: Amsterdam.
    i. Door J. W. J. Wellan en D. L. Helfrich. 1923.
    ii. 1916–1925. Door J. W. J. Wellan. 1928.

vi. Indonesian languages and literatures

G. OCKELOEN, Catalogus van boeken en tijdschriften uitgegeven in Ned. Oost-Indie van 1870–1937. Batavia &c. [1940]. pp.[vii].1016.25. [10,000.]*

CATALOGUS van in Ned.-Indie verschenen boeken in de jaren 1938–1941 en enkele aanvullingen op de gestencilde catalogus verschenen in 1939. Deel 1: Nederlandsche uitgaven. Batavia &c. 1942. pp.322. [3000.]

G. OCKELOEN, Catalogus dari boekoe-boekoe [buku-buku] dan madjallah-madjallah jang diterbitkan di Hindia Belanda [Indonesia]. Batavia, Amsterdam [Bandung].
    1870–1937. [1940]. pp.viii.612. [6000.]
    1937–1941. 1950. pp.115. [2300.]
    1945–1949. 1950. pp.140. [2500.]
    1950–1951. 1952. pp.312. [4000.]
    1952–1953. 1954. pp.276. [3000.]

POERBATJARAKA, P. VOORRHOEVE and C. HOOYKAS, Indonesische handschriften. Lemlaga kebudajaan Indonesia: Bandung 1950 pp.[iii].210. [750.]

BUKU KITA, Djakarta, Gunung Agung, 1955–56. [continued as:]
BERITA BIBLIOGRAFI (Biographical news.) Diterbitkan dari bulan ke bulan oleh n.v. (p.t.). Gunung Agung. Djakarta.
    ii. 1956. pp.232. [3000.]
    iii. 1957.
    iv. 1958.

v. 1959. pp.xiii. 279. [3500.]

vi. 1960. pp. .19.14.13. .14.16.14.14.12. ii.

vii. 1961. pp.16.16.16.16.16.16.20.20.20.20. 20. 20. [3000.]

viii. 1962. pp.24.24. .24.24.24.24. . . . 24.

ix. 1963.

x. 1964. (Indonesian books news.) pp.56.48. .56.48.48.48.48.48.

xi. 1965. pp.64.52.56.51. [1200.]

xii. 1966. pp.128.60. [1100.]

xiii. 1967.

xiv. 1968.

xv. 1969.

xvi. 1970. pp.51.55.61.60.54.61. [1624.]

in progress.

BERITA bulanan dari kantor bilografi nasional. Bandung [Djakarta].

i. 1953.

ii. 1954.

iii. 1955.

iv. 1956.

v. 1957.

vi. 1958. pp.4. .4.4.4.4. . .4.4.4.4. [563.]

vii. 1959. pp.8.4.4.8.4.4. . .20.

viii. 1960. pp.16.8.4.4.4.4.4.4.16. [1600.]

ix. 1961. pp. .8.8.8. ff.45.

x. 1962. pp.8.4.8. . .8.

[*continued as:*]

BIBLIOGRAFI nasional Indonesia: Kantor bibliografi nasional: Departemen pendidikan dasar dan kebudajaan.

xi. 1963. pp.8.8.7.8. [600.]

xii. 1964. pp.18.10.

in progress?

BIBLIOGRAFI nasional Indonesia. Kumulasi 1945–63. Diusahakan oleh: Projek perpustakaan nasional dan Biro perpustakaan dep. P.D. dan K. Djakarta 1965. pp. [330]+[326.] [11,405.]

A[NDRIES] TEEUW and H. W. EMANUELS, A critical survey of studies on malay and bahasa Indonesia. Koninklijk instituut voor taal-, land- en volkenkunde: Bibliographical series (no.5): 's-Gravenhage 1961. pp.[iv].176. [2500.]

JOHN M. ECHOLS, Preliminary checklist of indonesian imprints during the japanese period (March 1942–August 1945). Cornell university: Modern Indonesia project: Bibliography series: Ithaca 1963. pp.v.56. [250.]*

DAFTAR buku 20 tahun Penerbitan Indonesia 1945–1965. Diterbitkan oleh: Ikapi-O.P.S. Penerbitan: Pusat, Djakarata, n.d. pp.xii.416. [1200.]

DAFTAR pustaka bahasa dan kesusastraan Indonesia termasuk Bahasa-bahasa dan kesusastraan Nusantara. Jakarta 1968. pp.xxvi.223. [3000.]*

vii. *Regional languages and literatures*

Balinese

J[AN LOURENS ANDRIES] BRANDES, Beschrijving der javaansche, balineesche en sasaksche handschriften aangetroffen in de nalatenschap van dr H. N. Van der Tuuk, en door hem vermaakt aan de Leidsche universiteitsbibliotheek. Batavia 1901–1926. pp.x.284+v.262+vii.370+[v].129. [1658.]

H. H. JUYNBOLL, Supplement op den Catalogus van de sundaneesche handschriften en Catalogus van de balineesche en sasaksche handschriften der Leidsche universiteits-bibliotheek. Leiden 1912. pp.xvi.224. [Balinese: 501.]

Batak

P[ETRUS] VOORHOEVE, The Chester Beatty library. A catalogue of the batak manuscripts, including two javanese manuscripts and a balinese painting. Dublin 1961. pp.167.pls.9. [54.]

LIBERTY MANIK, Batak-handschriften. Verzeichnis der orientalischen handschriften in Deutschland. Wiesbaden 1973. pp.x.253. [501.]

Buginese

B. F. MATTHES, Kort verslag aangaande alle mij in Europa bekende makassaarsche en boeginesche handschriften, vooral die van het Nederlandsch bijbelgenootschap te Amsterdam. [Amsterdam] 1875. pp.viii.101. [250.]

Celebes

C. C. MACKNIGHT, Notes on south Celebes manuscripts. Department of history: Australian national university: Canberra [1963]. pp.iii.ff. [78].iii. [75.]

Javanese

L[ODEWIJK] W[ILLEM] C[HRISTIAAN] VAN DEN BERG, Verslag van eene verzameling maleische, arabische, javaansche en andere handschriften, door de regeering van nederlandsch Indie aan het Bataviaasch genootschap van kunsten en wetenschappen ter bewaring afgestaan. Batavia &c. 1877. pp.xii.62. [400.]

A. C. VREEDE, Catalogus van de javaansche en madoereesche handschriften der leidsche universiteets-bibliotheek. Leiden 1892. pp.ix.434-[javanese: 750.]

—— Supplement . . . door H[ermann] H[endrik] Juynboll. 1907–1911. pp.xvii.280+xvii.552. [500.]

J[AN LOURENS ANDRIES] BRANDES, Beschrijving der javaansche, balineesche en sasaksche handschriften aangetroffen in de nalatenschap van dr. H. N. Van der Tuuk, en door hem vermaakt aan de Leidsche universiteitsbibliotheek. Batavia 1901–1926. pp.x.284+v.262+vii.370+[v].129. [1658.]

E. M. UHLENBECK, A critical survey of studies on the languages of Java and Madura. Bibliographical series (7): Koninklijk instituut voor taal-, land-en volkenkunde: 's Gravenhage 1964. pp.viii.207. [1050.]

THEODORE G. TH. PIGEAUD, Lieterature of Java: catalogue raisonné of javanese manuscripts in the library of the university of Leiden and other public collections in the Netherlands. Koninklijk instituut voor taal-, land- en volkenkunde, Leiden: The Hague 1967–70. pp.xx.325+xv. 972+xvii. 441. [very large number.]

MUDJANATTISTOMO, Katalogus manuskrip Kraton Jogjakarta. Lembaga bahasa nasional: Jogjakarta 1971.

Macassar

B. F. MATTHES, Kort verslag aangaande alle mij in Europa bekende makassaarsche en boeginesche handschriften, vooral die van het Nederlandsch Bijbelgenootschap te Amsterdam. [Amsterdam] 1875. pp.viii.101. [250.]

Madurese

A. C. VREEDE, Catalogus van de javaansche en madoereesche handschriften der Leidsche universiteits-bibliotheek. Leiden 1892. pp.ix.434. [madurese: 25.]
— — Supplement ... door H. H. Juynboll. Deel I. Madoereesche handschriften, oud-javanische inscripties en oud- en middeljavaansche gedlichten 1907. pp.xviii.280. [madurese: 200.]
a second supplement, 1911, sets out no madurese works.

Menak

R. M. NG. POERBATJARAKA, Beschrijving der handschriften. Menak. [Koninklijk bataviaasch genootschap van kunsten en wetenschappen: Bandoeng 1940. pp.[iii].115. [60.]

Multatuli [pseud. Eduard Douwes Dekker]

JULIUS PÉE, Bibliografie over Multatuli. Levende talen (no.14): Brussel [1945]. pp.[ii].18. [400.]

A[RIE] J[ACOBUS] DE MARE, Multatuli-literatuur. Lijst der geschriften van en over Edvard Douwes Dekker. Leiden 1948. pp.[viii].220. [2030.]

Sumatra

P[ETRUS] VOORHOEVE, Critical survey of studies on the languages of Sumatra. Bibliographical series (1): Koninklijk instituut voor taal-, land- en volkenkunde: 's Gravenhage 1955. pp.55. [205.]

P[ETRUS] VOORHOEVE, Südsumatranische handschriften. Verzeichnis der orientalischen handschriften in Deutschland (band xxix): Wiesbaden 1971. pp.viii.70. [44.]

Sundanese

H. H. JUYNBOLL, Catalogus van de maleische on sundaneesche handschriften der Leidsche universiteits-bibliotheek. 1899. pp.xxiii.356. [sundanese: 23.]

H. H. JUYNBOLL, Supplement op den Catalogus van de sundaneesche en sasaksche handschriften der Leidsche universiteits-bibliotheek. Leiden 1912. pp.xvi.224. [sundanese: 127.]

COLLECTION of sundanese manuscripts in the National library of Australia. MS 1673. Canberra 1966. ff.[17]. [130.]*

STRAITS SETTLEMENTS

MEMORANDA of books registered in the "Catalogue of books printed in the Straits Settlements" under the provisions of ordinance no.xv [ordinance no.2 (book registration); the printers and publishers ordinance] during the quarter. Singapore.

    1887. ff.[4]. [23.]
    1888. ff.[4]. [24.]
    1889. pp.[6]. [22.]
    1890. pp.[8]. [29.]
    1891. pp.[8]. [26.]
    1892. pp.4.4.4.2. [42.]
    1893. pp.4.4.3.3. [39.]
    1894. pp.5.2.2.2. [39.]
    1895. pp.4.2.1.3. [34.]
    1896. pp.2.2.2.2. [22.]
    1897. pp.2.2.2.1 [19.]
    1898. pp.[5]. [19.]
    1899. pp.[6]. [20.]
    1900. pp.2.4.7.3. [72.]
    1901. pp.4.3.3.2. [33.]
    1902. pp.3.2.1.2. [27.]
    1903. pp.4.1.3.2. [38.]
    1904. pp.1.1.4.4. [34.]
    1905. pp.2.2.2.2. [29.]
    1906. pp.2.1.2.2. [20.]
    1907. pp.4.1.2.2. [32.]
    1908. pp.3.3.5.4. [47.]
    1909. pp.4.1.2.1. [24.]
    1910. pp.2.2.1.2. [22.]
    1911. pp.1.2.2.3. [30.]
    1912. pp.3.5.4. [40.]
    1913. pp.3.2.3.4. [32.]
    1914. pp.5.3.5.7. [57.]
    1915. pp.5.4.3.4. [47.]
    1916. pp.5.5.6.3. [53.]
    1917. pp.4.4.3.3. [39.]
    1918. pp.5.4.4.6. [68.]

1919. pp.4.3.2.3. [40.]
1920. pp.3.2.1.2. [31.]
1921. pp.3.4.2.2. [36.]
1922. pp.6.4.3.5. [62,]
1923. pp.3.2.3.5. [46.]
1924. pp.3.4.4.5. [54.]
1925. pp.4.2.5.6. [66.]
1926. pp.5.4.3.4. [60.]
1927. pp.3.3.7.5. [61.]
1928. pp.5.6.6.10. [102.]
1929. pp.9.5.5.6. [93.]
1930. pp.8.6.9.5. [107.]
1931. pp.8.7.8.12. [133.]
1932. pp.8.10.10.10. [143.]
1933. pp.8.5.12.6. [118.]
1934. pp.8.7.8.7. [120.]
1935. pp.7.14.6.11. [145.]
1936. pp.13.14.17.3. [168.]
1937. pp.11.11.13.14. [157.]
1938. pp.13.14.15.16. [154.]
1939. pp.30.21.14.13. [213.]
1940. pp.15.11.12.14. [155.]
1941. pp.4.10. [69.]

SIR WILLIAM GEORGE MAXWELL, A chronological table of ... the imperial acts ... the indian acts ... and ... the ordinances of the Straits Settlements. ... Ninth edition. Revised by A. B. Voules. Singapore 1916. pp.[ii].ii.279.[xiv]. [2250.]

— — Thirteenth edition. The chronological table of Straits Settlements laws. ... Revised by J. V. Mills. 1925. pp.[ii].iv.492. [3500.]
from this date new editions have appeared annually with more frequent corrections slips.

INDEX of Straits Settlements laws on 1st July 1933. Compiled in Deputy public prosecutors office, Penang. Singapore 1934. pp.[ii].100. [2500.]

C. H. WITHERS PAYNE, The malayan digest being a complete digest of every case in the colony of the Straits Settlements and the Federated Malay States reported from 1808. Singapore 1936. pp. [ix].305. [1504.]

D. K. WALTERS, Index to the municipal ordinances of the Straits Settlements. Singapore 1937. pp.iii.–xxiii.198. [6000.]

A CHRONOLOGICAL and alphabetical list of emergency legislation in force on 18th December 1940. Singapore 1941. pp.[vii].50. [500.]

WILLIAM R. ROFF, Bibliography of malay and arabic periodicals published in the Straits Settlements and the Peninsular Malay states 1876–1941, with an annotated union list of holdings in Malaysia, Singapore and the United Kingdom. London oriental bibliographies (vol.3): London 1972. pp.[v].74. [197.]

[PATIENCE ANNE EMPSON], Papers of James W. W. Birch and sir Ernest W. Birch. MSS. Ind. Ocn. s 242. Oxford university colonial records project: [Oxford 1972]. ff.8. [3 boxes, 10 files.]★

MALAYSIA

i. *General*
ii. *Regions, Topography*
iii. *Subjects*

i. *General*

PRICE list of maps & plans. Survey department: Kuala Lumpur 1924. pp.[7]. [75.]
— [another edition]. [1936]. pp.[iv].36. [500.]

I. H. N. EVANS, Catalogue of works dealing with linguistics & ethnography in the library of the Federated malay states museums at Kuala Lumpur and Taiping. Kuala Lumpur 1925. pp.148. [2500.]

[K. E. SAVAGE-BAILEY], Raffles library historical maps of Malaya (Mills collection). Singapore 1926. pp.[ii].26. [208.]

C. H. WITHERS PAYNE, The malayan digest, being a complete digest of every case in the colony of the Straits Settlements and the Federated Malay States reported from 1808. Singapore 1936. pp. [ix].305. [1504.]

J. H. ROBSON, A bibliography of Malaya. Also a short list of books relating to North Borneo and Sarawak. Kuala 1939. pp.48.

BASHĪR A[ḤMAD] MALLĀL and NĀZIR A[ḤMAD] MALLĀL, Mallal's digest of malayan case law. Being a comprehensive digest of all decisions of the superior courts of Malaya from 1808–1939. Singapore 1940. pp.xxiv.coll.592. [1500.]

FLORENCE S[ELMA] HELLMAN, British Malaya and British North Borneo: a bibliographical list. Library of Congress: Division of bibliography: Washington 1942. pp.66. [773.]★
— — [another edition]. 1943. pp.[iv].103. [980.]★

THE MALAYAN campaign: a list of references. Library of Congress: Washington 1943. ff.11. [109.]★

BIBLIOGRAPHY of Malaya. Behavior science bibliographies: HRAF-Malayia research project: University of Chicago. New Haven 1956. pp.55. [350.]★

KARL J[OSEF] PELZER, Selected bibliography on the geography of southeast Asia. Part III. Malaya. Yale university: Southeast Asia studies: New Haven 1956. pp.[vi].162. [2250.]★

H[AROLD] A[MBROSE] R[OBINSON] CHEESEMAN, Bibliography of Malaya, being a classified list of books wholly or partly in english relating to the Federation of Malaya and Singapore. 1959. pp. xi.234. [3500.]

BOOKS and periodicals banned in the Federation of Malaya ... between 7th July, 1948, and 19th August, 1960. Compiled by the library staff of the University of Malaya in Kuala Lumpur. [1300.]*

L. A. MILLS, British Malaya 1824–67, edited for reprinting, with a bibliography of writings in English on British Malaya, 1786–1867, by C. M. Turnbull ... Journal of the Malayan branch, Royal asiatic society (vol. xxxiii, part 3): Singapore 1960, pp.424. [1000.]

PIERRE FISTIÉ, La Fédération de Malaisie et Singapour. Fondation nationale des sciences politiques: Centre d'étude des relations internationales: États des travaux (ser. B, no.23): 1961. pp. 155–185. [208.]

WILLIAM R. ROFF, Guide to malay periodicals, 1876–1941, with details of known holdings in Malaya. Papers on Southeast asia subjects (no.4): Singapore 1961. pp.46.

BEDA LIM, Malaya: a background bibliography. Journal of the malayan branch, Royal asiatic society (vol.xxxv, parts 2 & 3): Singapore 1962.

BOOKS about Malaysia. National library: Singapore 1963. pp.22. [190.]
BOOKS about Malaysia and Singapore. 1965. pp.40. [350.]
BOOKS about Singapore & Malaysia. 1967. pp.65. [369.]
BOOKS about Singapore. 1970. pp.48. [276.]

KWAI LIEW CHEONG, Malaysia; a selected annotated bibliography. Library school: Wellington 1963. ff.iv.22. [61.]*

BIBLIOGRAFI negara Malaysia. Malaysian national bibliography. Arkib negara Malaysia: Kuala Lumpur.
1967. 1969. pp.xi.129. [600.]

L. J[OHN] HARRIS, Guide to current malaysian serials. University of Malaya library: Kuala Lumpur 1967. pp.xiii.73. [500.]

M. B. HOOKER, A source book of adat, chinese law & the history of common law in the Malayan peninsula. Malaya law review: Monograph (no.1): Faculty of Law: University of Singapore 1967. pp.xli. 211. [1946.]

INDEKS majallah kini Malaysia Singapura dan Brunei. Index to current malaysian singapore and brunei periodicals. Joint standing committee on library cooperation and bibliographical services: Kuala Lumpur, Singapura.*
1967. pp.113. [1000.]
1968. pp.xxi.168. [2135.]
no more published.

LIBRARY catalogue. The British association of Malaya. London 1967. pp.28. [800.]*

MALAYSIANA collection. Ipoh free public library [Ipoh] 1967. pp.ii, 102. [677.]*
— First supplement, Jan. 1968–Feb. 1971. Ipoh [1971]. ff.ii.pp.54. [282.]*

CATALOGUE of microfilm. National archives of Malaysia. Petaling Jaya 1968. pp.6. [17.]

CATALOGUE of the Singapore/Malaysia collection. Prepared by the Cataloguing department. University of Singapore library: Boston 1968. pp.xxiii.757. [15,882 cards.]

NEWSPAPERS in the University of Malaya library, Kuala Lumpur. Occasional list (4): 1968. pp.9. [136.]*

MALAYSIA & Singapore. Selected reading lists for advanced study: Commonwealth institute; London 1969. pp.17. [117.]*

RAMA SUBBIAH, Tamil malaysiana: a check list of tamil books and periodicals published in Malaysia and Singapore. University of Malaysia library: Kuala Lumpur 1969. pp.78. [900.]

SENARAI penerimaan. Accessions list. 1957–1967. Arkib negara Malaysia. Kuala Lumpur? 1969. pp.xvii.185. [large number.]

ACCESSIONS list: Indonesia, Malaysia, Singapore and Brunei. Library of congress: National program for acquisitions and cataloging: Djakarta. Vol. 5, no.9/10 &c. 1970 &c.

P[ATRICIA] LIM PUI HEN, Newspapers published in the malaysian area. Occasional paper (no.2): Institute of southeast asian studies: Singapore 1970. pp.157–198. [446.]

KARL J. PELZER, West Malaya and Singapore: a selected bibliography. Behavior science bibliographies: Human relations area files: New Haven 1971. pp.vi.394. [5000.]

MARGARET ROFF, Official publications of Malaysia, Singapore and Brunei in New York libraries. Southern asian institute: Columbia university: Occasional bibliographical papers (no.1): New York 1971. pp.45. [800.]*

DAFTAR buku2 terbitan Malaysia; disusun oleh Pustaka Antara. Kuala Lumpur 1972. pp.vi.390. [4250.]

CUMULATIVE list of Malaysia, Singapore and Brunei serials, september 1970–december 1972 &c. Library of congress office: Djakarta.
each list supersedes the previous issue.

ROHANI ZAINAL ABIDIN, Malaysia 1963–1969: a select bibliography. New Zealand library school: Wellington 1970. ff.[ii].iii.25. [73.]*

LIM HUCK TEE and D. E. K. WIJASURIYA, Index malaysiana; an index to the Journal of the Straits branch, Royal asiatic society and the Journal of the Malayan branch, Royal asiatic society, 1878–1963. Malaysian branch, Royal asiatic society: Kuala Lumpur 1970. pp.[iv].395. [7500.]

SURATAN Swettenham: Swettenham papers (SP. 12). Arkib negara Malaysia: Kuala Lumpur 1970. pp.11.

SURATAN Hervey. Hervey papers (SP.16). Arkib negara Malaysia: [Kuala Lumpur 1970]. pp.[v].5. [65.]*

TAN Cheng Lock papers: a descriptive list. Institute of southeast asian studies: Singapore 1972. pp.viii.112. [2000.]*

YEE SIEW-PUN, An index to chinese-language newspaper reporting on Singapore and Malaysian affairs: a pilot project covering the period january–march 1965 in Nanyang siang pau and Sin chew jit poh. Nanyang university: Singapore 1973.

ii. Regions. Topography

Malacca

[T. J. HARDY], Catalogue of church records, Malacca, 1642–1898. Singapore 1899. pp.22. [500.]
— — [reprint]. Catalogue [&c.]. ... [Royal asiatic society: Malayan branch: Singapore 1937]. pp.24.

Eastern Malaysia

CONRAD PATRICK COTTER, WILHELM G. SOLLHEIM and THOMAS R. WILLIAMS, North Borneo, Brunei and Sarawak: a bibliography of English language, historical, administrative and ethnographic sources. [n.p. 1963?] ff.33.5. [750.]*

CONRAD P. COTTER and SHIRO SAITO, Bibliography of english language sources on human ecology, eastern Malaysia and Brunei. Department of asian studies: University of Hawaii: Honolulu 1965. ff.xxv.348+349–755. [7317.]

Borneo, Sabah

THE LIBRARY of his excellency sir George Grey, K.C.B. Philology. Vol.II. Part IV (continuation). Polynesia and Borneo. 1859. pp.[iv].77–154. [Dayak language: 8.]

LABUAN and the Indian archipelago. [Colonial office (no.28 of a series of lists of works in the library): 1860]. pp.4. [60.]

BORNEO and New Guinea. Public library: Far eastern book and journal lists (no.14): Newark, N.J. [1921]. single leaf. [Borneo: 7.]

J. H. ROBSON, A bibliography of Malaya. Also a short list of books relating to North Borneo and Sarawak. Kuala 1939. pp.48.

FLORENCE S[ELMA] HELLMAN, British Malaya and british north Borneo. A bibliographical list. Library of Congress: Division of bibliography: Washington 1942. pp.66. [773.]*
— [another edition]. 1943. pp.[iv].103. [980.]*

BIBLIOGRAPHY of British Borneo. Human relations area files: Behavior science biliographies: New Haven 1956. pp.[ii].23. [125.]*

A. A. CENSE and E. M. UHLENBECK, Critical survey of studies on the languages of Borneo. Bibliographical series (2): Koninklijk instituut voor taal-, land- en volkenkunde: 's-Gravenhage 1958. pp.82. [323.]

CONRAD P[ATRICK] COTTER, Reading list of english language materials in the social sciences on British Borneo, with critical annotations. Honolulu 1960. ff.vii.88. [550.]*

JOHN BASTIN, Western language historical sources in the british Borneo territories. Department of history: University of Malaya: Kuala lumpur 1962. ff.27. [167.]*

MICHAEL B. LEIGH and JOHN M. ECHOLS, Checklist of holdings on Borneo in the Cornell university libraries. Data paper (no.62): Southeast Asia program: Department of asian studies: Cornell university: Ithaca 1966. ff.62. [750.]*

JOYCE CHALLIS, Annotated bibliography of economic and social material in Sabah (north Borneo) and Sarawak. Part I: government publications. Research bibliography series (no.4): Economic research centre: University of Singapore 1969. ff.ii.29. [76.]*

[GRAEME POWELL], Sabah: a bibliography of the dispute between Malaysia and the Philippines. National library of Australia: Canberra 1969.

Sarawak

J. H. ROBSON, A bibliography of Malaya. Also a short list of books relating to North Borneo and Sarawak. Kuala 1939. pp.48.

JOYCE CHALLIS, Annotated bibliography of economic and social material in Sabah (north Borneo) and Sarawak. Part I: government publications. Research bibliography series (no.4): Economic research centre: University of Singapore 1969. ff.ii.29. [76.]*

iii. Subjects

anthropology

P[ETER] SUZUKI, Critical survey of studies on the anthropology of Nias, Mentawei and Enggano.

Koninklijk instituut voor taal-, lund- en volkenkunde: Bibliographical series (no.3): 's-Gravenhage 1958. pp.[vii].87. [500.]

demography

SAW SWEE-HOCK, The demography of Malaysia,
Singapore and Brunei; a bibliography. Centre of
asian studies: University of Hong Kong 1970.
pp.v.39. [328.]*

economics

LIM TAY BO and S. J. GILANI, A critical review of
literature (originating mainly in Malaya) on
balanced economic and social development.
Department of economics: University of Malaya
in Singapore: Singapore 1961.*

JOYCE CHALLIS, Annotated bibliography of
economic and social material, West Malaysia.
Part I: government publications. Research bibliography series (no.2): Economic research centre:
University of Singapore 1968. pp.[iii].152. [450.]*

education

WANG CHEN HSIU CHIN, Education in Malaysia;
a bibliography. Reference department: University
of Singapore library: Singapore 1964. pp.35.
[451.]*

geology

D[EREK] J[OHN] GOBBETT, Bibliography and
index of the geology of west Malaysia and
Singapore. Geological society of Malaysia:
Bulletin (no.2): Kuala Lumpur 1968. pp.iii.152.
[600.]

nutrition

P[ENG] C[HONG] LEONG, Nutrition bibliography
of Malaya. Pacific area bibliographies: Honolulu
1952. pp.vii.23. [90.]

Raffles

JOHN BASTIN, Sir Thomas Stamford Raffles,
with an account of the Raffles-Minto manuscript
collection presented to the India office library on
17 July 1969 by the Malaysia-Singapore commercial association. Ocean steam ship company
limited: Liverpool 1969. pp.22.pls.12. [47.]

world war II

MILITARY operations, World war II. Malaya.
Imperial war museum: Library: [1954]. pp.2.
[33.]*

iv. Malay literature and language

[GEORGE KAREL NIEMANN], De maleische handschriften in het Britisch museum. [s.l. 1873]. pp.6.
[24.]

L[ODEWIJK] W[ILLEM] C[HRISTIAAN] VAN DEN
BERG, Verslag van eene verzameling maleische,
arabische, javaansche en andere handschriften,
door de regeering van nederlandsch Indie aan het
Bataviaasch genootschap van kunsten en wetenschappen ter bewaring afgestaan. Batavia &c.
1877. pp.xii.62. [400.]

H. H. JUYNBOLL, Catalogus van de maleische en
sudaneesche handschriften der Leidsche universiteits-bibliotheek. 1899. pp.xxiii.356. [malay: 378.]

—— Supplement-catalogus der maleische en
minangkabausche handschriften. By [P.] S. van
Ronkel. 1921. pp.xxxiii.316. [malay: 509.]

PH. S. VAN RONKEL, Catalogus der maleische
handschriften in het Museum van het Bataviaasch
genootschap van kunsten en wetenschappen.
Verhandelingen van het Bataviaasch genootschap
van kunsten en wetenschappen (deel lvii):
Batavia, 's Hage 1909. pp.xix.546. [919.]

RICHARD GREENTREE and EDWARD WILLIAMS
BYRON NICHOLSON, Catalogue of malay manuscripts and manuscripts relating to the malay
language in the Bodleian library. Oxford 1910.
pp.vi.coll.20. pp.[ii]. [12.]

A[NTOINE] CABATON, Catalogue sommaire des
manuscrits indiens, indo-chinois & malayo-poly-
nésiens. Bibliothèque nationale: 1912. pp.[vi].320.
[malayo-polynesian: 244.]

'THE PRINTS and books enactment, 1915'.—The
following memoranda ... are published for
general information in pursuance of section 13
of the said enactment. [Feddrated Malay States
1915 &c.].
*in progress; these memoranda are issued sometimes
in separate form, sometimes in rhe F.M.S. government gazette, sometimes in the form of letters.*

PH. S. VAN RONKEL, Bericht aangaande de jongste
aanwinst van maleische handschriften in het bui-
tenland (Cambridge). Koninklijke akademie van
wetenschappen: Mededeelingen (ser. A, vol.lix,
no.8): Amsterdam 1925. pp.16. [22.]

G. OCKELOEN, Catalogus dari boekoe-boekoe
dan madjallah-madjallah jang diterbitkan di
Hindia Belanda dari tahoen 1870–1937. Batavia
&c. [1940]. pp.[vi].612. [7000.]*

C. SNOUCK HURGRONJE, Katalog der malaiischen
handschriften der Königlichen hofbibliothek in
Berlin. (Cod.Or.8015 der Leidener universitätsbibliothek). Nich im handel. [Leiden 1950.]
pp.xvi.268. [60.]
photographic reproduction of ms.

CURRENT list of publications. Federation of
Malaya: [Kuala Lumpur] July 1955. pp.[iii].20.
[400.]

— [another edition]. January 1958. pp.28. [500.]

H[AROLD AMBROSE] R[OBINSON] CHEESEMAN, Bibliography of Malaya, being a classified list of books . . . in english relating to the Federation of Malaya and Singapore. British association of Malaya: 1959. pp.xi.234. [4000.]

A[NDRIES] TEEUW and H. W. EMANUELS, A critical survey of studies on malay and bahasa Indonesia. Koninklijk instituut voor taal-, land- en volkenkunde; Bibliographical series (no.5): 's-Gravenhage 1961. pp.[iv].176. [2500.]

JOSEPH H. HOWARD, Malay manuscripts; a bibliographical guide. University of Malaya library: Kuala Lumpur 1966. pp.96. [1000.]

WILLIAM R. ROFF, Autobiography & biography in malay historical studies. Occasional paper (no.13): Institute of southeast asian studies: Singapore 1972. ff.21. [30.]*

*WILLIAM R. ROFF, Bibliography of malay and arabic periodicals published in the Straits Settlements and the Peninsular Malay states 1876–1941, with an annotated union list of holdings in Malaysia, Singapore and the United Kingdom. London oriental bibliographies (vol.3): London 1972. pp.[v].74. [197.]

BRUNEI

CONRAD P. COTTER and SHIRO SAITO, Bibliography of english language sources on human ecology, eastern Malaysia and Brunei. Department of asian studies: University of Hawaii: Honolulu 1965. ff.xxv.348+349–755. [7317.]

INDEKS majallah kini Malaysia Singapura dan Brunei. Index to current malaysian singapore and brunei periodicals. Joint standing committee on library cooperation and bibliographical services. Kuala lumpur, Singapura 1967 &c.

SAW SWEE-HOCK, The demography of Malaysia, Singapore and Brunei; a bibliography. Centre of asian studies: University of Hong Kong 1970. pp.v.39. [328.]*

MARGARET ROFF, Official publications of Malaysia, Singapore and Brunei in New York libraries. Southern asian institute: Columbia university: Occasional bibliographical papers (no.1): New York 1971. pp.45. [800.]*

SINGAPORE. [see also MALAYA]

CATALOGUE of government publications. Colony of Singapore. 1949. pp.44. [1000.]

LIST of regulations, etc. presented pursuant to ordinances. Legislative assembly: Singapore 1959 &c.
in progress.

COMMUNIST literature in Singapore. Legislature assembly: Singapore sessional paper (Cmnd.14 of 1959): Singapore 1959*.

YEH SIEW KEE, Singapore; a list of publications and periodical articles arranged by subject. Library school: Wellington N.Z. 1962.

CHECK list of current serials in the National library, Singapore. Compiled by the Catalogue section. National library: Singapore 1967. pp.40.

LIM U WEN, Check list of current serials in the university of Singapore library. Singapore 1967. ff.[iv]. pp.112. [5500.]*

INDEKS majallah kini Malaysia Singapura dan Brunei. Index to current malaysian singapore and brunei periodicals. Joint standing committee on library cooperation and bibliographical services. Kuala Lumpur, Singapura 1967 &c.

SINGAPORE national bibliography. National library: Singapore.*
    1967. pp.xvi.155. [784.]
    1968. pp.xxii.141. [745.]
    1969. pp.xxiii.194. [881.]
    1970. pp.xxiii.185. [845.]
in progress.

CATALOGUE of the Singapore/Malaysia collection. Prepared by the Cataloguing department. University of Singapore library: Boston 1968. pp.xxiii.757. [15,882 cards.]*

MALAYSIA & Singapore. Selected reading lists for advanced study: Commonwealth institute: [London] 1969. pp.17. [117.]

JOYCE CHALLIS, Annotated bibliography of economic and social material in Singapore. Part I: Government publications. Research bibliography series (no.1): Economic research centre: University of Singapore 1969. ff.[iii].ii.86. [254.]*

SAW SWEE-HOCK, The demography of Malaysia, Singapore and Brunei: a bibliography. Centre of asian studies: University of Hong Kong 1970. pp.v.39. [328.]*

KARL J. PELZER, West Malaysia and Singapore: a selected bibliography. Behavior science bibliographies: New Haven 1971. pp.vi.394. [5000.]*

MARGARET ROFF, Official publications of Malaysia, Singapore and Brunei in New York libraries. Southern asian institute: Columbia university: Occasional bibliographical papers (no.1): New York 1971. pp.45. [800.]*

LENA U-WEN LIM, Physical planning in Singapore & Malaysia; a bibliography and index. Singapore 1972.*

STEPHEN H. K. YEH and MARGARET W. N. LEONG, Annotated urban bibliography of Singapore. Singapore 1972. ff.[iii].94. [275.]*

CHECK list of current serials in the University of Singapore library. Singapore 1967. pp.107. [4].

CHECKLIST of current serials in the library, may 1972. Library bulletin (no.4): Institute of southeast asian studies: Singapore 1972. ff.ii.30. [1000.]*

PHILIPPINE ISLANDS

i. *Bibliographies*
ii. *General*
iii. *Printing. National bibliography*
iv. *Cartography and topography*
v. *Foreign relations*
vi. *History*
vii. *Official publications*
viii. *Academic writings*
ix. *Periodicals*
x. *Other subjects*
xi. *Persons*
xii. *Philippine languages and literatures*

i. *Bibliographies*

[ASKEL GUSTAV SOLOMON JOSEPHSON], Bibliographies of the Philippine Islands. Bulletin of bibliography pamphlets (no.7): Boston 1899. pp.8. [43.]

CHARLES O[RVILLE] HOUSTON, Philippine bibliography. 1. An annotated preliminary bibliography of philippine bibliographies (since 1900). University of Manila: Manila 1960. pp.[ii].69.23. [155.]

SHIRO SAITO, The Philippines; a review of bibliographies. Occasional paper (no.5): East-west center library: Honolulu 1966. ff.iv.79. [215.]

GABRIEL A. BERNARDO, Bibliography of philippine bibliographies, 1593–1961. Edited by Natividad P. Verzosa. Occasional papers of the Department of history: Bibliographical series (no.2): Ateneo de Manila university: Quezon city 1968. pp.xiv.192. [xvii.] [1160.]

ii. *General*

CH[ARLES] LECLERC, Bibliotheca americana. Histoire, géographie, voyages, archéologie et linguistique des deux Amériques et des Îles Philippines. 1878. pp.[iii].xx.739. [2638.]
[—] — Supplément no.1. 1881. pp.[iv].103. [391.]
[—] — Supplément no.2. 1887. pp.110. [591.]
a photographic reprint of the whole was issued, Paris 1961.

W[ENCESLAS] E[MILIO] RETANA, Epítome de la bibliografía general de Filipinas. ... Obras que posee el autor. Madrid 1895–1898. pp.84+57+48+98. [1167.]

W[ENCESLAS] E[MILIO] RETANA, Catálogo abreviado de la bibioteca filipina. Madrid 1898. pp.xxxviii.655. [1697.]

THOMAS COOKE MIDDLETON, Some notes on the bibliography of the Philippines. Free library: Bulletin (no.4): Philadelphia 1900. pp.58. [125.]

A[PPLETON] P[RENTISS] C[LARK] GRIFFIN, A list of books (with references to periodicals) on the Philippine Islands ... with chronological list of maps ... by P[hilip] Lee Phillips. Library of Congress: Washington 1903. pp.xv.397. [4000.]
also issued in Senate document, 57th congress, 2nd session, no.74.

W[ENCELAS] E[MILIO] RETANA, Aparato bibliográfico de la historia general de Filipinas deducido de la colección que posee en Barcelona la Compañía general de tabacos de dichas islas. Madrid 1906. pp.xcvii.463+464–1064+1065–1801. [4623.]
reprinted Manila 1964.

JAMES ALEXANDER ROBERTSON, Bibliography of the Philippine Islands, printed and manuscript, preceded by a descriptive account of the most important archives and collections concerning Philippina. Cleveland 1908. pp.437. [4000.]
150 copies printed; also issued as vol.liii of The Philippine Islands, 1493–1898.
reprint, New York 1970.

THE PHILIPPINE Islands. For eastern book and journal lists (no.16): Public library: Newark, N.J. [1921]. single leaf. [18.]

A SHORT list of recent references on the Philippine islands (economics, history, natural resources, travel). Library of Congress: [Washington] 1924. ff.9. [83.]*
— [supplement]. A list [&c.].1933.ff.25.[325.]*
— [supplement]. A selected list [&c.]. Compiled by Ann Duncan Brown. 1935. pp.43. [585.]*

[ICHIRŌ MITAMURA], Bibliography of the Philippine islands. Institute of the Pacific: Tokyo 1941. pp.[v].291. [3058.]

SOUTHEAST Asia and the Philippines. A selected list of political, economic and cultural sources. Department of state: Division of library and reference services: Bibliographic list (no.33): [Washington] 1950. ff.9. [100.]*

LUISA and MODESTA CUESTA, Catálogo de obras iberoamericanas y filipinas de la Biblioteca nacional de Madrid. Catálogo de archivos y bibliotecas [vol.i]: Madrid 1953. pp.vii.322. [3364.]

FILIPINIANA in Jesuit libraries in the Philippines. Quezon City.
in progress.

LETICIA SANTOS-DOMINGO, List of filipiniana in the library of the University of Manila. Manila 1954. pp.27.*

FRED EGGAN, *ed.*, Selected bibliography of the Philippines. Preliminary edition. Human relations area files: Behavior science bibliographies: New Haven 1956. pp.vi.138. [xii]. [1000.]*

FRED[ERICK RUSSELL] EGGAN and E. D. HESTER, Selected bibliography of the Philippines. . . . Preliminary edition. Human relations area files: Behavior science bibliographies: New Haven 1956. pp.vi.138. [900.]*

CLASSIFIED list of filipiniana books and pamphlets in the main library, University of the Philippines, as of December, 1958. Quezon city 1959. pp.vi.358. [2959.]*

PACÍFICO M. AUSTRIA, GLORIA S. QUIROS and CONSOLACIÓN B. REBADAVIA, *edd.* Classified list of filipiniana books and pamphlets in the main library, university of the Philippines. Quezon City 1959. pp.[ii].vi.358. [2959.]

CLASSIFIED list of filipiniana books and pamphlets in the Filipiniana section, Far Eastern university, as of December, 1960. Manila 1960.ff.v. 254. [1866.]*

CLASSIFIED list of filipiniana holdings of the Ayala y compañía library. Makati 1961. ff.x.74.35. [770.]*

200 copies reproduced from typewriting.

BEYER library. Typescript on Philippine ethnography, folklore, customary law, and archaeology. Compiled under the direction of E. D. Hester, by the staff of the Asia Foundation-Beyer Project. Chicago 1962. pp.187.

CATALOGUE of filipiniana materials in the Lopez memorial museum. Pasay city 1961.71. ff.viii. 262+vii.181+vii.140+vii.161+ix.195. [7908.]*

MAXIMA M. FERRER, *ed.* Union catalog of philippine materials of sixty-four government agency libraries of the Philippines. University of the Philippines: Interdepartmental reference service: Manila 1962. pp.xvi.718. [10,277.]

PHILIPPINE bibliography 1963–1964. University of the Philippines library: Diliman, Rizal 1965. ff.v.142. [764.]*

UNIVERSITY of California library holdings on the Philippines. 1967. ff.63. [1200.]*

MICHAEL P. ONORATO, *ed.* Philippine bibliography (1899–1946). Santa Barbara 1968. pp.vii. 35. [460.]

FILIPINIANA 68—University of the Philippines: Quezon city 1969.

SELECT philippine publications for college use. Xavier university library: Cagayan de Oro city 1971 &c.
    i. 1971. pp.48.52.60.44. [150.]
    ii. 1972. pp.62.40.48.28. [200.]
    iii. 1973.
in progress.

*MAXIMA MAGSANOC FERRER, Union catalogue of philippine materials. Quezon city.
    i. A–O. 1970. pp.x.xlviii.877. [11,440.]

ISAGANI R. MEDINA, Filipiniana materials in the National library. Quezon city 1972. pp.xviii.353. [2524.]

iii. *Printing. National bibliography*

T[RINIDAD] H. PARDO DE TAVERA, Noticias sobre la imprenta y el grabado en Filipinas. Madrid 1893. pp.48. [100.]

J. T. MEDINA, La imprenta en Manila desde sus orígenes hasta 1819. Santiago de Chile 1896. pp.xcvi.280. [420.]
300 copies printed.
— — Adiciones e ampliaciones. 1904. pp.xi. 207. [145.]
— — Adiciones y observaciones . . . por W[enceslas] E[milio] Retana. Madrid 1897 [*on cover:* 1899]. pp.[iv].coll.275.pp.[iv]. [212.]
    206 copies printed.
— — Adiciones y continuación. Por . . . Angel Angel Pérez y Cecilio Güemes. Manila 1904 [*on cover:* 1905]. pp.[iv].lxvii.621. [1500.]
    reprinted, Amsterdam 1964.

JOSÉ TORIBO MEDINA, Brevísimo epítome de la imprenta en Manila (1593–1810). Madrid 1896. pp.32. [404.]
100 copies printed.

W. E. RETANA, Tablas cronológica y alfabética de imprentas é impresores de Filipinas (1593–1898). Madrid 1908. pp.115. [342.]
    150 copies printed.

W. E. RETANA, Orígenes de la imprenta filipina. Investigaciones históricas, bibliograficas y tipográficas. Madrid 1911. pp.204. [108.]
    127 copies printed.

BOOKS copyrighted, published in the Philippines, 1945–57. Bureau of public libraries: Manila 1957. pp.143.

GABRIEL A. BERNARDO, Philippine national bibliography, 1955–1959.

EARLY philippine imprints in the Lopez memorial museum. 1961. pp.viii.45. [44.]

COPYRIGHTED books in the Philippines, 1945–1963. National libray: Manila.

iv. *Cartography and topography*

w[ENCESLAS] E[MILIO] RETANA, Bibliografía de Mindanao (epítome). Madrid 1894. pp.71. [174.] *50 copies printed.*

PEDRO TORRES LANZAS, Relación descriptiva de los mapas, planos, etc., de Filipinas existentes en el Archivo general de Índias. Madrid 1897. pp.56. [139.] *200 copies printed.*

CATALOGUE of charts, maps, coast pilots, tide tables and current tables of the Philippine islands. Coast and goedetic survey: Manila [Washington] 1903 &c.

KARL J[OSEF] PEIZER, Selected bibliography on the geography of southeast Asia. Part II. The Philippines. Yale university: Southeast Asia studies: New Haven 1950. ff.[i].ix.76. [1000.]★

CARLOS QUIRINO, Philippine cartography (1320–1899). Manila [1959]. pp.vii.140. [1250.] *100 copies printed.*

JOSEFA B. ABRERA, An annotated bibliography of the history of the sugar industry in Panay and Negros. Occasional papers of the Department of history and government: Bibliographical series (no.1): Ateneo de Manila 1963. ff.iv.143. [833.]

ROBERT E. HUKE, Bibliography of philippine geography, 1940–1963: a selected list. Geography publications at Dartmouth (no.1): Department of geography: Dartmouth college: Hanover, N.H. 1964. pp.[iv].84. [1500.]★

WILLIAM HENRY SCOTT, Cordillera bibliography. Sagada social studies (no.14): Sagada 1970. ff.70. [800.]★

ALFREDO T. TIAMSON, Mindanao-Sulu bibliography, containing published, unpublished, manuscripts and works-in-progress. A preliminary survey and W. E. Retana's Bibliografia de Mindanao (1894). Davao city 1970. pp.xvii. 344. [2500.]

[LETICIA R. MALOLES], A guide to the map collection of the Filipiniana division. Bibliography division: [National library]: TNL research guide series (no.1): Manila 1971. ff.[iv].36. [71.]★

v. *Foreign relations*

LIST of references on the american occupation of the Philippine Islands. Library of Congress: Washington 1906. ff.15. [150.]★

— [supplement]. Select list of references on the Philippine Islands. 1911. ff.7. [65.]★

SELECT list of references of the independence of the Philippines. Library of Congress: Washington 1913. ff.7. [65.]★

— [another edition]. Philippine Islands, with special reference to the question of independence. 1931. ff.25. [297.]★ *there are intermediate editions.*

M[ARY] ALICE MATTHEWS, Philippine independence. Select list of books and articles... published since 1930. Carnegie endowment for international peace: Library: Select bibliographies (no.9): Washington 1939. ff.7. [80.]★

PHILIP M. HAMER, *ed.* Materials in the National archives relating to the Philippine Islands. National archives: [Reference information circular (no.1): Washington] 1942. pp.6. [very large number.]★

KENNETH MUNDEN, Records of the Bureau of insular affairs relating to the Philippine Islands, 1898–1935. A list of selected files. National archives: Special list (no.2): Washington 1942. pp.xii.91. [very large number.]★

THE PHILIPPINES during the japanese regime, 1942–1945. An annotated list of the literature published in or about the Philippines during the japanese occupation. Office of the Chief of counter-intelligence: [Manila] 1945. pp.[52.]★

vi. *History*

J[OSE] T[ORIBIO] MEDINA, Bibliografía española de las Islas Filipinas (1523–1810). Santiago de Chile 1897. pp.3–556. [667.] *200 copies printed.* *reprinted Amsterdam 1966.*

T[RINIDAD] H. PARDO DE TAVERA, Biblioteca filipana, ó sea catálogo razonado de todos los impresos... relativos a la historia... etc., de las Islas Filipinas, de Joló y Marianas. Washington 1903. pp.439. [2850.] *also issued in Senate document, 57th congress, 2nd session, no. 74.*

w[ENCESLAS] E[MILIO] RETANA, Aparato bibliografico de la historia general de Filipinas, deducido de la colección que posee en Barcelona la Compañía general de tabacos de dichas Islas. Madrid 1906. pp.[vii].xlvii–xcix.463+[iii].465–1064+[iii].1065–1803. [4623.] *262 copies printed.*

LIST of references on the influence of the friars on the economic life and thought of the Philippine Islands. Library of Congress: Washington 1922. ff.3. [22.]★

CATÁLOGO de los documentos relativos a las Islas Filipinas existentes en el Archivo de Índias de Sevilla. Compañía general de tabacos de Filipinas: Barcelona.

    i. 1493–1572. Por Pedro Torres y Lanzas. 1925. pp.[ii].cccv.211. [1809.]

ii. 1573–1587. 1926. pp.iii–cccxliv.189. [1645.]
iii. 1588–1595. 1927. pp.iii–ccclv.131. [1047.]
iv. 1595–1602. 1928. pp.iii–cclxv.191. [1613.]
v. 1602–1608. Por Francisco Nevas. 1929. pp.iii–cclxxiii.223. [1340.]
vi. 1608–1618. Por F. Navas del Valle. 1930. pp.iii–cccxvii.281. [2372.]
vii. 1618–1635. 1931–1932. pp.iii–ccxliv.207 +447. [5630.]
viii. 1636–1644. 1933. iii–ccxc.253. [2156.]
ix. 1644–1662. 1934. pp.iii–ccxxv.327. [2792.]
500 copies printed of most of the volumes.

ROB[ERT] STREIT and JOHANNES DINDINGER, Bibliotheca missionum. Sechster band. Missionsliteraturn Indiens, der Philippinen, Japans und Indochinas 1700–1799. Internationales institut für missionswissenschaftliche forschung: Aachen 1931. pp.32.616. [2005.]
—— Neunter band. Missionsliteratur der Philippinen 1800–1909. 1937. pp.36.996. [2500.]

KENNETH MUNDEN, Records of the Bureau of insular affairs relating to the Philippine islands 1898–1935; a list of selected files. National archives: Washington 1942. pp.xii.91. [large number.]*

PHILIP SELZNICK and ARTURO GUERRERO, The Philippines during the japanese regime, 1942–1945. An annotated list of the literature published in or about the Philippines during the Japanese occupation. Office of the chief of counterintelligence: Philippine research and information section: General headquarters: Armed forces of the Pacific: [Manila] 1945. pp.ii+44.*

PAUL S. LIETZ, Calendar of philippine documents in the Ayer collection of the Newberry library. (Short title list of transcripts from philippine documents in the Spanish archives. Chicago 1956. pp.xvi.259. [1120.]

DORIS VARNER WELSH, A catalogue of printed materials relating to the Philippine islands, 1519–1900, in the Newberry library. Chicago 1959. pp.viii.179. [1938.]

THOMAS POWERS, Balita mula Maynila (news from Manila). University of Michigan: Michigan historical collections and the Center for south and south east asian studies: Ann Arbor 1971. [40.]

vii. *Official publications*

EMMA OSTERMAN ELMER, Checklist of publica-, tions of the government of the Philippine islands September 1, 1900, to December 31, 1917. Philippine library and museum: Manila 1918. pp.288.

CHECKLIST of Philippine government documents, 1950. Library of Congress: Washington 1953. pp.vii.62. [755.]*
a catalogue of documents issued in 1950.

PHILIPPINE government publications. Department of education: Bureau of public libraries: Documents, gifts and exchange section: Manila 1958–9. ff.112+. [1455.]*

CHECKLIST of Philippine government publications. National library: Department of education: Manila.
1962. ff.21. [250.]
1963. ff.22. [250.]
1964. ff.91. [1181.]
1965–66.ff.91. [1431.]

ANDREA C. PONCE and JACINTO C. YATCO (part II: JACINTA Y. INGLES and URSULA G. PICACHE), List of Philippine government publications, 1945–1958. University of the Philippines: Institute of public administration: Library: Manila 1959–1960. ff.[i].iv.132+[viii].151. [3000.]*

CONSOLACIÓN B. REBADAVIA, Checklist of Philippine government documents 1917–1949. University of the Philippines: Library: Quezon City 1960. pp.[ii].xv.817. [6469.]*

MAXIMA M. FERRER, *ed.* and ELVIRA C. CERVANTES, *asst. ed.*, Union catalogue of philippine materials of sixty-four government agency libraries of the Philippines. Manila 1962. pp.xvi.718. [10,277.]

AN ANNOTATED bibliography of official statistical publications of the Philippine government. Office of statistical coordination and standards: Manila 1963. pp.25.

CHECKLIST of Philippine government publications, 1967–68. National library: Public documents, exchange and gifts division: [Manila 1968?] ff.101. [1467.]*

RICHARD S. MAXWELL, Preliminary inventory of the records of the Bureau of insular affairs. Record group (350): U.S. National archives: Washington 1960. pp.32.

RICHARD S. MAXWELL, Preliminary inventory of the records of the Office of the U.S. high commissioner to the Philippine islands. Recorded group (126): U.S. National archives: Washington 1963. pp.v.24. [large number.]

viii. *Academic writings*

PUBLICATIONS of the educational institutions and organizations in the Philippines. Unesco national commission of the Philippines. Publication (no.5): Manila 1954. pp.47.

MAURO GARCIA and PILAR CRUZ GARCIA. A list of publications of the Institute of science and technology, 1901–1953. Institute of science and technology: I.S.T. bibliographic series, Bulletin (no.2): Manila 1954. pp.5.46.*

INDEX of the published works of the faculty members of the University of Santo Tomás, Manila, Philippines. Indice de las obras publicados por profesores de la Universidad de Santo Tomás de Manila, Filipinas: Santo Tomás 1956. pp.89.

GENERAL index of academic works. U. Santo Tomás: Manila.
1960.
1965.

THESES abstracts. University of the Philippines: Graduate school of arts and sciences: [Quezon City].
i. 1947–1954. 1962. pp.ix.118. [100.]
ii. 1954–1956. pp.192. [115.]
iii. 1956–1959. pp.164. [119.]

RESEARCH works and other publications of the faculties. University of the Philippines: Quezon city.
1957–1959. pp.vi.173. [1500.]
1959–1961. pp.viii.263. [2500.]
1961–1963. pp.vii.299. [3000.]
in progress?

COMPILATION of graduate theses prepared in the Philippines, 1913–1960. National science development board: Manila.
1913–1960. pp.[viii]. 437. [4355.]
1961–1965. pp.ix.320. [1632.]

CONCEPCION S. BAYLON, Guide to doctoral dissertations on microfilm (1937–1968) in the Filipiniana division: TNL research guide series (no.3): [National library]: Manila 1971. ff.vii.92. [218.]*

LIST of theses and dissertations available in the Filipiniana division. [National library: Manila 1970?].ff.54. [600.]*

ix. *Periodicals*

W[ENCESLAS] E[MILIO] RETANA, El periodismo filipino. Noticias para su historia (1811–1894). Apuntes bibliográficos. Madrid 1895. pp.[vii]. 648. [142.]
largely printed on one side of the leaf.

UNION list of serials of selected special libraries in the Philippines (preliminary listing). University of the Philippines: Institute of public administration: Manila 1953. ff.vii.192. [1900.]*

CONCORDIA SANCHEZ [*and others*], Union list of serials of government agency libraries of the Philippines. University of the Philippines: Institute of public administration: Inter-departmental reference service: Manila 1955. pp.xii.623. [6000.]
— — Revised ... edition ... by Maxima M. Ferrer [*and others*]. 1960. pp.xxii.911. [8000.]

DONN V[ORHIS] HART and QUINTIN A. EALA, An annotated guide to current Philippine periodicals. Yale university: Southeast Asia studies: Bibliography series: [New Haven] 1957. pp.xxi.116. [325.]*

[LOURDES Y. COLLANTES *and others*], Union checklist of filipiniana serials in the libraries of the university of the Philippines. University of the Philippines: Library: Research guide (no.3) Quezon City 1962. ff.[ii].vi.287. [1701.]*

UNION list of serials of government agency libraries of the Philippines. Revised & enlarged edition. Inter-departmental reference service: Institute of public administration: University of the Philippines: Manila 1960. pp.xxii.914. [10,000.]

FRANK H. GOLAY, Annotated guide to philippine serial publications in the Cornell university library. Cornell university: Ithaca 1962. pp.72. [300.]*

SHIRO SAITO, Philippine newspapers in selected american libraries; a union list. Occasional paper (no.6): East-west center library: [Honolulu] 1966. ff.xi.46. [197.]

INDEX to philippine periodicals. Inter-departmental reference service: Institute of public administration: University of the Philippines: Manila.*
i. Edited by Maxima D. Ferrer. 1955–1956. pp.x.459. [9000.]
ii. Edited by Maxima D. Ferrer and Dolores D. Sadang. 1956–1957. pp.iv.670. [13,000.]
iii. Edited by Maxima D. Ferrer and Soledad M. Eugenio. 1957–1958. pp.vi.463. [9000.]
iv. Edited by Maxima D. Ferrer and Venancia T. Guillermo. 1958–1959. pp.v. 341. [7000.]
v. 1959–1960. pp.vi.381. [7500.]
vi. 1960–1961. pp.vii.384. [7500.]
vii. 1961–1962. pp.xi.435. [8500.]
viii. 1962–1963. pp.xii.537. [10,500.]
ix. 1963–1964. pp.xii.301. [12,000.]
x. 1964–1965. pp.xi.276. [10,000.]
xi. 1965–1966. pp.xii.373. [15,000.]
xii–xiii. 1966–1968. 1971. pp.xii.972. [38,000].
xiv. 1968–1969. Edited by Venancia T. Guillermo. 1972. pp.xii.649. [25,000.]
in progress.

GUIDE to Philippine periodical literature. [Silliman university, Dumaguete City].
[i]. 1955.
[ii]. 1956. [By] P. D. Dimaya [and G. D. Diega]. pp.66.257–292.34. [2000.]
[*continued as:*]
Philippine periodical index.

[iii]. 1958. Compiled by G. D. Diega and
E. P. Banas. pp.65–99.183–240.305–346.
[iv]. 1959. pp.141–176.246–279.376–411.
[2000.]
[v]. 1960.
in progress; not published for 1957.

x. *Other subjects*

Agriculture

EDUARDO R. ALVARADO, Philippine agricultural
bibliography. Part I. Check list of books, circulars, and miscellaneous publications of the Bureau
of agriculture. Bureau of agriculture: Manila
1926. pp.38. [350.]
no more published.

BASILIO HERNANDEZ, Philippine bibliography
of the nine major crops of the Philippines: rice,
sugar cane, abaca, coconut, tobacco, corn,
maguey, coffee and cacao. Bureau of science
library: Manila, P.I. 1933. ff.[i].ii.pp.132. [1500.]*

BASILIO HERNANDEZ and LAUREANA ESTRELLA
[VILLANUEVA], Philippine bibliography of the
minor crops of the Philippines. Department of
agriculture and commerce: Bureau of science:
Manila 1934. ff.[iii].ii.[i].166.iii. [2000.]

LIST of available publications. Department of
agriculture and commerce: Manila 1936. pp.41.
[400.]

ENGRACIO BASIO and ANDRES AQUINO, A bibliography of the published contributions in agriculture from 1909 to 1950. College of agriculture
and central experiment station library, University
of the Philippines: Los Banos: 1952. pp.iii.403.*

QUINTIN A. EALA [*and others*], List of references
on coconut available in the Scientific library,
Institute of science and technology. Institute of
Science and Technology, Manila 1955. pp.56.*

QUINTIN A. EALA, Classified list of references on
coconut (*cocos nucifera*) available in the Scientific
library. Institute of science and technology:
Manila 1956–1957. pp.151.*

BEATRIZ SOLER and PILAR CRUZ GARCIA, Classified
list of references on abaca (Manila hemp) musa
textilis available in the Scientific library. Institute
of Science and Technology: Manila 1956.
pp.34.*

ENRIQUE T. VIRATA, [*and others, edd.*] Agrarian
reform; a bibliography. Community development research council: University of the Philippines: Diliman, Quezon city 1965. pp.xv.239.
[1013.]

Astronomy

MIGUEL SELGA, The publications of the Observa-
tory of Manila. Government of the Philippine
Islands: Manila 1929. pp.21. [400.]

Biography

HELEN DUDENBOSTEL JONES, Biographical sources
for foreign countries. III. The Philippines. Library
of Congress: General reference and bibliography
division: Washington 1945. ff.v.pp.60. [306.]*

Botany

ELMER D[REW] MERRILL, A discussion and bibliography of Philippine flowering plants. Bureau of
science: Popular bulletin (no.2): Manila 1926.
pp.239. [1750.]

CATALINA A. NEMENZO, The flora and fauna of
the Philippines, 1851–1966. An annotated bibliography. Natural and applied science bulletin
(vol.21,nos.1 and 2): University of the Philippines: Quezon city.
i. Plants. 1969. pp.xv.307. [1493.]

BIBLIOGRAPHY of philippine bryology. Publication, National museum of Ceylon (3): Colombo
1967. pp.19.

Civil service

GREGORIO A. FRANCISCO, An annotated bibliography on the philippine civil service. University
of the Philippines: Institute of public administration: Manila 1953. ff.[i].iv.27. [200.]*

Community development

FELICIDAD V. CORDERO. An annotated bibliography on community development in the
Philippines from 1946–1959. Community development research council: University of the
Philippines: Diliman, Rizal.
i. Content and methodology. ff.ii.ii.436.
[2500.]*

ROBERT A. BULLINGTON, A review of com-
munity-oriented ecological research in the
Philippines. Ohio university: Center for international studies: Papers in international studies:
Southeast Asia series (no.19): Athens, Ohio 1971.
ff.ix.31. [50.]*

Drama and stage

W[ENCESLAS] E[MILIO] RETANA, Noticias histó-
rico-bibliográficas de el teatro en Filipinas desde
sus origenes hasta 1898. Madrid 1909. pp.184.
[100.]

Economics

ALEJANDRINO G. HUFANA and RONY V. DIAZ, An
annotated bibliography of philippine social services. Volume I: Economics. University of the
Philippines: Social science research center: Manila
1956. pp.x.525. [2895.]

BELEN ANGELES and RACHEL CABATO, A bibliography of periodicals and statistical sources on the philippine economy. Institute of economic development and research: School of economics: University of the Philippines: Quezon city 1970. ff.[iii].65.xiii. [246.]*

English literature

LEOPOLDO Y. YABES, Philippine literature in english 1898–1957. A bibliographical survey. University of the Philippines: Quezon City 1958. pp.[iv].343–434. [877.]
300 copies printed.

ALBERTO S. FLORENTINO. Midcentury guide to philippine literature in english. Manila 1963. pp.96. [500.]

Ethnology

C. P. WARREN, Negrito groups in the Philippines: preliminary bibliography. Philippine studies program: University of Chicago 1959. ff.ii.16. [450.]*

SHIRO SAITO, Preliminary bibliography of philippine ethnography. Ateneo de Manila: Manila 1968. pp.388.

SHIRO SAITO, Philippine ethnography. A critically annotated and selected bibliography. East-west bibliographic series: Honolulu 1972. pp. xxxi.512. [484.]

Finance

SELECTED references on public finances of the Philippine commonwealth. Library of Congress: Washington 1944. ff.3. [31.]*

Folk-lore

E. ARSENIO MANUEL, Philippine folklore bibliography; a preliminary survey. Philippine folklore society: Paper (no.1): Quezon city 1965. pp.xvii. 125. [2000.]

Geology

JUAN S. TEVES, Bibliography of philippine geology, mining and mineral resources. Bureau of mines: Bibliography series (no.1): Manila 1953. pp.v.155. [2846.]

Government

AJIT SINGH RYE. A selected bibliography on studies in government reorganization. Institute of Public Administration, University of the Philippines; Manila n.d. pp.12.*

Law

VICENTE J. FRANCISCO, Legal bibliography Manila 1950. pp.xvi.346.

LETICIA PACIS-NEBRIDA and AVELINO P. TENDORO, An annotated philippine legal bibliography. Institute of public administration: University of the Philippines: Manila 1954. pp.37.

Malaria

DAVID [W.] WALKER, A selected bibliography on malaria in the Philippines. Institute of science and technology: Bulletin (no.1): Manila 1953. pp.41. [750.]

Mines and mining

CIRILO B. PEREZ and LAUREANNA ESTRELLA, Bibliography on mines and mining in the Philippines. Department of agriculture and commerce: Scientific library division: Manila 1934. ff.[i].3. 130. [1400.]*
a copy in the Library of Congress contains a few ms. additions.
— — [another edition]. Bureau of sciences Scientific library: Bibliographic contribution: (no.1): 1937. pp.100. [1635.]

Muslims

THOMAS M. KIEFER and STUART L. SCHLEGEL, A selected bibliography: Philippine Moslems. Chicago 1965. ff.16. [150.]*

Natural resources

KOICHI SUZUKI [and others]. Bibliography of natural resources of south Asia: Philippine Islands. National Resources Institute: Tokyo 1942. pp.452.

BIBLIOGRAPHY of survey on resources in southern Asia: the Philippines. Shigenkagaku kenkyujo: Tokyo 1942. pp.391.61.

Numismatics

MAURO GARCIA, Philippine numismatic literature; a bibliography. 1961.

Planning

AN ANNOTATED bibliography of philippine planning. Institute of planning: University of the Philippines: Manila 1968. pp.203.

Religion

ROBERT B. VON OEYEN, *jr.*, Philippine evangelical protestant and independent catholic churches: an historical bibliography of church records, publications and source material located in the Greater Manila area. Bibliography series (no.1): Asian center: University of the Philippines: [Quezon city] 1970. pp.330.

SALVADOR PONS Y TORRES, El clero secular filipino, apuntes bibliográficos y biográficos. Manila 1900. pp.141.

Science

C. S. SEMILLA, List of philippines publications in the Scientific library, Institute of science and technology. Institute of science and technology: Manila 1954. pp.61.xii.

CONCORDIA SANCHEZ [and others], Union catalog of philippine publications on science and technology. National institute of science and technology: Division of documentation: Manila 1962. pp.xiv. [800.] [3545.]

Social sciences

AN ANNOTATED bibliography of philippine social sciences. Compiled under the supervision of Cecilio Lopez. Social science research center: University of the Philippines: Quezon city.
  i. Economics, by Alejandrino G. Hufana and Rony V. Diaz. 1956. pp.x.525. [2895.]
  ii. part i: Sociology, by Reginaldo F. Arceo. 1957. pp.vi.153. [286.]
  iii. part i: Political science, by Flora Celi-Lansang. 1960. pp.viii.175. [1321.]

Statistics

AN ANNOTATED bibliography of official statistical publications of the Philippine government Office of statistical coordination and standards: Manila 1963. pp.25.

Sugar

JOSEFA B. ABRERA, An annotated bibliography of the history of the sugar industry in Panay and Negros. Occasional papers of the Department of history and government: Bibliographical series (no.1): Ateneo de Manila 1963. ff.iv.143. [833.]

Trade and manufactures

LIST of references on philippine-american trade and economic relations which are available in the university of the Philippines library. [Manila] 1937. ff.[ii].134.[135].43.21. [1508.]*

PEDRO B. AYUDA, Filipiniana materials. Export bibliographic trade lists of Pedro B. Ayuda & company, Manila [1971]. pp.146–149. ff.170–180. pp.197–262. 10.17.30.17. [1863.]*

Zoology

CASTO DE ELERA, Catálogo sistemático de toda la fauna de Filipinas. Manila 1895–1896. pp.ix.701 + [iii].676 + [iv].942.lxiv. [75,000.]

xi. Persons

Aguinaldo, Emilio

[ISAGANI R. MEDINA], Preliminary bibliography on Emilio Aguinaldo. National historical commission: Manila 1969. pp.76. [600.]

Jimenez, P.

JAIME CARLOS DE VEYRA, Estudio bibliográfico. El Belarmino del P. Jimenez. Manila n.d. pp.12.

Magsaysay, Ramón

RAMÓN MAGSAYSAY. A bibliography. University of the Philippines: Institute of public administration: Library: Manila 1957. pp.[ix].185. [3500.]*

Quezon, Manuel L.

MANUEL L. QUEZON, a bio-bibliography. Bureau of public libraries: Manila 1962. ff.170.

MANUEL L. QUEZON, a register of his papers in the National library. Rare books and manuscripts room: Filipiniana division: National library: Manila [1968]. ff.41. [201.]*

xii. Philippine languages and literatures

FERDINAND BLUMENTRITT, Vocabular einzelner ausdrücke und redensarten, welche dem spanischen der Philippinischen Inseln eigenthümlich sind. ... Mit einem anhange: bibliotheca philippina. Alphabetisch geordnete sammlung einer anzahl von druckschriften und manuscripten ... die auf die Philippinen bezug haben. [Leitmeritz 1882]. pp.viii.132. [1000.]
— — [supplement]. II. theil. [1885]. pp.[viii].64. [600.]
privately printed.

DORIS VARNER WELSH, Checklist of philippine linguistics in the Newberry library. Chicago 1950. pp.vi.176. [1154.]

BOOKS copyrighted, published, in the Philippines: 1945–1957. Bureau of public libraries: Manila [1957]. ff.[ii].143. [1447.]*

LEOPOLDO Y. YABES, Philippine literature in english 1898–1957. A bibliographical survey. University of the Philippines: Quezon City 1958. pp.[iv].343–434. [877.]
300 copies printed.

ESTHER M. RONQUILLO, Tagalog 'Awits' and 'Corridos'. A study with prose translations and a comprehensive bibliography of available works. University of the Philippines: Quezon city 1953.

PILAR CRUZ GARCIA, A list of dictionaries in tagalog and other philippine languages. Institute of science and technology: Scientific library: Manila [1958]. ff.11. [109.]*

JACK H. WARD, A bibliography of philippine linguistics and minor languages. With annotations and indices based on works in the library of Cornell university. Linguistics series (v): Data paper (no.83): Southeast Asia program: Cornell university: Ithaca 1971. pp.viii.549. [6600.]*

NOBLEZA C. ASUNCION-LANDÉ, A bibliography of philippine linguistics. Ohio university center for international studies: Papers in international studies, Southeast Asia series (no.20): Athens, Ohio 1971. pp.xxiii.147. [1977.]*

Iloko

LEOPOLDO Y. YABES [and JOSÉ RESURRECCIÓN CALIP], A brief survey of Iloko literature . . . with a bibliography of works pertaining to the Iloko people and their language. Manila 1936. pp.x.156. [1999.]
privately printed.

Mindanao

W[ENCESLAS] E[MILIO] RETANA, Bibliografia de Mindanao (epítome). Madrid 1894. pp.71. [174.]
50 copies printed.

THAILAND

i. *General*
ii. *Tai languages*
iii. *Siamese manuscripts*

i. *General*

[SIR] E[RNEST] M[ASON] SATOW, Essay towards a bibliography of Siam. Singapore 1886. pp.xiv.103. [500.]

SIAM. Far eastern book and journal lists (no.17): Public library: Newark, N.J. [1922]. single leaf. [21.]

BIBLIOGRAPHY of Siam. Bibliography of British North Borneo, Sarawak and Brunei. Koto shogyo gakko toshokan: Taihoku 1934. pp.17.

BETH DICKERSON [and others], Bibliography of Thailand. A selected list of books and articles with annotations. Cornell university: Department of far eastern studies: Southeast Asia program: Data paper (no.20): Ithaca 1956. ff.iv.64.5. [400.]*
re-issued in 1957.

LIST of Thai government plublications [sic] covering the years B.E. 2497 (1954), B.E. 2498 (1955), B.E. 2499 (1956). National library: Department of fine arts: Bangkok [1957]. ff.[iii].32. [850.]*

TOSHIO KAWABE [and others], Bibliography of thai studies. Tokyo university of foreign studies: Institute of foreign affairs: Tokyo 1957. pp.ii.75. [720.]*

JOHN BROWN MASON and H. CARROLL PARISH, Thailand bibliography. University of Florida: Libraries: Department of reference and bibliography: Bibliographic series (no.4): Gainesville 1958. pp.vii.247. [2500.]*

LIST of Thai government publications [sic]. Thammasat university: Institute of public admin-istration: Research division: Bangkok 1958. ff.[i].4.43. [1250.]*

ACQUISITIONS list of thai government publications. Prepared by Cornell research center . . . Bangkok, Thailand. 1958. ff.18. [350.]*

RICHARD A. GARD. A select bibliography for the study of Buddhism in Thailand in western languages. Compiled at the request of the Mahmakuta library, Mahmakuta University, Bangkok 1958. pp.17. [70.]*

LIST of thai government publications covering the years 1954, 1955, 1956. National library: Bangkok 1958. [ff.iv.]pp.31. [1200.]

NATIONAL bibliography 1958. National library: Bangkok.
in progress? apart from a title page in english, all is in thai.

BIBLIOGRAPHY of material about Thailand in western languages. Compiled by the central library of Chulalongkoon university. Bangkok B.E. 2503 (A.D. 1960). pp.vii.326. [6000.]

THE WORLD of books. Books currently published in Thailand. (Bannaphiphop.) Phranakon 1962 &c.
in progress; entirely in thai.

AMARA RAKSASATAYA and VEERAVAT KANCHANADUL, Bibliography on social sciences in Thailand. Institute for advanced projects: East–west center: University of Hawaii. Honolulu.
   i. Sources in Thai language. Author and title classification. 1963. pp.148.

EDUCATION of Thailand: a bibliography. Compiled by the library staff. College of education: Prasarnmitr 2506 [1963]. pp.43. [450.]

DAN FENNO HENDERSON, Bibliography of english language material on the law of Thailand. Seattle, University of Washington: School of law: Seattle 1963. ff.9. [128.]*

SUGGESTED reading list on Thailand. Military assistance institute: Library: Arlington, Va. 1963. pp.36. [350.]*

LA THAILANDE. Direction de la documentation: Notes et études documentaires (no.3020): Paris 1963. pp.48.

FRANCES A. BERNATH, Catalogue of thai language holdings in the Cornell university libraries through 1964. Data paper (no.54): Southeast Asia program: Department of asian studies: Cornell university: Ithaca 1964. pp.v.236. [4921.]*

INDEX to thai newspapers 1964. pp.vii.710. [18,000.] *in thai.*

STATISTICAL bibliography: an annotated bibliorgaphy of thai government statistical publications. National office of statistics: Office of the Prime minister: [Bangkok 1964]. pp.[ix]. 175. [240.]

LAWAN VAJRATHON and SOMPHIT YŌTSĒNĪ, Index to thai periodical literature, 1960–1963. [Bangkok 1964.] pp.xiii.613. [3000.]

A COMPILATION of reports and publications. U.S. operations mission to Thailand: [Bangkok 1965]. pp.i.95. [350.]

AMARA RAKSASATAYA [*and others*], Thailand: social science materials in thai & western languages. National institute of development administration. Bangkok 1966. pp.xi.378. [6000.]

WOODWORTH G. THROMBLEY, WILLIAM J. SIFFIN and PENSRI VAYAVANANDA, Thai government and its setting, a selective annotated bibliography. National institute of development administration: [Bangkok 1967]. pp.x.514. [2500.]

DAVID K. WYATT, Thai-language books; a checklist. Second revised edition. Centre of south east asian studies: School of oriental & african studies: London 1967. pp.14. [645.]*

IRA BITZ, A bibliography of english-language source materials on Thailand in the humanities, social sciences and physical sciences. Center for research in social systems: American university: Washington 1968. pp.viii.272. [5000.]

CONSTANCE H. WILSON, A reference guide to selected materials for research in the social sciences in Thailand. De Kalb [1968?]. ff.7. [25.]*

LIST of scientific reports (scientific and technical literature) relating to Thailand. Thai national documentation centre: Bangkok.
  i. 1964. [ff.ii].pp.126. [1263.]
  ii. 1965. [ff.iii].pp.69. [2115.]*
  iii. 1969. pp.95. [2110.]*
  iv. 1971. pp.[vi].43. [1394.]*
  v. 1973. Compiled by Nonphanga Chitrakorn.pp.iv.99. [2012.]*

FIRST guide to the literature of the aquatic sciences and fisheries in Bangkok, Thailand, by Committee on fishery literature. Kasetsart university fishery research bulletin (no.2): Bangkok 1965. pp.46. [500.]

ANNIE E. GRIMES, An annotated bibliography on the climate of Thailand. U.S. Department of commerce: National oceanic and atmospheric administration: Environmental data service: NOAA technical memorandum EDS BC–105: Silver spring, Md. 1971. pp.viii.73. [220.]

CHAKRIT NORANITHIPHADUNGKARN and THAWEE SUANMALEE, Bibliography on development administration; a selective collection of english language materials. Research center: National institute of development administration Bangkok 1970. ff.iv.113. [1500.]

PERIODICALS and newspapers printed in Thailand between 1844–1934; a bibliography. Serials unit: National library: Department of fine arts. Bangkok 1970. pp.[xii].72. [450.]

DAVID K. WYATT, Preliminary checklist of Thailand serials. Southeast Asia program, Cornell university: Ithaca 1971. ff.ii.139. [1000.]*

BIBLIOGRAPHY on water resources in Thailand. Applied scientific research corporation of Thailand: Bibliographical series (no.1): Bangkok 1970. ff.52. [220.]*

WOODWORTH G. THROMBLEY and WILLIAM J. SIFFIN, Thailand politics, economy and sociocultural setting; a selective guide to the literature. Bloomington, London 1972. pp.xxi.148. [800.]

UNION catalogue of thai materials. I. Institute of developing economies: Tokyo 1972. pp.xxxii. 413. [2500.]

ii. *Tai languages*

H. L. SHORTO, JUDITH M. JACOB and E. H. S. SIMMONDS, Bibliographies of mon-khmer and tai linguistics. London oriental bibliographies (vol.2): 1963. pp.x.88. [931.]

iii. *Siamese manuscripts*

MARQUIS [EDMÉ CASIMIR] DE CROIZIER, Notice des manuscrits siamois de la Bibliothèque nationale. 1887. pp.85. [62.]

GEORGE COEDÈS, Catalogue des manuscrits en pāli, laotien et siamois provenant de la Thailande. Royal library, Copenhagen: Catalogue of oriental manuscripts, xylographs &c. in danish collections: Copenhagen 1966. pp. x. 116.]115.]

KLAUS WENK, Thai-handschriften. Verzeichnis der orientalischen handschriften in Deutschland (band ix): Wiesbaden 1963–1968. pp.xiii.88 + xii.34. [243.]

PACIFIC OCEAN AND REGION. OCEANIA

PACIFIC OCEAN AND REGION. OCEANIA

i. *Bibliographies*
ii. *General*
iii. *Explorers*
iv. *Cartography*
v. *Periodicals*
vi. *Academic writings*
vii. *Other subjects*
viii. *Miscellaneous*
ix. *Pacific/Oceanic languages*
x. *Pacific territories and languages*

i. *Bibliographies*

IDA [EMILY] LEESON, A bibliography of bibliographies of the south Pacific. South Pacific commission: 1954. pp.x.61. [376.]

ii. *General*

CATALOGUE des ouvrages donnés par M. V[ictor] Schoelcher, sénateur. Bibliothèque nationale: 1884. pp.99. [1776.]

A LIST of books, California and the Pacific, in the library of Augustin S. Macdonald. Oakland, Cal. 1903. pp.77. [1750.]

GEORGE A. BARRINGER, Catalogue de l'histoire de l'Océanie. Bibliothèque nationale: Département des imprimés: 1912. pp.169.[iii]. [1000.]

A CATALOGUE of 1017 books, maps, pamphlets, &c. relating to Australia, New Zealand and the south seas, . . . collected by mr. George Calvert. [*c*.1920]. pp.[ii].56. [880.]
— Addenda. [1922]. single leaf. [29.]

RAYMOND LESLIE BUELL, Problems of the Pacific. A brief bibliography. World peace foundation: Pamphlets (vol.viii, no.1): Boston 1925. pp.34.

L. JORE, Essai de bibliographie du Pacifique. 1931. pp.[iv].235. [1750.]

A LIST of current research projects dealing with China, Hawaii, Japan, Philippine islands, Russia and/or the U.S.S.R., Pacific islands and miscellaneous subjects of importance to the Pacific area. Institute of Pacific relations [*afterwards:* American institute of Pacific relations]: New York [San Francisco].★
　1934.
　1935.
　1936. pp.[ii].27. [300.]
　　[*continued as:*]
Current research projects dealing with subjects relating to the Pacific area.
　1937–1938. pp.[iv].40. [400.]
　　[*continued as:*]

The Pacific area in american research.
　1939.
　1940. ff.[i].iii.40. [416.]
　1941.

LIVRES sur les établissements français de l'Océanie et sur les mers adjacentes dans la collection Kroepelien. Oslo 1934. pp.21. [700.]

CATALOGUE of the australasian collection of books and pictures formed by the late James Edge Partington. With a memoir by Harry G. Beasley. London 1934. pp.[iv]. 178.xi. [2682].

SELECTED list of references on Oceania. Library of Congress: Washington 1922. ff.5. [61.]★
— [supplement]. 1936. ff.9. [101.]★

G. GIDEL and E. PÉPIN, La France dans le Pacifique. Liste des accords diplomatiques et juridiques. Centre d'études de politique étrangère: [1936]. pp.30. [200.]

PUBLICATIONS on the Pacific. Institute of Pacific relations: New York &c. 1936. pp.42. [150.]
limited to the publications of the Institute.

EXPLORING the Pacific. Readings suggested in connection with club programs. Pacific house bibliographies (vol.ii): San Francisco [1938]. pp. 85. [1000.]

AMERICA and the Pacific. Readings suggested in connection with study programs. Pacific house bibliographies (vol.iii): San Francisco [1938]. pp. 92. [1000.]

OUR debt to the Pacific. A bibliography for high schools and junior colleges. Pacific house bibliographies (vol.i): San Francisco [1938]. pp.30. [400.]

BIBLIOGRAPHIE de l'Océanie. Extrait du Journal de la Société des océanistes. Paris.
　1939–1944. Par Édouard Reitman. pp.187–231. [1400.]
　1945. Par Édouard Reitman & Patrick O'Reilly. pp.289–317. [750.]
　1946. Par Patrick O'Reilly. pp.173–200. [800.]
　1947. Par Patrick O'Reilly & Marie Serqueiew. pp.205–244. [1000.]
　1948. Par Patrick O'Reilly. pp.233–269. [900.]
　1949. pp.293–335. [1100.]
　1950. pp.327–370. [1100.]
　1951. pp.329–361. [950.]
　1952. pp.413–448. [950.]
　1953. pp.231–263. [800.]
　1954. pp.181–220. [1000.]
　1955. pp.379–410. [750.]
　1956. pp.117–147. [750.]
　1957. pp.171–204. [850.]

1958. Par Patrick O'Reilly & Renée Heyum.
   pp.427–467. [1000.]
1959. pp.143–189. [1150.]
1960. pp.89–140. [1250.]
1961. pp.155–207. [1300.]
1962. pp.327–391. [1650.]
1963. Par Renée Heyum. pp.121–184. [1650.]
1964. pp.187–244. [1450.]
1965. pp.135–195. [1500.]
1966. pp.173–236. [1550.]
1967. pp.167–236. [1750.]
1968. pp.405–455. [1250.]
1969. pp.291–336+67–101. [2000.]
1970. pp.365–426. [1550.]
in progress.

C[LYDE] R[OMER] H[UGHES] TAYLOR, A select list of books relating to New Zealand and certain Pacific islands, 1912–1939. Alexander Turnbull library: Bibliographical list (no.6): Wellington 1940. pp.12. [250.]
—— [another edition]. A select list ... 1912–1945 ... (no.9): 1948. pp.3–18. [500.]

MARY C[ATHERINE] GRIER, Oceanography of the north Pacific ocean, Bering sea and Bering strait: a contribution toward a bibliography. University of Washington: Publications: Library series (no.2): Seattle 1941. pp.xxiii.290. [2929.]

PHILIP M. HAMER, *ed.* Materials in the National archives relating to the southern and western Pacific areas. National archives: [Reference information circular (no.2): Washington] 1942. pp.14. [large number.]*

WERNER B[RUNO] ELLINGER and HERBERT ROSINSKI, Sea power in the Pacific, 1936–1941. A selected bibliography of books, periodical articles, and maps from the end of the London naval conference to the beginning of the war in the Pacific. Princeton 1942. pp.iii–xiv.80. [600.]

SELECTED list of recent references on the south seas, with special attention to the american islands. Library of Congress: Washington 1943. ff.14. [146.]*

HELEN F[IELD] CONOVER, Islands of the Pacific. A selected list of references. Compiled ... under the direction of Florence S[elma] Hellman. Library of Congress: Division of bibliography: Washington 1943. ff.[iii].181. [1747.]*
—— [another edition]. 1943. pp.[v].155. [1747.]*
—— Supplement. 1945. pp.[iii].68. [390.]*

[PERCY] EVANS LEWIN, The Pacific region: a bibliography of the Pacific and east indian islands, exclusive of Japan. Royal empire society: Bibliographies (no.11): 1944. pp.[iv].76. [1500.]

A CLASSIFIED catalogue of books in foreign languages in the Toyo bunko 1917–1956. Tokyo.
   i. 1917–1936. I. General reference works.
      I. Asia, east Asia and the Pacific. 1944.
      pp.xix.402.2. [Pacific: 137.]

ALICE WOODHOUSE, Descriptive works on some Pacific island groups in the Alexander Turnbull library. Alexander Turnbull library: Bibliographical list (no.7): Wellington 1944. pp.17. [275.]*

AN ANNOTATED bibliography of the south-west Pacific and adjacent areas. Allied geographical section, Southwest Pacific area: [*s.l.*] 1944.
   i. The Netherlands and british east Indies and the Philippine islands. pp.[vii].317. [2500.]
   ii. The mandated territory of New Guinea, Papua, the British Solomon islands, the New Hebrides and Micronesia. pp.[viii]. 274. [2200.]
   iii. Malaya, Thailand, Indo China, the China coast and the Japanese empire. pp.[vii]. 256. [2200.]
— Supplement. 1945. ff.[i].vi.pp.693. [2000.]*

A. L. OLSSON, A bibliography of the historical, political and commercial relations between New Zealand and Oceania (excluding island dependencies and mandated territories), from 1840 to 1947. Library School, Wellington: 1947. ff.17 [200.]*

C[LYDE] R[OMER] H[UGHES] TAYLOR, A Pacific bibliography: printed matter relating to the native peoples of Polynesia, Melanesia and Micronesia. Polynesian society: Wellington 1951. pp.xxix. 492. [9000.]
— Second edition. Oxford 1965. pp.xxx.692. [20,000.]

CELSUS KELLY, Calendar of documents, spanish voyages in the south Pacific from Alvaro de Mendaña to Alejandro Malaspina, 1567–1794 and the franciscan missionary plans for the people of the austral lands 1617–1634. Compiled from manuscripts and other documents in the archives and libraries of Spain, America, Rome, Paris, London, Sydney &c. Madrid 1965. pp.xxviii.470. [1215.]

SELECT bibliography and catalogue of publications and maps relating to trust territories in the Pacific. United Nations: Trusteeship council (T/INF/25): [New York] 1952. pp.11. [135.]*

ERNEST J. FREI, Bibliographies of southeast Asia and the Pacific areas. Bibliographical society of the Philippines: Occasional papers (no.1): Quezon City 1958. pp.34. [300.]

FLOYD M. CAMMACK and SHIRO SAITO, Pacific island bibliography. New York 1962. pp.421. [1727.*]

limited to works in the library of the university of Hawaii.

[PATIENCE ANNE EMPSON], Papers of brigadier C. F. C. Macaskie, MSS Pac. s 71. Oxford university colonial records project [Oxford 1968]. ff.[ii].3. [8.]*

BIBLIOGRAPHY of symposium papers. Tenth Pacific science congress: Honolulu, Hawaii, 1961. Pacific science association: Honolulu 1966. pp.95. [750.]*

CATALOGUE of manuscripts of Australia and the Pacific in the Mitchell library, Sydney. Sydney 1967–1969. pp.[vii].283+[vii].500. [1971.]

UNION catalogue of New Zealand and Pacific manuscripts in New Zealand libraries: Interim edition. Alexander Turnbull library: Wellington 1968–1969. ff.[iii]. pp.113+ii.185.ix. [3500.]*

COMMONWEALTH in the Pacific. National book league and the Commonwealth institute: [London] 1969. pp.47. [256.]

WILLEM C. H. ROBERT, Contributions to a bibliography of Australia and the South Sea islands. Second edition, revised and enlarged. Amsterdam 1969. pp.x.275+xi.227+x.401+xiii. 382. [4507.]*

PHYLLIS MANDER-JONES, *ed.*, Manuscripts in the British isles relating to Australia, New Zealand and the Pacific. Canberra 1972. pp.xxiii.697. [large number.]

DICTIONARY catalog of printed books. The Mitchell library, the public library of New South Wales. Boston 1968. 38 vols.

PACIFIC islands and trust territories. United States Department of the army: Washington 1971.

ROLF DU RIETZ, Bibliotheca polynesiana: a catalogue of some of the books in the polynesian collection formed by the late Bjarne Kroepelien and now in the Oslo university library. Oslo 1969. pp.lxix.455. [1368.]

HANS-JÜRGEN CWIK, Deutschsprächige publikationen des jahres 1969 über Asien und Ozeanien. Publications of 1969 on Asia and Oceania in german language. Documentatio Asiae (no.1): Institut für asienkunde: Dokumentationsleitstelle: Hamburg 1971. pp.[iii].ii.70. [571.]*

iii. *Explorers*

CELSUS KELLY, Calendar of documents, Spanish voyages in the south Pacific from Alvaro de Mendaña to Alejandro Malaspina 1567–1794 and the franciscan missionary plans for the peoples of the austral lands 1617–1634. Compiled from manuscripts and other documents in the archives and libraries of Spain, America, Rome, Paris, London, Sydney &c. Franciscan historical studies (Australia) in association with Archivo ibero-americano (Madrid): Madrid 1965. pp. xxviii.470. [1037.]

Cook, James

JAMES JACKSON, James Cook. . . . Cartographie et bibliographie. [1879.] pp.60. [525.]

BIBLIOGRAPHY of captain James Cook. Public library: Sydney 1928. pp.172. [2500.]
— — [another issue]. 1928. [1929]. pp.4.xi.7–172.
the 'opening address' added, and interleaved.

[SIR] MAURICE HOLMES, An introduction to the bibliography of captain James Cook. 1936. pp.61. [108.]
200 copies printed.
— [another edition]. Captain James Cook, . . . A bibliographical excursion. 1952. pp.103. [157.]
500 copies printed.

S[YDNEY] A[LFRED] SPENCE, Captain James Cook. . . . A bibliography of his voyages. . . life, conduct & nautical achievements. Mitcham 1960. pp.51. [400.]
300 copies printed.

ROLF DU RIETZ, Captain James Cook. A bibliography of literature printed in Sweden before 1819. Upsala 1960. pp.[ii].28. [19.]
300 copies privately printed.

M. K. BEDDIE, *ed.*, Bibliography of captain James Cook, R.N., F.R.S., circumnavigator. 2nd edition. Library of New South Wales: Sydney 1970. pp.xvi.894. [4808.]

Lapérouse, Jean François de Galaup, comte de

EDWARD WEBER ALLEN, Jean François Galaup de Lapérouse. A check list. [San Francisco] 1941. pp.[iv].18. [175.]

iv. *Cartography*

LIST of charts for the Pacific station, furnished from the Hydrographic office. Bureau of navigation: Washington 1872. pp.65. [1000.]
— [another edition]. Catalog of charts and plans issued to vessels of the United States navy on the Pacific station. Hydrographic office: 1934. looseleaf. [variable.]

[J. L. POWER], Catalogue of maps in the Intelligence division, War office. . . . Vol.IV. America, West Indies, and Oceania. 1891. pp.[ii].iii.301. [Oceania: 500.]

CLIFFORD H[ERBERT] MAC FADDEN, A bibliography of Pacific area maps. Institute of Pacific relations. Shanghai 1940. pp.xxiii.107. [290.]

reissued San Francisco 1941 as no.6 of the Studies of the Institute's American council.

ASIA, Australia, and the Pacific map catalog. Army map service: Washington [1954]. *consists largely of key-maps.*

LAWRENCE C. WROTH, The early cartography of the Pacific. Papers of the Bibliographical society of America (vol.38, no.ii): New York 1944. pp. 87–268, pls.xxii. [104.]

v. *Periodicals*

EXPERIMENTAL bibliographical service covering representative periodicals in the chinese, japanese, russian and dutch languages, with special reference to problems of the Pacific area. Institute of Pacific relations: I.P.R. bibliographies [no.1]: New York 1937. pp.[iv].39. [98.]

INDEX to periodicals, July 1949–December 1951. Public library of New South Wales: Sydney 1955. pp.[iii].xii.360. [4000.]*

H. ROTH, South Pacific government serials; a select list. University of Auckland library: Bibliographical bulletin (4): Auckland 1967. pp.21. [150.]*

FRITZ FEUEREISEN and ERNST SCHMACKE, Die presse in Asien und Ozeanien; ein handbuch für wirtschaft und werbung. München-Pullach 1968. pp.303. [Oceania: 43.]

ASIEN und Ozeanien behandelnde zeitschriften und ihre bestände in bibliotheken der bundesrepublik Deutschland (ZGV Asien) zusammengestellt und als manuskript gedruckt vom Institut für asienkunde. —Dokumentations-leitstelle-. Hamburg 1970. pp.iv.181. [Oceania: 31.]

JEAN GUIART [*and others*], Oceania I à XXXIV (1930–1964). Centre documentaire pour l'Océanie: serie, Bibliographies analytiques (i): Paris 1966. ff.ii. [124]. [4]. 14.23. [888.]*

vi. *Academic writings*

RÉPERTOIRE des thèses de sciences sociales sur le Pacifique sud. Commission du Pacifique sud: Document technique (no.102): Nouméa 1957. pp.x.85. [100.]

DIANE DICKSON and CAROL DOSSOR, World catalogue of theses on the Pacific islands. Pacific monographs: Canberra 1970. pp.xii.123. [1250.]

vii. *Other subjects*

Anthropology

C[LYDE] R[OMER] H[UGHES] TAYLOR, A Pacific bibliography. Printed matter relating to the native peoples of Polynesia, Melanesia and Micronesia.

Polynesian society: Memoirs (vol.xxiv): Wellington, N.Z. 1951. pp.xxix.492. [11,000.]

RECHERCHES en sciences sociales dans les îles du Pacifique. Commission du Pacifique sud: Document technique (no.20 &c.): Nouméa.

1951. ... (no.20).
1953. ... (no.52). pp.vi.34. [60.]
1956. ... (no.98). pp.[v].60. [120.]
1959. ... (no.127). pp.[v].70. [150.]
1961. ... (no.135). pp.[v].47. [100.]

IDA LEESON, Bibliographie des "cargo cults" et autres mouvements autochtones du Pacifique sud. Commission du Pacifique sud: Document technique (no.30): [Sydney] 1952. pp.[iii].16. [150.]*

IRWIN HOWARD, W. EDGAR VINACKE and THOMAS MARETZKI, Culture & personality in the Pacific Islands. A bibliography. Anthropological society of Hawaii: Honolulu 1963. pp.[ii].iv.110. [1000.]*

Archaeology

COWA survey (COWA bibliography). Current publications in old world archaeology. Area 21 — Pacific islands (New Guinea, Melanesia, Micronesia and Polynesia). Cambridge, Mass.*

1. 1958. pp.7.6. [55.]
    [*continued as:*]
COWA surveys and bibliographies.
2. 1960. pp.7.5. [68.]
3. 1965. pp.12.8. [137.]
4. 1970. pp.3.15. [282.]

Bible

D. G. DANCE, Oceanic scriptures: a revision of the oceanic sections of the Darlow and Moule historical catalogue of printed bibles, with additions to 1962. London [1964?] no pagination. [712.]*

Botany

ELMER D[REW] MERRILL, A botanical bibliography of the islands of the Pacific. United States national herbarium: Contributions (vol.xxx, part 1): Washington 1947. pp.v.404. [3850.]

Co-operation

A BIBLIOGRAPHY of co-operation in the South Pacific. Revised edition. South Pacific commission: Technical paper (no.51): Noumea 1953. pp.v.12. [103.]*

CATALOGUE of the SPC library on co-operation. Revised edition of Technical paper no.121. Technical paper (no.138): South Pacific commission: Noumea 1963. pp.iv.306. [3500.]* *originally published in 1955; revised edition 1959.*

Education

CAMILLA H[ILDEGARDE] WEDGWOOD, L'éducation dans les îles du Pacifique. Une bibliographie sélective. Commission du Pacifique sud: Document technique (no.99): Nouméa 1956. pp.viii.80. [772.]*

Geology

CATALOGUE of translations of japanese geological literature of the Pacific islands. United States army forces, far east: Geological surveys branch: [s.l.] 1954. pp.[v].34. [350.]*
— [another edition]. Catalogue of translations of japanese geologic, soils and allied literature [&c.]. [Compiled by Roy C. Kepferle]. 1959. ff.iii.96. [1000.]*

ANNOTATED bibliography of geologic and soils literature of western north Pacific islands. United States army forces far east: Office of the engineer: [s.l.] 1956. pp.[iii].884. [7500.]*

Housing

A SELECTIVE and annotated bibliography of tropical housing. South Pacific commission: Technical paper (no.76): Noumea 1955. ff.v.38. [250.]*

Land tenure

AN ANNOTATED bibliography on land tenure in the british and british protected territories in South east Asia and the Pacific. Colonial office: [London] 1952. pp.164. [2100.]*

Law

A BIBLIOGRAPHY of the laws of Australia, New Zealand, Fiji and the western Pacific from the earliest times. Sweet & Maxwell's legal bibliography (vol.vi): 1938. pp.vii.144. [1500.]

Marists

PATRICK O'REILLY, Essai de bibliographie des missions maristes en Océanie occidentale. 1932. pp.32.

Medicine

M[ANDAYAM] O[SURI] T[IRUNARAYANA] IYENGAR, ed. Bibliographie analytique de la filariose et de l'éléphantiasis. Commission du Pacifique sud: Document technique (no.65 &c.): Nouméa.*
   i. Épidémiologie de la filariose dans la région du Pacifique sud.... (no.65): 1955. pp.vii. 66. [115.]
   ii. Études sur les moustiques de la région du Pacifique sud, par M. O. T. Iyengar.... (no.88): 1956. pp.xi.128. [426.]
   iii. Symptomatologie, etiologie, anatomie pathologique et diagnostic des filarioses à Wuchereria Bancrofti et W. Nalayi....

(no.109): 1958. pp.xv.283. [899.]
   iv. Traitement.... (no.124): 1959. pp.xii. 175. [490.]
   v. Filarioses à W. Bancrofti et à W. Malayi. Lutte et prophylaxie.... (no.129): 1960. pp.viii.102. [195.]

REVUES médicales que reçoit la Commission du Pacifique sud. Commission du Pacifique sud: Circulaire d'information technique: Santé (no.41): Nouméa 1960. pp.4. [99.]*

W. NORMAN-TAYLOR, Annotated bibliography on medical research in the south Pacific. South Pacific commission: Technical paper (no.142): Noumea 1963. pp.viii.371. [1150.]*

Missions

ILDEFONSE ALAZARD, Essai de bibliographie picpucienne: missions de l'Océanie orientale. Annales des sacrés-coeurs: Braine-le-Comte 1912. pp.23. [211.]
— — Supplément. 1931. pp.20.

PATRICK O'REILLY, Essai de bibliographie des missions maristes en Océanie occidentale. 1932. pp.32.

Nutrition

ROBERT JOSEPH FANNING, Pacific islands nutrition bibliography. Pacific area bibliographies: Honolulu 1951. pp.ix.70. [225.]

Planning

DIANA CHANG, Asia and Pacific planning bibliography. University of Hawaii libraries and Pacific urban studies and planning program: Honolulu.*
   i. 1971. pp.29. [500.]
   ii. 1971. pp.29. [500.]
   iii.
   iv.
   v. 1974. pp.226. [2500.]

Population

INTERNATIONAL population census bibliography: Oceania. Census bibliography (no.3): Population research center: Department of sociology: University of Texas: Austin 1966. pp.viii.[99]. [400.]*
— Supplement 1968. Census bibliography (no. 7). [Oceania: 50.]

Salmon

G. H. MAXFIELD, Pacific salmon literature compilation, 1900-1959 instructions and index. Bureau of commercial fisheries biological laboratory: Seattle 1967. pp.20.

Science

E[DGAR] AUBERT DE LA RUE, Les sciences naturelles dans les îles australes françaises, de leur découverte à 1945. Bibliographie. 1966. pp.28.

Social sciences

RÉPERTOIRE des thèses de sciences sociales sur le Pacifique sud. Commission du Pacifique sud: Document technique (no.102): Noumea 1957. pp.x.85. [100.]

Trochus

R[ENÉ] GAIL and L. DEVAMBEZ, Bibliographie analytique du Troca (Trochus niloricus, Linn.). Commission du Pacifique sud: Nouméa 1958. pp.[i].iii.29. [50.]

World war II

SECOND world war. Pacific theatre: military operations. Imperial war museum: Library: [1953]. pp.11. [150.]

MILITARY operations — Pacific theatre. (English language only). Imperial museum: Library: [1958]. pp.17. [200.]*

viii. Miscellaneous

LIST of references on the Panama-Pacific exposition. Library of Congress: Washington 1914. ff.6. [66.]*
— Additional references. 1915. ff.2. [17.]*

LIST of references on the Pacific mail steamship company. Library of Congress: [Washington] 1916. ff.3. [26.]*

WERNER B. ELLINGER and HERBERT ROSINSKI, Sea power in the Pacific, 1936–1941. A selected bibliography of books, periodical articles, and maps from the end of the London naval conference to the beginning of the war in the Pacific. Princeton 1942. pp.iii–xiv.80. [600.]

ix. Pacific/Oceanic languages

LIST of grammars, dictionaries, etc. of the languages of Asia, Oceania, Africa in the New York public library. New York 1909. pp.201. [6000.]

A CHECK LIST of the books printed in the Hawaiian and other Pacific island dialects in the library of sir R. L. Harmsworth. [1938]. pp.31. [150.]

H[ANS] R[UDOLF] KLIENEBERGER, Bibliography of oceanic linguistics. London oriental bibliographies (vol.i): 1957. pp.xiii.144. [2166.]

x. Pacific territories and languages

Aneityum

JOHN A. FERGUSON, A bibliography of the New Hebrides and a history of the mission press. Part I.

Aneityum, Futuna, and Erromanga. Sydney 1917. pp.36. [200.]
20 copies privately printed.

Aniwa

JOHN A. FERGUSON, A bibliography of the New Hebrides and a history of the mission press. Part II. Tauna, Aniwa, Efate. Sydney 1918. pp.52. [300.]
20 copies privately printed.

Australian territories

ANNOTATED bibliography of select government publications on australian territories 1951–1964. Canberra 1965. pp.55. [460.]

Australian aborigines

R. ETHERIDGE, Contributions to a catalogue of works, reports, and papers on the anthropological, ethnological and geological history of the australian and tasmanian aborigines. Part I. Department of mines: Geological survey of New South Wales: Memoirs (Palæontology, no.8): Sydney 1890–1895. pp.vii.31+vii.49+vii.40. [1500.]
incomplete; no more published.

GEORGE F[RASER] BLACK, List of works relating to the aborigines of Australia and Tasmania. Public library: New York 1913. pp.56. [1400.]

ARNOLD R. PILLING, Aborigine culture history. A survey of publications 1954–1957. Wayne state university: Studies (no.11): Detroit 1962. pp.ix. 219. [600.]

JOHN GREENWAY, Bibliography of the australian aborigines and the native peoples of Torres strait to 1959. Sydney &c. 1963. pp.xv.420. [10,283.]

BERYL F. CRAIG, Arnhemland peninsular region (including Bathurst and Melville islands). Australian institute of aboriginal studies: Canberra 1966. pp.viii.205. [1044.]*

BERYL F. CRAIG, Cape York. Australian institute of aboriginal studies: Canberra 1967. pp.viii.233. [960.]*

BERYL F. CRAIG, Kimberley region: an annotated bibliography. Australian aboriginal studies (no. 13): Bibliography series (no.3): Canberra 1968. pp.x.209. [887.]*

BERYL F. CRAIG, Central australian and Western desert regions; an annotated bibliography. Australian aboriginal studies (no.31): Bibliography series (no.5): Canberra 1969. pp.xi.351. [2205.]

BERYL F. CRAIG, North-west-central Queensland; an annotated bibliography. Australian aboriginal studies (no.41): Bibliography series (no.6): Canberra 1970. pp.xiii.137. [774.]

ALDO MASSOLA, Bibliography of the Victorian aborigines. From the earliest manuscripts to 31 December 1970. Melbourne 1971. pp.[vi].95. [2000.]

N. J. B. PLOMLEY, An annotated bibliography of the tasmanian aborigines. Royal anthropological institute: Occasional paper (no.28): 1969. pp.xix. 143. [850.]*

LESLIE R. MARCHANT, A list of french naval records and illustrations relating to australian and tasmanian aborigines, 1771 to 1828. Australian aboriginal studies (no.21): Bibliography series (no. 4): Canberra 1969. pp.[vi].83. [500.]*

Australian languages

W[ILLIA]M HEINRICH IMMANUEL BLEEK, The library of his excellency sir George Grey, K.C.B. Philology. Vol. II.—Part I. Australia. 1858. pp.[iv].44. [87.]

AUSTRALIAN aboriginal languages. National library of Australia, Canberra: Select bibliographies: Australian series (no.7): Canberra 1962. ff.9. [96.]*
— Supplement 1966. ff.3. [23.]*

Banks islands

N. L. H. KRAUSS, Bibliography of the Banks islands, western Pacific. Honolulu 1971. pp.10. [152.]*

Cook islands

DONALD STANLEY MARSHALL, A working bibliography of the Cook islands. Department of anthropology: Auckland university college: Auckland 1951. ff.16. [314.]*

H. BOND JAMES, A bibliography of publications in Cook islands Maori. South pacific commission: Sydney 1953. pp.iii.28. [134.]*

Easter island

LIST of references on Easter island. Library of Congress: Washington 1914. ff.5. [55.]*

Efate

JOHN A. FERGUSON, A bibliography of the New Hebrides and a history of the mission press. Part II. Tanna, Aniwa, Efate. Sydney 1918. pp.52. [300.]
20 copies privately printed.

Ellice islands

E. F. KUNZ, An annotated bibliography of the languages of the Gilbert islands, Ellice Islands, and Nauru. Public library of New South Wales: Sydney 1959. pp.ix.202. [Ellice Islands: 19.]*

N. L. H. KRAUSS, Bibliography of the Ellice islands, western Pacific. Honolulu 1969. pp.13. [204.]*
reprinted 1971.

Erromanga

JOHN A. FERGUSON, A bibliography of the New Hebrides and a history of the mission press. Part I. Aneityum, Futuna, and Erromanga. Sydney 1917. pp.36. [200.]
20 copies privately printed.

Fiji

LIST of references on the Fiji islands. Library of Congress: Washington 1923. ff.11. [160.]*

A BIBLIOGRAPHY of the laws of Australia, New Zealand, Fiji and the western Pacific from the earliest times. With lists of reports of cases, digests and collections of statutes and rules. Sweet & Maxwell: legal bibliography (vol.vi): 1938. pp. vii.144. [1500.]

PATRICK O'REILLY, Imprints of the Fiji catholic mission, including the Loreto press 1864–1954. 1958. pp.3–61. [121.)
160 copies printed.

PRELIMINARY inventory. Central archives of Fiji and the Western Pacific high commission.
   1. Records of the Cakobau government, the ad-interim government and the provisional government. June 1871–September 1875. By S. Tuinaceva. ff.[.] [.]
   2. Records of the Land titles commission, Rotuma. 1882–1883. ff.[9]. [16.]*

CATALOGUE of microfilm of library material. Central archives of Fiji and the Western Pacific high commission: Suva 1966. ff.[ii].8.ii. [27.]*
— Catalogue of microfilm. Library series. Revised and enlarged. 1967 &c. f.p,
   in progress.

CATALOGUE of microfilm of archives material. Central archives of Fiji and the Western Pacific high commission: Suva 1966. ff.[ii].6. [6.]*

S. BAKSH, Serial publications of the government of Fiji. Suva 1967. ff.14.*
— Revised and enlarged by L. S. Qalo. Serial publications catalogue (no.2): Suva 1970. ff.16. [122.]*

CATALOGUE of microfilm. Archives series, revised and enlarged. Central archives of Fiji and the West Pacific high commission: Suva 1968. ff.9.ii. [18.]*

PHILIP A. SNOW, A bibliography of Fiji, Tonga, and Rotuma. Preliminary working edition. Canberra 1969. pp.xliii.418. [10,129.]*

R. F. DUBERAL and P. RODDA, Bibliography of the geology of Fiji, including published and unpublished references, up to november 1968. Department of geological surveys: [Suva 1969]. pp.[iv.].81. [503.]★

Fijian language

SIR G[EORGE] GREY and W[ILLIAM] H[EINRICH] I[MMANUEL] BLEEK, The library of his excellency sir George Grey, K.C.B. Philology. Vol.II. — Part III. Fiji Islands and Rotuma. 1859. pp.13–33. [Fiji language: 42.]

Futuna

JOHN A. FERGUSON, A bibliography of the New Hebrides and a history of the mission press. Part I. Aneityum, Futuna, and Erromanga. Sydney 1917. pp.36. [200.]
20 copies privately printed.

Gilbertese language

E. F. KUNZ, An annotated bibliography of the languages of the Gilbert islands, Ellice islands, and Nauru. Public library of New South Wales: Sydney 1959. pp.ix.202. [gilbertese: 324.]★

Guam

A[PPLETON] P[RENTISS] C[LARK] GRIFFIN, A list of books (with references to periodicals) on Samoa and Guam. Library of Congress: Washington 1901. pp.54. [Guam: 75.]

CHARLES F. REID, *ed.*, Bibliography of the island of Guam. New York 1939. pp.102. [2000.]

Hawaii

WILLIAM MARTIN, Catalogue d'ouvrages relatifs aux Îles Hawaii. 1967. pp.[iii].vii.92. [650.]

JAMES F[ROTHINGHAM] HUNNEWELL, Bibliography of the Hawaiian islands. Boston 1869. pp.[ii].17.ff.19–75. [1000.]
100 copies privately printed.
reprinted New York 1962.

[C. M. HYDE], Catalogue of the bound books in the library of the Hawaiian historical society. Honolulu 1897. pp.29. [500.]

A[PPLETON] P[RENTISS] C[LARK] GRIFFIN, List of books relating to Hawaii (including references to collected works and periodicals): Library of Congress: Washington 1898. pp.26. [245.]

BRIEF list of references on the Japanese in Hawaii. Library of Congress: Washington 1914. ff.4. [38.]★

[BERNICE JUDD], Voyages to Hawaii before 1860. A study based on historical narratives in the library of the Hawaiian mission children's society. Honolulu 1929. pp.109. [193.]

CURRENT Hawaiana. (Quarterly [A quarterly bibliography]). Honolulu.★
i. 1944–1945. ff.[25]. [300.]
ii. 1945–1946.
iii. 1946–1947. ff.12.8.8.7. [700.]
iv. 1947–1948. ff.14.8.11. [750.]
v. 1948–1949. ff.14.13.9.9. [1000.]
vi. 1949–1950. ff. . .8.9. [1000.]
vii. 1950–1951. ff.11.9.10.9. [1200.]
viii. 1951–1952. ff.11.9.9.10. [1200.]
ix. 1952–1953. ff.9.9.7. [1000.]
x. 1953–1954. ff.11.9.8.10. [1200.]
xi. 1954–1955. ff.10.9.9.11. [1200.]
xii. 1955–1956. ff.9.8.8.9. [1200.]
xiii. 1956–1957. ff. .9.8.9. [1200.]
xiv. 1957–1958. ff.10.9.9. . [1200.]
xv. 1958–1959. ff.10.8.8.8. [1200.]
xvi. 1959–1960. ff.12.8.11.16. [1300.]
xvii. 1960–1961. ff.16.14.18.18. [1400.]
xviii. 1961–1962. ff.20.17.18.20. [1500.]
xix. 1962. ff.15.15.20. [1000.]
xx. 1963. pp.20.15.15.17. [1400.]
xxi. 1964–1965. Janet E. Bell, editor. pp.83. [1600.]
xxii. 1965–1966. pp.47.[21]. [1400.]
xxiii. 1966–1967. pp.65. [1300.]
xxiv. 1967–1968. pp.93. [1800.]
xxv. 1968–1969. pp.89. [1800.]
xxvi. 1969–1970. pp.87. [1750.]
xxvii. 1970–1971. Yasuto Kaihara, editor. pp.97. [1900.]
xxviii. 1971–1972.
xxix. 1972–1973. pp.101. [2000.]
in progress.

MARGARET TITCOMB and ANITA AMES, Index to Hawaiian annual, 1875–1932. Bernice P. Bishop museum: Special publication (24): 1934.

AMOS P[ATTEN] LEIB, Hawaiian legends in English. An annotated bibliography. Honolulu 1949. pp.[v].118. [1000.]

OFFICIAL publications of the territory of Hawaii 1909–1959. Public archives: Honolulu 1962. pp.250.

MILDRED TERAUCHI and DANIEL W. TUTTLE, Hawaian politics 1945–1961. A selected bibliography. University of Hawaii: Department of government: Honolulu 1962. ff.ii.7. [50.]★

DICTIONARY CATALOG of the hawaiian collection. University of Hawaii library: Boston 1963. pp.iv.822+822+826+808. [78,805 cards.]★

MITSUGU MATSUDA, The japanese in Hawaii, 1868–1967: a bibliography of the first hundred years. Hawaii series (no.1): Social science research institute: University of Hawaii: Honolulu 1968. pp.xiv.222. [883.]★

P. QUENTIN TOMICH, Mammals in Hawaii: a synopsis and notational bibliography. Bernice P. Bishop special publication (57): Honolulu 1969. pp.v.238. [700.]

GEORGE PARARAS-CARAYANNIS, Catalog of tsunamis in the Hawaiian islands. World data center A, tsunami: U.S. Department of commerce: Washington 1969. pp.94. [1200.]*

Hawaii, university of

BIBLIOGRAPHICAL list of the publications by members of the faculty [List of publications: Publications distributed by the university of Hawaii publications division; Bibliography issue, university publications; Bibliography]. Honolulu.
1925–1927. pp.11. [100.]
1928.
1929. pp.[4]. [20.]
1930.
1931.
1932.
1933.
1934.
1935. ff.2. [50.]*
1936. ff.[2]. [70.]*
1937.
1938.
1939–1943. pp.54. [1000.]
1943–1944. pp.15. [125.]
1944–1952. Edited by Charles S. Bouslog. pp.174. [2500.]
1952–1954. pp.64. [750.]
1954–1956. pp.64. [750.]
1956–1959. pp.52. [900.]
in progress.

Hawaiian language

A CHECK LIST of the books printed in the Hawaiian and other Pacific island dialects in the library of sir R. L[eicester] Harmsworth. [1938]. pp.31. [150.]
privately printed.

HAWAIIAN language. [Newberry library:] Edward E. Ayer collection: [Chicago 1941]. pp. [33]. [301.]*

Hawaiian subjects
English

STANLEY M. TSUZAKI and JOHN E. REINECKE, English in Hawaii; an annotated bibliography. Oceanic linguistics: Special publication (no.1): [Honolulu] 1966. pp.ix.63. [300.]*

Entomology

J[AMES] F[RANKLIN] ILLINGWORTH, Early references to hawaiian entomology. Bernice P. Bishop museum: Bulletin (no.2): Honolulu 1923. pp.63. [225.]

Geology

NORAH D[OWELL] STEARNS, Annotated bibliography and index of geology and water supply of the island of Oahu, Hawaii. Division of hydrography: Bulletin (no.3): Hawaii 1935. pp.[iv].74. [436.]

GORDON ANDREW MACDONALD, Bibliography of the geology and water resources of the island of Hawaii. Division of hydrography: Bulletin (no. 10): Honolulu 1947. pp.191. [1000.]

Printing

JOURNAL of a canoe voyage . . . by hon. Gorham D. Gilman, and the history of the hawaiian mission press, with a bibliography of the earlier publications, by Howard M. Ballou and George R. Carter. Hawaiian society: Papers (no.14): Honolulu 1908. pp.44. [76.]

Water

NORAH D. STEARNS, Annotated bibliography and index of geology and water supply of the island of Oahu, Hawaii. Division of hydrography: Bulletin (no.3): Hawaii 1935. pp.[iv].74. [426.]

GORDON ANDREW MACDONALD, Bibliography of the geology and water resources of the island of Hawaii. Division of hydrography: Bulletin (no.10): Honolulu 1947. pp.191. [1000.]

Johnston island

N. L. H. KRAUSS, Johnston island (central Pacific ocean) bibliography. Honolulu 1969. pp.8. [69.]*

Line islands

N. L. H. KRAUSS, Bibliography of the Line islands, central Pacific. Honolulu 1970. pp.18. [317.]*

Maoris

[A. HAMILTON], Hand-list of certain books and papers containing information relating more or less directly to the Maori of New Zealand. Dominion museum: Wellington 1911. pp.30. [1000.]

A[LEXANDER] W[YCLIF] REED, The Maori and his first printed books. Reed's Raupo series (no.4): Wellington [1935.] pp.3–22. [15.]

Maori language and literature

SIR G[EORGE] GREY and W[ILLIAM] H[EINRICH] I[MMANUEL] BLEEK, The library of his excellency sir George Grey, K.C.B. Philology. Vol.II. — Part IV. New Zealand, the Chatham Islands and Auckland Islands. 1858. pp.[iii].76. [524.]

HERBERT W[ILLIAM] WILLIAMS, A bibliography of printed Maori to 1900. Dominion museum: Monograph (no.7): Wellington, N.Z. 1924. pp. xvi.198. [1100.]

—— Supplement. 1928. pp.24. [100.]

—— A supplement to the Williams bibliography of printed Maori. [By] A. D. Somerville. Wellington [N.Z.] [1947]. ff.[47]. [400.]*

A[LEXANDER] W[YCLIF] REED, The Maori and first printed books. Reed's Raupo series (no.4): Dunedin &c. [1935]. pp.3–22. [25.]

H. BOND JAMES, A bibliography of publications in Cook islands Maori. South pacific commission: Sydney 1953. pp.iii.28. [134.]*

R. N. ERWIN, Sir Apirana Ngata; a preliminary bibliography of his printed work. Library school: National library service: Wellington 1964. pp.62. [349.]*

C[LYDE] R[OMER] H[UGHES] TAYLOR, A bibliography of publications on the New Zealand Maori and the Moriori of the Chatham islands. Oxford 1972. pp.xii.161. [4350.]

Revision and "updating" of the section "New Zealand and Maori" in the compiler's Pacific bibliography.

Marquesas

LIST of references relating to Tahiti and Marquesa Islands. Library of Congress: Washington 1906. ff.7. [42.]*

LIST of references on the Marquesas Islands. Library of Congress: Washington 1914. ff.7. [72.]*

Melanesia

N. L. H. KRAUSS, Bibliography of Kilmailau atoll (Carteret islands), Melanesia. Pacific islands studies and notes (no.11): Honolulu 1973. pp.4. [44.]*

N. L. H. KRAUSS, Bibliography of Mortlock atoll (Tauu), Melanesia. Pacific islands studies and notes (no.10): Honolulu 1973. pp.6. [69.]*

N. L. H. KRAUSS, Bibliography of Nissan atoll (Green island), Melanesia. Pacific islands studies and notes (no.13): Honolulu 1973. pp.8. [106.]*

N. L. H. KRAUSS, Bibliography of Nuguria atoll (Fead islands), Melanesia. Pacific islands studies and notes (no.12): Honolulu 1973. pp.4. [57.]*

N. L. H. KRAUSS, Bibliography of Tasman atoll (Nukumanu), Melanesia. Pacific islands studies and notes (no.9): Honolulu 1973. pp.4. [51.]*

Micronesia

E[DWIN] H[ORACE] BRYAN, Bibliography of micronesian entomology. National research council: Pacific science board: [s.l.] 1943. ff.43. [500.]*

HUZIO UTINOMI, Bibliography of Micronesia (Bibliographia micronesica: scientiae naturalis et cultus). Translated by Mitsuno Fukuda [and others]. Edited and revised by O. A. Bushnell [and others]. Pacific area bibliographies: Honolulu 1943. pp.xiv.157. [5000.]

HUZIO UTINOMI [FUJIO UCHINOMI], Bibliographia micronesica scientiae naturalis et cultus. Tokyo 1944. pp.[ii].3.211. [3500.]

—— [another edition]. Bibliography of Micronesia (bibliographia micronesica: scientiae naturalis et cultus). Edited ... by O. A. Bushnell. Pacific area bibliographies: Honolulu [1952]. pp.xiv.157. [3000.]

MARIE HÉLÈNE SACHET and F[RANCIS] RAYMOND FOSBERG, Island bibliographies, Micronesian botany, land environment and ecology of coral atolls, vegetation of the tropical Pacific islands. Compiled under the auspices of the Pacific science board. National academy of sciences: National research council: Publication (no.335): Washington 1955. pp.[iii].v.577. [7500.]*

—— Supplement 1971. pp.ix.427. [6500.]*

CIMA bibliography. Pacific scientific information center: Bernice P. Bishop museum: Honolulu 1963. pp.[12]. [120.]

SIM bibliography. Pacific scientific information center: Bernice P. Bishop museum: Honolulu 1964. ff.[14]. [150.]*

TRIPP bibliography. Pacific scientific information center: Bernice P. Bishop museum: Honolulu 1966. pp.11. [150.]*

Nauru

E. F. KUNZ, An annotated bibliography of the languages of the Gilbert islands, Ellice islands, and Nauru. Public library of New South Wales: Sydney 1959. pp.ix.202. [Nauru: 52.]*

N. L. H. KRAUSS, Bibliography of Nauru, western Pacific. Honolulu 1970. pp.14. [179.]*

New Caledonia

LÉON VALLÉE, Essai d'une bibliographie de la Nouvelle-Calédonie et dépendances. 1883. pp. [iii].68. [400.]

PATRICK O'REILLY, Petit essai bibliographique des ouvrages exécutés à Nouméa et à Saint-Louis et sortis des presses de l'imprimerie catholique de la mission de Nouvelle-Calédonie, 1885–1939. Nouméa 1951. pp.[iii].viii.48. [137.]

200 copies printed.

PATRICK O'REILLY, Calédoniens. Répertoire bio-bibliographique de la Nouvelle-Calédonie. Société des Océanistes: Publications (no.3): 1953. pp.x.307. [1500.]

PATRICK O'REILLY, Bibliographie méthodique, analytique et critique de la Nouvelle-Calédonie. Société des Océanistes: Publications (no.4): 1955. pp.x.364. [4182.]

New Guinea

E[DWARD] C[ALDWELL] RYE. A bibliography of New Guinea. 1884. pp.50.

BORNEO and New Guinea. Far eastern book and journal lists (no.14): Public library: Newark. N.J. [1921]. single leaf. [New Guinea: 10.]

K[LAAS] W[ILHELM] GALIS. Bibliographie van Nederlands Nieuw-Guinea. [Voorburg-Vierhouten 1951]. pp.61. [1000.]*
— — Derde . . . uitgave. Den Haag 1962. pp. [iv].275. [5000.]*

SELECTED list of references to publications in the Science library on the fauna and flora of New Guinea and the Melanesian Islands. Science library: Bibliographical series (no.705): 1951. ff.2. [23.]*

OVERZICHT van de literatuur betreffende Nieuw-Guinea aanwezig in de bibliotheek van het Ministerie voor uniezaken en overzeese rijksdelen. 's-Gravenhage.*
i. Bocken en periodieken. 1952. pp.[iii].84. [500.]
ii. Kaarten (zowel van nederlands- als van australisch Nieuw-Guinea). 1953. pp.[iii]. 60. [500.]

THE TERRITORY of New Guinea as a trust territory. Commonwealth national library, Canberra: Select bibliographies: Australian series (no. 4): Canberra 1953. ff.15. [110.]*

[EVAN ROBERTSON GILL], New Guinea. Catalogue of books relating to New Guinea (but with special reference to Papua) in the library of Evan R. Gill. Liverpool 1957. ff.[ii].51. [ii].51. [750.]*

THE TERRITORY of Papua and New Guinea; a select book list. Department of territories: Canberra 1959. ff.13. [81.]*

PENELOPE RICHARDSON, Current field research in the territory of Papua and New Guinea: ff.20. [New Guinea research unit. Port Moresby? 1963.] [93.]*

WILLIAM A. MCGRATH, New Guineana or Books of New Guinea 1942–1964: a bibliography of books printed between 1942 and 1964 relating to the territory of Papua and New Guinea. Port Moresby 1965. pp.iv.88. [868.]*

NEW GUINEA bibliography: a subject list of books published in the New Guinea area and books dealing wholly or partially with a New Guinea

subject, published overseas. The library: University of Papua and New Guinea: Boroko, Papua. 1967 &c.
in progress.

COLIN FREEMAN [and others], New Guinea periodical index: guide to current literature about the New Guinea islands. The library: University of Papua and New Guinea: Boroko 1968 &c.
in progress.

COLIN FREEMAN and (vol.ii &c.) NANCY LUTTON, New Guinea periodical index. Guide to current periodical literature about the New Guinea islands. Annual cumulation. The library: University of Papua and New Guinea: Boroko.
[i]. 1968. pp.[xvi]. 104. [1000.]*
ii. 1969. pp.[xv]. 103. [1000.]*

C[OLIN] FREEMAN, Karkar or Dampier island, Madang district, New Guinea. New Guinea bibliography (no.3): Library, University of Papua and New Guinea: Boroko 1968. pp.5. [53.]*

CURRENT New Guinea periodical publications. A preliminary checklist. Library: University of Papua and New Guinea: Boroko 1968. pp.15. [150.]*

AN ETHNOGRAPHIC bibliography of New Guinea. Department of anthropology and sociology: Australian national university: Canberra 1968. pp.ix.318+110+235. [8500.]*

EDWARD P. WOLFERS, A bibliography of bibliographies relevant to a study of Papua and New Guinea. [Port Moresby 1968.] ff.17. [162.]*

S. C. YOCKLUNN, Government publications of Papua and New Guinea. A quarterly list of titles received by the library of the Administrative college of Papua and New Guinea. January–June 1968 &c.
in progress: from no.8 published anonymously.

C[OLIN] FREEMAN, Normanby or Duau island, Papua. New Guinea bibliography: Library, University of Papua and New Guinea: Boroko 1969. pp.4. [45.]*

S. C. YOCKLUNN, The Charles Barrett collection of New Guineana; an author checklist. Second, complete edition. Administrative college of Papua and New Guinea: Port Moresby 1969. ff. vii.64. [598.]

BARBARA MAINSBRIDGE, A bibliography of transport in Papua New Guinea 1971. Compiled for Marion W. Ward. New Guinea research unit: The Australian national university: Port Moresby 1971. ff.46. [611.]*

New Hebrides

JOHN H. FERGUSON, A bibliography of the New Hebrides and a history of the mission press. Sydney 1917–1918. pp.36+52. [500.]
20 copies privately printed.

PATRICK O'REILLY, Hébridais. Répertoire bio-bliographique des Nouvelles-Hébrides. Société des océanistes: Publications (no.6): 1957. pp.x.292. [1000.]

PATRICK O'REILLY, Bibliographie méthodique, analytique et critique des Nouvelles-Hébrides. Société des océanistes: Publications (no.8): 1958. pp.xii.306. [3016.]

Niué

N. L. H. KRAUSS, Bibliography of Niué, south Pacific. Honolulu 1970. pp.16. [206.]*

Ocean island

N. L. H. KRAUSS, Bibliography of Ocean island (Banaba), western Pacific. Honolulu 1969. pp.7. [78.]*
reprinted 1971.

Papua [see also *New Guinea*]

[EVAN ROBERTSON GILL], New Guinea. Catalogue of books relating to New Guinea (but with special reference to Papua) in the library of Evan R. Gill. Liverpool 1957. ff.[ii].51. [750.]*

Papuan languages

SIR GEORGE GREY, Philology. Vol.II. . . . Part II. Papuan languages. Cape Town 1858. pp.12. [21.]
the remaining parts of this work are entitled The library of his excellency sir George Grey, K.C.B. Philology.

Phoenix islands

N. L. H. KRAUSS, Bibliography of the Phoenix islands, central Pacific. Honolulu 1970. pp.13. [230.]*

Pitcairn island

LIST of references on Pitcairn island with special reference to the mutiny of H. M. S. Bounty. Library of Congress: Washington 1922. ff.6. [56.]*

Polynesia

E[LMER] D[REW] MERRILL, Bibliography of poly-nesian botany. Bernice P. Bishop museum: Bulletin (no.13): Honolulu 1924. pp.68. [1292.]

POLYNESIAN botanical bibliography 1773–1935. Bernice P. Bishop museum bulletin (144): Honolulu 1937. pp.194. [2000.]

LIST of books in the Polynesian society library 1 April 1965. Held on behalf of the Polynesian society by the Alexander Turnbull library. Wellington 1965. ff.33. [750.]*

Polynesian languages

THE LIBRARY of his excellency sir George Grey, K.C.B. Philology. Vol.III. — Part IV: (continuation). Polynesia and Borneo. 1859. pp.[iv].77–154. [polynesian languages: 225.]

A[NTOINE] CABATON, Catalogue sommaire des manuscrits indiens, indo-chinois & malayo-poly-nésiens. Bibliothèque nationale: 1912. pp.[vi].320. [malayo-polynesian: 244.]

Rotuma

SIR G[EORGE] GREY and W[ILHELM] H[EINRICH] I[MMANUEL] BLEEK, The library of his excellency sir George Grey, K.C.B. Philology. Vol.II. — Part III. Fiji Islands and Rotuma. 1859. pp.13–33. [50.]

Samoa

A[PPLETON] P[RENTISS] C[LARK] GRIFFIN, A list of books (with references to periodicals) on Samoa and Guam. Library of Congress: Washington 1901. pp.54. [Samoa: 600.]
— — [supplement]. Select list of references on Samoa. 1911. ff.16. [71.]*
— — Additional references. 1931. ff.4. [51.]*

WILLIAM DITTO LEWIS, Calendar of the George Handy Bates samoan papers at the university of Delaware. Wilmington 1942. pp.41. [350.]

N. L. H. KRAUSS, Bibliography of Swains island, american Samoa. Honolulu 1970. pp.7. [87.]*

N. L. H. KRAUSS, Bibliography of Rose atoll, american Samoa. Pacific islands studies and notes (no.5): Honolulu 1972. pp.6. [70.]*

Santa Cruz islands

N. L. H. KRAUSS, Bibliography of the Santa Cruz islands, western Pacific. Honolulu 1969. pp.8. [97.]*

Society islands

DONALD STANLEY MARSHALL, A working bibliography of the Society islands — particularly Tahiti. Department of anthropology: Auckland university college: Auckland 1951. ff.48. [857.]*

Solomon islands

P[ATRICK] O'REILLY and H[UGH] M. LARACY, Bibliographie des ouvrages publiés par les missions maristes des iles Salomon et en particulier par les presses missionaires de Visale, Honiara, Banony

Bay et Tsiroge. Publications de la Société des océanistes (no.29): 1972. pp.68. [205.]

N. L. H. KRAUSS, Bibliography of Choiseul, Solomon islands. Pacific islands studies and notes (no.7): Honolulu 1972. pp.8. [121.]*

N. L. H. KRAUSS, Bibliography of Ontong Java, Solomon islands. Pacific islands studies and notes (3): Honolulu 1971. pp.7. [112.]*

N. L. H. KRAUSS, Bibliography of Rendova, Solomon islands. Pacific islands studies and notes (no.8): Honolulu 1972. pp.5. [66.]*

N. L. H. KRAUSS, Bibliography of Rennell and Bellona, Solomon islands. Pacific islands studies and notes (no.4): Honolulu 1971. pp.11. [168.]*

N. L. H. KRAUSS, Bibliography of San Cristobal, Solomon islands. Pacific islands studies and notes (no.6): Honolulu 1972. pp.8. [120.]*

N. L. H. KRAUSS, Bibliography of Sikaiana atoll, Solomon islands. Pacific islands studies and notes (no.2): Honolulu 1971. pp.5. [68.]*

N. L. H. KRAUSS, Bibliography of Tikopia, Solomon islands. Pacific islands studies and notes (no.1): Honolulu 1971. pp.7. [110.]*

Tahiti

GEORGES L. HARDING and BJARNE KROEPELIEN, The tahitian imprints of the London missionary society, 1810–1834. Oslo 1950. pp.95. [118.]

PATRICK O'REILLY and RAOUL TEISSIER, Tahitiens. Répertoire bio-bibliographique de la Polynésie française. Société des océanistes: Publications (no.10): 1962. pp.xvi.538. [2500.]

PATRICK O'REILLY, ÉDOUARD REITMAN, Bibliographie de Tahiti et de la Polynésie française. Publications de la Société des océanistes (no.14): Paris 1967. pp.xvi.1047. [10,501.]

Tanna

JOHN A. FERGUSON, A bibliography of the New Hebrides and a history of the mission press. Part II. Tanna, Aniwa, Efate. Sydney 1918. pp.52. [300.]
20 copies privately printed.

Tokelau or Union islands

N. L. H. KRAUSS, Bibliography of the Tokelau or Union islands, central Pacific. Honolulu 1969. pp.11. [135.]*
reprinted 1971.

Torres islands

N. L. H. KRAUSS, Bibliography of the Torres islands, southwest Pacific. Honolulu 1971. pp.4. [47.]*

Wake island

N. L. H. KRAUSS, Wake island (western Pacific) bibliography. Honolulu 1969. pp.13. [133.]*
reprinted 1971.

Yap

BRIEF list of references on the island of Yap. Library of Congress: [Washington] 1922. ff.3. [28.]*

EAST ASIA (FAR EAST)

i. *Bibliography*
ii. *General*
iii. *Periodicals*
iv. *Persons*
v. *Foreign relations. History*
vi. *Cartography*
vii. *Subjects*

i. *Bibliography*

KIMPEI GOTO, *ed.*, Bibliography of bibliographies of east asian studies in Japan. Bibliography (no.3): Centre for east asian cultural studies: [Tokyo] 1964. pp.iv.190.xvi. [822.]

TOKIHIKO TANAKA, A survey of bibliographies in western languages concerning east and south-east asian studies. Bibliography (nos. 4, 5): Centre for east asian cultural studies: Tokyo 1966–1969. pp.v.227.+xiii.163. [1809.]

G. RAYMOND NUNN, East Asia; a bibliography of bibliographies. Occasional paper (no.7): East west center library: Honolulu 1967. ff.x.92. [495.]*

A BIBLIOGRAPHY of indexes and abstracts on asian studies in the library of University of British Columbia. Prepared by Asian studies division. Reference publication (no.39): List of catalogued books (Supplement, no.4): University of British Columbia library: Vancouver 1972. pp.ii.ff.47. [250.]

ii. *General*

F. A. SCHIEFNER, Каталог книг и рукописей на китайском, манчжурском, монгольском, тибетском и санскритском языке в библиотеке Азиатского денартемента. Санкт-Петербург 1844.

MAURICE COURANT, Catalogue des livres chinois, coréens, japonais, etc. Bibliothèque nationale: Département des manuscrits: Paris (1900–) 1902–12. pp.vii.499+823+232. [9080.]

APPLETON PRENTIS CLARK GRIFFIN, Select list of books (with references to periodicals) relating to the far east. Library of Congress: Washington 1904. pp.74. [1000.]

BERTHOLD LAUFER, Descriptive account of the collection of chinese, tibetan, mongol, and japanese books in the Newberry library. Newberry library: Chicago 1913. pp.ix.42. [1216.]

LIST of recent books on the far east. Library of Congress: Washington 1916. ff.6. [54.]*
— [another edition]. 1928. ff.10. [116.]*

ORIENTALIA [Chinese, japanese, and other east asiatic books] added ... 1919/20 [–1939/40]. Library of Congress: [1920–]1941.

THE FAR EAST. Public library: Far eastern book and journal lists (no.1): Newark, N.J. [1921]. single leaf. [21.]
— [revised edition] ... (no.27): [1922]. single leaf. [16.]

CATALOGUE of the asiatic library of Dr. G. E. Morrison, now a part of the Oriental library, Tokyo, Japan. Tokyo 1924. pp.[iii].802+551. [20,000.]

[CHARLES ANDRÉ JULIEN], Les civilisations d'extrême-orient. Histoire, littérature, beaux-arts. Bibliographie pratique. [1927]. pp.19. [150.]

ANTONIO R. RODRÍGUEZ MOÑINO, Bibliografía hispano-oriental. Apuntes para un catálogo de los documentos referentes a Indias orientales (China, Japón, Cochinchina, etc.) que se conservan en las colecciones de la Academia de la historia. Madrid 1931. pp.[iii].61. [153.]

K.B.S. bibliographical register of important works written in japanese on Japan and the far east published during the year 1932. Kokusai bunka shinkokai: Tokyo 1937. pp.[ii].vii.166. [1250.]

BULLETIN of far eastern bibliography. American council of learned societies: Committees of far eastern studies: Washington.*
    i. 1936. Edited by Earl H. Pritchard. ff.[225]. [2872.]
    ii. 1937. ff.[ii].261. [3518.]
    iii. 1938. ff.[i].249. [3422.]
    iv. 1939. ff.[i].204. [3033.]
    v. 1940. ff.[i].131.[i].20. [2238.]
continued in The Far eastern quarterly (*Menasha, Wis.*), *and the* Journal of asian studies.

CUMULATIVE bibliography of asian studies 1941–1965. Association of asian studies. Boston.
    Subject bibliography. 1970. pp.xvi.749+iv.725+iv.752+iv.734. [90,000.]
    Author bibliography. 1969. pp.xi.716+724+788+766. [90,000.]
    Bibliography of asian studies. General editor: Richard C. Howard.
now published independently of the J.A.S.
— Cumulative bibliography of asian studies. 1966–1970.
    Author bibliography. 1972. [74,000.]
    Subject bibliography. 1972. [80,000.]
    Bibliography of asian studies 1971. pp.xxii.514. [15,059.]
published annually and cumulated, the details of annual volumes covered in the cumulations are not set out.

[HISASHI AMAAKI], Bibliography of the far eastern tropics, Taihoku college of commerce: Taihoku 1938. pp.[ii].5.230 [*sic*, 246]. [3500.]

ROBERT J. KERNER, Northeastern Asia. A selected bibliography. Contributions to the bibliography of the relations of China, Russia, and Japan, with special reference to Korea, Manchuria, Mongolia, and eastern Siberia, in oriental and european languages. University of California: Northeastern Asia seminar: Publications: Berkeley 1939. pp.xxxix.675+xxxi.621. [13,884.]*

A SELECTED list of books on the far east, 1940–1941. Library of Congress: Washington 1941. ff.3. [25.]*

AIMEE DE POTTER, Postwar reconstruction in the far east. A selective bibliography. Institute of Pacific relations: American council: American council paper (no.9): New York [1942]. ff.[i].16. [100.]*

WHAT do you know about the far east? A bibliography. Canadian institute of international affairs. Toronto 1942. pp.[ii].28. [450.]*

[MARGARET B. DAVIS], Bibliography of the far east prepared for senior high-school libraries. National education association of the United States: Research division: Washington 1942. pp.26 [173.]*

DOROTHY BORG and HUGH BORTON, The far east. A bibliography. American library association: Book list (vol.xxxviii, no.14, part 2): Chicago 1942. pp.[ii].289–294. [100.]

A BIBLIOGRAPHY on the far east. Institute of Pacific relations: San Francisco &c. [1942]. pp.[8]. [60.]

[CHRISTIAN OTTOMAR ARNDT], The far east. An annotated list of available ... curricular material. Office of education: Washington 1943. ff.[i].11. [75.]*
— — [another edition]. An annotated list of available units, courses of study, and other curricular material dealing with the far east. Office of education: Division of comparative education: [Washington] 1944. pp.14. [100.]*

A CLASSIFIED catalogue of books in foreign languages in the Toyo bunko 1917–1956. Tokyo.
i. 1917–1936. I. General reference works. II. Asia, east Asia and the Pacific. 1944. pp.xix. 402.2. [8000.]

FAR EASTERN bibliographies 1947. American institute of Pacific relations: New York [1948]. ff.[19]. [250.]*

FAR EAST digest. Summaries of current periodical material on the far east. Institute of Pacific relations: New York 1948 &c.*
in progress.

POINT FOUR, far east. A selected bibliography of studies on economically underdeveloped

countries. Department of state: Division of library and reference services: Bibliography (no.57): Washington 1951. pp.[ii].46. [450.]*

FRENCH books on the far-east (1651–1951). [Haut commissariat de France en Indochine: Direction des archives et bibliothèques: &c. Singapore 1952]. pp.[ii].19. [59.]
an exhibition catalogue.

GENE Z. HANRAHAN, An annotated bibliography of selected chinese, japanese and english source material available at the Hoover library, Stanford university. 1952.ff.13. [29.]*

EXTERNAL research; a listing of recently (currently) completed studies.
Far east and Asia general. 1954–1955; 1956. ERS 5.5 & 6.5; 5–6.7)
China. 1954–1955; 1956. (ER 2.5, 2.7)
Japan. 1954–1955; 1956; 1957. (ER 4.5, 4.7, 4.9)
Far east. 1958. (ER 2.11)
East Asia. 1959–Fall 1963–Winter 1964 (ER 2. 13–21, odd numbers only)
Asia. A list of current social science research by private scholars and academic centers. 1964–1968. (ER 2.22–27)
no more published.

HERMANN BOHNER, Arbeiten und veröffentlichungen ostasien betreffend. Osaka 1955. pp.52. [52.]

MITSUKO KUNIYOSHI, Far east. Pacific air forces: PACAF basic bibliographies: Komaki 1957. pp. [ii].ii.57. [500.]*

A SELECTED bibliography of books ... about Asia. National commission for the United nations educational, scientific and cultural organization: Washington 1957. pp.v.47. [200.]

[SAITO HIROSHI and IWASAKI FUKUO], Recent trends of east asian studies in Japan with bibliography. Centre for east asian cultural studies: Tokyo [1962]. pp.vi.329. [1465.]

THEODORE E. KYRIAK, Catalog cards in book form to United States joint publications research service translations 1957–. Research and microfilm publications: Annapolis 1962 &c.
in progress.

HIROTAKE ARAI, MORIO GIBU, Catalog of the Glen Shaw collection at the East-west center library. East-west center library publications (no.8): Honolulu 1967. ff.ii.pp.239. [2953.]

EDITH EHRMAN, WARD MOREHOUSE, Preliminary bibliography on East Asia for undergraduate libraries. University of the state of New York: The State education department: Center for international programs and services: Foreign area materials center: New York 1967. pp.x.475. [2970.]

CHINA, Japan and Korea. Classification schedule, classified listing by call number, alphabetical listing by author or title, chronological listing. Harvard university library: Widener library shelf list (14). Cambridge, Mass. 1968. pp.[vi].494. [15,300.]

EAST asiatic library. University of California, Berkeley, Author-title catalogue. Radicals 1–214. Boston, Mass., 1968. pp.viii.703+vi.749+v.755 +vi.779+vi.709+iv.709+vi.748+viii.744+viii. 723+viii.727+vi.712+iv.466. [178,797 cards.]
— Alphabetical supplement. Vol.12, pp.467–762+718. [21,260 cards.]
— Subject catalog. pp.v.717+723+743+705 +746+714. [91,300 cards.]

CHAOYING FANG, The Asami library; a descriptive catalogue. Edited by Elizabeth Huff. Berkeley and Los Angeles 1969. pp.x.424. [900.]

FRANK J. SHULMAN, Recently microfilmed dissertations on east Asia. [Ann Arbor 1969.] ff.17. [270.]*

BULLETIN du Centre de publication de l'U.E.R. Asie orientale.
   1. 1970. pp.34. [18.]
in progress.
DONALD GILLIN, EDITH EHRMAN and WARD MOREHOUSE, East Asia: a bibliography for undergraduate libraries. Occasional publication (no.10): Foreign area materials center: University of the State of New York and National council of associations for international studies: Williamsport, Penn. 1970. pp.xvi.130. [2114.]

JOHN T. MA, East Asia: a survey of holdings at the Hoover institution on war, revolution and peace. Stanford 1971. pp.iv.24. [250.]

MILTON W. MEYER, Northeast Asia; an introductory bibliography. [Los Angeles 1971.] ff.[iv]. pp. 25. [600.]*

FAR EAST: an exhibition of resources in the University of Chicago library. The Joseph Regenstein library, march–june 1973.

iii. *Periodicals*

JOURNALS on the far east. Far eastern book and journal lists (no.28): Public library: Newark, N.J. [1922]. single leaf. [15.]

[MARTHA R. MCCABE and CHRISTIAN OTTOMAR ARNDT], An annotated list of periodicals on the far east for teachers and librarians. Office of education: Washington 1943. ff.[i].9. [60.]*

M. S. BATES, An introduction to oriental journals in western languages with an annotated bibliography of representative articles. Publications (series B): Institute of chinese cultural studies: University of Nanking: Nanking 1933. pp.65. [375.]

THOMAS C. KUO and JOHN W. CHIANG, East asian periodicals and serials; a descriptive bibliography. East asian library: University of Pittsburgh: 1970. ff.iv.142. [600.]

iv. *Persons*

Cohn, William

BIBLIOGRAPHY. Dr. William Cohn. In honour of his seventy-fifth birthday, 22 June 1955. Oxford [1955]. pp.39. [232.]

Cordier, Henri

PRINCIPALES publications de m. Henri Cordier. [1892]. pp.4. [125.]
— [another edition]. Leide 1907. pp.8. [250.]

BIBLIOGRAPHIE des œuvres de Henri Cordier. 1924. pp.viii.151. [1000.]

Gulik, Robert Hans van

BIBLIOGRAPHY of Dr. R[obert] H[ans] van Gulik (D.Litt.). Boston university libraries: Mugar memorial library: "Robert van Gulik collection": Boston [1970?]. pp.82. [165.]*

Maspero, Gaston Camille Charles

HENRI CORDIER, Bibliographie des œuvres de Gaston Maspero. 1922. pp.xvii.154. [1500.]

Polo, Marco

SHINOBU IWAMURA, Manuscripts and printed editions of Marco Polo's travels. National diet library: Tokyo 1949. pp.24. [50.]

Schefer, Charles Henri Auguste

HENRI CORDIER, In memoriam Charles Schefer, 1820–1898. [s.l. 1898]. pp.[ii].xiv. [39.]

Schjøth, Fredrik

LIST of consul general Fredrik Schjöth's translations from chinese and manchu. Oslo 1958. ff.[i]. 7 [26.]*

Siren, Osvald

OSVALDO Siren octogenario die sexto aprilis A.D. MCMLIX. Stockholm 1960. pp.xvi.46. [465.]

Varthema, Lodovico de

HENRI CORDIER, Deux voyageurs dans l'extrême orient au XVᵉ et au XVIᵉ siècles. Essai bibliographique. Nicolò de' Conti—Lodovico de Varthema. Leide 1899. pp.[ii].25. [Varthema: 40.]

Waley, Arthur

ARTHUR WALEY 1889–1966; a memorial exhibition of his work. Introductory note by Edmund Blunden. British Council: London 1967. pp.[10]. [22.]

FRANCIS A. JOHNS, A bibliography of Arthur Waley, 1968. pp.xi.187. [350.]

v. *Foreign relations. History*

HAROLD S. QUIGLEY, An introductory syllabus on far eastern diplomacy. Institute of Pacific relations: American council: Chicago 1931. pp.vi.40. [250.]

MERIBETH E[LLIOTT] CAMERON, The United States and eastern Asia. American association of university women: [Washington 1950]. pp.[ii].12. [100.]*

[JOHN R. TURNER ETTLINGER], Marco Polo to Perry. An exhibition portraying western knowledge of the far east during six centuries. Columbia university: New York [1955]. pp.ii.29. [69.]*

ANDREW MALOZEMOFF, Bibliographical essay and bibliography. Russian far eastern policy 1881–1904. Berkeley &c. 1958. pp.31. [400.]

FERRÉOL DE FERRY, La série d'extrême-orient du fonds des archives coloniales conservé aux Archives nationales (Registres C¹1 à C¹27). Direction des archives de France: 1958. pp.208. [2000.]

vi. *Cartography*

MAPS of the far east. Public library: Far eastern books and journal lists (nos.38–43): Newark, N.J. [1922]. ff.[6]. [92.]

CATALOG of nautical charts and publications. Region 9. East Asia. Hydrographic office: Washington 1962. pp.[37]. [1000.]

vii. *Subjects*

Archaeology

RICHARD K[ING] BEARDSLEY, JOHN B. CORNELL and EDWARD NORBECK, Bibliographic materials in the japanese language on far eastern archaeology and ethnology. [University of Michigan:] Center of japanese studies: Bibliographical series (no.3): Ann Arbor 1950. pp.ix.74. [1063.]

FAR EAST. Council for old world archaeology: COWA surveys and bibliographies: Cambridge, Mass.*

i. 1959. pp.43. [503.]
ii. 1961. pp.14.45. [551.]
ii. Far east: Japan. 1962. pp.5.14. [149.]
iii. 1964. pp.7.37. [506.]
iv. 1969. pp.9.49. [669.]

NORTHERN ASIA, Council for old world archaeology: COWA surveys and bibliographies: Cambridge, Mass.*

i. 1957. pp.8. [77.]
ii. 1960. pp.9.7. [74.]

Biology

N. S. ROMANOV, Указатель литературы по рыбному хозяйству дальнего востока за 1923–1956 гг. Академия наук СССР: Отделение биологических наук: Ихтиологическая комиссия: Москва 1959. pp.292. [3690.]

N. S. ROMANOV, Annotated bibliography on far eastern aquatic fauna, flora and fisheries. Translated from russian. Israel program for scientific translations: Jerusalem 1966. pp.391. [3690.]

Botany

V[LADIMIR] L[EONTEVICH] KOMAROV, Библиография к флоре и описанию растиельнойти дальнего востока. Государственное русской географическое общество: Записки юожно уссурийского отдела (vol.ii): Владивосток 1928. pp.278. [1202.]

ELMER D[REW] MERRILL and EGBERT H[AMILTON. WALKER, A bibliography of eastern asiatic botany] Harvard university: Arnold arboretum: Jamaica Plain, Mass. 1938. pp.xlii.719. [35,000.]

— Supplement 1, by EGBERT H[AMILTON] WALKER, American institute of biological sciences: Washington 1960. pp.xl.552. [10,000.]

Land tenure

EAST & Southeast Asia: a bibliography. A bibliography of materials dealing with east and southeast Asia in the Land tenure centre library. Training and methods series (no.14): Madison 1971.

Music

[K. T. WU and SHIO SAKANISHI], Books on east asiatic music in the library of congress (printed before 1800). Reprinted from the Supplement to the Catalog of early books on music. [Washington] 1944. pp.121–133. [56.]

WALTER GERBOTH, Music of east and southeast Asia: a selected bibliography of books, pamphlets, articles and recordings. University of the state of New York: Albany 1963. pp.v.23. [303.]*

Numismatics

[JOHN ROBINSON], Oriental numismatics. A catalog of the collection of books relating to the coinage of the far east presented to the Essex institute. Salem, Mass. 1913. pp.102. [506.]
300 copies printed.

ARTHUR BRADDAN COOLE, A bibliography on far eastern numismatics and an union index of currency, charms and amulets of the far east. California college in China: College of chinese studies: Peking 1940. pp.[iii].v.422. [1500.]

HOWARD FRANKLIN BOWKER, A numismatic bibliography of the far east: a check list of titles in european languages. American numismatic society: Numismatic notes and monographs (no.101): New York 1943. pp.[iv].144. [981.]

Printing

A MILLENNIUM of printing in China, Korea and Japan; an inaugural exhibition. Konung Gustaf VI Adolfs bibliotek för östasiatisk forskning: The royal library: Kungl. bibliotekets utstallningskatalog (nr 65): Stockholm 1972. pp.32. [73.]

Sino-tibetan languages

ROBERT SHAFER, *ed.*, Bibliography of sino-tibetan languages. Wiesbaden, 1957–63. pp.xi.211. +ix.141. [4500.]

Trade and manufactures

SELECT list of references on trade with the Far east. Library of Congress: Washington 1910. ff.5. [22.]*

BUSINESS in the far east. Public library: Far eastern book and journal lists (no.2): Newark, N.J. [1921]. single leaf. [17.]
— [revised edition]. Business with the far east ... (nos.29–30): [1922]. ff.[2]. [42.]

Tripiṭaka

SAMUEL BEAL, The buddhist Tripiṭaka as it is known in China and Japan. A catalogue and compendious report. 1876. pp.[iv].117. [1000.]

BUNYIU NANJIO, A catalogue of the chinese translation of the buddhist Tripiṭaka, the sacred canon of the Buddhists in China and Japan. Oxford 1883. pp.xxxvi.coll.480. [1850.]

[SIR] E[DWARD] DENNISON ROSS, Alphabetical list of the titles of works in the chinese buddhist Tripiṭaka, being an index to Bunyiu Nanjio's catalogue and to the 1905 Kioto reprint of the Buddhist canon. Archeological department of India: Calcutta 1910. pp.[iv].xcviii. [1750.]

ALFRED FORKE, Katalog des pekinger Tripiṭaka. Ostasiatische sammlungen der Königlichen bibliothek (vol.i): Berlin 1916. pp.[ii].vii.218. [1246.]

PRABODH CHANDRA BAGCHI, Le canon bouddhique en Chine: les traducteurs et les traductions. Tome 1er. Université de Calcutta: Sino-Indica (vol.i): Paris 1927. pp.[iii].lii.436. [2500.]
no more published.

CHINA

i. *Bibliography*
ii. *Periodicals*
iii. *General*
iv. *Emigration*
v. *Foreign relations*
vi. *History, Geography*
vii. *Other subjects*
viii. *Chinese language*
ix. *Chinese literature*

i. *Bibliography*

SSŬ-YÜ TÊNG and KNIGHT BIGGERSTAFF, An annotated bibliography of selected chinese reference works. Yenching journal of chinese studies: Monograph (no.12): Peiping 1936. pp.vi.271. [300.]
— — Revised edition. Harvard-Yenching institute studies (vol.xii): Cambridge, Mass. 1950. pp. x.326. [400.]

DONALD LESLIE and JEREMY DAVIDSON, Author catalogues of western sinologists. Guide to bibliographies on China and the far east. Department of far eastern history: Research school of pacific studies: Australian national university: Canberra [1966]. pp.lvii.259. [1000.]*

LI, Tze-chung and WANG, In-ian, A guide to Chinese reference books.

ANDREW J. NATHAN, Modern China, 1840–1972; an introduction to source and resource aids. Michigan papers in chinese studies (no.14): Ann Arbor 1973. pp.vi.96. [500.]*

ii. *Periodicals*

S. A. POLEVOY, Периодическая пепать в Китаѣ. Извѣстія Восточнаго института (том xlvii): Владивосток, 1913. pp.xi. 191. [487.]

JOURNALS on the far east and novels of China. Public library: Far eastern book and journal lists (no.28): Newark, N.J. [1922]. single leaf. [journals: 15.]

[ROSWELL SESSOMS BRITTON], Directory of Peking daily papers. Yenching university: Department of journalism: Peking 1925. pp.[ii].v.27. [60.]

UNION catalogue of books in European languages in Peiping libraries. ... Volume four (Union list of serials). National library of Peiping and the National academy of Peiping: Peiping 1931. pp.[vi].179.12. [3800.]

ROSWELL S[ESSOMS] BRITTON, 中國報紙 The chinese periodical press, 1800–1912. Shanghai 1933. pp.[vii].152. [200.]

CHINA publishers' directory. A practical guide to newspapers and periodicals. Shanghai 1934. pp.123. [900.]

NEWSPAPER directory of China (including Hongkong). With check list of newspapers and periodicals published in Japan, Chosen, Java, Sumatra, Borneo, Siam, Singapore and Federated Malay States. Shanghai 1931. pp.[iii].52. [500.]
— [third edition]. 1935. pp.[v].201. [1000.]
this edition is limited to China.

MOUSHENG [MOU-SHÊNG] LIN, A guide to leading chinese periodicals. China institute in America: New York [1936]. pp.30.[iv]. [157.]

RICHARD L[OUIS] WALKER, Western language periodicals on China. (A selective list). Yale university: Institute of far eastern languages: New Haven 1949. pp.i.30. [189.]★

CHINESE communist periodicals believed published as of Dec. 1, 1955. Publications procurement unit: American consulate general: Hong Kong 1955. pp.21. [340.]★

CHINESE scientific and technical serial publications in the collections of the Library of Congress. Library of Congress: Science and technology division: Washington 1955. pp.vii.55. [700.]★
— Revised edition. 1961. pp.v.107. [1100.]

CHINESE communist periodicals believed published. American consulate general: [Hong Kong].★
    1955. pp.21. [88.]
    1956. pp.24. [142.]
    1957. pp.58. [714.]

CHINESE communist periodicals available on subscription. American consulate general: [Hongkong 1956]. pp.7. [125.]★

Y[VES] HERVOUET, J[OHN] LUST and R[OGER] PELISSIER, Catalogue des périodiques chinois dans les bibliothèques d'Europe. École pratique des hautes études: Le Monde d'outre-mer passé et présent: Bibliographies (no.2): La Haye &c. 1958. pp.[v].102. [600.]

LESLIE T. C. KUO and PETER B. SCHROEDER, Communist chinese periodicals in the agricultural sciences. Department of agriculture: Library list (no.70): Washington 1960. pp.24. [115.]★

LIST of communist chinese scientific and technical periodicals. [Library of Congress:] Aerospace information division: AID report (no.61–21): [Washington] 1961. ff.[ii].63. [247.]★

JOURNALS in science and technology published in Japan and mainland China. A selected list. Library of Congress: Science and technology division: Washington 1961. pp.iii.47. [400.]★

CHINESE mainland journals: current NLM holdings. National library of medicine: Washington 1961. ff.[i].15. [69.]★

WILLIAM C. C. HU, Holdings of chinese journals of the Asia library. University library, University of Michigan. 1961. ff.41. [280.]★

LIST of mainland chinese magazines contained in the microfile of Union research institute, January 1961. Union research institute: Hong Kong 1961. pp.33. [300.]★

G. RAYMOND NUNN, Chinese periodicals. International holdings 1949–1960. Preliminary data paper. [Ann Arbor] 1961. ff.87. [2000.]★

[RICHARD S. HOWARD], Index to learned chinese periodicals. Compiled in the east asian library, Columbia university. Boston 1962. pp.vi.215. [4605.]★

CATALOGUE of mainland chinese magazines and newspapers held by the Union research institute. Kowloon [1962]. pp.[v].64.116. [1000.]★

CHINESE periodicals in British libraries, Handlist no.1. (Preface signed: E. D. Grinstead.) London [1962]. pp.41.3.8.
— Handlist no.4. By Bill Brugger [*and others*]. British museum: London 1972. pp.v.199. [3000.]★

CURRENT holdings of mainland chinese journals in the M.I.T. libraries. Second edition. Chinese science project: Massachusetts institute of technology libraries: Cambridge, Mass. 1963. pp.[42]. [198.]★

BERNADETTE P. N. SHIH and RICHARD L. SNYDER, International union list of communist chinese serials. Scientific, technical and medical, with selected social science titles. Cambridge, Mass. 1963. pp.[148]. [874.]

JOHN LUST and WERNER EICHHORN, Index sinicus; a catalogue of articles relating to China in periodicals and other collective publications 1920–1955. Cambridge 1964. pp.xxx.663. [19,734.]

LIST of scientific and technical periodicals received from China. National lending library of science and technology: Boston Spa 1964. pp.ii.54. [164.]★

FRANK H. H. KING, *ed.* and PRESCOTT CLARKE, A research guide to China-coast newspapers, 1822–1911. East Asian research center: Harvard university. Harvard east asian monographs (18). Cambridge Mass. 1965. pp.x.235. [200.]*

DAVID Y. HU, A guide to chinese periodicals. Bibliographical series (i): Bibliographical series of east asian collection: Washington university library: Saint Louis, Missouri 1966. ff.[ii].30. [214.]*

ROBERT L. IRICK, An annotated guide to Taiwan periodical literature, 1966. Chinese materials and research aids service center: Taipei 1966. pp.102.

TSIEN TCHE-HAO and J. TSIEN, La république populaire de Chine; revue des revues. Centre de recherches sur l'U.R.S.S. et les pays de l'est: Strasbourg 1966. pp.54. [143.]*

GARNETT ELMER BIRCH, Western language periodical publications in China, 1828–1949. Honolulu 1967. pp.166.

INDEX to titles of english news releases of Hsinhua news agency 1967. Union research institute: Hong Kong [1968]. pp.[i].459. [12,500.]

CATALOGUE of Mainland Chinese magazines and newspapers held by Union Research Institute. 3rd ed. Kowloon 1968. pp.[i].149. [1218.]

INVENTAIRE des périodiques reçus par la bibliothèque et les centres de documentation. Centre de documentation sur l'extrême-orient, section Chine: Paris 1968. pp.44. [450.]*

LIST of chinese journals in the Lu Hsün library of the Oriental institute of the Czechoslovak academy of sciences, Prague. [Prague 1969?] ff.67. [330.]*

JAMES CHU-YUL SOONG, The Red flag (Hung ch'i), 1958–1968: a research guide. Association of research libraries: Center for chinese research materials: bibliographical series (no.3): Washington 1969. pp.xviv [*sic*].312. [2000.]

[CHINESE communist periodicals and newspapers. Hoover institution. Stanford 1970?] pp. 378. [997.]*

[SUSAN PRENTICE], Chinese periodicals. The Australian national university library: Canberra 1970. pp.77. [300.]*

CHRISTINE HERZER, Die volksrepublik China; eine annotierte zeitschriftenbibliographie 1960–1970. Schriften des instituts fur asienkunde in Hamburg (band 31): Wiesbaden 1971. pp.346. [1000.]

HU CHI-HSI, Bibliographie annotée des principaux articles et documents parus dans les périodiques de la République soviétique chinoise du Jiangxi 1931–1934. Matériaux pour l'étude de l'extrême-orient moderne et contemporain: Travaux (6): La Haye, Paris 1971. pp.120. [313.]

INDEX to the Survey of China mainland press, Extracts from China mainland magazines, and Current background. American consulate general: Hong Kong 1950–1968.
in progress?

INDEX to Current background. United States consulate general: Hong Kong.
1950–1962.
1965–1968.
in progress?

INDEX to Selections from China mainland magazines. United states consulate general: Hong Kong.
1955–1962.
1965–1968.
in progress?

MARIE-ROSE SÉGUY and JEAN-CLAUDE POITELON, Périodiques en langue chinoise de la Bibliothèque nationale. Catalogue de périodiques par langues et pays: 1972. pp.xiv.163. [521.]

INDICE dei periodici in lingua cinese e giapponese. I. Biblioteca nazionale centrale: Roma 1973. ff.[v]. pp.184. [1500.]*

CHINESE periodicals in the libraries of the Australian national university, the University of Sydney and the University of Melbourne: a union list of holdings at 31 march 1973.

iii. *General*

HONG-KONG—China. [Colonial office (no.29 of a series of lists of works in the library): 1860]. pp.2. [30.]

CATALOGUE of books relating to China and the east. [?Calcutta *c.*1870]. pp.29. [987.]

HENRI CORDIER, A catalogue of the library of the North China branch of the Royal Asiatic Society. Shanghai 1872. pp.viii.86. [950.]
—— Catalogue of the library of the China branch . . . (including the library of Alex. Wylie, esq.) systematically classed. Third edition. [By Joseph Haas]. 1894. pp.xviii.282.ii. [1400.]
—— List of additions. [By Emil S. Fisher]. 1899. pp.[vii].79. [750.]

P. G. and O. F. VON MÖLLENDORFF, Manual of chinese bibliography, being a list of works and essays relating to China. Shanghai &c. 1876. pp. viii.378. [4639.]

HENRI CORDIER, Bibliotheca sinica. Dictionnaire bibliographique des ouvrages relatifs à l'empire

Chinois. École des langues orientales vivantes: Publications (vols.x–xi): 1878–1885. pp.[iii].xv. coll.868.pp.869–874 + [iii].coll.875–1396.pp. 1399–1408. [12,500.]

corrections by O. F. von Möllendorff appear in The China review (Hongkong 1882), x.396–402.

— — Supplément.... (3rd ser., vol.xv). [1893–] 1895. pp.[iii].coll.1409–2232. pp.2233–2243. [9000.]

— — Deuxième édition. 1904–1908. pp.xvi. coll.764 + pp.[iii].coll.765–1576 + pp.[iii].coll. 1577–2380 + pp.[iii].coll.2381–3236. pp.3239–3252. [50,000.]

— — — Supplément et index. 1922–1924. pp. [iii].coll.3253–4428.coll.4429–4440. [20,000.]

the index was not published; the whole of this edition was photographically reprinted in 1938.

— HENRI CORDIER, A rough index to the Bibliotheca sinica. Toyo bunko: Tokyo 1926. pp.2.34.

— BIBLIOGRAPHY of China. Being a rough index to Cordier's "Bibliotheca sinica". Columns 1–4428. Hankow club library: China class. 1926. pp.14.

— — — Author index. Columbia university: East asiatic library: New York 1953. ff.iv.84.*

— — T'ung-li Yüan, China in western literature. A continuation of Cordier's Bibliotheca sinica. Yale university: Far eastern publications: New Haven 1958. pp.xix.802. [14,000.]*

HENRI CORDIER, Half a decade of chinese studies (1886–1891). Leyden 1892. pp.[ii].36. [400.]

— — Les études chinoises (1891–1894). Leide 1895. pp.89. [500.]

— — — (1895–1898). 1898. pp.141. [1000.]

— — — (1899–1902). 1903. pp.78. [350.] *100 copies printed.*

BOOKS on China. Essex institute: Special catalogue (no.1): Salem, Mass. 1895. pp.[iii].19. [750.]

— [another edition]. Catalog of books on China in the Essex institute. By Louise Marion Taylor. 1926. pp.ix.392. [3500.]

BOOKS, pamphlets, parliamentary reports and magazine articles on China in the reference and lending libraries. Free libraries: occasional lists (no.1): Birmingham 1901. pp.20. [1500.]

MARGARET WINDEYER, China and the far east, 1889–99. Contribution toward a bibliography. New York state library: Bulletin (no.59=Bibliography no.25): Albany 1901. pp.563–679. [1000.]

FLORENCE AYSCOUGH, Friendly books on far Cathay (being a bibliography for the student). Shanghai 1921. pp.[ii].58. [200.]

LIST of recent references on China. Library of Congress: Washington 1922. ff.3. [33.]*

CATALOGUE of the asiatic library of dr. G[eorge] E[rnest] Morrison, now a part of the Oriental library, Tokyo. Tokyo 1924. pp.[iii].8.802 + [ii]. 551. [20,000.]

FREDERICK WELLS WILLIAMS and FRANK W. PRICE, The best hundred books on China. Yale university library: New Haven 1924. pp.20. [100.]

J. C. VAN SLEE, Catalogus van de chineesch-indische boekverzameling. Athenaeum-bibliotheek: Deventer 1925. pp.40. [China: 200.]

CHINA: some recent writings. Library of Congress: [Washington] 1926. ff.7. [69.]*

WILBUR LAURENT WILLIAMS, A survey course in the civilizations of the far east. China. Syllabus and bibliography. First revised edition. Columbia university: New York 1927. pp.47. [400.]*

DAS BUCH in China und das buch über China. Buchausstellung veranstaltet von der Preussischen staatsbibliothek und dem China-institut. Frankfurt a.M. 1928. pp.xiii.152. [1433.]

CATALOGUE of chinese government publications in the Metropolitan library, Pei-hai park, Peking. 1928.

[in chinese.]

БИБЛИОГРАФИЧЕСКИЙ бюллетень. Центральная Библиотека Китайской Восточной Жел. Дор: Библиографическое Бюро: Харбин.

   i. 1927–1928. [Edited by N. V. Ustryalov and E. M. Chepurkovsky]. pp.[ix].112. [2500.]

   ii. 1928–1929. pp.[x].142. [3000.]

   iii. 1930. pp.40.

   iv. 1931. pp.64.

   v. 1932. pp.375. [2000.]

J[OSEPH] PERCY BRUCE, China. National book council: Book list (no.128): 1930. pp.[3]. [80.]

P[ETR] E[MELIANOVICH] SKACHKOV, Библиография Китая. Систематический указатель книг и журнальных статей о Китае на русском языке 1730–1930. Коммунистическая академия: Научно-исследовательский институт по Китаю: Москва &c. 1932. pp.xxiii. 844. [11,000.]

— — [another edition]. Академия наук СССР. Институт народов Азии: 1960. pp.692. [19,551.]

CHARLES S. GARDNER, A union list of selected western books on China in american libraries. Second edition. American council of learned societies: Committee on chinese studies. Washington 1938. pp.xi.111. [371.]
reprinted New York 1970.

CHINA. Compiled by the China campaign committee. Second edition. National book council: Book list (no.128): 1942. pp.[4]. [120.]

ARTHUR W. HUMMEL, Toward understanding China. American library association: Chicago 1942. pp.6. [30.]

MARION HORTON, China. Books for children and young people. American library association: Chicago [1942]. pp.6. [50.]

WHAT to read about China. East and west association: [New York] 1942.*
  i. General bibliography. [80.]
  ii. A list of the armed forces. [13.]
  iii. A list for women's clubs [17.]
  iv. A list for business men. [20.]
  v. A list for high school students. [20.]
  vi. A list for college students. [33.]
  vii. A list for labor unions. [15.]
  viii. A popular list. [16.]
  ix. A list for boys and girls. [45.]

CHINA: the country and the people. Public library: Boston 1944. pp.[4]. [21.]

A. J. VAN BORK-FELTKAMP, Franz Weidenreich 1873–1948. Koninklijke vereeniging Indisch instituut: Mededeling (no.lxxxi): Afd.volkenkunde (no.30): Amsterdam 1948. pp.16. [217.]

JOHN KING FAIRBANK and KWANG-CHING LIU, Bibliographical guide to modern China: works and documents in chinese. Harvard university: Cambridge, Mass. 1948. pp.107. [1000.]*
— — [another edition]. Modern China. A bibliographical guide to chinese works, 1898–1937. Harvard-Yenching institute studies (vol.i): Cambridge, Mass. 1950. pp.[ii].xviii.608. [1200.]*

JOHN KING FAIRBANK, Bibliographical guide to modern China: works in western languages. Harvard university: Cambridge, Mass. 1948. ff.80. [600.]*

RUDOLF LÖWENTHAL, Bibliography of russian literature on China and adjacent countries, 1931–1936. Harvard university: Russian research center: Cambridge 1949. ff.[i].iii.93. [750.]*

S. V. KAZAKOV and M. A. KISELEVA, Китайска народная республика. Краткий рекомендательный указатель литературы. Государственная библиотека СССР им. В. И. Ленина: Москва 1950. pp.37.

S. B. THOMAS and KNIGHT BIGGERSTAFF, Recent books on China, 1945–1951. American institute of Pacific relations: New York 1951. ff.16. [75.]*

УСПЕХИ Китайской народной республики. Рекомендательный. Государственная библиотека СССР им. В. И. Ленина: Москва 1952. pp.80.

JOHN KING FAIRBANK and MASATAKA BANNO, Japanese studies of modern China. A biblio-

graphical guide to historical and social-science research on the 19th and 20th centuries. Harvard-Yenching institute: Rutland, Vt. &c. 1955. pp. xviii.331. [750.]

S. V. KAZAKOV, Успехи Китайской Народной Республики. Рекомендательный указатель литературы. Издание второе. Государственная . . . библиотека СССР имени В. И. Ленина: Москва 1955. pp.68. [175.]

MIROSLAV KAFTAN, Čína. Bibliografický seznam literatury. Universita: Knihovna: Čteme a studujeme (1955, no.2): Praha 1955. pp.40. [150.]

[PIET VAN DER LOON], Revue bibliographique de sinologie. Ecole pratique des hautes-études (VIe section): Paris &c.
  i. 1955. pp.194. [473.]
  ii. 1956. pp.251. [656.]
  iii. 1957. pp.393. [955.]
  iv. 1958. Rédacteur: Donald Holzman. 1964. pp.494. [966.]
  v. 1959. Rédacteur: Donald Holzman. Rédacteur adjoint: Michel Cartier. 1965. pp.468. [862.]
  vi. 1960. 1967. pp.404. [692.]
  vii. 1961. 1968. pp.435.7. [768.]
  viii. 1962. Rédaction: Michel Cartier. 1969. pp.497. [859.]
  ix. 1963. 1971. pp.491. [893.]
  x. 1964. 1973. pp.540. [901.]

TUNG-LI YUAN, Economic and social development of modern China. A bibliographical guide. Human relations area files: Behavior science bibliographies: New Haven 1956. pp.[ii].viii.130.v. 87.[xii]. [2500.]*

INDEX to the classified files on communist China held by the Union research institute. Second edition: Kowloon, Hong Kong 1962. pp.ix.197. [3000.]*

P[ETR] E[MILIANOVICH] SKACHKOV and I. K. GLAGOLAVA, Китайская художественная литература. Библиография русских переводов и критической литературы на русском языке. Всесоюзная государственная библиотека иностранной литературы: Москва 1957. pp.167. [1823.]

LUTZ NOACK, Neues China. Eine empfehlende bibliographie. Deutsche bücherei: Sonderbibliographien (no.9): Leipzig 1957. pp.71. [482.]
limited to works in german.

CHINA. A selected list of references. American institute of Pacific relations: New York 1957. ff.23. [350.]*
— Second edition. 1957. ff.26. [400.]*

JEAN CHESNEAUX, La Chine contemporaine. Fondation nationale des sciences politiques: Centre d'étude des relations internationales: États des travaux (ser. B, no.13): 1958. pp.384–411. [144.]

PETER A. BERTON [and others], The control of sources for the study of contemporary China; a preliminary bibliographic survey. n.p. 1959. ff.xi· 152. [large number.]*

PETER [ALEXANDER MENGUEZ] BERTON and PAUL LANGER, Soviet works on China. A bibliography of non-periodical literature, 1946–1955. University of southern California: School of international relations: Far eastern and russian research series (no.2): Los Angeles 1959 [1960]. pp.158. [389.]*

G[ALINA] P[ETROVNA] BOGATOVA [and others], Китайская Народная Республика. Рекомендательный указатель литературы 1949–1959. Государственная публичная библиотека: Научно-методический отдел библиотековедения и библиографии: Москва [1959]. pp.64. [200.]

A SELECTED and annotated bibliography of the republic of China 1958–1959. National central library: Taipei 1960. pp.[ii].v.127. [100.]

A LIST of the books on modern China held by the Hoover library. Toyo bunko: Seminar on modern China: Tokyo [c.1960]. ff.   +[i].266.7. [.]*

TUNG-LI YÜAN, Russian works on China, 1918–1960, in american libraries. Yale university: Far eastern publications: New Haven 1961. pp.xiv. 162. [1348.]*
an earlier edition appears in Monumenta sinica (1959), xviii.388–430.

RICHARD SORICH, Contemporary China. A bibliography of reports on China published by the United States joint publications research service. New York 1961. pp.[iii].100. [1000.]*

RICHARD HARRIS, Modern China. National book league: Reader's guides (4th ser., no.5): Cambridge 1961. pp.32. [125.]

CHARLES O. HUCKER, China. A critical bibliography. Tucson 1962. pp.x.126. [2285.]

COMMUNIST China: ruthless enemy or paper tiger? A bibliographic survey. Department of the army: [Washington] 1962. pp.vi.137. [1000.]

SUGGESTED reading list on China. Military assistance institute: Library: Arlington, Va. 1963. pp.36. [250.]*

THEODORE E. KYRIAK, China; a bibliography, and Guide to contents of a collection of United States joint publications research service translations in the social sciences emanating from communist China. Vols.1–3,i & ii. Research microfilms: Annapolis (New York) 1962–1964.
[Continued as:]

— China & Asia (exclusive of near east). Bibliography — index to U.S. JPRS research translations. Vol.III no.3 — VI No.12. 1964–1968.
[Continued as:]
— Bibliography — index to current U.S. JPRS translations. China & Asia exclusive of near east. Vol.VII — VIII. 1968–1970.
[Continued as:]
— Bibliography and index to the United States joint publications research service (JPRS) translations. Vol.9 &c. 1971. &c.
in progress.

C. A. VAN DEN BERG-VAN DE GEER, China: gids van boeken, tijdschriften en gramofoon platen — aanwezig in de bibliotheek van de Technische hogeschool te Delft. China: guide of books, periodicals and records in the library of the Delft technological university. Delft 1965. pp.x.49. [200.]*

BIBLIOGRAPHY of the national research professors & recipients of research grants 1960–1965. N[ational] C[ouncil] on S[cience] D[evelopment] review 1965. [Taiwan, 1965.] pp.[ii].210. [1800.]

RICHARD HARRIS, Modern China. Second edition: National book league in association with the Book development council. [London] 1965. pp.29. [110.]

CATALOG of current research publications on modern China. Published bi-monthly by Modern China historical materials center [Taipeh].
    1i. Jan.–Feb. 1966. pp.12. [55.]
    1ii. March–April 1966. pp.12. [70.]
    1iii. May–June 1966. pp.12. [80.]
    1iv. July–August 1966. pp.12. [70.]
    1v. Sept.–Oct. 1966. pp.12. [86.]
    2i.
    2ii. March–April 1967. pp.17. [903.]
    2iii. May–June 1967. pp.16. [96.]
    2iv. July–August 1967. pp.20. [111.]
    3i. Jan.–Feb. 1968. pp.16. [20.]
in progress?

PETER [ALEXANDER MENGUEZ] BERTON and EUGENE WU, Contemporary China; a research guide. Edited by Howard Koch, Jr. Joint committee on contemporary China of the American council of learned societies and the Social science research council. Hoover institution bibliographical series (xxxi): Hoover institution on war, revolution and peace: Stanford Univ.: Stanford, Cal. 1967. pp.xxix.695. [2226.]

DAVID L. WEITZMAN, Chinese studies in paperback. Berkeley 1967. pp.vi.82. [300.]*

MODERN China studies; international bulletin.
    i. August 1970. Current post-graduate research. pp.viii.87. [450.]
    ii. February 1971. pp.vii.155. [664.]

iii. August 1971. Newsletter 1971/2. pp.v.60.
iv. February 1972. Current post-graduate research. pp.vii.189. [1000.]
v. August 1972. Newsletter 1972/3. pp.v.46.
vi. February 1973. Current post-graduate research. pp.viii.184. [800.]
vii. August 1973. Newsletter 1973/4. pp.vii. 76.
in progress.

HOWARD K. SPRIGGLE, China: old and new. Darby, Penna. 1970. ff.[v].98. [2000.]★

E[RICH] ZÜRCHER, List of Chinese books dealing with the Chinese people's republic in the library of the Sinological institute, Leiden university. Leiden 1970. ff.ii.148. [1184.]★

CHUN-SHU CHANG, Premodern China; a bibliographical introduction. Michigan papers in chinese studies (no.11): Ann Arbor 1971. pp.iii. 183. [1100.]

MILTON W. MEYER, China: an introductory bibliography. Los Angeles 1971. pp.3.10.14.13.16. [1400.]★

FRANK J. SHULMAN, A bibliography of western-language doctoral dissertations regarding the Canton area and Hong Kong, prepared especially for the Canton delta conference, the University of Washington. University of Michigan: Ann Arbor 1971.ff.6.

LEONARD H. D. GORDON and FRANK J. SHULMAN, Doctoral dissertations on China. A bibliography of studies in western languages, 1945–1970. Association for asian studies: Seattle and London [1972]. pp.xviii.317. [2217.]

HELMUT MARTIN, Chinakunde in der Sowjetunion nach sowjetischen quellen. Mitteilungen der Instituts für asienkunde Hamburg (45). Hamburg 1972. pp.[iv].209. [large number.]

K. L. PRATT and D. W. S. GRAY, *edd.* China: an index to european visual and aural materials. 1973. pp.xvii.129. [957.]★

A CLASSIFIED collection of pamphlets in foreign languages in the Toyo bunko acquired during the years 1917–1971. Toyo bunko: Tokyo 1972. pp. [iv].ii.[iv].328. [5000.]

ANDREW J. NATHAN, Modern China, 1840–1972; an introduction to source and resource aids. Michigan papers in chinese studies (no.14): Ann Arbor 1973. pp.vi.96. [500.]★

iv. *Emigration*

A[PPLETON] P[RENTISS] C[LARK] GRIFFIN, Select list of references on chinese immigration. Library of Congress: Washington 1904. pp.31. [400.]

[—] — [supplement]. Chinese immigration: a bibliographical list. 1929. ff.6. [67.]★
[—] — — 1934. ff.8. [93.]★

ROBERT ERNEST COWAN and BOUTWELL DUNLOP, Bibliography of the chinese question in the United States. San Francisco 1909. pp.68. [450.]

LIST of references on chinese immigration, 1912–1919. Library of Congress: [Washington] 1919. ff.6. [74.]★

NANCY FOON YOUNG, The chinese in Hawaii; an annotated bibliography.

v. *Foreign relations*

WORKS on the diplomatic relations of the United States and China. Library of Congress: Washington [1908]. ff.3. [9.]★

A LIST of references on relations between the United States and China, 1900–1912. Library of Congress: Division of bibliography: [Washington] 1912. pp.10. [131.]
— Supplement. 1934. ff.9. [93.]★

LIST of references on the open door policy in China. Library of Congress: [Washington] 1915. ff.4.
— [another edition]. 1921. ff.12. [156.]★

ORDERS in council, rules of court, and regulations. [Foreign office]: 1930. pp.45. [1000.]
a list of orders &c. made by british authorities.

U.S. interference in foreign affairs, with special reference to China and Japan. Library of Congress: Washington 1931. ff.3.

HOWARD C[ROSBY] RICE, SHIH-KANG TUNG and FREDERICK W. MOTE, East & west. Europe's discovery of China, & China's response to Europe, 1511–1839. A check-list of the exhibition in the Princeton university library. Princeton, N.J. 1957. ff.xi.94. [184.]★

LIDIA FERENCZY-WENDELIN, Kinai-magyar bibliográfia. Országos Széchényi könyvtár:Új bibliográfiai füzetek (vol.iv): Budapest 1959. pp.334. [3000.]

ROBERT L. IRICK, YING-SHIH YÜ and KWANG-CHING LIU, American-chinese relations, 1784–1941. A survey of chinese-language materials at Harvard. Harvard university: Department of history: Committee on american far eastern policy studies: Research aids for american far eastern policy studies (no.3): Cambridge 1960. pp.[ii]. xxv.296. [2000.]★

NAOSAKU UCHIDA, The overseas Chinese. A bibliographical essay. Hoover institution: Bibliographical series (no.7): [Stanford] 1960. pp.ix.134. [679.]★

VALENTIN H. RABE, American-Chinese relations, 1784–1941: books and pamphlets extracted from the shelf lists of Widener library. Research aids for american far eastern policy studies (no.1): Committee on american far eastern policy studies: Department of history: Harvard university, Cambridge, Mass. 1960. pp.xxvi.126. [2500.]*

KWANG-CHING LIU, Americans and Chinese. A historical essay and bibliography. Cambridge, Mass. 1963. pp.x.211. [large number.]

KUO TING-YEE, Sino-Japanese relations, 1862–1927. A checklist of the Chinese Foreign Ministry archives. James W. Morley, editor. The East Asian Institute: Columbia University: New York [1965]. pp.[viii]. 228.xv. [1250.]

LO HUI-MIN, Foreign Office confidential papers relating to China and her neighbouring countries, 1840–1914; with an additional list, 1915–1937. Maison des sciences de l'homme: Matériaux pour l'étude de l'Extrême-orient moderne et contemporain: Travaux (4). The Hague, Paris 1969. pp. 280. [1000.]

VIMLA SARAN, Sino-Soviet schism. A bibliography, 1956–1964. School of international studies: Jawaharlal Nehru university. Bombay, etc. [1971]. pp.xv.162. [2030.]

PAUL HO, The People's republic of China and international law; a selective bibliography of Chinese sources. Library of congress, Washington 1972. pp.xiii.45. [632.]*

vi. History, Geography

LIST of references on the partitioning of China. Library of Congress: Washington 1902. ff.2. [8.]*

LIST of references on the revolution in China 1911–1912. Library of Congress: Washington 1912. ff.5. [63.]*

LIST of references on China under republican form of government. Library of Congress: Washington 1914. ff.5. [76.]*
— [supplement]. 1920. ff.6. [74.]*
— — List of recent references [&c.]. 1922. ff.4. [60.]*

CHINA and its history. Public library: Far eastern book and journal lists (no.8): Newark, N.J. [1921]. single leaf. [15.]
— [new edition] ... (no.35): [1922]. pp.4. [21.]

THEODORE [DEODATUS NATHANIEL] BESTERMAN, A bibliography of lord Macartney's embassy to China 1792–1794. 1928. pp.8. [25.]
the British museum pressmarks are added in ms. to the copy in that library.

L. G. GOODRICH and H. F. FENN, A syllabus of the history of chinese civilization and culture. New York 1929.
— — Sixth edition. 1958. pp.3–62. [600.]

CHU SHIH CHIA, A catalog of chinese local histories in the Library of Congress. Library of Congress: Asiatic division: Washington 1942. pp.xi. 552.21. [3000.]
the text is in chinese.

LIEN-SHENG YANG, Topics in chinese history. Harvard-Yenching institute studies (vol.iv): Cambridge, Mass. 1950. pp.xii.57. [750.]

E-TU ZEN SUN and JOHN DE FRANCIS, Bibliography on chinese social history; a selected and critical list of chinese periodical sources. Institute of far eastern languages: Yale university: New Haven 1952. pp.xiii.150. [176.]*

FREDERICK W. MOTE, Japanese-sponsored governments in China, 1937–1945. An annotated bibliography compiled from materials in the chinese collection of the Hoover library. Hoover institute and library: Bibliographical series (vol.iii): Stanford 1954. pp.viii.68. [383.]*

JOHN KING FAIRBANK and MASATAKA BANNO, Japanese studies of modern China: a bibliographical guide to historical and social-science research on the 19th and 20th centuries. Harvard-Yenching Institute: Cambridge, Mass. 1955. pp.xvii.331. [900.]
re-issued 1971.

CHUNG-LI CHANG and STANLEY SPECTOR, Guide to the memorials of seven leading officials of nineteenth-century China. Washington university: Far eastern and russian institute: Publications on Asia: Seattle 1955. pp.xv.457. [6000.]*

宋代研究文獻目錄　　　東京
宋史提要編纂協力委. [on cover:] A classified catalogue of japanese books and articles concerning the Sung. 1957. pp.[x].250. [5572.]

HANS H[ERMANN] FRANKEL, Catalogue of translations from the chinese dynastic histories for the period 220–960. University of California: Institute of international studies: Chinese dynastic histories translations: Supplement (no.1): Berkeley 1957. pp.[iii].295. [1000.]*

YVES HERVOUET, Catalogue des monographies locales chinoises dans les bibliothèques d'Europe. École pratique des hautes études: Le monde d'outre-mer passé et présent: Bibliographies (no.i): 1957. pp.100. [1500.]

CHARLES O. HUCKER, Chinese history. A bibliographic review. American historical association. Service center for teachers of history: Publication (no.15): Washington [1958].pp.[ii].42.[200.]

HANS H. FRANKEL, Catalogue of translations from the chinese dynastic histories for the period 220–960. Chinese dynastic histories translations (supplement no.1): Institute of international studies: University of California: Berkeley and Los Angeles 1957. pp.295. [2500.]*

ROBERT L. IRICK, YING-SHIH YÜ and KWANG-CHING LIU, American-chinese relations, 1784–1941. A survey of chinese-language materials at Harvard, Harvard University: Department of history: Committee on american far eastern policy studies: Research aids for american far eastern policy studies (no.3): Cambridge 1960. pp.[ii].xxv.296. [2000.]*

ABSTRACTS of japanese books and articles concerning the Sung. Japanese committee for the Sung project: Toyo bunko: Tokyo 1961. pp.xi.842. [large number.]

BIBLIOGRAPHY of social science periodicals and monograph series: Mainland China, 1949–1960. Foreign manpower research office: Bureau of the census: Foreign social science bibliographies (series P-92, no.3): Washington 1961. pp.iv.32. [119.]*

ALBERT FEUERWERKER and S. CHENG, Chinese communist studies of modern chinese history. East asian research center: Harvard university: Cambridge Mass. 1961. pp.xxv.287. [500.]*

MICHAEL O'QUINLIVAN, An annotated bibliography of the United States marines in the Boxer rebellion. United States marine corps: Marine corps historical bibliographies (no.4): Washington 1961. pp.9. [70.]*

ALLEN B. COLE, Forty years of chinese communism; selected readings with commentary. Service center for teachers of history: Washington, D.C. 1962. pp.ii.43. [126.]

CHUN-TU HSUEH, The chinese communist movement 1937–1949. An annotated bibliography of selected materials in the chinese collection of the Hoover institution on war, revolution, and peace. Hoover institution bibliographical series (xi): Stanford 1962. pp.x.312. [863.]*

SSU-YU TENG, Historiography of the Taiping rebellion. East asian research center: Harvard university: Cambridge Mass. 1962. pp.vii.180. [900.]*

KWANG-CHING LIU, American and Chinese. A historical essay and a bibliography. Cambridge [Mass.] 1963. pp.xi.211. [2000.]

CHOW TSE-TUNG, Research guide to the may fourth movement: intellectual revolution in modern China 1915–1924. Harvard east asian series (13): Cambridge Mass. 1963. pp.xv.297. [876.]*

PING-KUEN YU, Chinese history: index to learned articles 1902–1962. East Asia institute: Hong Kong 1963. pp.xxxi.573. [10,325.]

NAI-RUENN CHEN, The economy of mainland China 1949–1963: a bibliography of materials in english. pp.xxvii.297. [7300.]*

JEAN CHESNEAUX and JOHN LUST, Introduction aux études d'histoire contemporaine de Chine 1898–1949. Maison des sciences de l'homme: Materiaux pour l'étude de l'Extrême-Orient moderne et contemporain: Travaux (ii). Paris, La Haye 1964. pp.148. [250.]

ROBERT HARTWELL, A guide to sources of chinese economic history A.D. 618–1368. Committee on far eastern civilizations: University of Chicago [1964]. pp.xv.257. [1119.]

JOSEPH JIANG, Chinese bureaucracy and government administration; an annotated bibliography. Research translations: Institute of advanced projects: East-west center: [Honolulu] 1964. ff.[ii].ii.157. [561.]*

CHUN-JO LIU, Controversies in modern chinese intellectual history: an analytic bibliography of periodical articles, mainly of the may fourth and post-may fourth era. East asian research center: Harvard university: Cambridge Mass. 1964. pp.viii.207. [347.]*

CHOI SO-JA, Union list of western books on modern chinese history at major libraries in Seoul (as of Oct. 1965). Korean research center: Seoul 1966. pp.[v].71. [1600.]

EDWARD J. M. RHOADS [and others], The chinese red army, 1927–1963; an annotated bibliography. East asian research center: Harvard university: Cambridge, Mass. 1964. pp.xiv.188. [600.]*

JOHN DZEN-HSI LOWE, A catalogue of the official gazetteers of China in the university of Washington. Bibliotheca asiatica, 1. Zug, Switzerland, 1966. pp.7.72. [1000.]

DONALD LESLIE and JEREMY DAVIDSON, Catalogues of chinese local gazetteers. Guide to bibliographies on China and the far east: Department of far eastern history: Research school of pacific studies: Australian national university: Canberra 1967. pp.xliii.125. [111.]*

RICHARD BAUM, Bibliographic guide to Kwangtung communes 1959–1967. Union research institute: Hong Kong 1968. pp.[iii].236. [1750.]

RONALD DIMBERG, EDWARD L. FARMER and ROBERT L. IRICK, A Ming directory –1968; scholars, Taiwan publications. Chinese materials and research aids service center: Taipei 1968. pp.ii.39. [199.]

WOLFGANG FRANKE, An introduction to the sources of Ming history. Kuala Lumpur 1968. pp. xxv.347. [722.]

TRANSLATIONS on the geography of mainland China. United States department of commerce: Joint publications research service: Translations on communist China (no.10): Washington 1968. pp.232.

YVES HERVOUET, Bibliographie des travaux en langues occidentales sur les Song parus de 1946 à 1965. En appendice: Bibliographie des travaux en langue russe, par Ludmila Kurshinnikova. Collection sinologique de l'université de Bordeaux (vol. 1): Bordeaux 1969. pp.xxi.139.28. [600.]

THOMAS C. T. KUO, JOHN CHIANG and FRANCIS CHOW, The chinese local history — a descriptive holding list. Pittsburgh, 1969. ff.[iv].87. [250.]

CHI WANG, Chinese history; selected works in english. Department of history: Georgetown university: 1970. pp.vi.105. [1126.]

P[ING] K[UEN]YU, YU-NING LI and YU-FA CHANG, The revolutionary movement during the late Ch'ing: a guide to chinese periodicals. Center for chinese research materials: Association of research libraries: Washington 1970. pp.xvi.168. [large number.]

HU CHI-HSI, Bibliographie annotée des principaux articles et documents parus dans les périodiques de la République soviétique chinoise du Jiangxi 1931-1934. Matériaux pour l'étude de l'Extreme-Orient moderne et contemporain: Travaux (6): La Haye, Paris 1971. pp.117. [300.]

STEWART E. FRASER and HSU KUANG-LIANG, China: the cultural revolution: its aftermath and effects on education and society: a select and partially annotated bibliography. Institute of education, University of London and International center: George Peabody college for teachers. Education libraries bulletin (supplement 16): London 1972. pp.102. [350.]*

LO HUI-MIN, Foreign office confidential papers relating to China and her neighbouring countries 1840-1914, with an additional list 1915-1937. Matériaux pour l'étude de l'Extrême-orient contemporain: Travaux (4): The Hague, Paris 1969. pp.280. [2500.]

VIMLA SARAN, ed., Documentation on China 1963-1965. School of international studies: Jawahar Lal Nehru university: New Delhi 1971. pp.iv. 346. [2538.]*

ENDYMION [PORTER] WILKINSON, The history of imperial China; a research guide. East asian research center: Harvard university: Cambridge, Mass. 1973. pp.xxi.213. [large number.]

PAPERS relating to the Chinese maritime customs 1860-1943 in the library of the School of oriental & african studies. 1973. pp.[ii].13. [large number.]*

A PRELIMINARY bibliography of gazetteers treating the Ning-shao region of Chekiang. Compiled under the direction of G. William Skinner. ff.xiii. 36. [452.]*

vii. *Other subjects*

Agriculture

MAO YUNG, Bibliography of chinese literature on agriculture. University of Nanking: Library: Publications (no.1): Nanking 1924. pp.[226]. [3000.]
the text is in chinese.

LESLIE T. C. KUO and PETER B. SCHROEDER, Communist chinese periodicals in the agricultural sciences. Department of agriculture: Library list (no.70): Washington 1960. pp.24. [115.]*

LESLEY T. C. KUO and PETER B. SCHROEDER, Communist chinese monographs in the USDA library. Department of agriculture: Library list (no.71): Washington 1961. pp.87. [800.]*

LESLIE T. C. KUO and PETER B. SCHROEDER, Communist chinese periodicals in the agricultural sciences. Library list (no.70) revised: United States department of agriculture, National agricultural library, Washington D.C. 1963. pp.ii.33. [132.]*
first issued December 1960.

WILLIAM J. C. LOGAN and LESLIE T. C. KUO, Chinese agricultural publications from the republic of China since 1947. Library list no.81: National Agricultural library, United States Dept. of agriculture, Washington, D.C. 1964. pp.ii.55 [257.]*

[WILLIAM J. C. LOGAN], Publications on chinese agriculture prior to 1949. Library list (no.85): National agricultural library: Washington 1966. pp.ii.142. [888.]*

K. P. BROADBENT, The development of chinese agriculture 1940-1970. Annotated bibliography (no.3): Commonwealth bureau of agricultural economics: Farnham Royal [1971?]. pp.iv.29. [225.]

Architecture

BRIEF list of references on japanese and chinese architecture. Library of Congress: Washington 1925. ff.4. [44.]*

Art

CHINESE art. Far eastern book and journal lists (no.11): Public library: Newark, N.J. [1921]. single leaf. [19.]

CHINESE art. National book council. Book list (no.146): 1935. pp.15. [250.]

Bible

IGNATIUS KOEGLER, Notitiae s.s. Bibliorum Judæorum in imperio sinensi. Editio altera, auctior. Seriem chronologicam atque diatriben de sinicis s.s. Bibliorum versionibus addidit Christophor. Theophil. de Murr. Halae ad Salam 1805. pp.83. [25.]

Biography

EUGENE [WÊN-CHIN] WU, Leaders of twentieth-century China. An annotated bibliography of selected chinese biographical works in the Hoover library. Hoover institute and library: Bibliographical series (no.iv): Stanford 1956. pp.vii.106. [450.]*

RONALD SULESKI, A guide to some lesser known figures in modern China. Center for chinese studies: University of Michigan [1970]. pp.50. [150.]*

Botany

LIOU-HO and [J. A.] CLAUDIUS ROUX, Aperçu bibliographique sur les anciens traités chinois de botanique, d'agriculture, de sériculture et de fungiculture. Lyon 1927. pp.39. [75.]

Ch'u tz'ū

TSUNG-I JAO, 楚辭書錄　饒宗頤著 Bibliography of Chü Tzŭ. Hong Kong 1956. pp.[10]132.2.

Communism

[HAROLD ROBERT ISAACS and KUO-CHÜN CHAO], Draft survey of materials relating to communism in China, 1927–1934. [Stanford 1948]. ff.57. [500.]*

JOHN KING FAIRBANK and E-TU ZEN [I-TU JÊN] SUN, Chinese communist publications. An annotated bibliography of material in the Chinese library at Harvard university. Harvard university: Russian research center: Cambridge 1949. ff.iv. 122. [3000.]*
privately reproduced from typewriting.

C. MARTIN WILBUR, JOAN J. FELDMAN and SOPHIE LOU, Chinese sources on the history of the chinese communist movement. An annotated bibliography of materials in the East asiatic library of Columbia university. Columbia university: East asian institute studies (no.1): New York 1950. ff.[iii].pp.56.ff.[ii]. [300.]*

ICHIRŌ SHIRATO and C. MARTIN WILBUR, Japanese sources on the history of the chinese communist movement. Columbia university: East asian institute: Studies (no.2): New York 1953. pp.viii.69. [441.]

WRITINGS of the members of the Central committee of the chinese communist party. Columbia university: East asiatic library: New York 1952. ff.vii.41. [550.]*

CHUN-TU HSÜEH, The chinese communist movement. An annotated bibliography of selected materials in the chinese collection of the Hoover institution. Stanford university: Hoover institution on war, revolution and peace: Bibliographical series (vol.viii &c.): [Stanford].*

    1921–1937. ... (vol.viii): 1960. pp.viii.131. [359.]

    1937–1949. ... (vol.xi): 1962. pp.x.312. [863.]

ALLAN BURNETT COLE, Forty years of chinese communism. Selected readings with commentary. American historical association: Service center for teachers of history: Publication (no.47): Washington [1962]. pp.[iv].43. [200.]

Confucianism

LIST of references on chinese philosophy, especially Confucianism. Library of Congress: Washington 1917. ff.4. [36.]*

Drama and stage

LIST of references on the chinese drama and theatre. Library of Congress: Washington 1923. ff.6. [72.]*

DANIEL SHIH-P'ENG YANG, An annotated bibliography of materials for the study of the Peking theatre. Wisconsin China series (no.2): Madison 1967. pp.ix.98. [160.]*

Economics

PUBLICATIONS in english on economic and social China of the Nankai institute of economics, Nankai university. Tientsin 1937. pp.[ii].10. [40.]

HELEN F[IELD] CONOVER, China. A selected list of references on contemporary economic and industrial development, with special emphasis on post-war reconstruction. Library of Congress: General reference and bibliography division: [Washington] 1945. pp.[vi].102. [924.]*
—— Revised edition. 1946. pp.118. [1102.]*

T'UNG-LI YÜAN, Economic and social development of modern China. A bibliographical guide. Human relations area files: Behavior science bibliographies: New Haven 1956. pp.[ii].viii.130. v.87. [2000.]*

BIBLIOGRÁFIA Kina gazdaságáról. Magyar tudományos akadémia: Közgazdaságtudományi intézet: Budapest 1957. pp.[ii].iii.25. [250.]*

Education

JOHN ISRAEL, The chinese student movement, 1927–1937; a bibliographical essay based on the resources of the Hoover institution. Hoover institution bibliographical series (vi): Stanford university 1959. pp.v.29. [130.]*

Entomology

YOSHO ÔUCHI, Bibliographical introduction to the study of chinese insects. Shanghai science institute: Department of biology: Studies (Entomological report, no.1): Shanghai 1934. pp.[v]. 533. [3500.]
also forms vol.ii of section iii of The journal of the Shanghai science institute.

Finance

N. G. TRETCHIKOV, Библиография финансов Китая. Юридический факультет: Харбин [1930]. pp.[vi].70. [1085.]

Formosa

HENRI CORDIER, Bibliographie des ouvrages relatifs à l'île Formose. Chartres 1893. pp.59. [650.]
150 copies printed.

FORMOSA and JAVA. Far eastern book and journal lists (no.15): Public library: Newark, N.J. [1921]. single leaf. [Formosa: 6.]

臺灣文獻資料目錄臺灣省立臺北圖書館編 臺 北 臺灣省文獻委員會 [on cover:] Catalogue of books relating to Taiwan in the Provincial Taipei library. [Taipeh 1958]. pp.[ii].16.2.172.6. [2000.]

Geology

CHUNG YU WANG, Bibliography of the mineral wealth and geology of China. 1912. pp.[vii].63. [750.]

CATALOGUE of the library of the National geological survey of China. Peking 1927. pp.iii.45. [400.]

C[HI] C[HÊN] LIU, Catalogue of the library of the National geological survey of China. Maps and atlas, series A. [Peking] 1928. pp.viii.89. [500.]

LIST of publications of the National geological survey of China. Peiping 1930. pp.[ii].16. [150.]
— [another edition]. Publication list. 1934. pp.[ii].32. [300.]

T. I. YOUNG [TSUN-I YANG], Bibliography of chinese geology. National academy of Peiping: [Peiping] 1935. pp.[iii].xi.241. [2500.]

HSIAO-FANG LI, Bibliography of chinese geology. Bibliography of geology and geography of Sinkiang. National geological survey of China: Nanking 1947. pp.vii.216. [1750.]

Illustrated books

A GUIDE to the chinese and japanese illustrated books exhibited in the King's library. British museum: 1887. pp.16. [100.]

[HSI-HUA FU], Exposition d'ouvrages illustrés de la dynastie Ming. Centre franco-chinois d'études sinologiques: Pékin 1944. pp.xvi.168. [145.]

Islam

CLAUDE L. PICKENS jr., Annotated bibliography of literature on Islam in China. Society of friends of the moslems in China: Hankow 1950. pp.[v]. 72. [509.]

Jesuits

[PHILIPPUS COUPLET], Catalogus patrum Soc. Jesu, qui . . . ab anno 1581. vsque ad 1681. in imperio Sinarum Iesu Christi fidem propagarunt. Ubi singulorum nomina . . . libri sinicè editi recensentur. E sinico latinè redditus [and composed] a p. Philippo Covplet. Parisiis 1686. pp.42. [250.]

LOUIS PFISTER, Notices biographiques et bibliographiques sur les Jésuites de l'ancienne mission de Chine, 1552–1773. Variétés sinologiques (vols.lix.–lx): Chang-hai 1932–1934. pp.[ii].xxv. 561+[iii].561 bis–1108.ff.44. [5000.]
this work, completed in 1886, was based on a chinese compilation by Han Lin and Chang Kêng, edited by Ferdinand Verbiest.

Law

FU-SHUN LIN, Chinese law past and present: a bibliography of enactments and commentaries in english text. East asian institute: Columbia university: New York 1966. pp.xliii.419. [3500.]*

TAO-T'AI HSIA, Guide to selected legal sources of mainland China: a listing of laws and regulations and periodical legal literature with a brief survey of the administration of justice. Library of congress: Washington 1967. pp.ix.357. [946.]

PRELIMINARY union list of materials on chinese law, with a list of chinese studies and translations of foreign law. Prepared for the Sub-committee on chinese Law of the joint committee on contemporary China of the American council of learned societies and the Social science research council. Harvard law school: Studies in chinese law (no.6): Cambridge, Mass. 1967. pp.[iii].919 + Corrigenda, pp.[i].9. [9200.]

JAMES CHU-YUL SOONG, Political and legal research (*chen-fa yen-chiu*), 1954–1965: a research guide. Centre for chinese research materials: Association of research libraries: Washington 1970. pp.98. [512.]

Mao, Tsê-tung

GUIDE to the writings of Mao Tse-tung in the east asiatic library. Columbia university: New York [1951]. ff.16. [200.]*
— Supplement 1. 1952. ff.8. [100.]*

CATALOGUE of the works of Mao Tse-tung. Peking 1970. pp.57.

JEROME CH'EN, ed., Mao papers; anthology and bibliography. London 1970. pp.xxxiii.221. [560.]

AUSTIN C. W. SHU, On Mao Tse-tung; a bibliographic guide. Asian studies center: Michigan state university: East Asia series: Occasional paper (no.2): East Lansing 1972. pp.x.78. [800.]*

Mathematics

CHIA KUEI TSAO, Bibliography of mathematics published in communist China during the period 1949–1960. Contemporary chinese research mathematics (vol.1): American mathematical society: Providence 1961. pp.83. [1160.]

T'UNG-LI YÜAN, A bibliography of chinese mathematics 1918–1960. Washington 1963. pp.x. 154. [2000.]*

Medicine

FRANZ HUEBOTTER, A guide through the labyrinth of chinese medical writers and medical writings. A bibliographical sketch. Kumamoto, Japan 1924. ff.[ii].74. [100.]
70 copies reproduced from handwriting.

BIBLIOGRAPHY of the publications from the laboratories and clinics of the Peking [Peiping] union medical college and hospital. Peking [Peiping].
1915–1925. Compiled by Ernest Carroll Faust. pp.[v].149. [500.]
1926–1927. pp.[v].21. [200.]
1927–1928. pp.[v].24. [200.]
1928–1929. pp.34. [200.]
1929–1930. pp.38. [250.]
1930–1931. pp.36. [250.]
1931–1932. pp.36. [250.]
1932–1933. pp.30. [200.]
1933–1934. pp.32. [200.]
1934–1935. pp.39. [250.]
1935–1936. pp.42. [300.]

1936–1937. pp.43. [300.]
1937–1938. pp.45. [300.]
1938–1939. pp.40. [250.]
1939–1940. pp.40.[xxv]. [250.]
the issue for 1939–1940 includes an author index for 1935–1940.

CHINESE mainland journals: current NLM holdings. National library of medicine: Washington 1961. ff.[i].15. [69.]*

KAN LAI-BING, Parasitic infections of men and animals. A bibliography of articles in chinese medical periodicals 1949–1964. Hong Kong 1966. pp.xiii.120. [950.]

Military arts and science

COMMUNIST China, a strategic survey. A bibliography. DA pamphlet (550–9): Washington 1966. pp.143.
— Communist China: a bibliographical survey. 1971. pp.253.

EDWARD J. M. RHOADS [*and others*]. The Chinese Red Army, 1927–1963; an annotated bibliography. East Asian Research Center, Harvard university: Cambridge, Mass. 1964. pp.xiv.188. [682.]

Mineralogy, mining

WANG CHUNG-YU, Bibliography of the mineral wealth and geology of China. 1912. pp.[vii].63. [750.]

Missions

ALEXANDER WYLIE, Memorials of protestant missionaries to the Chinese, giving a list of their publications and obituary notices of the deceased with copious indexes. Shanghae 1967. pp.vi.331. [1000.]

ROB. STREIT and JOHANNES DINDINGER, Bibliotheca missionum. Siebenter band. Chinesische missionsliteratur 1700–1799. Internationales institut für missionswissenschaftliche forschung: Aachen 1931. pp.24.544. [2030.]
— — Zwölfter band. 1800–1884. 1958. pp.xviii. 745. [1217.]
— — Dreizehnter band. 1885–1909. 1959. pp.xx.807. [752.]
— — Vierzehnter band. 1910–1950. 1960–1961. pp.xviii.810 + xviii.614 + xx.453. [1500.]

CLAYTON H. CHU, American missionaries in China: books, articles and pamphlets extracted from the subject catalogue of the Missionary research library. Research aids for american far eastern policy studies (no.2): Cambridge Mass. 1960. pp.xxiv.509. [7000.]*

Music

GLEN W[ILLIAM] BAXTER, An index to the Ch'in ting tz'u p'u. Harvard-Yenching institute: Cambridge [Mass.] 1951. ff.viii.71. [1321.]*

TSAI-PING LIANG, ed. Bibliography on chinese music. Chinese national music association: Taipei 1956. pp.49.[xxvii]. [368.]

FREDERIC LIEBERMAN, Chinese music; an annotated bibliography. New York 1970. pp.xi.157. [1483.]*

Palaeontology

PIERRE TEILHARD DE CHARDIN and PIERRE LEROY, Chinese fossil mammals. A complete bibliography. Institut de géo-biologie (no.8): Pékin 1942. pp.iv.142. [130.]

Peiping

A BIBLIOGRAPHY of readings on Peiping for tourists. Compiled by the library of the College of chinese studies, cooperating with California college in China. Peiping 1936. pp.[ii].6. [62.]

Philosophy

A. K'AI-MING CH'IU, A classified catalogue of chinese books in the chinese-japanese library of the Harvard-Yenching institute at Harvard university. [Vol.ii]. Philosophy and religion. Cambridge [Mass.] 1939. pp.[ii].ii.201–347. [2750.]

WING-TSIT CHAN, An outline and a bibliography of chinese philosophy. Hanover, N.H. 1953. ff.62. [750.]*
— — [third edition]. An outline and an annotated bibliography [&c.]. Yale university. Far eastern publications: New Haven 1959. pp.vi.127. [1500.]*
— [Another edition.] Yale university 1961. pp.vi.127.20. [500.]*

WING-TSIT CHAN, Chinese philosophy, 1949–1963. An annotated bibliography of mainland China publications. Honolulu, Hawaii [1967]. pp.xiv.290. [969.]

Population

THE POPULATION and manpower of China: an annotated bibliography, by Foreign manpower research office, Bureau of the census, under contract with office for social science programs, Air force personnel and training research center: Air research and development command. International population reports (series P-90, no.8): Washington 1958. pp.iv.132. [300.]*
— [another edition.] New York [1968]. pp. iii.132. [608.]

Printing

HENRI CORDIER, L'imprimerie sino-européenne en Chine: bibliographie des ouvrages publiés en Chine par les européens au XVIIe et au XVIIIe siècle. Paris 1901. pp.ix.75. [395.]

Railways

SELECT list of references on railroads in China. Library of Congress: Washington 1913. ff.7. [69.]*
— Additional references. 1923. single leaf. [4.]*

RUSSIAN bibliographies on the Chinese eastern railway. Harbin 1935. pp.[i].8. [107.]

Science

LIST of scientific periodicals in the library of the Shanghai science institute. [Shanghai] 1934. pp. [ii].2.83. [600.]

CHINESE scientific and technical serial publications in the collections of the Library of Congress. Library of Congress: Science and technology division: Washington 1955. pp.vii.55. [700.]*
— Revised edition. 1961. pp.v.107. [1400.]

JOURNALS in science and technology published in Japan and mainland China. A selected list. Library of Congress: Science and technology division: Washington 1961. pp.iii.47. [400.]*

LIST of communist chinese scientific and technical periodicals. [Library of Congress:] Aerospace information division: AID report (no.61–21): [Washington] 1961. ff.[ii].63. [247.]*

LIST of scientific and technical periodicals received from China. National library for science and technology, Boston Spa, Yorkshire. 1964. pp.ii.54. [155.]*

AMY C. LEE and D. C. DJU CHANG, A bibliography of translations from mainland chinese periodicals in chemistry, general science and technology published by U.S. joint publications research service, 1957–1966. National academy of sciences: Washington 1968. pp.xviii.161. [445.]*

CHI WANG, Nuclear science in mainland China; a selected bibliography. Library of congress: Washington 1968. pp.vii.70. [615.]*

Shantung

LIST of references on the Shantung question. Library of Congress: Washington 1919. ff.6. [83.]*

Shen, Yen-ping

V. V. KUNIN, Мао Дунь. Всесоюзная государственная библиотека иностранной литературы: Писатели зарубежных стран. Москва 1958. pp.48. [301.]

Sinkiang

T. L. [T'UNG-LI] YUAN and H[IROSHI] WATANABE, Classified bibliography of japanese books and articles concerning Sinkiang. Tokyo 1962. pp. [vii].94. [1166.]

Social sciences

Современная китайская литература по общественным наукам.
in progress?

BIBLIOGRAPHY of social science periodicals and monograph series: republic of China, 1949–1961, by Foreign manpower research office, Bureau of the census, under grant from Office of science information service, National science foundation. Foreign social science bibliographies (series P-92, no.4). pp.iv.24. [64.]*

MODERN chinese society: an analytical bibliography.
  i. Publications in western languages 1644–1972; edited by G. William Skinner. pp.lxxviii.802. [13,059.]
  ii. Publications in chinese 1644–1969; edited by G. William Skinner and Winston Hsieh. pp.lxxvi.801. [11,215.]
  iii. Publications in japanese 1944–1971; edited by G. William Skinner and Shigeaki Tomita. pp.lxix.531. [7169.]

Taoism

L[ÉON] WIEGER, Taoïsme. Tome 1. Bibliographie générale. 1. Le canon (patrologie). 11. Les index officiels et privés. [Hien-hien] 1911. pp.338. [1464.]

Technology

JOURNALS in science and technology published in Japan and mainland China. A selected list. Library of Congress: Science and technology division: Washington 1961. pp.iii.47. [4000.]*

LIST of communist chinese scientific and technical periodicals. [Library of Congress:] Aerospace information division: AID report (no.61-21): [Washington] 1961. ff.[ii].63. [247.]*

Trade

LIST of references on the industrial development of China (with special reference to trusts and monopolies). Library of Congress: Washington 1915. ff.4. [48.]*

LIST of references on commerce between the United States and China. Library of Congress: Washington 1916. ff.3. [25.]*

LIST of references on the chinese consortium. Library of Congress: [Washington] 1921. ff.3. [29.]*

LIST of recent references on commerce between the United States and China. Library of Congress [Washington] 1923. ff.10. [99.]*

LIST of references on the chinese boycott. Library of Congress: Washington 1932. ff.6. [64.]*

Travel

TRAVEL and social life in China. Public library: Far eastern book and journal lists (no.9): Newark, N.J. [1921]. single leaf. [25.]
— [another edition] . . . (no.36): [1922]. single leaf. [24.]

Tung

K['AI] HO and H[U] LIU, Bibliography on tung tree and tung oil. Government testing bureau: Hankow 1937. pp.vii.175. [1400.]

CULTIVATION of tung oil trees, aleurites spp. Science library: Bibliographical series (no.324): 1937. ff.9. [172.]*

viii. Chinese language

STEPHANUS FOURMONT, Linguae sinarum mandarinicae hieroglyphicae grammatica duplex, latinè & cum characteribus sinensium. Item sinicorum regiae bibliothecae librorum catalogus . . . Lutetiae Parisorum 1742. pp.[x].xl.[iv].iv.516. [389.]

L[OUIS MATHIEU] LANGLÈS, Notice des ouvrages élémentaires manuscrits, sur la langue chinoise, que possède la Bibliothèque nationale. [c.1800]. pp.13. [15.]

V[ICTOR HERMANN] ANDREAE and JOHN GEIGER, 目總廣書法文字漢. Hán-tsé-wên-fă-chōu-kouang-tsōng-mōu. Bibliotheca sinologica. Uebersichtliche zusammenstellung als wegweiser durch das gebiet der sinologischen literatur. Frankfurt a.M. 1864. pp.xi.109.[iii].32. 16. [1000.]

COUNT [CIPRIANO MUÑOZ Y MANZANO] DE LA VIÑAZA, Escritos de los Portugueses y Castellanos referentes á las lenguas de China y el Japón. Congreso internacional de orientalistes: Lisboa &c. 1892. pp.140. [254.]
150 copies printed.

CHINESE language. Public library: Far eastern book and journal lists (no.13): Newark, N.J. [1921]. single leaf. [15.]

ROBERT SHAFER, *ed.* Bibliography of sino-tibetan languages. Wiesbaden 1957. pp.xi.211. [3500.]

MAURICE H. TSENG, Recent chinese publications on the chinese language. An annotated bibliography. Yale university: Institute of far eastern languages; New Haven 1961. pp.[ii].iii.45. [110.]*

WINSTON L. Y. YANG and TERESA S. YANG, A bibliography of the chinese language. New York 1966. pp.xiv.171. [1860.]*

WILLIAM S. Y. WANG and ANATOLE LYOVIN, CLIBOC: Chinese linguistics bibliography on computer. Princeton–Cambridge studies in Chinese linguistics (vol.1): Cambridge 1970. pp. 513. [3000.]

ix. Chinese literature

[ANDREAS MÜLLER], Catalogus librorum sinicorum Bibliothecæ electoralis brandenburgicæ [Andreæ Mülleri Greiffenhagii]. [Cologne 1683]. pp.[6]. [150.]
not limited to chinese books.
— — Anderer theil des Catalogi der sinesischen bücher bey der Churfürstl. brandenburgischen bibliothec. Cöln an der Spree 1683. pp.[28]. [5.]

PAVEL KAMENSKY and STEPHAN LIPOVTSOV, Каталогъ китайскимъ и японскимъ книгамъ, въ библіотекѣ Императорской академіи наукъ хранящимся . . . вновъ сдѣланый.
[St. Petersburg c.1815]. pp.57. [324.]

[JEAN PIERRE] ABEL RÉMUSAT, Mémoire sur les livres chinois de la Bibliothèque du roi, . . . avec des remarques critiques sur le catalogue publié par E. Fourmont, en 1742. 1818. pp.60. [30.]

JULIUS KLAPROTH, Verzeichniss der chinesischen und mandschuischen bücher und handschriften der Königlichen bibliothek zu Berlin. Paris 1822. pp.x.188. [75.]
200 copies printed.

— — Wilhelm Schott, 御書房滿 漢書廣錄 Verzeichniss der chinesischen und mandschu-tungusischen bücher und handschriften der Königlichen bibliothek zu Berlin. Eine fortsetzung des . . . Klaproth'schen Verzeichnisses. Berlin 1840. pp.[iii].iv.102. [2000.]

S[AMUEL] KIDD, Catalogue of the chinese library of the Royal asiatic society. 1838. pp.[iii].59. [250.]
500 copies printed.

A[LEXANDER] WYLIE, Notes on chinese literature: . . . and a list of translations from the chinese, into various european languages. Shanghai &c. 1867. pp.[ii].viii.xxviii.260. [2000.]
not limited to translations.

JOSEPH EDKINS, A catalogue of chinese works in the Bodleian library. Oxford 1876. pp.[ii].coll.46. [299.]

[SIR] R[OBERT] K[ENNAWAY] DOUGLAS, Catalogue of chinese printed books, manuscripts and drawings in the library of the British museum. 1877. pp.viii.344. [4500.]
— — Supplementary catalogue. 1903. pp.[iii]. 224. [3000.]

W. F. MAYERS, Bibliography of the chinese imperial collections of literature. Hongkong 1878. pp.25. [7.]

BUNYIU NANJIO, A catalogue of japanese and chinese books and manuscripts lately added to the Bodleian library. Oxford 1881. pp.[iii].coll.5–28. [75.]

HENRI CORDIER, Essai d'une bibliographie des ouvrages publiés en Chine par les Européens au xviie et au xviiie siècle. 1883. pp.[ii].52. [196.]

[G. SCHLEGEL], Catalogue des livres chinois qui se trouvent dans la bibliothèque de l'université de Leide. Leide 1883. pp.iv.28. [234.]
— — Supplément. 1886. pp.12. [50.]

[AUGUSTE LESOUËF], Catalogue des livres et manuscrits chinois collectionnés par A. Lesouëf. Leide 1886. pp.40. [100.]
100 copies privately printed.

A GUIDE to the chinese and japanese illustrated books exhibited in the King's library. British museum: 1887. pp.16. [Chinese: 30.]

HENRY F. HOLT, A catalogue of the chinese manuscripts in the library of the Royal asiatic society. (Cover title: Catalogue of chinese printed books . . .) London 1889 (cover). pp.v.117. [562.]

[JOHN PHILIP EDMOND], Bibliotheca lindesiana. Catalogue of chinese books and manuscripts. Aberdeen [printed] 1895. pp.xi.90. [475.]
100 copies privately printed.

HERBERT A[LLEN] GILES, A catalogue of the Wade collection of chinese and manchu books in the library of the university of Cambridge. Cambridge 1898. pp.viii.169. [chinese: 796.]
— — Supplementary catalogue. 1915. pp.vi.30. [125.]

MAURICE COURANT, Catalogue des livres chinois, coréens, japonais, &c. Bibliothèque nationale: Département des manuscrits: 1900–1912. pp.[iii]. vii.499+[v].823+232. [9080.]
limited to chinese books; no more published.

DAITARO SAEKI, Catalogue of Ta-jih-pên-hsü-ts'ang-ching. Kyoto 1915. pp.viii.215. [2021.]

CHINESE collection, Library of Congress. . . . Part II—stroke index of independent works. [Washington 1918]. ff.[v].58.6. [2498.]

— Third edition. Title index to independent chinese works in the Library of Congress. . . . Newly compiled [by Berry Armstrong Claytor]. 1932. ff.[i].iii.15.xxxi.211 + [i].213–454.40. [13,419.]
a reduced photographic reproduction of the ms. catalogue cards.

RIKICHI KUROSAWA, Imperial chinese art. A catalogue of writings and paintings by the chinese emperors, empresses and princes dating from the T'ang dynasty to the end of the Ch'ing dynasty, A.D. 618–1912. Shanghai 1919. pp.[vi].xx.[xvi].215. [350.]

RELIGION, education and literature of China. Public library: Far eastern book and journal list (no.10): Newark, N.J. [1921]. single leaf. [20.]

NEW CHINA and novels of China. Public library: Far eastern book and journal lists (no.12): Newark, N.J. [1921]. single leaf. [22.]
— [new edition]. New China . . . (no.37): [1922]. single leaf. [17.]

JOURNALS on the far east and novels of [or rather, concerning] China. Public library: Far eastern book and journal lists (no.28): Newark, N.J. [1922]. single leaf. [novels: 17.]

[CHONG MAN-KHAI *and others*], Inventaire du fonds chinois de la bibliothèque de l'École française d'extrême-orient. [Edited by Henri Maspero and Léonard Aurousseau]. Hanoi.
  i. A–Hou. 1929–1931. pp.viii.644.ii. [5347.]
  ii. 1. Hou-K'iao. 1935–1937. pp.645–932. [2264.]
  iii. 1. Lie-Lu. 1941–1943. pp.[ii].933–1462. [1636.]
  iii. II. Ma-Mou, 1951. pp.1463–1658.163. [5548.]

BOOKS on China. Library: North China union language school cooperating with California college in China: Peiping 1931. pp.ii.359. [7000.]
— Supplement 1. 1934. pp.86. [2000.]

BERNHARD KARLGREN, Chinese books in swedish collections. Högskolas årsskrift (vol.xxxvii, no.6): Göteborg 1931. pp.26. [406.]

CHARLES S[IDNEY] GARDNER, A union list of selected chinese books in american libraries. American council of learned societies: Washington 1932. pp.v.50. [228.]*

A CLASSIFIED catalogue of the Mollendorff collection deposited in the library by Mr. Chu Chi-chien. National library of Peiping: Peiping 1932. pp.[v].285.65. [2000.]

P[ING] Y[AO] YÜ, Title index to the Ssŭ k'u ch'üan shu. Compiled . . . under the supervision of I[rvin] V[an Gorder] Gillis. Peiping 1934. pp. [422]. [11,124.]

QUARTERLY bulletin of chinese bibliography. Edited . . . by the National library of Peiping. Chinese national committee on intellectual co-operation: Shanghai.
  i. 1934. pp.[iii].276. [4000.]
  ii. 1935. pp.[iii].240. [3500.]
  iii. 1936. pp.[iii].277. [4000.]
  iv. 1937. pp.[iii].172. [2500.]
continued in a more general form.

TSAO TSU-PING, An analytical author index to tsung shu in the University of Nanking library. Nanking 1935. pp.[2].2.32.20.558.[2]. [large number.]

A. K'AI-MING CH'IU, A classified catalogue of chinese books in the chinese-japanese library of the Harvard-Yenching institute at Harvard university. Cambridge [Mass.].
  [i]. Classics. 1938. pp.[ii].iii.199. [3000.]
  [ii]. Philosophy and religion. 1939. pp.[ii].ii.201–347. [2750.]
  [iii]. Historical sciences. 1940. pp.[ii].vii.349–829. [7500.]

SELECTED chinese books, 1933–1937. Edited by the National library of Peiping. [Peiping] 1939. pp.[i].64. [900.]
printed on one side of the leaf.

PIH SHUT'ANG [SHU-T'ANG PI], Catalogo di opere in cinese tradotte dall'italiano o riguardanti l'Italia. Centro culturale italiano: Saggio di bibliografia (no.1): [Peking] 1942. pp.[ii].79. [202.]

DEUX siècles de sinologie française. (Exposition des principaux ouvrages d'auteurs français publiés au XVIIIe et au XIXe siècle et rassemblés á Pékin. Catalogue.) Centre franco-chinois d'études sinologiques: Pekin 1943. pp.xii.75. [75.]

LIONEL GILES, Six centuries at Tunhuang. A short account of the [sir Aurel] Stein collection of chinese mss. in the British museum. China society: 1944. pp.50. [100.]

PHILOBIBLON. A quarterly review of chinese publications. National central library: Nanking.
  i. 1946–1947. Editor: C. S. Ch'ien. pp.93.80.60.48. [1500.]
  ii. 1947–1948. pp.74.52.35. [1000.]

[GORAN MALMQVIST and SÖREN EGERÖD], Gunnar Martins samling av kinesisk och japansk litteratur. Kungl[iga] bibliotek: Stockholm 1947. ff.[110]. [282.]*

JOSEPH SCHYNS [*and others*], 1500 modern chinese plays and novels. Peiping 1948. pp.lviii.484. [1500.]

CATALOGUE of the Pei-t'ang library. Lazarist mission, Peking: Peking 1949. pp.xxxiii.1334. [4101.]

JAMES ROBERT HIGHTOWER, Topics in chinese literature. Outlines and bibliographies. Harvard-Yenching institute: Studies (vol.iii): Cambridge 1950. pp.ix.130. [500.]
— — Revised edition. 1953. pp.ix.141. [500.]

MARTHA DAVIDSON, A list of published translations from chinese into english, french, and german. Part 1: Literature, exclusive of poetry. (Tentative edition). American council of learned societies: Ann Arbor 1952. pp.xxix.179. [1512.]★
— Part 2: Poetry. (Tentative edition). American council of learned societies: Ann Arbor [1957]. pp.[v].181–462. [3898.]★

HERBERT FRANKE, Orientalistik. 1. Teil. Sinologie. Wissenschaftliche forschungsberichte, Geisteswissenschaftliche reihe. (Band 19.) Bern 1953. pp.216. [2000.]

REVUE bibliographique de sinologie. Ecole pratique des hautes etudes (VIe section): Paris, La Haye.
1. 1955. Rédacteur: Piet van der Loon. 1957. pp.194. [473.]
2. 1956. 1959. pp.251. [656.]
3. 1957. 1962. pp.393. [955.]
4. 1958. Rédacteur: Donald Holzman. 1964. pp.494. [966.]
5. 1959. Rédacteur: Donald Holzman. Rédacteur adjoint: Michel Cartier. 1965. pp.468. [862.]
6. 1960. 1967. pp.404. [692.]
7. 1961. 1968. pp.435. 7. [768.]
8. 1962. Rédaction: Michel Cartier. 1969. pp.497. [859.]
9. 1963. 1971. pp.491. [893.]

LIONEL GILES, Descriptive catalogue of the chinese manuscripts from Tunhuang in the British museum. 1957. pp.xxv.334. [8102.]

P[ETR] E[MILIANOVICH] SKACHKOV and I. K. GLAGOLEVA, Китайская художественная литература. Библиография русских переводов и критической литературы на русском языке. Всесоюзная государственная библиотека иностранной литературы: Москва 1957. pp.167. [1823.]

CHUNG-MIN WANG, 國會圖書館藏 中國善本書錄 A descriptive catalog of rare chinese books in the Library of Congress. Edited by T. L. [T'ung-li] Yuan. Washington 1957. pp.[vi].666+667–1306. [1777.]

SELECTED bibliography of the Republic of China. National central library: Taipei 1957. pp.[i].59. [600.]

JOHANNES SCHUBERT, Publikationen des modernen chinesisch-tibetischen schrifttums. Deutsche akademie der wissenschaften zu Berlin: Institut für orientforschung: Veröffentlichung (no.39): Berlin 1958. pp.56. [77].

LIST of consul general Fredrik Schjöth's translations from chinese and manchu. Oslo 1958. ff.[i]. 7. [26.]★

CATALOGUE of chinese classical books. Kowloon 1959. pp.[iv].60. [250.]★

JAMES I. CRUMP, Selected anthologies of chinese literature. [Ann Arbor 196–?]. pp.23. [21.]★

THE MONTHLY list of chinese books. National central library, Taipei. 1960 &c.
in progress.

LOUIS DE LA VALLÉE POUSSIN, Catalogue of the tibetan manuscripts from Tun-huang in the India office library. ... With an appendix on the Chinese manuscripts by Kazuo Enoki. 1962. pp. xviii.299. [chinese: 136.]

LIBRARY catalogue of the School of oriental and african studies, university of London. Chinese catalogue. Boston 1963. pp.[ii].646+[ii].664+ [ii].819+[ii].744+994.
— First supplement.
Chinese catalogue. 1968. pp.598+608+368 +viii.369–652.

UNIVERSITY of California, Los Angeles, Dictionary catalog of the university library 1919–1962. Boston 1963.
vol. 127. Chinese collection A–Lim. pp.866. [18,168 cards.]
— 128. Chinese collection Lin–Z. pp.803. [16,860 cards.]

WALTER FUCHS, Chinesische und mandjurische handschriften und seltene drucke, nebst einer standortliste der sonstigen mandjurica. Verzeichnis der orientalischen handschriften in Deutschland (xii.1): Wiesbaden 1966. pp.xiii.160. [373.]

LIU TS'UN-YAN, Chinese popular fiction in two London libraries. Hong Kong [1967?] pp.xv.375. [132.]

AKIRA YUYAMA, Indic manuscripts and chinese blockprints (non-chinese texts) of the oriental collection of the Australian national university library, Canberra. Occasional paper (no.6): Centre of oriental studies: the Australian national university: Canberra 1967. pp.viii.124. [large number.]

TIEN-YI LI, Chinese fiction. A bibliography of books and articles in Chinese and English. New Haven, Conn. 1968. pp.xiv.356. [2200.]

THE LIBRARY catalogs of the Hoover institution on war, revolution and peace, Stanford university.

Catalog of the chinese collection. Boston, Mass. 1969.

1. A- Chia-S. pp.x.745. [15,641.]
2. Chia-T- China-Hist. 1643. pp.751. [15,756.]
3. China-Hist.1644 — Ch'iu-S. pp.739. [15,515.]
4. Ch'iu-T — Chung-kuo M. pp.739. [15,528.]
5. Chung-kuo N — Fir. pp.750. [15,749.]
6. Fis — Hsu chi-K. pp.734. [15,414.]
7. Hsu Chi-L — Kol. pp.749. [15,719.]
8. Kom -Lin, Yu-S. pp.734. [15,397.]
9. Lin Yu-T — Num. pp.733. [15,387.]
10. Nun — Shan. pp.731. [15,338.]
11. Shao -Tam. pp.733. [15,374.]
12. Tan—Wang, Chu-H. pp.731. [15,345.]
13. Wang Chu-I—Z. pp.744. [15,617.]

SHIH-KANG TUNG, Chinese microfilms in Princeton university: a checklist of the Gest oriental library. Center for chinese research materials: Association of research libraries: Washington 1969. pp.57. [361.]*

TSUNG-I JAO, A descriptive bibliography of rare books in the Fung-ping-shan library. University of Hong Kong: Hong Kong 1971.

MARIÁN GÁLIK, Preliminary research-guide, germen [sic] impact on modern chinese intellectual history. Herausgegeben von Wolfgang Hauer. Seminar für 'ostasiatische sprach- und kulturwissenschaft: Munchen 1971. pp.v.120. [1858.]*

JAMES CHU-YUL SOONG, Chinese materials on microfilm available from the library of Congress. Center for chinese research materials: Association of research libraries: Bibliographical series (no.11): Washington 1971. pp.xiii.82. [large number.]

WOLFRAM EBERHARD, Taiwanese ballads; a catalogue. Asian folklore and social life monographs (vol.xxiii): Taipei 1972. pp.ix.171. [197.]*

CATALOGS of the Far eastern library, university of Chicago. Chicago 1973.
Author/title catalog of the chinese collection. pp.vii.771 + 817 + 744 + 775 + 783 + 788+699+820. [60,000.]
Author/title catalog of the japanese collection. pp.v.810+777+839+820. [35,000.]
Classified catalog and subject index of the chinese and japanese collections. pp.cxxxix. 558+785+691+726+722. [94,700.]

COLLECTIONS of chinese books in Japan: a catalogue of catalogues of chinese books in public and private collections. Studies on Asia in japanese (ii). Toyo bunko: Tokyo.

BORIS BORISOVICH VAKHTIN [and others], Каталог фонда китайских ксилографов Института востоковедения АН СССР. Москва 1973. pp.402+591+502. [3665.]*

JAPAN

i. *Bibliography*
ii. *General*
iii. *Periodicals*
iv. *History*
v. *Cartography*
vi. *Foreign relations*
vii. *Japanese in other countries*
viii. *Official publications*
viiia. *Social life and topography*
ix. *Other subjects*
x. *Japanese language*
xi. *Japanese literature*

i. *Bibliography*

EMILE GASPARDONE, Les bibliographies japonaises. Maison franco-japonaise: Tokyo 1933. pp.29–116. [large number.]
Extrait du Bulletin de la Maison franco-japonaise (tome iv).

KEITARO AMANO, MICHIMUNE MADENOKOJI and KATSUKO YAMAGUCHI, Catalogue of reference books in european languages in Kansai university. Suita, Osaka 1960. pp.16.222. [2500.]

A SURVEY of japanese bibliographies concerning asian studies. Compiled and published by Centre for east asian cultural studies. Tokyo 1963. pp.iii. 200.xvii. [1200.]

GUIDE to japanese reference books. Chicago 1966. pp.[x].303. [2575.]

HIROSHI MORI, List of japanese bibliographies; the holdings of the Asia library of the university of Michigan: Supplement of the monthly selective list of current acquisitions, vol.vi, no.1 (July 1966). Asia library, the university of Michigan: Bibliographical series (no.iii). ff.[ii]. pp.95. [1550.]*

ii. *General*

LÉON PAGÈS, Bibliographie japonaise ou catalogue des ouvrages relatifs au Japon qui ont été publiés depuis le xve siècle jusqu'à nos jours. 1859. pp.[iv].68. [730.]
see also next entry.

FR[IEDRICH] VON WENCKSTERN, A bibliography of the Japanese empire. Being a classified list of all books, essays and maps in european languages relating to Dai Nihon . . . from 1859–1893 . . . to which is added a facsimile-reprint of: Léon Pagès, Bibliographie japonaise. Leiden 1895. pp.xiv.338. [6000.]
—— from 1894 to the middle of 1906 . . . with additions . . . to the first volume and a supplement to Léon Pagès. . . . Added is a list of the swedish

literature on Japan by miss Valfrid Palmgren. Tokyo &c. 1907. pp.iii–xvi.487.28.23. [10,000.]

—— 1906–1926. ... Compiled by Oskar Nachod. 1928. pp.iii–xvi.384+[iv].385–832. [9575.]

reissued as an independent work:

——— Bibliographie von Japan, 1906–1926. Leipzig 1928. pp.xvi.384+[iv].385–832. [9575.]

——— 1927–1929. 1931. pp.iii–xv.411. [4020.]

——— 1930–1932. ... Aus dem nachlass ergänzt und herausgegeben von Hans Praesent. 1935. pp.xv.351. [4803.]

———1933–1935. [By] H. Praesent and Wolf Haenisch. 1937. pp.x.452. [6978.]

——— 1936–1937. Von W. Haenisch und H. Praesent. 1940. pp.569. [8245.]

reprinted 1970.

HELEN KILDUFF GAY, Reading list on Japan. University of the state of New York: State library bulletin (Bibliography no.6): [Albany] 1898. pp. 119–135. [100.]

LIST of works in the New York public library relating to Japan. [New York 1906]. pp.79. [3000.]

HENRI CORDIER, Bibliotheca japonica. Dictionnaire bibliographique des ouvrages relatifs à l'empire Japonais. Publications de l'École des langues orientales vivantes (5e série, tome viii): 1912. pp. xii.coll.762. [3500.]

SELECT list of references on Japan. Library of Congress: Washington 1913. ff.8. [92.]*

SELECT list of references on the Japanese question. Library of Congress: Washington 1913. ff.13. [69.]*

LIST of references on Japan and her future expansion. Library of Congress: Washington 1918. ff.2. [16.]*

CATALOGUE of the library of the Asiatic society of Japan. [Tokyo] 1919. pp.[iv].57. [750.]

JAPAN. Public library: Far eastern book and journal lists (no.7): Newark, N.J. [1921]. single leaf. [27.]

Z[OTIK] N[IKOLAEVICH] MATVEEV and A. D. POPOV, Библиография Японии. Государственный дальневосточний университет: Восточный факультет: Труды (vol.i, no.2): Владивосток 1923. pp.6.[ix].117.15. [1500.]

BRIEF list of references on Japan as a world power. Library of Congress: Washington 1923. ff.3. [37.]*

CATALOGUE of foreign books in the Tokyo imperial university 1923–1935. Vol.1. General & miscellaneous. pp.104. [5000.]

— supplement 1. 1935–1936. pp.395. [20,000.]

A SHORT bibliography on Japan in english. Kokusai bunka shinkōkai: Tokyo 1934. pp.[iii].37. [4000.]

— Third edition. A short bibliography of english books on Japan. 1936. pp.[iv].44. [400.]

BIBLIOGRAPHIE abrégée des livres relatifs au Japon en français, italien, espagnol et portugais. Kokusai bunka shinkōkai: K.B.S. publication (ser. B, no.31): Tokyo 1936. pp.[ii].iv.53. [400.]

MIKINOSUKE ISHIDA, A list of books on Japan in european languages published during the year 1936. pp.15. [163.]

[MIKINOSUKE ISHIDA *and others*], Catalogue of the K.B.S. library; a classified list of works in western languages relating to Japan in the library of the Kokusai bunka shinkokai. K.B.S. publications series (A. no.6): Tokyo 1937. pp.xxi.203. [3000.]

K. B. S. bibliographical register of important works written in japanese on Japan and the far east published during the year. Kokusai bunka shinkōkai: Tokyo.

    1932. 1937. pp.[ii].vii.166. [1250.]
    1933. 1938. pp.[ii].ix.180. [1300.]
    1934. 1940. pp.[ii].ix.211. [1400.]
    1935. 1942. pp.ix.211. [1400.]
    1936. 1942. pp.ix.204. [1200.]
    1937. 1943. pp.[ii].ix.217. [1250.]
    1938. 1949. pp.[ii].iv.113. [750.]

A GUIDE to japanese studies. Kokusai bunka shinkokai: Publications (series A, no.3): Tokyo 1937. pp.[iv].ix.264. [500.]

[MIKINOSUKE ISHIDA], Catalogue of the K.B.S. library. A classified list of works in western languages relating to Japan. Kokusai bunka shinkōkai: Publications (ser. A, no.6.): Tokyo 1937. pp. xxi.205. [2750.]

[MASAHARU ANESAKI, *ed.*], Kurze bibliographie der bücher über Japan in deutsch, holländisch, dänisch, schwedisch und norwegisch. Kokusai bunka shinkokai: Publications (ser. A, no.45): Tokyo 1938. pp.[ii].v.66. [500.]

F. M. TRAUTZ, *ed.* Bibliographischer alt-Japan-katalog, 1542–1853. Deutsches forschungsintitut: Kyoto 1940. pp.xxxviii.415. [1624.]

DOCTORAL dissertations on Japan, accepted by american universities, 1912–1939. Japan institute: New York 1940. ff.vii.17. [89.]*

HUGH BORTON, SERGE ELISSÉEFF and E[DWIN] O[LDFATHER] REISCHAUER, A selected list of books and articles on Japan in english, french, and german. American council of learned societies: Committee on japanese studies: Washington 1940. pp.[ii].x.142. [842.]

— — [another edition]. Harvard-Yenching institute: Cambridge 1954. pp.xiv.272. [1781.]

KATALOG der bücherei des Japaninstituts zu Berlin. . . . Erster teil: werke in europäischen sprachen. [Berlin 1941]. ff.[ii].154. [3000.]*

LÉVAI GABOR, Japán magyar könyvészete. Keletázsiai dolgozatok. Budapest 1943. pp.56. [822.]

A CLASSIFIED catalogue of books in foreign languages in the Toyo Bunko 1917–1936. Vol.1: i. General reference works; ii. Asia, east Asia and the Pacific. Toyo Bunko: Tokyo 1944. pp.xix.402.2. [8000.]

NELSON R. BURR, The Japanese empire. Library of congress: General reference and bibliography division: Biographical sources for foreign countries (vol.4): Washington 1945 [reissued 1946]. pp.v.114. [375.]

CATALOG of materials on Japan in western languages in the National diet library, April 1948–December 1962. pp.[vii].306.74. [2100.]*

SELECT list of material on japanese peace treaty, signed at San Francisco, September 8, 1951. Commonwealth national library: Select bibliographies: General series (no.1): Canberra 1952. ff.5. [50.]*

G[ODFREY] RAYMOND NUNN, JUNE OTSUKI and YUKIHISA SUZUKI, Books on Japan 1941–1954 in western languages in the general library of the university of Michigan. Ann Arbor 1954. ff.[ii].27. [500.]*

HYMAN KUBLIN, What shall I read on Japan? Second edition. Japan society: New York [1955]. pp.16. [100.]

— 8th edition, revised. New York [1965]. pp.18. [96.]

— An introductory guide. Tenth edition. Japan society: New York 1971. [111.]

BIBLIOGRAPHY of the humanistic studies and social relations. Higher education and science bureau: Ministry of education: [Tokyo.]*

    i. 1952. 1955. pp.[ii].146. [3000.]
    ii. 1953–1954. 1956.pp.[iii].222. [4000.]
    iii. 1955. 1957. pp.[iii].185. [3000.]
    iv. 1956. 1958. pp.[vi].207. [3500.]
    v. 1957. 1959. pp.[viii]. 197. [3500.]
    vi. 1958. 1960. pp.viii.293. [5500.]
    vii. 1959. 1961. pp.[x].233. [4000.]
    viii. 1960. 1962. pp.[x].220. [5000.]
    ix. 1961. 1963. pp.[viii].230. [5500.]
no more published.

JAPAN bibliographic annual. The latest list of old and new books on Japan in english. Japan writers society: [Tokyo].

    1956. Compiled by Katsuji Yabuki. pp.ix.378. [3600.]
    1957. pp.viii.177. [1175.]
includes an index to both volumes.

A CLASSIFIED catalogue of books on the section XVII, Japan, in the Tōyō bunko acquired during the years 1917–1956. Tokyo 1957. pp.[iii].xx.304. [5000.]

JEAN LEQUILLER and PIERRE FISTIE, Le Japon depuis 1945. Fondation nationale des sciences politiques: Centre d'étude des relations internationales: États des travaux (ser. B, no.11): 1957.pp. 890–912. [134.]

V[IKTOR] A[LEKSEEVICH] VLASOV [and others], Библиография Японии. Литература изданная в Советском Союзе на русском языке с 1917 по 1958 г. Академия наук СССР: Институт народов Азии [&c.]: Москва 1960. pp.328. [6249.]

IVAN MORRIS, Japan. National book league Reader's guides (4th ser., no.2): Cambridge 1960. pp.40. [125.]

TENG SSU-YÜ, MASUDA KENJI and KANEDA HIROMITSU, Japanese studies on Japan & the far east. A short biographical and bibliographical introduction. [Hong Kong] 1961. pp.x.486. [5000.]

BERNARD S. SILBERMAN, Japan and Korea; a critical bibliography. Tucson, Arizona 1962. pp. xiv.120. [1933.]

KIICHI MATSUDA, Catalogo dos documentos sobre o Japão existentes na Europa meridional. [1964]. pp.viii.437. [8000.]

A SELECTED list of books on Japan in western languages (1945–1960). Studies on Asia abroad (i): Information center of Asian studies: Toyo bunko: [Tokyo] 1964. pp.vi.74. [967.]

A CLASSIFIED list of books in western languages relating to Japan acquired by the K.B.S. library during the years 1935–1962. Kokusai bunka shinkokai: Tokyo 1965. pp.ix.316.124. [5294.]

VLADIMIR SERGEEVICH GRIVNIN, N. F. LESHCHENKO, M. V. SUTYAGINA, Библиография Японии. Литература, изданная в России с 1734 по 1917 г. Москва 1965. pp.379. [7897.]

K.B.S. BIBLIOGRAPHY of standard reference books for japanese studies with descriptive notes. Kokusai bunka shinkokai. Tokyo.

    1. Generalia. 1971. pp.vii.154. [277.] Revised edition.

2. Geography and travel. 1966. pp.ix.164. [284.]

3. History & biography. 1965. pp.xi.197+ xi.218+xvi.257. [1385.]

4. Religion. 1966. pp.[ix].181. [327.]

5-A. History of thought. 1965. pp.xiii.239+ xii.167. [593.]

5-B. Education. 1966. pp.[xiv]. 184. [435.]

6-A. Language. Revised edition. 1972. pp. [vii].217. [270.]

6-B. Literature. 1966–1968. pp.vii.122+xii. 249+ix.150+xiv.153+xvi.252. [1626.]

7-A. Traditional art and architecture. Revised edition. 1971. pp.xi.167. [435.]

7-B. Theatre, dance and music. 1966. pp.vii. 182. [250.]

8. Manners and customs, & folklore. 1966. pp.v.101. [243.]

9-A. Politics. 1970. pp.x.178. [565.]

9-B. Law. 1968. pp.xi.165+xiii.242. [877.]

10. Economics. 1969. pp.x.165+x.196. [963.]

CATALOG of materials on Japan in western languages in the National diet library formerly in the collections of the Ueno library 1872–1960. Tokyo [1966.] pp.vi.166. [4000.]★

C. A. VAN DEN BERG-VAN DE GEER, Japan; gids van boeken tijdschriften en documentaire gramofoonplaten aanwezig in de Biblioteek van de Technische Hogeschool te Delft. Guide of books, periodicals and documentary records in the library of the Delft technological university. Delft 1967. pp.viii.67. [306.]

A CLASSIFIED catalogue of the Ichikawa & Saito collection of the Osaka prefectural library. 1967. pp.[viii].114. [800.]

NAOMI FUKUDA, Union catalog of books on Japan in western languages. International house library: Tokyo 1967. pp.iv.543. [10,000.]★
reprinted 1968.

CATALOGUE of the Toyo bunko (the oriental library) publications. Tokyo [1968?]. pp.xxx. [286.]

[HANS-BERND GIESLER], Japan bibliographie. Deutsch-japanisches wirtschaftsbüro Hamburg-Düsseldorf [1968]. pp.42. [1050.]

FRANK J. SHULMAN, Japan and Korea. An annotated bibliography of doctoral dissertations in western languages 1877–1969. American library association: Chicago 1970. pp.xix.340. [2615.]

CLASSIFIED catalog of foreign books in the Naikaku bunko. English books. [Tokyo? 1972]. pp.3.458. [11,672.]

NIPPONALIA: books on Japan in european languages in the library of Kyoto university of foreign studies. Kyoto gaikokugo daigaku: Kyoto 1972. pp.xlvi.326. [2584.]

iii. *Periodicals*

LIST of foreign periodicals received at the Kyoto imperial university. [Kyoto] 1909. pp.[ii].34.

[M. G. HAGUENAUER], Bibliographie des principales publications éditées dans l'Empire japonais. [Maison franco-japonaise: Bulletin: série française (vol.iii, no.3–4):] Tokyo 1931. pp.[ix].iii. 250. [459.]
many pages are blank.
— — Supplément no.I. 1932. pp.[iv].28. [40.]
— — Supplément no.II. 1933. pp.[v].42. [101.]
printed on one side of the leaf.
— — Supplément no.3. [By Takuzō Obasa].... (vol.vi,no.4): 1934. pp.[ii].vi.203. [600.]

YÜ SHIH-YÜ, A bibliography of orientological contributions in thirty-eight japanese periodicals, with indices. Harvard-Yenching institute sinological index series (suppl.no.6): Peiping 1933. pp.343. [large number.]

CATALOGUE of periodicals written in european languages and published in Japan. Kokusai bunka shinkōkai: [Tokyo] 1936. pp.[v].51. [275.]

JAPANESE periodicals containing electrical papers. Science library: Bibliographical series (no.241): 1936. single sheet. [17.]★

YÜ SHIH-YÜ and LIU HSÜAN-MIN, A bibliography of orientological contributions in one hundred and seventy-five japanese periodicals, with indices, in Harvard-Yenching institute sinological index series (suppl.no.13): Peiping 1940. pp.xliv. pp.6. 198.131.125.35. [large number.]

BIBLIOGRAPHIE des principales publications périodiques de l'Empire japonais. Maison franco-japonaise: Bulletin (vol.xii, nos.2–4): 1941. pp. [ii].vi.375. [1000.]

[HANS ECKARDT], Bibliographischer katalog ausgewählter japanischer zeitschriften. Deutsches forschungsinstitut: Kyoto 1942. pp.[xi].409. [1300.]

BASIC data on all established japanese newspapers and magazines receiving official paper rations. Revised edition. SCAP [Supreme commander for the allied powers]: Civil information and education section: [Tokyo 1949]. pp.iii.226. [2000.]

A LIST of scientific periodicals from japanese learned organizations. [Mombushō: Daigaku gakujutsukyoku]: Tokyo 1949. pp.[iii].58. [1158.]★
reproduced from handwriting.

LIST of scientific periodicals published in Japan. No.1. Association for science documents information: Meguroku 1953. pp.[ii].14. [800.]★

DIRECTORY of japanese learned periodicals. National diet library: [Tokyo 1953]. pp.vii.220. [994.]
— [another edition]. 1958. pp.[132]. [1500.]*

BIBLIOGRAPHICAL list of japanese learned journals. Humanities and social sciences. Ministry of education: Bureau of higher education and science: Science information section: Tokyo.*
    i. 1956. pp.[vi].3.35. [300.]
    ii. 1959. pp.xvi.347. [2000.]
in progress?

BIBLIOGRAPHICAL list of japanese learned journals, natural sciences. Department of education: Higher education and science bureau: Tokyo 1957 &c.

JION KONDŌ, 日本医・歯・薬学雑誌総覧 近藤慈恩編著 東京大学書房 Union catalogue of medical, dental and pharmaceutical periodicals in Japan. 1958. pp.[ii].4.3.2. 2.503. [3680.]

I. I. MORRIS, PAUL C. BLUM, The transactions of the Asiatic society of Japan. Comprehensive index. A classified list, followed by author and subject indexes, of papers appearing in the Transactions of the Asiatic society of Japan, 1872–1957. Transactions of the Asiatic society of Japan (3rd series, vol.6): Tokyo 1958. pp.vii.96. [538.]

GEORGE S[CHLEGEL] BONN, Japanese journals in science and technology. An annotated checklist. Public library: New York 1960. pp.xv.119. [660.]

[PETER B. SCHROEDER], Japanese serial publications in the National agricultural library. Department of agriculture: National agriculture library: Library list (no.72): Washington 1962. pp.iii.172. [1118.]*

ROBERT M. SPAULDING, *jr.*, Bibliography of western-language dailies & weeklies in Japan, 1861–1961. ff.21. [175.]*

DIRECTORY of japanese scientific periodicals, 1962. Natural sciences, medical sciences and industry. National diet library: Tokyo 1962. pp.229.

JAPANESE scientific and technical serial publications in the collections of the Library of Congress. Washington 1962. pp.v.247. [1500.]*

BIBLIOGRAPHY of social science periodicals and monograph series: Japan 1950–1953, by Foreign demographic analysis division, Bureau of the census. Foreign social science bibliographies (series P-92, no.20). [Washington, D.C. 1965.] pp.iv.346. [2112.]

DIRECTORY of japanese scientific periodicals 1967. National diet library: Tokyo [1967]. pp.xii.660. [4929.]

[KOZEN TACHIBANA, *ed.*,] A catalogue of the periodicals in foreign languages in the Toyo bunko acquired during the years 1917–1966. Tokyo 1967. pp.[viii].135. [2000.]

SIGRID M. MANDAHL and PETER W. CARNELL, Check-list of japanese periodicals held in british university and research libraries. Sheffield university library 1968. pp.iv.65+iv.96. [2449.]*

YASUMASA KURODA, A guide to social and behavioral science journals in Japan. Occasional papers of research publications and translations: Annotated bibliography series: Translation series: East-west center: [Honolulu] 1969. ff.v.157. [880.]*

INDICE dei periodici in lingua cinese e giapponese. Biblioteca nazionale centrale: Roma 1973. ff.[v]. pp.184. [1500.]*

iv. *History*

SELECT list of references on the political history of Japan. Library of Congress: Washington 1907. ff.5. [26.]*

JAPANESE HISTORY. Public library: Far eastern book and journal lists (no.3): Newark, N.J. [1921]. single leaf. [12.]
— [another edition]. ... (no.31): single leaf. [17.]

BIBLIOGRAPHIE japonaise concernant l'histoire nationale. Suivie d'une liste des principaux ouvrages parus &c. Commission nationale de coopération intellectuelle du Japon: [Tokyo].
    1924–1926. pp.28. [139.]
    1927–1929. pp.20. [71.]
the titles are given in japanese and french.

F. JOUÖN DES LONGRAIS, L'Âge de Kamakura. Sources (1150–1333). Tome III. Archives. Tokyo &c. 1950. pp.xxiv.451. [1500.]

JOHN W[HITNEY] HALL, Japanese history. A guide to japanese reference and research materials. University of Michigan: Center for japanese studies: Bibliographical series (no.4): Ann Arbor 1954. pp.xi.165. [1551.]*

CECIL H. UYEHARA, Checklist of archives in the japanese ministry of foreign affairs, Tokyo, Japan, 1868–1945 microfilmed for the library of congress 1949–1951. Washington 1954. pp.xii. 262. [3700.]

HISTORICAL documents relating to Japan in foreign countries: an inventory of microfilm acquisitions in the library of the Historiographical institute (Shiryo Hensan-jo), the university of Tokyo: Tokyo. [large number.]

    i–v. The Netherlands. 1963–1966. pp.xix. 252 + xiv.233 + xiii.252 + xv.359 + xiv. 90+xiv.90.

vi–viii. The United Kingdom. 1966–1967. pp.xxiii.198 + xviii.416 + xviii.474.

ix–x. The United States of America. 1968. pp.xxxvi.490 + xxv.412.

xi. Switzerland, German democratic republic, Federal republic of Germany, Sweden. 1968. pp.xxiv.182.

xii. The Vatican city, Italy, Portugal, Spain, the united Mexican states. 1969. pp.xxxvi. 271. ff.5.

xiii. France. 1965. pp.xv.96.

xiv. Australia, India, the republic of Indonesia. With addenda to the United Kingdom & France. 1969. pp.xx.142. xxxviii. ff.2.

1263 reels, 720,536 exposures.

READINGS on the modernization of Japan: a selected bibliography. Ministry of foreign affairs: Japan reference series (no.7–68): [Tokyo] 1968. pp.22. [206.]

INDEX for japanese history; a guide to reference and research materials. School of oriental studies: Canberra university college. pp.33.

ALLIED occupation of Japan 1945–1952; an annotated bibliography of western language materials. 1974.

v. *Cartography*

GEORGE H[ARRY] BEANS, A list of japanese maps of the Tokugawa era. Tall tree library: Publication (no.23): Jenkintown [Pa.] 1951. pp.[v].51. [500.]
—— Supplement A. ... (no.24): 1955. pp.[vii].53. [400.]
—— Supplement B. ... (no.25): 1958. pp.[v].67. [500.]
100–150 copies printed.

vi. *Foreign relations*

CHARLES H. HUNT and WILLIAM T. MONTGOMERY, Russo-japanese war. Some interesting publications relating to the peoples and countries mainly concerned. Free library and museum: Bootle 1904. pp.6.

JAMES A[LEXANDER] ROBERTSON, Bibliography of early spanish japanese relations. Compiled from manuscripts and books in the Philippine library, Manila. Asiatic society of Japan: Transactions (vol.xliii, part 1): [Tokyo] 1915. pp.[iv]. iv.170. [250.]

DOROTHY PURVIANCE MILLER, Japanese-american relations. A list of works in the New York public library. New York 1921. pp.67. [2500.]

THE UNITED STATES and Japan. Selected references to books and periodicals. Public library:

Brief reading lists (no.22): Boston 1921. pp.[iv]. 20. [250.]

JAPAN's foreign relations. Public library: Far eastern book and journal lists (no.34): Newark, N.J. [1922]. single leaf. [24.]

[SHIGETOMO KODA]. A short list of books and pamphlets relating to the european intercourse with Japan. Hibiya library: Tokyo 1930. pp.[iii]. 32. [1000.]

ROB[ERT] STREIT and JOHANNES DINDINGER, Bibliotheca missionum. Sechster band. Missionsliteratur Indiens, der Philippinen, Japans und Indochinas 1700–1799. Internationales institut für missionswissenschaftliche forschung: Aachen 1931. pp.32.616. [2005.]
reprinted 1964.

—— Zehnter band. Missionsliteratur Japans und Koreas 1800–1909. 1938. pp.32.565. [1475.]

JAPAN's foreign policy. Library of Congress: Washington 1933. ff.6. [78.]*

HELEN F[IELD] CONOVER, Japan — economic development and foreign policy. A selected list of references. Compiled ... under the direction of Florence S[elma] Hellman. Library of Congress: Division of bibliography: Washington 1940. pp. 36. [403.]*

V[LADIMIR VASILEVICH] LUCHININ, Русско-японская война, 1904–1905 гг. Библиографический указатель книжной литературы на русском и иностранных языках. Государственная библиотека СССР: Военный отдел: Москва 1940. pp.144. [1218.]

BACKGROUND bibliography on Japan and the far east. Library of Congress: Washington 1946. ff.31. [352.]*

SELECT list of material on japanese peace treaty, signed at San Francisco, September 8, 1951. Commonwealth national library: Select bibliographies: General series: Canberra 1952. ff.5. [50.]*

CECIL H. UYEHARA, Checklist of archives in the japanese ministry of foreign affairs, Tokyo, Japan, 1868–1945, microfilmed for the Library of Congress, 1949–1951. Washington 1954. pp.xii.262. [large number.]

FREDERICK W. MOTE, Japanese-sponsored governments in China, 1937–1945. An annotated bibliography compiled from materials in the chinese collection of the Hoover library. Hoover institute and library: Bibliographical series (vol. iii): Stanford 1954. pp.viii.68. [383.]*

[WOLFGANG and ELISABETH BICHMANN], Deutsche Japan-bibliographie 1945–1953. Asien-bücherei: Frankenau/Hessen 1954. ff.[ii].35. [315.]*

ANDREW C. NAHM [CH'ANG-U NAM], Japanese penetration of Korea, 1894–1910. A checklist of japanese archives in the Hoover institution. Hoover institution on war, revolution and peace: Bibliographical series (no.5): [Stanford] 1959. pp.v.103. [large number.]*

TENG SSU-YÜ, MASUDA KENJI and KANEDA HIROMITSU, Japanese studies on Japan & the far east. A short biographical and bibliographical introduction. [Hong Kong] 1961. pp.x.486. [5000.]

BERNARD S. SILBERMAN, Japan and Korea. A critical bibliography. Tucson 1962. pp.xiv.122. [1933.]

vii. *Japanese in other countries*

BRIEF list of references on the Japanese in Mexico. Library of Congress: Washington 1914. single leaf. [5.]*

LIST of references on Japanese in America. Library of Congress: Washington 1916. ff.16. [244.]*
— [another edition]. 1920. ff.26. [358.]*
— — Supplement. 1924. ff.10. [131.]*

BIBLIOGRAPHY of Japanese in America. War relocation authority: [Washington 1942].*
  i. Periodical articles, January 1941–November 1942. ff.13. [200.]
  ii. Books and pamphlets, 1937–1942. pp.[ii]. 6. [125.]

HELEN [GERTRUDE] DUBENBOSTEL JONES, Japanese in the United States. A selected list of references. Library of Congress: General reference and bibliography division: Washington 1946. ff.iv.36. [268.]*

EDWARD N. BARNHART, Japanese american evacuation and resettlement. Catalog of material in the general library. University of California: Berkeley 1958. pp.[ii].xxxii.177. [2000.]

BIBLIOGRAPHY on War relocation authority, Japanese and japanese-Americans. War relocation authority: Washington.*
  i. 1942–1943. pp.[37]. [600.]
  ii. 1942–1943. pp.[ii].38. [500.]
  iii. 1942–1943. pp.[ii].32. [350.]
  iv. 1943–1944. pp.[37]. [400.]

viii. *Official publications*

KANCHŌ kankō tosho mokuroku. Naikaku insatsu-kyoku. Tokyo 1927–1937.
[*continued as:*]

Kanchō kankō tosho geppō. 1938–1943.
Kanchō banko-butsu sōgō mokuroku. Shibu toshokan bu: Tokyo 1952. pp.650.
covers the period 1945–1950.

LIST of japanese government publications in european languages. Revised and enlarged edition. National diet library: Tokyo 1959. pp.82.

viiia. *Social life and topography*

SELECT list of references on Japan: social life and customs. Library of Congress: Washington 1905. ff.4. [22.]*

TRAVEL and social life in Japan. Public library: Far eastern book and journal lists (no.4): Newark, N.J. [1921]. single leaf. [23.]

TRAVEL in Japan. Public library: Far eastern book and journal lists (no.32): Newark, N.J. [1922]. single leaf. [15.]

SOCIAL, industrial and political life of Japan. Public library: Far eastern book and journal lists (no.33): Newark, N.J. [1922]. single leaf. [17.]

ROBERT B[URNETT] HALL and TOSHIO NOH, Japanese geography. A guide to japanese reference and research materials. University of Michigan: Center for japanese studies: Bibliographical series (no.6): Ann Arbor 1956. pp.x.128. [1254.]*

MASATO MATSUI, KATSUMI SHIMANAKA, Research resources on Hokkaido, Sakhalin and the Kuriles at the East west center library. Occasional paper (no.9): Honolulu 1967. pp.vii.266. [1.] [1978.]*

ROBERT B[URNETT] HALL and TOSHIO NOH, Japanese geography; a guide to Japanese reference and research materials. Revised edition. Ann Arbor 1970. pp.iii.233. [1486.]*
first published in 1956.

ix. *Other subjects*

Academic writings

DOCTORAL dissertations on Japan, accepted by american universities, 1912–1939. Japan institute: New York 1940. ff.vii.17. [89.]*

Aeronautics

TECHNICAL report. Catalog of aeronautical and allied technical documents. . . . Selective listing of captured german and japanese material [vols.iii–vi: Desk catalog of german and japanese air-technical documents]. Headquarters air material command: Wright field, O. 1947–1948. pp.[ii].iii.634 + [viii].846 + [vi].919 + [vi].717 + [vi].692 + [vi]. 879. [45,000.]*

Ainus

MARTIN GUSINDE and CHIYE SANO, An annotated bibliography of ainu studies by japanese scholars. Nanzan university: Collectanea universitatis catholicae Nanzan (3rd ser.): Nagoya 1962. pp.[v]. ix.109. [349.]

Anthropology

RENÉ SIEFFERT, Études d'ethnographie japonaise. Maison franco-japonaise: Bulletin (n.s.ii): Tōkyō 1953. pp.[i].203. [378.]

[SEIICHI IZUMI], Cultural anthropology in Japan. Committee for the publication of cultural anthropological studies in Japan. Tokyo 1967. pp. 6.112. [587.]
titles are given in english and japanese.

RICHARD K. BEARDSLEY, NAKANO TAKASHI, Japanese sociology and social anthropology: a guide to japanese reference and research materials. Center for japanese studies: bibliographical series (no.10). Ann Arbor 1970. pp.viii.258. [4500.]*

Architecture

BRIEF list of references on japanese and chinese architecture. Library of congress: Washington 1925. ff.4. [44.]*

Art

[EDWARD FAIRBROTHER STRANGE], Japanese art. I. Japanese books and albums of prints in colour. [II. Books relating to japanese art] in the National art library. 1893. pp.94+39. [1000.]

JAPANESE art. Public library: Far eastern book and journal lists (no.5): Newark, N.J. [1921]. single leaf. [19.]

BRIEF list of references on japanese art. Library of Congress: Washington 1922. ff.5. [51.]*

Biography

NELSON R. BURR, Biographical sources for foreign countries. IV. The Japanese empire. Library of Congress: General reference and bibliography division: Washington 1945. pp.[ii].v.114. [375.*]

Botany

HARVEY HARRIS BARTLETT and HIDE SHOHARA, Japanese botany during the period of wood-block printing. . . . An exhibition of japanese books & manuscripts, mostly botanical, held at the Clements library [Ann Arbor]. Los Angeles 1961. pp.vi.271. [112.]

Buddhism

BANDŌ SHŌJUN [and others], A bibliography on japanese buddhism. Tokyo 1958. pp.xiii.181. [1660.]

PIERRE BEAUTRIX, Bibliographie du bouddhisme zen. Institut belge des hautes études bouddhiques: série "bibliographies" (no.1): Bruxelles [1969]. ff.iv.2–114. [746.]*

Communism

PAUL F[RITZ] LANGER and A. RODGER SWEARINGEN, Japanese communism. An annotated bibliography of works in the japanese language . . . 1951–52. Institute of Pacific relations: New York 1953. pp.xii.95. [242.]*

CECIL H. UYEHARA, Leftwing social movements in Japan. An annotated bibliography. Tufts university: Fletcher school of law and diplomacy: Tokyo &c. [1959]. pp.444. [2000.]

Drama and stage

LIST of references on japanese pantomimes. Library of Congress: Washington 1915. ff.2.[13.]*

SHIO SAKANISHI, MARION H[ELEN] HADDINGTON and P[ERCIVAL] D[ENSMORE] PERKINS, A list of translations of japanese drama into english, french, and german. American council of learned societies: Washington 1935. pp.viii.89. [550.]*

RENÉ SIEFFERT, Bibliographie du théâtre japonais. Maison franco-japonaise: Bulletin (no.iii): Tōkyō 1954. pp.[iii].154. [700.]

Economics

A LIST of periodicals and yearbooks dealing with the economic problems of Japan. Japan institute: New York 1941. ff.[iii].25. [150.]*

CHARLES F[REDERICK] REMER and SABURO KAWAI, Japanese economics. A guide to japanese reference and research materials. University of Michigan: Center for japanese studies: Bibliographical series (no.5): Ann Arbor 1956. pp.xi.91. [1191.]*

HENRY ROSOVSKY, HARRY NISHIO and KONOSUKE ODAKA, Quantitative japanese economic history. An annotated bibliography and a survey of U.S. holdings. University of California: Center for japanese studies [&c.]: [Berkeley 1961]. pp.[ii]. viii.173. [476.]*

BIBLIOGRAPHY on economic planning, with special reference to long-term project. [National diet library: Tokyo 1963.] pp.xiv.208. [3500.]
— supplement 1967. pp.xvii.102. [1500.]

RYUTARO KOMIYA, A bibliography of studies in english on the japanese economy. Research institute for the japanese economy: faculty of economics, university of Tokyo (Research materials series, no.3): Tokyo 1966. pp.52. [554.]

JAPANESE annual bibliography of economics. Third division, Japan science council: Tokyo.*

    i. 1967. 1971. pp.27. [800.]
    ii. 1968. 1971. pp.30. [900.]
    iii. 1969. 1972. pp.30. [900.]
    iv. 1970. 1973. pp.39. [1000.]

Education

BRIEF list of references on japanese schools and colleges. Library of Congress: Washington 1923. ff.2. [18.]*

WALTER CROSBY EELLS, The literature of japanese education 1945–1954. Hamden, Conn. 1955. pp. viii.210. [1428.]*

RYOJI ITO, L'éducation au Japon. Unesco: Revue analytique de l'éducation (vol.viii, no.4): 1956. pp.13. [50.]

HERBERT PASSIN, Japanese education: guide to a bibliography of materials in the english language. East asian institute: School of international affairs: Columbia university: [New York] 1965. pp.81–101. [466.]
reprinted from Comparative education review (vol.9, no.1, February 1965).

Engineering

P[ENELOPE] C. R. MASON, A classified directory of japanese periodicals: engineering and industrial chemistry. Aslib: London 1972. pp.160. [1580.]*

Fishing

EDWARD NORBECK and KATSUNORI SAKURADA, A romanized bibliography of publications in japanese on japanese fishing communities.[Salt Lake City] 1954. ff.[ii].23. [227.]*

Forestry

S. KURATA [and others], A bibliography of forest botany in Japan (1940–1963). Tokyo 1966. pp.xiii. 146. [4500.]

Geology

LIST of publications of the Imperial geological survey of Japan (1880–1932). Tokyo 1932. pp.[ii]. 2.2.58. [750.]
— (1880–1952). 1952. pp.[ii].124. [1000.]

Hearn, Lafcadio

MARTHY HOWARD SISSON, Lafcadio Hearn. A bibliography. Bulletin of bibliography pamphlets (no.29): Boston 1933. pp.30. [450.]

P[ERCIVAL] D[ENSMORE] and IONE PERKINS, Lafcadio Hearn. A bibliography of his writing. Boston &c. 1934. pp.xix.444. [2500.]
200 copies printed.

WILLIAM TARG, Lafcadio Hearn: first editions and values. Chicago 1935. pp.52. [83.]

Illustrated books

A GUIDE to the chinese and japanese illustrated books exhibited in the King's library. British museum: 1887. pp.16. [100.]

[EDWARD FAIRBROTHER STRANGE], Japanese art. I. Japanese books and albums of prints in colour in the National art library: South Kensington. 1893. pp.94. [750.]

THÉODORE DURET, Livres & albums illustrés du Japon. Bibliothèque nationale: Département des estampes: 1900. pp.[iii].322. [581.]

KENJI TODA, Descriptive catalogue of japanese and chinese illustrated books in the Ryerson library of the Art institute of Chicago. [Chicago 1931.] pp.xxxiii.466.
— Supplement: Index of the titles in chinese and japanese characters and errata. pp.xv. — Addenda. pp.3. [1057.]

YUTAKA SHIMIZU, Nara picture books. Translated by Richard Zumwinkle. Los Angeles 1960. pp.46. [160.]

C. H. MITCHELL and OSAMA UEDA, The illustrated books of the Nanga, Maruyama, Shijo and other related schools of Japan; a bibliography. Los Angeles 1972. pp.623. [1200.]*

Inventions

INDEX to classification of patents of invention, nos.1–45, 570, 1885–1923, with classification scheme and numerical list. Patent office: Tokyo 1924. pp.282. [45,570.]

Labour

SOURCES of information on labor in Japan. Bureau of labor statistics. U.S. Department of labor.

Law

BIBLIOGRAPHY of the studies on law and politics (1952). Higher education and science bureau: Ministry of education: [Tokyo] 1955. pp.83. [985.]*

REX COLEMAN, An index to japanese law 1867–1961: preliminary draft of all books, pamphlets, articles, essays, statutes, case and other legal materials concerning japanese law in the english language. Harvard law school: Cambridge, Mass. [1964]. pp.181.

YASUHEI TANIGUCHI, Bibliography of books and articles on japanese administration of justice and civil procedure in western languages. Kyoto 1971. ff.19. [164.]★

Medicine

CURRENT list of japanese medical journals. Army medical library: [Washington 1949]. ff.11. [150.]★

JAPAN science review. Medical sciences Abstracts. Edited by Science council of Japan & Ministry of education, Japan. Tokyo.
    i. 1953. pp.[iii].564. [1128.]
    ii. 1954. pp.[iii].446. [892.]
    iii. 1955. pp.[iii].378. [756.]
    iv. 1956. pp.[iii].354. [708.]
    this publication was merged into that set out next below.

JAPAN science review. Medical sciences. Bibliography. Edited by Science council of Japan & Ministry of education, Japan. Tokyo.
    i. 1953. pp.[viii].263. [4107.]
    ii. 1954. pp.[viii].453. [6963.]
    iii. 1955. pp.[viii].682. [11,259.]
    iv. 1956. pp.[iii].733. [12,226.]
    v. 1957. pp.[viii].849. [11,065.]
    vi. 1958. pp.[ix].502+[xi].494. [12,105.]
    vii. 1959. pp.[xi].402+[xi].416+[xi].394. [14,383.]
    viii. 1960–1961. pp.[xix].486+[xv].395+[xix].370+[xix].425. [18,313.]★
    ix. 1961–1962. pp.[xv].449+[xvii].339+[xvii].326+[xv].353. [14,918.]★
    x. 1962–1963. pp.[xvii].325+[xvii].300+[xvii].259+[xvii].262. [10,657.]★
    xi. 1963. pp.[xiii].273+[xiii].302+[xiii].249+[xiii].253. [10,122.]
    xii. 1964. pp.[xiii].230+[xiii].267+[xiii].230+[xiii].229. [8248.]
    xiii. 1965. pp.[xi].189+[xi].239. [3595.]
    no more published.

JION KONDŌ, 日本医·歯·薬学雑誌総覧 近藤慈恩編著 東京 大学書房 Union catalogue of medical, dental and pharmaceutical periodicals in Japan. 1958. pp.[ii].ii.4.3.2. 2.503. [3680.]

Music

LIST of references on japanese music. Library of Congress: Washington [?1905]. ff.3. [15.]★

CATALOGUE of the W. H. Cummings' collection in the Nanki music library. [Tokyo] 1925. pp.[iii].iv.70. [500.]
covers the period 1600–1800.

LIST of acquisition [*sic*]. Musashino college of music: Library: Tokyo.★
    i. 1957–1958. pp.[iii].43. [750.]
    ii. [1958–1959]. pp.[iv].91. [1250.]
    iii. 1959–1960. pp.[iv].113. [1500.]
    iv. 1960–1961. pp.[iv].119. [1500.]
    v. 1961–1962. pp.[iv].193. [2000.]
    vi. 1962–1963. pp.[iv].151. [1750.]
    vii–xii.
    xiii. 1969–1970. pp.[iv].173. [2600.]
    xiv. 1970–1971. pp.[iv].169. [2500.]
    xv. 1971–1972. pp.[iv].102. [1500.]
    in progress.

LITTERAE rarae liber primus. Musashino academia musicae: Biblioteca: Tokio 1962. pp.[v].142. [600.]

Navy

BRIEF list of references on the navy of Japan. Library of Congress: Washington 1918. ff.2. [18.]★

Philosophy

DONALD HOLZMAN [*and others*], Japanese religion and philosophy. A guide to japanese reference and research materials. University of Michigan: Center for japanese studies: Bibliographical series (no.7): Ann Arbor 1959. pp.x.102. [992.]★

Political science

PUBLICATIONS of political science in Japan. Edited by the Japanese political science association. Tokyo.
    1.
    2. 1966 (1967). pp.93. [542.]
    3. 1967 (1968). pp.94. [668.]
    4. 1968 (1970). pp.109. [651.]
    5. 1969 (1970). pp.92 [+errata slip]. [647.]
    6. 1970 (1971). pp.102. [650.]

Population

[KENTARO NOMURA], Literature on population problems in Japan (1945–1951). Japanese national commission for Unesco [&c.]: [*s.l.*] 1952.pp.[vii]. 67.20. [1250.]

Printing

[SIR] ERNEST MASON SATOW, The Jesuit mission press in Japan, 1591–1610. 1888. pp.vii.54. [14.] *privately printed.*

Religion. See also Buddhism, Shinto

JOHANNES LAURES, Kirishitan bunko: a manual of books and documents on the early christian mission in Japan, with special reference to the principal libraries in Japan, and more particularly to the collection at Sophia university, Tokyo. With an appendix of ancient maps of the far east, especially Japan. Third, revised & enlarged edition. Monumenta nipponica monographs (no. 5): Sophia university: Tokyo 1957. pp.xxiv.537. [1507.]

DONALD HOLZMAN [and others], Japanese religion and philosophy. A guide to japanese reference and research materials. University of Michigan: Center for japanese studies: Bibliographical series (no.7): Ann Arbor 1959. pp.x.102. [992.]*

ARIMICHI EBISAWA, Christianity in Japan: a bibliography of japanese and chinese sources. Committee on asian cultural studies: International christian university: Tokyo.

i. 1543–1858. 1960. pp.xxvii.171. [3648.]

FUJIO IKADO and JAMES R. MCGOVERN, A bibliography of christianity in Japan: protestantism in english sources 1859–1959. Committee on asian cultural studies: International christian university: Tokyo 1966. pp.xvii.125. [1000.]

H. BYRON EARHART, The new religions of Japan: a bibliography of western-language materials. Monumenta nipponica monograph: Tokyo [1970]. pp.xi.96. [810.]

Science

CATALOGUE of scientific periodicals in the College of agriculture, Kyoto imperial university. Kyoto 1935. pp.[vi].140. [1394.]

CATALOGUE of the scientific periodicals and allied serials in the Osaka imperial university. Osaka imperial university: Library: Bibliographical series (no.1): Osaka [1937]. pp.[iv].115. [2300.]

CATALOGUE of foreign scientific serial publications in the various Institutions in Japan. Third edition. National research council: Tokyo 1938. pp.[iii].viii.25.827. [12,500.]

A LIST of scientific periodicals from japanese learned organizations. [Mombushō: Daigaku gakujutsukyoku]: Tokyo 1949. pp.[iii].58. [1158.]*
reproduced from handwriting.

LIST of scientific periodicals published in Japan. No.1. Association for science documents information: Meguroku 1953. pp.[ii].14. [800.]*

BIBLIOGRAPHICAL list of japanese learned journals, natural sciences. Department of education: Higher education and science bureau: Tokyo 1957 &c.

GEORGE S[CHLEGEL] BONN, Japanese journals in science and technology. An annotated checklist. Public library: New York 1960. pp.xv.119. [660.]

JOURNALS in science and technology published in Japan and mainland China. A selected list.

Library of Congress: Science and technology division: Washington 1961. pp.iii.47. [400.]*

JAPANESE scientific and technical serial publications in the collections of the Library of Congress: Washington 1962. pp.v.247. [1500.]*

DIRECTORY of japanese scientific periodicals, 1962. Natural sciences, medical sciences and industry. National diet library: Tokyo 1962. pp.229.

DIRECTORY of japanese scientific periodicals. National diet library: Tokyo 1967. pp.xii.660. [4929.]

Shimazaki, Toson

V. S. GRIVNIN, Симадзаки-Тосон. Всесоюзная государственная библиотека иностранной литературы: Писатели зарубежных стран: Москва 1957. pp.40. [256.]

Shinto

GENCH KATŌ, 神道書籍目錄 加藤玄智編 A bibliography of Shintō ... from the oldest times till Kei-ō 4 (1868). [1938]. pp.8.7.2.646.2.

KARL REITZ, Die angaben des Engishiki zum Ainihi no Matsuri. Bibliographie ausländischer shintoforschung. Tokyo 1946. pp.3–144. [304.]

GENCH KATŌ, 明治・大正・昭和神道書籍目錄(自明治元年至昭和 年) A bibliography of Shinto ... from Meiji 1 (1868) till Showa 15 (1940). [1953]. pp.8.2.8.707.2.

GENCHI KATŌ, KARL REITZ and WILHELM SCHIFFER, A bibliography of Shinto in western languages, Tokyo 1953. pp.[xi].58.7. [1218.]

JEAN HERBERT, Bibliographie du shintô et des sectes shintôîstes. Leiden 1968. pp.72. [1182.]

Sinkiang

T[UNG-] L[I] YUAN and H. WATANABE, Classified bibliography of japanese books and articles concerning Sinkiang. Tokyo 1962. pp.[vii].92. [1166.]

Sinology

KYŪSHIRŌ NAKAYAMA. Sinological researches in contemporary Japan.

Technology

GEORGE S[CHLEGEL] BONN, Japanese journals in science and technology. An annotated checklist. Public library: New York 1960. pp.xv.119. [660.]

JAPANESE scientific and technical serial publications in the collections of the Library of Congress. Washington 1962. pp.v.247. [1500.]★

Trade

REFERENCES on the industrial development of Japan (with special reference to trusts and monopolies). Library of Congress: Washington 1915. ff.4. [48.]★

FLORENCE S[ELMA] HELLMAN, The Japanese empire: industries and transportation. A selected list of references. Library of Congress: [Washington] 1943 [on cover: 1945]. pp.56. [598.]★

REPORTS on german and japanese industry. Classified list. Stationery office: 1945–1948.

World war II

JOHN CHARLES SHARP, In japanese hands. A list of books dealing with prisoners of war [&c.]. [Birmingham 1952]. pp.24. [200.]★
—— Complementary list.★
 [i]. 1953. pp.25–30. [50.]
 ii. [1954]. pp.31–45. [100.]
 iii. 1957. pp.46–63. [150.]

Yaoi, Hidetake

A LIST of publications by professor Hidetake Yaoi. [Tokyo] 1954. pp.[iv].42. [650.]

x. Japanese language

COUNT [CIPRIANO MUÑOZ Y MANZANO] DE LA VIÑAZA, Escritos de los Portugueses y Castellanos referentes à las lenguas de China y el Japón. Congreso international de orientalistas: Lisboa &c. 1892. pp.140. [254.]
150 copies printed.

JORDÃO A. DE FREITAS, Subsidios para a bibliographia portugueza relativa ao estudo de lingua japoneza. Coimbra 1905. pp.83. [16.]

ROBERT H[OPKINS] BROWER, A bibliography of japanese dialects. University of Michigan: Center for japanese studies: Bibliographical series (no.2): Ann Arbor 1950. pp.xi.75. [995.]★

JOSEPH K[OSHIMI] YAMAGIWA, Japanese language studies in the Shōwa period: a guide to japanese reference and research materials. University of Michigan: Center for japanese studies: Bibliographical series (no.9): Ann Arbor 1961. pp.x.153. [1473.]

JOSEPH K. YAMAGIWA, Bibliography of japanese encyclopaedias and dictionaries. Panel on far eastern language institutes of the Committee on institutional cooperation: Ann Arbor 1968. pp.ix. 139. [1092.]★

xi. Japanese Literature

PAVEL KAMENSKY and STEPAN LIPOVTSOV, Каталогъ китайскимъ и японскимъ книгамъ въ библіотекѣ Императорской академіи наукъ хранящихся ... вновь сдѣланный. [St. Petersburg, c.1815]. pp.57. [324.]

PH[ILIPP] FR[ANZ] DE [VON] SIEBOLD and J[OHANN J.] HOFFMANN, Catalogus librorum et manuscriptorum japonicorum a Ph. Fr. de Siebold collectorum, annexa enumeratione illorum, qui in Museo regio hagano servantur. Lugduni-Batavorum 1845. pp.[ii].vi.35.[xvi]. [594.]
125 copies privately printed.

BUNYIU NANJIO, A catalogue of japanese and chinese books and manuscripts lately added to the Bodleian library. Oxford 1881. pp.[iii].coll.5–28. [75.]

LÉON [LOUIS LUCIEN PRUNOL] DE ROSNY, Bibliothèque de Stockholm. Catalogue de la bibliothèque japonaise de [baron Nils Adolf Erik] Nordenskiöld. Paris 1883. pp.xxiv.359. [1000.]

[AUGUSTE LESOUËF], Catalogue des livres et manuscrits japonais collectionnés par A. Lesouëf. Leide 1887. pp.128. [208.]
100 copies privately printed.

A GUIDE to the chinese and japanese illustrated books exhibited in the King's library. British museum: 1887. pp.16. [japanese: 70.]

L[INDOR] SERRURIER, Bibliothèque japonaise. Catalogue raisonné des livres et des manuscrits japonais enregistrés à la bibliothèque de l'université. Leyde 1896. pp.xii.299. [1263.]
the title is misleading; this is a union catalogue of four Leyden libraries.

SIR ROBERT KENNAWAY DOUGLAS, Catalogue of japanese printed books and manuscripts in the British museum acquired during the years 1899–1903. 1904. pp.[iv].98. [1000.]

JAPANESE literature. Public library: Far eastern book and journal lists (no.6): Newark, N.J. [1921]. single leaf. [15.]

M. HAGUENAUER, Bibliographie des principles publications éditées dans l'Empire japonais. Maison franco-japonaise: Bulletin (sér. française, vol.iii): Tokyo 1931. pp.250. [500.]

CATALOGUE of the library of the Asiatic society of Japan. [Tokyo] 1935. pp.iv.251. [2500.]

[GÖRAN MALMQVIST and SÖREN EGEROD], Gunnar Martins samling av kinesisk och japansk litteratur. Kungl[iga] bibliotek: Stockholm 1947. ff.[110.] [282.]
reproduced from typewriting and manuscript.

JAPANESE collected works and series in the chinese-japanese library at Harvard university. Harvard-Yenching institute: Cambridge 1954. pp.32. 殊 K. [1027.]

BIBLIOGRAPHY of the humanistic studies and social relations. Department of education: Higher education and science bureau: [Tokyo].*
    i. 1952. 1955. pp.[ii]. 146. [3000.]
    ii. 1953–1954. 1956. pp.[iii].222. [4000.]
    iii. 1955. 1957. pp.[iii].185. [3000.]
    iv. 1956. 1968. pp.[vi].207. [2500.]
    v. 1957. 1959. pp.[viii].197. [3500.]
    vi. 1958. 1960. pp.viii.293. [5500.]
    vii. 1959. 1961. pp.[x].233. [4000.]
    viii. 1960. 1962. pp.[x].220. [5000.]
    ix. 1961. 1963. pp.[viii].230. [5500.]

JAPANESE literature in european languages. A bibliography complied [sic] by Japan P.E.N. club. [Tokyo 1957]. pp.iii–ix.69. [2000.]
— Another edition. 1961. pp.xii.98. [3000.]
— — Supplement. 1964. pp.v.8. [250.]

DON BROWN, Japanese literature in english 1955–56. An indexed list of new and reprinted translations. Tokyo 1957. pp.40. [250.]

RICHARD MÖNNIG, ed. Übersetzungen aus der deutschen sprache. Eine bibliographische reihe. Heft 14. Japan 1950–1956. Bonn 1959. pp.[iv].39. [1000.]

明治大正昭和翻訳文学目録
国立国会図書館編 東京 風間書房
[colophon:] List of foreign literary works done into japanese. National diet library: [Tokyo 1959]. pp.[vii].781. [25,000.]

JOSEPH K[OSHIMI] YAMAGIWA, Japanese literature of the Shōwa period: a guide to japanese reference and research materials. University of Michigan: Center for japanese studies: Bibliographical series (no.8): Ann Arbor 1959. pp.xii. 212. [7500.]*

C. OUWEHAND and S. KUSUNOKI, Rilke in Japan. Versuch einer bibliographie. 1960.

ERIC B[ERTRAND] CEADEL, Classified catalogue of modern japanese books in Cambridge university library. Cambridge [1962]. pp.xxix.558. [6000.]*

LIBRARY catalogue of the School of oriental and african studies, university of London. Japanese catalogue. Boston 1963. pp.760.*
— First supplement.
Japanese catalogue. 1968. vol.16, pp.653–718.

O[LGA] P[ETROVNA] PETROVA [vol.ii: G. D. IVANOVA] and V[LADIMIR] N[IKANOROVICH] GOREGLYAD, Описание японских рукописей, ксилографов и старопечатных книг. Академия

наук СССР: Институт народов Азии: Москва.
    1. 1963. pp.243. [166.]
    2. Филология. 1964. pp.231. [158.]
    3. Идеология. 1966. pp.173. [81.]
    4. 1969. pp.172. [112.]
    5. 1971. pp.132. [117.]

UNIVERSITY of California, Los Angeles. Dictionary catalog of the university library 1919–1962. Vols.125–127. Boston 1963.
    Vol. 127: Chinese collection A-Lim. pp.866. [18,190.]
    Vol.128: Chinese collection Lin-Z. pp.803. [16,860.]
    Vol.129: Japanese collection A-Z. Armenian Collection A-Z. pp.606.[Japanese: 11,391.]

MASATO R. MATSUI and HITOSHI INOUE, A classified catalogue of modern japanese literature (Meiji, Taisho, Showa) with periodical index in the Far eastern library, University of Washington. Seattle 1964. ff.[ii].39. [400.]

A CLASSIFIED catalogue of the Ichikawa & Saito collection of the Osaka prefectural library. Osaka 1967. pp.[viii].114. [1000.]

STANFORD University. Hoover institution on war, revolution and peace. The library catalogs of the Hoover institution on war, revolution and peace, Stanford University: catalog of the japanese collection. Boston 1969. 7 vols.

HIDE IKEHARA INADA, Bibliography of translations from the japanese into western languages from the 16th century to 1912. Sophia university: Tokyo 1971. pp.viii.112. [439.]

CLASSIFIED catalogue of pamphlets. Toyo bunko: Tokyo 1972.

YUKIO FUJINO, Modern japanese literature in western translations; a bibliography. International house of Japan library: Tokyo 1972. [4000.]

CATALOGS of the far eastern library, University of Chicago. Boston, Mass. 1973.
    Author/title catalog of the chinese collection.
    Author/title catalog of the japanese collection. [66,600 cards.]
    Classified catalog and subject index of the chinese and japanese collections. [94,700 cards.]

KOREA

    i. *Bibliography*
    ii. *General*
    iii. *Subjects*
    iv. *Korean literature*
    v. *Korean war, 1950–1953*

i. Bibliography

HESUNG CHUN KOH and JOAN STEFFENS, *edd.*, Korea; an analytical guide to bibliographies. Behaviour science bibliographies: New Haven 1971. pp.xviii.334. [500.]*

ANNOTATED bibliography of korean reference books. Compiled by Korean bibliographical center. Korean library association: Seoul 1971. pp.xiii.273. [2500.]
mostly in korean, but with a few titles in english.

BYONG-TAI YOON, A chronological table of korean bibliography to 1910. Korean library association: Seoul 1972. pp.ix.256. [5000.]

ii. General

BRIEF list of references on japanese policy in Korea. Library of Congress: [Washington] 1923. ff.4. [35.]*

HORACE H. UNDERWOOD, Occidental literature on Korea. [A partial bibliography . . . from early times to 1930]. Royal asiatic society: Korea branch: Transactions (vol.xx): Seoul 1931. pp.[v].198.xvi. [2882.]
a supplement by E. and G. StG. M. Gompertz appears in the Transactions (*1935*), *xxiv.21–48.*

ROB[ERT] STREIT and JOHANNES DINDINGER, Bibliotheca missionum. Zehnter band. Missionsliteratur Japans und Koreas 1800–1909. Internationales institut für missionswissenschaftliche forschung: Aachen 1938. pp.32.565. [1475.]

KOREA: a preliminary bibliography. Library of Congress: Washington 1950. ff.107. [632.]*

EDWIN G. BEAL, *ed.* Korea. An annotated bibliography of publications in far eastern languages. Library of Congress: Reference department: Washington 1950. pp.viii.167. [528.]*

HELEN DUDENBOSTEL JONES and ROBIN L. WINKLER, Korea. An annotated bibliography of publications in western languages. Library of Congress: Reference department: Washington 1950. pp.ix.155. [753.]*

WORKS on Korea. Columbia university: East Asiatic library: New York 1950. pp.[iii].22. [535.]*

KOREA: an annotated bibliography of publications in the russian language. Library of Congress: Washington 1950. ff.65. [436.]*

KOREA. House of commons: Library: Bibliography (no.67): [1950]. pp.11. [64.]*

ROBIN L. WINKLER, The Horace Allen manuscript collection at the New York public library. Research monographs on Korea (series H. no.1): Hamilton, N.Y., South Pasadena, Cal. 1950. pp. 12. [47.]*

ALBERT PARRY, JOHN T. DOROSH and ELIZABETH GARDNER DOROSH, Korea: an annotated bibliography of publications in the russian language. Library of congress: Reference department: Washington 1950. pp.xi.84. [436.]*

ANDOR TISZAY, Korea harca a békéért. Ajánlott müvek bibliográfiája. Fovárosi könyvtar: Bibliográfiai osztály: Budapest 1952. pp.40. [30.]

B[ENJAMIN] H. HAZARD [*and others*], Korean studies guide. University of California: Institute of east-asiatic studies: Berkeley &c. 1954. pp.xii. 220. [491.]*
— — Russian supplement . . . by Robert L. Backus. 1958. pp.xii.211. [893.]*

MIROSLAV KAFTAN, Lidově demokratické země Asie: Korea-Vietnam-Mongolsko. Vyberovy seznam literatury. Universita: Knihovna: Čteme a studujeme (1956, no.2): Praha 1956. pp.16. [100.]*

RIN PAIK [*and others*], Guide to korean reference books 1910–June 1958. Yonsei university: Library [&c.]: Seoul 1958. pp.[i].vii.92. [250.]

ANDREW C. NAHM [CH'ANG-U NAM], Japanese penetration of Korea, 1894–1910. A checklist of japanese archives in the Hoover institution. Hoover institution on war, revolution and peace: Bibliographical series (no.5): [Stanford] 1959. pp. v.103. [large number.]*

SOON HI LEE [SUN-HI YI], Korea: a selected bibliography in western languages. Catholic university of America: Washington 1959. ff.[ii]. vii.55. [500.]*

J[EFFERSON] MCREE ELROD, An index to english language periodical literature published in Korea. 1890–1940. Yonsei university: Seoul 1960. pp.v. 214. [6000.]*

KEY PAIK YANG, Reference guide to korean materials, 1945–1959. Catholic university of America: Washington 1960. ff.[ii].xii.131. [991.]*
limited to works in the Library of Congress.

BIBLIOGRAPHY of korean studies . . . 1945 to 1958. Korea university: Asiatic research center: Seoul 1961. pp.vii.410. [797.]
— 1959 to 1962. 1965. pp.vii.432. [863.]

BERNARD S. SILBERMAN, Japan and Korea. A critical bibliography. Tucson 1962. pp.xiv.122. [1933.]

G. ST. G. M. GOMPERTZ, The first sections of a revised and annotated bibliography of western literature on Korea from the earliest times until 1950. Based on Horace G. Underwood's "Partial bibliography of occidental literature on Korea". Transactions of the Korea branch of the Royal asiatic society (vol.40): Seoul 1963. pp.[iv].263. [2276.]

JEFFERSON MCREE ELROD, An index to english language newspapers published in Korea, 1896–1937. Yonsei university: Seoul 1966. pp.[vi].11.2.[64]. [2300.]

MUNAM CHON, An index to english periodical literature published in Korea, 1945–1966. Korean research center: [Seoul] 1967. ff.[ii].153. [2700.]*

SANGWOON KANG, A list of articles on Korea in the western languages 1800–1964. Seoul 1967. pp.xv.192. [5500.]
english titles only.

YOUNG ICK LEW, Korea on the eve of japanese annexation. Seoul 1967. pp.194.

WILLIAM E. HENTHORN, A guide to reference and research materials on korean history; an annotated bibliography. East-west center: Occasional papers: Annotated bibliography series: Translation series: [Honolulu] 1968. ff.iii.152. [612.]*

ARTHUR L. GARDNER, The Koreans in Hawaii; an annotated bibliography. Hawaii series (no.2): Social science research institute: University of Hawaii: Honolulu 1970. ff.v.83. [223.]*

FRANK J. SHULMAN, Japan and Korea. An annotated bibliography of doctoral dissertations in western languages 1877–1969. American library association: Chicago 1970: pp.xix.340. [2615.]

UNION catalog of books on Korea in english, french, german, russian, etc. International house of Japan library: Tokyo 1971. pp.iii.95. [1300.]*

CATALOGUE of contents of korean periodicals published in the end of Yi dynasty, 1896–1910. National assembly library: [Seoul 1967]. pp.[vii].138. [large number.]

SANGWOON KANG, A list of articles on Korea in the western languages 1800–1964. Seoul 1967. pp.15.192. [3500.]
contains articles published between 1890 and 1964 only.

AN ANNOTATED bibliography of the archives in the Central national library, Republic of Korea. [Seoul.]
I, 1. 1972. pp.[v].590. [7746.]
in korean.

iii. *Subjects*

Agriculture

[PETER BRETT SCHROEDER], Korean publications in the National agricultural library. Library list (no.79): National agricultural library: Washington 1963. pp.i.25. [189.]*

Anthropology

BERT A. GEROW, Publications in japanese on korean anthropology. A bibliography of un- catalogued material in the [Takeo] Kanaseki collection, Stanford university library. [Stanford 1952]. ff.iv.18. [225.]*

Botany

ALICE MARIA GOODE, An annotated bibliography of the flora of Korea. Catholic university of America: Washington 1955. ff.[v].65.3. [305.]*

Public administration

DONG-SUH BARK and JAI-POONG YOON, Bibliography of Korean public administration, 1945.9 — 1966.4. Graduate school of public administration: Seoul national university: Seoul 1966. pp.78. [2000.]

Science

BIBLIOGRAPHY of scientific publications of Korea. Vol.1, 1945–1965. Korea scientific and technological information center: Seoul 1966. pp.xvi.484. [10,664.]

Social sciences

BIBLIOGRAPHY of social science periodicals and monograph series: North Korea 1945–1961, by Foreign manpower research office, Bureau of the census ... Foreign social science bibliographies (series P-92, no.8): Washington 1962. pp.iv.12. [41.]*

BIBLIOGRAPHY of social science periodicals and monograph series: Republic of Korea 1945–1961. Foreign social science bibliographies (series P-92, no.8): United States bureau of the census: Washington 1962. pp.iv.48. [261.]

iv. *Korean literature*

MAURICE [AUGUSTE LOUIS MARIE] COURANT, Bibliographie coréenne. Tableau littéraire de la Corée contenant la nomenclature des ouvrages publiés dans ce pays jusqu'en 1890, ainsi que la description et l'analyse détaillées des principaux d'entre ces ouvrages. École des langues orientales vivantes: Publications (3rd ser., vols.xviii–xx): 1894–1896. pp.ccxvi.503 + x.539 + x.446.lxxviii.clxxix. [3240.]
—— Supplément ... (jusqu'en 1899). 1901. pp.x.122. [581.]

MARK NAPIER TROLLOPE, Corean books and their authors. [Short list of some korean books in the Chosen Christian college library]. [Edited by Charles Hunt]. Royal asiatic society: Korea branch: Transactions (vol.xxi): Seoul 1932. pp.[v].104. [100.]

O. P. PETROVA, Описание письменных памятников корейской культуры. Академия наук СССР: Институт востоковедения: Москва &c. 1956–63. pp.83+138. [236.]*

A CLASSIFIED catalogue of Korean books in the Harvard-Yenching institute library at Harvard university. Cambridge, Mass. 1962. ff.iii.194. [3160.]*

W[ILLIAM] E. SKILLEND, Kodae sosŏl: a survey of korean traditional style popular novels. London 1968. pp.268. [531.]

v. *Korean war, 1950–1953*

UNITED NATIONS effort against aggression in Korea: a selected list of references. Library of Congress: Washington 1952. ff.8. [71.]*

THE WAR in Korea, 1950–1953. A list of selected references. Imperial war museum: Library. [1955]. pp.9. [150.]*

MICHAEL O'QUINLIVAN, An annotated bibliography of the United States marines in the Korean war. United States marine corps: Historical branch: Marine corps historical bibliographies (no.6): Washington 1962. pp.[ii].ii.31. [287.]*

CARROLL H[ENRY] BLANCHARD, Korean war bibliography and maps of Korea. Korean conflict research foundation: [Albany 1964]. pp.iv.181. [7000.]

HONG-KYU PARK, The Korean war; an annotated bibliography. Marshall, Texas 1971. pp.iv.29. [121.]

TIBET

i. *General*
ii. *Tibetan languages and literature*

i. *General*

TIBET. Public library: Far eastern book and journal lists (nos.18–20): Newark, N.J. [1922]. ff.[3]. [51.]

HIMALAJA-bibliographie (1801–1933). Herausgegeben von der Deutschen Himalaja-expedition 1934 mit unterstützung des Vereins der freunde der alpenvereinsbücherei. München 1934. pp.48. [736.]

T. C. TSENG, Bibliography of chinese geology. Bibliography of geology and allied sciences of Tibet and regions to the west of the Chinshachiang. National geological survey of China: Nanking 1946. pp.viii.116. [1000.]

HSU GINN-TZE, A bibliography of the tibetan highland and its adjacent districts. Peking 1958. pp.vi.462. [5407.]

YOSHIMI YAKUSHI, Selected index of reports on Himalaya, Tibet and Central Asia to the Geographical journal (the Royal geographical society), vol.1 (1893) — vol.125 (1959). Kyoto 1960. pp.52. [527.]*

SIBADAS CHAUDHURI, Bibliography of tibetan studies, being a record of printed publications mainly in european languages. Asiatic society: Calcutta 1971. pp.[vii].232. [2032.]

YOSHIMI YAKUSHI, Catalogue of himalayan literature. Kyoto 1972. pp.343.

ii. *Tibetan languages and literature*

F. A. SCHIEFNER, Каталог книг и рукописей на китайском, манчжурском, монгольском, тибетском и санскритском языке в библиотеке Азиатского департемента. Санкт-Петербург 1844.

I. J. SCHMIDT and O[TTO] BÖHTLINGK, Verzeichniss der tibetischen handschriften und holzdrucke im Asiatischen museum der Kaiserlichen akademie der wissenschaften. St. Petersburg [c.1845]. pp.71. [500.]

[FREDERICK WILLIAM THOMAS], [*begins:*] The librarian ventures to represent ... the desirability ... of profiting by any opportunity ... for the extension of the collections of tibetan books in the India office library. [1904]. pp.13. [75.]
consists of lists of desiderata.

P[ALMYR ULDÉRIC ALEXIS] CORDIER, Catalogue du fonds tibétain. ... Deuxième[–Troisième] partie. Index du Bstan-Hgyur. Bibliothèque nationale: 1909–1915. pp.vii.402 + xi.562. [4000.]
no more published.

BERTHOLD LAUFER, Descriptive account of the collection of chinese, tibetan, mongol, and japanese books in the Newberry library. Chicago 1913. pp.ix.42. [1216.]

HERMANN BECKH, Verzeichniss der tibetischen handschriften. ... Erste abteilung. Königliche bibliothek: Handschriften-verzeichnisse (vol. xxiv): Berlin 1914. pp.x.192. [1500.]
no more published.

MARCELLE LALOU, Répertoire du Tanjur d'après le catalogue de P. Cordier. Bibliothèque nationale: 1933. pp.ix.243. [6500.]

JEAN FILLIOZAT, État des manuscrits sanscrits, bengalis et tibétains de la collection Palmyr [Uldéric Alexis] Cordier. Bibliothèque nationale: 1934. pp.19. [350.]

M[ARCELLE] LALOU, Inventaire des manuscrits tibétains de Touen-houang conservés à la Bibliothèque nationale (fonds Pelliot tibétain). 1939 &c.*

    i. 1939. pp.xvi.187. [849.]
    ii. 1950. pp.xv.97. [433.]
    iii. 1961. pp.xix.221. [934.]

iv.i. Les Mdo-mań. Par Marcelle Lalou. Buddhica: documents et travaux pour l'étude du bouddhisme (deuxième série: documents-tome iv). Paris 1931.

HAKIYU UI and others, *edd.*, A complete catalogue of the tibetan buddhist canons (Bkah-ḥgyur and Bstan-ḥgyur). Tohoku imperial university: Sendai 1934. ff.[iv]. pp.703.3. [4569.]
— A catalogue-index of the tibetan buddhist canons (Bkah-ḥgyur & Bstan-ḥgyur). 1934. ff.124.

R. DE NEBESKY WOJKOWITZ, Catalogue of the collections of tibetan blockprints and manuscripts in the National museum of ethnology (Rijks-museum voor volkenkunde), Leiden, Holland. Leiden 1953–5. pp.2.[ii].267.[vii]. [1578.]*

ROBERT SHAFER, *ed.* Bibliography of sino-tibetan languages. Wiesbaden 1957. pp.xi.211. [3500.]

R[ICHARD] O. MEISEZAHL, Die tibetischen hand-schriften und drucke des Linden-Museums in Stuttgart. Tribus (no.7): Stuttgart 1957. pp.vii. 166. [750.]

JOHANNES SCHUBERT, Publikationen des moder-nen chinesisch-tibetischen schrifttums. Deutsche akademie der wissenschaften zu Berlin: Institut für orientforschung: Veröffentlichung (no.39): Berlin 1958. pp.56. [77.]

B[IDIYA] D[ANDAROVICH] DANDARON, Описа-ние тибетских рукописей и ксилографов Бурятского комплексного научно-исследо-вательского института. Москва 1960. pp.72. [126.]

R[ICHARD] O. MEISEZAHL, M. HARDERS-STEIN-HÄUSER and GEORGE JAYME, Alttibetische hand-schriften der völkerkundlichen sammlungen der stadt Mannheim im Reiss-museum. Kopenhagen 1961. pp.[vii].48. [50.]

LOUIS DE LA VALLÉE POUSSIN, Catalogue of the tibetan manuscripts from Tun-huang in the India office library.... With an appendix on the Chinese manuscripts by Kazuo Enoki. 1962. pp.xviii.299. [tibetan: 765.]

R. O. MEISEZAHL, Tibetische Prajñāpāramitā-texte im Bernischen historischen museum. Sonderdruck aus der zeitschrift *Libri*, band 13, no. 3–4, 1964. Kopenhagen 1964. pp.42. [21.]

GOPI RAMAN CHOUDHARY, The catalogue of the tibetan texts in the Bihar research society, Patna. i. (Miscellaneous series). Edited by Aniruddha Jha. [1965.] pp.xvi.253. [1619.]

MANFRED TAUBE, Tibetische handschriften und blockdrucke. Verzeichnis der orientalischen handschriften in Deutschland (band xi): Wies-baden 1966. pp.xvi.374+vii.375–683+vii.685–996+vii.997–1296. [3000.]

THE CHESTER BEATTY library. A catalogue of the tibetan collection by David L. Snellgrove and a catalogue of the mongolian collection by Charles R. Bawden. Dublin 1969. pp.109. [tibetan: 160.]

JOSEF KOLMAŠ, Tibetan manuscripts and block-prints in the library of the Oriental institute, Prague. Dissertationes orientales (vol.16): Prague 1969. pp.112. [65.]

E. GENE SMITH, University of Washington tibetan catalogue (part 1): University of Washington: Seattle 1969. ff.iii.160. [350.]*

ZUIHO YAMAGUCHI, *ed.*, Catalogue of the Toyo Bunko collection of tibetan works on history. Classified catalogue of the Toyo Bunko collection of tibetan works (vol.1): Tokyo 1970. pp.xii.249. [200.]

ALAKA CHATTOPADHYAYA, MRINALKANTI GANGO-PADHYAYA and DEBIPRASAD CHATTOPADHYAYA, Catalogue of indian (buddhist) texts in tibetan translation: Kanjur & Tanjur (alphabetically arranged). Vol.1: Texts (indian titles) in Tanjur. Indo-tibetan studies: Calcutta 1972. pp.xiv.535. [5000.]
planned in three volumes.

MONGOLIA, MONGOLS

i. *General*
ii. *Mongolian literature*

i. *General*

E. N. YAKOVLEVA, Библиография Монголь-ской народной республики. Систематический указатель книг и журнальных статей на русском языке. Труды Научно-исследовательской ас-социации по изучению национальных и колониальных проблем (выпуск xviii): Мос-ква 1935. pp.230. [2422.]

БИБЛИОГРАФИЯ Бурят-Монголии за 1890–1936 гг. Бурят-Монгольский государствен-ный научно-исследовательский институт культуры и экономики: Москва &c.
i.
ii.
iii. Сельское, лесное, пушно-зверевое и рыбное хозяйство. Составии ... М. И. Помус. 1946. pp.535. [2527.]
iv. Здравоохранение. Составил В. В. Хижняков. 1940. pp.220. [977.]

KONST[ANTIN] KHRISTENKO, Указатель лите-ратуры о колмыцком народе (1728–1916 гг). Архивный отдел НКВД КалмАССР: [Stalin-grad] 1941. pp,68, [966.]

HUGO KNOEPFMACHER, Outer Mongolia. A selection of references. Public library: New York 1944. pp.13. [100.]

M. CHANG CHIH-YI, A bibliography of books and articles on Mongolia. [London] 1950. pp.49. [105.]

Reprinted from Journal of the Royal central asian society, vol.xxxvii, 1950.

V. F. TYULYAEVA, Монгольская Народная Республика. Библиография книжной и журнальной литературы на русском языке, 1935–1955 гг. Труды Монгольской комиссии (no.42): Москва 1953. pp.88. [1000.]

MIROSLAV KAFTAN, Lidově demokratické země Asie: Korea-Vietnam-Mongolsko. Výberovy seznam literatury. Universita: Knihovna: Čteme a studujeme (1956, no.2): Praha 1956. pp.16. [100.]★

BIBLIOGRAPHY of the Mongolian people's republic. Behavior science bibliographies: Far eastern and russian institute: New Haven 1956. pp.101.

V. I. SHUBINA, Бурят-Монгольская АССР. Библиографический указатель. Республиканская библиотска Бурят-Монгольской АССР: Улан-Удэ 1957. pp.97. [1250.]

R. L. BALDAEV and N. N. VASILEV, Указатель библиографий по монголоведению на русском языке, 1824–1960. Академия наук СССР: Библиотека: Ленинград 1962. pp.89. [201.]

R. L. BALDAEV and N. N. VASILEV, Библиография Монгольской Народной Республики. Книги и статьи на русском языке (1951–1961). Академия наук СССР: Институт народов Азии: Москва 1963. pp. 120. [1798.]

DENIS SINOR, Introduction à l'étude de l'Eurasie centrale. Wiesbaden 1963. pp.xxiv.371. [4403.]

ROBERT A. RUPEN, Mongols of the twentieth century. Indiana university publications: Uralic and altaic series (vol.37): Bloomington 1964. pp. xxii.510+xii.167. [2839.]

I[L'YA] I[OSIFOVICH] IORISH, Материалы о монголах, калмыках и бурятах в архивах Ленинграда. История, право, экономика. Академия наук ССР: Институт народов Азии: Москва 1966. pp.206. [589.]

Библиография работ по Монголии. Государственная публичная библиотека МПР. Улан-батор.
   i.
   ii.
   iii. 1962.

N[IMA] B[UDAEVICH] DUGAROV, Библиография литературы по бурятскому языкознанию. Академия наук СССР: Сибирское отделение: Бурятский научно-исследовательский институт: Улан-уде 1964. pp.165. [877.]★

ii. *Mongolian literature*

F. A. SCHIEFNER, Каталог книг и рукописей на китайском, манчжурском, монгольском, тибетском и санскритском языке в библиотеке Азиатского департемента. Санкт-Петербург 1844.

BERTHOLD LAUFER, Descriptive account of the collection of chinese, tibetan, mongol and japanese books in the Newberry library. Chicago 1913. pp.ix.42. [1216.]

WALTER HEISSIG, Die pekinger lamaistischen blockdrucke in mongolischer sprache. Materialien zur mongolischen literaturgeschichte. Göttinger asiatische forschungen: Monographienreihe zur geschichte, sprache und literatur der völker Süd-, Ost- und Zentralasiens (band 2): Wiesbaden 1954. pp.xv.220. [219.]

L. S. PUCHKOVSKY, Монгольские, бурят-монгольские и ойратские рукписи и ксилографы Института востоковедения. Академия наук СССР: Москва &c.
   i. История, право. 1957. pp.279. [272.]
in progress.

ПИСАТЕЛИ Советской Бурятии. Био-библиографический справочник. Улан-Удэ 1959. pp.188. [2000.]

LOUIS LIGETI, Catalogue du Kanjur mongol imprimé. Vol.I. Catalogue. Société Kőrösi Csoma: Bibliotheca orientalis hungarica (vol.iii): Budapest 1942–1944. pp.[iii].347. [1161.]

JADAMBA, Collection of mongolian manuscripts from the private library of his holiness Jebtsundamba Khutuktu in the State public library. Studia mongolica (tomus 1, fasciculus 6): Ulaanbaator 1959. pp.44. [?]
in mongolian.

WALTER HEISSIG, Mongolische handschriften, blockdrucke, landkarten. Verzeichnis der orientalischen handschriften in Deutschland: Wiesbaden 1961. pp.xxiv.494. [853.]

NICHOLAS POPPE, LEON HURVITZ, HIDEHIRO OKADA, Catalogue of the manchu-mongol section of the Toyo bunko. Tokyo, Washington 1964. pp.387. [525.]

T. RAJAPATIRANA, Index to the titles of works in the mongolian kanjur & tanjur. Part II: Mongolian titles. Department of south asian & buddhist studies: Faculty of oriental studies: Australian national university, Canberra [1969?]. pp.89. [1500.]★

THE CHESTER BEATTY library. A catalogue of the tibetan collection by David L. Snellgrove and a catalogue of the mongolian collection by Charles R. Bawden. Dublin 1969. pp.109. [mongolian: 52.]

WALTHER HEISSIG and CHARLES BAWDEN, Catalogue of mongol books, manuscripts and xylographs [in the Royal library and the National museum, Copenhagen]. Catalogue of oriental mss., xylographs, etc. in danish collections (vol.3): Copenhagen 1971. pp.li.305. [569.]

MANCHURIA, MANCHUS

i. *Bibliographies*
ii. *General*
iii. *Manchu literature*

i. *Bibliographies*

MINOROU TAGOUTCHI, Bibliographies en langue japonaise sur la Mandchourie de primaire et moyenne période de l'empire Meiji, 1868–1904. Dairen-bibliothèque: Recherches sur les bibliographies de Mandchourie et de Mongolie (no.3): Dairen 1935. pp.16.

MANCHURIA: a selected list of bibliographies. Library of Congress: Washington 1951. ff.15. [64.]★

ii. *General*

MINORU TAGUCHI, Histoire de l'étude de Mandchourie en France. Annexe: bibliographie de Mandchourie en langue française. Bibliothèque Dairen: Recherches sur les bibliographies de Mandchourie et de Mongolie (no.1): Dairen 1933. pp.24. [142.]
the preliminary text is in japanese.

WHAT to read about Manchuria. Chinese eastern railway economic bureau: Publications: Harbin 1933. pp.11. [75.]

MINOROU TAGOUTCHI, Ce qu'il faut lire de la Mandchourie en langue japonaise. Dairen-bibliothèque: Recherches sur les bibliographies de Mandchourie et de Mongolie (no.2): Dairen 1934. pp.23.

A LIST of recent references on Manchuria (with special reference to economic, financial, industrial and agricultural conditions). Library of Congress: Washington 1935. ff.12. [156.]★

JOHN L. MISH, The Manchus. A list of references in the New York public library. [New York 1947]. pp.5. [60.]

PETER A. BERTON, Manchuria. An annotated bibliography. Library of Congress: Reference department: Washington 1951. pp.xii.187. [843.]

JOHN YOUNG, The research activities of the South manchurian railway company 1907–1945. A history and bibliography. The East asian institute: Columbia university: New York 1966. pp.[x]. 682. [6284.]★

iii. *Manchu literature*

[LOUIS MATHIEU] LANGLÈS, Notice des livres tartars-mantchoux de la Bibliothèque nationale. [*s.l. c.*1820]. pp.26. [50.]

JULIUS KLAPROTH, Verzeichniss der chinesischen und mandschuischen bücher und handschriften der Königlichen bibliothek zu Berlin. Paris 1822. pp.x.188. [75.]

— — Wilhelm Schott, 御書房 "蒲" 藏書廣錄 Verzeichniss der chinesischen und mandschu-tungusischen bücher und handschriften der Königlichen bibliothek zu Berlin. Eine fortsetzung des … Klaproth'schen verzeichniss. Berlin 1840. pp.[iii].iv.120. [200.]

F. A. SCHIEFNER, Каталог книг и рукописей на китайском, манчжурском, монгольском, тибетском и санскритском языке в библиотеке Азиатского департамента. Санкт-Петербург 1844.

HERBERT A[LLEN] GILES, A catalogue of the Wade collection of chinese and manchu books in the library of the university of Cambridge. Cambridge 1898. pp.viii.169. [manchu: 87.]

WALTER FUCHS, Beiträge zur mandjurischen bibliographie und literatur. Deutsche gesellschaft für natur- und völkerkunde Ostasiens: Mitteilungen (supplementband xiv): Tōkyō 1936. pp.[vii]. 148. [500.]

LI TEH CH'I, Union catalogue of manchu books in the National library of Peiping and the library of the Palace museum. Edited by Yu Dawchyuan. [Peiping] 1933. pp.iii.126.i. [large number.]

[COLLECTION of manchu books, Tenri central library, 1955.] pp.16. [138.]
In japanese, but with a note in English.
The titles are given also in roman characters.

NICHOLAS POPPE, LEON HURVITZ, HIDEHIRO OKADA, Catalogue of the manchu-mongol section of the Toyo Bunko. Tokyo, Washington 1964. pp.387. [525.]

WALTER FUCHS, Chinesische und mandjurische handschriften und seltene drucke, nebst einer standortliste der sonstigen mandjurica. Verzeichnis der orientalischen handschriften in Deutschland (xii,1): Wiesbaden 1966. pp.xiii.160. [373.]

HONG KONG

HONG-KONG — CHINA. [Colonial office(no.29 of a series of lists of works in the library): 1860]. pp.2. [30.]

RETURN of books registered under ordinance 10 [section 6 of ordinance no.2] of 1888, during the quarter ended June 30th, 1888 [&c.]. Colonial secretary's office (*afterwards:* Secretariat for chinese affairs): Hongkong.

1888. pp.[6]. [21.]
1889. pp.[10]. [36.]
1890. pp.[12]. [55.]
1891. pp.[8]. [29.]
1892. pp.[10]. [29.]
1893. pp.[10]. [44.]
1894. pp.[13]. [63.]
1895. pp.[9]. [28.]
1896. pp.[9]. [34.]
1897. pp.[11]. [62.]
1898. pp.[14]. [80.]
1899. pp.[11]. [47.]
1900.
1901.
1902. pp.[6]. [36.]
1903. pp.[13]. [84.]
1904. pp.[11]. [59.]
1905. pp.[11]. [66.]
1906. pp.[13]. [65.]
1907. pp.[10]. [53.]
1908. pp.[11]. [56.]
1909. pp.[8]. [38.]
1910. pp.[11]. [53.]
1911. pp.[4]. [13.]
1912. pp.[8]. [40.]
1913. pp.[6]. [25.]
1914. pp.[9]. [49.]
1915. pp.[4]. [9.]
1916. pp.[9]. [52.]
1917. pp.[4]. [17.]
1918. pp.[7]. [36.]
1919. pp.[7]. [29.]
1920. pp.[8]. [35.]
1921. pp.[7]. [24.]
1922. pp.[8]. [41.]
1923. pp.2.3.3.4. [51.]
1924. pp.2.2.4.1. [38.]
1925. pp.[4]. [12.]
1926. pp.[8]. [27.]
1927. pp.1.1.4.3. [26.]
1928. pp.3.3.4.2. [47.]
1929. pp.4.2.4.3. [59.]
1930. pp.[8]. [36.]
1931. pp.2.3.1.5. [44.]
1932. pp.[6]. [21.]
1933. pp.5.3.4.1. [50.]
1934. pp.[9]. [31.]
1935. pp.1.4.2.2. [26.]
1936. pp.6.2.1.1. [43.]
1937. pp.2.6.1.3. [52.]
1938. pp.8.2.8.4. [81.]
1939. pp.6.4.6.7. [109.]
1940. pp.4.6.8.6. [92.]
1941. pp.7.3. [34.]
1946. pp.1.1.1. [12.]

1947. ff. . [61.]
1948. ff.[3].[2].13.14. [203.]
1949. ff.19.36.39.21. [808.]

MILITARY operations, World war II. Hong Kong. Imperial war museum: Library: [1954]. single leaf. [9.]★

BIBLIOGRAPHY of social science periodicals and monograph series: Hong Kong 1950–1961. By Foreign manpower research office: Bureau of the census: Foreign social science bibliographies (series P-92, no.7): Washington 1962. pp.iv.13. [45.]★

LIST of government publications. Hong Kong 1964 &c.
in progress?

J. M. BRAGA, A Hong Kong bibliography. Hong Kong 1965. pp.[iii].17. [350.]

M. I. BERKOWITZ and EDDIE K. K. POON, Hong Kong studies: a bibliography. Department of extramural studies: Chinese university of Hong Kong, 1969. pp.xvi.137. [960.]★

H. ANTHONY RYDINGS and NELLIE CHILDE, Directory of current research on asian studies in Hong Kong 1969–1970. Centre of asian studies: University of Hong Kong 1970. pp.iv.133. [800.]★

FRANK J. SHULMAN, A bibliography of western-language doctoral dissertations regarding the Canton area and Hong Kong, prepared especially for the Canton delta conference, the University of Washington. University of Michigan: Ann Arbor 1971. ff.6. [88.]★

FILM catalogue. Revised edition. Hong Kong government information services: Film library: Hong Kong 1973. pp.54.[ix]. [120.]

PAUL P. W. CHENG, An annotated guide to current chinese periodicals in Hong Kong.

RYUKYU ISLANDS

GEORGE H. KERR [*and others*], The Ryūkyū islands. A preliminary checklist of reference materials. National research council: Pacific science board: Washington 1952. ff.[i].vi.219. [2500.]★
50 copies reproduced from typewriting.

RYUKYU islands, with emphasis on the island of Okinawa: a selected list of references. Library of Congress: Washington 1952. ff.13. [111.]★

ROLF [ALBERT ALFRED] BINKENSTEIN, Beitraege zu einer kulturhistorischen bibliographie der Ryukyu (Okinawa)-inseln. [Berkeley, Cal. 1954]. ff.66. [425.]★

PHILIP M. BETTENS [*and others*], The Ryukyu islands. A reference list of books and articles in english, french and german. Hoover institute and library: [Stanford] 1954. ff.[i].ii.33. [400.]★

SHUNZO SAKAMAKI, Ryukyu. A bibliographical guide to okinawan studies, surveying important primary sources and writings in ryukyuan, japanese, chinese, 2nd korean. Honolulu 1963. pp.xv. 354. [2500.]

SHUNZO SAKAMAKI, Ryukyuan research resources at the University of Hawaii. Ryukyan research center research series (no.1): Social science research institute: University of Hawaii. Honolulu 1963. pp.vi.454. [4195.]★

NORMAN D. KING, Ryukyu islands; a bibliography. Department of the army pamphlet (550–4). [Washington] 1967. pp.iii.105. [2108.]

DOUGLAS G. HARING, Catalog of the Ryūkyū research collection. Syracuse university library and the Maxwell graduate school of citizenship and public affairs [1969]. pp.xvi.157. [2103.]

MACAO

C. R. BOXER and J. M. BRAGA, Algunas notas sôbre a bibliografia de Macau. Macau 1939. pp.30. [500.]

JAIME ROBARTS, Índice alfabético da legislação de província de Macau ... desde 1915 até junho de 1958. Macau 1958. pp.143. [2000.]

LUIZ GONZAGA GOMES, Catalogo dos manuscritos de Macau. Centro de estudos históricos ultra-marinos: Lisboa 1965. pp.148. [1344.]
Separata do No.31 do Boletim du Filmoteca ultramarina.

MARY C. SCHLOEDER, Salazar's Portugal (Angola, Goa, Macao, Mozambique, Portugal and Timor). ATMC monthly memo: [Washington?] 1968. ff.9★. [250.]
— — Addendum. 1968. ff.4. [100.]

TUN-HUANG

KEIKI YABUKI, Rare and unknown chinese manuscript remains of buddhist literature discovered in Tun-huang collected by sir Aurel Stein and preserved in the British museum. Tokyo 1930. ff.8.pls.104. [104.]

HENRI MASPERO, Les documents chinois de la troisième expédition de sir Aurel Stein en Asie centrale. British museum: London 1953. pp.xii. 268. pls.xl. [607.]

E[RIC] D. GRINSTEAD, Title index to the Descriptive catalogue of chinese manuscripts from Tunhuang in the British museum. British museum: London 1963. pp.41. [1800.]★

M. I. VOROB'EVA-DESATOVSKAYA [*and others*], Описание китайских рукописей дунхуанского фонда Института народов Азии. Академия наук СССР: Институт народов Азии: Москва 1963-7. pp.774+688. [2954.]★

ANNEMARIE VON GABAIN, Die drucke der Turfansammlung. Sitzungsberichte der deutschen akademie der wissenschaften zu Berlin: Klasse für sprachen, literatur und kunst, jahrgang 1967 (nr. 1): Berlin 1967. pp.40. [large number.]

A CLASSIFIED catalogue of japanese books and articles concerning Tunhuang documents. Committee for the studies of the Tunhuang documents: the Toyo Bunko: [Tokyo] 1959. pp.[viii].82. [984.]

CATALOGUE des manuscrits chinois de Touenhouang (Fonds Pelliot chinois). Bibliothèque nationale.
   i. nos.2001–2500. 1970. pp.xxxi.406. [500.]

HSI-HSIA (TANGUT)

Z. I. GORBACHEVA and E. I. KUICHANOV, Тангутские рукописи и ксилографы. Список отождествленных и определенных тангутских рукописей и ксилографов коллекции Института наровов Азии АИ СССР: Академия наук СССР: Институт народов Азии: Москва 1963. pp.172. [405.]

NA-KHI (MOSO)

JOSEPH FRANCIS ROCK, Na-khi manuscripts. Edited by Klaus L. Janert. Verzeichnis der orientalischen handschriften in Deutschland (vii): Wiesbaden 1965.   pp.xix.196.pls.31+vi.197–485. [541.]

U.S.S.R. IN FAR EAST

Amur

[F. BUSSE], Указатель литературы объ амурскомъ краѣ. С.-Петербургъ 1874. pp.iii. 42. [522.]

Far Eastern Province

I. M. DROVENKO [*and others*], Приморский край. Рекомендательный указатель литературы. Приморская краевая библиотека имени А. М. Горьского: Владивосток 1962. pp.116. [700.]

A. N. ASATKIN and V. A. SAMOILOV, Библиография Дальневосточного края 1890–1931. ... Том п. Геология, полезные ископаемые, палеонтология. Дальневосточный краевой исполнительный комитет: Москва 1935. pp.xl. 415. [2000.]

Irkutsk

L. E. ZUBASHEVA, Библиография Иркутской области. Физическая география. Иркутский государственный университет: Труды научной библиотеки (vol.13): Ленинград 1957. pp.177. [2358.]

P. P. BOROVSKY, Иркутская область за 40 лет (развитие народного хозяйства). Краткий аннотированный указатель литературы. Областная библиотека: Иркутск 1957. pp.35. [200.]

N[ONNA] K[ONSTANTINOVNA] POTAPOVA [*and others*], Что читать об Иркутской области. Указатель литературы. Иркутск 1958. pp.52. [750.]

Kamchatka

LIST of references on Kamacharka [*sic*]. Library of Congress: [Washington] 1920. ff.6. [49.]*

Tannu-Tuva

V. I. DULOV [*and others*], Библиография Тувинской автономной области, 1774–1958 гг.

Академия наук СССР: Совет по изучению производительных сил: Москва 1959. pp.168. [1750.]

Turukhansk

V[ASILY] N[IKOLAEVICH] UVACHAN, Енисейский Север. (Библиографический указатель). Красноярская краевая библиотека: Библиографический отдел: Красноярск 1959. pp.136. [1250.]

Yeniseisk

V[YACHESLAV] P[ETROVICH] KOSOVANOV, Библиография Приенисейского края ... [с. 1612 по 1923 год]. Красноярск.

i.

ii. Филология, чистые (точные) науки и прикладные знания. Енисейское губернское экономическое совещание: 1923: pp.[v.].xii.296.xv. [6088.]

iii. Искусства, литература, история, описательная география, картография и биографии. Средне-Сибирское государственное географическое об-во: 1930. pp.xvi. 348.xiv. [6317.]

Currie, J. C., 367
Curzon, Robert, 74
Cwik, H.-J., 55, 525

D

Dadashzade, M. A., 268
Daftar buku2 terbitan Malaysia; disusun oleh Pustaka Antara, 490
Daftar buku 20 tahun Penerbitan Indonesia 1945-1965, 483
Daftar kepustakaan, 478
Daftar pustaka bahasa dan kesusastraan Indonesia, 483
Dagher, J. A., 46, 139, 161, 165
Dahood, M. J., 116
Dai, Shen-yu, 66, 67, 68
Dalleggio d'Alessio, Eugene, 250
D'Alwis, James, 400, 402
Damle, Y. B., 359
Damodar Dasa, 310
Danandjaja, James, 481
Dance, D. G., 528
Danckwortt, Helga and Dieter, 33
Dandaron, B. D., 629
Dandekar, R. N., 297, 306, 366
Daneche-Pajouh, M. T., 184, 214, 215
Dani, A. H., 144
Danson, A. L., 350
Danvers, F. C., 304, 305, 372, 468, 469
Dao, N. X., 462
Das, A. R., 359
Das, Damodar, 310
Dasgupta, S. C., 300
Dashian, Jacobus, 271
Datta, K. K., 307
Datta, Rajeshwari, 320, 422
Dâver, Bülent, 233
David, Yonah, 115
Davidson, Jeremy, 562, 578
Davidson, Martha, 595
Davis, J. H., 456
Davis, M. B., 555
Davison, R. M., 134
Davityai, G. M., 270
Davuidova, M. I., 254
Dawson, W. R., 89, 91
Dayaram, Ganeshi, 312
De Bary, W. T., 54
de Benko, Eugene, 288
de Buck, H., 471
Decourdemanche, J. A., 177
de Francis, John, 576
de Graaf, H. J., 474
Dehérain, Henri, 139
Deinard, E., 99
Deinard, Ephraim, 110
Deissmann, G. A., 231
Delitzsch, Franz, 170, 204, 239
Deloncle, M. F., 172
De Mare, A. J., 485
Dembski, Wojciech, 185
Demiéville, P., 377
Democratic republic of Viet-Nam, 464
Deny, J., 153, 220
Derenbourg, Hartwig, 173, 175
Der Nersessian, Sirarpie, 274
Descriptive analysis of the Kashmir series, 401

Descriptive catalogue of ancient manuscripts, 398
Descriptive catalogue of books and publications registered in West Bengal, 328
Descriptive catalogue of the government collections of manuscripts, 392
Descriptive catalogue of the islamic manuscripts, 143
Descriptive catalogue of pali ... books in the Oriental library, 71
Descriptive catalogue of the sanskrit manuscripts of the Government oriental manuscripts library, 389
Descriptive catalogue of the sanskrit manuscripts in the Sanskrit university library, 398
Descriptive catalogue of sanskrit manuscripts in the library of the Asiatic society, 399
Descriptive catalogue of tamil manuscripts, 414
Descriptive catalogue of the tamil manuscripts, 413
Descriptive catalogue of the telegu manuscripts, 415
Descriptive catalogue of university (of Calcutta) publications, 314
Des Granges, comtesse Alix, 171, 205, 239
Deshpande, P. G., 377
De Silva, W. A., 433
Deutsch, Simon, 97
Deutsche Japan-bibliographie, 609
Deutsche übersetzungen asiatischer, orientalischer und afrikanischer autoren, 54
Deux siècles de sinologie française, 594
Devambez, L., 531
Devaraja Aiyar, S., 310
Devasthali, G. V., 396
Devéria, Théodule, 92
Devī Prasāda, 385
Devillers, Philippe, 473
Devlet plânlama teşkilati yayınları indeksi, 233
Deydier, Henri, 358
de Zoysa, Louis, 403
Dhabhar, E. B. N., 74, 198, 206, 210
Dhingra, Baldoon, 51
Dhīrajlāla Keṣvlāla Ṭhākura, 335
Dhuṇḍhirāja Dharmādhikāri, 386
Dia' Abou-Ghazi, 152
Diaz, R. V., 508, 511
Dickerson, Beth, 513
Dickinson, Benjamin, 228
Dickson, Diane, 527
Dictionary catalog of the hawaiian collection, 536
Dictionary catalog of the Khan library, 113
Dictionary catalog of the Oriental collection, the New York public library, 60
Dictionary catalog of printed books, 525
Dictionary catalog of the university library, university of California, 596, 622
Diega, G. D., 506, 507
Diehl, K. S., 302
Dienstag, J. I., 112

Dietrich, Manfred, 87, 95
Díez Macho, Alejandro, 102
Digest of the cases reported in the Punjab record, 348
Digest of Ceylon cases reported, 429
Digest of indian law cases, 311
Dighe, V. G., 335
Dik Keam, 460
Dimaya, P. D., 506
Dimberg, Ronald, 578
Dindinger, Johannes, 30, 305, 458, 473, 503, 586, 608, 623
Dinçer, Ferruh, 234
Directory of current scientific research projects in Pakistan, 427
Directory of japanese learned periodicals, 605
Directory of japanese scientific periodicals, 605, 618
Directory of Peking daily papers, 562
Direr, Françoise, 466
Disbury, D. G., 140
District officers' handy reference book (Bengal), 329
Diwan-Chand Obhrāi, 350, 361
Dju Chang, D. C., 588
Dmitrieva, L. V., 245
Do Van Anh, 460, 461, 465
Doan Thi Do, 462
Dobraca, Kasim, 185, 216, 245
Dobson, W. A. C. H., 49
Doctoral dissertations on Japan, 510
Documentatieblad, 22
Documentatio Asiae, 67
Documents on asian affairs, 50
Documents relatifs aux civilisations orientales, 71
Dodd, S. C., 130
Dodge, Bayard, 166
Dodwell, H., 343
Докторские и кандидатские диссертации, 56
Dokumentasi guntingan surat kabar mengenai biologi, 480
Donkin, W. C., 139
Dorn, Bernard, 58, 163, 170, 171, 201, 204, 205, 239
Dorosh, J. T., 126, 624
Dossor, Carol, 527
Dost, H., 136
Dotan, Uri, 134
Dotson, L. O., 442
Douglas, sir R. K., 592, 620
Dozy, R. P. A., 76
Draft survey of materials relating to communism in China, 581
Drakakis Smith, D. W., 135
Drovenko, I. M., 638
Dry farming in India, Egypt and South Africa, 155, 356
Duberal, R. F., 535
Dubester, H. J., 359, 424
Dubrovina, E. I., 256
Du Cauzé de Nazelle, marquis, 305
Dugarov, N. B., 631
Dukes, Leopold, 96
Dulov, 639
Dunlop, Boutwell, 574
Dünya edebıyatından tercümeler listesi, 251
Duparc, Johan, 469
Dupleix, J, F., 305

E

F

Filliozat, Jean, 395, 396, 405, 628
Film catalogue. Hong Kong government information services, 636
Films on Asia available in Canada, 63
Finck, F. N., 272
Findikoğlu bibliyografyası, 236
Finot, Louis, 459
Firdawsi celebration, 935–1935, 212
Firminger, W. K., 325, 326
Firouzabadi, Homa, 190
First guide to the literature of the aquatic sciences and fisheries in Bangkok, 515
First world war, 121, 157
Fischer, A., 58, 163
Fischer, H. T., 473, 474, 478
Fish, T., 86
Fisher, E. S., 566
Fisher, Joseph, 454
Fisher, M. L., 460
Fisher, M. W., 434
Fistié, Pierre, 489, 602
Fitzgerald, Edward, 200
Fleisch, Henri, 94
Fleischer, H. L., 72, 170, 204, 238, 239
Flemming, Barbara, 246
Fletcher, T. B., 364
Florentino, A. S., 509
Flügel, Gustav, 162, 171, 205, 239, 246
Fodor, Michael, 54
Folliot, A. A., 457
Following government publications are for sale at . . . Trivandrum, 351
Fonahn, Adolf, 199
Fontaine, A. L., 121, 150, 157
Forbes, Duncan, 74, 205
Forbes, Lesley, 62
Forke, Alfred, 562
Formosa and Java, 481, 583
Forrer, Ludwig, 133
Forrest, G. W., 334
Forshall, Josiah, 127
Fosberg, F. R., 540
Foster, R. C., 132
Foster, sir William, 305, 375
Fourmont, Etienne, 71, 139
Fourmont, Stephanus, 590
Fox, James and Irmgard, 482
Frähn, C. M., 162, 201, 247
Francis, sir F. C., 70
Francisco, G. A., 508
Francisco, V. J., 509
Frank, Othmar, 203
Franke, Herbert, 595
Franke, Wolfgang, 579
Frankel, H. H., 576, 577
Fraser, S. E., 579
Freeburger, A. R., 286
Freeman, C., 542
Frei, E. J., 441, 524
Freijate, Faёz, 188
Freimann, Aaron, 102, 104, 105, 110
Freitas, J. A. de, 619
French books on the far east, 556
Frewer, L. B., 78
Friedberg, Bernard, 105, 110
Friederich, R. H. T., 171
Friederici, Karl, 43
Friedlaender, Israel, 116
Friedman, Philip, 112

Fu, Hsi-hua, 584
Fuad, Kamal, 194
Fuchs, Walter, 596, 635
Fujino, Yukio, 662
Fuks, L., and Fuks-Manfeld, R. G., 102
Fukuda, Mirsuno, 540
Fukuda, Naomi, 603
Fukuo, Iwasaki, 556
Full digest of the Madras criminal cases, 361
Fuller, G. H., 221
Fulton, A. S., 163, 164, 167
Fürer-Haimendorf, Elizabeth, 288

G

G., 140
Gabain, Annemarie von, 256, 638
Gable, R. W., 420
Gabor, Lévai, 601
Gabrieli, Giuseppe, 46, 70, 75, 142, 179, 211, 242
Gachechiladze, M. A., 278
Gachet, 178, 210, 273
Gadzheva, T. D., 268
Gaffarel, Jacques, 106
Gafurov, B. G., 187, 216, 256
Gail, Rene, 531
Gálik, Marian, 597
Galis, K. W., 541
Gallent, C. G., 144
Gambier-Parry, T. R., 393, 395
Gamidova, A. M., 269
Ganda Singh, 350
Gandhi and the british raj, 307
Gandhi, J. N., 291
Gandhi, M. K., 377
Gangoly, O. C., 371
Gangopadhyaya, Mrinalkanti, 404, 630
Gangulee, N., 372
Garbe, Richard, 379
Garcia, Mauro and Pilar Cruz, 504, 510
Garcin de Tassy, 172
Garcin de Tassy, J. H., 381, 408, 418
Gard, R. A., 456, 514
Garde, P. K., 50
Gardner, A. L., 625
Gardner, C. S., 568, 593
Gardner, F. M., 306
Gardner, R. K., 462
Gardthausen, Victor, 137
Garnot, J. S., 89
Gaspardone, Émile, 462, 598
Gaster, Moses, 116
Gaudart, Edmond, 328, 351, 355
Gaur, Albertine, 410
Gautam, B. P., 373
Gay, H. K., 599
Gay, Jean, 149
Gaynullin, M. F., 257
Geddes, C. L., 145, 151
Gee, J. G., 465
Geiger, John, 590
Geissler, Friedmar, 55
General catalogue of all publications of the Government of Bombay, 335
General catalogue of the Punjab government publications, 349

General directory of the press and periodicals in Jordan and Kuwait, 169
General index of academic works. U. Santo Tomas, 505
General list of newspapers and periodicals published in Pakistan, 423
Gengaro, M. L., 101
Gennadi, G. N., 258
Geological bibliography of the former province of Sind, 422
Geologisch mijnbouwkundige bibliographie, 472
Georgiev, K., 224
Georgievskaya, I. A., 262
Gerboth, Walter, 449, 560
German, Sh. M., 27
German-Reed, T., 140
Geroneografeerde catalogus, 470
Gerow, B. A., 625
Gesenius, F. H. W., 96
Gestetner, Adolph, 108
Ghali, R. S., 166
Ghali, W. R., 160
Ghani, A., 427
Ghani, A. R., 218, 418, 422, 426, 427
Ghazikean, A. G., 270
Ghose, Sailen, 300
Ghoshal, U. N., 46
Ghouse, Mohammad, 187
Ghulam Qādir, Mawlay, 201
Giannini, Crescentino, 104
Gibson, M. D., 174
Gibu, Morio, 556
Gicher, Strakhill, 106
Gidel, C. A., 522
Gidwani, N. N., 293
Giesecke, H. H., 139
Giesler, H.-B., 603
Gilani, S. J., 493
Gilbert, W. H., 359
Gildemeister, Johann, 72, 400
Giles, H. A., 592, 595, 634
Gill, E. R., 541
Gillin, Donald, 557
Giniyatullina, A. K., 262
Ginzburg, Simon, 116
Gjandschezian, Levon, 272
Glagoleva, I. K., 570, 595
Glanville, S. R. K., 92
Glasenapp, Helmut van, 377
Gobbett, D. J., 493
Gobind Singh, 377
Gobineau, J. A., 205, 239
Goby, J. E., 152
Godchot, J. E., 133
Gode, P. K., 377, 392
Goeje, M. J. de, 76, 169
Goell, Yohai, 113
Goil, N. K., 69, 290
Goitein, S. D., 103
Gökalp, Ziya, 236
Gokarṇa-Nātha Miṣra, 346
Gökman, Muzaffer, 184, 214, 224, 232, 235, 236, 244
Golay, F. H., 506
Goldenthal, Julius, 97
Goldhammer, Leo, 120
Goldschmidt, Solomon, 109
Goldstein, Miron, 88, 91
Goldziher, Ignáz, 139
Golius, Jacobus, 169
Göllner, Carl, 223

Hebraica Ambrosiana, 102
Hebraica & judaica, 113
Hebraica at the university of Chicago, 113
Heerma van Voss, M. S. H., 89
Heinz, Wilhelm, 217
Heissig, Walther, 632, 633
Helfrich, D. L., 482
Heller, Bernard, 139
Hellman, F. S., 470, 488, 492, 523, 608, 619
Henderson, D. F., 514
Henning, W. B. H., 199
Henoch, H., 25
Henthorn, W. E., 625
Heper, Metin, 233
Herbert, Jean, 373, 378, 618
Herlitz, G., 122
Hermann, C. H., 43
Hernandez, Basilio, 507
Hernandono, 477
Hervouet, Yves, 563, 576, 579
Herzer, Christine, 565
Hester, E. D., 499
Heymowski, Adam, 186
Hewitt, A. R., 29
Heylingers, A. J. M., 342
Heyworth-Dunne, Gamal-Eddine (James), 144, 149, 153
Hickey, G. C., 461
Hicks, G. L., 479
Hidayat Hosain, M., 181
Hifny, S. M. el, 153
Hightower, J. R, 595
Hildenfinger, P. A., 118
Hill, S. C., 296, 305
Hill, W. C., 25
Hills, T. L., 21
Ḥilmy, prince Ibrāhīm, 151
Himalaja - bibliographie (1801–1933), 339, 627
Hincks, Edward, 92
Hinds, A. B., 220
Hintze, Fritz, 46
Hīrā-lāl, Rāi Bahādur, 393
Hīrālāl Rasikdās Kāpadiajā, 395, 408
Hiromitzu, Kaneda, 562, 602, 609
Hiroshi, Saito, 556
Hirsch, A. S., 469
Hirsch, E. E., 220
Hirschfeld, Hartwig, 99
Hirschhorn, H. J., 113
Historical documents relating to Japan, 606
Hitti, P. K., 180
Ho, K., 590
Ho, Paul, 575
Hobbs, C. C., 441, 445, 459
Hockings, Paul, 343
Hodgson, J. G., 419
Hodgson, W. B., 170, 204, 238
Hoe, Robert, 207
Hoenderkamp, Mariette, 476
Hoffmann, J. J., 620
Hofman, H. F., 250
Höfner, Maria, 94, 140
Hogg, H. W., 86
Hoghoughi, Ascar, 216
Hoheisel, J. D., 106
Hohlenberg, M. H., 97, 171
Holmes, Maurice, 526
Holmes, Winifred, 63
Holt, H. F., 592
Holzman, Donald, 570, 595, 616, 617

Holzman, Lore (Sander-), 399
Hommel, C. F., 149
Hong Kong–China, 566
Honsebrouck, P. van, 635
Hooker, M. B., 489
Hooykaas, C., 473, 482
Hooykaas, J. C., 468
Hopkins, J. F., 168
Hopwood, Derek, 135, 144, 145, 169, 180
Horigan, F. D., 124
Horne, N. P., 443
Horton, Marion, 568
Hospers, J. H., 94
Hosten, H., 456
Hottinger, J. H., 41
Hotz, A., 195
Houdas, Octave, 140
Houdas, Octave, 173
Houston, C. O., 497
Houtsma, M. T., 76, 169, 174, 240
Hovaguimian, Stepanos, 275
Howard, H. N., 135
Howard, Irwin, 528
Howard, J. H., 495
Howard, R. C., 554, 564
Hṛishikeṣa Ṣastri, 358, 368, 369, 373, 388, 390
Hsia, Tao-t'ai, 584
Hsieh, Winston, 589
Hsu Ginn-tze, 627
Hsu Kuang-ling, 579
Hsueh, Chun-tu, 577, 582
Hu Chi-hsi, 565, 579
Hu, David, Y., 565
Hu, W. C. C., 564
Huart, C. I., 140
Huart, C. I., 60, 163, 202, 247
Hucker, C. O., 571, 576
Huebotter, Franz, 585
Hufana, A. G., 508, 511
Hufnagel, W. F., 103
Huisman, A. J. W., 161
Huke, R. E., 501
Hultzsch, Eugen, 379, 388
Hulûsi, Şerif, 236
Hummel, A. W., 569
Hunnewell, J. F., 535
Hunt, C. H., 607
Hunter, sir W. W., 328, 387
Hurvitz, Leon, 632, 634
Husain, A. I., 411
Husain, Asad, 434
Hussein, M. A., 153
Hüttl-Worth, Gerta, 254
Hyde, C. M., 535

I

Iancoulesco, Victor, 236
Ibn Khaldūn, 189
Ibn Khayr al-Ishbilī, 163
Ibn al-Nadīm, 162, 166
Ibragimov, A. A., 267
Ibrahim, Zahida, 161
Ichikawa, Kenjiro, 444
Ikado, Fujio, 617
Ilahi, K. N., 426
Il'enko, E. M., 263
Ilkin, Selim, 231
Illingworth, J. E., 537
Iltis, J. C., 287

Imbonati, C. G., 106
Impex reference catalogue of indian books, 300
L'imprimerie hors l'Europe, 46
Inada, H. I., 622
Inanchinova, E. I., 258
Indeks majallah kini Malaysia Singapura dan Brunei, 489, 495, 496
Indeks selektif artikel 2 harian Bandung & Djakarta, 477
Inden, R. B., 286
Index to Chinese periodical literature on southeast Asia, 447
Index to the circular orders of the courts of Sudder dewanny adawlut, 323
Index to the circular orders passed by the Sudder dewanny adawlut, 323
Index to the classification of patents of invention, 614
Index to the classified files on Communist China, 570
Index to Current background, 566
Index of documents issued for general distribution by the Technical assistance administration, 32
Index excerpta of selected precedents of the Suddar dewanny court, 324
Index to the foreign & political department records, 306
Index India, 293
Index to indian legal periodicals, 308
Index to indian medical periodicals, 369
Index indo-asiaticus, 57, 285
Index of indonesian learned periodicals, 476
Index for japanese history, 607
Index to the leading decisions, 421
Index to learned chinese periodicals, 564
Index librorum orientalium et latinorum, 58
Index to papers in commemoration volumes, 300
Index to papers read at the Indian historical records commission sessions, 306
Index to periodicals. Public library, New South Wales, 527
Index to philippine periodicals, 506
Index of post-1937 european manuscript accessions, 286
Index of the published works of the faculty members of the university of Santo Tomas, 505
Index to Selections from China mainland press, 566
Index to the statute law of Cyprus, 227
Index of Straits Settlements laws, 487
Index to Survey of China mainland press, 566
Index to titles of english news releases of Hsinhua news agency, 565
Index to unrepealed central acts, 309
India. Far Eastern books and journal lists, 296

Kalaidovich, K. F., 207, 241
Kalandadze, Ts., 276
Kalaydjian, Ara, 275
Kalelkar, N. G., 399
Kalemkiar, Gregoris, 271, 272
Kali-Prasanna Vandyopadhyaya, 328
Kalia, D. R., 298, 382
Калидаса, 402
Kamāl, ud-Dīn Aḥmad, 176, 208
Kamalov, N. G., 275
Kambara, Tatsu, 433
Kamensky, Pavel, 591, 620
Kamil, Murad, 77
Kamp, Joseph van, 305, 430
Kan, C. M., 468
Kan, J. van, 306
Kan, Lai-bing, 586
Kan Siew Mee, 450
Kanakura, Yensho, 68
Kancho kanko &c., 609
Kandel', B. L., 67
Kang, Sangwoon, 625
Kanitkar, D. L., 300
Kanitkar, J. M., 357
Kanta, Surya, 292
Kantūrī, I'jāz Ḥusain, 203
Kapadia, H. R., 392
Kapadia, K., 302
Kaplan, M. M., 111, 116
Kaplony-Heckel, U., 93
Karachi university library periodical holdings, 423
Karagöz, A. R., 249
Karambelkar, V. W., 397
Karamianz, N., 271
Karatay, F. E., 165, 182, 211, 213, 215, 243, 245, 249
Karayalçın, Yasar, 222, 223, 225
Karimullin, A. G., 245, 262, 263
Karlgren, Bernhard, 593
Karmenyan, V. N., 270
Karmirès, I. N., 126
Karolyi, Zoltan, 377
Kasher, M. M., 112
Kāşī-Prasāda Jāyaswal, 394
Ḳāsim Naṣīr Raẓavī, 210
Kāsinātha Kunte, 386
Каталог арабских рукописей, 184
Katalog armenischen handschriften, 276
Katalog der ausstellung von handschriften aus dem islamischen kulturkreis, 142
Katalog der bibliothek des verewigten prof. Ludwig Blau, 111
Katalog der bücherei des Japaninstituts, 601
Katalog der handbibliothek der orientalischen abteilung, 60
Каталогъ книгамъ Эчмядзииской, 270
Каталогъ книгамъ, рукописямъ . . . на китайскомъ . . . языкахъ, 58
Каталогъ санскритскимъ . . . книгамъ, 76
Katalog rękopisów egipskich, 92, 93
Katalog rękopisów ormiańskich i gruzińskich, 274, 277
Каталог рукописей Матенадарана, 274
Katanov, N. F., 175, 207, 258
Katharate, A. V., 385
Kātib Chelebī, 246
Katō, Genchi, 618

Katrak, J. C., 198, 212
Katre, S. M., 392
Katsh, A. I., 101, 111
Katz, S. M., 34
Kaufmann, David, 110
Kaul, H. K., 376
Kaula, P. N., 369
Kavi Raja Shyamal Das Ji's private library, 295
Kaviraj, Gopinath, 402
Kawabe, Toshio, 513
Kawai, Saburo, 612
Kayzer, S. I., 265
Казахская ССР, 259
Казахстан, Библиография, 259
Kazakov, S. V., 569, 570
Kazancıgıl, Aykut, 232
Kazbekova, E., 260
Kazhdarova, E., 214, 245
Kāzimī, Aṣghār, 197
Kazmi, S. M. A., 424
Keddie, N. R., 362, 424, 427
Keith, A. B., 384, 387, 390, 404
Keldani, E. H., 156
Kelkar, A. G., 323
Kelley, Doug, 299
Kelly, Celsus, 524, 525
Kemp, Stanley, 291, 374
Kenji, Masuda, 562, 602
Kennedy, Raymond, 474, 478
Kensdale, W. E. N., 182
Kent, Laura, 304
Kepferle, R. C., 529
Kerner, R. J., 220, 555
Kerney, Michael, 174, 207, 241
Kerr, G. H., 636
Kesavan, B. S., 298, 382, 383
Keschischian, Mesrop, 272
Keyes, J. G., 463
Khabirova, N. S., 256
Khachatryan, A. E., 270
Khakhanov, A. S., 276
Khalidov, A. B., 184
Khalife, I. A., 182
Khān, Mu'īn ul-Dīn Aḥmad, 145
Khandwala, V. K., 363
Khanna, A. N., 350
Kharbanda, Mohan-Lal, 361
Kharbas, D. S., 344
Kharuzin, A. N., 258, 261
Khater, Antoine, 93
Khazars, 260
Khitrovo, V. N., 119
Khizhnyakov, V. V., 630
Khorganeants, Th., 270
Kristenko, Konstantin, 630
Khubua, Makar, 213
Художественная литература Казахстана, 260
Khusaynov, G. B., 257
Khvolson, D. A., 109
Kiang, Lu-Yu, 454
Kidd, Samuel, 591
Kiefer, T. M., 510
Kielhorn, Franz, 384, 385, 387
Kindersley, A. F., 335
King, F. H. H., 565
King, L. W., 86
King, N. D., 637
King, R., 151, 159
Kiratli, Metin, 233
Kireev, N. G., 234
Kirkland, E. C., 288
Kirpal Singh, 215, 398, 411, 417
Kiseleva, M. A., 569

Kitano, H. H. L., 69
Кітап летописі, 259
Kitch, E. M., 406
Klaproth, Julius, 591, 634
Klatt, Johannes, 44, 368
Kleinhaus, Arduino, 160
Kleiweg de Zwaan, J. P., 478
Klette, Anton, 72
Klieneberger, H. R., 531
Klimke, C., 136
Klimova, V. P., 258
Книги издательства Академии наук Азербайджанской ССР, 268
Knoepfmacher, Hugo, 630
Knyazhetskaya, E. A., 264
Kobidze, D. I., 203
Kocayusufpaşaoğlu, Necip, 223
Köcher, H. F., 107
Koda, Shigetomo, 608
Koegler, Ignatius, 581
Koh, H. C., 623
Kohut, G. A., 116
Kohler, Carl, 119
Koikulides, K. M., 120, 128, 175
Kokoropoulos, Panos, 137
Kokowzoff, Paul, 109
Koll, M. J., 465
Kolmas, Josef, 630
Koloniales schrifttum, 26, 27
Kolonien im deutschen schrifttum, 26
Komarov, V. L., 560
Komissarov, D. S., 218
Komiya, Ryutaro, 613
Kondo, Jion, 605, 615
König, G. M., 41
Konikoff, A., 121
Konogorov, P. F., 253
Kononov, A. N., 245
Kononova, A. N., 52
Konow, Sten, 295
Köprülü, M. F., 236
Koran in Slavonic, 147
Koray, Enver, 221
Korea: an annotated bibliography, 623
Korea. House of commons library, 623
Korea: a preliminary bibliography, 623
Korean publications in the National agricultural libraries, 625
Kormilitzin, A. I., 253
Kornrumpf, H. J., 225
Kosovanov, V. P., 640
Kosover, M., 118
Kossian (K'ōsean), Jakob, 272
Kostuigova, G. I., 218
Kotansky, Wieslaw, 50
Kotovskiy, G. G., 299, 301
Koychubaeva, B. K., 260
Kozicheva, N. A., 254
Kozicki, R. J., 287, 447
Krachkovsky, I. I., 140
Krader, Lawrence, 259
Krafft, Albrecht, 97, 170, 204, 239
Kraemer, Jörg, 73
Krauss, N. L. H., 533, 534, 538, 539, 543, 544, 545, 546
Krek, Miroslav, 166, 185
Kremer, Alfred, freiherr von, 173, 206, 240
Kṛishṇa Śāstri Chiplonkar, 402
Krishnamacharya, V., 396, 397
Krishnamūrti Aiyar, S., 361

Lou, Sophie, 581
Louca, Anouar, 187
Low, D. A., 287
Löwe, H. K., 234
Lowe, J. Dz., 578
Löwenthal, Rudolf, 145, 150, 569
Löwy, Albert, 109
Luard, C. E., 354
Luce, E., 456
Luchinin, V. V., 608
Luker, Thomas, 291
Lumbroso, Giacomo, 88
Lust, John, 563, 564, 578
Lüthi-Tschanz, K. J., 105
Lutton, Nancy, 542
Lutzky, Aaron, 116
Luyken, R., 479
Luzac & Co., 44, 45
Luzzatto, Aldo, 102
Luzzatto, Isaia, 117
Luzzatto, M. N., 116
Luzzatto, S. D., 108, 117
Lyons, Ursula, 183
Lyovin, Anatole, 591

M

Ma, J. T., 557
Macaskie, C. F. C., 525
McCabe, M. R., 557
Macdonald, D. B., 177, 242
MacDonald, G. A., 538
Macdonald, John, 183, 215
Macdonald, Teresa, 320, 431
MacFadden, C. H., 526
McGovern, J. R., 617
McGowan, Frank, 34
McGrath, W. A., 541
McGrigor, A. B., 119
MacGuckin de Slane, baron
    William, 173
Machwe, V., 52
Mackenzie, Colin, 356
MacKenzie, D. N., 193
McKinstry, John, 461
MacKnight, C. C., 484
McLean, C. S., 328
Macler, Frédéric, 128, 273, 276
McMurtrie, D. C., 296, 429
McNicoll, Geoffrey, 479
Macpherson, J. M., 309
Macro, Eric, 150, 160
McVey, R. T., 443
Maden tetkik ve arama enstitüsü
    dergisi makeleler bibliografyası,
    232
Madenokoji, Michimune, 598
Madhava Krishna Sarma, K., 396,
    397
Mādhavan Nair, 344
Madras state tamil bibliography, 414
Mager, Henri, 29
Magsaysay, Ramon, 512
Mahādeva Sitārāma Muṇḍle, 330,
    337
Mahalingam, T. V., 308
Mahapatra, Kedarnath, 397
Mahar, J. M., 301
Mahdavi, Yahya, 189
Mahdi, M. el, 168
Mahfuzul Haq, M., 181
Mahmood, E. M., 158

Mahmudov, H. Z., 268
Mai, Angelo, 91, 170, 204, 239
Mainsbridge, Barbara, 542
Majda, Tadeusz, 217, 246
Majewska, Barbara, 50
Makagiansar, M., 478
Makaliwe, W. H., 478
Makovelskiy, A. O., 268
Malaise, Michel, 90
Malakar, Dilip, 407
Malayan campaign, 488
Malaysia & Singapore, 490, 496
Malaysian collections, 490
Malik, I. A., 350
Mallal, B. A. and N. A., 488
Malmquist, Goran, 594, 620
Maloles, L. R., 501
Malozemoff, Andrew, 559
Malūr Raṅgāchārya, 380, 389, 391,
    412, 413, 414, 415
Mamatzashvili, M. G., 187, 217, 246
Mamed Arif Dadashzade, 268
Mameev, S. N., 252
Manaseryan, A. S., 270, 274
Manchuria: a selected list of
    bibliographies, 633
Mandahl, S. M., 606
Mandelbaum, D. G., 356
Mandelbaum, J. B., 112
Mander-Jones, Phyllis, 525
Māṇekji Bejanji Pithāvālā, 422
Manibhūshan Majirmdār, 328
Manik, Liberty, 484
Manindra-Mohana Vasu, 405
Manohar Bhaskar Arte, 374
Manoscritti e stampe venete, 188
Mansel, A. M., 231
Mansur, Abulhasan, 320
Mantran, Robert, 223
Manuel, E. A., 509
Manuel, R. A., 309
Manuel L. Quezon, a bio-biblio-
    graphy, 512
Manuscripts from indian collec-
    tions, 381
Manuscripts & papyri, 78
Manuscrits arabes de Rabat, 178
Manuscrits tamouls, 412
Manzoni, Giacomo, 104
Mao Tsê-tung, 585
Mao Yung, 580
Maouad, Ibrahim, 159
Map catalogue [Palestine], 121
Maps of the far east, 559
Maple, H. L., 89
March, A. C., 68
Marchant, L. R., 533
Mardirossian, N. B., 275
Maretzki, Thomas, 473, 474, 478,
    528
Margoliouth, D. S., 74, 129, 179
Margoliouth, George, 95, 99, 127
Maron, Stanley, 419
Marquardsen, Hugo, 25
Marr, N. Y., 276
Marsden, William, 58
Marshall, D. N., 216, 307
Marshall, D. S., 533, 544
Marsigli, 174
Martelli, V. A., 102
Martin, Gunnar, 594, 620
Martin, Helmut, 573
Martin, William, 535
Martineau, Alfred, 26, 355
Martinez, E. R., 116

Martinov, I. M., 136
Martinovitch, N. N., 211, 242
Martirodiredjo, Soedarminto, 476
Marucchi, Orazio, 92
Masihul Hassan, S., 383
Maslova, O. V., 251, 253, 254
Mason, J. B., 513
Mason, P. C. R., 613
Masoodul Hasan, 302
Maspero, Gaston, 558
Maspero, Henri, 593, 637
Massé, Henri, 219
Massignon, Louis, 140
Massola, Aldo, 533
Masson, Paul, 159
Mas'udi, 480
Materials in the National archives
    relating to the Netherlands East
    Indies, 470
    middle east, 133
    the Portuguese possessions, 31
Materials on the Pacific area in
    selected libraries of the Los
    Angeles region, 60
Матерıалы для изслѣдованıя . . .
    Brhatkatha, 402
Matsuda, Kiichi, 602
Matsuda, Mitsugu, 536
Matsui, Masato, 610, 622
Matsunami, Seiren, 399
Matthes, B. F., 434, 485
Matthews, M. A., 502
Matthews, Noel, 286, 444
Matveev, Z. N., 599
Maunier, René, 153
Maxfield, G. H., 530
Maxwell, R. S., 504
Maxwell, sir W. G., 487
Ma-yar, M. Q., 193
Mayer, H. E., 136
Mayer, L. A., 95, 145, 146, 148
Mayer, U. P., 28
Mayer, Walter, 87
Mayers, W. F., 592
Mayrhofer, Manfred, 85
Medical centre . . . Hebrew uni-
    versity, 125
Medina, I. R., 500, 511
Medina, J. T., 500, 502
Meek, C. K., 27
Mehendale, M. A., 399
Mehren, A. F. M., 71, 97, 205, 239,
    416
Mehta, C. C., 383
Mehta, M. M., 34
Meillier, M., 460
Meilman, M. N., 267
Meisezahl, R. O., 629
Mekinasi, A. M., 165
Melzig, Herbert, 221, 235
Memoranda of books printed . . .
    in Cyprus, 227
Memoranda of books registered in
    Punjab, 348
Memoranda of books registered . . .
    in the Straits Settlements, 486
Memoranda of books registered in
    the Hyderabad assigned districts,
    339
Memorandum of books registered
    in the Madras presidency, 339
Menant, Joachim, 86
Menasce, P. J. de, 192
Menge, P. E., 288
Menon, C. A., 410

Q

Qalo, L. S., 534
Qassim, N. M. A., 136
Qazi Mahmud ul-Haq, 417
Quadro delle opere di vari autori anticamente tradotte in armeno, 270
Quan, L. King, 49
Quarterly bulletin of chinese bibliography, 594
Quarterly check-list of oriental studies, 51
Qubain, F. I., 150
Quenzel, C. H., 298
Quezon, M. L., 512
Quigley, H. S., 559
Quirino, Carlos, 501
Quiros, G. S., 499
Quist, J. A., 472
Qureshi, A. M., 426
Quynh Bui, 463

R

Raadgever voor koloniale jeugdlectuur, 469
Rabbinovicz, R. N., 108
Rabe, V. H., 575
Rabindranath Tagore, 407
Rabino, H. L., 200
Raccolta cartografica, 25
Radī al-Dīn Ahmad ibn Ismā'īl, 165
Radlov, V. V., 237
Radzhievskaya, S. B., 245, 262
Rafikov, A. K., 224
Ragatz, L. J., 26, 27, 28
Raghavan, V., 372, 378, 397, 401
Raghu Singh, 425
Rahman, M. A., 426
Rai, Hira, 372
Rāi Bahādur Hirā-Lāl, 393
Rajapatirana, T., 632
Rajaratnam, S., 429
Rājendralāla Mitra, 384, 386
Rāma-chandra Nārāyana Dandekar, 366
Ramachandra Rao, T. B., 410
Ramachandran, K. S., 357
Rāmakrishna Gopāla Bhāndārkar, sir, 385, 386, 387, 388
Rāmanātha Sukula, 386
Rama Rao, B., 399
Ramaratnam, N., 313
Rama Subbiah, 414, 490
Ramaswami Shastri Siromani, K. S., 393
Ramdev, J. S., 377
Ramsey, R. W., 465
R'anā-Huseynī, Karāmat-e, 203
Rangāchārya, M., 389
Ranganathan, S. R., 285, 289
Rangoonwalla, Firoze, 364
Ranjee Singh, 302
Ranking, G. S. A., 59
Rāsavihārī Ghosha, 314
Rásonyi, László, 220
Ratan, S. K. L., 314
Ratanlāla Ranchhoddāsa, 335
Rath, Vimal, 362

Rattigan, H. A. B., 348
Rawdati, M. A., 185, 216
Reading list on colonial development, 27
Reading list. United Nations conference on the application of science and technology, 33
Reading lists on certain underdeveloped countries, 31
Readings on the modernization of Japan, 607
Realia, 468
Rebadavia, C. B., 499, 504
Reban, M. J., 462
Recent printed material (Palestine), 120
Recent studies ... on southeast Asia, 443
Recent trends of east asian studies, 556
Recherches en sciences sociales (Pacifique), 528
Records of the government of Bengal. Proceedings of the Committee of circuit, 327
Recueil égyptien périodique de la propriété industrielle, 156
Reddick, O. I., 304
Reed, A. W., 538
Reed, C. F., 448
Reese, I. C., 419
Reference catalogue of works upon the great pyramid, 88
References on the industrial development of Japan, 619
Regamey, C., 68, 381
Regel, Fritz, 130, 220
Register of the Palestine press, 121
Register op de uitgaven van het Koninklijk bataviaasch genootschap, 470
Regragui, A., 178
Rehatsek, Edward, 74, 205, 246
Reich, Bernard, 123
Reichert, Rolf, 188
Reid, C. F., 535
Reid, R. M., 357
Reider, Joseph, 115
Reimann, J. F., 71
Reinecke, J. E., 537
Reisen, Abraham, 117
Reitman, Édouard, 546
Reitz, Karl, 618
Religion, education and literature of China, 593
Remer, C. F., 612
Rémusat, J. P., 591
Renaud, H. J. P., 173
Renou, Louis, 366
Répertoire des thèses de sciences sociales, 527, 531
Repertorio delle attività italiane intese a promuovere e diffondere la conoscenza della civiltà orientale, 50
Report on the dutch records ... at Colombo, 430
Report on sanskrit mss., 385, 386
Report on a search for sanskrit manuscripts, 385, 386
Reports on german ... industry, 619
Reports on publications issued and registered in the several provinces of british India, 294

Republic of Vietnam (south Vietnam), 463
Rescher, Nicholas, 189, 190
Rescher, Oskar, 177
Research in the Annamalai university, 314
Research catalogue of the American geographical society, 21, 61
Research work of the university teachers, 314
Research works and other publications of the faculties, 1957–1959 (Philippines), 505
Résumé of the contents of the dutch diaries, 351
Résumé analytiques des travaux scientifiques ... en Égypte, 138
Retana, W. E., 497, 498, 500, 502, 505, 508, 513
Return of books (Hongkong), 635
Reviews of research on arid zone hydrology, 24
Revised catalogue of books in the Burma secretariat library, 455
Revised list of southeast Asia holdings in the Swen Franklin Parson library, 445
Revue bibliographique de l'Indo-Chine, 457
Revue bibliographique du moyen orient, 151
Revue bibliographique de philologie et d'histoire, 43
Revue bibliographique de sinologie, 570, 595
Revues médicales, 530
Reymond, E. A. E., 93
Reynolds, E., 348
Rhoads, E. J. M., 578, 586
Rhodes, E. F., 274
Riant, count P. E. D., 136
Ribera Tarrago, Julian, 163, 177
Ricci, S. M. R., de, 88
Rice, B. L., 387
Rice, D. S., 146
Rice, H. C., 574
Richardson, Joanna, 200
Richardson, Penelope, 541
Richer by Asia. West-east understanding, 51
Richter, Gustav, 73
Ricks, Thomas, 197
Riedel, W., 77, 179, 210, 242
Rieu, Charles, 170, 206, 240
Ritter, Helmut, 191
Rivkin, B., 117
Rivlin, H. A., 155
Riza Atay, A., 224
Roadarmel, G. C., 409
Robarts, Jaime, 637
Robert, W. C. H., 525
Roberts, W. E., 365
Robertson, Edward, 95, 179, 211
Robertson, J. A., 498, 607
Robinson, B. W., 76, 214
Robinson, John, 402, 405, 561
Robson, J. H., 488, 492
Rochas, H. J. A., 91
Rock, J. F., 638
Rockwell, W. W., 270
Rodriguez de Castro, Joseph, 107
Rodriguez Moñino, A. R., 47, 554
Roediger, Johannes, 162
Roff, Margaret, 490, 495, 496
Roff, W. R., 169, 487, 489, 495

Soler, Beatriz, 507
Sollheim, W. G., 491
Soltani, Poori, 197
Somalean, Sukias, 270
Somerville, A. D., 539
Sommer, F. E., 181
Somphit Yōtsēnī, 515
Sonnino, Guido, 105
Soong, J. C., 565, 585, 597
Sorich, Richard, 571
Soseliya, O., 276
Sources of information on labor in Japan, 614
Sourdel, Dominique, 141
Sourdel-Thomine, Janine, 141
South Asia social science abstracts, 289
South Asia social science bibliography, 289
Southan, J. E., 126
Southeast Asia and the Philippines, 442, 498
Southeast Asia, COWA, 288
Southeast Asia subject catalog. Library of congress, 446
Southeast asian newspapers, 447
Southeast asian periodicals and official publications, 447
Southern Asia, 287, 445
Southern Asia accessions list, 286, 442
Southern Asia publications, 285, 286, 442
Современная китайская литература, 589
Spaho, Fehim, 181
Sparks, Stanley, 361, 420, 425
Sparn, Enrique, 70
Sparvenfeld, J. G., 161, 201, 246
Spaulding, R. M., jr., 605
Special list of books in medieval hebrew poetry, 111
Spector, Stanley, 576
Spelnikov, V. M., 259
Spence, S. A., 526
Spencer, D. M., 363
Speransky, A. I., 126
Sperk, F. F., 255
Spies, Otto, 139
Spitz, A. A., 34
Sprenger, A., 58, 201, 205, 416
Spriggle, H. K., 573
Springer, Carl, 445
Spuler, Bertold, 47, 133
Sreekrishna Sarma, E. R., 380
Śrīdhara Rāmakrishna Bhāndārkar, 387, 390
Srinivasa Aiyar, A. S., 311, 314
Srinivasagopalachar, T. T., 395
Srī-Rāma Ṣarmā, 306
Ständer, Josef, 72
Standrod, G. L., 434
Starcke, S. G., 72
Startsev, I. I., 254
Statement of books printed in Ceylon, 428
Statement of important publications (Cochin), 337
Statement of particulars regarding books, ... published in the North-Western provinces, 351
Statistical bibliography: thai government statistical publications, 515
Staviskiy, B. Y., 256

Stchoukine, Ivan, 77, 148, 211, 231, 243
Stearns, N. D., 538
Steeper, H. F., 134
Stefanovich, V. N., 253
Steffens, Joan, 623
Stein, M. A., 388
Steinschneider, Moritz, 118
Steinschneider, Moritz, 96, 97, 98, 107, 113, 118, 119, 142, 164, 192
Stekelis, Miriam, 123
Stekelis, Mosheh, 120
Stepanov, A. Y., 264
Stepanova, A. A., 258
Stepanova, L. I., 299
Stepanova, N. A., 267
Stephanou, K. D., 228
Sternbach, L., 308
Sternstein, Larry, 445
Stevens, J. H., 151, 159
Stewart, Charles, 58
Stone, F. A., 232
Storey, C. A., 143, 147, 172, 202, 306
Strack, H. L., 98, 114
Strange, E. F., 611, 614
Streit, Robert, 47, 288, 305, 371, 455, 458, 473, 503, 586, 608, 623
Strelcyn, Stefan, 51, 92
Strizhevskaya, L. A., 406
Strouse, Leopold, 109
Strout, Elizabeth, 60
Stüber, J. W., 42
Stucki, C. W., 55, 56
Sturm, A. L., 222, 233
Subbarāu Seshagiri Hālkar, 453, 456
Subkhanberdina, Y., 260
Subrahmanya Sastri, P. P., 181, 390, 391, 394, 396, 409, 410, 412, 413, 414, 415, 417
Sud, K. K., 293
Sudhākara Dvivedī, 386
Sueter, E. B. F., 429
Suez crisis, 157
Suggested reading list on Burma, 454
Suggested reading list on China, 571
Suggested reading list on Laos, 461
Suggested reading list on Pakistan, 420
Suggested reading list on Thailand, 514
Suggested reading list on Vietnam, 463
Süheyl Ünver, A., 237
Suleski, Ronald, 581
Suleyman, Khamid, 262
Sultanbawa, M. U. S., 432
Sultanov, M. S., 268
Sun, E-tu Zen, 576, 581
Supplement to the Bengal district records, 351
Supplement to the Consolidated list of publications in the ECAFE library, 48
Suratan Hervey, 491
Suratan Swettenham, 491
Suri, V. S., 213
Survey of bibliographies ... concerning east and southeast asian studies, 441
Survey of japanese bibliographies, 53, 598
Sutugin, A. P., 267

Sutyagina, M. V., 602
Suzuki, Koichi, 510
Suzuki, Peter, 225, 231, 492
Suzuki, Yukihisa, 601
Sverchevskaya, A. K., 197, 218, 223
Svidina, E. D., 265
Swanson, D. C. E., 237
Swearingen, A. R., 612
Sweet, L. E., 137
Syām Bihāri Misra, 408
Syamasundara Dasa, 408
Systematische bibliographie der Palästina-literatur, 120
Systematische katalogus van tijdschrift- en dagbladartikelen, 471
Szajkowski, Z., 117

T

TRIPP bibliography. Pacific scientific information center, 540
Ta'avoni (Khaleghi), Shirin, 199
Tachibana, Kozen, 606
Tagirdzhanov, A. T., 194, 215, 217, 246
Taglicht, I., 114
Tagoutchi, Minorou, 633
Takaïchvili, E., 276
Takashi, Nakano, 611
Talantova, M. N., 27
Talass, M. A., 182
Talboys, D. A., 400
Talman, Michael, 71
Tal'man, R. O., 219
Talukdar, Alauddin, 425
Tamannai, Z. A., 419
Tamboer, K., 194
Tamim, Suha, 135
Tamkoç, Metin, 224
Tamney, J. B., 450
Tan Cheng Lock papers, 491
Tan Sok Joo, 455
Tanaka, Otoya, 195
Taner, Hasan, 232
Taniguchi, Yasuhei, 615
Tanilli, Server, 223
Tantet, Victor, 25
Taraporevala, V. D. B., 216, 307
Targ, William, 614
Tarhan, A. H., 237
Tarkatirtha, A. M., 397
Tarkarirtha, J. C., 398
Tarka-vedāntatīrtha, Birajmohan, 398
Tasbihi, M. H., 218
Taube, Manfred, 629
Taw Sein Ko, 455
Tawney, C. H., 390
Taylor, C. R. H., 523, 524, 527, 539
Taylor, John, 377
Taylor, William, 74, 356
Technical assistance, 31
Technical report, Catalog of aeronautical ... documents, 610
Teeuw, A., 483, 495
Teherani, A. B., 203
Teilhard de Chardin, Pierre, 587
Teissier, Raoul, 545
Тематический план изданий, 259
Tendoro, A. P., 510
Teng Ssu-yu, 562, 577, 602, 609